Opening NATO's Door

How the Alliance Remade Itself for a New Era

Ronald D. Asmus

A COUNCIL ON FOREIGN RELATIONS BOOK

COLUMBIA UNIVERSITY PRESS

NEW YORK

The Council on Foreign Relations, Inc., a nonprofit, nonpartisan national membership organization founded in 1921, is dedicated to promoting understanding of international affairs through the free and civil exchange of ideas. The council's members are dedicated to the belief that America's peace and prosperity are firmly linked to that of the world. From this flows the mission of the Council: to foster America's understanding of other nations—their peoples, cultures, histories, hopes, quarrels, and ambitions—and thus to serve our nation through study and debate, private and public.

From time to time books and reports written by members of the Council's research staff or others are published as "A Council on Foreign Relations Book."

Columbia University Press
Publishers Since 1893
New York, Chichester, West Sussex
Copyright © 2002 Columbia University Press
All rights Reserved

Library of Congress Cataloging-in-Publication Data

Asmus, Ronald D.
    Opening NATO's door : how the alliance remade itself for a new era / Ronald
D. Asmus.
        p.   cm.
    "A Council on Foreign Relations book."
    Includes bibliographical references and index
    ISBN 0–231-12776-6 (cloth : alk. paper)
    1. North Atlantic Treaty Organization—Membership.   2. United States—Foreign
relations—1989–   3. National security—Europe.   4. Peaceful change (International
relations)   5. Post-communism—Europe.   6. Intervention (International
law)   I. Title

UA646.3 A82 2002
355'.031091821—dc21

                                                              2002073637

Columbia University Press books are printed on permanent and durable acid-free paper
Printed in the United States of America

c 10 9 8 7 6 5 4 3 2

For Erik

CONTENTS

LIST OF ILLUSTRATIONS

FOREWORD

The North Atlantic Treaty Organization's invocation of Article 5 in the wake of the terrorist attacks on the United States on September 11, 2001 was a vivid reminder of how fundamentally our security environment has changed. The frozen certainties of the Cold War threat to Europe have given way to an entirely new set of challenges, much different, but no less menacing than those of the past.

The invocation of NATO's collective self-defense clause, for the first time ever in its history, and in response to a terrorist attack on the United States, also demonstrated how much the Alliance has changed since the demise of communism and the Soviet Union in the early 1990s. Originally founded in 1949 to deter Stalin from attacking Western Europe, NATO was then little more than a U.S. promise of protection to a Europe devastated and demoralized by war. But 53 years later, NATO's Article 5 commitment brought the old world to the aid of the new, to reverse the words of Winston Churchill. If ever one was looking for a demonstration of the undiminished vitality of the transatlantic relationship, this is it.

That NATO could respond so swiftly to the events of September 11 was no coincidence. Throughout the 1990s, the Alliance underwent the most far-reaching changes in its history. And Ron Asmus was one of the key architects of that adaptation. In addition to enlarging to Central and Eastern Europe, NATO reached out to build a new cooperative relationship with Russia, its erstwhile adversary. It also reoriented itself to face new threats beyond its borders and intervened to stop ethnic cleansing and genocide in Bosnia and Kosovo. And it embraced the European Union's efforts to build a European Security and Defense Policy as a step toward a fairer sharing of the transatlantic security burden. Initially a U.S.-West European alliance designed to meet the Russian threat, the Alliance was being transformed into the foundation for a new pan-European alliance between North America and a Europe whole and free.

Behind this transformation lay the conviction that NATO was not just a temporary Cold War creation designed by necessity to deter Russian power. Two world wars and fifty years of working together during the Cold War led both sides of the Atlantic to conclude that the virtues of their strategic partnership transcended the communist or any other specific threat. The Atlantic Alliance is the expression of a community of North American and European democracies based on common values and interests. As NATO heads of state put it in a declaration at their fiftieth anniversary summit in Washington in the spring of 1999, NATO must be adapted so that it is as good in meeting the threats of the 21st century as it was in fighting the Cold War.

In November 2002, at its summit meeting in Prague, NATO will confront a new set of challenges. It must now complete the vision of a Europe whole and free that stretches, in the words of President George W. Bush, from the Baltic to the Black Sea and enlarge to new members willing and able to shoulder the burdens of membership. The terrorist attacks on the United States have only reinforced the desire to consolidate peace and democracy in post–Cold War Europe. A strong and stable Europe is a key asset at a time when American and Western security is under attack elsewhere.

But the war on terrorism has also highlighted the continuing importance of allies and alliances. Today Western democracies face new, potentially existential threats to their security in the form of terrorism and weapons of mass destruction. Our Alliance must be modernized and adapted to face this threat if we are to live up to the principles NATO was founded on. This modernization must not be confined to developing new strategies or working methods. It must entail, above all, a commitment to build the necessary military capabilities. This is a challenge for NATO Allies as well as for those who aspire to join the Alliance. Our still-young century has already taught us a lesson we must heed as we continue NATO's modernization: that you cannot have defense on the cheap.

In *Opening NATO's Door*, Ron Asmus provides us with a definitive and insider's account of the first chapter in NATO's modernization after the end of the Cold War. He takes us behind the scenes in Washington and into the diplomatic corridors of Europe to tell the story of the debates that took place in the early and mid-1990s as the U.S. and its European allies grappled to define the

Alliance's post–Cold War strategic direction in the wake of communism's collapse. He shows how the initial impulse for NATO enlargement came from dissidents-turned-diplomats in Central and Eastern Europe and how it was eventually embraced by U.S. and European leaders. Above all, he provides us with an insider's view on how Washington's own views and those of its allies evolved as NATO grappled with how to turn enlargement from a noble idea into political reality.

Opening NATO's Door documents the diplomacy, some of it dramatic, that took place in the run-up to the NATO Brussels summit in January 1994 and, above all, during the run-up to the Madrid summit in July 1997. At the same time, he highlights how, from its inception, NATO enlargement was about more than just consolidating the peace in Central and Eastern Europe. His detailing of the intense negotiations that produced the signing of the NATO-Russia Founding Act documents the lengths to which the Alliance went to create a new relationship with Moscow and to give it a place in a new European security order. He offers some vivid insights into the political battle that took place both in public and behind the scenes in Washington and the building of a true bipartisan consensus for the ratification of enlargement by the U.S. Senate in the spring of 1998.

Above all, Ron underscores how the early proponents of enlargement were trying to develop a rationale for a new NATO that would bind the U.S. and Europe together as closely in the post–Cold War era as they had been during the fight against communism. For the United States, NATO enlargement became the centerpiece of a broader agenda—to transform and modernize the U.S.-European strategic partnership to deal with the threats of a new century. That strategy reflected an American commitment to the spread of democracy and Western values, the premium put on building new alliances in a globalized world and the fact that Washington looked to Europe whole and free as America's most natural partner likely to share those values and address those challenges.

NATO heads of state will doubtless draw some of the intellectual, political and diplomatic lessons from the events described in this book when they meet in Prague in November 2002. The questions they must grapple with—the scope of the next wave of NATO enlargement, how best to deepen NATO-Russia cooperation and how to build capabilities so that the Alliance serves as an effective tool in the war on terrorism—are the natural outgrowth of the debates and policies described in these pages.

Dean Acheson, one of NATO's founding fathers, once said that "the really successful international organizations are those that recognize and express underlying realities." In facing long-term, strategic challenges, there can be no substitute for long-term, strategic partners: Partners you can trust. Partners who trust you. That is the underlying reality which the North Atlantic Alliance has always been about.

Ron Asmus' fascinating account explains how NATO, by recognizing and expressing these "underlying realities" in post–Cold War Europe, transformed both itself, European security, and the transatlantic security partnership.

Ron Asmus played a key—indeed essential—role, both in and out of government, in ensuring that this effort was enormously successful. For that, I thank Ron and am grateful for the contribution this book makes to documenting this historic story.

Lord Robertson of Port Ellen
Secretary General of NATO
May 2002

ACKNOWLEDGMENTS

This book is the result of a decade's involvement in the intellectual and political battle over NATO enlargement. I would like to thank Jim Thomson at RAND for encouraging me to pursue my initial ideas on NATO enlargement and modernization in the early 1990s. One of RAND's many strengths is its analytical teamwork. I owe a great debt to Richard Kugler and Steve Larrabee for their personal friendship and intellectual collaboration. A special word of thanks also goes to Vice Admiral Ulrich Weisser. As a guest scholar at RAND and subsequent top aide to German Defense Minister Volker Ruehe, he contributed in many ways to RAND's early work on these issues. Our work together in and outside of government is a testimony to the spirit of the trans-Atlantic relationship.

It was an honor to serve my country under President Bill Clinton and Secretary of State Madeleine K. Albright from 1997 to 2000. I would like to thank Strobe Talbott and Jim Steinberg for helping to bring me into the State Department. For three years I had the opportunity to work with some of the best and the brightest diplomats the United States has: Eric Edelman, Dan Fried, Marc Grossman, Victoria Nuland, E. Anthony Wayne and Sandy Vershbow. Similarly, Jeremy Rosner was a true friend and colleague who helped me understand the nexus between policy and politics during the Senate ratification debate and afterward. Their support then and now has helped make this book possible. I hasten to add that opinions expressed in this book are mine alone and do not reflect any official position of the United States government.

Without the support of Les Gelb and the Council on Foreign Relations this book would never have become reality. The Council provided the environment and support that allowed me to translate the swirl of events of the last decade into a narrative for a broader audience. Dr. Zbigniew Brzezinski was kind enough to chair a Council study group whose members read and critiqued the initial draft chapters of this book. While they are too numerous to be named individually, their comments and feedback helped sharpen my thinking and arguments. I would also like to thank Madeleine Albright, Richard Holbrooke, Tony Lake, Jim Steinberg, and Strobe Talbott for their comments on earlier drafts of the manuscript.

Bruce Curley edited and helped shape my initial draft with an eye toward a broader audience. My Research Associate, Jessica Fugate, deserves special thanks for her tireless work in helping to organize my research, track down facts, and contribute in countless ways in transforming a mass of paper and ideas into this book. Leigh Gusts and her team at the Council's library deserve special thanks for their research support as well. I would also like to thank my Senior Executive Editor, Peter Dimock, at Columbia University Press, for his encouragement and advice on how to make this story accessible. Similarly, Leslie Bialler's editing helped tighten both my prose and my arguments.

A special word of thanks also goes to all of my friends and colleagues from Central and Eastern Europe. You are too numerous to mention. But NATO enlargement was your idea. You continued to believe in and fight for it even when many in the West said it was impossible. You served as an inspiration to all of us.

In today's world no book can be written without financial support. I would like to thank the United States Institute of Peace and the Carnegie Corporation, for providing generous grants to help support my research and writing while at the Council.

And, finally, a heartfelt thanks goes to my wife Barbara who for a decade has endured with patience and humor a steady stream of trips to, and visitors from, the region, as well as phone calls at all hours of the day (and night) by people wanting to discuss NATO enlargement. As I was leaving for yet another trip to Warsaw in the late 1990s, she said to me: "Make sure you get NATO enlargement right so that members of another generation of Americans, including our son Erik, will not give up their lives fighting in Europe twenty years from now." I am confident we did.

NOTE ON SOURCES

This book was written under an executive order signed by the Secretary of State granting the author access to the U.S. Department of State's archives. While it is not unusual for former officials to consult government records while writing historical accounts, it is unusual to cite these records as a professional historian would. In doing so, I have followed the precedent set by Philip Zelikow and Condoleezza Rice in *Germany Unified and Europe Transformed: A Study in Statecraft.*

My archival access was limited to the Department of State. However, those archives contain documents from other government agencies—e.g., the National Security Council or Department of Defense—circulated for interagency consultations or to U.S. Embassies abroad. The records I cite remain classified and will remain unavailable to the public for the time being. I am able to refer to them because the references themselves were determined not to reveal any secrets. Until they are declassified, scholars will have to take on faith that I have used the evidence fairly.

As a scholar, I recognize the dilemma that colleagues will not have immediate access to the same sources. But not to have cited my sources could have left the reader, as well as future scholars, even more frustrated. The issue of privileged access is not a new one. Papers or materials held by private persons or institutions are often made available with restrictions. The documents I have drawn on belong to the American people and will eventually be made available to the public. Scholars may, of course, request documents cited through the Freedom of Information Act.

The author's research has benefited from other sources as well. Strobe Talbott and Jeremy Rosner allowed me access to their private papers. Polish Foreign Minster Bronislaw Geremek granted me access to select documents from the Polish Foreign Ministry's archives. Alfred Moses and Nicholas Rey provided me access to personal diaries they kept from their days as U.S. Ambassador to Bucharest and Warsaw respectively. Stephen Biegun shared his personal files on NATO enlargement from his tenure working for Senator Jesse Helms (R- NC) on the Senate Foreign Relations Committee. Bruce Jackson granted me access to the archives of the Committee to Expand NATO. Similarly, Jan Novak allowed me to look through his private papers and correspondence, and Zbigniew Brzezinski allowed me to draw on several memos summarizing key conversations with administration officials. Each of these contributed in an important way to my research.

Finally, my research also included an extensive set of interviews with officials on both sides of the Atlantic. They included: Andrezj Ananicz, Ivan Baba, Allison Bayles, Steve Biegun, Samuel Berger, Marc Perrin de Brichambaut, Hank Brown, Martin Butora, Per Carlsen, Ashton Carter, Emil Constantinescu, Lynn Davis, Jorge Domecq, Thomas Donilon, Stephen Flanagan, Newt Gingrich, Mircea Geoana, Przemylsaw Grudzinski, Istvan Gyarmati, Hans Haekkerup, Richard C. Holbrooke, Wolfgang Ischinger, Geza Jeszensky, Rudolf Joo, Andrzej Karkoszka, Gyula Kodolanyi, John Kornblum, Laszlo Kovacs, Jerzy Kozminski, Anthony Lake, François de Lattre, Jean-David Levitte, Richard Lugar, Jean-Claude Mallet, Gebhardt von Moltke, Dick Morris, Robert Mroziewicz, Klaus Naumann, Pauline Neville-Jones, Jan Novak, Joseph Nye, Andrzej Olechowski, Sir David Omand, Gardner Peckham, William Perry, Carter Pilcher, Bruno Racine, Steve Rademaker, Gunnar Riberholdt, Jamie Rubin, Volker Ruehe, Klaus Scharioth, Elizabeth Sherwood-Randle, Jamie Shea, Marek Siewic, Ferenc Somogyi, James Steinberg, Karsten Voigt, Alexandr Vondra, Ulrich Weisser, and Sir John Weston.

INTRODUCTION

It was March 12, 1999 and I was walking across the tarmac at Andrews Air Force base to the plane of Secretary of State Madeleine K. Albright. As the senior representative of the State Department's European Bureau, I was flying with her to Independence, Missouri to celebrate the entry of the Czech Republic, Hungary, and Poland into the North Atlantic Treaty Organization (NATO). As the U.S. Secretary of State, Albright had the honor of receiving the protocols of accession officially marking the entry of these three countries into the Alliance. She had chosen the Harry S. Truman Library for the ceremony. It was her way of emphasizing that the U.S. and our European allies were continuing the original dream of Truman and NATO's founding fathers by enlarging the Atlantic Alliance to include countries from Central and Eastern Europe who, only a decade earlier, had broken loose from Soviet rule.

It was an important day for the United States and for the Administration of President Bill Clinton. The U.S. and its allies were extending a security guarantee to Central and Eastern Europe—a region that had been at the center of many of Europe's great conflicts in the past. It was the largest increase in the American commitment to Europe in decades—and came at a time when many people doubted the staying power of the U.S. in Europe and elsewhere around the globe. It was a testimony that America was not becoming isolationist but instead was renewing and expanding its commitment to alliance with the old continent and with the world more generally.

But NATO enlargement was only part of a broader effort to transform and modernize the Atlantic Alliance. Founded in 1949 to defend Western Europe from a Soviet threat, the Alliance was now being used to help unify Europe by opening its door to new members from the Baltic to the Black Sea. In parallel, NATO had reached out to establish a cooperative relationship with Moscow, its erstwhile adversary. While maintaining the core commitment to the collective defense of its members, the U.S. had also pushed NATO to embrace new military missions in response to new threats and to intervene militarily beyond its borders in defense of Western values and interests, starting in the Balkans.

These were some of the most far-reaching changes in NATO in decades. And it was all coming together in the spring of 1999. The enlargement of NATO's members and missions were the highlight of the Alliance's fiftieth anniversary summit scheduled for April 1999 in Washington, D.C. The vision was clear: a new NATO between the U.S. and a Europe whole and free committed to tackling the new threats of the 21st century. Enlargement was a centerpiece of a strategy to make NATO effective in meeting the challenges of the future as the Alliance had been in winning the Cold War. While none of us could foresee it at the time, these efforts helped to lay the foundation for NATO's invoking of Article V on September 11, 2001 in response to terrorist attacks on the United States.

It had not been easy or without controversy. At a time of general indifference to foreign policy following the end of the Cold War, NATO enlargement sparked one of the most passionate and fierce national security debates of the decade in the United States. The reasons went beyond the issue of the fate of those Central and East Europeans nations. Instead, the debate revolved around America's vision of Europe, relations with Russia, as well as NATO's future purpose now that communism was gone. Initially, much of the American foreign policy establishment opposed it; most Europeans were lukewarm at best; and the Russians were almost unanimous in their opposition to it. Critics claimed that it was a strategic blunder that would derail Russia's democratic reforms, provoke a new Cold War, and dilute or weaken America's premier military alliance. And they doubted President Clinton's commitment to this project and insisted that the U.S. public and Senate would never consent to extend a U.S. security guarantee to these countries.

But President Clinton overcame opposition to the idea—first in his own Administration, then among our European allies and, finally, in Russia—and successfully enlarged the Alliance. And he did so without the crisis in relations with Russia or the evisceration of NATO as a military alliance critics had predicted. Both major political parties supported NATO enlargement and the U.S. Senate ratified it by a vote of 80–19. In doing so, the Administration laid a cornerstone for a new NATO that reflected the realities and threats of a new Europe — an accomplishment that was likely to be one of the Administration's most enduring foreign policy legacies.

Why had the Clinton Administration done it? There were three key reasons. First, President Clinton was attracted early on to NATO enlargement as a means to help create a democratic, peaceful, and secure Europe whose future, as he often put it to visitors, could be better than the continent's bloody past. He believed that the U.S. had a unique chance to help do for Europe's eastern half what the generation of Truman and Acheson had done for the continent's western half. He wanted to extend NATO's security umbrella to lock in peace and democracy in Europe as a whole and complete the overcoming of Europe's Cold War divide that had started with the crumbling of the Berlin Wall ten years earlier. And he wanted to do so while also embracing and integrating a democratic Russia.

Second, the President believed that one of the great lessons of the 20th century was that the United States and Europe should stick together. Although the old Soviet threat had gone away, America's interest in an alliance with Europe had not. He wanted to modernize NATO in a way that would keep the U.S. and Europe tied together and the Alliance relevant in a way that publics on both sides understood. Clinton believed that there was perhaps no other part of the world with which the U.S. had more common values and interests. By locking in peace and security on the continent once and for all, the U.S. could create precisely the kind of stability in Europe that would better allow it to address new challenges elsewhere. This would in turn allow the U.S. and its European allies to focus on the new challenges they needed to confront together in the years and decades ahead in a globalized world.

Third, the Clinton Administration viewed the fight over NATO enlargement as part of the larger battle over what America stood for in the world. It was part of the broader foreign policy struggle over whether the United States would remain internationally engaged or retreat into a new kind of isolationism or unilateralism. President Clinton wanted to modernize the Alliance to deal with the threats of the future because he believed the U.S. should not go it alone but had to act together with its partners on the global stage. He wanted to reform NATO so that the American public would understand why it was still relevant in a new era and support its continuation. To be sure, not all opponents of enlargement were isolationist or unilateralist. But there were voices advocating a U.S. disengagement from Europe either to focus on domestic problems, or to free up American attention and resources to act elsewhere in the world. The Clinton Administration believed that these were the false and wrong choices.

As the Secretary of State's plane took off from Andrews Air Force base, I thought about the key individuals who had made this day possible. That vision and strategy were not the result of a sudden epiphany. Instead, they had evolved over time and resulted from intellectual and political battles waged and won. The idea of enlarging NATO had originated in Central and Eastern Europe where former dissidents turned diplomats and statesman saw it as the logical extension of their struggle against communism and the culmination of their fight for freedom, democracy, and national independence. It was then picked up by a handful of Western intellectuals and politicians who recast the issue in broader terms of the Alliance's overall future and survival. In doing so, they put the NATO enlargement issue front and center on the West's strategic agenda.

That debate fell into the lap of the Clinton Administration shortly after it assumed office in early 1993. And it was President Clinton who personally set the tone within the Administration by responding positively when first confronted with the issue by Vaclav Havel, Lech Walesa, and Arpad Goncz—the presidents of the Czech Republic, Poland, and Hungary—in the spring of 1993. Tony Lake, Clinton's first National Security Advisor, was perhaps the first proponent of NATO enlargement in the President's inner circle along with Sandy Berger. Warren Christopher, Albright's predecessor as Secretary of State, was initially cautious but gradually became a strong supporter, toiling in the diplomatic trenches to lay the groundwork for the successes that followed after his departure. Richard C. Holbrooke was brought back to enforce the President's will on a reluctant bureaucracy, especially the Pentagon, and to get reluctant allies on board. And Deputy Secretary of State Strobe Talbott, while initially skeptical, took on the arduous task of negotiating a new cooperative NATO-Russia relationship that would enable enlargement to move forward while avoiding a train wreck in Russia's relations with the West.

But this was also a very special moment for Albright. The daughter of a Czechoslovak diplomat driven from his homeland by Stalin, she was committed to using America's power and influence to overcome Europe's Cold War division. While much of the groundwork for NATO enlargement was completed during Clinton's first term in office, it was Albright who became the Administration's champion on enlargement and pulled together the ideas, the diplomacy, and the politics to successfully get the job done. Her tenacity helped keep the Atlantic Alliance on course. And her passion on the issue, knack for public diplomacy, and personal relationship with Republican Senator Jesse Helms allowed her to reach across the political aisle and build bipartisan support to ensure Senate ratification. To use a sports metaphor that Albright would have frowned on as "boy's talk," she came in as the quarterback in charge of the red zone offense to put the ball in the end zone.

But credit for NATO enlargement clearly extended across the political aisle and beyond the Administration. Without President George Bush's successful reunification of Germany in NATO, the Alliance would never have been able to reach out further to the East. The leaders of Central and East European ethnic groups helped draw early attention to the issue and elevated it on the agenda of both the

Administration and Congress . . . and played a key role in providing support in the ratification process. The Republican Party embraced enlargement as one of its goals in the Contract with America in the summer of 1994 at the same time the Clinton Administration was deciding to move forward on enlargement. The Clinton Administration disagreed with many Republicans on the overall strategy and timing of enlargement and, above all, on how to handle Russia and the NATO-Russia relationship. But at a time of growing partisanship in Washington, both parties came together to produce a bipartisan 80–19 vote on enlargement. Forty-five of those Senators were Republicans. It was an affirmation of a strong bi-partisan commitment to U.S.-European relations and trans-Atlantic cooperation.

As we flew toward St. Louis on a dreary March day in the spring of 1999, NATO was bracing to go to war in Kosovo. Albright had kept a grueling sched-ule in the preceding weeks trying to keep the NATO Alliance together and the Russians on board while the West ratcheted up the political and military pres-sure on Serbian leader Slobodan Milosevic to halt his barbaric "ethnic cleans-ing" campaign. She was in the front line of fire for what the press would soon dub "Madeleine's war." But it was time to put the problems of Kosovo aside for a day to welcome the Czech Republic, Hungary, and Poland into NATO. Albright's Chief-of-Staff, Elaine Shocas, tapped me on the shoulder and said Albright wanted to see me. As I entered her private cabin, she broke out into a smile and gave me a huge hug. "Madeleine"—as we all referred to her—had been waiting a long time for this day, and her ebullient mood showed it.

We were joined on the plane by the Foreign Ministers of these three coun-tries—Bronislaw Geremek of Poland, Jan Kavan of Czechoslovakia, and Janos Martonyi of Hungary. Each came up to Albright's cabin to spend a few private minutes with her and to congratulate her. Geremek, a former Solidarity dissi-dent and a close personal friend of Albright's, reminded her that during Poland's first post-communist election campaign, Solidarity had used an election poster with a picture of Gary Cooper from *High Noon* to symbolize the triumph of good over evil. "Madeleine," Geremek said, "this is the fulfillment of that dream." "NATO enlargement," he continued, "is the most important event that has happened to Poland since the onset of Christianity." This was a remarkable statement considering that it came from a Polish medieval historian of Jewish origin. After Geremek left the cabin, Albright turned to me and said: "Ron, it doesn't get any better then this. We are making history."

At the ceremony at the Truman Library, each of the three Foreign Ministers spoke eloquently about what NATO membership meant to them and their na-tions. The table used for the signing ceremony was the same one President Truman had used on March 12, 1947 to sign legislation that provided assistance to Greece and Turkey under the Marshall Plan to help defend them against a possible communist takeover—a first step in a U.S. commitment that would lead to the creation of NATO two years later. After the Foreign Ministers handed their signed protocols to Albright, she held them above her head in triumph and beamed. "Hallelujah," she proclaimed. "Never again will your fates be tossed around like poker chips on a bargaining table." NATO enlargement, she said, was erasing "the line drawn in Europe by Stalin's bloody boot." Looking at the three Foreign Ministers, she said to them: "You are truly allies; you are truly home."

I looked over at the Polish, Czech, and Hungarian delegations. A number of them had been imprisoned under communism in their fight for democracy and freedom. They had always dreamed of the day when they could join the West. For them this day was the culmination of a struggle that had started with the founding of Charter 77 or when a young Polish electrician by the name of Lech Walesa had jumped the fence at the Lenin shipyards in August 1981 in Gdansk to lead the strikes that would lead to the creation of Solidarity and eventually topple the Soviet empire in Central and Eastern Europe. When these Poles, Czechs, and Hungarians had initially raised the issue of joining NATO in the early 1990s, many in the West had dismissed them as hopeless romantics. But they had persevered. They had always been part of the West in spirit. Now they were joining its premier military alliance. It was the fulfillment of their dreams and their triumph as well. Many of them were in tears.

Returning home from Independence on the evening of March 12, I also thought about how my own life had become intertwined with the NATO enlargement debate. Central and Eastern Europe had been a part of my life since childhood. My parents were German immigrants, driven by the aftermath of war and destruction to start a new life in Milwaukee. My family had roots in various parts of Central and Eastern Europe—Bohemia, Pomerania, Lower Saxony, and Silesia. My first exposure to Central and Eastern European politics came at home in the evenings when I would listen to my grandmother tell me about what Berlin, Warsaw, Prague, and Budapest had been like before World War II destroyed and divided Europe.

My education continued on to the soccer field. Our local soccer league—organized along ethnic lines with German, Polish, Italian, Czech, Hungarian, and Serbo-Croatian teams—reflected the large number of Central and East European immigrants who had landed in Milwaukee. While children kicked the ball around the field, parents yelled at them and each other in a multitude of tongues, only to retire to the tavern afterward to talk about life in the old country. Like many young Americans, I went to Europe to study during my college years. During that time, I visited the battlefields where World War II had been fought and the concentration camps where millions of Jews and other victims had perished. I saw the reality of Europe's division in a divided Berlin where I searched for the home in which my grandmother had lived in the 1930s.

That reality—complete with barbed wire, armed towers manned by soldiers with guard dogs, and orders to shoot to kill—was a pivotal experience that changed my life and future career path. Simply put, it horrified me. I began to ask questions: How could this have been allowed to happen? How long would it endure? What could be done to end it? To the great consternation of my parents, I returned home to announce that I was abandoning a planned engineering degree and instead wanted to study European and Russian History and International Relations.

My first job after graduate school was with Radio Free Europe (RFE) in Munich, Germany. There was hardly a better microcosm of Central and Eastern Europe for a young American interested in the region. Many of the most knowledgeable experts on communist affairs in the world worked at or visited RFE. Solidarity was on the rise in Poland. It and other dissident movements in Central and Eastern Europe were signs that the Soviet bloc was starting to crumble. The émigrés and experts there taught me a great deal about the aspirations and fears of the people of this region. Several colleagues would return to their native countries following communism's collapse and reappear in my life as diplomatic counterparts after I joined the State Department.

In the late 1980s I joined RAND, the leading think tank in the U.S. at the time on European security issues. It was an exciting time: the Berlin Wall would soon fall and much of the conventional wisdom on European security went out the window. RAND was a beehive of debate over future U.S. strategy toward Europe and Russia. The Czech Republic, Poland, and Hungary had turned to RAND for assistance in developing new national security strategies. Working with them provided a unique window into their thinking and aspirations to join NATO. Many of our new colleagues and friends were as pro-western and committed to the values NATO was pledged to defend as any of us. How could the U.S. say "no" to their desire to join the Alliance?

During the 1992 Presidential campaign, I was attracted to then Governor Bill Clinton's "New Democrat" philosophy. I joined one of several groups of foreign policy experts attached to the campaign. The purpose of such ragtag groups was as much to keep us would-be foreign policy advisors feeling involved as producing anything of use to the campaign. But the battle lines on NATO enlargement were already being drawn. Several colleagues and I argued that the U.S. should enlarge NATO as the natural extension of the American commitment to democracy and integration in Europe, while others argued that such a move would alienate Moscow and that the Central and East Europeans should be encouraged to look to European structures instead. Such discussions foreshadowed the debate that would unfold in the years to come.

The selection of Clinton's initial national security team did not fill me with confidence that the issues I cared about were high on the Administration's agenda. Along with two RAND colleagues, Steve Larrabee and Dick Kugler, I decided to go public with the case for enlarging NATO in an article in *Foreign Affairs* in the fall of 1993 that quickly became a *cause célèbre* in policy-making and diplomatic circles. German Defense Minister Volker Ruehe, the first major West European politician to publicly advocate NATO enlargement, now turned to RAND for help in developing his ideas. So did the Polish government. The debate over NATO's future was launched and my colleagues and I were in the center of it.

In late December 1993, the phone rang while I was at home in Santa Monica. On the line was Rose Gottemoeller, a former RAND colleague then at the National Security Council. She was calling on behalf of Strobe Talbott who was about to become Warren Christopher's new Deputy at the State Department. Rose had just returned from Moscow with Vice President Gore and Talbott. During a stopover in Bonn, Richard Holbrooke had recommended me for a job. Talbott wanted to know if I could come to Washington as soon as possible for an interview.

I had met Holbrooke some months earlier. He was known for his audacity. He was also keen on getting me into the Administration. He once sent me a postcard saying: "Ron, I will be in touch to let you know how you can best serve your country." It was vintage Holbrooke. But Talbott's interest left me even more curious. I had met him at several seminars but did not know him well. He was reported to be the leading opponent of NATO enlargement in the Administration's inner circle. Why would he want to hire me? As I walked into the lobby of the State Department two days later, I couldn't help but wonder what I was getting myself into.

But Talbott and I had an immediate personal and intellectual rapport. I quickly realized that his views were different than the caricature presented in the media—including on NATO enlargement. At one point he remarked that while he had not read all of my writings, he did know one article quite well, the *Foreign Affairs* article that he had been arguing about for the past three months. I could not help but ask him: "Strobe, if you have been fighting my ideas for all of these months, why do you want to hire me?" He answered: "Because we have a Russia policy but we do not yet have a European policy. And we need to have both and they need to fit together. We need to find a way to meld our European and Russian policy requirements. I want you to help me figure out how to do that."

The job offer did not work out. When Talbott offered me a less senior slot, I declined. I knew Washington well enough to understand that rank mattered if one wanted to have an impact. Talbott sat me down in one of the Department's ornate seventh-floor rooms to make a final pitch. He pointed out that I had no previous government experience and asked me to consider taking a staff position with a promise of a promotion down the road. When I noted that his lack of government experience had not prevented him from getting a very senior post, he laughed and said: "But you haven't known the President for twenty-five years either." As we parted, he told me: "You will end up working for this Administration before it is over. I will make sure of that." He later hired me as a consultant to the Department so that we could stay in touch.

With Clinton's reelection in November 1996 and the nomination of Madeleine Albright as Secretary of State, that time had arrived. I knew Albright through my former RAND colleague, Jim Steinberg, who was about to become President Clinton's Deputy National Security Advisor. She was looking for someone to be her point person on NATO enlargement. Talbott and Steinberg convinced her I should be it. I joined the Clinton Administration later that spring as a Deputy Assistant Secretary of State in the State Department's European Bureau under Assistant Secretary John Kornblum and, subsequently, Marc Grossman. On my first day on the job, Talbott took me to see Albright. "Ron," she told me, "I am looking to you to help us enlarge NATO, work out this deal with the Russians, and come up with a strategy for the Baltic States."

Talbott took me back to his private office. He told me that he would look to me personally to be his representative on all issues related to NATO enlargement. I was to have direct and personal access to him. But Talbott underscored the need to work NATO enlargement and NATO-Russia in tandem and with equal commitment. "You need to commit to bringing the same amount of intellectual commitment and passion to the building of a NATO-Russia relationship as you have brought to NATO enlargement," he told me. "It is what the President, the Secretary, and I all want." As he put it, we needed to think "bi-lobally" — with one lobe of the brain working on enlargement and the other on NATO-Russia. It was a phrase I would hear many times over the next three years.

A Deputy Assistant Secretary, or DAS in the nomenclature of the U.S. government, is a key link between the political leadership and the working level of the State Department. He or she is not in the innermost circle of power, but is senior enough to observe and at times participate in high-level policy decisions and to help carry them out. For the next three years I was part of the senior staff at Albright's and Talbott's sides as the United States enlarged NATO, negotiated the NATO-Russia Founding Act, and steered enlargement through the U.S. Senate. I was the U.S. negotiator for the U.S.-Baltic Charter and was part of the team that put together a new strategic concept for the Alliance's fiftieth-anniversary summit in the spring of 1999 and NATO's air campaign in Kosovo. For someone who had spent his professional career writing about NATO and European affairs, it was a unique perch from which to witness how policy really is made.

As we returned from Independence and prepared to land at Andrews Air Force base, I realized it was time to leave the world of diplomacy. Much of what I had set out to accomplish when I joined the Administration had been achieved. Poland, Hungary and the Czech Republic were free and safe in NATO. We had laid the foundation for a more modern Atlantic Alliance that was reshaping itself for a new era, changes that would be embraced at the Alliance's Fiftieth Anniversary Summit the following month.

Most importantly, the Europe my son would grow up to visit would be a different and better one. The line that had cruelly and artificially divided families, countries, and an entire continent for half a century was being erased. Whereas I as a young student had traveled across a continent divided by barbed wire and guard dogs, my son would never think twice about visiting Berlin, Warsaw, or Budapest. He would never know the divided Europe I had grown up with and what it was like to cross a Cold War boundary where great armies stood in an ideological and military standoff for some four decades. Thank God, I thought to myself.

Rarely does one have the opportunity to contribute intellectually to the origins of a major policy initiative as well as to implement it in practice. I was fortunate to have that opportunity. This book is a history of that experience—the intellectual origins of the NATO enlargement debate, the diplomacy that turned those ideas into real policies, and the politics that shaped the battles and final outcome. This story is told from the perspective of someone who was involved in that debate—as a scholar, policy activist and a diplomat. It does not attempt to cover every aspect of the debate, though I have tried to be comprehensive in my treatment of many issues. Additional insights will undoubtedly emerge as the memoirs of many of the key participants are published, the archives of other countries open, and as other scholars in the United States and abroad unearth additional insights.

This book is also unique in one final regard. My library at home has one section for memoirs and another for scholarly studies. They are very different genres. But this book seeks to combine the two. It is written first and foremost as a diplomatic and intellectual history. But my perspective has inevitably been shaped by the fact that I participated in the debates and was a witness to many of the events described in these pages. I have tried to use my personal experience to capture the passion, drama and occasional messiness of the diplomacy as it happened. For me personally, this was the most honest and accurate way to tell this story. I hope it will contribute to a deeper understanding of how Europe's divide was overcome.

R.D.A.
Washington, D.C.,
May 2002

Opening NATO's Door

Book I

THE ORIGINS

On October 3, 1990, tens of thousands of Germans had gathered in front of the Reichstag in Berlin to celebrate the final step in the official unification of Germany. Less than a year earlier, on November 9, 1989, the world had watched with amazement as the Berlin Wall—*the* symbol of Germany and Europe's partition—crumbled when East German border guards, confused over their precise orders, had opened the border to allow a gathered crowd of East Germans to cross over to West Berlin. What started out as a trickle soon became a torrent as joyous Germans began to tear down the hated wall that had divided their country, and no one stopped them. It was the beginning of the end of the division of Germany. Ten months later Germany was unified—and in NATO.

I was among those standing in front of the Reichstag, a young American academic who had returned to Berlin to witness this event for both personal and intellectual reasons. My grandmother had lived in Berlin in the 1930s. I had been a Research Fellow at the Free University in West Berlin while writing my doctoral dissertation on the division of Germany. During the course of my research, I had visited East Berlin many times. My first job out of graduate school had been as a cub research analyst on East Germany at Radio Free Europe before joining RAND. The German Democratic Republic, as East Germany was officially known, was one of the most repressive regimes in the Soviet bloc. Now, it along with the Soviet bloc was disappearing! Rarely has someone witnessed the vanishing of one of his academic research topics with a greater sense of satisfaction.

But it was not only the division of Germany that was passing from the scene. A mindset and way of thinking about European security was being shattered as well. During the post–World War II period, the belief that security in Europe was built on the partition of Germany and the continent had increasingly become conventional wisdom in the West. While both Washington and Moscow claimed that they wanted to overcome Europe's divide, the reality was that many people had not only become comfortable with but even saw virtue in a divided continent. In a widely read book in the late 1970s called *Europe Between the Superpowers: the Enduring Balance*, for example, A. W. DePorte wrote that the division of Europe had created a security system that was quite stable and stood independently of its Cold War origins.[1] One of our best known diplomatic historians, John Lewis Gaddis, had titled his study of the Cold War, *The Long Peace*, reflecting the widespread view that the Cold War, while certainly unsatisfactory in many ways, had nevertheless created a degree of stability in a part of the world where two world wars had originated.[2]

NATO had originally been created to deter a Soviet military threat posed by Stalin and to provide a security umbrella under which Western Europe could rebuild and integrate. It had brought peace and stability to Europe's western half, but left the continent's eastern half in the Soviet orbit. The Alliance's founding fathers had held out the hope that one day the Soviet Union would mellow and release its grip on the eastern half of the continent and allow Europe to again come together. But as the Cold War division of Europe deepened in the 1950s and 1960s, the existence of two opposing military alliances — NATO and the Warsaw Pact — increasingly seemed to reinforce the continent's division as opposed to fostering the overcoming of that divide.

In Central and Eastern Europe that system was known as Yalta — a metaphor for an unjust division of Europe that had left the eastern half of the continent under Soviet domination. While different in their origins and nature, NATO and the Warsaw Pact were increasingly seen as confirming Europe's division into hostile military camps. The rise of détente in the 1970s in Europe was in many ways an effort to ameliorate the impact of that division. While governments in West and East continued to support their alliance affiliations, unofficial voices started to bubble up, questioning whether western policy was effective and arguing that these two military alliances were part of the problem and had to be abolished if Europe's divide was to be overcome. On both the left and the right, *Ostpolitik* was accompanied by calls for a drawdown or even withdrawal of U.S. and Soviet troops and the loosening of alliance ties in order to help knit Europe back together.

I was part of a generation of Western academics raised with the conventional wisdom that a divided Germany and continent was a more or less permanent feature of Europe's geopolitical landscape. When I opted to write my doctoral dissertation on overcoming the division of Germany in the mid-1980s, several colleagues suggested that I consider a less esoteric and more topical issue. No one imagined that by the time I had completed my thesis that division would be no more. Conventional wisdom not only underestimated Moscow's willingness to let go of its satellites. It also misjudged the strong desire among the people of what was then still called Eastern Europe to liberate themselves and become part of the West. It was a lesson I would remember in the years ahead as the NATO enlargement debate raged and cautious diplomats argued that fulfilling Central and East European aspirations to join the Alliance was simply not politically or strategically feasible.

The fall of the Berlin Wall also raised the question of NATO's future. For decades academics had debated what would happen to the Atlantic Alliance if and when Moscow mellowed—to use the original phrase from George Kennan—and relaxed the Soviet grip on Central and Eastern Europe. Would Washington choose to remain in Europe or declare victory and go home, too? Did our European allies want us to stay or go? If NATO was supposed to survive, what would be its purpose in a Europe where the Soviet threat had disappeared? In the fall of 1990 what had previously seemed like a very theoretical consideration was becoming a very real policy challenge. Communism in Central and Eastern Europe was collapsing in front of Western eyes—and would soon collapse in the USSR as well. A priority of the new noncommunist governments in the region was the withdrawal of Soviet troops. The Warsaw Pact's days were numbered. The question of what would happen to NATO was not far behind.

1. AN AMBIGUOUS PLEDGE

October 3, 1990 had provided part of an answer. Germany was officially reunified—as a member of NATO. German Chancellor Helmut Kohl had decided to push for German unification shortly after the Berlin Wall fell—and to do so in NATO and with an ongoing U.S. military presence on German soil. The West German constitution allowed East Germany to accede to the Federal Republic, and thereby become part of the network of alliance commitments that West Germany already enjoyed. Getting Moscow to agree to German unification in NATO was among the greatest foreign policy accomplishments of President George Bush and his national security team. Many had deemed its mission impossible when the Wall first came down. But the Bush Administration had pulled off a diplomatic coup by convincing Soviet President Gorbachev that Europe and Russia, would be better off with a unified Germany in NATO rather than outside of it.[3]

It was also the first step in overcoming Europe's divide—and in retooling NATO for the post–Cold War era. Faced with the prospect of NATO disappearing and the U.S. disengaging, the instinct of nearly every government in Europe was to opt to maintain the Alliance in some new form, if only as an insurance policy. German unification in NATO was the first post–Cold War enlargement of the Alliance and an early sign that NATO's role in Europe was growing, not shrinking. To what degree German unification was thought of as a precursor of NATO's subsequent enlargement to Poland, the Czech Republic, and Hungary is less clear—and remains a bone of contention even today. Moscow would subsequently claim that it had received assurances from the United States, France, and the United Kingdom that NATO enlargement would go no further than eastern Germany. Former senior officials of the Bush Administration have denied that charge, and at least some have suggested that it was at least implicitly the first step in a broader opening of the Alliance to the East.[4]

The dispute centers on a discussion that took place in Moscow between Soviet President Gorbachev and U.S. Secretary of State James Baker on February 9, 1990. The Berlin Wall had fallen exactly three months earlier. The issue on the table was Germany's future. It had become increasingly clear that events on the ground were moving faster than anticipated and that the train to a unified Germany was leaving the station. Many of Germany's neighbors, including some of its closest European allies, had deep reservations about the prospect of a unified Germany. President George Bush and the United States had decided to support German aspirations but hoped to secure a unified Germany in NATO. Baker's mission to Moscow was to convince Gorbachev that Moscow was better off with a unified Germany in NATO than an independent, neutral Germany outside of it.

Following an opening introductory summary by Gorbachev on the Soviet domestic scene, Baker went right to the issue of Germany's foreign policy future. "The unification process is moving much faster than anyone anticipated last December," he told the Soviet President. The internal aspects of unification were for the Germans to decide, he emphasized. But Germany's future foreign policy alignment was an issue where the views of the country's neighbors had to be considered. As two of the victorious powers over Germany in World War II, the USSR and the U.S. had a legal voice in determining the country's foreign policy orientation.

"I want you to know one thing for certain," Baker continued. "The President and I have made clear that we seek no unilateral advantage in this process." The U.S. was not proposing to keep a unified Germany in NATO to gain a strategic edge over Moscow, but rather to ensure European stability, an interest the two countries shared. The U.S. favored a unified Germany in NATO, Baker underscored, because it was not sure that a neutral Germany would remain nonmilitaristic. Germany's NATO membership was also the mechanism to ensure an ongoing American military presence in Europe. "All our allies and East Europeans we have spoken to have told us that they want us to maintain a presence in Europe," Baker told the Soviet leader. "I am not sure whether you favor that or not. But let me say that if our allies want us to go, we will be gone in a minute."

Gorbachev seemed open to Baker's logic. But he delivered a long, somewhat rambling account of how many different views and voices one could find among the Germans themselves over how unification should take place. "We understand the need for assurances to the countries to the East," Baker continued. "If we maintain a presence in a Germany that is a part of NATO, there would be no extension of NATO's jurisdiction for forces of NATO one inch to the East. At the end of the day, if it is acceptable to everyone, we could have discussion in a two plus four context that might achieve this kind of outcome. Maybe there is a better way to deal with the external consequences of German unification. And if there is I am not aware of it."

After Gorbachev responded, Baker broke in to ask the key question: "Let's assume for the moment that unification is going to take place. Assuming that, would you prefer a united Germany outside of NATO that is independent and has no U.S. forces or would you prefer a united Germany with ties to NATO and assurances that there would be no extension of NATO's current jurisdiction eastward?" Gorbachev responded that he was "giving thought to all of these options" and that the Soviet political leadership was going to be holding a seminar on the issue shortly and went on to say: "Certainly any extension of the zone of NATO is unacceptable." Baker responded: "I agree."

But to what? Was Gorbachev referring to the extension of NATO to eastern Germany or further eastward to other Central and East European countries? And what exactly was Baker agreeing to? Just to extend NATO to eastern Germany? Or was he saying that NATO would never enlarge further eastward? The issue was left hanging. Gorbachev went on to say that he favored the presence of U.S. troops and that he did not want to see a replay of Versailles when it came to Germany's future. He concluded by saying: "What you have said to me about your approach and your preference is very realistic. So let's think about that. But don't ask me to give you a bottom line right now."[5]

Gorbachev eventually acquiesced to German unification in NATO, albeit with special provisions limiting the deployment of non-German NATO forces on the soil of what had been East Germany. The issue of NATO's further eastward enlargement was never again raised. While Washington and Moscow would spend months and many hours of negotiations going over the details of a settlement for a unified Germany, neither Gorbachev nor Foreign Minister Eduard Shevardnadze again raised the issue or sought further assurances to limit NATO's future enlargements. In the summer of 1990, NATO revised its military strategy and publicly stated that it no longer considered the Soviet Union a threat, changes that made it easier for Moscow to argue back home that German unification in NATO was part of the transformation of the Alliance and that it was no longer the Cold War foe it had once been. The Bush

Administration received credit for a truly historic diplomatic accomplishment. In the West, Soviet leader Gorbachev was hailed as a far-sighted statesman. At home, his conservative critics accused him of selling out and suggested that Moscow could and should have gotten a much better deal.[6]

In the mid-1990s, Russian leaders would resurrect the Baker-Gorbachev conversation of February 9, 1990 and claim that they had received a U.S. pledge to not enlarge NATO to Central and Eastern Europe. Washington would, in turn, reject this charge and insist that this conversation was limited to the future of Germany, not Central and Eastern Europe. U.S. diplomats noted that Gorbachev and Shevardnadze never returned to this issue in the numerous subsequent conversations both sides had on German unification, and that Moscow had subsequently recognized the right of all countries in Europe to choose their own alliance affiliations in the Charter of Paris. Moreover, American diplomats insisted, the U.S. and the USSR were discussing Germany's future in their unique roles as victorious powers over a defeated Nazi Germany in World War II. They were exercising those residual legal rights and obligations to help determine the foreign policy and security orientation of a unified Germany. There were no similar rights for Central or Eastern Europe.[7]

Such nuanced diplomatic points aside, the reality was that no one in either Washington or Moscow was thinking about further NATO expansion in the spring and fall of 1990. Indeed, the issue had not yet been raised by the Central and East Europeans. These countries would not embrace that goal for another two years. Better than anyone, they understood at the time that Germany's unification in NATO was not the first step of a Western strategy to bring them into the Alliance. Germany's security was one thing; Central and Eastern Europe's was another. Krzysztof Skubiszewski, Poland's Foreign Minster at the time, subsequently wrote:

> The position of the Alliance at the time was clear: from its perspective, the admission of new members was absolutely out of the question. Although the unification of Germany resulted in a territorial expansion of the Alliance, it did not simultaneously, involve an increase in the number of members. In reality, the various guarantees extended by the West to the USSR in relation to the settlement of the German problem eliminated, under the circumstances, the option of admitting new members. The German issue aside, the Alliance reacted with prudence to the changes in Central Europe. The USSR's consent to the envelopment by the Alliance of the whole (that is, unified) Germany drew the limit to the Soviet concessions and the West fully approved of that state of affairs. Thus the solution adopted in the case of Germany made the openness of the Alliance somewhat illusory. On the other hand, it could not have been ruled out that at some point the United States would acknowledge its interest in the enlargement, while Germany—America's most important partner in

Europe—having remained within the Alliance, would not want to be for-ever its eastern outpost; in other words that it would support Poland's membership. However, that was a matter of further developments, which at the onset of the 1990s did not yet appear.[8]

2. DISMANTLING YALTA

If it had been up to NATO alone, enlargement might very well have stopped at the eastern German border—not because of any secret understanding with Moscow, but simply because there was no impetus in the West to expand the Alliance's borders further eastward. The fact that Moscow had agreed to German unification in NATO was considered a near miracle by all. No one wanted to push the envelope any further. Instead, Western policy focused on shoring up the Soviet leader, as the best way to ensure that the USSR would stay on a pro-Western reformist track—especially as it became clear that he was en-gaged in his own power struggle at home.

Instead, the push for NATO to move further East would come from Central and East European leaders themselves. Once they were confident they had re-gained their national independence and dismantled the structures of Soviet dom-ination, they would start to look for ways to integrate with the West. And as they worked their way though the options, they soon settled on the goal of becoming NATO members and increasingly came to see it as the natural culmination of their desire to be fully integrated and secure in the West. To reach that goal, they would have to persevere in overcoming the hesitance and objections of nearly every Alliance member's capital in Western Europe and North America.

But those aspirations to join NATO, which became so strong in the region in the mid and late 1990s, were not immediately apparent in the initial wake of communism's collapse in the fall of 1989. Joining NATO had not been a de-mand during previous anti-Soviet rebellions in Hungary in 1956, the Prague Spring in 1968, or part of Solidarity's platform in Poland in 1981. Nor was the issue of joining NATO widely discussed in the underground literature of the op-position movements in these countries in the 1980s. It was simply beyond the scope of imagination even for anti-communist dissidents.

It also reflected a bitter lesson drawn from the failure of anti-Soviet uprisings in 1956 and 1968—namely that Western support for overcoming Europe's divide was largely rhetorical and that the West, too, had become increasingly comfort-able with the status quo in a divided Europe. Opposition strategists in Central and Eastern Europe, having concluded that they could not rely on the West for their liberation, now embraced the notion of trying to roll back communism from below. Following the Helsinki Final Act in 1975, groups like Charter 77 emerged in Czechoslovakia committed to building civil society outside of the control of the communist authorities. Polish intellectual dissidents also concluded that the overall strategic balance had cemented Europe's division and Poland's subjugation. It was the origins of what would eventually become Solidarity's main strategy—avoid directly threatening the official trappings of Soviet domination or communist rule in Poland and instead hollow out communist rule from within. Implicit in this strategy was the assumption that foreign policy issues would not be questioned lest they gave the communist authorities or Moscow a pretext to intervene.[9]

By the early 1980s the lack of any real prospect in overcoming the division of Europe and the apparent willingness of many in the West to acquiesce in this state of affairs was nevertheless leading to growing frustration in the region. As Milan Kundera wrote in a widely read essay, the tragedy of Central Europe was that it had been forgotten and "vanished from the map of the West." [10] Renewed East-West tension in the wake of the 1979 Soviet invasion of Afghanistan, the election of President Ronald Reagan, and the deployment of Euromissiles all had their echo in the region. Against this backdrop Ronald Reagan and his hard-line policies were extraordinarily popular in parts of Central and Eastern Europe—precisely because they were seen as challenging the status quo. Solidarity leaders saw a parallel between their strategy to roll back communism from below in Poland and Reagan's efforts to roll back Soviet power on the global scene. A common joke at the time was that Reagan was probably more popular in Warsaw than in any other European capital—with the exception of Thatcherite London. As Adam Michnik pointed out, Polish workers had no sympathy for Republican domestic polices. But they were pleased that Reagan was trying to change the rules of the game on Central Europe.[11]

Other Central and East European dissidents, however, were sympathetic to the anti-Yalta undertones of the peace movement and its call for the abolition of *both* alliances as a best way for their nations to regain their independence. In his book *Antipolitics*, the Hungarian writer Gyorgy Konrad blamed both superpowers for acquiescing in the existing status quo and division of the continent. The status quo in Central Europe, he argued, represented "the petrification of an exceptional state of postwar occupation." NATO and the presence of U.S. military forces in Western Europe only served to legitimate the Yalta system as much as Soviet forces and the Warsaw Pact, he claimed. His book called on Europeans in both halves of the continent to detach themselves from their respective superpowers and ask them to withdraw their troops to help create a unified Europe.[12]

These Central and East European dissidents, certainly not naïve about Soviet intentions, rejected the view that both superpowers were somehow moral equivalents. They pointed out to Western peaceniks that true peace was required both within societies between rulers and the ruled, as well as peace between states, something that existed in West European democracies but did not exist in their societies. As Vaclav Havel wrote, it felt a bit surreal to pontificate about the future of alliances and European security architecture when one was more worried about being arrested by the secret police.[13]

But they nevertheless had some sympathy for Western peace activists precisely because they were among the few circles in the West reaching out and talking about a strategy to overcome Yalta. In 1985 a group of Czechoslovak dissidents from Charter 77 issued a document called the Prague Appeal, which called on the peace movements to recognize that peace must exist not only between states but also between the state and its citizens. It said that German unification would be an important step in overcoming the continent's division — the first statement of its kind in Central Europe. But it also called for the dissolution of both the Warsaw Pact and NATO and the withdrawal of Soviet and American forces to help create a unified Europe.[14]

These debates over how best to dismantle Yalta were overtaken by the sudden collapse of communism in the fall of 1989. It took nearly everyone by surprise, including the political opposition in many of these countries. During the summer of 1988, Polish and Czech dissidents had met conspiratorially in the Tatra mountains on the Polish-Czech border near the town of Rychlebske Hory. They spent much of their time worried they would be arrested at any moment. The following summer Adam Michnik showed up in Prague as an elected member of parliament, brimming with confidence that the winds of change were blowing. He told his Czechoslovak friends that within the year they, too, would be free. No one on the Czech side believed him. But within a matter of months Hungary was opening its border to the West, the Berlin Wall was coming down, and the Velvet Revolution was taking place. By the end of the year, Vaclav Havel had gone from dissident playwright to President of Czechoslovakia.[15]

Initially, the new democratic elites of Central and Eastern Europe focused on securing democratic governance and dismantling the vestiges of communist and Soviet control. National independence was their top priority — and that meant first and foremost negotiating the withdrawal of Soviet troops from their soil and dismantling the formal structures of the Soviet imperial system: the Warsaw Pact and the Council of Mutual Economic Assistance (CMEA). Within a matter of months, Czechoslovakia and Hungary had reached agreements with Moscow on the withdrawal of Soviet troops from their soil by the end of 1991. Poland moved more slowly, both because it was relying on Moscow's support for a final settlement on its western border with a unified Germany, and because it would serve as the transit route for the withdrawal of the bulk of the Red Army from Germany as well.[16]

But Soviet troop withdrawals were only the first step. The next step was dismantling the Warsaw Pact itself. In May 1990, Jozsef Antall was elected the Prime Minister of Hungary. Antall was a schoolteacher but had been banned from teaching after his role, as a young man, in the 1956 anti-Soviet uprising. He became the curator of a small museum on the history of medicine that served as a haven for members of the political opposition. He now emerged as the leader of the Hungarian Democratic Forum and was elected Prime Minster committed to withdrawing Hungary as soon as possible from the Warsaw Pact. At the time, Moscow was still hoping to somehow preserve the Pact on a new basis, plans for which were to be discussed at a Warsaw Pact summit in Moscow in early June 1990. Antall, with Havel's support, managed to get Gorbachev at the last second to agree to simply review the future of the Pact without prejudice to the final outcome.

The new language decided nothing, but gave the Central Europeans political cover to subsequently push for more radical change. When, during the summer and fall months, Soviet draft proposals for a reform of the Warsaw Pact started to circulate, former dissidents now turned diplomats in the Czech Republic, Poland and Hungary stepped up their consultations—often relying on contacts and friendships forged in the political underground—to come up with a common front on the need to dissolve, not reform, the Pact. They formed the Visegrad group, named after the city in Hungary where they established their cooperation. In November Lech Walesa replaced Jaruzelski as President of Poland, putting former dissidents at the helms of all three countries. In January 1991, Visegrad Foreign Ministers gathered in Budapest to publicly announce their desire to dissolve the Warsaw Pact. When the Visegrad heads of state met in early February, they were publicly joined by Romania and Bulgaria. Moscow was now confronted with a unanimous view among its former allies.

Recognizing the handwriting on the wall, Gorbachev agreed to dissolve the integrated military structure of the Pact while still hoping to preserve it as a political entity. This step was taken in Budapest in late February 1991. Central and East European participants reported that several of the Soviet generals actually had tears in their eyes during the session. The Soviet delegation did not attend the press conference and at one point suggested that the proceedings not be published.[17] But Moscow had not yet fully given up on keeping these countries in their orbit. Soviet Foreign Minister Bessmertnykh told his colleagues that while Moscow had agreed to dissolve the Pact, it would not tolerate these countries joining either the European Community (EC) or NATO. Between December 1990 and March 1991, the Soviets tabled drafts of new bilateral treaties with these countries that contained clauses not to join new alliances, embark on military or intelligence cooperation, or allow the deployment of foreign troops or transit rights by third parties.[18] They refused, with the exception of Romania.

On July 1, Czechoslovak President Vaclav Havel presided over the final dissolution of the Warsaw Pact in Prague. Soviet Vice President Gennady Yanayev called for NATO to follow and dissolve itself as well. But the final communiqué issued by the Pact instead simply called for a "transition to all-European structures." The Central and East Europeans refused to say anything that implied that NATO should follow suit. At a news conference, Havel noted the symbolism of signing the Pact's death warrant in Czechoslovakia: "Prague, once the victim of the Warsaw Pact, has become the city where the Warsaw Pact is meeting its end as an instrument of the Cold War." In the words of Jozsef Antall: "A bad marriage has ended, now friendship can begin."[19] Yalta was dead. The question now was, what would replace it?

3. ALIGNING WITH THE WEST

Having dismantled the pillars of past Soviet rule, these countries now turned to the goal of locking in and consolidating their newly won freedom and independence. Rejoining the West had been an important *leitmotif* of the revolutions of 1989. The institutions these countries initially turned to in order to achieve that goal were not NATO, but the Organization for Security and Cooperation in Europe (OSCE) and the European Union (EU).[20] The OSCE was the one institution to which these countries already belonged. It also had a strong moral standing in Central and Eastern Europe given the role the Helsinki Final Act had played in defending human rights and inspiring opposition to communism. And it espoused the vision of a pan-European peace order uniting both halves of Europe that these countries were looking for.

In the spring of 1990, Czechoslovak Foreign Minister Jiri Dienstbier proposed the creation of an OSCE-based "European Security Commission" that would eventually replace NATO and the Warsaw Pact.[21] Speaking at the Council of Europe that May, Havel himself echoed the same message, noting that while NATO had a better chance than the Warsaw Pact to become the core of a new European security order, it, too, needed to change everything from its doctrine to its name.[22] In justifying his proposal in an article, Dienstbier argued that simply switching membership in the Warsaw Pact for membership in NATO would be the wrong approach. "Replacing previous membership in the Soviet sphere of influence with integration into another sphere of influence would hardly improve the security situation of Central Europe."[23]

Such proposals clearly went too far for many in the West, as well as in Central and Eastern Europe. Western governments, including the United States, viewed the OSCE as a complement to NATO, not an institution that would supplant it.[24] But they, too, were looking to the OSCE as a lead institution for addressing the security problems in the eastern half of the continent and for putting the two halves of Europe back together. The OSCE summit in Paris in November 1990 not only issued the "Charter of Paris," reflecting a vision of a new, democratic and undivided Europe, but also took a number of steps to institutionalize the OSCE as a forum for political dialogue between the two halves of Europe.[25] But it quickly proved unrealistic to expect an institution armed with little more than moral suasion and few resources or capabilities at its disposal to provide security to the eastern half of the continent or to carry the burden of overcoming Europe's Cold War divide.

If the OSCE was too weak, the EU was too slow. The initial hopes of many Central and East Europeans in the early 1990s that the EU would rapidly open its political and economic doors to embrace them were quickly dashed. In early 1990 the EU negotiated new "Europe Agreements," which provided limited market access as well as political consultations for these countries, but carefully avoided any hard commitments to membership.[26] There were differences within the EU on whether the priority should be "deepening" integration in Western Europe or "broadening" to embrace Central and Eastern Europe. The forces in favor of deepening were led by France, where President François Mitterrand spoke of a process to integrate these countries into the EU that could take "decades."[27] While Brussels was also promising to reinvigorate the Western European Union (WEU) as a potential European-only defense arm, the Central and East Europeans soon concluded that relying on the EU as the primary framework for Western integration and to address their security needs was not going to work.

There were two other problems with the EU. One was its failure in Bosnia where the EU had stumbled in trying to play a lead role in stemming the conflict after war broke out in the spring and summer of 1991. The other problem with the EU was that it did not involve the Americans. The Central and East Europeans trusted the United States. They were among the most pro-American countries in Europe in spite of—or perhaps because of—decades of communism. They did not necessarily trust the major European powers with which they had their own mixed histories. Their goal was to get the Russians out and the Americans in.

That was not what the EU had on offer. Indeed, not all West Europeans even shared that goal. When senior French diplomats came to Paris in the spring of 1991 to prepare a joint conference between Presidents Havel and Mitterrand, the divergence in their thinking became apparent. As one senior Czechoslovak official put it: "I soon realized that the French wanted the Americans out and the Russians in—and we wanted it the other way around." In his speech at the conference, Havel noted in Mitterrand's presence that it was crucial that the link between North America and Europe remain in the future.[28]

That left NATO. It had been demonized for decades by communist propaganda as the citadel of American imperialism and aggression. Almost none of the new democratic elites knew much about it or had ever stepped foot in NATO headquarters. It was mysterious if not forbidden fruit. The Central and East Europeans nevertheless gravitated toward it for a mix of reasons. In some cases, it was fear of Russia reasserting its influence. For others it was as much about involving the Americans in Central Europe to balance other European powers, and in particular, a unified Germany.[29] Above all, it was about having a security anchor to help consolidate a pro-Western democratic orientation in what historically had been a rough geopolitical neighborhood. It reflected a desire to be part of the one institution that had the military muscle to provide real security in a pinch.

I was exposed to Central and East European thinking on these issues as part of a team of RAND experts invited to assist these countries in the early 1990s. Along with the National Defense University (NDU), RAND was among the first western think tanks on the ground in the region helping these new democratic governments establish civilian control over the military and develop new national security strategies. In June 1990, RAND co-hosted the first of several workshops in the region, starting with the Polish Ministry of Defense in Warsaw—the first of its kind. Soviet troops were still in Poland but the new Solidarity-led government had started to reach out to the U.S. The conference took place in the hall where the Warsaw Pact had been established. Sitting in chairs once occupied by the likes of former Soviet communist party head Leonid Brezhnev, and where Soviet marshals had deliberated on Warsaw Pact plans to invade Western Europe, one could not help but feel a sense of history.

The American delegation included the then Commander-in-Chief of U.S. Forces in Europe, Air Force General James McCarthy, and Army Lieutenant General John Shalikashvilli, who would go on to become NATO's Supreme Allied Commander—Europe (SACEUR) and, subsequently, President Clinton's Chairman of the Joint Chiefs of Staff. It was the first time McCarthy had been east of the Iron Curtain, while it was the Polish-born Shalikashvilli's first trip back to Poland since his childhood. The Polish delegation contained an uneasy mix of former Solidarity activists and old guard Soviet-trained generals. But the new tone in Polish foreign policy was soon apparent. We sat there in amazement as former Solidarity dissidents-turned-diplomats explained how they had always shared the goals and values the West had fought for in the Cold War—and asked whether it might be possible to join the institution created to defend them: NATO.

During a panel discussion I chaired, a Polish general stood up to ask whether it was possible for U.S. forces to be stationed on Polish soil to help provide them with security. I looked at General Shalikashvilli who was sitting next to me on the panel. Neither of us knew what to say. In the car on the way back to the hotel a number of the American participants got into a heated argument over the issue of possible Polish membership in NATO. The debate among the Americans continued at the bar. It was the first time I met several individuals— Eric Edelman and Dan Fried—who would become close colleagues when I joined the State Department seven years later. That evening we stayed up late with our new Polish friends drinking vodka and trying to explain a RAND briefing on how the U.S. might help secure Central Europe's newly won freedom by defending Poland.[30]

As the final negotiations on the dissolution of the Warsaw Pact were moving forward in the spring of 1991, these countries stepped up their official efforts to reach out to NATO. Initially they sought only closer ties with the Alliance, not membership. That was what the Alliance had to offer and was all they dared to hope for. Already in June 1990 the Alliance had established liaison relationships with the former members of the Warsaw Pact. But given the insecurity they felt, the leap from wanting to have closer ties with NATO to actually becoming a member of the Alliance was not huge. Initially, it was the Hungarians under Prime Minister Jozsef Antall who were in the lead in articulating their desire to develop the closest possible relationship with NATO. But the Czechs were not far behind. In late 1990 and early 1991, a number of President Havel's close advisors—Michael Zantovsky, Alexandr Vondra, and Karel Schwarzenberg—began to argue in favor of abandoning Dienstbier's OSCE-based scheme and embracing NATO instead.

In February 1991, Vondra, Havel's chief foreign policy advisor at the time, told a visiting Political Committee delegation from NATO that the OSCE was not going to be enough and that Prague was looking for a security guarantee. He argued that the deteriorating situation in the Balkans and the Persian Gulf, as well as the rise of nationalism in the Balkans and elsewhere, were all signs of growing instability that could affect Czechoslovakia. Neutrality was not an option and it had become clear that EU membership was not in the cards either. He suggested that NATO consider some kind of special treaty or declaration with Czechoslovakia to provide that guarantee. The reaction was not enthusiastic. As Jiri Dienstbier, who was also in the meeting, recalled in his memoirs: "The guests raised the question that would make the issue of the expansion of the Atlantic Alliance so problematic for years to come: how would the Soviet Union accept any kind of special agreement between NATO and Central European countries?" Vondra responded by arguing that NATO should say that such a step was designed to promote stability and not aimed against anyone.[31]

Dienstbier made the same proposal to NATO Secretary General Manfred Woerner in late February while in Brussels to prepare Havel's upcoming trip to NATO headquarters. But Woerner told him that NATO would not agree because of the likely Soviet reaction. Therefore, when Havel visited the Alliance in early March, the first head of state from a Central and East European state to do so, he was careful not to push the envelope too far. He opened his remarks to the NATO ambassadors by apologizing for the lies that his predecessors had spread about the Alliance during the Cold War and thanking the Alliance for its role in saving Europe from totalitarianism. But he also warned that Czechoslovakia and the other countries were in danger of sliding into a security vacuum that could jeopardize the new democracies of the region and that the dangers his country faced were common threats shared by all those around the table.

"We know that for many different reasons we cannot become full members of NATO at present," Havel continued. "At the same time, however, we feel that an alliance of countries united by a commitment to the ideal of freedom and democracy should not remain permanently closed to neighboring countries which are pursuing the same goals. History has taught us that certain values are indivisible: if they are threatened in one place, they are directly or indirectly threatened everywhere." In the meantime, he concluded, "we would welcome it if a lasting system could be set up soon for cooperation and exchange of information between Czechoslovakia and NATO. We wish to intensify our dialogue on security matters."[32] The issue was now openly on the table.

Poland was paradoxically still the most cautious of the three Visegrad countries in articulating its NATO aspirations. While Solidarity had been the first democratic opposition movement to come to power in the region, it had agreed to leave the Presidency and the key ministries handling internal and external security in communist hands so as not to provoke Moscow. While such arrangements were quickly overtaken by events, they nevertheless remained intact and slowed down Poland's articulation of its desire to build closer ties with NATO. Warsaw also felt obliged to seek Moscow's support during the negotiation on German unification until it was sure that the Oder-Neisse border issue had been resolved once and for all. Poland was also a key transit route for withdrawing the Red Army from Germany as well as the sizeable number of Soviet forces on its territory. Moscow had withdrawn its troops from Hungary and Czechoslovakia by the end of 1991, but the final units of the Red Army did not leave Poland until September 1993. Although Walesa had replaced Jaruzelski as the elected President of Poland in December 1990, during the spring of 1991 the official Polish position continued to be in favor of neutrality, which Walesa and Skubiszewski both stated during the Polish President's trip to Washington, D.C. in the spring.[33] One month later he reiterated: "Poland is not putting itself forward as a candidate for NATO membership," emphasizing that Warsaw only wished to have closer contacts with the Alliance.[34]

But in the spring of 1991 the first political voice, the right-wing Center Alliance, an opposition party, called for Polish membership in NATO. That summer and fall, a group of post-Solidarity intellectuals, frustrated by what they viewed as the government's timidity on the NATO question, established the Atlantic Club to lobby more actively for Polish membership in the Alliance. In January 1992, a new center-right Polish government under Prime Minister Jan Olszewski came to power and took a clear stance in favor of full NATO membership. But in March Walesa was still flirting publicly with ideas such as NATO-II or "NATO-bis" in which the Central and East European states would organize themselves as a group of countries with a special and close relationship with, but not membership in the Alliance.

Two factors now pushed the Central and East Europeans over the threshold to push for full NATO membership. One was the war in Bosnia, which broke out in the summer of 1991 and immediately sent reverberations across the continent. In Central and Eastern Europe it served as a reminder that Europe's nationalistic demons were still alive in the post-communist world. While the Balkans certainly had their own special circumstances, many Central and East European leaders looked at what Milosevic was doing and recognized it as the kind of manipulated nationalism they knew from their own histories. They knew that the danger of what the Hungarian writer Gyorgy Konrad called a new "ethnic Cold War" existed in their region as well. "Yugoslavia is a miniature central Europe," Adam Michnik wrote. "What is happening in the Balkans could be a warning shot for it could happen here. We have the same psychological makeup, only our traditions and ethnic situation are somewhat different."[35] This only reinforced the Central and East Europeans to anchor their fledgling democracies firmly in the West.

The other factor was the aborted coup by Soviet hard liners in Moscow in the summer of 1991. On August 19, 1991 Russia awoke to hear on the music of Chopin and Tchaikovsky on the airwaves, the classic harbinger of grave news in the USSR. An announcement followed that President Mikhail Gorbachev was sick and unable to perform his duties and that a special committee, called the Committee for the State of Emergency, had assumed power. At the time, Boris Yeltsin was President of the Russian Federation, one of the USSR's 15 republics, and involved in his own power struggle with the Soviet President. Yeltsin appeared in front of the Russian White House to declare the ouster unconstitutional and called for a general strike. He then proceeded to go outside and climb up on a Russian tank to show his defiance. That picture would make history. It signaled the beginning of the end of the failed coup and Yeltsin's political ascendancy as a protector of Russian democracy.[36]

The aborted coup in Moscow affected Central and East European thinking in two ways. The initial announcement of the coup had sent shivers down the spines of many in the region and reminded them of how vulnerable their newly won freedom and independence might be. Central and East European leaders had immediately consulted among themselves and requested clear signals of support from both Washington and NATO headquarters in Brussels. While many Western officials considered the language of the U.S. and NATO response strong, it only reminded the Central and East Europeans how vulnerable they were and that that they did not have any meaningful security guarantees. Having close ties with NATO in a pinch, they concluded, meant little. They decided they could not afford to run that risk again.

Equally important, the failed coup set into motion a chain of events culminating in the USSR's collapse by year's end, when Mikhail Gorbachev presided over the lowering of the hammer and sickle in the Kremlin and stepped down as Soviet President. The dissolution of the Soviet Union was a geopolitical earthquake as profound as the collapse of the Soviet empire in Central and Eastern Europe had been two years earlier. Both the outer and the inner Soviet empires were now gone. Russian military power would be withdrawn another 1,000 kilometers eastward. A second band of newly independent states would now emerge between NATO and Russia. It gave these countries new geopolitical room for maneuver. As Polish Foreign Minister Skubiszewski put it: "It took the 1991 August coup in Moscow and the break-up of the Soviet Union—events that came out of the blue and had nothing to do with Poland—to open up certain chances."[37]

At a NATO summit in Rome in November 1991, the Alliance unveiled its own post–Cold War new look by issuing a new strategic concept and by launching the North Atlantic Cooperation Council (NACC) to reach out to the countries of the former Soviet bloc. But the collapse of the Soviet Union quickly outpaced these changes as well. The Alliance's new strategic concept was drawn up for a world in which the USSR still existed and in which one of NATO's primary roles was to deter a residual Soviet threat. Similarly, the NACC was premised on the assumption that the countries of Central and Eastern Europe would be content with closer institutional cooperation with NATO short of membership.

Both were soon overtaken by events. The collapse of the USSR gave the countries of Central and Eastern Europe new leeway and emboldened them to put their NATO aspirations directly on the table. Meeting in Prague on May 6, 1992, Czech President Vaclav Havel, Polish President Lech Walesa and Hungarian Prime Minister Jozsef Antall now declared that their goal was actual full-fledged membership in NATO.[38] By the end of the year that goal of full NATO membership was written into the official national security strategies of the Czech Republic, Hungary, and Poland. Their quest for NATO was now official.

By the spring of 1992, the debate over NATO enlargement was starting to bubble up in the public domain. Testifying before the Polish Senate in February 1992, former National Security Advisor Zbigniew Brzezinski suggested that the question of Poland's eventual membership in NATO "now needs to be put officially on the table."[39] At a conference in Warsaw one month later, Secretary General Woerner acknowledged that while enlargement was not now on the Alliance's agenda, there was no reason why it could not be at some point in the future.[40] At the spring NATO Ministerial in June in Oslo, Deputy Secretary of State Larry Eagleburger noted that at some point NATO might have to expand, but made it clear that this issue was not part of the current agenda.[41]

In the run-up to what would become George Bush's final trip to Poland and Central and Eastern Europe as President, Administration officials debated whether or not the President should open his speech with a perspective on eventual NATO enlargement. Language was drafted for a speech the President would give in Warsaw's Castle Square on July 5, 1992.[42] But Bush's key advisors could not agree and the language was never used. Instead, the issue of whether or not to enlarge NATO to Central and Eastern Europe would be left to the next President of the United States, Bill Clinton.

Book II

THE DEBATE BEGINS

NATO enlargement was undoubtedly one of the farthest things from Bill Clinton's mind as he was inaugurated President of the United States on January 20, 1993. The governor of the small southern state of Arkansas, he had been elected on an agenda of domestic renewal after the end of the Cold War. Throughout the Presidential campaign, Clinton had focused like a laser beam on U.S. domestic weaknesses. "Putting People First" was his campaign slogan. The campaign's infamous battle cry, "It's the economy stupid!" was, at least in part, a criticism of President George Bush's neglect of domestic issues and his focus on international affairs. Having won the Cold War, America seemed to be looking inward and ready to retreat from its international commitments, including in Europe.

If Europe was not a top priority when President Clinton assumed office, it soon became one. By the end of the President's first year in power the issue of the continent's future was front and center on the Administration's agenda. Bloodshed in the Balkans, growing instability in Russia, and the clear desire of the countries of Central and Eastern Europe to anchor themselves to the West forced the Administration to confront some tough questions: what was America's post–Cold War vision of Europe and the trans-Atlantic relationship? Were the U.S. and its allies prepared to go to war to stop ethnic cleansing in Bosnia? Was Washington willing to extend security guarantees to stabilize Central and

Eastern Europe? How could the Administration reconcile its desire to secure Central and Eastern Europe with supporting democratic reform in Russia? Perhaps most important, what was NATO's purpose in a world where communism no longer existed and Russia was increasingly a partner and not an adversary?

These issues led to a far-reaching debate within the ranks of the Administration. Its outcome was a set of policy decisions that, over the President's two terms in office, led to some of the most far-reaching changes in the Atlantic Alliance since its founding more than forty years earlier. Rather than scale back the U.S. commitment to and engagement in Europe, the Administration extended NATO's umbrella over Central and Eastern Europe—initially to the Czech Republic, Hungary, and Poland but with the perspective of eventually covering all countries from the Baltic to the Black Sea—and reached out to build a new cooperative relationship with Russia, the Alliance's former adversary.

In parallel to opening NATO's door to Central and Eastern Europe, Washington and its allies updated the Alliance's mission to embrace the security of the continent as a whole along with the need to address new threats that could come from beyond member's immediate borders. Initially created as an Alliance between North America and Western Europe to deter the Soviet Union, NATO was being transformed into an alliance committed to building an undivided, democratic and secure Europe and protecting its members from the new threats of the post-Cold Ear era. The process of enlarging NATO's membership and missions culminated at the Alliance's fiftieth anniversary summit in the spring of 1999. In March the first former Warsaw Pact countries—Poland, the Czech Republic, and Hungary—acceded to the Alliance. That same month, NATO launched its air campaign in Kosovo and, at the Washington summit, adopted a strategic concept that set a new strategic direction by pointing to the need for the Alliance to confront new threats beyond its borders. Alliance leaders set a simple benchmark for the future: NATO must be as effective in dealing with future threats as it was in meeting the Soviet threat during the Cold War.

Enlarging and modernizing NATO was not part of a preexisting grand design President Clinton and his national security team harbored when they entered office in 1993. Although the President had spoken of the need to update America's key alliances during the campaign, few if any of Clinton's top aides were focused on the issue or had a clear vision or strategy for NATO's future, and the intellectual, political, and diplomatic path to these decisions were neither easy nor without controversy. Recasting NATO involved major, and at times dramatic, fights and negotiations with the Russians, our European allies, and within the U.S. where it produced a passionate debate over what the Alliance was for in the post–Cold War world. While it would take a number of years for the Administration's policies to be fully developed, diplomatically implemented, and politically ratified by the U.S. Senate, the origins of those policies can be traced back to the debate that took place within the Administration during Clinton's first year in office.

1. RUSSIA FIRST

During his Presidential campaign, Clinton had singled out two specific areas of President Bush's European policy for criticism: Russia and Bosnia. Concerning Russia he had accused Bush of being too timid in supporting reform and squandering a historic opportunity. In office, the new President moved to turn that rhetoric into reality. "Upon his election, President Clinton decided that we should make an early, all-out effort to engage Russia's reformers and support their efforts," wrote Warren Christopher after he left the State Department. "Our assessment was that America's national interest lay squarely in supporting the process of reform—and that this was the key payoff of the end of the Cold War."[1] Speaking in Chicago in mid-March 1993, Christopher described supporting Russia's transition to democracy as the "greatest security challenge of our time." If the great challenge after World War II had been integrating Germany into the West, he continued, the challenge facing the United States after the end of the Cold War was consolidating Russia's democratic transition and its eventual integration into the Western community of nation states.[2]

At a time when the President was devoting the majority of his time to domestic issues, Russia stood out as the Administration's top foreign policy priority—and an area where Clinton was directly and personally involved. His first trip out of the country was to meet Yeltsin in Vancouver in April 1993. The trip's goal, the President stated, was to establish a "strategic alliance" with Russian reformers. "Nothing could contribute more to global freedom, security and prosperity than the peaceful progression of Russia's rebirth."[3] To back that up, the President fought—and won—an early battle on Capitol Hill to get a $1.6 billion package of assistance for the struggling Russian economy. At Vancouver, the two Presidents established the Gore-Chernomyrdin Commission (GCC) to develop across-the-board American support for Russia's democratic transformation. The scope and intensity of the effort were without precedent in U.S.-Russian relations.[4]

The architect of the Administration's Russia policy was Strobe Talbott, Ambassador-at-Large for the Newly Independent States (NIS). Clinton and Talbott were friends from their student days at Oxford where they shared a strong interest in Russia. Talbott had gone on to a successful journalist career with *Time* magazine, publishing several influential books on Russia and arms control issues. He had also lived in and traveled throughout Central and Eastern Europe. His first overseas assignment as a journalist was actually in the Balkans, an experience that he would draw on as the Administration wrestled with Bosnia and Kosovo in the years ahead. Both during the campaign and in the early months of the Administration, his expertise, zeal, and personal relationship with the President made him a driving force, making Russia the President's top priority at a time when reform in Moscow seemed to hang in the balance.

On Russia, there was a strategy, an architect and, most importantly, a Presidential commitment. There was nothing similar when it came to Europe and NATO. Asked by Senator Joseph Lieberman (D-CT) in his confirmation hearings in January 1993 about his vision for NATO's future, Representative Les Aspin (D-WI), Clinton's nominee for Secretary of Defense, candidly responded that this was "a very, very important and critical question for which I have no immediate answer."[5]

The European security issue where Clinton had staked out a clear public position was Bosnia. In the summer of 1992, Americans and Europeans woke up to the worst fighting in Europe in forty years. Horrors that most Europeans believed were gone forever returned as the world saw shocking film of emaciated prisoners in Bosnia looking through barbed wire fences—scenes reminiscent of Nazi concentration camps from World War II. An ugly new phrase entered the modern English political vernacular: ethnic cleansing. It was, in Richard Holbrooke's words, "the greatest collective security failure of the West since the 1930s."[6]

During the campaign, Clinton had accused President Bush of not standing up to aggression in Bosnia and being too timid in defending democratic values.[7] In office, the Administration had to turn those bold words into policy. The President asked his national security team to review all policy options, including those previously ruled out of bounds by his predecessor. But the Clinton team soon found itself beset by the same divisions that had paralyzed the Bush Administration. Bosnia was what Secretary Christopher called "the problem from hell." The Administration was ambivalent about the diplomatic approach on the table, the Vance-Owen Plan, which it believed to be unenforceable and morally flawed.[8] But it was unable to formulate a better alternative allies would support. Whereas Clinton's neo-Wilsonian National Security Advisor Tony Lake argued for intervention, Secretary of Defense Aspin and the Chairman of the Joint Chiefs of Staff, Colin Powell—a Bush Administration holdover— wanted to keep the United States' military role as limited as possible.[9]

As the spring unfolded, the violence in Bosnia escalated and the pressure on the President to "do something" increased. More and more, White House meetings ranged beyond the specifics of Bosnia policy and spilled over into a broader debate about the use of force and the U.S. role in Europe and beyond. One high-ranking official noted at the time: "It was group therapy—an existential debate over what is the role of America, etc."[10] Powell was less charitable. These initial meetings, he subsequently wrote, "continued to meander like graduate-student bull sessions or the think tank seminars in which many of my new colleagues had spent the last twelve years while their party was out of power."[11]

On May 1, 1993, Clinton decided to support what his advisors had dubbed the "lift and strike" option—i.e., a plan to lift the arms embargo to allow the Bosnians to arm and defend themselves while using Western air power to deter the Serbs from trying to take military advantage of Bosnia's vulnerabilities in the short-term. The President and his advisors knew that European allies strongly opposed this proposal, but hoped that the public outrage over recent Serbian massacres along with the Bosnian Serb rejection of the Vance-Owen mediating effort might permit Washington to sell a more aggressive policy. But the President was not yet prepared to put his full authority and that of the United States on the line. Instead, Christopher was asked to go to Europe to sound out the allies on the approach: "You've been a great lawyer and advocate all these years," he told Christopher, "now you've really got your work cut out for you."[12]

Christopher's trip to Europe was a failure. There were no takers among the allies who quickly sensed that the Administration's support for its own initiative was half-hearted. Ray Seitz, U.S. Ambassador in London, described Christopher's meeting with British Prime Minister John Major, Foreign Secretary Douglas Hurd and Defense Secretary Malcolm Rifkind:

> Christopher pulled out his papers, tapped them carefully into order and started to lay out the American proposal. His words had all the verve of a solicitor going over a conveyance deed. I watched the faces of the three ministers opposite me, trying to catch the little flickers of disbelief as the plan unfolded. . . . When the presentation was over, the British sat in silence. There was some clearing of throats and a few sideways glances. 'Well, ah, yes . . . ' Major, Hurd and Rifkind each asked two or three what-if questions. There were long pauses. Christopher had no real answers. After a couple of sterile hours, the meeting adjourned. . . . The atmosphere was downbeat and awkward. I suggested to the Prime Minister that he take Christopher aside and tell him straight that, leaving apart the wisdom of the American plan, he couldn't possibly deliver his skeptical cabinet to such a risky proposal. It was, in the jargon, a non-starter. This the Prime Minister proceeded to do.[13]

Christopher returned from the trip, as one colleague put it, with "bullet holes all over him."[14] He reported that the only way to get the allies to agree with Washington's preference was to use "the raw power approach." Not even the most vocal supporters of intervention in the Administration favored that. U.S. policy now shifted from intervention to containment—the latter being the European preference. The trip's failure would contribute to the impression that the President was not fully engaged on foreign policy issues, that the Administration did not have a coherent European policy and, worst of all, that it could be rolled and would back down if faced with strong opposition. In late

May, an unnamed senior Administration official, soon identified as Undersecretary of State Peter Tarnoff, defended U.S. policy on Bosnia by stating that the U.S. was not inclined to get involved in every conflict in Europe, a fact America's allies would have to get used to. Christopher immediately moved to counter the impression that the Administration was disengaging from Europe.[15] But commentators were starting to question America's staying power in Europe and NATO's future. James Chace, author of a prominent biography of Dean Acheson and NATO's origins, claimed in *The New York Times* that "the dominant fact of the Administration's foreign policy so far is the collapse of the Western alliance.[16]

The NATO enlargement issue first appeared on Bill Clinton's radar screen in conjunction with the budding crisis over Bosnia and growing doubts about the Alliance's future. When he attended the opening of the Holocaust Museum in Washington in late April 1993, the parallel between the Holocaust and the ethnic slaughter in Bosnia was on everyone's mind. After the Second World War, a generation of Western leaders had said "Never again!" pledging that they would never again stand aside as a people was singled out for destruction on racial or religious grounds. At the dedication ceremony of the museum, Elie Wiesel turned to Clinton and said: "Mr. President, I cannot not tell you something. I have been in the former Yugoslavia last fall. I cannot sleep remembering what I have seen. As a Jew, I am saying that we must do something to stop the killing in that country. Something, anything must be done to stop the bloodshed there. Mr. President, it will not stop unless we stop it."[17]

Many of the heads of state of Central and Eastern Europe were in town. The Holocaust had also taken place on their soil and they were there, too, to mark the opening of the museum. The Museum's opening served as a potent reminder of Europe's past demons and the dilemma of being smaller nations located between Germany and Russia. It only added to the sense of urgency these leaders felt in terms of anchoring their countries to the West.[18] While the museum opening was a private event, many Central and East European leaders had asked to see the new American President. Few if any had established meaningful high-level contacts with the incoming Administration.

Over the course of the next two days the President met the leaders of Poland, the Czech Republic and Hungary—Lech Walesa, Vaclav Havel, and Arpad Goncz respectively. It was their first and perhaps best chance to make their case on NATO enlargement. They had a common view. Their countries were vulnerable. They still feared Russia. They did not trust the major West European powers. They trusted America. They wanted to join NATO to ensure that their countries would never again fall victim to the twin evils of nationalism and geopolitics that had produced so much tragedy in their part of Europe—and that were rearing their ugly heads in the Balkans.

The White House, as often was the case in the early months of the Administration, was running notoriously behind schedule—on so-called

"Clinton time." When the leaders finally did get to see the President, they put diplomatic niceties aside and underscored the same message: they wanted to join the West. Havel was the first to meet with Clinton on April 20. "Our main problem is that we feel as if we are living in a vacuum," he told Clinton. "That is why we want to join NATO. In addition, in our values and spirit, we are part of Western Europe." All of Central Europe was debating how best to integrate with the West, he continued. "The issue is not that we are faced with imminent threats. Rather, we are in the process of undergoing an image transformation — a reshaping of our identity." By securing democracy in Central Europe, Havel concluded, the West would set a powerful precedent that would allow reform to spread eastward. "Entry into NATO and the EC is central to expanding democracy, not just to Central Europe, but also to the NIS."[19]

The next day Walesa was blunter. "We are all afraid of Russia," he told the President. At times, Walesa continued, he was afraid to turn on the radio for fear of what the most recent news from Moscow might be. "It is important to remember that this is the first time in history that the Soviet army has withdrawn from territory peacefully," Walesa continued, "If Russia again adopts an aggressive foreign policy, that aggression will be directed against Poland and Ukraine." Poland was also scared, he continued, "by the prospect of having a powerful Germany on one side and a powerful Russia on the other." It was an illusion to think that the West could reform Russia without stabilizing and integrating Central Europe first. Success in Central and Eastern Europe would spread eastward, Walesa insisted, not the other way around. The problem was that Western Europe was not willing to open its doors to Central and Eastern Europe. The West, Walesa argued, had achieved "the biggest victory in history" by winning the Cold War, "but we are not capitalizing on it. Only the United States could change that," he concluded.[20]

None of the delegations came away from those meetings sensing they had a major impact on the President's thinking. But they had. Afterward, the President would turn to his National Security Advisor, Tony Lake, and comment on how impressed he was by their desire and commitment to join NATO. According to Lake, President Clinton asked: "Tony, why can't we do this?"[21] As Sandy Berger, Lake's Deputy at the time and eventual successor as National Security Advisor recalled: "The issue of enlargement was first sharply posed to the President during the opening of the Holocaust Museum in April 1993. Both Havel and Walesa took the President aside and made a very strong pitch for the opening and enlargement of NATO to their countries. Today we think of both the EU and NATO as magnets for these countries. At that time, however, there was only one magnet for them — the NATO magnet. It was the number one, two and three priority of all of these governments. Being in NATO was not only a security issue for them; it was also about being part of the West. That began the discussion."[22]

The President would often refer back to the strong and positive impression these Central and East European leaders had made on him. Asked in mid-June whether NATO's inability to stop the bloodshed in Bosnia hadn't shown that the Alliance was obsolete, Clinton responded that his meeting with the Central and East European Presidents had given him "the clearest example I know . . . that NATO is not dead." He added: "When they came here a few weeks ago for the Holocaust dedication, every one of those Presidents said that their number one priority was to get into NATO. They know it will provide a security umbrella for the people who are members."[23] Shortly thereafter the new Dutch Ambassador to Washington, Adriaan Jacobovits, presented his credentials to the President. He told Jacobovits that he had been thinking about the security of Central and Eastern Europe ever since these leaders raised NATO expansion with him at the Holocaust Memorial Museum opening. He admitted that U.S. policy was not yet formed but that this was an issue he was interested in actively pursuing.[24]

President Clinton did not decide to enlarge NATO in April 1993. But he displayed a positive predisposition and an open mind. "It was not so much a policy as an attitude," as Lake subsequently put it. NATO enlargement resonated with two of Clinton's core convictions—a commitment to expand and consolidate democracy and his belief in the importance of modernizing America's alliances in a globalized world. As a "New Democrat," Clinton believed expanding democracy should be a key foreign policy priority—a position Lake elevated to a central tenant of the Administration's foreign policy in the fall of 1993.[25] Clinton frequently talked to visitors about the unique historical chance to build a Europe that was democratic, secure, and undivided. Bringing the eastern half of the continent into the institutions that had created peace and prosperity in the western half of the continent, including NATO, flowed from this vision.

Clinton also saw NATO enlargement as a way to re-anchor the U.S. in a new partnership with the old continent for the future. He was not wedded to the traditional theology of the trans-Atlantic relationship and at times impatient with the advice he received from traditional NATO hands whose cautious views on Alliance reform had been shaped by the Cold War. The President wanted to update and modernize NATO to assume new roles that the American public could relate to and support, thereby insuring its future relevance. Using NATO to help consolidate democracy and a new peace in Central and Eastern Europe was one of those. Stopping ethnic conflict beyond the Alliance's borders was another. Toward the end of his term, the President increasingly pointed to the growing threat posed by weapons of mass destruction as well as terrorism as a challenge that NATO had to start to confront as well. In short, Clinton saw an enlarged and modernized NATO as the natural adaptation of the Alliance to a more globalized world in which the United States and Europe formed a natural coalition to meet these new threats. Locking in peace and stability in Europe once and for all would allow the U.S. to focus its attention on other issues and areas of the world knowing the continent was secure and with a greater likelihood that European allies would now be willing to take on new responsibilities further afield. The President's thinking was often well beyond the conventional wisdom of experts in or outside the government. As Tony Lake put it to his staff in a meeting during Clinton's early months in office: "He thinks differently than you" on these issues.

Unlike many conservatives, however, Clinton did not back NATO enlargement as part of a policy of neo-containment toward Russia. On the contrary, building a new cooperative relationship with a democratic Russia remained a leitmotif for him throughout his tenure in the Oval Office. While he certainly recognized the potential for Russian reform to fail, he did not consider Russia a near-term military threat and remained firmly committed to supporting democratic reform in Moscow throughout his years in office. Assisting Central and Eastern Europe on the one hand and Moscow on the other was not something he viewed in zero-sum terms. Instead, he saw them as parallel tracks in an effort to build a unified Europe that could eventually include Russia as well. And he wanted a strategy that would allow the Alliance to enlarge to consolidate democracy on the continent, support democratic reform in Moscow, and lay the basis for addressing the new threats of the post–Cold War world.

Clinton's views on NATO enlargement were also shaped by the broader political battle in the U.S. over the future of American foreign policy. He had come to power at a time when the pressures on the U.S. to scale back its international commitments were considerable, and he considered NATO enlargement a litmus test of whether the U.S. would remain internationally engaged and defeat the isolationist and unilateralist sentiments that were emerging in the U.S. Meeting with Italian Prime Minister Carlo Ciampi in the White House Oval Office on September 17, Clinton told him: "The U.S. cannot signal a withdrawal from Europe. NATO looking eastward will help explain the need for NATO to our domestic electorates. I believe that the U.S. must lead, but we must do so by reasoning with our allies and finding a common position," he told Ciampi. "Because of our economic problems, a peculiar isolationist strain is emerging in the U.S." He was determined to fight it. "We have learned the hard lessons from the 1920s and '30s. Others in the U.S. say that we should go it alone and lead through unilateral actions. But this will hurt NATO, the UN and other institutions. The challenge is for me to sell to our people and to Congress the need for our engagement in the world. The U.S. will lead, but through a partnership. This is a very big challenge. We need a common position at the NATO summit."[26]

Critics would claim that Clinton's support for NATO enlargement was driven by the domestic desire to court voters of Central and East European origins. But there is little hard evidence that such considerations were either the catalyst or the driving force in his thinking. The President's interest in enlargement came early in his first term before reelection was on the horizon. Neither of Clinton's two key pollsters during this period—Stan Greenberg and Dick Morris—conducted polling on NATO enlargement.[27] Both of Clinton's two national security advisors, Tony Lake and Sandy Berger, insist that political considerations were not central in this decision. "What drove this was the President's sense of the transformation of Europe and the integration of Central Europe into the West—his vision of the opportunity to create for the first time in history a Europe that was free, democratic and secure," Berger claimed. "NATO enlargement would have happened had there not been one ethnic American of Central and East European origin in the Midwest."[28]

But politics were not completely absent in the debate either. As Lake later put it: "The politics of NATO enlargement were like sex in the Victorian age: no one talked but everyone thought about it."[29] The President and his advisors were well aware there also was a domestic constituency that favored enlargement—and which was vocal in making its views known vis-à-vis the White House and Capitol Hill. At a time when Administration policy was not yet fully settled, the growing pressure from conservative Republicans in the summer of 1994 to support NATO enlargement undoubtedly reinforced the hand of those in the Administration who favored enlargement. It was a clear incentive for the Administration to move forward and not to waver or backslide on this issue, and increasingly so, especially as the 1996 Presidential elections approached.

More broadly, Clinton was under pressure to prove his and his party's foreign policy credentials. Not only had the Democrats been out of power for twelve years, but also they were still viewed by the public as less competent than Republicans on national security issues. Clinton's critics repeatedly portrayed him as weak on foreign and defense policy. U.S. leadership on NATO was a traditional benchmark by which an American President's foreign policy stature was measured, and Democrats were keenly aware of Republican efforts to paint the Administration as mismanaging the Atlantic Alliance. All of these factors and pressures combined to make NATO enlargement a highly political issue, which both sides attempted to exploit for their own purposes.

President Clinton's early interest in NATO enlargement was initially not widely shared in the U.S. government. Tony Lake was perhaps the only person among the President's close advisors who supported it from the outset. He faced strong opposition from the State and Defense Departments, and from his own senior staff. There were several reasons. A number of key Clinton advisors considered building a new strategic relationship with Russia—a goal Clinton had just declared to be his top foreign policy priority—a more pressing and important national security concern. NATO enlargement was widely seen as threatening to undercut those objectives by playing into the hands of anti-democratic and anti-Western forces in Moscow. That view existed in the upper echelons of the State Department as well as the Pentagon.

Before entering office a number of senior Democratic defense officials, who subsequently assumed key positions in the Defense Department, had developed a new concept of "cooperative security" for Europe in which military cooperation with Moscow was a key part. Security in post–Cold War Europe, they argued, should be built by de-emphasizing old alliances and instead expanding institutionalized collaboration with former enemies.[30] Such cooperation was to be at the cutting edge of transforming political relationships across the continent. "Our new links to the Russian military were crucial to realizing an undivided Europe. Russia's empire and war machine were much reduced, but it still had the world's largest nuclear arsenal and a power and position in Eurasia that made its participation in the emerging European security system essential," Bill Perry and Ash Carter subsequently wrote. "Our objective was to promote common action between our militaries where Russian and American interests converged, building a foundation of cooperation that would survive the inevitable differences."[31]

Opposition to enlargement was not limited to Russia hands or arms control experts, however. It was also widely shared among senior State Department officials responsible for European and NATO affairs. In their view, NATO was the "crown jewel" of U.S. policy in Europe, an elite club whose cohesion needed to be protected—above all at a time of trans-Atlantic strain over Bosnia. Enlargement was seen as extending NATO's responsibilities, but without adding the resources needed to fulfill those commitments. America's European allies were seen as largely unsupportive. Its political viability at home was not clear either. Were Americans truly prepared to go to war for Warsaw or Budapest? Would the U.S. Senate expand the U.S. defense pledge to Europe when there were very real pressures to scale back America's overseas commitments? As Christopher prepared for his first visit to NATO headquarters in late February 1993, senior State Department officials made sure it was not mentioned as an issue the Secretary needed to address.[32]

The U.S. military, too, had its reasons for being wary. With the collapse of the Soviet threat, they viewed their posture in Europe as a waning asset. Secretary Aspin had launched a review of U.S. global force commitments. Entitled the Bottom-Up Review (BUR), it barely mentioned Europe and instead shifted U.S. defense planning toward a greater focus on the Persian Gulf and Asia.[33] The U.S. military was looking for ways to reduce its engagement in Europe—not to increase it. Talk about using NATO to project stability did not sound like a real military mission to many senior uniformed officers. Given the weak military capabilities of those countries seeking NATO membership, the prospect of enlargement was seen as yet another unwelcome burden for the U.S. military at a time when their forces and budgets were being reduced.

Thus, when the President asked "why not enlargement," senior U.S. officials felt confident they could list very real reasons why the answer was "no" or at least "not now." When Woerner suggested to NATO Ambassadors in early June that enlargement might be a topic of discussion at an upcoming NATO Foreign

Ministers' meeting in Athens, he was told that the issue was too controversial.[34] In a letter to his NATO counterparts, Christopher made it clear that Washington also opposed raising the issue: "As we intensify our efforts at NATO outreach, we need to be clear about our objectives. While we should keep open the perspective of eventual membership, we do not believe that opening public discussion of possible expansion would serve a good purpose at this time. Raising this possibility for specific countries can only imply a less favored position for others. Eventual expansion of NATO, to which the U.S. is open in principle, needs deliberate study within the alliance at the appropriate time. Let us not force the pace, and let us avoid raising public expectations that cannot be met."[35]

Christopher's speech in Athens laid out a five-part agenda for NATO reform, but enlargement was not part of it. Instead, he focused on the crisis of the moment—Bosnia—and proposed several initiatives to strengthen the Alliance's peacekeeping capabilities. While he addressed the need for "continent-wide security," his emphasis was on strengthening the NACC. "At an appropriate time," he stated in public, "we may choose to enlarge NATO membership. But that is not now on the agenda."[36] His talking points for the Foreign Ministers lunch were blunter. While noting that some allies wanted to discuss expansion, they stated: "Our view is different. We are concerned about the destabilizing effects if we begin an early debate, or an early process of expansion. . . . We can begin to sort through them privately out of public exposure. But the less said about this in public, the better. We should not even say that NATO is studying this."[37]

But the Athens meeting was a mess. NATO was still reeling in the wake of the Bosnia crisis. Christopher's reform proposals came across as half steps that tinkered with the status quo, a Band-Aid offered at a time when the Alliance was in danger of hemorrhaging. During a press conference the Secretary was peppered with questions about why the Administration had gone back on its previous tough rhetoric on Bosnia, whether its subsequent proposals on Bosnia were "spineless," and whether the Clinton team had the moral authority and capacity to lead the NATO alliance.[38] Christopher knew he had to do something—and soon—if Washington was to regain control of the Alliance. He called Lake to get his agreement to announce a Presidential trip to Europe and a NATO summit. When the National Security Advisor said that the Administration did not yet know what it wanted from such a summit, Christopher replied that the best way to get a policy was to schedule a summit as an action-forcing event. Lake acquiesced and Christopher announced that Clinton planned to make his first trip to Europe around the end of the year.

2. MAKING THE CASE

If the Administration was trying to avoid a public debate on NATO enlargement, there were others in the West trying to ensure that one took place. In the spring and summer of 1993, the first high-level advocates of NATO enlargement on both sides of the Atlantic stepped forward to advocate expansion as part of a broader transformation of the Alliance for the post–Cold War era. The case they put forward had been developed through informal collaboration over several years. It was calculated to challenge the dominant conventional wisdom and present an alternative policy framework for NATO's future. And it succeeded.

The first major Western politician to break the public taboo on the subject was German Defense Minister Volker Ruehe who made the case for enlarging NATO in March 1993 in a speech at the International Institute of Strategic Studies (IISS) in London. He was joined in June by Senator Richard G. Lugar (R-IN) who called on NATO to enlarge both its membership and its missions to stabilize the continent as a whole and become the core of a new post–Cold War European security order. Finally, in September, two RAND colleagues, Steve Larrabee and Richard Kugler, and I published an article entitled, "Building a new NATO" in *Foreign Affairs* that made the case for enlargement part of a more thorough overhaul of the Alliance. I knew Ruehe and his key advisors from the years I had spent in Germany. Although a Democrat, I had a close re-lationship with Senator Lugar and had helped him draft his speech as well. The debate over NATO enlargement had begun — and I found myself in the middle of it.

My own thinking on NATO had crystallized in the early 1990s while working at RAND. Along with several colleagues, I had concluded that enlarging NATO was the logical continuation of the policies that the U.S. had pursued through-out the post-war period, and that it was necessary not only to stabilize Central and Eastern Europe but to ensure that NATO remained relevant and survived. Making NATO enlargement the centerpiece of a new U.S. policy toward Europe promised to achieve those objectives. Although I considered myself a "New Democrat" and had volunteered for Bill Clinton's Presidential campaign, the selection of his initial national security team left me convinced that NATO enlargement was nowhere near the top of the Administration's agenda. I had therefore asked Larrabee and Kugler to join me in writing an article for *Foreign Affairs* that made the public case for enlargement. It was, initially, not a popular one. Many of our colleagues thought it was an off-the-wall idea, that would go nowhere. On more than one occasion, I was taken aside to suggest that I tone down my views lest I damage my career prospects.

In the spring of 1993 we shared an early version of the draft with several trusted colleagues on both sides of the Atlantic to test our arguments. Among them was Vice Admiral Ulrich Weisser, one of Germany's most fertile strategic minds who had become the top advisor to German Defense Minister Volker Ruehe. Weisser had been involved in several major debates in German security policy during his career. As a young officer he had helped draft Helmut Schmidt's 1977 Alastair Buchan Memorial Lecture that kicked off the debate on

Intermediate Nuclear Forces (INF). Fifteen years later, he was at Helmut Kohl's side when the Chancellor pushed through Euromissile deployment before the German Bundestag in the face of massive political protests.[39] We had met in the late 1980s and stayed in touch over the years. Weisser had been a guest scholar at RAND and we had become friends, collaborating informally since on NATO reform issues.

In the fall of 1992, Weisser became head of the Policy Planning staff for Volker Ruehe. Ruehe was a political heavyweight and represented a younger generation of more confident postwar German leaders less afraid to assert German interests at a time when it was still largely taboo. He was also ambitious. Coalition politics dictated that in the ruling coalition between Christian and Free Democrats, the latter had a firm lock on the Foreign Ministry. As a result, the ambitious young Christian Democratic politician took the defense portfolio. But Ruehe was still determined to play a role on broader foreign policy issues. He was looking for an issue and advisors that would help him to do so.

Ruehe and Weisser were a perfect match. "The Admiral," as Weisser was re-ferred to, shared Ruehe's conviction that Germany had to come out of the shad-ows and more openly define its own national interests. Shortly after assuming his job as head of the Defense Ministry's Policy Planning staff, Weisser had briefed Ruehe on the major tasks he faced as Defense Minister. He went through the difficult but largely technical challenges facing the Bundeswehr after German unification. Knowing none of these tasks would fully satisfy Ruehe's foreign policy interests and political ambitions, he added one addi-tional issue of possible interest for the Minister: the debate over NATO enlarge-ment and new missions. The Minister was interested indeed. He asked Weisser to prepare a speech to help launch this debate.

Ruehe was convinced that Germany had a vital interest in expanding NATO and the EU eastward to protect itself from any potential instability in Central and Eastern Europe.[40] From Germany's own postwar history he knew that the NATO umbrella could play a key role in consolidating democracy and fostering reconciliation and integration with neighboring countries. As foreign and secu-rity policy spokesperson for the Christian Democrats in the 1980s, Ruehe had traveled through Central and Eastern Europe and met the dissidents who would subsequently play a key role in toppling communism. He believed Germany had a moral obligation to help them as their efforts had paved the road to German unification.[41] During a visit to Bonn in early 1993, Weisser told me confidentially that Ruehe would soon make a major speech supporting NATO enlargement. We could not have had a better European spokesman, I thought.

Consulting neither the Foreign Office nor the Chancellor, Ruehe called for NATO to enlarge at the annual Alastair Buchan lecture at the IISS on March 26—on the same podium from which Helmut Schmidt had launched the

NATO debate on Euromissiles in 1977. NATO, the Minster emphasized, had to adapt to a completely new set of strategic challenges: unifying Europe, redefining burdens across the Atlantic, and coming up with a new concept for dealing with crises in and beyond Europe. Never before in Europe's history, Ruehe said, was there such an opportunity to overcome Europe's divide and unify the continent. He could not "see one good reason for denying" the countries of Central and Eastern Europe membership in NATO and the European Union. It was time, Ruehe concluded, for the Alliance to open the perspective of NATO enlargement to these countries.[42]

The reaction to the speech was icy. As Weisser would subsequently write: "Whereas those Ambassadors among the well-represented diplomatic corps from East European countries reacted enthusiastically, the body language and gestures of those representatives of the British 'strategic community' as well as that of the NATO Ambassadors in attendance signaled their skepticism if not outright open opposition to Ruehe's speech."[43] On the plane during the flight back to Cologne, one of Ruehe's top military advisors remarked that it had been a mistake to give the speech and it would take Germany years to recover from the damage caused by the Minister's comments. He was mistaken. Within several years every one of Ruehe's core ideas would be embraced by the U.S. and would become official Alliance policy.

Back in Washington, Senator Lugar, one of the most respected voices on Capitol Hill on foreign policy in general, and Europe and Russia in particular, read Ruehe's speech with great interest. Lugar also thought the U.S. and its allies were being too timid in responding to the changes in Europe since the end of the Cold War. Traveling through Europe and the former Soviet Union, he had been struck by the fragility of the new democracies of Central and Eastern Europe and their intense desire to find a connection to the West. Lugar was convinced that the West had to lock in the gains of the end of the Cold War before they were frittered away. He was also convinced that NATO had to be overhauled if it was to remain relevant and have public support at home. The Gulf War had convinced him that NATO had to be prepared to assume new missions outside of Europe in the future.

Watching the Clinton Administration stumble in its first months in office on Bosnia and NATO, Lugar decided it was time to deliver a wake-up call to the Administration on the Alliance's importance. In late March 1993 Ken Myers, Lugar's key foreign policy advisor, phoned me. The Senator, too, had read the draft of our forthcoming article and wanted to discuss NATO's future with us. Kugler, Larrabee, and I met with Lugar several weeks later. The Senator laid out his own thinking on NATO and asked us to help him develop some ideas for a major speech. Over the next two months we worked with his staff to prepare a speech intended to get the Administration's attention and force a public debate on NATO's future.

In late June Lugar spoke before the Overseas Writers Club in Washington.[44] He argued that the Clinton Administration had its priorities wrong in focusing solely on supporting reform in Russia. The real issue was whether the U.S. and its allies could create a security order for a unified Europe whole and free—or whether it ran the risk that Europe would once again come apart at the seams. The West, Lugar argued, had to project stability beyond NATO's current borders to those areas in the east and south where the seeds of future conflicts in Europe lie. It needed to embrace both new members and new missions as part of a new strategic bargain between the U.S. and Europe to stabilize all of Europe. "If NATO is to survive, then it must be transformed from an alliance for collective defense against a specific threat into an alliance in the service of shared values and common strategic interests," Lugar emphasized. The Alliance had to go "out of area or out of business." That phrase quickly caught on as a kind of battle cry for those advocating that the Alliance open its doors to Central and Eastern Europe.

The speeches by Ruehe and Lugar were important not only because of the stature each of these men enjoyed in the strategic community. Intellectually, they also recast the debate in a way that made it more difficult for critics to dismiss NATO enlargement as an idea that was not serious. The issue was no longer defined in terms of whether the West should or should not help the Central and East Europeans by bringing them into the Alliance, but rather in terms of how to preserve security in Europe as a whole and revitalize NATO. Enlargement was no longer portrayed as an anti-Russia move but rather as a pro-stability strategy that would unite Europe, keep the U.S. engaged, and give the Alliance a new lease on life. The emphasis was now on Western, including American, interests—not only those of Central and Eastern Europe. It was a more potent set of arguments that was harder for the opponents to knock down and which resonated with Americans concerned about preserving a strong trans-Atlantic relationship.

The debate received a further boost with the appearance of our article in *Foreign Affairs* entitled "Building a New NATO."[45] The article made a forceful case in favor of enlargement as part of a seven point plan for overhauling the Alliance. The reaction in much of the strategic community, as well as most parts of the U.S. government, was initially hostile. I got a personal whiff of this over the summer when I presented a RAND briefing on enlargement to a group of senior Pentagon officials headed by Lieutenant General Barry McCaffrey, at the time head of strategy in the Joint Chiefs of Staff (JCS). McCaffrey was a tough-talking, highly decorated Gulf War veteran who glowered at me throughout the presentation. After I finished, he made it crystal clear that he opposed any mention of NATO enlargement: "I don't want these God damn countries in my alliance until my daughter is the Chairman of the JCS—and that is not going to happen for a long time to come." The reception we received at the State Department was not much different.

But the intellectual and political battle was being waged on many fronts. And there were signs that we were winning in other places, including at the highest levels of the Administration. One day in early August, Larrabee and I dropped in to see Jennone Walker, Lake's Senior Director for European Affairs at the NSC staff. We both knew Walker, and had worked with her on the 1992 Presidential campaign. We knew she strongly opposed enlargement and we had no illusion that we were in for a hard sell. She listened politely to us but made it clear that she and the vast majority of her colleagues disagreed with us. To our surprise, she then added with a note of exasperation in her voice: "There are only two people in this government who agree with you—the President and Tony Lake." Larrabee started to argue with her when Walker was pulled away to take an urgent phone call. I nudged him and whispered: "That is not a bad start. Let's declare victory and go home." It was the first we had heard of the President's and Lake's interest in the issue.

Shortly thereafter I made my first acquaintance with Dick Holbrooke—and discovered that he, too, was sympathetic to enlargement. I was invited to speak at a State Department-sponsored seminar in Washington on August 13, 1993 to help prepare Holbrooke for his posting as U.S. Ambassador to Germany. Along with the then Principal Deputy Assistant Secretary of State for European Affairs, Jim Dobbins, I participated in a panel discussion on future German foreign policy. While enlargement was not officially on the agenda, our *Foreign Affairs* piece was the talk in foreign policy circles and Dobbins immediately criticized my views on enlargement. After he had finished, Holbrooke looked at me and said: "Ron, you have been attacked. Would you like to defend yourself?" Dobbins and I debated the issue until Holbrooke broke in: "Jim, I think Ron has the better arguments. Maybe you better go back and rethink."

But the center of gravity of thinking in the Administration was still moving in another direction. The announcement of the President's trip to Europe had led to the first serious Administration review of existing U.S. policy toward Europe and NATO. An Inter-agency Working Group (IWG) was established in mid-June to develop a set of summit initiatives by the fall. The going-in assumption was that NATO enlargement was off the agenda. Following Lugar's speech, the State Department's European Bureau circulated a copy of Christopher's remarks reminding everyone that the Administration opposed even discussing enlargement. A framework paper circulated by the State Department in early July concluded that the Administration needed to preempt pressures to discuss the issue: "To tie these issues to the summit would put expanded membership on NATO's immediate agenda, with divisive and potentially destabilizing consequences in the East." A NSC paper circulated two days later agreed.[46]

Over the summer the IWG came up with several summit initiatives. One was a proposal to create more mobile and flexible command structures and forces so that NATO could more easily deploy forces beyond its borders to deal with future Bosnias through so-called Combined Joint Task Forces or CJTFs. A second was expanding work on NATO's European Security and Defense Identity (ESDI) designed to respond to the growing impetus for European integration and support a European option of acting militarily without the U.S. if need be. Third, the Defense Department proposed a counter proliferation initiative to underscore the Alliance's commitment to confront new emerging threats in the future.

The fourth and final initiative was the Peacekeeping Partnership, later dubbed the Partnership for Peace (PfP). It was the IWG's answer to Christopher's call in Athens for "continent-wide security."[47] PfP was the brainchild of General John Shalikashvilli, commonly referred to by his colleagues as Shali. Shali was NATO's Supreme Allied Commander-Europe (SACEUR) at the time but was in line to replace Colin Powell as the Chairman of the Joint Chiefs of Staff in Washington. As SACEUR, he was not normally a participant in internal Washington policy deliberations. But the fact that he was Powell's anointed successor and had been the Chairman's representative to the Bush Administration's working group on the same set of issues allowed him to play a key role.

Shali believed the time was not right for NATO to enlarge. He felt that NATO members, including the U.S., were not prepared to extend new security guarantees to potentially unstable new members, that the Central and East Europeans were not ready to assume the responsibilities of membership and that Moscow would inevitably view NATO enlargement as aimed against it. But Shali also recognized the NACC's inadequacies and the growing pressure for Washington and the Alliance to "do more." Shali took the ideas circulating in the interagency process and packaged them in a way that squared the circle among boosting NATO's engagement with Central and Eastern Europe, avoiding alienating Russia, and not saddling the U.S. military with new commitments. Peacekeeping was one way to connect the dots among the different political imperatives. It was a new mission for NATO. By working together with these countries, NATO would inevitably develop a much closer set of relationships with these countries, allowing them to get what Alliance officials called "NATO dirt under their fingernails."

In early August Shali proposed that NATO reaffirm that it was not a closed shop, expand the NACC by developing a charter as well as a vigorous work plan, and establish a NATO "Peacekeeping Partnership" for countries prepared to participate in future peacekeeping operations. The idea was to turn the NACC into an operational organization in its own right—a new all-European concord that could lay the groundwork for eventual NATO enlargement down the road but without prematurely opening up a debate on this thorny issue.[48] NSC Senior Director Jennone Walker quickly embraced it as a way to bridge the differences within the government on the issue and provide an alternative to the growing pressure to consider enlargement. Joseph Kruzel, who joined the

Pentagon in August as the Deputy Assistant Secretary of Defense responsible for NATO issues, but would lose his life in a car crash during a peace mission to Bosnia one year later, renamed it the Partnership for Peace (PfP), after the debacle in Somalia later that fall made the peacekeeping label less politically radioactive.[49]

But there were several people in the Clinton Administration who wanted to go further. One was National Security Advisor Tony Lake. When Walker reported to Lake early in the summer that enlargement was now "off the table" as a possible summit initiative, he responded that the issue was very much on the table in his eyes and those of the President. Another was Christopher's chief-of-staff at the State Department, Tom Donilon, who was convinced that U.S.-European relations were in serious trouble and that the NATO summit had to launch a new vision and strategy to stabilize the trans-Atlantic relationship. He wanted something politically more attractive than what the interagency process was producing. He was instantly attracted to the case for NATO enlargement. As he later recalled, "It wasn't even a close call. Honor, history, national interest and strategy all argued for NATO enlargement."[50]

The arguments of Ruehe, Lugar, and RAND provided ammunition for those in the Administration pushing for more ambitious policies. Donilon read Lugar's speech and had received an advance copy of our RAND article from Undersecretary of State Lynn Davis. Davis was an old NATO hand from previous stints in government and think tanks. As a RAND Vice President, she had directed some of RAND's early work on NATO enlargement. While not directly responsible for Alliance policy, she was one of Secretary Christopher's confidants. Along with Steve Flanagan and Hans Binnendyk, from the Policy Planning staff, she became the voice in Christopher's immediate entourage making the intellectual case for NATO enlargement.[51]

With the public debate on NATO enlargement gaining momentum over the summer, Assistant Secretary of State for European and Canadian Affairs Steve Oxman sent Secretary Christopher a memo in late July reiterating the European Bureau's case against enlargement.[52] On August 12, Oxman spoke at the Atlantic Council where he opposed enlargement and argued that there were less risky ways to address the issues Lugar and others had raised.[53] That same day Davis and Policy Planning head Sam Lewis took exception to Oxman's views. In a memo to Christopher they wrote: "We, and others in the interagency and expert communities, believe it will not be possible to defer a debate on the expansion and fundamental transformation of the Alliance, nor would it be in our interest to do so. Indeed, avoidance of this issue will undermine NATO by reinforcing the growing perception that the Alliance is only marginally involved in addressing Europe's new security problems. It would also feed growing disillusionment with the West and democratic reforms in

Central and Eastern Europe. This mood could trigger new instability in that region, with dangerous ripple effects across the continent."[54]

NATO, they argued, had to be bolder. Just as the U.S. extended a security guarantee to Western Europe in 1949 to safeguard their postwar recovery, so, too, the Alliance now had to open a similar perspective to Central and Eastern Europe. NATO's mission, they argued, had to be broadened from the guardian of Western Europe to the guardian of democracy throughout Europe. "Just as the U.S. extended a security guarantee to Western Europe in 1949 to safeguard their post-war recovery and avoid a Third World War, so too, we must work together with our allies to provide a similar security umbrella to those states for whom we struggled to liberate from Communism." They urged Christopher to go beyond the IWG proposals and PfP to consider establishing a clear perspective for NATO membership, identifying the criteria these countries had to meet to qualify, and a commitment to consult in crisis consultations.

It was against this backdrop that policymakers in the West received the sensational news on August 25, 1993 that Russian President Boris Yeltsin and Polish President Lech Walesa had signed a communiqué stating that Moscow did not object to Poland joining NATO. The news came as a complete surprise as Russian Foreign Minister Kozyrev had rejected the idea only two days earlier.[55] Now an official Polish-Russian communiqué noted that Poland's desire to join NATO "was met with understanding" by Yeltsin. The key sentence read: "In the long term, such a decision taken by a sovereign Poland in the interests of overall European integration does not go against the interests of other states, including the interests of Russia."[56] In the press conference, Yeltsin added that "the ice of distrust" between the two countries had melted and that the days were over when Moscow would dictate to Warsaw what it should do.[57]

While Russian and some Western commentators subsequently downplayed Yeltsin's remarks, suggesting that the Russian leader had only agreed to the language, as one European diplomat put it, "à la vodka"—i.e., after a long drinking session with Walesa—the key Polish participants in these discussions have insisted that Yeltsin was sober and knew exactly what he was doing during the critical conversations. Indeed, Walesa had already laid out both his intent and his strategy in a meeting with Senator Lugar, who, coincidentally, was in Warsaw on August 24, 1993—only a few hours before the Russian leader arrived in Warsaw. He told Lugar that he understood Western nervousness about Russian views on enlargement but that he was going to try to convince Yeltsin that Poland in NATO was better for Russia than a security vacuum in the region. He added that he had already spoken with Kiev and that Ukraine would not oppose Polish membership in NATO. "We are not looking for a confrontation," Walesa told Lugar, "we are only seeking to guarantee Polish security." The Polish President rehearsed with Lugar the arguments he was planning to use with Yeltsin.[58]

After his arrival, Yeltsin and Walesa had a one-on-one dinner and went for a long private walk. Yeltsin's visit had been advertised as an opportunity to turn the page in Polish-Russian relations. Walesa, picking up on Yeltsin's theme of a new start, asked whether Moscow would accept Poland's independent choice when it came to its security policy. He argued that Warsaw could either look westward and to the EU and NATO, or turn eastward and form an alliance with Ukraine. The latter suggestion harked back to the days of Pilsudski and his proposals for a Polish-Ukrainian federation after the Polish-Russian war of 1919–1920, and was clearly anti-Russian. Warsaw's preference, Walesa continued, was to integrate with the West. If Russia and Poland were to truly make a new start, it was important to clarify this issue so that it would not burden the new start both leaders were striving for.

Yeltsin responded that he accepted Polish sovereignty and independence and that it was up to Poland to decide what path to take. Warsaw, he said, was outside of Russia's immediate sphere of influence. The Russian President then went on to describe his own vision of Russia and its relations with its neighbors. Moscow had to move beyond the artificial structures of the past and rebuild a more genuine set of relations within the Commonwealth of Independent States (CIS). Russia's economic revitalization, Yeltsin added, would bring the CIS countries back—but on a more genuine and natural basis. Although the two men would subsequently drink, the Polish side insists that Yeltsin was sober when this conversation took place.

The head of the Polish negotiating team in August 1993 was Deputy Foreign Minister Robert Mroziewicz. He recalls how the Polish and Russian drafting teams, who had been waiting in the Polish Foreign Ministry all evening, were told around midnight that the two Presidents had reached an agreement in principle which now needed to be translated into communiqué language. They ordered pizza, found some vodka and scotch, and proceeded to sit down to try to draft a communiqué. At around 3:00 A.M. the two negotiating teams agreed on a text with the standard understanding that it would be reviewed by delegation heads the following morning.

That next morning the two delegations met for a final session in the Presidential Belvedere Palace. Polish participants recall Russian Foreign Minister Kozyrev and Defense Minister Grachev looking surprised by the draft communiqué and becoming angry at the language, having apparently seen the draft only shortly before the meeting started. They asked for a break in the meeting and started arguing with Yeltsin in front of the Polish delegation that he should not accept that language. Polish participants had seen this before. At the last Walesa-Yeltsin meeting in Moscow in 1992, Grachev had lost his temper and started shouting at the Russian President over some important issues associated with the Russian troop withdrawal from Poland. At that time, Yeltsin had acted as if he had a headache and told the Defense Minister to shut up.

When the plenary session resumed, Walesa noted that Poland's decision to seek NATO membership was its choice but that it was helpful to address the issue in the joint communiqué to "clear the air." Russian Defense Minister Grachev argued that the language in the communiqué was dangerous for Yeltsin. NATO, he said, was still seen as a "monster directed against Russia" and such a statement would be exploited by the nationalist opposition. Similarly, Kozyrev insisted that it was not in Poland's interest to isolate Russia by joining the Alliance. But Walesa interjected. He turned to Yeltsin and said that both he and the Russian President, as democratically elected heads-of-state, were in charge and that Yeltsin should not listen to his "advisors." If they, as Presidents, had decided something, he continued, there was no reason to change it. Yeltsin agreed. The two sides agreed to some final, modest wording changes. The communiqué was issued with the key section on Poland's NATO aspirations intact.[59]

The news had an electrifying impact on Poles who believed they had cleared the way for NATO to enlarge. Polish papers on the morning of August 26 proclaimed a diplomatic breakthrough and Russia's "agreement" to Poland's joining NATO. Symbolically, they showed a picture of Yeltsin bowing at the monument to the victims of the Katyn massacre. The country seemed to be seized with "NATO-mania." "Now the West has no argument to say no to Poland," stated Walesa's press spokesman Andrzej Drzycimski. "Until now the West has been using the argument, 'We don't want to upset the Russians.' Now we will see the true intentions of the West towards Poland," he added.[60]

Yeltsin arrived in Prague the next day—coincidentally the 25th anniversary of the Soviet invasion of Czechoslovakia. There, he had a similar conversation with Czech President Vaclav Havel, who explained that the Czech Republic, along with the other Visegrad countries, wanted to be part of the West, including institutions such as the European Union and NATO. Such aspirations were not aimed against Russia, he insisted, but designed to create stability in the region. Yeltsin responded that he understood those aspirations and that Russia, too, would like to be part of those Western structures. Yeltsin responded that he no longer wanted to behave like the former Soviet Union and try to tell other countries what they had to do. "It's your free choice," the Russian President said. Havel asked Yeltsin, and the Russian President agreed, to repeat that statement at the press conference. Following the conversation, however, Yeltsin's aides (again) angrily tried to convince Yeltsin not to make such a public statement with the result that the Russian President avoided the issue in public.[61]

Several days after the Walesa-Yeltsin meeting, Polish Foreign Minister Skubiszewski jotted down his own analysis and thoughts, which he attached to the Foreign Ministry's summary of the Polish-Russian plenary session. He concluded that Polish diplomacy had scored a major triumph by including the key language on its NATO aspirations in the joint communiqué. Warsaw had in all likelihood succeeded in its objective of putting the NATO enlargement issue on the agenda for the upcoming NATO summit. The ball, he concluded, was now in NATO's court. But it was also important for the West to move quickly to take advantage of this diplomatic opening since the Russian concessions could be only temporary. It was far from clear, he added, that Russia had fully abandoned its hope of someday pulling Poland back into its sphere of influence.

But the Western reaction was muted at best. Many Western capitals found the news difficult to believe and even more difficult to respond to. The reaction in Warsaw and Prague to Western diffidence was, in turn, one of dismay. On August 31, Polish Prime Minister Hanna Suchocka, speaking before the diplomatic corps in Warsaw, said that "failure to act on the admission of Central European states [to NATO] will force them to seek alternative security arrangements and weaken the effectiveness of the European security system" by fueling anti-Western sentiments.[62] The next day Walesa wrote NATO leaders urging them to seize the historical moment and extend invitations to the Visegrad countries to join the Alliance at the upcoming summit. That letter would go unanswered for weeks as Washington and its allies mulled over how to respond.[63] For years afterward, the former leader of Solidarity would complain that he had created a historical opportunity that Western leaders had failed to recognize or grasp.

3. "WE NEED A PERSPECTIVE"

Over the summer of 1993 NATO enlargement had gone from an issue that was ostensibly "not on the agenda" to one that was on the front page of nearly every major newspaper in Europe. And while the Yeltsin-Walesa statement did not publicly shift Western policy, it had a considerable impact behind the scenes, especially regarding the thinking of Manfred Woerner. The NATO Secretary General had privately long been sympathetic both to the strategic case for enlargement and the moral argument that the West had an obligation to assist the Poles, Czechs, and Hungarians after the role they had played in toppling communism. But Woerner's job was to represent and reflect the views of the Alliance as a whole—and he knew that most allies were not ready to support NATO enlargement. In his meeting with Christopher in Washington the previous March, for example, Woerner had mentioned the difficulties in expanding NATO ties with the East in light of Russian opposition and had suggested it might be easier for the EU to take the lead in reaching out to these countries.[64]

But Woerner was also increasingly worried about the sense of drift in the Alliance and in U.S. policy toward NATO since the Bush Administration. In the spring he had told Christopher that whereas he was confident that the EU would still exist in ten years, he was not sure about NATO. Over the summer Woerner confided his growing concerns over NATO's future to Ambassador Hunter. He told him that he thought the Bush Administration had been lax in its leadership of the Alliance after the Gulf War. Absent U.S. leadership, Europe could not cope with Bosnia or stabilizing Central and Eastern Europe. He was impressed with Clinton and wanted to encourage him to stake out a leadership role in the Alliance. But Woerner still urged caution. In a meeting in Bavaria on August 5, 1993, he argued that a bold move on enlargement was premature as there was no Alliance consensus on the issue and it ran the risk of undercutting Russian reform. He emphasized that the upcoming summit should focus on re-structuring the Alliance to deal with new missions like Bosnia, not enlargement.[65]

Following the Yeltsin-Walesa meeting, however, Woerner changed his mind. After calling in Klaus Scharioth, a German diplomat who became the director of Woerner's Private Office the last week of August 1993, Woerner asked him for his thoughts on the agenda for NATO's upcoming summit. Scharioth, who had joined the staff the previous spring and had spent the intervening months getting up to speed, replied that the most important task facing the West was stabilizing and integrating Central and Eastern Europe. The EU could not do it alone and NATO would have to play a key role by enlarging. The summit was the best place to launch the process. Recognizing that Russia would oppose such a move, Scharioth suggested creating a special NATO-Russia consultative track to ad-dress Moscow's concerns and overcome Russian paranoia about the Alliance.

Woerner asked a number of pointed questions, but it was clear to Scharioth that he was thinking along similar lines. He asked him to write up his arguments in a short paper for him and to share it with no one. Scharioth wrote three pages listing the arguments for a limited NATO enlargement to the Visegrad coun-tries coupled with a dual track strategy for engaging Russia.[66] On September 2, Woerner told Hunter that Yeltsin's comments in Warsaw and Prague had changed the political landscape. Whatever Yeltsin had intended in his meeting with Walesa, NATO now had to seize the moment. After much reflection, Woerner continued, he had concluded that a historic opportunity had arisen and that NATO must provide a clear perspective on enlargement. If NATO did not grasp this moment, Woerner asked, would it ever come again? In his per-sonal view, he continued, the Alliance should admit all of the former Warsaw Pact countries from Poland to Romania, although he recognized that this would have to happen in several stages. Hunter immediately sent back a cable inform-ing Washington of Woerner's change of heart.[67]

One week later, Woerner went public with his support for NATO enlarge-ment at the annual IISS conference at the Hilton Hotel in Brussels on September 10. By this time the NATO enlargement debate was the rage in the strategic community. At first glance Woerner's speech, which was entitled "The Slogan 'Out of Area' or 'Out of Business' is Out of Date: We are Acting Out of Area and we Very Much Are in Business," seemed an obvious counter to the ar-guments put forward by Lugar and RAND.[68] But in the hotel foyer Woerner's press spokesman, Jamie Shea, came over to Larrabee and me with an advance copy of the speech, smiled, and said: "I think you are going to like what he has to say."

It quickly became clear that the Secretary General, while nominally taking issue with the view that NATO was in jeopardy, had actually joined the ranks of those calling for far-reaching change in the Alliance. The collapse of communism, he noted, had left Europe with a paradox: it faced less of a threat but also had less peace than during the Cold War. The West could no longer afford to be passive in the face of growing disorder in Europe but had to draw the lessons from its failures in Bosnia and elsewhere—"or it will wither away." Far from being irrelevant, he insisted, NATO was needed more than ever—to sustain the trans-Atlantic link, to prevent Europe from sliding back into nationalism, and to address new conflicts beyond NATO's borders. The Alliance's primary future mission should be to project stability to the East. "In my view," he stated, "the time has come to open a more concrete perspective to those countries of Central and Eastern Europe which want to join NATO and which we may consider eligible for future membership. This should be one of the major subjects of the forthcoming NATO summit." Woerner had publicly switched sides on the enlargement issue.

In Washington, Davis had already sent Christopher a second memo on September 7 arguing that the Administration should seize this historic window of opportunity created by the Walesa-Yeltsin statement to launch NATO enlargement. PfP was inadequate as the centerpiece of the upcoming summit, she insisted. The issue was not how to ensure that these countries could contribute to future peacekeeping operations, she argued, but rather President Clinton's vision was for the trans-Atlantic relationship and whether the U.S. would lead a fundamental transformation of the Alliance. PfP lacked the historical vision and political dimension that was desperately needed—and failed to answer the key question of what the U.S. and NATO's role in Europe should be after the end of the Cold War.

"The fundamental task for the President is to develop a rationale for why Americans still need to play a major role in Europe's evolution, beyond support for reform in Russia," Davis wrote. "The answer is that American leadership will be required both to build democracy and to prevent the dangers of revived nationalism." There was a growing possibility that democracy and pro-Western reform efforts in Central and Eastern Europe could fail and that dangerous forms of nationalism and conflict could return. "If the summit skirts the question of expansion, disillusionment with the West and the prospect of reform will deepen in many of these states," she wrote. "Interest in NACC could diminish further because it would tend to confirm that this body is a permanent second-class status rather than a way station to full integration with the West, especially as the obstacles to European Community membership expand. Pressures could arise in Germany for a re-nationalization of its security and defense policy."

The U.S. should set for itself and its allies the goal of making the prospect of war and conflict in Central and Eastern Europe as inconceivable as it had become in Western Europe after World War II. As before, extending a U.S. security umbrella and supporting the European integration process across Europe would be key ingredients for success. Davis suggested the Administration commit to a phased strategy of enlargement that autumn and seek agreement at the 1994 January summit on a set of criteria and blueprint on the way ahead. This would provide for expansion by 1998 to a limited number of countries in Central and Eastern Europe with a second phase of full membership reserved for those who would subsequently show themselves to be capable of contributing to NATO's defense missions. "The vision is bold, but it is one with built in safeguards and pauses. There is risk in trying to transform NATO, but there is also risk of NATO loosing credibility if it does not move more forcefully to address the Eastern security problem."[69]

Davis' case to Christopher was buttressed by a memo written by Dr. Charles Gati, a leading scholar on Central and Eastern Europe who had been brought on as a senior member of the Policy Planning staff. Gati's memo challenged the assumption that liberal democracy was slowly but surely taking hold in Central and Eastern Europe. Instead, he warned that post-communist authoritarian forces were gaining ground and that there was a real danger that countries in the region would, if not firmly anchored to the West, succumb to creeping authoritarianism. If Western policy were not more forthcoming in its embrace of pro-democratic forces, he predicted, "in two to three years Slovakia will have embraced Right authoritarianism of the Franco-Salazar variety," adding that Poland and Hungary were in danger of sliding in the same direction. The key was Poland, where elections were approaching. "Only Western engagement can provide the hope that the people of Central Europe need to foster their growing stakes in the West," he concluded. Donilon was so impressed by the memo that he walked in and gave it to Christopher for immediate reading.[70]

On September 7 Christopher held a lunch for his senior staff, including Strobe Talbott. Davis made the case in favor of a more ambitious U.S. approach. To the surprise of many in the room, Christopher agreed with her. On the issue of Russia, Dennis Ross chipped in. Although he was Christopher's special Middle East coordinator, Ross had been head of the Policy Planning staff in the Baker State Department and involved in the 2 + 4 negotiations with Moscow on German unification. He argued that getting Moscow to acquiesce to enlargement, while difficult, was not impossible. He emphasized that the West had to make clear to the Russians early on how committed it was and then work to define terms Moscow could accept. Christopher asked Davis to circulate her memo for interagency discussions.[71]

There was hardly a Russian expert in or outside the U.S. government who thought NATO enlargement could be done without risking serious damage to relations with Moscow. Strobe Talbott, the Administration's top Russia hand, was no exception. He had not been closely involved in the Administration's early enlargement discussions, but Davis' second memo and Christopher's green light on enlargement gave him pause. He had by coincidence been meeting with his Russian counterpart, Deputy Foreign Minister Mamedov, in London on August 25 and had mentioned that NATO enlargement was becoming an issue back in Washington. Mamedov rolled his eyes and said: "Only our worst enemies would wish that topic on us. NATO, in Russian, is a four-letter word. Let's concentrate on the merely very difficult and not adding ourselves Mission Impossible." Later that afternoon the two men were interrupted by a news bulletin announcing that Yeltsin had just stated that he had no objections to Poland's joining NATO. Mamedov was speechless.[72]

Talbott has been portrayed as the key opponent to NATO enlargement in the Administration's ranks. His promotion to Deputy Secretary of State in early 1994 and his subsequent role as the Administration's diplomatic point man in implementing enlargement made the question of what he thought when about enlargement, and his exact role in the Administration's deliberations in the fall of 1993, an important part of this story. Talbott himself has disputed that he was an outright opponent of NATO enlargement. He has written that he never fundamentally opposed enlargement or had a subsequent "turnabout" or "change of heart" on the issue. Instead, he has insisted that he believed that the arguments in favor of admitting new members outweighed those against from the outset—but he also felt that enlargement should only be pursued in parallel with the development of a cooperative strategy with Russia and Ukraine.[73]

Talbott often gave credit to one of his closest aides, Eric Edelman, for helping him keep an open mind on enlargement. Edelman was first Talbott's Deputy in the State Department's Newly Independent States bureau, S/NIS. After Talbott became Deputy Secretary, Edelman became his chief of staff before becoming U.S. Ambassador to Finland. He was as erudite as he was practical. With a Ph.D. in diplomatic history, he was well read in both European and Russian history. His memos to Talbott often contained references to political theory or recent scholarly articles that he recommended Talbott read in his spare time. Following the appearance of the RAND article advocating NATO enlargement in *Foreign Affairs*, Talbott called Edelman—who was in Czech language training preparing to go to Prague in the number two slot in the U.S. Embassy—to ask for his views. Talbott was so impressed by Edelman's arguments in favor of NATO enlargement that he asked him to write up his thoughts and send them to him.[74]

But Talbott opposed the strategy Lake, Davis, and RAND were pushing—a view he labeled the "fast track" approach. And in the world of bureaucratic politics and warfare, timing was everything. What mattered in the fall of 1993 was not that he might be in favor, intellectually, of enlarging at some future point, but rather that he was opposed bureaucratically to moving forward at that point in time. In Talbott's words: "I was opposed to the idea of "fast-track" admissions per se, since I believed that the stakes were too high and the complexities too great to move precipitously; enlargement should be a deliberate process, not a quick one."[75] At the time, he was supported by the U.S. Ambassador in Moscow, Thomas Pickering, who argued that Russians would inevitably interpret NATO enlargement, even if couched in terms that did not explicitly exclude Moscow, as directed against them and could produce the kind of Russian policies it presumably was designed to guard against.[76]

The fall of 1993 was a dramatic point in the ongoing power struggle in Moscow between Yeltsin and his rivals. The fight over Russia's future would soon escalate into a shoot out as Yeltsin ordered the military to storm the Russian White House in early October after it had been taken over by his opponents. Arriving in Ankara at the beginning of a long trip through the former Soviet Union, Talbott followed up on Christopher's decision to table the State Department's pro-enlargement position in interagency deliberations with a cable outlining his views. "With a Department position on NATO expansion now in place, I see it as an important part of my job to ensure that our policies toward NATO and the former Soviet Union are fully coordinated and mutually reinforcing. To that end, we must ensure that what we eventually propose is seen by key countries of the former Soviet Union as enhancing their security and their sense of belonging in Europe."

"At our lunch on Monday," Talbott wrote, "I urged that we take no steps that could fuel a conservative, perhaps even aggressive backlash in Russian foreign policy. The key here is to present our expansion plan in a way that stresses eventual inclusion rather than near-term exclusion of Russia—and that is seen to enhance regional stability and security for all states in the area. Just as important," he continued, "we must be very careful not to pull this off in a way that makes Ukraine feel it is being left out in the cold with its furry neighbor to the north; otherwise we could inadvertently—and disastrously—give hardliners in Kiev new arguments for their case that Ukraine needs a nuclear deterrent. These two points argue strongly that any inclusion of new members in NATO must be coupled with concrete steps to improve the security position of the Big Two in the FSU."[77]

But the U.S. government did not have a common position. Although the State Department had now adopted a more positive view, strong opposition to NATO enlargement continued to come from the Pentagon. Whereas Secretary of Defense Aspin was drawing the opposite conclusion from Christopher. Aspin, too, had attended the IISS conference in Brussels. But unlike Woerner, he was an enlargement skeptic. Hunter had taken advantage of the Secretary's visit to organize a barbecue and discussion of enlargement at his residence that included Aspin, Shalikashvilli, Hunter, Kruzel and other members of the DoD team. Shali presented his thinking to Aspin at a time when DoD was looking for a way to contain the building momentum for enlargement. Aspin endorsed PfP and the DoD position was set in favor of PfP and against moving forward on enlargement.

On September 13, the State Department presented its new position in favor of enlargement at a meeting of the IWG. But any discussion was short-circuited when Assistant Secretary of Defense Chaz Freeman asserted that Aspin and Shalikashvilli strongly opposed enlargement on the grounds that it would dilute NATO, and accused the State Department of focusing too much on the interests of the Central and East Europeans as opposed to those of the U.S.[78] Later that day Christopher met with Kozyrev and briefly mentioned to him that he wanted to discuss the issue of NATO enlargement in greater detail when U.S. thinking was further along. The interests of the U.S. and Russia, Christopher underscored, were not necessarily antithetical in this matter and he hoped that Moscow and Washington could approach the question together.[79]

On the final leg of his trip to Russia and Central Asia, Talbott stopped at NATO Headquarters in Brussels. Woerner took him aside to make the case for the Alliance offering a NATO enlargement perspective to send the message to Central and Eastern Europe that "you belong to us." Talbott demurred, saying that Washington had not reached a final decision, but nonetheless underscored the need not to "slam the door" on Russian reformers."[80]

Talbott also found the United States' European allies as divided as Washington was on the enlargement question. The mainstream allied view at the time was that Central and Eastern Europe should focus first on getting into the European Union, not NATO. This was seen as a more "natural" and politically easier way for them to integrate into the West, with Alliance membership coming later if at all. Washington's key NATO allies—Germany, the United Kingdom, and France—each had their own specific reasons for being cautious if not opposed to enlargement.

London was worried that NATO enlargement, which it initially saw as a German idea, would dilute the Alliance and the U.S. commitment to Europe. British defense officials worried about the defense implications of extending new Article V commitments; and London was not yet sure about what they called the "existential issue"—was the British public willing to go to war for Poland? Throughout the summer and fall of 1993 British diplomats, while acknowledging that the Alliance might one day have to enlarge, emphasized that was an issue for the future. In June, Foreign Secretary Hurd warned that NATO "must not let rhetoric run ahead of reality" on enlargement.[81] Speaking before the House of Commons in October 1993, UK Defense Minister Malcolm Rifkind remarked that the Alliance "must not be tempted into hasty or ill-thought-out decisions" and had to find ways to enhance the security of all European nations, including Russia. A democratic and peaceful Russia, he concluded, "is the great prize to be won."[82]

If London was worried about enlargement diluting NATO, Paris was worried about it possibly strengthening the Alliance. Enlarging NATO was, in the words of one senior French official, like "giving NATO vitamins." France's instincts were to integrate Central and Eastern Europe through European, not trans-Atlantic, institutions. In the spring of 1993, Paris proposed the Balladur plan for Central and Eastern Europe. As the debate over NATO membership picked up steam in the summer and fall, Paris also pushed for the expansion of WEU associate membership to these countries. As France's new Defense Minister François Leotard said: "To knock at NATO's door is to knock at America's door and ask for American guarantees. That is understandable, but it is not our conception. We want the request for security to be directed to the countries of Europe."[83] The French Ambassador to NATO, Jacques Blot, told Ambassador Hunter in Brussels that he doubted the U.S. would support NATO enlargement since it was only a matter of time before the U.S. left Europe.[84]

Germany's position was key, but it was speaking with different voices. Following Ruehe's speech German Foreign Office officials had rushed to tell their U.S. counterparts that he did not speak for the German Foreign Office. Chancellor Kohl was not on board either. In late September 1993, Richard Holbrooke arrived as the new U.S. Ambassador to Germany. He immediately cabled back to Washington: "In my first meetings yesterday, three top German officials, including Chancellor Kohl, disassociated themselves from Defense Minister Ruehe's views on NATO's future." He quoted the Chancellor as having given him the following message at a private dinner the previous evening: "NATO can exclude taking in countries of Eastern Europe. At the NATO summit in January, we must talk of restructuring and reorienting NATO. We must tell these East European countries that they can count on our support, but not membership." Afterward, German National Security Advisor Bitterlich emphasized to Holbrooke that Ruehe was "on his own" on the expansion issue.[85]

All eyes were now on Moscow. Yeltsin had returned home from Warsaw and Prague to a barrage of criticism for his comments in Warsaw. In private Russian officials started to walk back his remarks. Mamedov now suggested to Talbott that Yeltsin's remarks had been highly cynical and had only agreed to Walesa's request in Warsaw because he thought the West would never act on it. On September 3 he previewed with U.S. embassy officials the contents of a draft Yeltsin letter on enlargement that showed that the Russian position was turning against enlargement.[86] The U.S. Ambassador to Moscow, Tom Pickering, warned Washington not to interpret Yeltsin's comments in Warsaw as a green light and insisted that Moscow still overwhelmingly opposed NATO enlargement.[87] Shortly thereafter, Kozyrev told Pickering that Moscow did not oppose enlargement, but that Russia should be the first to join.[88]

In mid-September 1993, Yeltsin's letter arrived in Washington and several other European capitals. It reaffirmed that Moscow did not consider NATO an enemy and recognized the rights of the Central and East Europeans to choose their own alliances. But Yeltsin also insisted that relations between Russia and NATO should always be "a few degrees warmer" than those between the

Alliance and Central and Eastern Europe. Instead of NATO enlarging, he proposed that the Alliance and Russia offer reciprocal security guarantees to Central and Eastern Europe and that the two sides work together to create a new pan-European security system. Russia, Yeltsin wrote, did not exclude wanting to join NATO herself but that "for the time being" this was only a theoretical possibility.[89] The letter leaked to the press in Central and Eastern Europe where it created an uproar.

The existence of harder-line views in Moscow soon became clear in late November when Yevgeny Primakov, then head of the Federal Security Bureau (FSB), the Russian Federation's successor to the KGB, issued his own study entitled "Prospects for NATO Expansion and Russia's Interests. Foreign Intelligence Service Report," in which he painted a much more dire threat posed by enlargement.[90] At a press conference on November 25, Primakov argued that NATO remained a threat to Russian national interests and would require the Russian military to rethink its force posture and defense budget. In introducing the report to the press, Primakov was blunt in his view: "What is being put before us is entirely unambiguous. Once there was confrontation between the two blocs. One of these has ceased to exist and the other is extending its influence into the area of the former Warsaw Treaty Organization. This is believed to be a reliable guarantee of security? We do not believe that."[91]

Primakov's target was Kozyrev. The future Russian Foreign Minster was already maneuvering to position himself as Kozyrev's successor and as someone who could be more effective in standing up to the West. It also reflected the policy dilemma Russian policymakers faced: Could Moscow have more influence over NATO and Western policy by working with the West? Or should it try to fight enlargement? Kozyrev favored the former; Primakov the latter. Kozyrev believed Russia could maximize its influence toward the Alliance by engaging the West. Primakov dismissed that approach as "capitulationist." In the fall of 1993, Yeltsin was still following the Kozyrev line. Meeting with Woerner in December, Yeltsin shocked the Secretary General when he said that he considered the prospect of Russia joining NATO a "realistic" one. His only worry, he added, was what the Chinese would think about Russia joining NATO.[92]

4. THE PARTNERSHIP FOR PEACE

The Clinton Administration was internally deadlocked on NATO enlargement. A Deputies Committee meeting on September 15 failed to find common ground, as did discussions between Christopher, Aspin, and Lake in the so-called CAL channel.[93] The Pentagon opposed enlargement and preferred to keep PfP as a stand-alone initiative, but was willing to live with a link if it was kept general and noncommittal.[94] Lake and Christopher wanted a specific commitment to enlargement, the announcement of criteria, and an "associate membership" as well as PfP. As NSC Senior Director Jennone Walker suggested in a note to Lake on September 23: "My admittedly imperfect proposed compromise is to say we expect and want NATO to expand to include new democracies; the pace will vary depending on applicants readiness and with due regard to security and stability throughout Europe (code for not disregarding Russian/Ukrainian/others' concerns); and meanwhile Partnership participation will immediately produce a qualitative change in NATO's engagement in the east while preparing states for possible eventual NATO membership."[95]

The debate was overshadowed by the brewing political crisis in Moscow which now escalated into violence and bloodshed. On September 21, Yeltsin announced he was suspending parliament and calling for new elections. His opponents in the Duma immediately voted to have him removed from office. Two days later, armed men linked to Yeltsin's opposition raided a Moscow military unit for weapons and killed several militiamen. On September 25, Interior Ministry troops surrounded the Russian White House. The entire world watched on CNN as the bloody battle for Russia's future was fought out over the next week, culminating in Yeltsin's order to the Russian military on October 3 to shell the holed-up parliamentarians in the Russian White House to force them to surrender.

That same weekend, NATO Secretary General Woerner arrived in Washington to discuss the goals for the upcoming NATO summit. In his meetings he pulled the Scharioth paper out of his pocket to make the case for NATO enlargement. On October 5, he told Christopher that he saw a rare historical opportunity to anchor Central and Eastern Europe once and for all to the West and urged him to recommend setting the enlargement process in motion without specifying who would be able to join, and when. Christopher responded that the U.S. was thinking positively about expansion but had not reached a final decision.[96] On the plane back to Brussels, Woerner told his staff that he felt this had been his most productive trip to Washington in years and that he believed that he had helped convince the Americans to say "yes" to enlargement. When Les Aspin arrived in Brussels two weeks later with the Partnership for Peace proposal, Woerner would ask his staff: What happened back in Washington?

Several things had happened. Events in Moscow had made the differences in the top echelons of the Administration over enlargement more, not less, intractable. A Principals Committee meeting was called for October 18 to settle them. Christopher scheduled a final meeting with his top aides for Saturday, October 16 to go over the position he would take. On October 15, Davis again urged him to support enlargement. "We are close to losing the ability to lead the Alliance on NATO's future," she wrote. "Western Europeans are becoming increasingly critical and uncertain of our resolve to remain seriously engaged in Europe. Reform in Central and Eastern Europe is under growing challenge, while America's interest is focused elsewhere. . . . Russia stands on the brink with instability casting fear around its periphery," Davis wrote. "We have little time before the December NATO Ministerials. I urge you to move to a decision early in the week on NATO expansion and the character of the Peacekeeping Partnership."[97]

On Saturday morning, October 16, Christopher went over the pro and con arguments on enlargement one last time with his senior staff. Both Davis and Donilon left the meeting believing he had decided to support launching NATO enlargement. New talking points were tasked making the argument that the NATO summit had to send a clear signal on expansion and establish associate membership status as an intermediate step toward that goal.[98] Later that afternoon, Davis left town on a long scheduled trip. Talbott, on the other hand, returned from a conference in St. Louis that afternoon. Donilon called to brief him on the results of the Secretary's meeting. He immediately decided to write Christopher his own memo, making the case against Davis's view and in favor of a slower, more gradual approach. He delivered his memo in person at the Secretary's home the next day, a Sunday.

Talbott's memo argued that the coming fortnight was a critical test of the U.S. ability to reconcile its policies on NATO, Russia, and coaxing Ukraine to abandon its nuclear weapons. At the core of that test, he insisted, was whether the Administration would put Poland, the Czech Republic, and Hungary on a "fast track" to NATO membership. While endorsing the integration of Central Europe into the West in principle, Talbott wrote: "We must not advance that goal at the expense of our support for reform further East, especially in Russia — which, after all, the President keeps saying is our No. 1 priority. A NATO-plus-V3 strategy, even if it is only an implicit one, risks putting our East Europe policy and our NIS policy in zero-sum competition with each other."

Russian reformers, Talbott wrote, viewed the NATO enlargement issue as a crucial test of Washington's commitment to the U.S.-Russian "strategic alliance" announced earlier in the year. Talbott referred to an op-ed by Vaclav Havel that had appeared that day in *The New York Times* arguing that NATO enlargement, by consolidating democracy in Central and Eastern Europe, would actually shore up Russian democrats. He told Christopher that he disagreed with the Czech President. "I fear — and certainly Yeltsin is telling us — that we'd be doing just the opposite." It would be harder for the U.S. to sustain, in Russian reformers' minds, the claim to be Moscow's key partner if Washington was seen as treating Yeltsin as a second-class partner after Havel and Walesa. "The key principle, as I see it, is this," Talbott argued. "An expanded NATO that excludes Russia will not serve to contain Russia's retrograde, expansionist impulses; quite the contrary, it will further provoke them."

Instead, Talbott argued for a slower and more general approach. "My recommended bottom line is this: take the one new idea that seems to be universally accepted, the Partnership for Peacekeeping, which truly is inclusive, and make that, rather than expanded NATO membership (which is at least implicitly exclusive) the centerpiece of our NATO position." In conclusion he wrote: "We can hold out the possibility that our Peacekeeping Partners might, in the future, be eligible for membership, but we should avoid criteria and talk of associate status." He pointed to a cable sent in by Ambassador Hunter arguing for making PfP the summit's centerpiece.[99]

But Talbott also laid out his fallback position: "Since I'm being so blunt in this memo, I might as well go all the way and lay out my fallback. If, despite the appeal I'm making here, our Administration decides to proceed on a NATO-plus-V3 fast track, then let's take Yeltsin up on his proposal for a security arrangement of some kind between the Russian Federation and NATO." Talbott, who would become the Administration's architect in NATO-Russia negotiations three years later, ended with a sentence that was almost prophetic: "Perhaps (imagine my squinting and crossing my fingers) by being maximally responsive to him on that, we can offer him consolation, or an "offset," for what we'll be giving the V3. I'm not sure this would do the trick, although it would help minimize the dangers and damage I'm concerned about."[100]

Talbott's memo persuaded Christopher to reconsider his position. On Monday, October 18, he called in his top aides to inform them that he had opted to support Talbott's slower and more general approach on enlargement at the PC. With Christopher now favoring the slow track option along with Aspin and Shalikashvili, Lake was isolated as the only person favoring a more ambitious approach at the Principals Committee meeting that afternoon. PfP became the Administration's summit centerpiece. An NSC memo summarizing the Principals' conclusions noted that: "The summit should make a commitment in principle to NATO expansion but without articulating criteria, specifying timing or likely candidates for membership or establishing the concept for associate status. The path to membership," it continued, should be described as an "evolutionary process" with active participation in PfP as an important step in preparing states for the possibility of full membership in the future." It was an ambiguous compromise, a decision not to decide that had kicked the can down the road on this issue.[101]

Christopher now outlined the official U.S. position to his NATO Foreign Minister colleagues. The U.S. wanted the summit to "send a clear, politically effective message of NATO's relevance to European security in post–Cold War Europe," he wrote. Washington's goal was to "qualitatively transform NATO's relationship with the new democracies of the East." PfP was an effort to provide a framework for military cooperation that would demonstrate "in tangible terms NATO's intention to forge new security relationships with the nations to the East." The summit "should formally open the door to an evolutionary process of NATO expansion" without setting a timetable or criteria for membership. "A summit statement of principles opening the door to future enlargement,"

Christopher concluded, "would be seen as a victory for pro-Western forces in the former communist countries without, in our judgment, risking destabilizing consequences in the area."[102]

With a common position and a plan for consultations in place, Christopher and Aspin left for Europe—Christopher to Budapest and Moscow and Aspin to the annual fall informal NATO Defense Ministers meeting in the northern German city of Travemuende. But modern diplomacy is made as much through public presentation as through carefully worded diplomatic correspondence. Aspin arrived on the ground in Europe first, and it was his comments to the media that made the first news. He emphasized that NATO was not close to making any decisions about enlargement.[103] The U.S. delegation circulated a paper that was also cool on enlargement. "Rather than forcing a premature consideration of formal membership at this time," the paper stated, "the partnership focuses instead on real elements of defense cooperation." At some point, the paper concluded, "as critical uncertainties about European security are resolved, and nations continue to evolve toward pluralistic, democratic states, then the question of expanded membership in NATO can be addressed."[104]

German Defense Minister Ruehe was the host at Travemuende. He had sent Weisser to Washington in advance to check out where the policy debate in Washington was going. Weisser reported that support for enlargement was strongest in the White House and State Department but that the Pentagon was opposed and viewed PfP as an alternative to enlargement. Armed with this report, Ruehe approached his colleague and friend, Danish Defense Minister Hans Haekkerup, to discuss how they could ensure that the meeting and the unveiling of PfP send a positive signal on enlargement. The two men agreed to argue both in the meeting and in public that it was critical that NATO make clear that PfP was not an alternative to enlargement but rather a stepping-stone to that goal.[105] Woerner, sensing an embarrassing rift between the U.S. and several allied delegations, stepped in to bridge the gap. In summarizing the meeting before the press, he underscored that PfP had received the full support of the Ministers but that it was not an alternative to NATO enlargement.[106] Later that day, the Ministers visited the Marienkirche in the neighboring city of Lubeck where Woerner gave an impassioned speech on the need for NATO to reach out to Central and Eastern Europe to overcome the legacy of the Cold War.

On the Secretary of State's plane en route to Budapest, Christopher's staff saw press reports on Aspin's conservative remarks on PfP coming over the wire. They immediately woke up sleeping reporters to provide their own briefing to ensure that the more forward-leaning State Department interpretation of PfP also made the news. *Washington Post* diplomatic correspondent Tom Lippman recalls being aroused from sleeping and suddenly offered a detailed briefing on PfP—despite being told earlier that such a briefing was not going to happen. On background, a "senior State Department official" emphasized that PfP "would qualitatively transform NATO's relations with the new democracies in the East" and open the door to eventual NATO enlargement.[107] Back in Washington, Lake went before the press to clarify the confusion generated by conflicting reports coming from Travemuende and Budapest.[108] It was an inauspicious launch for the U.S. initiative.

In Budapest, Christopher's job was to reassure the Central and East Europeans that PfP was an important step in their direction they should support. It was a tough sell. Only two weeks earlier, Hungarian Prime Minster Joszef Antall, who was dying of cancer, had written Clinton a personal letter from the hospital following the bloody events in Moscow. He underscored that his government was supportive of Yeltsin and the democratic forces in Moscow but called on Clinton to "accelerate the NATO integration of the country so that membership be attained as soon as possible" in light of the growing conflict in the Balkans and instability in Russia.[109]

Arriving in Budapest, Christopher tried to put the best foot forward on the U.S. initiative by tying PfP to NATO's eventual expansion. At the press conference with Hungarian Foreign Minister Geza Jeszenszky, Christopher stated that "we have proposed a framework for considering expansion involving a partnership for peace." Asked whether PfP met Hungary's need, Jeszenszky responded that "the very idea that the principle that there is a possibility and even a need for expansion is something that we welcome" and that PfP was "a good start."[110]

From Budapest, Christopher traveled to Moscow. Driving in from the airport the U.S. delegation passed the charred, hulking structure of what had once been the Russian White House. Christopher was helicoptered out to Yeltsin's dacha in Zavidovo where the Russian President was recuperating from health problems and recent political events. As Christopher recalled, it was clear that Yeltsin was in pain and that his movements were stiff and almost robotic.[111] After discussing the President's upcoming trip to Moscow, Christopher raised the NATO issue. Washington did not want to exclude Russia from being a full participant in European security, he stated. That was one reason why the President had decided to propose PfP, which would be open to all members of the NACC. Yeltsin broke in to ask whether it was correct that countries from Central and Eastern Europe and the former Soviet Union would be treated on an equal footing and that there would be no invitations for new members at the upcoming NATO summit.

When Christopher responded "yes," Yeltsin became animated and called the Partnership a "brilliant idea" and a "stroke of genius." He underscored that the most important thing for Moscow was to ensure equal status for all countries, including Russia, on the basis of partnership. Yeltsin reiterated that PfP was "a great idea, really great" and asked Christopher to tell President Clinton that he was thrilled by this initiative. Christopher added that in due course the Alliance would enlarge but that this would be pursued over time based on PfP. But Yeltsin was no longer paying attention.[112] On the helicopter ride back to Moscow, Talbott tried to tell Kozyrev that the enlargement issue had simply been deferred, not resolved, but the Russian Foreign Minster pretended not to be able to hear over the engine noise. Both Yeltsin and Kozyrev had nothing but words of praise in public for PfP, portraying it as having put off NATO enlargement. As Christopher concluded in his memoirs: "In retrospect, it is clear that his enthusiasm was based upon his mistaken assumption that the Partnership for Peace would not lead to eventual NATO expansion."[113]

If Moscow was relieved, Warsaw, Prague, and Budapest were not. The tone of Christopher's Hungarian hosts also became more critical as soon as the Secretary of State had left town. Defense Minister Lajos Fur told the Hungarian media that he was not sure what PfP meant for Hungary except that it did not give Budapest what it wanted—namely a security guarantee.[114] Jeszenszky, a historian by training, delivered a speech shortly thereafter entitled "The Lessons of Appeasement" in which he pointed to the West's appeasement of Hitler in the late 1930s and to its acquiescence to Stalin's sphere of influence in Eastern Europe after World War II. Referring to the Latin saying *Vincere scis Hannibal, victoriam uti nescis* (You know how to win, Hannibal, but not how to use your victory), Jeszenszky argued that there was a thin line between "offering genuine friendship (or partnership) and inviting disaster by giving too much away without guarantees for proper behavior. . . . If the lessons of appeasement are not drawn," he added, "we may well see our hopes dashed again."[115] It was hardly a ringing endorsement.

Assistant Secretary of State for European Affairs Steve Oxman had stayed behind in Budapest to further brief the Deputy Foreign Ministers of Poland, the Czech Republic and Hungary following Christopher's departure. Although the U.S. record of that conversation suggests that they were starting to come around to the U.S. position by the end of the evening, several of the Central European participants have a different recollection.[116] The head of the Polish delegation, Deputy Foreign Minister Andrzej Ananicz, recalls asking himself whether PfP was part of a strategy to overcome or to perpetuate Yalta. Over coffee he asked the U.S. Assistant Secretary of State the question directly. Oxman's answer left him worried that PfP ran the risk of becoming an alternative track to enlargement where Poland might be stranded in a kind of strategic limbo. He reported to Foreign Minister Olechowski and President Lech Walesa that PfP was not only inadequate but also dangerous.[117]

These countries were disappointed with PfP because, from their perspective, it looked more like a potential dead end than a first step toward NATO membership. It offered no commitment, plan, or roadmap for eventual NATO membership. Their main concern was not peacekeeping capabilities but their own defense and security needs. Central and East Europeans did not find the official arguments reassuring about why NATO could not be more explicit about NATO enlargement reassuring either. As two senior Polish officials wrote: "NATO's reluctance to embrace the East Central European states reminds some in these capitals of the live-in lover, enjoying the benefits of affection but anxious to avoid the onerous commitments of marriage."[118] If the West was unwilling to stand up to Moscow when it was weak, they asked, what would it do if Russia became strong again? When ultra-nationalist Vladimir Zhirinovsky emerged as the big winner in the Russian Duma elections in December, it sent shivers down the spines of many in these countries. Along with the communists, nationalists now had more than twice as many votes as the parties supporting Yeltsin.

Nowhere was this anxiety greater than in Poland. Walesa and Olechowski now decided that PfP was not acceptable and that it had to push Washington for more. While they knew there was a risk of overplaying their hand, they knew also that Washington needed their stamp of approval. As a senior State Department official admitted to *The Washington Post*, Central and East European opposition to PfP would be devastating: "If they don't believe in the partnership, then it serves no purpose." [119] Thus was born a Polish strategy to try to make PfP into something Warsaw could accept. Polish officials differentiated between what they called PfP I and PfP II. PfP I was Aspin's PfP at Travemuende. PfP II would include a clearer political commitment that it was a first step to actual NATO membership.[120]

Over the next three months Poland played the one card it had—Washington's need for its support of PfP—to try to stretch the U.S. initiative to meet its own political needs. In mid-December Olechowski arrived in Washington to tell Christopher that he had come to "knock again" at the door of NATO membership. Poland did not want to accelerate the NATO enlargement process but Warsaw's support for PfP was linked to whether it was or was not a path to NATO membership. If Washington made clear that PfP was a path to NATO membership, it would be Warsaw's highest priority. If not, political support for Poland's participation in PfP would be lacking.[121] Arriving back in Warsaw, Olechowski publicly stated that Poland would not sign PfP if it was "just a second Yalta."[122] On December 22, he sent Christopher a letter reiterating that Poland would support PfP only if it included a clear membership perspective to countries that met NATO standards and were willing and able to defend its values.[123]

Poland had two unique assets to draw on. One was Lech Walesa. Having faced down the Soviets, the former Solidarity leader was no novice when it came to remaining stubborn and fighting for his views. Ambassador Nicholas Rey, a Democratic Polish-American businessman from Wall Street, experienced Walesa's tactics firsthand when he arrived in Warsaw in late December to assume his new duties. He knew that many Poles still blamed U.S. President

Franklin Delano Roosevelt and the Democratic Party for their betrayal at Yalta and he was determined to show them that they were wrong to distrust the Clinton Administration. While presenting his credentials to President Walesa on December 22, Walesa pulled him into a small back room for a private conversation. Sitting knee-to-knee with Rey, Walesa lectured him on the dangers of Russian neo-imperialism. Walesa told him: "Mr. Ambassador, we have to cage the bear." When Rey summoned his courage to point out to the Nobel prize winner and hero of Solidarity that a cornered bear could be dangerous, Walesa responded: "So long as it is caged it does not matter."[124]

The second asset Poland had was the Polish-American community. With some 10 million members, it was the largest of all the Central and East European ethnic communities and it had well-connected individuals working behind the scenes. At the top of that list was Jan Nowak, who as a young man had been a courier between the Polish underground resistance and London and Washington. In that role he had met Churchill and Anthony Eden and warned them about Stalin's designs on Central Europe—unsuccessfully.[125] After the war, Nowak became the head of Radio Free Europe's Polish service where for 25 years he was regarded as one of the best sources on what was happening behind the Iron Curtain. He later returned to Washington where he became an interlocutor of a series of U.S. Presidents, Republican and Democrat alike. As Berger recalled, "it was not so much a question of their numbers but also the impact of their arguments. People like Jan Nowak, a Polish-American leader, affect your thinking—because of his experience, his life story and the logic and power of his arguments."

Having witnessed Poland regain its independence in 1989, Nowak was determined that the West not make the same mistakes again. The Administration's tepid response to Yeltsin's letter of mid-September set off alarm bells for him. He turned to the media to draw attention to the issue. Shortly thereafter, an article appeared by Rowland Evans and Robert Novak in entitled "Ghost of Yalta," warning that PfP was "a sweetheart deal offering Russia virtual hegemony over most of the former Soviet Union and denying Eastern Europe entry into NATO."[126] On November 30, 18 ethnic groups of Central and East European origin met in Washington to coordinate a lobbying effort in favor of enlargement. On December 6 they founded the Central and East European Coalition (CEEC). That same day the Polish-American Congress (PAC) sent a letter to Polish-Americans urging them to call and write the White House to protest against what they called "Yalta II."[127]

On December 21, National Security Advisor Tony Lake met with former NSC Advisor Zbigniew Brzezinski to discuss the President's upcoming trip to Europe. Brzezinski told Lake that the Administration's policy lacked clarity and vision. He urged that Clinton set the specific goal of achieving for Central and Eastern Europe, and in particular, Poland, what George Bush had achieved for a unified Germany—membership in NATO. Lake responded that he agreed with Brzezinski and that the State Department's narrow interpretation of PfP was not the last word on the subject. Lake added that he expected some movement on the enlargement issue in the President's speech in Brussels. Lake also assured him that the concept of democratic enlargement that he had spelled out at Johns Hopkins University's School of Advanced International Studies (SAIS) in Washington, D.C. in September was still the core of the Clinton Administration's foreign policy and that it applied to Europe.[128]

At an internal NSC staff meeting later that day to review the materials being prepared for the President, Lake erupted in anger at some of the papers his staff had prepared. He complained that they did not recognize the historic moment the U.S.-European relationship was at or how the U.S. initiatives fit together into a coherent vision. He referred to his breakfast meeting with Brzezinski and their discussion about the "big picture." He told his staff that they needed to be bolder and to address the Central European anxiety by making it clear that there was a path for them to integrate into the West. Referring to PfP he asked his staff: "You have given me a wonderful instrument in PfP but where is the President's vision?" He sent most of the papers back to be reworked. One paper went forward to the President unchanged. It described why the Central and East Europeans were interested in joining NATO in the first place.

Book III

ACROSS THE RUBICON

1994 was the year the Clinton Administration crossed the Rubicon in deciding to enlarge NATO. That decision took place not in one clear or decisive stride, but rather through a series of policy steps that cumulatively set the Administration on course to open NATO's door to Central and Eastern Europe. In a NATO summit in January, the U.S. and its allies embraced the goal of NATO enlargement in principle. President Clinton then met with the Visegrad heads-of-state in Prague, where he stated that enlargement was "no longer a question of whether but when and how."

But making a decision in principle and implementing it in practice were not the same thing. Indeed, the key issues in the debate were precisely those issues that NATO leaders had dodged: why, when, and how would the Alliance enlarge? Would it enlarge to extend a security umbrella over the region and fill in a security vacuum, in tandem with the EU's eventual enlargement, or only in response to the emergence of a new Russian threat, should one arise? Neither the declaration by NATO heads of state in Brussels nor Bill Clinton's statement in Prague had answered those questions. The reason for the silence on these issues was quite simple: there was not yet consensus on the way ahead.

In the course of the year, however, the Clinton Administration started to fill in the blanks on these key questions, at least in its own internal deliberations. It would take the rest of the year for the Administration to consolidate that decision and to resolve the final differences within its own ranks. By the end of the year that opposition had been overcome, a strategy had developed, and the U.S. had started to move forward with NATO enlargement.

This is perhaps the most important, yet also the murkiest, period in the Administration's internal deliberations and the one that future historians are likely to debate. The decision to enlarge NATO was ambiguous and opaque, at times deliberately so, and it was a decision that hardly qualified as a model of executive branch decisionmaking. Preoccupied with its domestic agenda and foreign policy crises in places like Haiti, Somalia, and Bosnia, the Administration never held a second top-level Principals Committee meeting to make a final decision to move forward on NATO enlargement. Nor did Clinton receive or sign the kind of official action memorandum that normally accompanies a major foreign policy decision in the U.S. government's interagency process.

Instead, one of the most far-reaching decisions on future U.S. strategy toward Europe emerged from behind-the-scenes bureaucratic combat, subtle public high-level policy proclamations, and growing political pressure from Republican opponents on Capitol Hill. Future historians will debate whether these vagaries reflected sloppy decisionmaking or deliberate Machiavellian bureaucratic behavior—or some combination of both. Even today key figures involved in the process at the time do not fully agree exactly when the Administration made the decision to enlarge NATO. But one thing is clear. While public debate over expanding the Alliance would continue unabated for several years to come, the Administration had crossed its own Rubicon.[1]

The first step in this shift came in January 1994 when Alliance heads-of-state embraced the goal of NATO enlargement and launched the Partnership for Peace (PfP) at a summit in Brussels. In Prague several days later, President Clinton announced at a meeting with the four Visegrad heads of state that NATO enlargement was no longer a question of "whether" but "when" and "how." That statement was the result of an intense set of discussions among the President and his key aides in the run up to Clinton's first trip to Europe and reflected the President's desire to send a clear message that PfP was the start of a process that would open NATO's door to new members.

Yet, it was one thing to endorse enlargement in principle and quite another to set into motion the practical steps to make it happen. PfP was being launched at NATO with no agreement or even direct consideration of how it might actually lead to NATO enlargement. The issues of why, when, or how the Alliance would enlarge were never even raised at the January meeting of NATO leaders. Would enlargement take place before or after the EU's own enlargement? In two years or in ten? Or, would it take place only if a new Russian threat were to emerge? Instead of answering such questions, the summit had simply kicked the can down the road.

In the spring of 1994 National Security Advisor Lake made the first step in answering such questions when he quietly asked his staff to prepare a memo for the President that provided a rationale, a framework, and a timeline for NATO enlargement—i.e., a plan. Lake presented the memo to the President in late June. In Europe several weeks later, the President publicly called on the Alliance to take the next steps in the enlargement process. Ambassador Richard C. Holbrooke was brought back to Washington in the autumn of 1994 to work in Bosnia and impose the President's will to enlarge NATO on a recalcitrant bureaucracy. In September, Clinton told Russian President Boris Yeltsin for the first time that he was committed to enlarging NATO, but that the process would be gradual and that he would respect Russian interests and sensitivities.

The President's decision to push ahead with enlargement was reinforced by conservative Republican pressure on the Administration to be more outspoken. In the summer of 1994, Republicans embraced NATO enlargement as a key foreign policy goal in the Contract with America and tabled legislation on Capitol Hill calling on the Administration to identify specific candidates and set a public timeline for enlargement. After the Republican landslide victory in the November 1994 midterm congressional elections, the enlargement issue moved from the world of strategic seminars and internal Alliance debates to the political arena.

The shift in U.S. policy on NATO enlargement that took place in the course of the year had a cascading effect on attitudes across the European continent. Allies in Western Europe were caught by surprise, as many had concluded that PfP was intended to dodge the enlargement issues for some time to come. Many were reticent to follow the U.S. lead. The result was a compromise, in which an official NATO study on enlargement was launched in December at the annual Foreign Minister's meeting. Even this small half-step, however, elicited an angry outburst from Russian President Boris Yeltsin. Moscow's hostile reaction, in turn, convinced enlargement skeptics in the Clinton Administration, led by new Secretary of Defense Bill Perry, to make one final appeal to the President to reverse course. But the President stood by the decision to press forward.

To be sure, NATO enlargement was not yet a done deal. Many of the biggest hurdles still lay ahead. A cloud of uncertainty continued to hang over the Administration's policy as it slowly moved forward with enlargement, struggled to find its footing in Bosnia as well as to steady an increasingly topsy-turvy relationship with Moscow. Critics repeatedly questioned the depth of the President's support. Many predicted Washington would buckle under Russian pressure, weak allied support, or intellectual opposition at home. But the Administration would hold firm.

1. AN AMBIGUOUS DECISION

In early January 1994, Bill Clinton prepared to depart on his first trip as President to Europe and Russia. It was his first major opportunity to lay out his vision of a post–Cold War trans-Atlantic relationship and to highlight how his policies toward Europe and Russia meshed. The trip's itinerary was designed to underscore his commitment to building a Europe undivided, democratic, and secure. His first stop was the NATO summit in Brussels. It was followed by a meeting in Prague with the heads of state of the four Visegrad countries. From there the President would stop briefly in Kiev on his way to Moscow. A brief and final stop was scheduled in Minsk, the capital city of Belarus, to seal an arms reduction deal that rid Ukraine and Belarus of the nuclear warheads inherited from the breakup of the USSR.

Tony Lake knew that the President was leaning toward enlargement. As National Security Advisor, his job was not only to make sure the President knew about differences on key issues in his national security team, but also to implement the President's own will. Lake was determined that the President's trip send a clear message on America's willingness to lead in opening NATO's door to the East. Sending a positive message on enlargement was central to the President's vision of a modern, updated Alliance. In the run-up to the trip, Lake and his Deputy, Sandy Berger, talked to President Clinton at length about NATO's future and what was at stake for the United States. It was those discussions and the subsequent trip that crystallized Clinton's support for enlargement.

As Sandy Berger noted, "The catalytic event was the President's trip to Europe in January 1994." Berger went on: "In preparation for that trip there were a series of discussions between the President and Tony Lake and myself about the concept of NATO enlargement. The President's view, which Tony and I supported, was that while Article V and collective defense needed to remain at NATO's core, the Alliance's membership and missions needed to be revised to maintain its relevance and the trans-Atlantic link as well as to provide a magnet for the East. That trip was a very important event and the President's statement in Prague publicly endorsed NATO enlargement for the first time. That statement was the result of a dialogue that had taken place between the President, Tony and me on enlargement."[2]

The more immediate problem facing the Administration was shoring up Central and East European support for PfP. In early January, Christopher had written his Central and East European counterparts urging them to embrace and exploit PfP's potential to build closer relations with NATO, but the response was not the desired one.[3] Nowhere was skepticism greater than in Warsaw. Olechowski complained privately that PfP made NATO membership appear like a "vanishing point" on the horizon.[4] Walesa unleashed his harshest public criticism yet, publicly lambasting PfP as a "major tragedy" bordering on appeasement. He insisted that by not standing up to Moscow, the West was only fueling Russian imperial tendencies. "If the West allows small things like this today, it will allow bigger things tomorrow. . . . We kept crying and shouting in 1939 but they only believed us when the war reached London and Paris. The situation is very similar today."[5]

Warsaw's support was critical for PfP's success. To get it, the Administration turned to three individuals in its ranks of Central European origin—Czech-born Madeleine K. Albright, Polish-born General John Shalikashvilli and Hungarian-born Charles Gati—to visit the region and lobby for the U.S. initiative. But their main mission was to get Walesa to endorse PfP—and to do so before the President arrived in Prague. On the day the trip was announced, Shalikashvilli defended PfP in a press briefing and made it clear that he viewed it as an alternative to NATO enlarging in the near-term. He argued that enlarging NATO could be "destabilizing" by drawing "a new line of division" in Europe that could fuel nationalist feelings in Russia. While PfP did not have NATO membership as its specific endpoint, he argued that it would start a process at the end of which all parties "would be in a much better position to seriously discuss" actual enlargement. Having counseled prudence, he said that the debate had already shifted and was now less about "whether" the Alliance should expand than "how" and "when." It was meant as a description of where the debate stood, not as a policy statement.[6]

When Albright, Gati and Shalikashvilli met with Walesa in Warsaw on January 7, the Polish President delivered a blunt message: PfP was "doomed to fail." The U.S., he insisted, was missing a historic opportunity to build a lasting peace in Europe. He urged Washington to make a "quick, short leap" to expand NATO and accomplish that goal. PfP, he complained, was more like crawling than leaping. Admitting that it would be "ridiculous" for him to reject PfP, he insisted that this U.S. initiative would only encourage Russian imperial tendencies. "To tame the bear," he told his U.S. guests, "you must put him in a cage and not let him run free in the forest."

It was already too late to stop Moscow from asserting its control in the CIS, Walesa continued. Enlarging NATO was only going to get harder with time if the West remained too preoccupied with Russian concerns. NATO should just enlarge and not pay any attention to what Moscow said. "Let the Russian Generals get upset," he proclaimed, "they won't start a nuclear war." Failure to act now could close the door permanently. American attempts at "finesse and nobility" were of little help when dealing with Russian blackmail, he told the U.S. delegation. "If the West does not leap now, it never will," he concluded.

Albright responded by telling Walesa that the U.S. had supported Poland during the long struggle against communism and it would continue to do so now. She recalled how impressed she had been watching him calm down striking Polish workers at a steel factory in 1981 and urged him to show the same pragmatism now. PfP could be the "leap" Walesa was looking for if he embraced it and exploited its potential. Shali added that the U.S. had not flinched in dealing with Moscow during the Cold War and that it would not flinch now or in the future. Both Albright and Shali told Walesa that the U.S. had a "direct and material interest" in Poland's security and would not abandon it—language that came close to sounding like a promise to come to Poland's defense.

Walesa was still not impressed. The U.S. had followed a brilliant strategy in winning the Cold War, he noted, but Washington was now making a mistake. Poles were among the most pro-American people in the world, but there were already nationalistic voices saying that Warsaw should stop begging the West to integrate them. He would consider carefully what to say when President Clinton came to Europe, Walesa continued, but as a "friend of America" he felt compelled to remain stubborn in his opposition. Foreign Minister Olechowski added that one could fill the Presidential library with "beautiful, idealistic statements" on Western intentions, but not one contained what Poland needed—a meaningful commitment on a timetable or roadmap.[7]

Afterward, Olechowski pulled Albright and Shali aside and repeated that there was a growing feeling arising in Poland of being spurned by the West. To turn public opinion around, PfP had to be seen as opening the door to Poland's eventual membership in NATO. If nothing else, "my job is on the line," he quipped. PfP in its current form was based on nothing more than "promises, promises and promises." What Poland needed, he said, was a U.S. assurance that it could join if and when it met all the criteria. "If at the end of the day, we look like a duck and quack like a duck, we want assurance that we will be called a duck," he concluded.[8]

The argument continued over dinner where Olechowski was joined by former Solidarity dissident and head of the Democratic Union party, Bronislaw Geremek, as well as the head of the post-communist Democratic Left alliance, Aleksandr Kwasniewski.[9] Kwasniewksi told the American guests that he had won the recent parliamentary elections, and that Geremek—who was seated next to him—had lost in part because of the West's reluctance to embrace Poland. Geremek nodded in agreement. Both men urged Washington to think in historic terms. Solidarity had succeeded by daring to do what others said could not be done. And Helmut Kohl had unified Germany by ignoring the nay-sayers, too. Washington had to use a window of opportunity that might last only months, not years.

Albright responded that Clinton cared deeply about Poland's security and wanted to move forward. But that would not happen if Poland refused to engage and continued to view PfP as a detour from its goal. The U.S. knew that it had to deliver with PfP, she continued, and that its own credibility was on the line. Shalikashvili added that it was simply not possible at this point to bring Poland into NATO in the short-term. The 16 members of the Alliance would never agree to it. The U.S. had brought the Alliance to the point where it was debating not the "whether" but "when." But it did not want to make promises it could not deliver and repeat the mistakes of the 1930s when allies extended security guarantees they later did not implement.[10]

Back in the U.S., Vice President Al Gore was defending the President's policy against similar criticism. The Vice President, stepping in for Clinton, who was attending his mother's funeral, delivered a major speech in Milwaukee. In it, Gore rejected criticism that the U.S. was neglecting the security of Central and Eastern Europe with PfP. "The security of the states that lie between Western Europe and Russia affects the security of America," Gore said. America had not spent years supporting Solidarity just to lose democracy in Poland; nor had it celebrated the Velvet Revolution just to watch it die from neglect, Gore insisted. "We prevailed in the Cold War for their sake and ours," the Vice President stated, "And now, we must prevail for their sake and ours in building a broader, democratic peace throughout Europe." PfP, he insisted, was meant to help these countries integrate into the West and to build the cooperation that could lead to NATO membership.[11]

The evening before, Berger and Dan Fried spent several hours in a heated roundtable discussion with the leaders from the U.S. ethnic communities of Central and East European origin. Participants on both sides subsequently recalled the meeting as a vivid moment in the enlargement debate. While the ethnic communities' leaders voiced their criticism of the Administration's policy as too deferential to Russia, they also sensed an openness on Berger's part and a commitment to Central and Eastern Europe that they had not expected. Berger, in turn, recalls being impressed by the group's sophistication and their arguments. He was disappointed by his inability to convince them that they should trust the Administration. Both sides would look back at this meeting as an important step in starting a dialogue on enlargement between the Administration and the ethnic communities that would deepen in the years ahead.[12]

On January 8, the President departed for Europe. As Air Force One crossed the Atlantic, Clinton sat down with Christopher, Lake, and Talbott, to talk about enlargement. Talbott, worried about the President's inclination to tailor his remarks to what his audience wanted to hear, emphasized the need to avoid pro-enlargement statements in Brussels and Prague that would only create additional problems in Moscow. Lake, in turn, warned against making PfP sound like a "treadmill" that would never lead to enlargement, and underscored that what was needed was a sense of "something real, of genuine momentum." Christopher, in turn, cautioned against making it sound "like a moving sidewalk that just keeps moving ahead at the same speed no matter what." In his words, "The direction is not in question, but we've got to be able to control the pace." Talbott noted the need for consistency: "Just remember, it's all zero-sum between Prague and Moscow. Give joy in one place and it translates into fear and loathing in the other. Any nuances of difference in the way you handle this thing from one stop to the other will be scrutinized and interpreted to death."[13]

Clinton's first European trip was filled with the typical combination of substance and pageantry. In Brussels the President received a new saxophone from the country that invented the instrument. In Prague, he drank Pilsner beer with

Havel and played the saxophone in a Prague jazz club. In Moscow, he enjoyed a dinner of more than 20 courses, including moose lips and vodka in Yeltsin's dacha while rubbing shoulders with local Muscovites in the Arbat. Throughout the trip, he mingled with crowds of curious onlookers.

But the tone of the trip was set soon after his arrival in Brussels. Clinton staked out a claim for a younger generation of leaders on both sides of the Atlantic to redefine the U.S.-European partnership for a new era. Over the past half century, he told his audience, the trans-Atlantic community had realized only half of the triumph of the Second World War. But there was now an opportunity to complete that vision by integrating Europe's new democracies into the West. "For history," the President noted, "will judge us as it judged with scorn those who preached isolationism between the world wars, and as it has judged with praise the bold architects of the trans-Atlantic community after World War II."[14]

The President picked up on the theme at the NATO summit the next day: "I believe our generation's stewardship of this grand alliance, therefore, will most critically be judged by whether we succeed in integrating the nations to our east within the compass of Western security and Western values." NATO's founders had "always looked to the addition of new members who shared the Alliance's purposes and who could enlarge its orbit of democratic security," he added. "So let us say here to the people in Europe's East, we share with you a common destiny and we are committed to your success. The democratic community has grown, and now it is time to begin welcoming these newcomers to our neighborhood."[15]

More specifically, the President said, "the Partnership for Peace sets in motion a process that leads to the enlargement of NATO." But he also made it clear that he was not proposing enlargement in the immediate future. A rapid move on enlargement, he said, could draw a new line further eastward or foreclose the possibility of a democratic Russia and Ukraine. The President defended PfP against the accusations that it was too little too late. PfP was not a half-hearted compromise, he insisted; it was the right thing to do precisely because it enabled the Alliance to work toward enlargement while still reaching out to Russia.

On January 11, the President arrived in Prague for his first visit there since his student days. The previous day Warsaw announced that it would join PfP but labeled it "too small a step in the right direction."[16] That evening Clinton met with Czech President Vaclav Havel, explaining that two factors were key in his decision to support PfP. The first was what was politically possible. There was no consensus among NATO allies to extend formal security guarantees to the region for the time being.

But his thinking was also shaped by what was in Europe's own long-term interest, Clinton continued. Using a phrase he would repeat over and over again, the President said that he viewed PfP as a way to work for the best possible future in European security while preparing for the worst. PfP allowed NATO to prepare for eventual membership without alienating Russia or pushing Ukraine back into Moscow's orbit. The U.S. President emphasized that he believed Russia was too weak economically and militarily to be a near-term military threat. But if he was wrong, he added, PfP would have better prepared the Alliance to move quickly to extend membership as a deterrent to Moscow. Havel replied that he understood the President's logic but that it was essential to publicly state that PfP was a first step to full membership. The President agreed.[17]

The next day the President fulfilled that pledge. Following his meeting with the Visegrad heads of state, the President used a press conference to reaffirm that PfP was the beginning of a process that could lead to NATO membership. "While the Partnership is not NATO membership, neither is it a permanent holding room. It changes the entire dialogue so that now the question is no longer whether NATO will take in new members, but when and how."[18] They were the same words Shalikashvilli had used a week earlier. But coming from the President in that setting made it an unmistakable tilt toward a firmer U.S. commitment to moving forward sooner rather than later. Those words would become a battle-cry for those who wanted to move ahead on enlargement quickly. "Finally," Lake exclaimed, "we've got a Presidential marker."

The following morning Clinton met with Walesa. He told him that he had been thinking about enlargement since their first meeting at the opening of the Holocaust Museum. He saw PfP as a door to eventual full NATO membership for Poland while protecting those countries that were not ready for NATO today but might be at some future point. He also did not want to draw a new dividing line in Europe that would isolate states of the former Soviet Union. He understood that Walesa and many Poles had a different view. And he recognized that Russian behavior might make it necessary to draw a new line in Europe at some point. But, Clinton continued, he wanted to see whether it was possible to enlarge NATO gradually and to build a system that brought security to all of Europe, including Russia. If Washington was wrong and Moscow attempted to reassert its influence, the U.S. would do "the right thing" and bring Warsaw into NATO. He asked Walesa to commit to making the most of PfP.

Walesa responded that PfP was a fine initiative, but that Poland had a different view of the problem. It had learned the hard way that opportunities should be acted upon lest they vanish. "Guarantees," he told Clinton, "do not create facts; it is facts that create guarantees." The West needed to create facts on the ground. There was a historic opportunity to include Poland in the West. This is what Russian generals feared and why they spoke in such threatening tones. If this was their attitude now, one could only imagine what it would be once Moscow was stronger. Yeltsin had promised him not to block Polish entry into NATO, but the West had not acted on it and Yeltsin had subsequently changed his mind.[19] After Walesa left the room, Ambassador Rey told President Clinton he had just heard the Polish primal scream born of a thousand years of history and fifty years of personal experience.

After stopping briefly in Kiev to meet with President Kravchuk at the airport, Clinton arrived in Moscow. The trip's main goal was to reaffirm the framework for a U.S.-Russian partnership built on a Russian commitment to reform in the wake of the failed putsch attempts in Moscow and the disastrous results of the recent Duma elections. Foreign policy was discussed at a dinner held at Yeltsin's dacha on January 13. Upon his arrival, Yeltsin presented Clinton with a blue porcelain figure of the President holding a saxophone, and then had a real one brought out for him to play. Over dinner the two Presidents discussed everything from Russian politics to Yeltsin's tennis game as well as foreign policy issues such as Bosnia, Iraq and Europe.

Yeltsin told the President that the U.S.-Russian political relationship was the most important factor in Russia's foreign policy. He admitted that he was sometimes criticized for being too pro-American and allowing the West too much influence in Russia. But he wanted Clinton to know how much he appreciated his personal support and that of the U.S. "This is my personal view and it is a frank one, but it should be clearly understood on your side. We have great respect for you, for your work and for what you are doing." Russians knew, he added, that "you have come to Russia not to confront us," but "with a sense of support for Russia."

Yeltsin sketched out his vision of a future in which the U.S., Russia and the Europeans formed a kind of cartel working together on global security. While Yeltsin insisted that he supported PfP, it became clear that he did so as an alternative to NATO enlargement. If NATO were to enlarge, he told Clinton, Russia had to be the first country to join. But he quickly conceded that, "In truth, Russia is not yet ready to join NATO." He also noted that he had to consider the reaction of Russia's neighbors. Had the CIA, he teased Clinton, already done a report on the Chinese reaction to Russia joining NATO? At one point Yeltsin looked over at Talbott and raised his glass in a toast to him for being a true friend of the Russian people. His remarks left little doubt that Talbott had earned these words because he was seen as having championed PfP as an alternative to enlargement. Lake gave Talbott a wry look of amusement as he joined in the toast.

Clinton responded, telling Yeltsin by saying that there was now an unprecedented historical chance to build a unified Europe free of conflict for the first time since the rise of the nation state. That's why, the President continued, the U.S. and Russia had to work together in places like Bosnia and through partnerships like PfP. The U.S. wanted to work toward a situation where all countries in Europe had equal security. "If your efforts are successful and our own relationship of trust and confidence endures, that will be the key to gaining this objective," Clinton concluded. Yeltsin responded: "I agree with all that you have said.

The two of us have a unique potential as partners. If we decide to do something together, even in the face of obstacles, it can be done if we have your support," he added. "If we continue to work together as you suggest, we can do much to ensure peace and stability for Europe and for the rest of the world."[20]

The next day Clinton touched only lightly on NATO in a joint press conference with the Russian president. But the press zeroed in and asked Yeltsin about enlargement. He responded that NATO enlargement was fine so long as Russia was among the first to join. Europe must not be redivided "into black and white," as he put it. He was strongly opposed to admitting some countries but not others. "I'm against that; I'm absolutely opposed to it. That's why I support the President's initiative for Partnership for Peace." Clinton demurred, saying that NATO "plainly contemplated an expansion" at some future point, but PfP was "the real thing now."[21]

As the President returned home, commentators on both sides of the Atlantic tried to sort out what exactly the U.S. and its allies had or had not agreed to about NATO enlargement. Most people left the chambers of the North Atlantic Council on January 11 knowing that the issue of enlargement was now on the agenda and that NATO would enlarge at some point in time. But many assumed that NATO would only come back to this issue several years hence when PfP had been fully developed, the EU's timetable for enlargement was much clearer, and when the West had a better sense of where Russia was headed. Some Alliance officials thought this would take two to three years, others four to five years, and still others believed or hoped it would be much longer, perhaps up to a decade.

Even within the Administration's senior ranks, individuals came away from the trip with different views on just what had been decided. Lake, for example, was convinced that the President had already made the strategic decision to enlarge NATO. Referring to the Prague statement, Lake recalled: "When the President makes a speech like that, it's policy."[22] Others such as Bill Perry—who became Secretary of Defense on February 3, 1994—and the Defense Department believed that the President had merely launched PfP but had not yet made a final decision to enlarge. While enlargement was likely to happen at some future point, it was, in Perry's view, a separate issue that would be dealt with later and require another debate and decision.[23] When the Administration's NATO interagency working group (IWG) reconvened in the spring of 1994 to follow up on the summit's decisions, its focus was exclusively on getting PfP up and running. There was no discussion of actually enlarging NATO.

Even proponents of enlargement had their doubts about the Administration's future course. National Security Council aide Dan Fried, for example, recalls coming back on the plane from Europe and feeling that the momentum for NATO enlargement had been contained and that the opponents of enlargement had carried the day. Madeleine Albright, talking to some of her colleagues on the airplane trip across the Atlantic from Bucharest, expressed her own doubts about the way ahead: "I guess we did a good job of selling PfP to them. I only wish I believed in it. I only wish it were real." In a memo to the President in late January, she warned about the lingering sense of disappointment in Central and Eastern Europe—a part of the world, she pointed out, that was unabashedly pro-American. That disappointment was caused, she noted, by a sense that the West was both naïve about Russia and too slow and too timid to open its doors to the region's nations. She urged the President to pay more attention to the region and to consider a range of policy steps—precisely because enlargement seemed a distant prospect.[24]

2. SHIFTING GEARS

In the spring of 1994 the focus at NATO headquarters in Brussels was on launching the Partnership for Peace. With the implementation of this new initiative came a flurry of new diplomatic and military activities.that led to a leap in the level of interaction between the Alliance and the nations of Central and Eastern Europe. Within 10 weeks of the Brussels summit, NATO briefing teams had visited 16 countries to explain how PfP would operate. Former communist military officers who had spent years trying to decipher what was going on in the Alliance now found themselves sitting in new offices at NATO headquarters and the Partnership Coordination Cell at SHAPE headquarters in Mons receiving NATO's advice on future joint operations. To those accustomed to the hostility and secrecy of the Cold War, it was nothing less than a miracle.[25]

This did not mean that the Central and East European countries had given up on trying to join NATO. They had not. But they realized that PfP was the only game in town and the best way to build a track record demonstrating their commitment. By the time NATO Foreign Ministers met in Istanbul for their annual spring ministerial meeting in June, some 20 Partner countries had signed up for PfP.[26] The first PfP exercises took place in Poland in September, an exercise named Cooperative Bridge 94 involving troops from thirteen nations—six of them NATO members, six former Warsaw Pact countries and Ukraine. NATO Supreme Allied Commander (SACEUR) George Joulwan declared it a step toward realizing "the vision of a new Europe, a peaceful and cooperative Europe from the Atlantic to the Urals."[27] German Defense Minster Volker Ruehe, sitting beside his Polish colleague Piotr Kolodziejczyk, noted the presence of German troops on Polish soil and said: "Anyone who knows even a little bit about history knows that this is not a routine event when Polish and German soldiers are working together."[28]

The exception to this trend was Russia. Despite Yeltsin's promises to Clinton, getting Moscow to sign up for PfP was easier said than done. Yeltsin was under growing pressure to adopt a more assertive stance toward the West in a Duma now dominated by nationalists and communists. During mid-March Duma hearings, Vladimir Lukin, Chairman of the Duma's International Affairs Committee, compared PfP to the proposition of a rapist to a girl he has cornered: she can resist or submit but the result will be the same.[29] Even harsher voices came from the Russian military. The notoriously hard line Lt. General Leonid Ivashov, then Secretary of the Council of Defense Ministers of the CIS, blasted PfP as a covert program to expand NATO by "hook or by crook" and the means for NATO to establish its strategic influence in Central and Eastern Europe right up to Russia's borders.[30]

Christopher felt the cooler political winds coming from Moscow at a meeting with Kozyrev at the Vladivostock airport on March 14. Although the two men usually worked in English, the Russian Foreign Minister pulled out a lengthy document and insisted on reading it line-by-line in Russian. He stated that while the U.S.-Russian partnership was of immense value to Moscow, there was a growing feeling that it was too unequal. Russian nationalists were exploiting this sense politically against Yeltsin. While the Russian President did not want to yield to the nationalists, he needed a strategy to deny them this card. Moscow and Washington needed to decide in advance the areas where they would cooperate or act independently. Above all, Moscow wanted U.S. understanding for its policies in the CIS. Yeltsin was not trying to restore the former USSR, Kozyrev insisted, but had the right to enjoy stability on its borders. If the U.S. supported Russian-led peacekeeping and economic integration in the CIS, Moscow would back the U.S. with peacekeeping in Haiti, Central America, Asia, or Africa.

Christopher replied that President Clinton, too, faced growing criticism of his approach to Russia. Americans were asking whether Yeltsin would stick to a reformist course, treat Russia's neighbors as independent states, and even whether a partnership was still viable. He noted that he had answered "yes" to all three questions in recent congressional testimony. But the glue holding the partnership together had to come from consultations that created real common ground, not some artificial agreement in advance. Following the meeting, Christopher cabled back to the President that the U.S.-Russian relationship was in a new phase. Washington and Moscow were like a newlywed couple. The honeymoon was over and they had survived their first squabbles. The question was whether they could move beyond these and build a more mature partnership.[31]

Russia's quest for a special status with NATO nevertheless continued. Yeltsin reiterated to German Chancellor Kohl his need for an agreement underscoring that Russia was different than other PfP members—in Yeltsin's words "a great country with a great army with nuclear weapons"—to satisfy Russian public opinion.[32] Finding that formula fell to U.S. Secretary of Defense Bill Perry and Russian Defense Minister Pavel Grachev. The two men were a study in contrasts. Grachev was a combat veteran of the airborne forces and the Soviet military campaign in Afghanistan. He had earned Yeltsin's respect by standing by him during the October 1993 parliamentary putsch attempt. In contrast, Perry was a civilian and soft-spoken intellectual who looked as if he was straight out of a university—which he was.[33]

But the two men established a solid working relationship. Perry was a true believer in the Partnership for Peace and repeatedly urged Grachev to grasp the opportunities PfP held for Russia to redefine its relations with the U.S. and its European neighbors. "Bill had a phrase," recalled Ash Carter, one of Perry's closest confidantes and the then DoD Assistant Secretary dealing with US-Russian relations. "Play a lead role. Don't just hang back and sulk or you will be marginalized. If you want to be a leader in your neighborhood you have to act in a way that others will voluntarily follow you. That is the kind of Russia you should want to try to be and PfP can help you become that."[34]

In late March Perry left Moscow with a commitment from Grachev that Moscow would sign up for PfP by the end of the month.[35] That promise was immediately put on hold when NATO launched its first airstrikes against Serb positions in Bosnia. Criticized in the West as ineffective "pinpricks," NATO's actions created an uproar in Moscow and led to new demands for Yeltsin to stand up to the West.

In late May, however, Grachev arrived at the NATO Defense Ministers meeting in Brussels to announce that Moscow would sign up for PfP "without preconditions." But he also called for a "full blooded strategic partnership" and a separate document recognizing Russia's special status. Moscow, Grachev insisted, was not seeking "a warmer place in the sun" than other PfP partners, but a relationship "adequate to its weight" as a nuclear superpower with territory stretching from Europe to the Pacific. "What we suggest is not to limit the sphere of partnership," Grachev told his NATO counterparts, "but to enrich it with cooperation between Russia and NATO, not only in military areas but on other important issues." Agreement on this broader framework was needed before Russia could sign up for PfP, he insisted, and circulated a "parameters paper" detailing Russian thinking in this regard.[36]

NATO and Russian officials now worked out a compromise whereby Russia would sign on to PfP on the same terms as other Partners, but that both sides would also issue a short, general joint document on Russia's relationship with NATO outside of PfP.[37] At the NATO Foreign Ministers meeting in Istanbul in mid-June, Kozyrev promised Christopher a Russian signature on PfP before Clinton and Yeltsin met at the G-8 Naples summit in early July.[38] The next day Kozyrev told his NATO colleagues that he would soon return to Brussels to sign the PfP Framework Agreement.[39] Following his departure, however, the meeting deteriorated as the Russian delegation withdrew its support for compromise communiqué language, precipitating a five-hour long haggling session. One

Alliance official noted that he had "not seen negotiating tactics like this from Russia since we settled the terms for German unification nearly five years ago."[40]

Two weeks later, Kozyrev nonetheless returned to NATO headquarters for a carefully choreographed ceremony marking Russia's officially joining PfP. As agreed, NATO also issued a "Summary of Conclusions" referring to Russia as a "major European, international and nuclear power," thereby allowing Kozyrev to claim that NATO recognized Russia's unique role and special weight in European security.[41] Kozyrev stated that there were "no insurmountable obstacles" to developing a working NATO-Russia partnership. But the headaches in sorting out relations with NATO also led him to quip: "It is one thing if a small poodle tries to walk through these gates but quite another when an elephant like Russia tries to do the same thing."[42]

Meeting with Christopher and NATO Ambassadors, Kozyrev returned to the need to improve NATO's image in Russia but also warned the Alliance against making a "victorious march eastward."[43] As an unnamed U.S. official said following the Brussels signing ceremony: "This is just the beginning. We will see how Russia operates. Will they try to throw their weight around? Try to tell NATO what to do? Or be a true partner?"[44] Back in Moscow Russian communist party chief Gennady Zyuganov called Russia's signing up for PfP the "capitulation of Russian diplomacy and a betrayal of Russian interests" comparable to Operation Barbarossa, Hitler's invasion of the Soviet Union in 1941. Communists and nationalists failed by only nine votes to pass a resolution in parliament declaring Russia's signature on PfP "null and void."[45]

While the Alliance focused on launching PfP, Tony Lake was thinking about how to move forward on NATO enlargement. Clinton had accepted an invitation to visit Warsaw in July and Lake wanted the President to be able to show visible progress on enlargement by then. Lake knew that the normal interagency process was too divided to produce the results he wanted. He embarked on his own process, using his knowledge that the President wanted to move forward on this issue. Instead of trying to force a consensus, he used his own staff to develop a new approach and selectively shared it with other key members of the President's national security team. Once he had the President's support for a new direction, he was willing to again open up that process—but with the strategic direction now established by the President.

In March 1994 the President queried his staff about a report on Russian pressure on Central and East European countries to drop their bid to join NATO. When NSC staffers Dan Fried and John Beyerle sent forward a memo summarizing where things stood on PfP, Lake rejected it and called Fried into his office. He told him that he wanted a paper not on PfP but on how to enlarge NATO. Fried was taken aback. He asked Lake whether he realized that nearly the entire bureaucracy was still hostile to the idea. Lake responded: "That's my problem, not yours. You give me the policy. I'll give you the protection you need."

Fried knew he needed intellectual and bureaucratic allies to pull this off. He asked Nick Burns, the NSC's Senior Director for Russian, Ukranian, and Eurasian Affairs, for his help. Burns replied: "OK, let's do this right. Let's do this together." As neither Fried nor Burns were NATO hands, they sought out Alexander "Sandy" Vershbow, then the Principal Deputy in the State Department's European Bureau but scheduled to become the new NSC Senior Director for European Affairs in June. While Vershbow had loyally represented the European Bureau's critical approach to enlargement in the past, Fried knew that he was actually a closet supporter of enlargement. Vershbow agreed to be a ghost contributor to the memo pending his transfer to the NSC.

What came to be known as the NSC troika—Fried, Vershbow, and Burns (later replaced by Coit Blacker and Steven Pifer)—was born. These three NSC Senior Directors—responsible for NATO, Central and Eastern Europe, and Russia respectively—would work as a team over the next three years as the U.S. developed its strategy on NATO enlargement and a NATO-Russia relationship. Backed by Lake and Berger, their cooperation enabled the NSC to speak with a single voice in the interagency process. Following the Madrid summit in 1997, each of them would be promoted to Ambassadorial rank, partly in recognition of their work on NATO enlargement. National Security Advisor Berger gave them a signed copy of one of their early strategy memos on NATO enlargement noting how successful they had been in carrying it out.

In developing this strategy, the NSC troika also turned to their own contacts in the strategic community, including RAND. In May 1994, I heard of the troika and their memo during a visit to the NSC. Along with Larrabee and Kugler, I had gone to see Vershbow and Fried to present a RAND briefing we had completed for German Defense Minster Ruehe on the "how" of enlarging NATO. Vershbow and Fried welcomed us with open arms and showed an intense interest in our work. They told us they were preparing a memo to the President on the issues our briefing raised and asked whether we would help them develop their ideas. We were delighted. It was the start of a close professional and personal relationship with Vershbow and Fried that culminated in the spring of 1997 when I became their counterpart on NATO enlargement issues at the State Department.[46]

Lake's tasking resulted in the first NSC memo to the President laying out a strategy on how to enlarge NATO. Entitled "Advancing our European Security Agenda: Working with Russia and the Central and East Europeans (CEE)," the memo argued that it was time to start to remove the ambiguity surrounding U.S. policy and to be clear about the Administration's objectives—at home, in Europe, and with Moscow. It was no longer sustainable to advocate NATO enlargement in principle but refuse to discuss the when and the how. Similarly, it was insufficient to tell the Central and East Europeans privately that the Administration was prepared to enlarge if an authoritarian, aggressive Russian regime returned to power but not discuss the scenario for enlarging NATO in the absence of a new Russian threat. After all, the memo noted, the United States wanted Russian reform to succeed, not fail.

Above all, the memo noted the need to start to lay out a positive vision of NATO enlargement that could be accomplished while continuing to support democratic reform in Russia. It identified the Visegrad states as the leading candidates for NATO membership. While not excluding other Central and Eastern European countries, it noted that the process had to start with the most feasible candidates if it was to start at all. The memo also underscored the need to be honest and recognize that while the U.S. should not *a priori* exclude Russia from joining NATO, such membership was unlikely even in the longer term. It was therefore necessary to create a separate cooperative relationship with Russia as NATO expanded as the best way to include Moscow in a new European security order.

The memo also laid out a national timeline for enlarging NATO. It argued that the President should use his first term to lay the groundwork at home and abroad and prepare candidate countries for enlargement, with actual decisions on invitations being made at the start of the President's second term. The option of moving faster if events in Russia took a turn for the worse would, of course, be maintained. The memo recognized that the Administration would come under pressure from the Central and East Europeans to move faster and to be more explicit publicly about its intentions. It was nonetheless important to retain some ambiguity and move incrementally, the memo concluded, if Washington hoped to pursue these goals without precipitating a new crisis with Moscow.

This memo provided a remarkably prescient guide to U.S. policy on NATO enlargement over the next several years. While laid out in an intellectual straw-man fashion, it contained all the key elements of the Administration's future strategy. It also foreshadowed the political problems the Administration would later face. By remaining publicly ambiguous on the timetable for enlargement and by refusing to commit to specific countries, the Administration may have made its work within the Alliance and with Moscow easier. But it also left itself open to accusations at home that it was not fully committed to enlargement and inadvertently contributed to a widespread perception that the issue was still up for grabs long after the Administration had internally decided to move forward.

Lake kept the memo at close hold, but shared it with select senior officials at both State and Defense for their input before forwarding it to the President. One of those was Talbott, who had since been promoted to Deputy Secretary of State. In the spring and summer of 1994 Talbott moved from opposing what he considered a NATO enlargement "fast track" to supporting enlargement on a slower time line and with stepped up efforts to build a parallel NATO-Russia relationship that could mute Moscow's concerns. In a speech at Oxford University in January 2000, Talbott justified his and the Clinton Administration's support of NATO enlargement by invoking the teachings of Isaiah Berlin, an intellectual figure who was a major influence on him and a generation of scholars who had studied communism and the Soviet Union. Talbott recalled that a core theme in Berlin's teachings was "the unavoidability of conflicting ends" and the belief that final or perfect answers to difficult questions rarely exist. Berlin's writings had taught him, he noted, that the essence of statecraft was recognizing the necessity of choice and the fact that every choice could also entail an irreparable loss.

The Administration, Talbott said, ran that risk with NATO enlargement. It ran the risk of alienating Russian democrats engaged in a life-and-death struggle over reform and their country's future orientation. But not enlarging and adapting NATO to a new post–Cold War world also entailed risks to American interests and European security. The Administration made the decision to enlarge the Alliance while trying to mitigate Berlin's "unavoidability of conflicting ends." In Talbott's own words: "Seven years ago, at the beginning of this Administration, we faced a choice about the future of NATO. Given most Russians' fears that NATO is irredeemably hostile to their interests, many in Europe and in the U.S. felt that we should retire the Alliance with honor.

"But we said that would leave us without the means of deterring or if necessary defeating threats to our common security. Okay, said others, then we should keep NATO in business but freeze it in its Cold War membership. But we said that would mean perpetuating the Iron Curtain as a permanent fixture on the geopolitical landscape and locking newly liberated and democratic states out of the security that the Alliance affords. So instead, we chose to bring in new members while trying to make real a post–Cold War mission for NATO in partnership with Russia."[47]

This evolution in Talbott's thinking resulted from a combination of factors. An old truism in Washington is where you stand depends in part on where you sit. As Deputy Secretary of State, Talbott was no longer responsible only for U.S. policy toward Russia and the successor states of the former Soviet Union, but NATO and Europe as well. Whatever misgivings he had previously harbored on enlargement, Talbott knew that the President wanted to enlarge NATO. He also knew the President remained committed to supporting Russian democratic reform and integrating Russia into the West. His new portfolio, background, and relationship with the President inevitably made him the person that Clinton and Christopher turned to in order to figure out how to do both.

Talbott was now also exposed firsthand to the determination of countries like Poland to join NATO. In April 1994, he visited Warsaw to prepare the ground for the President's upcoming trip. President Walesa treated him to another lecture on Western naïveté in dealing with Russia.[48] Talbott also attended a quasi-public meeting in the Parkova Hotel with "Poland Inc." — the elite of the Polish political class, policymakers, intelligentsia, and other influential groups in Poland. He made it clear that he understood their concern about a security vacuum in Central and Eastern Europe, that this vacuum needed to be filled, and that PfP was an important step to achieving that and the path to Poland's future NATO membership. Polish participants in this meeting found Talbott more realistic on Russia and supportive of NATO enlargement than expected. "Strobe," according to U.S. Ambassador Nicholas Rey, who accompanied Talbott to the meeting, "demonstrated that he was not naïve about Russia and was not the enemy."[49]

Talbott also had an intellectual openness and curiosity unusual among the senior echelons of government. He was not afraid to change his mind if he became convinced of the merits of another position. He intentionally recruited people with different positions into his inner circle of lieutenants and encouraged debate among them, believing that the resulting tension would produce better policy. After becoming Deputy Secretary, Talbott started reaching out to proponents of NATO enlargement to hear their views. In his mind, the Administration already had the right Russian strategy. But it did not have a clear European strategy, let alone the right integration of the two. Talbott wanted to find that balance.

As Talbott often remarked to his staff, he wanted a policy that was "bilobal"—i.e., one that used the two lobes of the brain to integrate policy toward Europe and Russia into a common and consistent approach.[50] But Talbott's interest in moving forward was best reflected in the person he turned to as his alter ego in finding the balance between enlarging NATO and cementing a new relationship with Russia—Richard Holbrooke. Along with Tom Donilon, Christopher's chief-of-staff, Talbott was key in convincing Christopher to offer Holbrooke the job of Assistant Secretary of State for European Affairs. Equally important, Talbott helped convince Holbrooke to take the job. Neither was an easy sell. While Christopher wanted a strong person to take over the European portfolio, Holbrooke's ambition, steamroller tactics, and *modus operandi* were hardly his style. Similarly, Holbrooke was not eager to return to Washington for the same job he had held twenty years earlier. While interested in the issues, he feared he would lack the authority to get the job done.[51]

But Bosnia was spinning out of control and the Administration desperately needed a stronger hand on European policy to handle this crisis. Throughout the spring and summer Talbott and Donilon worked on Christopher and Holbrooke to finalize the latter's return to Washington. It was while sitting on a balcony of a hotel in Rome that spring that the Secretary of State finally agreed to bring Holbrooke back. "I'll hire him," Christopher told Donilon, "but he's your problem to manage." Talbott, in turn, helped convince Holbrooke to take the job. While he was brought back to Washington as Assistant Secretary first and foremost to deal with what Christopher had dubbed "the problem from hell"—Bosnia—Holbrooke also told Talbott that he was prepared to take the job only if the two men also had a common position on NATO enlargement. He also told Talbott that the Deputy Secretary had to overcome the perception that he was only interested in Russia. There was no better way to do so, he argued, than to take the lead on NATO enlargement, especially as he was publicly identified as the Administration's leading opponent of the policy.

Being Ambassador in Bonn had only hardened Holbrooke's commitment to enlargement.[52] Talbott knew that Holbrooke was more forward leaning on NATO enlargement than he was. But he felt that Holbrooke's creativity and forcefulness were essential if the Administration was going to get it done in practice. The two men were in almost daily contact on the phone throughout the spring and summer as Holbrooke prepared his return to Washington. They debated how to harmonize the Administration's European and Russian policies over the summer of 1994, with Holbrooke repeatedly arguing that Talbott's handling of enlargement would be a key test of whether he would be seen as more than a "single issue" person.

As Holbrooke subsequently wrote: "Strobe and I agreed that we should try to reach a common position on NATO enlargement before I returned, and that he was perceived as its main opponent. . . . He needed no persuading that the countries of Central Europe needed the reassurance of an American commitment to their security; the issue was whether or not this could be accomplished without wrecking the emerging U.S.-Russian relationship. By the time I returned to Washington Strobe and I had reached a common position: it was possible to bring new members into NATO, slower than the Kissingers and the Brzezinskis wanted but faster than the Pentagon and some others desired."[53]

Talbott's memos to Christopher in the fall of 1994 reflected this shift in his thinking. "A year ago we said that the expansion of NATO would depend in part on the "security environment" in Europe. By that we meant—and we were clearly understood to mean—that if Russia "went bad," we'd hasten the entry of CEE states to protect them," he wrote Christopher in mid-September. "That remains a valid theme in our doctrine and contingency planning," he continued, "but it must not stand alone as a reason to expand NATO." Instead, the Administration needed to make the case for NATO to expand in a way that supports Russian reform. "An expanded NATO in an integrated Europe," he concluded, "is not a contradiction. But keeping it from becoming one requires conceptual sophistication, deft statesmanship, consistency, patience—and disciplined interagency considerations of tactics and strategy alike."[54]

Lake's memo went to the President in late June with Talbott's comments and blessing. It emphasized that U.S. policy had to articulate a clear rationale for NATO expansion that underscored that such a move would not constitute a threat to any other country and would not depend on a catastrophic failure of reform in Russia. Instead, it argued, the Administration had to begin making the case that expansion would be stabilizing and reduce the security vacuum or blank spot in the center of Europe. The memo concluded that the President's July trip to Warsaw should be used to initiate the process, but do so in a fashion that did not precipitate new problems in relations with Russia. It recommended that President Clinton publicly reaffirm the case for NATO expansion and lay down a marker on the need to move forward without getting into specifics in his upcoming trip.

Looking back, Sandy Berger would point to this memo as the decisive one — the President now formally endorsed enlargement. "There are some decisions [in government] that are top-down and others that are bottom-up. This was a decision that was both," Berger argued. "The top-down part came from the President. The fundamental concept of enlargement was something he believed in. What came from the bottom-up were the how, the when and the what. Perhaps the reason there was not an orderly decision making process in the bureaucracy was that the President had made his decision. The President believed in this — and Tony and I believed in it, too. We did not feel the need to formalize it."[55]

The fact that U.S. policy was shifting gears became evident during Clinton's Warsaw visit in early July 1994. Polish officials had lobbied hard for some sign of movement on NATO enlargement, arguing that Warsaw needed to counter a widespread sentiment among Poles that they would again be "betrayed" by the West. "Now it is your time to be more concrete," Olechowski told Ambassador Rey.[56] Opposition leader and Solidarity icon Bronislaw Geremek was equally emphatic with U.S. officials: "Words are most important," he said. "We need words that Poland will be a member of NATO." When former Deputy Foreign Minister Jerzy Kozminski arrived in Washington as Warsaw's new Ambassador in mid-June, he, too, underscored the need to take "a clear step forward from Prague" during Clinton's trip.[57]

Speaking before the Polish Sejm on July 7, Clinton inched beyond simply repeating that enlargement was not a question of whether but when and how. Instead, he started to lay out in public the rationale for enlargement contained in the Lake memo, stating that enlargement would not depend on the emergence of a new threat in Europe but should be viewed as "an instrument to advance security and stability" in the region. Poland, he also underscored, was likely to be among the first to join when NATO expanded.[58] At the press conference with Walesa, the President took a further step when he stated that he had always supported enlargement, that PfP had been a first step toward enlargement and that "now what we have to do is to get the NATO partners together and to discuss what the next steps should be."[59] The last part of that sentence was not in his talking points. Watching the President speak, Lake turned

to Fried and said: "He's making policy; he's making policy."[60] At a press conference in Berlin several days later, Clinton repeated his message.[61]

Returning to Washington, Lake seized upon the President's remarks and
queried his staff how best to follow up. On July 15, Senior Director Sandy
Vershbow sent Lake a memo entitled "NATO Expansion—Next Steps" in
which he proposed launching exploratory discussions in September with key allies on the issues of criteria and a timetable to be followed by a broader discussion in the Alliance as a whole. He also suggested using the December
Ministerial to launch a NATO enlargement study to start spelling out in greater
detail U.S. and allied thinking on a NATO-Russia relationship. Lake agreed.[62]

3. PRESSURE FROM THE RIGHT

This shift in Administration policy took place against the background of, and
was reinforced by, growing political pressure from conservative Republicans
and the so-called "ethnics"—Americans of Central and East European origin—
in the course of 1994 for the Administration to commit more explicitly to NATO
enlargement. Prior to the summer of 1994, congressional and public interest in
NATO's future and questions such as enlargement on Capitol Hill was almost
nonexistent. NATO had faded from the political radar screen as an issue with
the end of the Cold War. A handful of Republican and Democratic Senators
such as Senator William Roth (R-DE) and Senator Joseph Lieberman (D-CT)
introduced resolutions on NATO's future, including enlargement, as early as
1992. Both resolutions died in Committee due to lack of interest and support.[63]

In the spring and summer of 1994, however, the issue of NATO enlargement
moved back to the center of attention on Capitol Hill. It was a time of growing
partisanship in American politics. The Clinton Administration had come to
power with Democratic majorities in both the House and the Senate. But the
Republicans were launching an aggressive campaign to regain control under
the leadership of minority leader Newt Gingrich. Republicans in the House
were putting together a series of attacks on the Administration's domestic and
foreign policies. And high on the Republican hit list were the Administration's
policies on Russia and NATO.

In the spring and summer of 1994, a small but influential group of
Republicans on Capitol Hill started to rachet up the pressure on the
Administration to adopt a clearer stance in favor of NATO enlargement and a
tougher policy toward Moscow. Their interest in these issues was rooted in both
substance and politics. Republicans, especially from the Reagan wing of the
party, had a long tradition of supporting freedom and independence in Central
and Eastern Europe throughout the Cold War and the rise of Solidarity in
Poland in the 1980s. Many of them viewed NATO enlargement as a logical ex-

tension of that tradition. Not all Republicans were part of this tradition—nor did all major figures or voices in the Republican party support enlargement. Opponents ranged from Realpolitik figures such as Brent Scowcroft, George Bush's former National Security Advisor, to the neo-isolationist and nativist Pat Buchanan. But in the early 1990s the Reaganite wing of the Republican party with its strong anti-Yalta tradition held sway in powerful leadership positions in both the House and the Senate.

Republicans also considered the embracing of NATO enlargement as good politics. There was a modest but real constituency for enlargement among Americans of Central and East European origin. They were centered in so-called "battleground states" in the Midwest. It was a constituency that usually voted Republican but one where Clinton had registered strong gains among so-called "Reagan Democrats" in 1992. It was a constituency the Republicans wanted to bring back to their fold. In the spring of 1994, it was also a constituency whose leadership was increasingly disappointed with the Clinton Administration's approach on Europe and Russia, which it viewed as too pro-Moscow and unresponsive to its concerns. In early 1994, the Central and East European Coalition (CEEC) approached key Republican Senators and Congressmen seeking their support in stepping up the political pressure on the Administration on enlargement. Gingrich and his key lieutenants sensed a political opportunity. "NATO enlargement was," as Gingrich subsequently recalled, "the right thing to do for foreign policy and ideological reasons and it was the right thing to do for political reasons."[64]

The main vehicle for Republican pressure was legislative. Republican Senators and Members of the House started to introduce one piece of legislation after another promoting a clearer commitment to NATO enlargement by singling out the Visegrad countries as the strongest candidates for membership, setting a target goal of 1999 for the first candidate countries, and authorizing the President to provide defense equipment to assist these countries in their defense modernization efforts. When such legislation was being discussed in Committee, various groups of the CEEC would organize calls, letters or simply line up outside of a congressman's office or hearing room to ensure that their views were known. They never failed to mention that there were about ten million Americans of Polish origin and an additional ten million from other Central and Eastern Europe countries who could cast votes in the next election. These efforts culminated in the NATO Participation Act in October 1994.[65]

The Republican push on enlargement can be traced to a handful of individuals who took up this issue as a personal crusade in the spring of 1994. One of them was Senator Hank Brown (R-CO). A soft-spoken junior Senator on the Senate Foreign Relations Committee, Brown was not a foreign policy heavyweight. But he was passionate on the issue of NATO enlargement. As a college student at the University of Colorado, Brown had studied Central European history with a Polish émigré Professor by the name of Edward Rozek who had fought the Nazis during, and the communists after, World War II before heading West. Brown came away from his classes ashamed that the United States and its allies had done so little to stand up for the cause of Polish freedom and independence after the end of World War II. For Brown, supporting NATO enlargement was a matter of national honor given what he viewed as America's failure to stand up for these countries in the past.

Speaking before the Senate in the summer of 1994, he stated:

The year before I was born the world saw Poland disappear as it was engulfed by Germany and the Soviet Union. Many important historians looking back on those events cite the perception created by democracies of the world that they would not stand with Poland as the impetus behind the Nazi invasion. Because our support was ambiguous, because those of good faith, who believe in democracy did not stand together, each country fell separately to the totalitarian aggressors. . . .

Other members will recall the valiant struggle of the Polish underground during World War II against the Nazi invaders. As the end neared, the Soviet Army asked these partisans to surrender and negotiate for control over the country, for the bringing of democracy and stabilization to Poland. The Polish underground leaders were reluctant to do so and only agreed to surrender to the Soviet authorities after the United States urged and assured them that they would be well treated. . . . The tragedy of history is that those valiant leaders of the Polish underground were arrested, were imprisoned and eventually executed. . . .

And what did the United States do? Tragically, little. I do not want, for this generation, for it to be said that we did not do what we could to make sure that these same events do not happen again.[66]

Brown was also appalled by the overall Western response to Central and Eastern Europe after the fall of the Berlin Wall. He often pointed to the response of the United States to Western Europe after World War II and the subsequent creation of the Marshall Plan and NATO—a historic time when Washington had opened its markets, supported European integration, and extended a security umbrella over these countries via NATO. In contrast, he felt that after the watershed events of 1989, both the EU and NATO were timid and shortsighted in reaching out to Central and Eastern Europe. Above all, Senator Brown was suspicious of Russian intentions. He became convinced that PfP and what he saw as the Administration's "go-slow" policy designed to deal with Russian sensitivities was a mistake that could lead to the same kind of historical blunder that had allowed Moscow to assert its control over the region in the late 1940s and early 1950s.

In February 1994, following the NATO summit, Brown decided to introduce legislation that would clarify what he considered to be the fuzziness in U.S. policy. Politically, he was determined to do exactly what the Administration was still loath to do in public: differentiate between Central and Eastern Europe and Russia and put the former on an explicit track to full NATO membership. Practically, he wanted to make these countries eligible for excess defense equipment purchases that could be used to increase their defense capabilities and make their forces interoperable with their NATO neighbors. Brown now submitted the first of several amendments proposing to name the Visegrad countries as the leading candidates to join NATO and make them eligible to purchase excess defense equipment. It was the first move in a game of political and legislative chess. Brown and his allies tried to attach their amendment to almost any piece of legislation. The Administration would counter by insisting that such legislation was unnecessary or politically premature.

But Brown also enlisted the support from a handful of Democratic Senators who were pro-enlargement—including Paul Simon (D-IL) and Barbara Mikulski (D-MD). Simon, one of the most independent-minded and liberal members of the Senate, represented a state with one of the largest communities of Central and East European origin. Senator Barbara Mikulski was herself a proud Polish-American. She shared Brown's view that the United States had failed these countries in the past and had an obligation to assist them in their efforts to integrate themselves into the West. She often told the story of how her grandmother had been a strong supporter of President Franklin D. Roosevelt but that after Yalta she turned her picture of FDR on its side. For Brown, Simon and Mikulski, NATO enlargement was not only a political and strategic interest. It was also a chance for the U.S. to help undo the tragedy that had befallen Central and Eastern Europe after the Second World War.

Similar efforts were underway among Republicans in the House of Representatives. Leading them was Republican Congressman Benjamin Gilman (R-NY). In the spring of 1994, Gilman was the ranking minority member of the House Foreign Affairs Committee. A centrist Republican, he embraced NATO enlargement because he believed it was the right policy and because he wanted to show that the Grand Old Party was still internationalist. Gilman introduced his bill, entitled the NATO Expansion Act, in April. While welcoming PfP, it, too, argued it was time to recognize the Visegrad countries as candidate countries and set the goal of bringing them into NATO by 1999.[67] Gilman justified his bill by arguing "there is genuine doubt in the Administration and elsewhere about where the Congress stands on the vitally important question of expanding NATO to include the new democracies of Central Europe."[68] A third and similar piece of legislation entitled the NATO Revitalization Act was introduced by Representative Henry Hyde (R-IL) in early May. It too called on the

Administration to establish specific benchmarks and a timetable on enlargement.[69]

The real breakthrough came with the Contract with America in August 1994—literally a few weeks after President Clinton had given the green light on enlargement in Warsaw. The brainchild of Gingrich, the Contract became the vehicle for the so-called Republican Revolution of November 1994 and the end of the Democrats' control of the House of Representatives and the Senate for the first time in 40 years. Unveiled in the summer of 1994, the Contract with America became the Ten Commandments for the "Gingrich Revolution." NATO enlargement was one of its key planks and those congressmen who rode to power on the Contract's coattails were signed up to it. Along with a commitment to National Missile Defense (NMD) and limits on the U.S. contribution to peacekeeping, NATO enlargement was one of the Contract's few national security priorities. It specifically called for the United States to reaffirm its commitment to NATO after the end of the Cold War, to enlarge to democracies in Central and Eastern Europe, and to reorient the Alliance to meet new threats. It set the goal of bringing Poland, the Czech Republic, and Hungary into NATO by January 1999.[70]

The background materials published with the Contract underscored the gap between Republican and Administration thinking. Whereas enlargement proponents in the Administration were articulating a rationale centered on integration and emphasizing a step was not necessarily aimed against Russia, the Contract with America underscored a harder-edged rationale for enlargement as a hedge against Russian neo-imperialism. The Administration was portrayed as being romantic and "soft" on Russia, with PfP portrayed as a naïve attempt to build a liberal collective security system in Europe that would render NATO ineffective as a military alliance. "The countries of Eastern Europe know only too well what Russia is capable of," the materials continued, adding that "Russia still has to prove that it will observe its new boundaries which goes against its centuries old imperial tradition and the belief of many within its military and government." The U.S., it concluded, should expand the frontier of freedom eastward without asking Moscow for permission.[71] NATO enlargement had moved from the world of strategic intellectuals and seminars to center stage in American politics.

Republicans would subsequently claim that their leadership on Capitol Hill, backed up by the political muscle of the "ethnics," eventually pressured the Clinton Administration to embrace NATO enlargement.[72] They point out that the Administration opposed their legislation on the Hill and refused to publicly endorse leading candidate countries or set a target date for enlargement as proof that the Administration had not yet made up its mind on, or even opposed, NATO enlargement. Senior Clinton Administration officials, on the other hand, insist that the President had embraced enlargement well before the Republicans on Capitol Hill discovered the issue, and that Republican legislation had little if any impact on their thinking. They claim that they opposed Republican efforts to legislate policy on enlargement for other reasons—executive privilege, the need to take into account the concerns of key allies as well as those Central and East European countries not included in Republican-backed legislation, and the need to manage relations with Moscow. At least one senior Clinton Administration official recalls that a Republican congressman involved in the Contract admitted in private that Clinton was moving to embrace enlargement and that Republicans did not want to be outflanked on this issue.

The record shows that the President had indeed decided to move forward on NATO enlargement prior to the launch of the Contract with America in the summer of 1994, or the final passing of the NATO Participation Act late that fall. But the White House's strategy on enlargement was just that—internal and confidential. Republican pressure to move forward on enlargement came exactly at a point when the final debates over how to move forward were still being fought out in the Administration's ranks. Its public posture was far less clear. Under the circumstances, Republican pressure reinforced enlargement proponents in the Administration and made any prospect of backing down increasingly difficult— if not impossible. As Gingrich himself put it: "They might have done it anyway but we made it impossible for them not to do it."[73]

There was a more basic political disconnect, however, as both sides approached the enlargement issue with very different premises. The Clinton team had come to power with its top priority being the consolidation of democracy in Russia. The President embraced NATO enlargement as part of a broader strategy to consolidate democracy in Central and Eastern Europe, and as part of a strategy to modernize the Alliance for the future by shifting its focus toward new threats. It viewed an enlarged NATO and a new partnership with a democratic Russia as equally important pillars in a new pan-European security structure. It saw its main challenge as finding a way to enlarge NATO without changing or undermining the President's support for Russia. It therefore wanted to move slowly and cautiously to manage the tensions between those two policies.

Republican critics, on the other hand, increasingly criticized the Administration's approach to Russia as fundamentally flawed and interpreted the Administration's more cautious approach to NATO enlargement as being overly influenced by what it considered too much deference to Russian concerns. Conservative critics believed that Russia did pose a threat to these countries and that Washington and its allies should move expeditiously and irrespective of Russian concerns. Their rationale for enlargement was different and explicitly tied to a policy of neo-containment. Many of them agreed with the views of leaders such as Lech Walesa who argued that NATO should just go ahead and create facts by enlarging, and deal with Moscow later. Administration statements about enlargement as part of NATO's overall transformation and the need to focus on new missions were often seen as either misguided liberal thinking, or a simple reluctance to stand up to Moscow on this issue.

Republicans, in short, did not believe the Administration was serious about NATO enlargement. They believed that in the end the President's desire to maintain relations with Moscow would win out. They wanted to force it to do what they considered to be the right thing. From the Administration's viewpoint, the Republican embrace of NATO enlargement in the Contract with America was part of an effort to condemn the Administration's foreign policy, not cooperate with it. It was seen as a hostile act, not as an attempt to build bipartisan support. The Administration's rationale for enlargement was different than the one being proposed by the Republicans. There was little trust or common ground and the Republican antipathy toward Clinton was already strong. As Gingrich put it, "even if the President had spoken out more clearly in favor of enlargement we would not have believed him because he simply lacked credibility."[74]

Finally, Republicans were increasingly determined to use this issue politically to criticize the Clinton Administration and paint it as "soft" on Russia and incapable of handling a major national security issue such as NATO. The Democrats had been out of power for more than a decade and were seen as inexperienced. President Clinton's critics were seeking to exploit the issue of his draft record in Vietnam, the controversy over gays in the military, and any other real or perceived foreign policy weaknesses to question his competence as commander-in chief. The public still viewed Republicans as more competent on such issues as national security and defense. NATO and the management of the United States' premier military alliance was widely seen as a benchmark of a President's foreign policy skill and acumen. By criticizing the President on this issue, Republicans hoped to further discredit the Administration's overall foreign policy competence and standing—and the White House knew it.

By the fall of 1994, Republicans and Democrats would start to compete over who could do a better job on NATO enlargement. An early example of this competition took place in October 1994 when President Walesa attended the annual meeting of the Polish-American Congress in Buffalo, New York. At the dinner banquet Senator Hank Brown presented the Republican Party as the champion of Poland and the NATO enlargement cause. Madeleine Albright, who was on the stage with Brown, was furious and rewrote her speech on the spot to challenge Brown's assertions that the Administration was soft on the issue. Leaving the podium, she turned to U.S. Ambassador Rey with fire in her eyes and said, "We have got to do this." NSC Senior Director Fried pulled aside Walesa's Chief of Staff Mieczyslaw Wachowski and said to him: "Do you now understand that the Administration is serious about this?" Wachowksi, known for his skepticism and argumentative nature, replied soberly: "Yes, we now understand this is real."

Republican support for NATO enlargement was also critical for two additional reasons. First, it gave the Central Europeans additional leverage vis-à-vis the Administration. It was an open secret that Republicans on the Hill were in close contact with the Central Europeans and used their reactions to Administration policy moves as a guide to whether or not to attack U.S. policy. They would frequently check with Central European Ambassadors whether or not they were satisfied with an Administration policy. If they were not, the Republicans would try to turn up the heat. For its part, the Administration knew that if the Poles were happy, the Republicans were likely to be content as well.

Second, Republican support also started to challenge the widespread assumption that the U.S. Congress was unlikely to support enlargement. One major argument against enlargement throughout the 1993 debate was precisely the contention that it was not ratifiable on Capitol Hill. This view was also widespread among allies in Europe. Gingrich's ability to tap into the party's Reaganesque legacy, his authority, and the weight of the Contract locked in the Republican Party's support of enlargement at this crucial early stage in the debate. The fact that Republicans were pushing the Administration to move further and faster on enlargement changed the political calculus and lineup and suggested that domestic support for enlargement was stronger than many had assumed. This issue was not going to go away or to be managed outside of the public spotlight.

4. HOLBROOKE'S RETURN

Richard Holbrooke's return to Washington in late summer 1994 consolidated the Clinton Administration's decision to move forward with NATO enlargement. Holbrooke was essential in turning the strategy laid out in Lake's NSC memo into actual U.S. policy. He was a relentless negotiator, willing and able to use every scrap of leverage to achieve his objective. He was capable of cajoling, browbeating, or charming his way to his desired goal—and often would try all three methods in the course of a single conversation. Within three months, Holbrooke had bulldozed through the shift in both U.S. and NATO policy.

Roger Cohen of *The New York Times* once described Holbrooke in the following terms: "His appetite goes beyond the [dining] table. It is a force of nature. It gulps down movies . . . books. It zaps restlessly from channel to channel. . . . It leads him to carry on two or even three telephone conversations at once. . . . The appetite fills rooms and disrupts meetings. It is in short, a devouring zest for life that sweeps over people, embracing them in its intrusive warmth or crushing them in its roughshod power, complicating his life and sometimes putting his [Dean] Ruskian ideal of service and self-effacement grotesquely at odds with the baroque reality of being Richard Holbrooke."[75]

Holbrooke's commitment to NATO enlargement had deepened during his tenure in Bonn. His presence and his activism were felt in Washington shortly after he arrived. During his confirmation hearings, he defended PfP but underscored his interest in setting a clearer course on NATO enlargement.[76] Following his confirmation he called in members of his senior staff who had opposed enlargement in the past. He made it clear that that they had a choice: get on board or get another job. He also asserted the State Department's right to chair the Interagency Working Group (IWG) on NATO policy. He wanted to make it clear that he was in charge.

Holbrooke returned briefly to Berlin to attend a ceremony marking the withdrawal of the U.S., British, French, and Russian troops. He had put together a "New Traditions" conference designed to emphasize the new bonds that could tie the U.S. and Germany together even as the American military presence was declining. It was his grand finale as Ambassador to Germany. Vice President Gore was supposed to attend, but had torn his Achilles' tendon and had to address the conference by video from Washington. As a skilled bureaucratic infighter, Holbrooke understood that if Gore repeated Clinton's remarks from Warsaw on the need for the Alliance to now take the next steps on enlargement, they would be locked in as U.S. policy. The Pentagon also understood this, and therefore wanted to walk back what it saw as off-the-cuff comments that it had not agreed to. What Gore would say in Berlin now became an issue of an intense bureaucratic wrestling match.

Shortly before the conference, Holbrooke had accompanied Chancellor Kohl to Chicago where Germany's soccer team was playing in the World Cup. Holbrooke spoke to Ruehe's right hand, Vice Admiral Weisser, who assured him that if Gore repeated Clinton's language on the Alliance taking the next steps on enlargement, Ruehe would second it. Holbrooke now went all out to get the key language in the speech over the Pentagon's objections, discussing it with Gore personally. Even from a distance in Berlin, Holbrooke intervened by sending his deputy, John Kornblum, to seek out Gore's national security advisor, Leon Fuerth, and to intercede with Gore himself to explain why the key language had to remain in the speech over the Defense Department's objections. Gore followed Holbrooke's advice. Speaking the next day, the Vice President repeated the key language on the need for the Alliance to begin discussions on NATO enlargement that fall.[77] Ruehe immediately supported the Vice President. Bill Perry, who was also on stage with Ruehe, was caught off guard and tried to suggest that Gore had not meant to imply that negotiations needed to start immediately.[78]

The Defense Department was furious. Holbrooke had outmaneuvered them and they knew it. But the Pentagon stood by the long-standing bureaucratic principle that existing policy stood until it was officially revised. In their view, a new policy decision to actually move forward with a specific strategy on enlargement had not yet been made. It required their approval, too. Holbrooke was seen as trying to make policy over their heads and over-interpret what the President and Vice President had said. The shootout took place when Holbrooke circulated a State Department paper laying out a strategy for enlarging NATO and called an IWG meeting on September 22, 1994 to discuss it. More than 30 senior officials gathered around a horseshoe-shaped table in the conference room of the State Department's European Bureau, including Assistant Secretaries of Defense Joseph Nye and Ashton Carter, Deputy Assistant Secretary Joseph Kruzel and the newly appointed Army Lieutenant General Wesley Clark.[79]

Many of the attendees watched in astonishment as Holbrooke insisted that he had a mandate from the President to enlarge NATO—and the sole purpose of the meeting was to discuss how to implement that decision. As far as he was concerned, the debate within the Administration on this issue was over. He had not returned to the job he had held 20 years earlier to waste his time with inter-agency squabbles, he told the assembled crowd. Anyone who had problems with enlargement should address their concerns to the President, he concluded. Holbrooke then went around the table and either demolished or simply ignored the arguments of the Pentagon representatives. As he came around to the end of the u-shaped table, he turned to Wes Clark. The two men would become close friends, working together to bring peace to the Balkans in the years to come. But this was their very first encounter. When General Clark questioned Holbrooke's claim, he asked him if he was questioning his Commander-in-Chief. That, he added, would be "insubordination." Clark turned red with anger and demanded that Holbrooke retract the accusation. The participants sat in stunned silence. This was clearly not your average interagency meeting.

But Holbrooke was right. The President did want to enlarge the Alliance. One day earlier, Holbrooke had sat in on a discussion Clinton had on enlargement with a skeptical Jacques Chirac, then Mayor of Paris. After Chirac queried Clinton on NATO enlargement, the President first turned to Christopher, who responded: "If we handle this carefully and relatively slowly, NATO expansion can be accomplished. An abrupt, precipitous move right now to take in three or four countries could cause difficulties." Enlargement was not, as the Secretary put it, "a weekend project" but one that would require several years to lay the foundation for NATO and with Moscow. "This is an area for moving carefully, not taking the plunge," he noted.

The President then jumped into the conversation, "How and when we expand the Alliance while we—all of us in the West—manage our relations with Russia depends in part on whether we believe we can make the future differently from the past. Poland and Hungary and others want to be in NATO because they believe that the impulse of the Russian empire will reassert itself." Yeltsin wanted Russia to be able to settle disputes along its borders and be adequately represented as a great power, the President continued, but he "does not believe there will be a new impulse toward empire building after he is gone—at least not in terms of geographic expansion." Clinton continued that the Russian President did see NATO expansion "as forcing him to react and reawakening forces in Russia he is trying to keep down." Therefore, the President concluded, the Alliance should expand but "in a careful way, so as to leave open the possibility that the future will be different, rather than recreating the certainty of the past."[80]

One week later Boris Yeltsin arrived in Washington. One year after his bloody confrontation with the Russian Parliament, Yeltsin wanted to project the image of a country that had moved beyond the violent confrontation of the previous autumn. He arrived in the U.S. determined to present himself as a confident leader ready to build on his personal relationship with President Clinton. As he stated in his memoirs:

I was completely amazed by this young, eternally smiling man who was powerful, energetic and handsome. For me, Clinton was the personification of the new generation in politics. He lent hope to the idea of a future without wars, without confrontations, and without the grim ideological struggles of the past.

I understood that this personal human contact with me was important for Clinton, too. In his view my political steps were connected with the fall of communism, which had been the main threat to America in the twentieth century. Clinton was ready to meet me halfway. No other President came to Moscow so many times. . . . No other President engaged in such intensive negotiations with the leaders of our country or provided us with such large-scale aid, both economic and political.[81]

The "Bill and Boris" relationship was in full bloom. The two leaders cultivated a relaxed and informal image of two good friends doing business in shirtsleeves. The event was so down home that *kasha*, the traditional Russian peasant fare, found its way onto the White House state dinner menu. Before the Russian President's arrival, Administration officials briefing the press hinted that the enlargement issue was likely to come up. The press was told that President Clinton planned to discuss with Yeltsin "the future security structure of Europe"—including NATO expansion and Russia's place in that structure.[82]

Before arriving in the United States, Yeltsin had stopped in London for talks with British Prime Minister John Major. The White House immediately received a readout from 10 Downing Street. The Russian leader, Major reported, was concerned that the U.S. was accelerating NATO enlargement, and had urged London to help rein in American "eagerness" on the issue. Yeltsin did not argue that the Visegrad countries should never join NATO, but insisted that their entry in the next few years would cause a severe reaction in Russia. Major said that he had reassured Yeltsin that enlargement would be gradual, was not aimed against Russia, and that it would not take place for several years. Yeltsin, he reported, seemed relieved and indicated that he would have no difficulty with enlargement on that kind of timetable.[83]

Clinton had prepared himself to discuss NATO enlargement with Yeltsin by rehearsing his talking points with his senior aides. As the visit unfolded, however, the Russian President did not raise the issue. Finally, Clinton himself brought it up at the end of a private lunch the two leaders had in the East Wing of the White House on September 28. Over coffee, Clinton said: "Boris, one last thing. On NATO, please note I have never said we shouldn't consider Russia for membership or a special relationship with NATO. So when we talk about expanding NATO, we're emphasizing inclusion, not exclusion. My objective is to work with you and others to maximize the chances of a truly united, undivided and integrated Europe. There will be an expansion of NATO, but there's no timetable yet. If we started tomorrow to include the countries that want to come in, it would still take several years until they are qualified and others said yes. The issue is about psychological security and a sense of importance to these countries. They're afraid of being left out in a gray area or purgatory."

"So we're going to move forward on this. But I'd never spring it on you. I want to work closely with you to get through it together," the President continued. "As I see it, NATO expansion is not anti-Russian; it's not intended to be exclusive of Russia, and there is no imminent timetable. And we'll work together. I don't want you to believe that I wake up every morning thinking only about how to make the Warsaw Pact countries a part of NATO—that's not the way I look at it. What I do think about is how to use NATO expansion to advance the broader, higher goal of European security, unity and integration—a goal I know you share."

Yeltsin replied, "I understand, and I thank you for what you've said. If you're asked about this at the press conference, I'd suggest you say that while the U.S. is for the expansion of NATO, the process will be gradual and lengthy. If you're asked if you'd exclude Russia from NATO, your answer should be 'no.' That's all." Washington considered it a pale green light to proceed cautiously. Clinton then asked Talbott, who was taking notes, to explain a public dispute that had taken place between Perry and Ruehe in Berlin over whether NATO's door should or should not be open for Russia. Talbott summarized Perry's view as "we're not ruling it out" and Ruehe's as "never." Yeltsin responded: "Good for Perry. He is smarter than Ruehe."[84]

Washington's key allies had picked up on the Clinton Administration's shifting priorities as well. Many of them were surprised. They were not all happy. The United Kingdom was the first to pick up on the shift behind the scenes in Washington. It now found itself caught between its preference for a go-slow approach on NATO enlargement and a determination not to repeat the mistake of getting on the wrong side of U.S. policy as it had on the issue of German unification. As London concluded that President Clinton was committed to moving forward, it made clear that it was not prepared to stand in the way.[85] In mid-October, Holbrooke visited London to discuss NATO enlargement. British officials told him that London "accepts and welcomes" enlargement but that the pace should not be forced and urged Washington to proceed in a way that did not upset relations with Moscow.[86]

France was the most ambivalent of Washington's allies about the U.S. policy shift. In the summer of 1994 French officials had told their U.S. counterparts that they assumed that Central and Eastern Europe would first be integrated into the EU and NATO integration would come gradually at the end of that process—i.e., in about a decade.[87] When Undersecretary of State for Political Affairs Peter Tarnoff visited Paris in mid-September he was immediately queried whether the U.S. now wanted to move faster. He responded "yes." His French interlocutors underscored their preference for a more gradual approach.[88] "What," one French official asked, "has happened in the past year to make this so urgent?" But by mid-October 1994, Paris, too, was signaling that while it was not enthusiastic, it could go along with enlargement so long as it proceeded in tandem with EU enlargement and Washington did not provoke a crisis with Russia.[89]

Germany was the key. In a *tour d'horizon* with Holbrooke before his return to Washington in early September, Kohl had laid out his views on America's future role in Europe to the departing U.S. Ambassador. Europe was fortunate to have in President Clinton a leader from a generation less burdened by World War II and the Cold War, Kohl said. He criticized the previous Bush Administration's hostility to European integration as "old think" he had disagreed with. "Please tell your colleagues and the President," he stated, "that there are certain times, in both domestic politics and foreign affairs, when windows of opportunity open. Most people fail to notice at all, and the results only show years later." The current period was one of those windows, the Chancellor noted. The U.S. and Germany needed to set a course that would ensure the trans-Atlantic relationship for the future and lock in security and stability in Europe as a whole.

Kohl made it clear that he saw NATO as the critical European defense institution for the foreseeable future, not the EU. The EU, the Chancellor said, was unable to deal with defense issues. The French were becoming "milder" in their opposition to the Alliance, he noted, and went so far as to speculate that Paris might rejoin the Alliance's integrated command. But the biggest challenge the U.S. and Germany had to tackle together was Central Europe, the Chancellor continued. There was no simple answer. He pointed to the anxieties of countries like Hungary and Poland. They were determined to get into NATO and did not care what price the West might pay in overall relations with Russia. NATO enlargement was inevitable, he concluded. But the West needed a balanced approach that took Moscow's concerns into account.[90]

In mid-October, a second NSC strategy paper listed five U.S. objectives for the end of the year: launching a formal Alliance review on a framework for expansion; an initial sketch of benchmarks for potential new members; an expanded PfP program for future members and nonmembers alike; an expanded NATO-Russia relationship; and a strengthened OSCE to underscore Western willingness to include Russia in a new European security architecture.[91] In early November, a U.S. briefing team toured Brussels as well as individual national capitals to propose that the December Foreign Ministers meeting launch an official NATO study on the "why" and the "how" of enlargement, but set aside the more controversial "who" and "when." This would allow the Alliance to answer the myriad of questions involved in actually enlarging the Atlantic Alliance but leave the politically controversial issues of which countries might enter, and when, for later.[92]

Two problems loomed on the horizon, however. One was Bosnia where trans-Atlantic differences were again reaching the breaking point.[93] The other was Russia. The President's exchange with Yeltsin notwithstanding, there were signs that Moscow was not at all comfortable with the direction the U.S. and NATO were headed. The U.S. Embassy in Moscow was reporting signs of growing Russian nervousness that the U.S. was going to pursue a tough line—which the Republican landslide victory in the November mid-term elections only reinforced.[94] On November 14, the newly arrived Russian Ambassador to NATO, Vitaly Churkin, zeroed in on NATO expansion in a courtesy call to Ambassador Hunter. He argued that if the Alliance launched the next stage in the enlargement process before the NATO-Russia relationship was up and running, it ran the risk of undercutting the latter even before it got started.[95] The storm clouds were starting to gather.

Christopher and Talbott were counting on the President's relationship with Yeltsin to keep Russian anxieties in check—and that meant meeting with him at the upcoming OSCE summit in Budapest at the end of the year. Clinton had promised the Russian President he would come if there was important work to do. But the U.S. President's domestic advisors were insisting that he travel less and focus on his domestic agenda. In mid-October Christopher and Talbott weighed in urging the President to attend the summit. "We are on the verge of being able to lay out a sweeping vision of a 'new European architecture' that would build on your January Brussels speech," Christopher wrote the President.[96] Talbott argued that the Administration had a chance for a diplomatic breakthrough that would also inoculate Clinton against Republican charges that the Administration was soft on enlargement. "If we get this right— and at the right time, which means very soon—we can seize control over this issue in a way that essentially takes it away from the Republicans in '96. That doesn't mean that Poland will be in NATO by then. But it does mean that we will have a plan in place and a process underway that will make it difficult for anyone to attack the President for failing to deliver on his promise or for giving the Russians a veto over NATO expansion."[97]

The Republican sweep of Congress in the November mid-term elections left the White House in shock and only made the President's domestic advisors more adamant that he not go to Budapest. On November 7, Talbott, supported by Lake and Christopher, sent a note directly to Clinton pleading with him to attend: "Chief," he wrote, "believe me, this is an absolute, total, no-question-about-it MUST. You gotta go. If you go, it'll do a lot of good, diplomatically and politically; if you don't, it'll cause big problems on both fronts." Budapest was a "launching pad" for our "tough but doable" goal of harmonizing NATO expansion with support for Yeltsin: "If you give Budapest a miss, you'd appear to be abandoning the field to Yeltsin, Kohl and others; we'd miss the chance to establish a CSCE 'second track' that must parallel the NATO expansion track. Yeltsin (who's under huge pressure to come out against NATO expansion) would feel vulnerable at home and, frankly, let down by you, since you agreed when he was here that you'd meet in Budapest 'if there's serious work to be done,' which there sure is."

5. ACROSS THE RUBICON

On December 1 Christopher and his NATO colleagues announced that the Alliance would "initiate a process of examination to determine how NATO will enlarge, the principles to guide this process and the implication of membership." They were careful to underscore that it was still "premature" to discuss a timeframe for enlargement or which countries would be invited to join. In other words, the study would answer the "why" and the "how" but not yet the "who" or the "when" of enlargement. Finally, NATO emphasized its interest in closer relations with Moscow and ensuring that enlargement contributed to the stability and security of the entire Euro-Atlantic region—code for ensuring that Russian security interests did not suffer. While it was at a pace that seemed glacial to some, the Alliance had finally taken its first official step in a process explicitly designed to enlarge NATO.[98]

And everyone knew it. The Central and East Europeans were delighted. They realized that enlargement was not yet a done deal, but the process was finally moving forward. In Brussels, Olechowski joked to a somewhat startled Christopher that he wanted to kiss him out of gratitude to Clinton for finally turning words into deeds.[99] As he later recalled: "This was the moment that I thought there was a turning point."[100] Czech Foreign Minister Zielenic termed the meeting "one of the most important in NATO's modern history" and noted that "after eighteen months of hesitation NATO members have clearly assumed a more active approach to expansion."[101]

Moscow knew it, too. And its reaction was quite different. Later that same day Kozyrev met with NATO's Foreign Ministers for what was supposed to be a carefully choreographed event where he signed two key documents inaugurating expanded NATO-Russia cooperation.[102] Although the Russian side had been briefed on the enlargement statement in advance, at the last second Kozyrev refused to play along with the agreed script. He stunned his NATO colleagues by suddenly announcing that he had just spoken to Yeltsin and that it was "impossible" to sign the documents in light of the decisions NATO had taken earlier in the day on enlargement. Moscow now wanted a "pause" to clarify NATO's intentions.[103] As one Russian paper put it, "Mr. Da" had suddenly become "Mr. Nyet."[104]

The story only got worse. Two days later in Budapest more than 50 heads of state gathered for the OSCE summit. The President had overruled his domestic advisors and agreed to go to Budapest after all. But it required him to fly through the night for a brief stop of several hours on the ground before returning to Washington. Although Christopher and Holbrooke had gone directly from Brussels to Budapest to meet the President, there was no opportunity to discuss the implications of Kozyrev's surprise performance in Brussels. The tight schedule also left no time for Clinton and Yeltsin to meet before either of them spoke publicly.

Instead of the trip becoming the successful bookend of his European policy for the year Christopher and Talbott had promised, it became a diplomatic nightmare. Following Clinton's address, Yeltsin gave a dramatic speech in which he criticized the U.S. for moving ahead with NATO enlargement. Washington, he said, was "sowing the seeds of distrust" and not taking Russian interest into account. "Europe, not having yet freed itself from the heritage of the Cold War, is in danger of plunging into a Cold Peace," he warned.[105] President Clinton felt ambushed and was furious as he jetted back across the Atlantic. Talbott would later say it was one of the worst days of his diplomatic career. One week later Moscow invaded Chechnya, dealing yet another setback to U.S.-Russian relations.

In the days following Budapest, American diplomats scurried to find out what was behind the Russian leader's outburst.[106] Had Moscow deliberately sandbagged Washington in an attempt to derail enlargement? Or had there been a breakdown in communication? Talbott was dispatched to Moscow to find out what had happened and why. Yeltsin's National Security Advisor Dimitri Ryurikov told him Yeltsin had reacted so harshly because he felt Washington no longer trusted him. The Republican victory in Congress, along with the NATO enlargement study decision were seen as evidence that U.S. policy toward Russia was hardening. Ryurikov compared Yeltsin to a businessman who has just discovered that his partner has taken out an insurance policy in case their joint venture fails. He claimed that Moscow had believed that NATO enlargement had been stopped in the fall of 1993 and that PfP was a kind of alternative, only to now discover it was moving forward. Moreover, Washington's European allies were also telling Moscow it was the U.S., not them, that was rushing the pace.[107]

In a separate meeting, Kozyrev told a somewhat different story. He admitted that Yeltsin had been unconcerned about reports that the U.S. was pushing forward on NATO enlargement, saying he trusted the assurances Clinton had given him. Kozyrev admitted that he himself had called the Russian President before Brussels and had spun him up over the language in the NAC communiqué. When Yeltsin then saw television reports of the NAC meeting, he had become angry, saying: "What's happening to my friend Clinton? Why is he doing this to us?" He had then been unable to keep Yeltsin in check at Budapest where the Russian President had personally rewritten his speech at the last minute to attack the U.S. President, Kozyrev admitted.

"The combination of the content of the Brussels communiqué itself, and the tone of what Clinton said in Budapest made us feel that you were triumphing, you'd scored a diplomatic victory over us, you were ramming this through over Russian objections," Kozyrev replied.

Talbott responded angrily that Clinton had consistently stood by Yeltsin when many in the West were ready to write him off. The NATO communiqué reflected exactly the kind of strategy the President had discussed with Yeltsin in September and did not represent a sudden shift in U.S. policy. But he added that Yeltsin's behavior had certainly made it harder to support a policy of engagement with Russia. Kozyrev replied that Yeltsin did not want, and Russia could not afford, a new Cold War. What was now needed, he added, was to find a way to include Russia in decisions regarding NATO's future and a new European security architecture.[108] That job now fell to Vice President Al Gore, who arrived in Moscow for a previously scheduled meeting of the Gore-Chernomyrdin Commission.

Meeting with Chernomyrdin and Kozyrev over breakfast, Gore underscored that the U.S. remained committed to a vision of an undivided Europe that included Russia. Moscow's protests, Gore added, were based on the assumptions that NATO would expand quickly and without a *modus vivendi* with Russia. Neither was true. Enlargement was going to be a slow, deliberate process consistent with what Clinton had told Yeltsin in September. Chernomyrdin shot back, "that is your view, but the Baltics and the others have already started to pack up their bags for NATO as a result of the communiqué." He noted that while both sides spoke of a slow and deliberate process, they meant something very different. Moscow wanted a timeline of 10, 15 or 20 years for enlargement, but could perhaps live with 5–7 years. Gore responded progress could be much more rapid. But the way out of the dilemma, he underscored, was for NATO and Russia to accelerate work on creating a new NATO-Russia relationship.[109]

Yeltsin himself received Gore in a hospital where he was recovering from surgery. Yeltsin was clearly determined to send the political message that U.S.-Russian relations were alive and well. "Despite all the talk, the reports in newspapers and the gossip," he said, "Russia and America remain partners. Bill Clinton and I remain partners. It will take more than we've been through to ruin that." But he then went straight to the NATO enlargement issue and his suspicion that the U.S. was accelerating its policy under Republican pressure. When Gore insisted that Clinton's September commitment stood and there had been no change of policy, Yeltsin challenged this and argued that the NATO communiqué had changed Alliance policy. But he asked the Vice President: "Can you assure me that in 1995 it will be solely a matter of working out the concept?" Gore responded in the affirmative. Yeltsin asked what Clinton would do if the Poles pressured him to move in 1995? Gore repeated that the U.S. only had plans to study the enlargement issue, not to actually expand, in the upcoming year.

But Gore also underscored that NATO would, at some point, enlarge. Yeltsin replied by asking: "What then is Russia's relationship with NATO?" When Gore responded that the U.S. had not ruled out eventual Russian membership either, Yeltsin answered, "Nyet, nyet , that doesn't make sense. Russia is very, very big and NATO is quite small." The Vice President then used the image of two space ships docking in parallel to imitate NATO and Russia coming close together. Yeltsin responded enthusiastically "Da, Da." Gore added: "We need a process that brings three things together: our bilateral partnership, Russia's relationship with NATO, and NATO expansion. It must be gradual."

"Yes," said Yeltsin. "In parallel! Simultaneous, simultaneous! But not like this." And with his hands, he demonstrated one spacecraft moving toward the other but the other moving off in the other direction. As the conversation was ending, the Russian President said to Gore, "We are being advised to step up the pressure on Clinton. Please convey to him that we will never do that, that Russia will remain the U.S.'s partner to the end."[110]

Yeltsin's outburst in Budapest also forced a final clarification of the battle lines within the Clinton Administration on NATO enlargement. Secretary of Defense Bill Perry was in Moscow with the Vice President. He had been on the road dealing with growing tension in the Persian Gulf and Korea and had not been closely involved in the internal U.S. deliberations on enlargement. But he had been in Brussels after Yeltsin's Budapest outburst and came away convinced the decision to launch the enlargement study was a mistake. In his view, PfP had just been launched and the U.S. had not yet had a chance to engage the Russian military, or to make any progress in changing hostile Russian attitudes toward NATO. Perry believed that there was a reasonable chance that PfP could start to change those attitudes—and that it was important to do so *before* NATO started to enlarge.[111]

Returning to Washington, Perry asked for a meeting to make his case. On December 21 he joined Gore, Talbott, Christopher, Lake, and Berger in Clinton's private study in the White House to discuss the way ahead.[112] The Secretary of Defense argued that moving ahead on enlargement was a mistake, that a Presidential decision had never been made, and that it was wrong to make policy through a communiqué. He recommended that the U.S. return to the original go-slow approach based on PfP for several more years. But Clinton made it clear that he had decided to move forward with enlargement. As Perry later described it, the President "felt that right was on the side of the East European countries that wanted to enter NATO soon, that deferring expansion until later in the decade was not feasible and that the Russians could be convinced that expansion was not directed against them."[113] Looking back, Perry acknowledged he realized during the meeting that in Clinton's mind the decision to enlarge NATO had already been made some time ago, something he should have known earlier but did not.[114]

But Clinton also underscored that he wanted to move forward slowly on enlargement and with a maximum effort to address Russia's concerns. Gore and Christopher argued that it was going to take at least three to five years to get NATO and candidate countries ready in any case which left time to first establish a parallel NATO-Russia relationship that could defuse tension with Moscow. Gore pointed out that such an approach would be criticized by the Republicans and the leaders of the ethnic groups who wanted a clearer public commitment and timetable on enlargement, but that the Administration would simply have to absorb such criticism. It was agreed to keep the Administration's policy ambiguous and to avoid setting a public timetable. The way to manage the tension of supporting the Central and East Europeans and also assisting Yeltsin was, as Gore put it, to take refuge in "parallelism." He proposed that a Deputies level process be set up to work both the NATO enlargement and NATO-Russia tracks and suggested the Administration find a way to insulate itself from the political pressure generated by both the Republicans and ethnic lobby to move faster. Ambiguity was key to avoiding open conflict on the issue at home and abroad. The President concluded: "The policy is right. But we need to work with the Russians."[115]

In the days following the meeting, Talbott would sit down with Perry to explore the Secretary of Defense's concerns. He subsequently sent Christopher a memo summarizing Perry's views on the following terms: "What is bugging him about our approach to NATO expansion and the Brussels communiqué, quite simply, was that he doesn't agree with our policy. In his view, NATO should not take on new members unless Russia goes bad; we should hold open the possibility of adding new members only as a hedge against the failure of Russian reform and a return of the Russian government to the geopolitical offensive. In the meantime, we should put all our emphasis on developing PfP, in lieu of Alliance expansion." Talbott went on to add that this was a defensible position intellectually that others had taken previously as well. "Trouble is, it's not our Administration policy—and hasn't been for just over a year now."[116]

The Deputy Secretary noted that the Administration had been committed to expanding NATO since the President's trip to Europe the previous January. "In other words, we've rejected, as a matter of policy, the notion of only expanding NATO if Russia turns bad." He had made the case to Perry that it was a mistake to justify expansion solely in terms of dealing with a resurgent Russia. "If we cast expansion in those terms, we'll give the CEE states a stake in portraying reform as having failed; and we'll give the Russians no choice but to see expansion—or any steps in that direction—as a vote of no-confidence in them. Yet there will have to be steps toward expansion, of the kind we're contemplating in 95; otherwise the President's rhetoric of 94; will look very hollow indeed."

As 1994 drew to a close, Clinton wrote Yeltsin to reiterate his commitment to a strong U.S.-Russia partnership. He noted that the last year had been a difficult one for both of them, but insisted that both leaders could look back with pride at what they had accomplished together. He assured Yeltsin that he stood by his September commitment on NATO enlargement: enlargement would proceed gradually and openly and the U.S. would develop a partnership with Russia in parallel to this process. "I know you share my view that the European security issue is almost without question the most important and sensitive issue we will confront together. I believe we have now laid a solid foundation for dealing with the many questions and complexities that lie ahead. I look forward to keeping this in the forefront of the personal discussions in the year ahead."[117]

On December 29, Yeltsin replied that Gore's visit to Moscow had helped eliminate the "serious misunderstandings" from Budapest. His understanding of their September conversation on NATO enlargement, he emphasized, was that NATO would not act hastily but rather put in place a full-scale NATO-Russia partnership before proceeding with enlargement. Yeltsin suggested accelerating efforts to reach a parallel agreement on a NATO-Russia relationship along with the completion of the NATO enlargement study. He invited Clinton to Moscow in May and suggested that Christopher and Kozyrev meet early in the New Year to come up with some ideas for the two leaders to discuss.[118] Washington breathed a sigh of relief. The Russian President no longer seemed focused on stopping enlargement, but instead on accelerating work on building a NATO-Russia relationship. Now Washington had to fill both tracks with substance.

Book IV

ESTABLISHING THE DUAL TRACK

The Clinton Administration had decided to enlarge NATO—but slowly, cautiously, and with an expanded effort to engage Moscow. This dual track approach was seen as the way to manage the tension between the President's commitments to secure Central and Eastern Europe yet support Russian democratic reform. By moving gradually, the Administration also hoped to buy time to overcome allied doubts about enlargement, work out a cooperative NATO-Russia relationship, and assemble the various other pieces of its strategy—all without precipitating a controversial debate at home, in Europe, or with Moscow.

Russian and allied reticence weren't the only factors that led the Administration to opt for this approach. Moving gradually also gave NATO breathing space to focus on the considerable amount of homework it needed to complete before it could enlarge—both in the Alliance and with candidate countries in Central and Eastern Europe. Those voices calling for a faster approach often overlooked the fact that enlarging the Alliance to Central and Eastern Europe was a major undertaking. A blueprint for how to deal with the political and military modalities did not yet exist, and first needed to be created. Institutionalizing a cooperative NATO-Russia relationship was also *terra incognita* that needed to be explored. The Alliance set for itself the goal of completing both the NATO enlargement study and the parameters for a new NATO-Russia relationship by the end of the year.

As the spring of 1995 unfolded, it became clear that this latter goal was going to be harder to achieve than expected. Yeltsin was under growing political pressure at home to directly oppose the Alliance's eastward expansion. As the nationalistic and anti-NATO tone in Russia increased, the Russian President started to inch away from his commitment to NATO-Russia cooperation. In May, President Clinton convinced him to finally follow through on moving ahead with a NATO-Russia relationship—but only in return for a pledge that the U.S. would not move on enlargement until after the Russian Presidential elections in the summer of 1996.

At home, the Clinton Administration also found itself facing a growing controversy over enlargement. Conservative Republicans on Capitol Hill now accused the Administration of waffling on enlargement and capitulating to Russian pressure. They stepped up their attacks on the Administration's handling of both NATO and Russia and tabled legislation in an attempt to pressure the Administration to commit to specific candidates and a clear deadline. At the same time, opponents of enlargement stepped up their criticism. The latter included some of the most influential voices on defense issues in the President's own party such as Senator Sam Nunn (D-GA). The Administration found itself in a fierce political crossfire between those wanting to move faster on enlargement and those not wanting to move ahead at all.

The debate over NATO enlargement was not taking place in a vacuum. Against the backdrop of the war in Bosnia, the Alliance was staring into an abyss. Its inability to stop the bloodshed in the Balkans increasingly cast a shadow over the U.S.-European relationship. Ethnic cleansing threatened to undermine European security, while the inability of the most powerful Alliance in the world to stop the Bosnian Serb military threatened to make a mockery of the vision of a Europe whole and free. And for the Clinton Administration, Bosnia was a cancer eating away at America's credibility. Until the war in Bosnia was stopped, NATO was hardly in a position to credibly extend new security commitments to Central and Eastern Europe.

In the summer of 1995, the Clinton Administration shifted course in its Bosnia policy and decided to make an all out effort to end the bloodiest conflict in Europe since World War II. Following the election of French President Jacques Chirac in May 1995, the United States detected a greater European willingness to use force in Bosnia. With a ceasefire established on the ground, the U.S. launched a second major effort to negotiate a peace settlement among the warring parties at Dayton. The success at Dayton in the fall of 1995 not only brought peace to Bosnia, but also paved the way for NATO to enlarge. It restored a sense of purpose and confidence in the Alliance and reassured Washington's allies that it could credibly extend new security guarantees to Central and Eastern Europe. Above all, the U.S.-brokered deal on Russian participation in NATO's Implementation Force (IFOR) moved the idea of NATO-Russia cooperation from theory to reality.

By the end of the year, the NATO enlargement study was completed. NATO and Russian troops who once faced each other as Cold War adversaries were now preparing to deploy together to Bosnia. And the troops of former Warsaw Pact countries that desired NATO membership were preparing to operate side-by-side with NATO troops. It was a powerful example of how NATO was adapting to a new era and the challenge of projecting stability throughout Europe.

1. ESTABLISHING THE NATO TRACK

Washington's first challenge on enlargement in the spring of 1995 was to consolidate an Alliance consensus. While Holbrooke had steamrolled the allies into moving beyond PfP, many of them were not happy about the shift in U.S. and NATO policy and still had doubts about enlarging the Alliance. The NATO enlargement study commissioned by allied Foreign Ministers in December 1994 now became the vehicle for addressing those doubts. In late January 1995, the U.S. Ambassador to NATO, Robert Hunter, reiterated that European support for enlargement was still shallow. "Few allies are enthusiastic about expansion, and several will drag their feet on getting the necessary work done this year, whether out of inertia or out of a hope that, somehow they will not have to cross this particular Rubicon." Washington had to view the enlargement study, he argued, "not as a technical exercise of working through the details of a robust NATO decision, but primarily as a process of building political support for the taking of actual decisions on enlargement in terms of real countries and real dates"—with the goal being "to get allies used to the idea of having new allies, comfortable with the fact that the alliance which emerges afterwards will not somehow be weakened, and confident that enlargement will not help bring into being renewed threats to European security."[1]

One way to do so was for the Administration to underscore its own commitment to moving ahead. From the President on down, senior Administration officials such as Secretary of State Christopher and Secretary of Defense Perry now delivered major speeches presenting the Administration's case for enlargement as the centerpiece of a more general overhaul of the Atlantic Alliance to help shape a unified Europe.[2] In the spring issue of *Foreign Affairs*, Assistant Secretary of State Holbrooke argued that the U.S. had become a "European power" in a new sense and that NATO enlargement was part of recasting the Alliance as a permanent feature of a post Cold War Europe.[3] And in the summer, Deputy Secretary of State Talbott, still portrayed by some critics as an opponent, publicly argued in favor of NATO enlargement to help consolidate democracy and to promote stability in Central and Eastern Europe in an essay in *The New York Review of Books*.[4]

The Administration's increasingly strong public commitment helped to bring allies on board. In early January 1995, a team of senior British officials arrived in Washington for consultations. Their message was that London would support enlargement, but wanted assurances that the U.S. would take the defense component seriously and not compromise the integrated command structure. It was also important, British officials underscored, to be "realistic" and recognize that some PfP countries would not be able to join NATO for a long time, if at all.[5] Following a visit by Foreign Secretary Sir Douglas Hurd to Washington, British officials cautioned the Americans that while enlargement was not something to be undertaken in haste, they were on board.[6] In late January Hurd publicly endorsed the U.S. dual-track strategy and shortly thereafter British Defense Secretary Rifkind told Bill Perry that London was in "lockstep" with Washington on the issue.[7]

Germany was the key, however. In the White House on February 9, 1995, Kohl told Clinton that his goal was to broaden the trans-Atlantic link, not to push the U.S. out of Europe. "We need to enlarge to Central and Eastern Europe," Kohl stated. "The issue, of course, is Poland, not Hungary or the Czech Republic." His top priority, he noted, was Poland: "They are our closest neighbor." But Kohl was equally adamant of the need for a parallel NATO-Russia track. Enlargement "will not work" if the West used harsh, anti-Russia language. "It has always been our position that NATO enlargement only makes sense if it does not lead to increased hostility with the Russians," he told President Clinton. "Therefore, we can only do it if Russia—and Ukraine as well—are part of the process."

Kohl urged great caution when it came to the timing of NATO enlargement. He supported using the rest of the year to determine the "why" and the "how" of enlargement. He praised Clinton for maintaining ties with Yeltsin in spite of the Russian invasion of Chechnya and the growing criticism by Republicans of the Administratino's Moscow policy. The West could not, he continued, simply "lean back and say that Yeltsin is an autocrat, a traitor to the cause of democracy. . . . I don't know if Yeltsin will prevail. But I am sure that if we leave him in the lurch, matters will get much worse." Kohl urged Clinton to stand up to those Republicans urging the Administration to accelerate enlargement. "We should stick to our [current] policy line on NATO enlargement. Perhaps we are wrong—that is a risk we always run in politics—but the other risk would be greater."[8] After Kohl's departure, Christopher cabled all American Ambassadors in Europe underlining that there was now a common U.S.-German position on NATO enlargement. "We now hope," the cable concluded, "to move beyond the question whether the U.S. is pushing the process too rapidly" while "recognizing that there will be continued delaying attempts from other quarters."[9]

One of those quarters was Paris. It, too, was worried that the Clinton Administration was already moving too fast and was likely to succumb to conservative Republican pressure to move even faster on enlargement.[10] Meeting with Secretary Christopher in late January 1995, French Foreign Minister Alain

Juppé queried him several times whether the combination of Chechnya and Republican pressure would lead Washington to pick up the pace on enlargement and adopt a harsher course vis-à-vis Russia.[11] At the same time, the first signs of a reappraisal in French attitudes toward NATO were bubbling up to the surface. In late January, Juppe gave a major speech laying out a post–Cold War Gaullist vision. In it he stated clearly that European defense for the foreseeable future could not be built outside of NATO. The expansion of the EU and the WEU, he noted, "will bring with it sooner or later the expansion of the Atlantic Alliance."[12] The election of Jacques Chirac as President of France later that spring would accelerate France's reappraisal of its relations to NATO, including its position on enlargement.

In the meantime, at NATO headquarters, diplomats were busy hammering out early drafts of the enlargement study under NATO's Assistant Secretary General for Political Affairs, German Ambassador Gebhardt von Moltke. By early March, an initial round of "brainstorming sessions" had led to agreement on a set of core ideas. The first was that enlargement's rationale was to expand integration and stability in Europe eastward, and not a strategic response to a specific military threat from Russia. A second was that there would be no "second class" membership. New members would share both the benefits and risks of membership and be expected to adhere to existing NATO strategy and doctrine and participate in both collective defense obligations and also undertake new military missions beyond Alliance borders. Subsequent drafts started to fill in the blanks on the criteria new members were expected to meet, the modalities on how enlargement would take place, and how enlargement would relate to PfP. The Alliance blueprint for NATO enlargement was slowly taking shape and allies were buying into the process.[13]

The assumption that NATO enlargement was not driven by an imminent Russian military threat also shaped early Alliance thinking on enlargement's military implications. While during the Cold War NATO faced Soviet military superiority, it was now the Alliance that enjoyed the upper hand. The Alliance's conventional superiority and the strategic warning it enjoyed allowed NATO planners considerable flexibility in carrying out new security guarantees. While new allies would be covered by the Alliance's nuclear umbrella and integrated into alliance nuclear planning, there was no need to deploy nuclear weapons on the territory of new members.[14] Similarly, while the U.S. wanted new members to be fully integrated into NATO's multinational command structures, American defense officials concluded that there was also no *a priori* need for NATO to permanently deploy large numbers of troops on the territory of new members either.

Instead, NATO officials concluded that the Alliance could rely on the projection of military power into the region in a crisis to carry out its new defense obligations to new members under Article 5. To do this, it was essential that

NATO retained the right to deploy its forces to reinforce new members in a crisis or if the security environment changed for the worse. Relying heavily on reinforcement also meant the Atlantic Alliance would have to create the infrastructure so that forces of other allies could move in fast enough and in adequate numbers to defend new members in a crisis. In order to back this up, NATO defense planners would also need to routinely hold exercises on the territory of new members to demonstrate its reinforcement capabilities and to help the forces of these countries adapt to alliance standards.[15] But the bottom line was that NATO was capable of defending Central and Eastern Europe, and did not require the forward deployment of large numbers of allied troops has had been the case in West Germany during the Cold War.

By early March, Ambassador Hunter reported that the framework of the study was in place and that only a handful of political issues were left to resolve.[16] At the same time, the early draft suffered from many of the typical faults of a document drafted by Committee—it was too long, inconsistent, and written in bureaucratic code that was difficult for any layperson to comprehend. Washington wanted a document that was clear and accessible to the public, not one that only insiders would understand. After Holbrooke reviewed a draft in late March, he wrote a note to his principal deputy, John Kornblum: "John, I find this draft desperately didactic, diversionary, etc. It will cause us real problems with the pro-expansionists and raises too many hypotheticals. Can we still walk it back without an undue Euro-crise?"[17] U.S. diplomats were sent back to clean up the language and come back with a better, more accessible document.

On March 7, NATO Secretary General Claes met with President Clinton in the White House and assured the President that the enlargement study was on track and that NATO would complete its work by the end of the year. The most difficult question, the NATO Secretary General underscored, was what to do next. He warned President Clinton that if NATO moved to immediately try to tackle the question of the "who" and "when" of enlargement, it could "play into the hands of the Russian nationalists and communists" in the run up to Russian parliamentary elections at the end of the year and Presidential elections the following summer.

Claes was not the only one with an eye on the Russian electoral calendar. President Clinton looked, too. But it was politically dangerous to slow enlargement preparations until after the Russian elections in light of Republican criticism that the Administration was already waffling on the issue. Lake immediately pointed out that if such an assumption leaked it would appear as if Washington had given Moscow a veto over enlargement. "The consequence would be to destroy the psychological progress we have made in Central and Eastern Europe and it would exacerbate the domestic politics of NATO expansion," Lake underscored. Vice President Gore added: "We should never use the Russian elections as a reference date. It is not part of our decision-making process."

But the Russian elections *were* a reference point—especially as it became clear that Yeltsin had decided to run for reelection against communist leader Gennady Zuganov. No one in the room was more attuned to supporting Yeltsin than Bill Clinton. Claes responded that he was simply recognizing that a NATO decision on the "who" and "when" in December 1995 could play into the hands of the nationalist and communist parties. He added that the Alliance had legitimate internal homework to do that could be stretched out in a way to justify not tackling the "who" and "when" until after the Russian Presidential elections in mid-1996. "That's the way to do it," Clinton responded.[18]

When NATO Foreign Ministers met in late May, the enlargement study was on track. The issue barely made the news, having been overshadowed by the growing crisis in Bosnia and the Alliance's efforts to finally finish the NATO-Russia framework with Moscow.[19] Over the summer months of 1995, NATO officials wrapped up the final details for the study in time to meet their mid-September deadine. On September 28, NATO Secretary General Claes officially presented the study to a gathering of NATO and Partner Ambassadors at NATO headquarters. Claes highlighted the principles underpinning the study and the contribution enlargement could make to broader Euro-Atlantic stability. The Ambassadors from the Partner countries warmly welcomed and praised the study, with the head of the Polish delegation noting that critics of NATO enlargement now had to justify their claim that it would somehow endanger European security.[20]

The first track of the Administration's dual track strategy was in place. In Washington, on October 2, 1995, the Deputies Committee met to review next steps following the completion of the enlargement study. They concluded that NATO had to "maintain palpable and substantive momentum toward enlargement in 1996" but that no decisions on extending invitations should be made before the end of the year "given our interest in trying to ensure that enlargement plays as small a role as possible in the June 1996 Russian Presidential elections." Instead, they suggested that the U.S. propose to NATO intensified consultations with Partner countries seeking membership to familiarize them with what membership would actually entail. This would also allow NATO military authorities to look at the military capabilities of potential members.[21]

2. A PARALLEL TRACK WITH MOSCOW

Getting the NATO-Russia track up and running was more difficult but just as important. Supporting Moscow's integration into the West was crucial to the Administration in its own right. But ensuring that enlargement did not produce a blow-up with Moscow was also a *sine qua non* for keeping nervous allies on board. As Kohl had told Clinton in February, enlargement made sense only if it did not lead to increased hostility with the Russians. It was a view shared by many allies. Enlargement critics at home were also predicting a train wreck in relations with Moscow. There was no better way to disarm them than to successfully deliver a NATO-Russia deal. Clinton was cautiously optimistic. Asked in February 1995 by Dutch Prime Minister Wim Kok what he thought the chances were of getting the Russians on board, the President responded: "It will be difficult but at least in principle I think Russia can be bought off. . . . The Russians are still uneasy but if we make the most of Partnership for Peace and show good faith in dealing with Russia, then we can make progress on the timetable we have set."[22]

U.S. thinking was reflected in an internal Administration strategy paper circulated in early January 1995. The paper defined the Administration's goal as a formalized NATO-Russia arrangement that would reassure Moscow that NATO expansion to Central and Eastern Europe was neither directed against or aimed at marginalizing Russia in European security. To underscore this, it proposed that the Administration seek to negotiate a NATO-Russia "arrangement" in parallel to enlargement. The core of such an arrangement would be a consultative mechanism "with" but not "in" NATO. It would allow Russia to engage with NATO on a regular and ad hoc basis, to have timely input into Alliance decisions on Bosnia-type non-Article 5 operations, and to work out means of cooperation and in implementing those decisions.[23] But Washington also needed to protect NATO's only internal decisionmaking mechanisms from potential Russian mischief. The paper rejected, for example, Russia's demand that a NATO-Russia relationship be worked out prior to enlargement. Giving Russia a seat at the NATO table or some kind of "political membership," as some Russians had suggested, was also excluded.

In early January 1995, Talbott traveled to Brussels to share Washington's early thinking on a NATO-Russia strategy with Washington's allies. He met separately with Deputy Foreign Minister Mamedov to lay the groundwork for the upcoming Christopher-Kozyrev meeting in Geneva later that month. During a walk around the grounds of Truman Hall, the U.S. Ambassador to NATO's residence, Mamedov also pressed Talbott for a response to Yeltsin's invitation to Clinton to visit Moscow in early May for the fiftieth anniversary celebrations of the end of World War II. Talbott was noncommittal, and joked that his credibility as a Presidential travel agent had suffered a nearly mortal blow after what happened in Budapest the previous December.

Mamedov floated an even more explosive trial balloon. He suggested that the U.S. and Russia work out a secret deal, to be concluded by the end of the year, in which Russia would acquiesce to NATO enlargement. In return, NATO would have to take three steps. First, NATO would transform itself from a collective defense into a collective security organization—and revise the language of the 1949 Washington Treaty to that effect. NATO's historical task of deterring Russia as an aggressor would be cast onto the ash heap of history and the

Alliance would now commit itself to focusing on new missions, such as peace-keeping and counter-terrorism. Second, Russia would also be allowed into the decisionmaking mechanism of the Alliance, by either joining a "political committee" or through a binding consultative mechanism. Third, NATO would admit new members but only after this transformation of the Atlantic Alliance had taken place.

The two processes would be linked, Mamedov underscored: NATO expansion would proceed only if this internal transformation of NATO took place. This package, which the Russian side called the "reform" of NATO, would be concluded by the time of the completion of the NATO enlargement study in the fall of 1995. Such changes to NATO would be implemented over a three-to-five year period while the Alliance was preparing to bring in new members. As the "reformed NATO" was expanding, Russia would join "politically" or by some other formal arrangement. Mamedov also proposed a "confidential" exchange of letters on this work plan sometime after the upcoming Christopher-Kozyrev meeting, to be followed up with a "confidential" bilateral understanding by the two Presidents at the May summit.

Talbott sent an unmistakable signal for the Deputy Foreign Minster to take back to Moscow. "Your boss is on his way to making a huge mistake. You've given us a sneak preview of a disaster movie," he told Mamedov. Kozyrev was living in a "dangerous dream world" if he thought Washington would consider that kind of package. Clinton and Christopher were already taking a risk by being willing to go forward with a serious discussion on a NATO-Russia relationship against the backdrop of Chechnya and Russian behavior in other areas. "But this proposal could abort the whole process," Talbott continued. "Moreover, if it gets out that you're playing this sort of game, it could actually accelerate NATO expansion and exacerbate concerns that Russia is out to wreck the Alliance."[24]

Talbott sent Christopher a private memo on his conversation. Mamedov's trial balloon, he noted, crossed all of the Administration's red lines—the Russians might as well have proposed a U.S.-Russia summit in Yalta! But there was also a silver lining in what he was saying. The Russians were acknowledging that NATO was going to expand, and laying out their opening gambit on the terms of enlargement. The fact that this opening gambit was completely unacceptable to the U.S. was not surprising. That was a classic Soviet negotiating tactic. But the bottom line was that the Russians knew enlargement was coming and were willing to deal. In his upcoming meeting with Kozyrev, Christopher's task would be to defend Washington's own red lines while making it clear that Moscow's were unacceptable. Further, he had to convince Kozyrev that Moscow had little choice but to work out a special relationship with NATO before it expanded.[25]

Christopher and Kozyrev met in Geneva on January 17–18, 1995 for a private one-on-one dinner followed by a larger meeting of the full delegations the next day. Discussion of Moscow's invasion of Chechnya dominated much of the meeting. But Christopher told Kozyrev that NATO enlargement was inevitable, that the basic character of NATO was not going to change, and that nonmembers could not be involved in decisionmaking. While Russia was not a priori excluded from joining NATO, Christopher made it clear that this was not likely to happen any time soon. The real question, therefore, was how to build a positive relationship between NATO and Russia. It was important that both sides roll up their sleeves and start to try to develop that relationship. The most important thing, Christopher concluded, was for Russia to engage and work with NATO through PfP.

Kozyrev initially trotted out a half-hearted version of the NATO "reform" plan Mamedov had previewed for Talbott. But he soon switched gears and admitted that the real problem with NATO was the widespread view in Russia that the Alliance was still an "alien body." To make a NATO-Russia relationship work, the two sides needed to address several Russian concerns. He went on to list four issues. The first was to show the Alliance no longer saw Russia as an enemy. The second was how to change Russia's public perceptions of the Alliance. A third issue was what Kozyrev called the "organizational trap," Russia wanted to be a partner with NATO but found the Alliance's decisionmaking closed and cumbersome. Fourth, there was what the Russian Foreign Minister called the "natural nervousness" that occurs when a military alliance comes closer to a country's borders.

To address these concerns, Kozyrev emphasized, NATO need to take several steps. First, it needed to show that it was changing its Cold War orientation and be seen as an institution evolving away from an "exclusive military body." Second, the two sides needed to come up with an institutionalized consultative mechanism for joint decisionmaking, and leave open the option of eventual Russian membership. Third, NATO needed to reassure Moscow that it would not move conventional or nuclear forces eastward as it expanded. And fourth, he suggested that there be a "joint market" for armaments in Central and Eastern Europe to help the Russian defense industry.[26] It was the first time Washington got a clear list of Russian desiderata. British Foreign Secretary Hurd subsequently assessed Kozyrev's demands as follows: the first was straightforward, the last conceivable, the third not impossible and the second the most problematic.[27]

In early February 1995, Secretary of Defense Bill Perry took the next step by laying out in public the key elements of what a NATO-Russia partnership could consist of at the annual major "Wehrkunde" conference held in Munich. "Right now, a set of plans for Russia's cooperation within and outside of the Partnership for Peace awaits their signature," Perry stated. "We should build on these plans. For example, we could have a formal arrangement—perhaps eventually codified in a memorandum of understanding or a charter—for a number of cooperative arrangements." Such arrangements could include "some sort of Standing Consultative Commission to provide formal structure for our NATO-Russia relationship" as well as "a continuing dialogue on a variety of subjects, such as: counter-proliferation, cooperation on defense technology, transparency in defense policymaking, crisis management, and peacekeeping doctrine and tactics." While respecting each side's independence, such an approach, he concluded, "should give input into each other's decision-making and we should cooperate in implementing our decisions."[28]

U.S. and Russian officials had originally hoped to establish a framework for NATO-Russia cooperation by the spring of 1995 and to finalize an agreement by the end of the year. But the rising tide of anti-Western sentiment in Russia made that goal increasingly elusive. Throughout the spring, opposition to NATO enlargement grew across the political spectrum both in its breadth and intensity. The chorus of voices calling for a tougher line no longer came just from the far right or far left but from moderate and centrist Russians as well.[29] In late February 1995, Mamedov arrived in Washington for another round of consultations. He pushed for Clinton to attend the fiftieth anniversary V-E Day summit in Moscow. In an emotional appeal to Talbott, he argued that it was important that on this the sacred day for Russia, Yeltsin was standing on the podium in Red Square with western leaders like Clinton and Kohl, not anti-democratic pariahs like the Slovak Prime Minister Vladimir Meciar, or Belarussian President Aleksander Lukashenko. The future of reform in Russia, he warned, could be at stake.[30]

In a larger meeting with U.S. officials the next day, Mamedov reiterated that Moscow wanted a NATO-Russia agreement by the end of the year that could serve as a kind of security safety net for the 1996 political season in Russian politics. Such an agreement was within reach, he argued. Indeed, the elements were already on the table: a statement that NATO's mission had changed; a standing consultative mechanism as outlined by Perry at Wehrkunde; an explicit statement that Russia was not excluded from membership; no prohibition on the sales of Russian arms to new members; and "guarantees" that there would be no NATO conventional or nuclear forces deployed on the soil of new members. Mamedov claimed that he had no illusions about when Russia might be prepared to join the Alliance, noting that it might take "up to one-hundred years." But it was psychologically crucial that NATO's door be open to eventual membership.[31]

In mid-March 1995, after weeks of debate, President Clinton decided to attend the Moscow May summit to underscore his support for Yeltsin. The President also initiated an exchange of letters with the Russian President designed to answer some of the issues Kozyrev had raised with Christopher and start to create a common framework the two sides could work with. In a letter dated March 15, 1995, Clinton wrote that the U.S. and Russia had a common interest in building an inclusive and undivided Europe for generations to come. It was important to build on the existing foundation of institutions in Europe of which NATO was an essential one. The Alliance had already changed substantially since the end of the Cold War. The concept of containment no longer governed NATO's strategy and planning. Instead, the Alliance was focusing on new threats that could arise from ethnic and territorial disputes, weapons of mass destruction, and other post–Cold War risks. It was the President's way of signaling that NATO and the U.S. presence were here to stay but that the Alliance was changing in ways that Yeltsin could point to in order to answer his critics.

At the same time, President Clinton continued, a consensus among NATO member states now existed that enlargement would enhance stability in Europe. Clinton reminded Yeltsin that he had assured him the previous fall that Russia would not be excluded from eligibility to join the Alliance. The Alliance did not plan to make any decisions on enlargement "this year." Instead, it wanted to use this period to develop a relationship with Russia in parallel to the NATO enlargement study. The President underscored that good NATO-Russia relations could be achieved only if Russia cooperated with the Alliance, starting with the implementation of PfP. President Clinton enclosed an attachment laying out arguments on how NATO had changed. While ostensibly designed to assist President Yeltsin in making the case to the Russian public for a NATO-Russia rapprochement, it was really meant to counter the internal arguments from hard-line voices in Yeltsin's entourage.[32]

Clinton's letter, however, had not yet arrived in Moscow when Yeltsin himself joined the ranks of the critics, harshly criticizing Kozyrev for not being vigorous enough in opposing enlargement in a Kremlin meeting on March 14.[33] On March 17, Mamedov told Pickering that Yeltsin was again suspicious about a possible "acceleration of NATO expansion." Asked where Yeltsin was getting such mistaken perceptions, Mamedov responded that "some of your European allies are telling us again that you're pushing them harder on expansion than you're telling us, just as they claimed before Brussels and Budapest last year." He added that opposition to enlargement was growing across the Russian political spectrum and was likely to get stronger as elections approached. Kozyrev, he told Pickering, had been instructed to get a "straightforward" assessment of Washington's enlargement plans from Christopher.[34]

Two days later on March 23, Christopher and Kozyrev met in Geneva. Over dinner, Kozyrev expressed growing apprehension over NATO enlargement. He again admitted that Russian concerns were being driven largely by political rather than strategic considerations, but insisted it was critical that public discussion of enlargement be toned down given the changing political scene in Russia.[35] In a subsequent note to the President, Christopher wrote that Russia was clearly pursuing its own definition of national interest and the U.S. had to do the same."[36] But the roller-coaster ride on NATO-Russia talks continued. When U.S. Secretary of Defense Bill Perry arrived in Moscow in early April for talks on U.S.-Russian military cooperation, Grachev told him in private that he supported moving ahead with PfP. But in public the Russian Defense Minister threatened to abrogate key arms control treaties if NATO went ahead with enlargement.[37] Russian General Alexsandr Lebed went so far as to warn of a third world war if NATO enlarged.[38] While no one took it seriously, it was a further sign that Russian politicians were competing to out do one other with their anti-NATO rhetoric in trying to score points against Yeltsin.

3. THE MAY-FOR-MAY DEAL

By the spring of 1995 a long and growing list of disagreements over Bosnia, Chechnya, Iran, and NATO were casting an increasingly long shadow over U.S.-Russian relations. With the President committed to visiting Moscow in May, an increasingly frustrated Christopher turned to Talbott to ask how the U.S. could better bring its leverage to bear.

Talbott sent Christopher several memos in the ensuing weeks laying out his views on how the Administration should manage relations with Moscow, including NATO enlargement, against this deteriorating political backdrop. Russia, he wrote, was a country in a transition of uncertain duration, course, and destination. Russians had lost their defining ideology, the principles for organizing their state and society, and their international role. The 20th century had essentially been a series of disasters for the Russian people, he wrote. Russians were only beginning to realize that the transition to a new Russia was going to be long and very hard. And Yeltsin was facing the political backlash from that growing realization.

At the same time, Moscow needed all the help it could get from the West. Most Russians knew this. Many of them resented it. The U.S. was the western country most willing to champion Russia's inclusion and eventual integration into Western institutions. That was the source of Washington's leverage but also a source of frustration as it reminded Russians just how uneven the U.S.-Russia relationship had become. Talbott noted how much Yeltsin had liked Vice President Gore's metaphor comparing the U.S.-Russia relationship to two space stations docking—precisely because it retained the notion of them as co-equals. But it was also misleading, he noted. The U.S. and Russia were not equals and were not going to meet each other half way. Russia was either going move toward the West or it would flounder as the Soviet Union did.

But Talbott also argued that the U.S. should not abandon Moscow when confronted with unacceptable Russian behavior as conservative Republican critics were suggesting. Instead, Washington had to focus on influencing Moscow's behavior over the longer term, recognizing that Russia's course would be erratic. He suggested his own metaphor for U.S. policymakers. Washington, he argued, should view itself as the lighthouse on the horizon that could help guide Russian reformers to a safe harbor in the West. Russian reformers had their own vision of integrating with the West. What Washington could provide for them was a constant point of light and navigational assistance as they tried to reach western shores. Such assistance was needed not only during fair weather, Talbott underscored, but all the more so during rough seas to ensure that what he termed the "the rickety, leaky, oversized cannon-laden Good Ship Russia, with its erratic autocratic captain, semi-mutinous crew and stinking bilge (complete with black eye patches and peg legs)" had a clearly visible point on the horizon to steer by."[39]

Washington's leverage, Talbott continued, came from the fact that the U.S. controlled the pace of Moscow's integration with the West. Moscow knew that American willingness to champion Russia's integration into the West was conditional and subject to review. Yeltsin knew that if he went in the wrong direction on NATO, for example, the Alliance could accelerate enlargement. If he moved in the right direction, however, Russia would get more cooperation, international acceptance, and financial assistance. Washington and its allies therefore had to defend NATO's red lines but also keep holding the door open to cooperation — in spite of Moscow's regular anti-Western outbursts. Washington's ace in the hole, Talbott concluded, was Clinton's personal relationship with Yeltsin. The Russian President wanted to make Russia a normal Western country at peace with itself and its neighbors. Given the choice between isolation and integration, Yeltsin would choose integration. But he was increasingly surrounded by advisors whose orientation was anti-reformist if not openly revanchist. That meant Clinton had to involve the Russian President directly.[40]

In early April, the Deputies Committee met again to review what additional steps the U.S. might consider to respond to the demands Kozyrev had laid out to Christopher. In what became known as the "May-for-May" deal, the Deputies recommended that the U.S. reaffirm to Moscow that NATO actions in 1995 would be limited to completing the NATO study and briefing Central and East Europeans on its results if Moscow was prepared to take the next steps on PfP and work to reach closure on the framework of a new NATO-Russia relationship by December. When the Alliance would tackle the question of "who" or "when" in 1996 with both Russian and U.S. Presidential elections scheduled was left open.[41]

President Clinton had more immediate concerns. In a meeting with British Prime Minister John Major on April 4, he noted that Yeltsin was backing away from his previous assurances on NATO. "I thought that if we could get an understanding with the Russians [on NATO enlargement], we could achieve some level of comfort and tone down the rhetoric," Clinton told Major. "I thought we could proceed at a deliberate pace, but my current feeling is that

Yeltsin is mishandling the issue." But he also told Major that the fact Yeltsin was being driven in the wrong direction by Russian domestic politics made it all the more important to remain engaged with him in spite of the criticism he was facing from Republicans on this issue. "Anything we can do in May to get him more centered on the issue would be helpful," Clinton said. "When we stay away from Yeltsin, domestic politics begin to affect him."[42]

The next day President Clinton met with his foreign policy team in the Oval Office. Christopher tried to brace him for what he warned could be a difficult visit to Moscow. The Yeltsin he would meet in May would be "a different man from the one you dealt with in Vancouver, when he was worried about his own survival, and even from the one you dealt with here in Washington last September when he seemed prepared to be sensible about NATO," Christopher warned. The Russian President was consumed by domestic politics and the growing opposition to NATO enlargement. He had taken the NATO portfolio completely into his own hands. "Only he can decide the issue and he's got a lot of people around him pushing him the wrong way. You're going to have to deal with him yourself and make him understand that his current course is self-destructive. He may do another Budapest on you."[43]

Following a quick Talbott trip to Moscow to test the waters, President Clinton reconvened his foreign policy team on April 13. This time Clinton was worried about the depth of the allied commitment to NATO enlargement, too. "They aren't exactly sounding four-square behind me on this thing," he told his advisors. "They're probably sympathetic to some of the arguments they're hearing from the Russians. They worry that I'm being driven by the Polish-American vote in 1996 and the Republicans just aggravate that calculus." There was a danger that Moscow would isolate the U.S. and split the Atlantic Alliance. "We're getting double-boxed here—both by the Russians and the Europeans." It made a NATO-Russia understanding all that more difficult yet also more important to achieve. Talbott and Perry laid out the strategy for the summit and the run up to the NATO Ministerial in May. As the meeting was breaking up, Clinton pulled Talbott aside and said: "Strobe, I want you to bust your ass to get this thing fixed along the lines you and Bill [Perry] were talking about."[44]

For the third time that spring, Christopher and Kozyrev met on April 27, this time in the U.S. State Department's Madison Room for two hours. The U.S. Secretary of state noted that Yeltsin's response to President Clinton's letter had been positive and bore Kozyrev's fingerprints. The Russian Foreign Minster replied that they were bloodstains and reflected the blood he had shed to get the letter past hard-liners in Yeltsin's entourage. The answer to Russia's concerns about enlargement, Christopher countered, was an active NATO-Russia dialogue. "That's fine," said Kozyrev, "but I need an ally in Washington to make this work." Christopher responded: "You've got an ally in me and another one at 1600 Pennsylvania Avenue."[45]

Christopher then laid out the "May-for-May" deal. If Russia would commit to signing up for PfP at the spring NATO Ministerial, the U.S. would ensure that the Alliance would proceed "no faster and no slower" than already agreed, and put a fresh emphasis on inaugurating the NATO-Russia dialogue. The U.S. would avoid any suggestion that it was speeding up enlargement. In return, Moscow would avoid claiming it had slowed it down. Since NATO had yet to set a definite timeline for enlargement, the deal provided political cover for both sides. Christopher added that he expected the Alliance to be busy at the December 1995 Ministerial following up on the NATO enlargement study. While not saying so explicitly, Christopher was telling Kozyrev that the Alliance would not make any major decisions on the "who" or the "when" of enlargement until well into 1996—at the earliest.

Kozyrev underscored the need to avoid public statements that could aggravate the political situation in Moscow on NATO. "There is so much talk about the expansion of NATO and about the acceleration of that expansion," he stated, "that it is like an echo in a valley in the mountains that causes an avalanche." Christopher's approach, he noted, seemed "pragmatic enough" and that "there is really no other way to handle the issue." But he cautioned he was not sure he could deliver Yeltsin, and that Clinton would have to help get the Russian President on board. Western statements on enlargement were being used to torpedo Russian participation in PfP. Hard-liners in Moscow were urging the Russian President to try to halt enlargement by imposing "countermeasures" designed to scare off the West. It was essential to get momentum back into the NATO-Russia track. Only Yeltsin could give the green light on that.[46]

The next morning Christopher took Kozyrev to the White House for a brief meeting with the President to seal the agreement. Later that day, Clinton telephoned Yeltsin. He assured Yeltsin that enlargement was proceeding along the path the two Presidents had agreed to the previous September, and went on to describe the "May-for-May" deal in some detail. Just as the interpreter was beginning to translate Clinton's fairly long statement into Russian, Yeltsin hung up. After the connection was re-established, Yeltsin agreed to support the agreement in a preliminary basis but added that he wanted to clarify some details and insisted that the two men discuss it in greater detail in Moscow.[47]

President Clinton met with Yeltsin in Moscow on the margins of the fiftieth anniversary commemoration of the defeat of Nazi Germany. Talbott was the President's notetaker in these meetings and often fine-tuned Clinton's talking points at the last minute. This time he added a brief note to accompany the talking points entitled "May 10: The Moment of Truth." The summit, he said, was key to both strategies and crucial to President Clinton's vision of post–Cold War Europe: admitting new members to NATO and to developing a security relationship between the Atlantic Alliance and Russia. The best outcome that could be hoped for, Talbott wrote, was one in which President Clinton disabused

Yeltsin of his fears regarding NATO enlargement and secured Russia's membership in PfP. The start of a NATO-Russia dialogue could, by the end of the year, yield a framework for NATO-Russia relations.

The second-best outcome would be an inconclusive, but not acrimonious, exchange—no breakthrough—but also not a second Budapest. The Russians were motivated by a fear and a hope—the fear that Washington would accelerate expansion, and the hope that they could drive a wedge between the U.S. and its NATO allies to stop it. President Clinton had to convince them otherwise. The U.S. comeback, Talbott wrote, was to convince Yeltsin that NATO enlargement would proceed even if the Russians refused to permit progress on the NATO-Russia track—which would only further isolate Moscow. Talbott's note concluded: "Yeltsin has taken over this issue personally. It must be resolved at the Presidential level."[48]

On the morning of May 10, 1995, Clinton and Yeltsin met one-on-one in Saint Catherine's Hall of the Kremlin. Whatever open-mindedness Yeltsin had shown to the President the previous September was gone. Instead, the Russian President adamantly tried to persuade Clinton to halt, postpone or limit the future scope of NATO enlargement. "I see nothing in enlargement but humiliation for Russia," Yeltsin said. Many Russians were afraid of it and viewed enlargement as a new form of encirclement, he continued. "For me to agree to the borders of NATO expanding toward those of Russia would constitute a betrayal of the Russian people," Yeltsin stated. Wasn't it better to think about creating new pan-European structures with joint U.S. and Russian guarantees to Central and Eastern Europe? Wouldn't it be better to postpone enlargement until 2000 to calm down the situation, he asked? Finally, Yeltsin noted that some of Washington's key Western allies, such as France, did not support U.S. policy. But he also told Clinton he knew that British Prime Minister Major and German Chancellor Kohl "are under your influence" and had "tried to talk me into your approach."

Clinton replied that he wanted to first talk about the merits of enlargement and then the political problems it posed for Yeltsin. The real issue, he stated, was whether the U.S. would remain involved in European security after the Cold War to help promote a unified, integrated Europe. NATO, President Clinton argued, was also founded to keep the U.S. and Canada involved in European security. Although the Cold War was over and Russia no longer posed a threat to NATO, the U.S. still needed to be involved, he continued. Yeltsin interrupted to say he was not sure the U.S. still needed to be permanently involved in Europe. President Clinton countered: "Well, Boris, I believe we do. Yesterday's ceremony [commemorating V-E Day] was a reminder of why." According to Clinton, the issue was how to ensure that the U.S. stayed involved in Europe and that Russia, too, be integrated and allowed to play a role.

The U.S., President Clinton underscored, was committed to doing everything it could to open the doors of Western financial, political, and other insti-

tutions to Russia. But Russia had to walk through those doors itself and participate in PfP and build a positive NATO-Russia dialogue. Looking ahead,
Clinton proposed four steps. First, the U.S. and Russia should make the best out
of PfP—which required Moscow to join it. Second, the U.S. was willing to
make a clear statement that Russia should not be excluded from NATO membership. Third, the two sides should agree to work together to build a special
NATO-Russia relationship. Fourth, that "there be a very deliberate process for
review of NATO's membership—a process that's designed, among other things,
not to cause you problems in 1996." The President explained how NATO's consultation schedule would, in his words, "consume us for the first half of 1996."

Yeltsin then interjected: "The first half? Meaning what?" Clinton repeated
that NATO's own planned consultations would consume "a major portion of
1996" and that he, mindful of the political pressures facing Yeltsin, had tried to
structure the NATO processes accordingly. After a long pause, Yeltsin acknowledged he understood Clinton's line of reasoning. But, he continued, there was
not only a strategic but also a political issue: Russian parliamentary elections
were scheduled for late 1995 and Russian Presidential elections for mid-1996.
His electoral position heading into the 1996 elections was not good, he conceded. "One false move now could ruin everything," Yeltsin remarked. Could
the American President postpone any major decisions on enlargement until
after the Russian Presidential elections, he asked? It was Yeltsin's first unambiguous sign to Clinton that he would run for reelection in 1996, thus breaking
a vow he had made many times in public that he would not, again, seek public
office.

"If there is anything I can do to help you, I will," Clinton told Yeltsin. He
pointed out how he had stood by Yeltsin on many occasions as President, including coming to Moscow in spite of Chechnya. Clinton noted that he, too,
faced a difficult reelection campaign in 1996. Conservative Republicans were
pushing for rapid NATO enlargement, he said, adding that this would be an
issue in Midwestern states he had won in the 1992 Presidential elections by a
narrow electoral margin. "So here is what I want to do," President Clinton continued. "I've made it clear I'll do nothing to accelerate NATO enlargement. I'm
trying to give you now, in this conversation, the reassurance you need for '95
and '96. But we need to be careful that neither of us appears to capitulate. For
you, that means you're not going to embrace expansion; for me it means no talk
about slowing the process down or putting it on hold or anything like that."

Clinton suggested that if Yeltsin agreed to move forward on PfP and start the
NATO-Russia dialogue, he would control the timing of the enlargement process "so that nothing is done to cause you a problem." When Yeltsin replied that
expansion should be held back until after the Russian Presidential elections,
Clinton reiterated that if Yeltsin signed PfP and began the NATO-Russia dialogue, then "I can get you past the next election with no discussion of 'who' or

'when.'" Yeltsin then proposed a break. When the two leaders resumed their conversation, Yeltsin, who had huddled with his advisors during the break, said: "I accept your plan, especially what you said about delaying through the Presidential election in '96. But this is not something we should tell the press. Let's tell them that we discussed the issue—not conclusively, but we understood each other. . . . As for the political fallout, we can both absorb the punches we'll take." Clinton responded: "Good, so join PfP, too." Yeltsin responded: "Okay, we sign both documents."[49]

It was a breakthrough. In their joint press conference, Clinton remarked that progress had been made with regard to European security. "While there was not an agreement between us on the details on the question of the expansion of NATO," the American President stated, "Russia did agree to enter into the Partnership for Peace. And I committed myself in return at the meeting at the end of the month to encourage the beginning of the NATO-Russia dialogue which I think is very important." In response, Yeltsin added that one needed to look at the question of NATO enlargement in broader terms: While noting that one could not say the two Presidents had agreed on the subject, he underscored that they had had a long and positive meeting and that they would continue to consult when they next saw each other.[50]

Following President Clinton's departure from Moscow, U.S. officials started to hear rumors that opposition in Moscow was mounting and that the deal was in danger of unraveling. On May 23, Clinton wrote Yeltsin to firm up the understanding, describing it as an "act of statesmanship that would help open a new era in the history of Europe."[51] Nonetheless, Washington continued to receive reports that at a Kremlin meeting anti-reformist forces—led by Russia's SVR Chief Primakov, Presidential Advisor Baturin, Deputy Defense Minister Kokoshin, and the Executive Secretary of the Russian Security Council Lobov—made a last-minute attempt to scuttle the deal, sack Kozyrev, and embrace a hard-line strategy to try to stop enlargement.[52] The Russian press even reported that the Defense Ministry had convinced Yeltsin that NATO enlargement could be stopped with a "decisive no."[53]

On May 26, however, Yeltsin confirmed in writing to Clinton that the understanding the two men had reached in Moscow was still on.[54] NATO diplomats nonetheless awaited the arrival of Kozyrev at the Alliance's spring Ministerial in Noordwijk, the Netherlands with some trepidation. But Kozyrev signed Russia's Individual Partnership Program (IPP) and a second document entitled "Areas of Profound Dialogue between Russia and NATO," without incident. In his statement to NATO Ministers, he underscored the need for the Alliance to "transform" itself "from a military alliance to a political organization with corresponding changes in NATO institutions and basic documents." But it was a *pro forma* demand, not a precondition for moving forward.[55] As *The Economist* put it, Russia had "grunted" yes on NATO-Russia cooperation.[56]

Following the meeting, Christopher wrote the President that it was the "good" Kozyrev who had shown up in Brussels this time. The U.S. would have to continue to carry the burden of bringing the NATO-Russia relationship to life but, he concluded, Russia had crossed an important threshold toward integration with the West.[57]

But the U.S. was not out of the woods yet. At a major academic conference on European security held in Moscow in late June, First Deputy Defense Minister Andrei Kokoshin told the gathering: "We have a national consensus in Russia against NATO expansion."[58] The influential Russian Council on Foreign and Defense Policy issued a report arguing that Moscow could still stop enlargement by adopting a harsher anti-NATO line and allying itself with opponents of enlargement in the West. It pointed to enlargement critics in the West and claimed that proponents were still in a minority[59] The chief author of the Council's report, Sergei Karaganov, Director of the Institute of Europe, boasted to American diplomats that while Moscow's chances of stopping enlargement had been reduced because of the war in Chechnya, the odds were still in favor of Moscow stopping it. When reminded of Moscow's failure to stop NATO's Euromissile deployments in the early 1980s, his response was that this time Moscow would rely on mainstream conservative parties, not just on Greens and leftists, in pursuing its campaign.[60]

4. THE POLITICAL BATTLE HEATS UP

It was not only in Russia that the controversy over NATO enlargement was heating up. At home the Administration found itself caught in a political crossfire between those who wanted to enlarge NATO faster and those who did not want to enlarge it at all. What started out as a trickle grew into a torrent of criticism in the spring of 1995 as the enlargement issue exploded into one of the most divisive foreign policy debates since the end of the Cold War. At a time of general indifference over foreign policy issues, NATO enlargement sparked an increasingly fierce debate not only in the strategic community but also in the media and on Capitol Hill. Dueling op-eds in favor of and against enlargement appeared in many newspapers in what Administration officials referred to as the "op-ed war on enlargement." National Security Council Senior Director Dan Fried and Poland's Ambassador to Washington, Jerzy Kozminski, jokingly compared the debate to the old Stalinist thesis from the 1930s regarding the onset of communism: the closer you come to reaching the goal, the greater the intensity of the class struggle.

Several factors contributed to this escalation. In terms of substance, NATO enlargement generated so much controversy precisely because it raised issues that went beyond the question of the future of Central and Eastern Europe and whether and how to integrate those countries into the West. It also raised the issue of what kind of vision the U.S. had of Europe and NATO in a world absent a communist threat, as well as what kind of relationship the U.S. and Europe wanted to have with Moscow. In the U.S., the debate also became a kind of surrogate litmus test for many on the issue of whether the U.S. was stepping up its international engagement or retreating from it with the Cold War's end.

Democrats and Republicans often approached these issues with very different premises. President Clinton came to power focused on Russia as his top foreign policy priority. He had subsequently embraced NATO enlargement as well, not as an anti-Russia move but rather as part of a strategy to consolidate democracy in Europe's eastern half and modernize NATO to face new threats after the end of the Cold War. For many Democrats, they key issue was whether, and how, to reconcile enlargement with a commitment to democratic Russian reform, so that the U.S. could pursue both goals.

In contrast, Republicans were less trusting of Moscow and more wedded to the traditional view of NATO's role as a hedge against potential residual neo-imperial Russian impulses. They supported NATO enlargement first and foremost as a hedge against Russia and were skeptical about the Administration's broader efforts to transform the Alliance. They opposed Clinton's policy on Russia, and increasingly so in the aftermath of Moscow's invasion of Chechnya and the drift in Russian politics toward greater nationalism. They were much more comfortable in expanding but preserving the old NATO and talk of a "new NATO" made them nervous.

Moreover, relations between the Clinton Administration and the Republican leadership on Capitol Hill were going from bad to worse. Many Republicans did not like or trust President Clinton. They thought his policy on Russia was misguided and bordered on appeasement. In a hearing before the Senate Sub-Committee on Foreign Operations of the Appropriations Committee in mid-February 1995, Senator Mitch McConnell (R-KY) bluntly attacked the Clinton Administration's Russian policy and its main architect, Strobe Talbott.[61] Although President Clinton had embraced NATO enlargement, Republicans doubted his commitment and saw this as an opportunity to attack the Administration's foreign policy competence and credentials. As William Safire wrote in *The New York Times* in January 1995: "President Clinton is waffling on this central issue. He talks the talk of protecting Poland and other states at potential risk, but walks the walk of not offending Boris Yeltsin by failing to set out a timetable for new membership."[62]

Partisan politics and the approach of the 1996 U.S. Presidential election also played a role. The Republicans had put the NATO enlargement issue on their own masthead as one of the few foreign policy issues in the Contract with America. They sensed a political vulnerability and wanted to exploit this for all it was worth. On the opening day of the new Congress, Representative Benjamin Gilman, (R-NY), the new Chairman of the House International

Relations Committee, introduced the National Security Revitalization Act (NSRA). It called for a clear timetable, a list of leading candidates and greater resources to help Central and East European countries prepare for membership.[63] Senator Hank Brown (R-CO) tabled similar legislation in the Senate in mid-March. And Senator Richard Lugar (R-IN), Chairman of the European Sub-Committee of the Senate Foreign Relations Committee, announced that he would hold a series of hearings to help the Administration develop a plan on moving ahead on NATO enlargement.[64]

Meeting with Belgium Prime Minister Dehaene in mid-February 1995, Clinton admitted that he was under growing pressure from Republicans on Capitol Hill to accelerate enlargement. "Some of them," the President noted, "believe we should be moving faster on NATO expansion, partly because of domestic politics and partly because of their convictions." The Republican argument that NATO had to enlarge quickly before Russia regained its strength, Clinton added, was being fueled by the war in Chechnya and Polish President Walesa's stature. "I disagree with this," Clinton noted. "But there is pressure here from people arguing that we should take the historic opportunity now to move east." President Clinton encouraged Dehaene to make the European view clear that the Alliance was moving at the right pace in his talks on Capitol Hill. "Things might change. We could have a different conversation in six months. But for now I think we are on the right track." [65]

On March 1, 1995, Senate Majority leader Bob Dole (R-KS) broadened the attack on the Administration by calling for a "new realism" in dealing with Russia, including a clear timetable for NATO enlargement.[66] The end of communism in Russia, Dole argued, had not led to the end of Moscow's imperialist impulses. Dole claimed that the Clinton Administration was ignoring "the fact that President Yeltsin has made serious errors, has moved toward authoritarian rule, and has lost the political support of virtually all reform-minded Russians." When the Administration announced Clinton's visit to Moscow for the fiftieth anniversary of Victory in Europe (V-E) Day, Senator Jesse Helms (R–NC) criticized the decision as "the latest in a series of ill-advised foreign policy actions" that would "be interpreted as an endorsement of Russian aggression in Chechnya, nuclear sales to Iran and meddling by Russian agents in the affairs of former Soviet Republics."[67]

Such criticism again underscored that while both the Clinton Administration and Republican leaders favored enlarging NATO in principle, they did so with different rationales and conflicting strategies. Republicans preferred a *Realpolitik* rationale for enlargement based explicitly on the need to preempt any neo-imperial impulses or temptations by Moscow. They feared that the strategy of trying to build NATO-Russia cooperation would either stall the enlargement process or allow Moscow to obtain concessions that would render NATO enlargement meaningless. As Henry Kissinger put it: "I strongly favor

NATO expansion. The current policy of carrying water on both shoulders, of hinting at expansion to Eastern and Central Europe while trying to placate Russia with prospects of a protracted delay—of which the Moscow summit is a prime example—is likely to accelerate the disintegration of Western unity without reassuring Russia. NATO expansion requires a decision, not a study."[68]

But for every voice urging the Administration to move faster on NATO enlargement, there was another one calling on the Administration to postpone or roll back its decision. Opposition to NATO enlargement was centered on three core arguments. The first was that enlargement could alienate Moscow and that supporting Russian reform and cooperative U.S.-Russian relations should be a higher U.S. priority. The second was that enlargement could weaken and dilute the Alliance's political cohesion and military effectiveness. The third was that NATO enlargement should be opposed because it involved the extension of new commitments to countries and areas that were unstable or where the U.S. had little national interest and the American public would never support it.

Opponents included many of the remaining figures from the generation of U.S. strategists that had helped to found NATO—strategic icons such as Andrew Goodpaster, George Kennan, and Paul Nitze. While the Republican Party's platform supported NATO enlargement, a number of influential Republican strategists such as former NSC advisor Brent Scowcroft and former Undersecretary of Defense Fred Ikle did not.[69] Democratic skeptics included Harold Brown, former Secretary of Defense under President Jimmy Carter; Lee Hamilton (D-IN), the influential ranking Democrat of the House International Affairs Committee; and Senator Sam Nunn (D-GA), the ranking Democrat on the Senate Armed Services Committee.[70]

Opposition also ran deep among American diplomats. On May 2, 1995 a group of 15 retired senior diplomats who had served in Europe and Russia wrote U.S. Secretary of State Christopher criticizing Administration policy. "In our view," they wrote, "this policy risks endangering the long-term viability of NATO, significantly exacerbating the instability that now exists in the zone that lies between Germany and Russia and convincing most Russians that the United States is attempting to isolate, encircle and subordinate them, rather than integrating them into a new European system of collective security."[71] Hostility to NATO enlargement was just as strong in the academic community. In the spring and summer of 1995, nearly every major academic journal in international affairs carried articles criticizing the policy and urging the Administration to abandon its enlargement plans.[72] As former Clinton NSC aide Charles Kupchan wrote: "NATO expansion is a train wreck in the making."[73]

But perhaps no voice was more strident in opposing enlargement than *The New York Times*. Over the next few years this pillar of the East Coast establishment printed one editorial after another savaging Administration policy. In an opening salvo on the eve of President Clinton's trip to Moscow in May 1995, an

editorial stated: "Rooted in Cold War logic and driven partly by domestic politics, the idea of expanding NATO's defense perimeter eastward represents a failure of imagination. It would unwisely commit American troops in advance to
defend countries, with nuclear weapons if necessary, where no vital American
security interest may be involved."[74] The following day, *New York Times'* foreign
affairs columnist, Tom Friedman, wrote that the U.S. needed to keep its eye on
the big prize—which was Russia, and not ignore the costs enlargement would
entail.[75]

The President's own party was divided on the NATO enlargement issue.
Democratic Senators such as Joseph Lieberman (D-CT), Barbara Mikulski (D-
MD) and Paul Simon (D-IL) were among the earliest and strongest supporters.
Other key Democratic foreign policy figures on Capitol Hill, such as Senator
Joe Biden (D-DE)—who would later become the most passionate supporter of
enlargement and lead the Senate floor debate on ratification—had not yet
made up their minds.[76] But some prominent Democrats figures openly opposed
the Administration. At the top of that list was the most influential Democratic
thinker on defense policy in the U.S. Senate—Senator Nunn.

Nunn came out publicly against NATO enlargement in a speech at NATO's
Supreme Allied Command Atlantic (SACLANT) in June 1995. "I have missed
the logical explanation of why" the U.S. wants to enlarge, the Senator stated.
"Are we really going to be able to convince the East Europeans that we are protecting them from their historical threats, while we convince the Russians that
NATO enlargement has nothing to do with Russia as a potential military
threat?" The "number one security threat for America, for NATO and the
world," Nunn argued, was stopping the proliferation of weapons of mass destruction and controlling Russia's Cold War nuclear stockpiles—a goal that
NATO enlargement could undermine by producing a more paranoid and nationalistic Russia less willing to cooperate with the West. He warned that Russia
might respond by redeploying tactical nuclear weapons or putting its strategic
nuclear forces on a higher nuclear alert status. "This," he concluded, "is the
stuff that self-fulfilling prophecies and historic tragedies are made of."[77]

Nunn posed a political threat to the Administration of a different magnitude.
He was the ranking Democrat on the Senate Armed Services Committee and the
leading authority on defense issues in the Democratic Party. He had opposed
President Clinton on issues such as gays in the military—and won. His anti-enlargement arguments were essentially the same as those the Defense Department
and Secretary Perry had advanced in the Administration's internal debate one
year earlier. If Nunn were to lead a revolt against enlargement in the Democratic
Party, it would provide political cover for other Democrats to desert the President
on this issue and could reopen the debate within the Administration as well.

The growing volatility in the U.S. debate made Washington's West European
allies nervous, and no one more so than Chancellor Kohl. In late May Kohl

called Clinton to express his concern about the American debate. "I hear with concern what Dole is saying about you," Kohl said. "The subject [of NATO expansion] is being used to harm you," he said, noting that the Republicans and Polish-American lobby would be turning up the political heat on Clinton in the months ahead. Kohl told Clinton that he would be in Warsaw in several weeks where he would endorse Poland's NATO bid but also tell the Poles not to lobby the U.S. to move faster. "My intention is to tell those in charge that it won't help to light a NATO fire and that this would only cause problems for their friends in the U.S."

The German Chancellor added that he was "willing to be as helpful as I can." He had discussed this issue with Chirac, Kok and would be speaking with Major soon: "I think we have everyone in line," Kohl added. "We cannot let foreign policy become a blunt instrument of domestic policy." The President responded that he did not expect to have to deal with the NATO enlargement issue politically in the U.S. until after the Russian election and the final phase in the U.S. election. "My goal is for us to be seen as steady so that neither the Poles nor the Russians will make an issue out of it. We must keep the dialogue steady and deliberate so that we can get through June 1996 without any adverse consequences for Yeltsin or for us." Kohl responded: "Bill, I totally agree with you. I will do everything so that the Europeans follow this path."[78]

But if Washington's West European allies were concerned that the Clinton Administration might move too fast on enlargement, Central and East European leaders were concerned that the process was stalling.[79] In May 1995, Polish Ambassador to Washington, Jerzy Kozminski, returned to Warsaw to brief the Sejm's Committee on Foreign Affairs. Kozminski was struck by the audience's profound skepticism about the U.S. commitment, whether the European allies were really on board, and whether the Alliance would hold firm in the face of growing Russian opposition. The Committee's Chairman, Bronislaw Geremek, a former Professor familiar with the U.S. academic scene, wondered out loud why the overwhelming majority of American academics at institutions such as Harvard opposed NATO enlargement.[80] In mid July, Foreign Minister Bartoszewski remarked in public what many Poles thought in private: that they had a better chance to get into NATO under Republicans than Democrats, thereby eliciting a howl of protest from Assistant Secretary Holbrooke.[81]

The conflicting political pressures the Administration was subjected to surfaced following the release of the NATO enlargement study in September 1995. German Chancellor Kohl was on the phone a few days later again urging Clinton not to accelerate enlargement. "I see a major problem by things being said in Congress by a few people," Kohl told Clinton. "Yeltsin told me he didn't have any problems with you. But he is concerned that the Republicans will use the primaries to get Polish-American votes. You must make sure that things don't degenerate to irrationality." The Chancellor continued by saying that the impact of the U.S. elections on the NATO enlargement process had been discussed at an EU meeting by European heads-of-state. "The view is unanimous and clear. They want NATO enlargement, especially with a view towards Poland, which is Russia's main concern." The Chancellor added: "All colleagues agreed to support your steady hand, so to speak. . . . You have lots of support here. I can make that public. You must tell me when it would be useful."[82]

In the Oval Office several weeks later, Czech President Vaclav Havel told President Clinton that the U.S. and NATO needed to act now on enlargement. The region could not go on forever in the kind of uncertainty and vacuum that existed. While everyone wanted to have good relations with Russia, there were some issues on which one cannot yield, Havel continued. If the West postpones NATO enlargement to reassure Moscow, he argued, it was accepting Russia's logic that NATO was the enemy and that it was slowing down what was essentially an anti-Russia process. The real issue was how NATO could encourage Russia to change its thinking. Prolonging the vacuum in Central and Eastern Europe would only retard that adjustment, he concluded. President Clinton promised Havel that he would be firm with Yeltsin and that NATO enlargement would proceed as planned.[83]

On October 10, however, Senators Nunn and Kay Bailey Hutchison (R-TX) took to the Senate floor to call on the Clinton Administration to postpone NATO enlargement. They claimed that the 1995 NATO enlargement study had not answered the question about why the Alliance was enlarging, had understated the likely Russian reaction, and ignored what enlargement meant for the U.S. Senator Hutchison stated, "We are talking about American troops and American tax dollars." NATO enlargement, she emphasized, "is a strategic decision that must not be made in haste and must not be made before we answer the crucial questions" lest the U.S. and its allies are drawn "into regional border and ethnic disputes in which we have no demonstrable national security interest." In Nunn's words, the Administration was trying to "bridge the unbridgeable."[84]

5. BOSNIA AND NATO ENLARGEMENT

NATO enlargement would never have happened absent the U.S. and NATO's all-out and eventually successful effort to stop the war raging in Bosnia. The Administration's vision of a Europe democratic, secure, and undivided rang hollow so long as one part of Europe was involved in a fratricidal war that the West would or could not stop. NATO's claim that an enlarged Alliance should be the core of a new European security architecture was not credible as long as the most powerful alliance in the world was unable to halt the bloodiest war in Europe in 50 years. The same Alliance that was so badly fractured on questions of war and peace in the Balkans could not simply turn around and initiate the largest increase in NATO security commitments since 1949. As Richard Holbrooke wrote: "This new European security structure could not be built while part of it, the former Yugoslavia, was in flames."[85]

The U.S. decision to reengage in the Bosnia conflict was a turning point not only on the ground in Bosnia, but also in U.S.-European relations. It reinvigorated NATO and reestablished the Alliance's, and thereby Washington's, primary role in European security. As Ian Davidson wrote in *The Financial Times* following the conclusion of the Dayton negotiations in November 1995, the peace plan was not perfect, and it was not even clear if it would actually bring peace to Bosnia, but it was "having an electric effect on NATO" and ended the debate over whether NATO had a post–Cold War purpose.[86] As French Foreign Minister Herve de Charette put it: "America was back."

Bosnia also reinforced the growing conviction that NATO needed a post–Cold War overhaul. Senator Lugar's original battle cry that the alliance had to go "out of area or out of business" had been validated. While NATO's collective defense guarantee would remain the formal core of the Alliance, the need to respond to threats from beyond the Alliance's borders was a key challenge for the future. For enlargement proponents, Bosnia also validated the second part of Lugar's thesis—that NATO had to enlarge to Central and Eastern Europe to consolidate democracy *before* instability arose there. New NATO missions and members were increasingly seen as two sides of the same coin of Alliance reform. Each underscored NATO's need to transcend a Cold War Maginot Line mentality and project stability beyond its original borders.

Bosnia also validated the Partnership for Peace, which now provided an ideal framework to bring together allies and non-allies into an Implementation Force (IFOR). Of the initial 60,000 IFOR troops deployed in early 1996, one in six were from non-NATO countries. PfP countries contributed troops and, in the case of Hungary, permitted the transit and stationing of NATO troops on their soil, and host-nation support. Few things more vividly demonstrated how NATO could transcend past Cold War divisions than the sight of a Czech-mechanized battalion incorporated into a Canadian brigade subordinated to a British division—or a Polish airborne battalion serving as part of a Nordic-Polish brigade subordinated to a U.S. infantry division.

Above all, Bosnia underscored how the Alliance's relations with Russia were changing. NATO ground troops were deploying—for the first time in Alliance history—with Russian soldiers at their side as partners, not enemies. While both NATO and Russia had proclaimed that they no longer viewed each other as adversaries in 1991, the fact that U.S. and Russian soldiers were now working together on the ground in Bosnia was a mini-revolution. Nothing more graphically demonstrated how NATO was moving beyond its Cold War mindset and rationale.

The Clinton Administration's *volte face* in Bosnia took place in the summer of 1995. Instead of simply trying to contain the conflict, Washington launched an all-out effort to stop the war on the ground, and forge a peace settlement. This reversal resulted from a realization that the previous policy had failed, the violence in Bosnia was spreading and the risks of not acting—for Europe, NATO and overall U.S. foreign policy credibility, including the President's— had become greater than the risks of acting. Early on in the Clinton Administration, National Security Adviser Tony Lake had written the President a memo arguing that the Administration's "muddle-through" strategy in Bosnia could become a cancer not only in the region but on the Administration's entire foreign policy. In the summer of 1995, President Clinton concluded that this Bosnian cancer had to be stopped before it metastasized further.

This realization came slowly and only after the Administration and the Alliance stared into the potential abyss facing it in the Balkans.[87] The turning point came in the spring and summer of 1995 as the Administration realized its policy was failing. In May, Bosnian Serbs responded to NATO air strikes by taking several hundred UN troops hostage and chaining them to telephone poles to deter further NATO action. It was a short-term tactical victory for the Bosnian Serbs, but a strategic mistake. In Europe, the newly elected President of France, Jacques Chirac, was enraged. In one of his first telephone conversations with Clinton, Chirac interrupted the interpreter to tell the President emphatically that the Serbs were behaving like terrorists and that it was time to get tough. When Chirac visited the White House in mid-June, his message was clear: enough is enough. Clinton was rapidly reaching the same conclusion."[88]

President Clinton now gave Lake a green light to start thinking through what became known as the "endgame strategy." As Lake and his staff were developing their plan, the news arrived that the Bosnian Serbs had overrun the UN "safe area" of Srebrenica. It was a further shock to the U.S. and its allies. According to the International Committee of the Red Cross, 7,079 Bosnian Muslims were killed in Srebrenica between July 12–16, 1995. Most of the victims were unarmed and died in ambushes or mass executions. As Richard Holbrooke wrote: "For sheer intensity, nothing in the war matched, or would ever match, Srebrenica. The name would become part of the language of horrors of modern war, alongside Lidice, Pradour, Babi Yar and the Katyn Forest."[89]

The slaughter in Srebrenica helped tip the balance within the Administration in favor of intervention. On July 17, 1995, Clinton dropped by, unannounced, to a breakfast meeting at the White House to reinforce the point that the U.S. needed a new policy. In attendance were Lake, Christopher, Perry, Shalikashvili, Albright, and Berger. Clinton told his team he wanted a new policy. "I don't like where we are now. This policy is doing enormous damage to the United States and to our standing in the world. We look weak." The current policy, Clinton concluded, was unsustainable on the ground in Bosnia and was having a negative impact on U.S. standing in the world.[90]

In early August, the U.S. settled on a strategy combining carrots and sticks in an all-out effort to get a definitive end to the war. The plan called for using NATO air power to bring the Bosnian Serbs to the peace table. If that failed, the Clinton Administration would let UNPROFOR collapse and take a number of steps to protect the Muslims and Sarajevo, including lifting the arms embargo against the Bosnians. In early August Lake led a delegation to various European capitals to share the U.S. thinking. Unlike Christopher's ill-fated trip two years earlier, Lake was authorized to say that the President had made up his mind. Although there was some grumbling in France, most allies were enormously relieved that the U.S. was finally committing its prestige and power to get a settlement. As the Lake team concluded after one of their stops, "the big dog [in the Alliance] had barked."[91]

Richard Holbrooke was chosen to be the American President's envoy for the shuttle diplomacy in the Balkans that would begin the diplomatic push. He headed to the Balkans with a team that included Lieutenant General Wes Clark from the Joint Chiefs of Staff, the NSC's Colonel Nelson Drew, Deputy Assistant Secretary of State Robert Frasure and Deputy Assistant Secretary of Defense Joe Kruzel. Five days later, on August 19, on a dirt road on Mount Igman, which overlooked Sarajevo, a French armored vehicle carrying half the U.S. team rolled off the road and tumbled more than 1,000 feet down the mountainside, taking the lives of Drew, Frasure, and Kruzel.[92] Following the tragedy and a trip home to Washington to bury their colleagues and regroup, Holbrooke and his team arrived in Paris on August 28 to hear the news that a Bosnian mortar shell had landed in a marketplace in Sarajevo, killing 35 people.

As Holbrooke later wrote, it was the final outrage. While it was not the worst incident of the war, it came at a turning point in Western policy after Srebrenica, the launching of the diplomatic shuttle, and the tragedy on Mt. Igman. As a result, it appeared not only as a random act of terror against innocent civilians but "the first direct affront to the United States."[93] Two days later, the Alliance launched Operation Deliberate Force. It ultimately consisted of 3,515 sorties over two weeks flown by 293 aircraft from eight NATO countries. The avowed objective of the campaign was to get the Bosnian Serbs to lift the siege of Sarajevo, remove their heavy weapons, and allow freedom of movement around the capital. The unstated objective was to achieve the terms of the U.S. peace plan. Moreover, the NATO campaign overlapped with a Croatian military offensive that began in early August and contributed to a major shift in the balance of power and forces on the ground. By early October the Bosnian Serbs were in retreat. On October 5, President Clinton announced that a cease-fire would go into effect five days later.

NATO's actions were received with relief in Central and Eastern Europe. The impotence of the West to stop the bloodshed that ensued from the disintegration of the former Yugoslavia recalled vivid memories from their own recent history. As one Polish commentator put it, Central Europeans knew only too well what it was like to be treated as second-class Europeans whose fate was not worth fighting or dying for.[94] Donald Blinken, U.S. Ambassador to Hungary at the time, recalled how the failure of the U.S. to initially stop the Bosnian Serbs had an enormous impact in the region. "I was painfully aware," he wrote, "that U.S. prestige was visibly ebbing away, not only in Hungary and the new democracies of Central Europe but also in Western European capitals." Hungarians, he noted, draw parallels with their own past. "Sarajevo often reminded them of Budapest in late 1944 or 1956."[95]

The fact that the Bosnian conflict was ended through the reassertion of NATO's primacy, however, only reinforced the Central and East European's conviction that their security could only be secured with and through the Atlantic Alliance. A NATO-led peacekeeping force in Bosnia now offered these countries an opportunity to show that they could be good allies. Nowhere was this more true than in the case of Hungary. U.S. and NATO military officials had concluded that southern Hungary was their preferred choice for a staging ground for the deployment of U.S. and other NATO-led forces into Bosnia. But they were uncertain whether Hungary would be willing to put bases in this region at NATO's disposal. It was only four years after the uninvited troops of the former Soviet Union had departed and memories of occupation by foreign troops were still strong. The Hungarian minority in Serbia, Bosnia, and Croatia had also made Budapest cautious about how far it went in supporting the NATO effort.

In the fall of 1995, Hungarian Foreign Minister Laszlo Kovacs visited New York for the annual United Nations General Assembly. While in New York City, he spoke at a roundtable at the Council on Foreign Relations presided over by the Hungarian-born journalist Kati Marton who, since the previous spring, was married to Holbrooke. Although the Dayton negotiations were not yet over, Holbrooke, in town to visit with her, was already thinking about implementing the peace plan. He told Kovacs that Hungary had to be part of the effort on the ground to bring peace to Bosnia. Kovacs agreed. It was absurd, he told Holbrooke, to expect a country like Sweden in Northern Europe to send peacekeepers and for Hungary not to contribute. He promised Holbrooke he would recommend that Hungary provide a contingent of non-combat forces. Holbrooke also hinted that Hungary was being considered as a staging base for NATO forces to move into Bosnia. Kovacs carried the message back to Budapest.[96]

In Budapest, Ambassador Donald Blinken knew the Pentagon was considering using southern Hungary as a military staging base. When the first Pentagon team arrived in early November for informal talks with the Hungarian side,

Blinken was determined that this issue be turned into a success story in U.S.-Hungarian relations.[97] Over the next three weeks the U.S. and Hungarian sides finalized agreements on NATO's use of Hungarian bases. The normally fractious Hungarian parliament came together to shepherd through the necessary resolutions and approvals. The Dayton peace accords were signed on November 21, 1995. The day before Thanksgiving, the U.S. State Department officially requested the use of Hungarian facilities to deploy U.S. forces as part of IFOR. The following day the Hungarian parliament voted 312 in favor, one against, and with six abstentions to approve the request.

As Blinken summed it up: "By putting aside both domestic politics and residual fears following 45 years of Soviet occupation in just 48 hours time, Hungary demonstrated in a manner no words could match, that it was clearly prepared to be taken seriously as a candidate for NATO membership."[98] Hungarian officials soon had a clever motto to summarize their new relationship with NATO: "Hungary has not entered NATO but NATO has entered Hungary." Whatever local concerns had existed about the presence of American and NATO troops quickly dissipated. Indeed, public support increased for NATO in the region surrounding the Taszar base, and ended up being higher than average in the country as a whole.[99] Hungarians had cheered the departure of the Soviet troops four years earlier. Now they were quite content for the Americans to stay. The local mayor even commented that the U.S. and NATO forces might as well just stay until Hungary joins the Alliance.[100]

If the Central and East Europeans were relieved by NATO's actions, the Russians were furious—at least initially. It was another moment of *Sturm und Drang*. The rhetoric from Moscow exploded into one of the harshest attacks on the West in years—and it came from Yeltsin himself. In a letter to Clinton on September 7, Yeltsin denounced NATO's air campaign as "unacceptable" and as an "execution of the Bosnian Serbs." In a press conference the following day, he accused the West of ignoring Russia. "This is impossible. . . . This means a return to two camps that are at war with one another," he warned. If bombing the Serbs and dismissing Russian views continued, he added, "we will have to thoroughly reconsider our strategy, including our approach to relations with the North Atlantic Alliance."[101]

As the Bosnian conflict edged to a cease-fire, Talbott traveled to Moscow for consultations. He told Kozyrev that given the dreadful experience with UNPROFOR, a new Bosnian peacekeeping force would have to be NATO-led if the U.S. was going to participate. "We have to avoid a situation where only NATO is in charge," Kozyrev told Talbott. Russia's role in the Bosnian peace force would set a precedent for future European security arrangements, he continued, "so we must have an equal seat at the table." If the U.S. and Russia could not find a solution, "it will be ruinous to our future relations and our ability to cooperate in Europe," he said. The only way to reconcile conflicting U.S. and

Russian views was for Clinton to stay in regular touch with Yeltsin. "Put Boris Yeltsin's name on an auto-dial button in the Oval Office," he told Talbott and advised him to make good use of the Perry-Grachev channel as well. "All we want is to end this bloody goddamn war, and to end it in a way that's a visibly cooperative achievement," he told Talbott.[102]

For Washington, Bosnia was a chance to put into practice the theory that there was a new NATO interested in cooperating with Russia. If NATO could work with Russia in Bosnia, such concrete cooperation might gradually lead to a shift in Russia's attitude toward the Alliance more generally. But first the issue of who commanded whom had to be resolved. SACEUR George Joulwan had drawn up plans for a force of 50,000 to 60,000 troops divided into three different geographic zones headed by an American, British, and French division. Meeting with President Clinton on September 27, Kozyrev stated that Russia would not put its troops under NATO command. Clinton, in response, made it equally clear that the principle of unity of command in NATO was sacrosanct. On September 29, the NAC approved the IFOR mission and decided that NATO should be prepared to include non-NATO troops, including those of Russia. At the informal NATO Defense Ministers meeting in Williamsburg, Virginia on October 5–6, Perry received approval from his NATO counterparts to negotiate the terms of Russian participation with Defense Minster Grachev.

Arriving in Geneva on October 7, the U.S. delegation led by Perry and Talbott sat down for what in diplomatic parlance would qualify as "frank and candid" discussions with their Russian counterparts. While both sides agreed in principle on the desirability of Russian participation in IFOR, their positions seemed unbridgeable. Ash Carter and Bill Perry subsequently described the scene: "The mood at the table was surly from the outset. Those of us from the Pentagon who knew each other well greeted one another with uncharacteristic grimness. The Bosnian experts on both sides were glowering. Each Minister got right to the point." The Bosnian peace force, said Perry, "must be a NATO force, for military reasons. Grachev shot back that it could not be a NATO force, that Russia would not accept this. He gripped his throat with both hands: this is what would happen in Moscow, he said, to any Russian who agreed to such a humiliation. 'And therefore you, Dr. Perry, have me by the throat.' "[103]

At the end of a day of unsuccessful negotiations, Perry suggested that Grachev send a senior Russian military officer to General Joulwan at SHAPE to allow the Russian side to get a better feel for what NATO was planning. Grachev agreed. Perry also asked him to attend a U.S-Russia peacekeeping exercise in Fort Riley after the October 1995 Hyde Park summit. It would provide an opportunity for the two men to take another run at finding a solution. Perry was cautiously optimistic. Grachev had signaled a willingness to have a Russian General serve under a senior U.S. military commander so long as there was no direct link with the NATO chain of command. The reason was political.

Grachev had told Perry that placing Russian forces under NATO would be political dynamite for Yeltsin and could produce a communist victory in the upcoming parliamentary elections.

On October 23, 1995 Clinton and Yeltsin met at Franklin D. Roosevelt's estate in Hyde Park, New York. The setting could hardly have been more symbolic, recalling an era when the two countries were allies in the fight against Nazi Germany. As Yeltsin had mentioned to Clinton during a phone call on September 27, "NATO, NATO, NATO, NATO" was the most difficult issue that had to be resolved. Clinton opened the discussion with a friendly challenge to Yeltsin by saying their objective should be to "prove the pundits wrong" and show that they could still work together, including on Bosnia. Yeltsin responded enthusiastically, saying, "we can't let our partnership be shattered by a failure." He continued: "We need to end the discussion today with an agreement. If we don't agree, it'll be a scandal." The two Presidents went through their respective positions on a NATO-led force in Bosnia. Clinton explained the importance of unity of command and why a separate Russian sector in IFOR did not make sense.[104]

Yeltsin, in turn, sketched out on a piece of paper how he envisioned Russian forces being under U.S. but not NATO command. He reiterated that Russian forces could not be under NATO. "The Russian people," he said, "have an allergy against NATO." At the end of the conversation, Yeltsin told Clinton that if he agreed to the U.S. proposals, he would lose the 1996 Russian Presidential elections. "I'll be finished," he told Clinton who responded: "Let's not give up. Let's work on this." And he asked Yeltsin to agree to contribute "at a minimum" two battalions of Russian forces for non-combat tasks "in a liaison relationship with NATO." Yeltsin agreed and the two leaders decided that Perry and Grachev would be asked to explore what might be done "beyond that." In the subsequent plenary meeting, Yeltsin, as Carter and Perry would subsequently note, "gave a strong *da*, to the obvious discomfort of his staff" to the proposal.[105] The Russian President had, once again, responded with his gut instinct to align himself with the West.

In late October, Grachev was back in the U.S. to attend the joint peacekeeping exercise at Fort Riley, Kansas. The exercise symbolically underscored that American and Russian troops could work together on the ground if their leaders could sort out the chain-of-command issue. Between events, the two delegations reached agreement on an arrangement that would allow the Russians to participate in non-combat roles. Thus, they had achieved the minimum. But Perry and Grachev agreed to try for more—a full combat role for Russian forces. They asked U.S. General George Joulwan and Russian Colonel General Shevtsov to see what they could work out. Perry also invited Grachev to attend the November NATO Defense Ministers meeting to see for himself whether NATO was truly still the enemy of Russia.

In early November 1995, Joulwan and Shevtsov came up with a scheme that squared the circle. It hinged upon the difference between what military commanders call "operational control," or OPCON, and "tactical control," or TACON. Joulwan and Shevtsov now agreed that Joulwan, as overall commander, would exercise TACON through the divisional commander in the northern sector of Bosnia, while Shevtsov, as his deputy, would maintain OPCON. This enabled Moscow to say that they were not under the command of NATO, but under General Joulwan in his role of Commander-in-Chief of the U.S. Army in Europe. When Perry and Grachev arrived in Brussels in early December 1995, Joulwan and Shevtsov had prepared a briefing that started with a chart displaying the NATO emblem and the Russian flag. Underneath were the words: "Intended Outcome: NATO + Russia = Success."[106] As Joulwan wrote in a subsequent op-ed, the U.S. and Russia were no longer making Cold War but peace together in Europe.[107]

In late October, President Clinton spoke at a dinner honoring the Harry S. Truman Library Institute. Truman, President Clinton noted, had considered the creation of NATO one of his finest achievements. "What are we going to do to build on his achievement?" he asked. History, the President continued, had made it "possible for us to help to build a Europe that is democratic, that is peaceful, and that for the first time since nation states appeared on that continent is undivided." The U.S. and Europe needed to build a new trans-Atlantic community to meet new threats. That was why, the President continued, the U.S. had to deploy forces to Bosnia. And that was why NATO had to enlarge. "The end of the Cold War cannot mean the end of NATO, and it cannot mean a NATO frozen in the past because there is no other cornerstone for an integrated, secure and stable Europe for the future." It was essential to include the new democracies of Central and Eastern Europe and the former Soviet Union into NATO's community of shared values. NATO enlargement, Clinton pledged, would move forward "carefully, and deliberately and openly."[108]

In London on November 29, 1995, British Prime Minister John Major asked Clinton for his views on the timing of NATO enlargement. The American President replied that specific decisions on the "who" and the "when" should wait until after the Russian Presidential elections. Clinton talked about how Yeltsin had been driven toward a more hard-line position on NATO enlargement by Russian domestic politics, but that he continued to take a softer line in private, and still seemed committed to maintaining a cooperative relationship with the West. "At one point Yeltsin agreed with me," Clinton said, "but over a year [sic] he modified his position. There is a difference between his public posture and his private talks with me; between his rhetoric and his cooperative action. That shows he wants to build bridges without undermining his political base."

When Major asked Clinton whether he thought Yeltsin would run again for President, Clinton remarked, "Perhaps I am biased because I like him," but "if he can stay healthy and sober he might pull it off." Major agreed but noted that the Russian President had already had his third heart attack and was six years older than the average Russian male. Clinton responded: "When General Grant started winning battles, President Lincoln's advisors told him that Grant was a crude drunk. Lincoln replied: 'Find out what he drinks and give it to the rest of them.'"[109]

As December 1995 drew to a close, Russia again held parliamentary elections for the Duma. Whereas two years earlier it had been Zhirinovsky's right wing fascist party that had gained the largest vote, this time it was the left-wing communists that gained the upper hand. On Christmas Eve, Clinton pulled Talbott aside at a party and asked him for his assessment of the communists' strong showing in the Duma elections. "How many more of these elections is it going to take before they stop electing fascists and communists?" Clinton asked. "Lots," Talbott replied. "The main thing is that they keep having elections. Eventually they'll get it right." "Yeah," Clinton responded," I guess that's part of the deal, isn't it? Well, let's hope they're a little smarter in the Presidential electing next year."[110]

Book V

TOWARD A NEW NATO

In early December 1995, NATO Foreign and Defense Ministers gathered in Brussels for a rare joint meeting. They looked back at one of the most dramatic years in Alliance history. NATO had gone to war for the first time ever to help end nearly five years of ethnic conflict in Bosnia. Alliance ground troops were preparing to deploy for the first time ever beyond Alliance borders to help secure the peace in that war-ravaged country—alongside those of Moscow. As Secretary of State Warren Christopher told his colleagues, "For NATO this is, without exaggeration, a moment worthy of being called historic."[1]

NATO enlargement was not out of the spotlight. The drama of Bosnia and President Clinton's pledge to Boris Yeltsin to keep the issue out of the upcoming Russian Presidential elections had ensured that. But the Alliance's preparations were nonetheless moving ahead. The Alliance enlargement study had been completed on time and NATO now offered so-called "intensified dialogues" as the next step to those countries seeking membership. Following a meeting with Central and East European Foreign Ministers at the Ministerial, Christopher wrote Clinton underscoring the positive impact the prospect of enlargement was having in the region—and why it was essential that the process move forward in spite of Russian opposition and the doubts of some of Washington's allies. As Romanian Foreign Minister Melescanu had told the

Secretary: "The pace of enlargement may not meet all of our desires, but I believe it is proceeding in the most realistic way."[2]

Finally, France, which had emerged as a key ally in pushing a more muscular approach in Bosnia, now announced that it was prepared in principle to end its arms-length approach to NATO, bringing another chorus of cheers from the gathered Ministers.[3] That announcement offered the possibility of healing the rift that had been created when Charles de Gaulle pulled France out of the Alliance's military structures in the mid-1960s. The Clinton Administration's vision of a revamped and rebalanced NATO assuming a new post–Cold War mission by providing stability beyond its borders and across the continent was starting to take shape. As Christopher wrote the President, the decision to intervene in Bosnia was key in order to put the Alliance back on track: "Only a few months ago, many in Europe, as well as in the United States, questioned whether NATO had a continuing role to play after the Cold War. Now, NATO's role is universally acknowledged. It has found a vocation."[4]

But neither the U.S. nor its allies had time to rest on their laurels. Some 60,000 NATO-led forces had to successfully deploy to Bosnia to enforce a fragile peace. France's willingness in principle to fully return to the NATO fold needed to be explored. With Russian and U.S. Presidential elections scheduled for the summer and fall, NATO was not planning any major enlargement decisions. But the Alliance was quietly working to help prepare Central and East European countries for possible invitations. Last but certainly not least, NATO's search for a new *modus vivendi* with Russia remained elusive. While Yeltsin had chosen to work with NATO in Bosnia, Moscow was reluctant to take steps to institutionalize a broader NATO-Russia relationship lest they be interpreted as acquiescing to enlargement.

It was no easy task to bring these various pieces together into a coherent whole. At NATO's helm was a new Secretary General, former Spanish Foreign Minister Javier Solana. As a young socialist leader, Solana had demonstrated against NATO membership for Spain but had since become a strong supporter of the Alliance. He had spent several years in exile in the U.S. and had a keen understanding of the Anglo-Saxon mind set. His commitment to European unification was also deeply rooted. Coming from a country that itself had been isolated from the European mainstream, Solana instinctively understood the aspirations of Central and Eastern Europe. But like many European leftists, he shared the Administration's commitment to build a new relationship with a democratic Russia. Although a number of Republican Senators and members of Congress opposed his nomination, Solana turned out to be very much in synch with the Clinton Administration and became a central figure in the endgame on NATO enlargement.

1. ON THE BACK BURNER

Throughout much of the spring of 1996 NATO enlargement was kept on the back burner of Alliance work and intentionally so. Instead, this period was dominated by NATO's deployment of troops to Bosnia and the desire to explore France's interest in returning to the NATO fold. The latter was especially important to the Clinton Administration, which had reversed its predecessor's skepticism toward European integration and a greater European role in the Alliance. President Clinton had, from the outset, made it clear that he wanted to support European unity and integration. France's announcement was therefore welcomed with open arms in Washington.

The impetus for France's reintegration had come from President Jacques Chirac who, as the head of the Gaullist party, had performed the French political equivalent of Nixon going to China by reaching out to the Alliance whose integrated military structures de Gaulle had left in 1966. Several factors had led to this reassessment. Paris' vision of the EU assuming primary responsibility for European security after the Cold War had been tempered by the crisis in Bosnia and the difficulties in negotiating and ratifying the Maastricht Treaty. From his early days in office, Chirac saw both a need and an opportunity to rebalance the U.S.-European partnership through NATO as opposed to outside of it. The collapse of Soviet power had made Europe less dependent upon America for its security and refocused NATO on new missions in a way that could allow Europe to assume greater responsibility. If NATO's future was going to focus on peace support operations, these were areas where the Europeans could carry a larger share of the burden. Such a redefinition, Chirac calculated, could allow France to return to a more balanced and equal Alliance.[5]

U.S. diplomats had picked up on signs of France's new interest in NATO during the fall of 1995. The U.S. Ambassador to France, Pamela Harriman, reported that French officials had told their U.S. counterparts that they were considering returning to NATO's military structures. They cautioned against using the word "reintegration" given French domestic political sensitivities, preferring to talk about the Alliance's "renovation." Paris, they underscored, could not say it was returning to the "old NATO" but needed to be able to claim it was joining a "new and adapted" Alliance. They nonetheless made it clear they were aiming at "a major transformation of the structures of the Alliance." As one French official put it, "no options, not even radical ones" were excluded. How far Paris would go also depended on the Alliance: "The more it appears that NATO is changing and the Europeans are responsible for their own security, the closer France can move to NATO."[6]

When Chirac visited Washington in early February 1996, he underscored that the U.S. presence was still needed in Europe but that NATO also had to adapt to a new era. "France," he promised, "is ready to assume its full share of this renovation process," adding that he wished to "confirm the open-mindedness and availability with which France approaches this adaptation of NATO, including the military side, as long as the European identity can assert itself fully."[7] In private, Chirac dismissed the notion of an Alliance based on two pillars—one American and the other European. "Previously we talked about two pillars. I was one of those who invented that concept, but it was probably not a good idea," said Chirac. "The problem is how to find a system—a single system—that can work in the event that the U.S. does send troops and also if the U.S. does not send troops because you think that it [the crisis] is not worth it." But Chirac was optimistic: "I believe we can find a solution. I am not worried. We have made a big change, taken a big step and we are ready to discuss everything. There are no taboos."[8]

The vehicle for negotiating France's rapprochement with NATO was the European Security and Defense Identity (ESDI). It had been created in the early 1990s as a vehicle for European allies to organize themselves better under NATO's umbrella as well as to create the nucleus for Europe acting on its own in a future crisis if the U.S. refused to participate. ESDI now became the venue through which allies would try to hammer out a new arrangement that met French demands. The goal was to reach agreement on an overall principle and framework by the time NATO Foreign Ministers met in June, with details finalized by the end of the year. With such an understanding in place and with France reintegrated into NATO's military structures, the Alliance would also be in a much stronger position to enlarge eastward.

The Clinton Administration was delighted by this French shift. As Clinton told Solana in late February: "I think the French initiative is a positive thing. Chirac is very, well, French, but also a strong and imaginative leader who looks to the future. . . . We have never objected to a European security pillar within NATO, although we don't want Alliance equities to be compromised. I believe Chirac's proposal can be a good thing."[9] U.S. officials returned from early consultations in Paris in late February 1996 convinced that the French commitment to return to the Alliance was genuine, and that considerable common ground existed between the two countries.[10]

By late spring the U.S., France and other key allies had reached closure on several key principles. One was that NATO would remain the vehicle for Article 5 and defending Europe against future attack. A second was that ESDI would be built within, not outside of, the Alliance framework. A third was that when it came to addressing conflicts beyond Alliance borders, NATO would have what became known as the right of first refusal. This meant that allies would turn to the Alliance as the preferred framework for collective military action, but that there would also be a credible backup option for the European-only force under the Western European Union (WEU) to step in if NATO could not act. This last provision was critical. While European countries wanted the U.S. to remain involved in European security, they did not ever again want to find themselves in a position such as in Bosnia where the U.S. would not participate in a military operation and they did not have the ability to act on their own to stop a crisis in their own backyard.

To put meat on the bones of this proposal, London proposed creating a European Deputy SACEUR (D/SACEUR) who, in addition to being a traditional Deputy, would also be the personification of ESDI and the strategic commander of any WEU-led operation. If the U.S. did not want to participate in a military operation, NATO would step aside and the D/SACEUR would lead such an operation under the WEU. This concept built on the Alliance's Combined Joint Task Force (CJTF) initiative from the January 1994 NATO summit, which allowed military planners to put together and deploy mobile headquarters and forces in response to new crises in the post–Cold War world. Alliance planners also coined the concept of "separable but not separate forces." This meant that the U.S. and Europe would maintain a single pool of forces from which a smaller force package could be broken out or separated for a European-led operation. The WEU, therefore, did not have to develop its own planning capability, command structure and forces, but could instead draw on those of the Alliance. This would avoid duplication and ensure close trans-Atlantic ties.

With Russia's Presidential elections less than six months away, NATO's work on enlargement in the spring of 1996 was kept low-key and out of the public eye. As President Clinton told Secretary General Solana in March: "We should stay on the timetable that has been agreed, because it is designed to do the work that needs to be done in a low-key, unthreatening and transparent way. We also need to walk a tightrope and not unnecessarily inflame things in Russia or in Central and Eastern Europe. We should stay on the timetable and be almost boring, methodical, plodding, even bureaucratic. We need as much as possible to take away the emotional energy from the NATO enlargement issue in both Russia and Central and Eastern Europe, as well as among constituencies that support enlargement in the U.S. and Europe. In short, we should smile and plod ahead."[11]

The NATO bureaucracy did exactly that as it worked out the practical issues of actually preparing to enlarge the Alliance. Bilateral "intensified dialogues" were launched with those countries interested in knowing more about what enlargement would entail.[12] Candidate countries submitted papers detailing their membership credentials and responded to a range of questions regarding their military capabilities. NATO's Military Committee geared up to assess potential members' preparedness and their ability to contribute to Alliance defenses. NATO military staff started to travel to these countries for a hands-on look at the condition of infrastructure, port facilities, military bases, and airfields.

Work also started on two additional issues that were rapidly moving up on the Alliance's agenda. One was the cost of NATO enlargement. Widely varying estimates of what enlargement would cost were popping up in the West. These differences revealed very different assumptions regarding what enlargement would entail militarily and how broad or narrow a definition of costs the Alliance should embrace. Some of the high estimates assumed NATO should deploy forces on the territory of new members and also included the overall costs of bringing the militaries of these countries up to NATO standards. Others assumed that allies would not deploy forces on the territory of new members and that the costs of enlargement should be restricted to the much narrower definition of ensuring, for example, that NATO command, control, and communication capabilities existed. NATO officials were asked to come up with an agreed-upon cost assessment by the end of the year.[13]

The second issue was how to deal with those candidate countries not included in a first round of enlargement. By now nearly a dozen countries of widely varying levels of preparedness had declared an interest in NATO membership. While official debate on which countries would be invited for a first round had been put off for the future, the U.S. had pledged to manage enlargement in a fashion that contributed to overall European security, including the security of those countries not receiving invitations. In some ways, the issue of how to handle those countries not joining the Alliance was just as difficult as deciding who would be brought in. By this time, the Partnership for Peace was increasingly recognized as a great success and both the number and complexity of PfP exercises was increasing. NATO set up a special task force, called the Senior Level Group, to examine how to expand it into something called "PfP plus" for those countries not invited to join the Alliance.

In early June 1996, NATO Foreign Ministers gathered in Berlin for their spring meeting. With the first round of Russian Presidential elections just around the corner, talk of NATO enlargement was consigned to the realm of "ongoing work" in the official communiqué. Instead, the Ministers' main message was that "a new NATO" was emerging—an "adapted" Alliance that, while retaining its core functions, was better equipped to deal with crises beyond Alliance borders, more balanced across the Atlantic with a strengthened European pillar, and better equipped to cooperate with Russia.[14] Speaking before the North Atlantic Council on June 3, Christopher praised the progress the Alliance had made in building a new NATO for a new Europe.[15] French Foreign Minister de Charette hailed the Alliance compromise on a European pillar as "a great success for Europe" and hinted that France would now be willing to take the next steps in terms of returning to the NATO fold.[16]

2. SLEEPING WITH THE PORCUPINE

Negotiating a NATO-Russia *modus vivendi* remained a top American and NATO priority. Yeltsin's decision to deploy Russian troops to Bosnia was considered a breakthrough in Moscow's cooperation with the West. At the same time, the strong showing of the communists in the December 1995 Duma elections and Yeltsin's firing of several key reformers led to yet another wave of speculation about a possible Russian lurch toward authoritarian rule. On January 26, Yeltsin called Clinton to assure him of his commitment to a reformist course. "At this point," he told Clinton, "I guarantee to you the course of reform and democracy will stand." Yeltsin also noted that he had just sent a letter to Clinton on NATO. "The whole issue of enlargement will affect many aspects, including our election process," he concluded with an eye toward the upcoming Russian Presidential elections.[17]

Yeltsin's letter contained a litany of complaints about NATO enlargement. It claimed that the Alliance's decision to launch "intensified dialogues" with partner countries violated the understanding between the two Presidents on enlargement.[18] It was a reminder that while Yeltsin had opted to cooperate with NATO in Bosnia, he was still fighting enlargement and that the institutionalization of a broader NATO-Russia relationship was still held hostage, at least in Russian eyes, to the enlargement issue. On February 8, Clinton responded by reminding Yeltsin that they had agreed in the past "on the importance of advancing the integration of the Euro-Atlantic community to enhance regional stability and to assure an undivided Europe." The prospect of NATO enlargement, he argued, was already bringing enhanced stability to Central and Eastern Europe. "This is to Russia's advantage," Clinton wrote. "Boris, a new century is coming. The Russians, Europeans and Americans of the next century deserve to live without fear of the recurrence of this century's tragedies. NATO's enlargement, to which I am committed, will help ensure stability for future generations." Enlargement, the letter continued, "is part of a means to achieve our shared goal of a more stable Europe. And that goal includes a close, cooperative NATO-Russia relationship, to which I am also committed. We both share an interest in deepening Russia's integration into European structures. In the end, it is Russia's choice, but I stand ready to build a cooperative relationship between NATO and Russia."[19]

The Administration was convinced that Yeltsin's opposition was driven primarily by domestic political concerns, above all in an election year. This reinforced Clinton's determination to engage the Russian President to try to manage the enlargement issue. Yeltsin's uncertain health and political fortunes nevertheless left U.S. officials worried. The Russian President could be replaced by a harder-line leader, or by succumbing to those voices in his own entourage urging an all-out effort at trying to stop the Alliance. On January 9, those concerns were elevated when Yeltsin replaced Foreign Minister Kozyrev with Yevgeny Primakov, the head of Russia's foreign intelligence service. Interpreted as an attempt by Yeltsin to improve his nationalist credentials in the run-up to Presidential elections, it nevertheless raised the possibility of a tougher Russian approach to the West in general and on NATO in particular.

Primakov had been one of Kozyrev's most prominent critics. As Talbott wrote Christopher after his first official meeting with the new Foreign Minister, the contrast between the two men could not have been greater. Kozyrev was genuinely pro-Western and believed Russia's best hope lay in cooperating as closely as possible with the West. In contrast, Primakov had made his career by standing up to the West—"the man who could say *Nyet*." He was well known in the West for having defended Saddam Hussein during the Gulf War. In the Russian press he was portrayed as a "Eurasianist" who believed Russia, along with China, could form an independent alternative power to the West. Whereas Kozyrev cared about ideas, the currency Primakov cared about was power. The new Russian Foreign Minster, Talbott wrote, seemed to relish the prospect of diplomatic and political combat. "There's an honor-among-thieves twinkle in his eye when he says, as he did several times in our sessions something like, 'Come on, cut the crap.' "[20]

Primakov, Talbott continued, saw his job as masking Russian weakness while rebuilding Moscow's strength. By his desk, he kept a small bust of Prince Alexandr Gorchakov, a 19th-century Russian Foreign Minister under Czar Alexander II who had presided over Russia's recovery from its total defeat in the Crimean war. Partnership with the U.S. was not part of his lexicon. For Primakov, the U.S. was a problem to be managed, humored or outfoxed. It was not the country Russia would turn to for help or advice. "We're a lot of things in his calculations about how to do that [rebuilding Russian power], but emphatically not partners. We're not necessarily enemies in the sense that we were during more doctrinaire Soviet eyes during the Cold War, but we're certainly rivals, which, in his view, is the fitting role for a Great Power."[21]

When Christopher called Primakov to congratulate him, the Russian Foreign Minister went out of his way to emphasize that his appointment did not signal a dramatic shift in Russian policy and that Yeltsin had underscored to him the importance of maintaining good relations with Washington.[22] When Mamedov met Talbott in Bonn, Germany several days later, the Russian Deputy Foreign Minister urged him not to treat Primakov's appointment "like the second coming of the Soviet Union" and instead tried to convince the Deputy Secretary that the appointment was good for the U.S. "You should welcome the change," he told Talbott. Kozyrev's perceived softness in dealing with the West had compelled Yeltsin to show he could be tough—the opposite could be the case with Primakov. "Primakov," he told Talbott, "can make deals from political strength that Kozyrev couldn't make from weakness."[23]

While a number of op-eds in the American press lambasted Primakov's appointment, the internal U.S. reaction was initially one of "wait-and-see." An internal State Department strategy paper commissioned by Talbott on the prospects for U.S.-Russian in late January concluded: "While buckling our seatbelts for a rough ride during the months and years (and decades) ahead, we should stay the course" and remain engaged with Moscow. "Yeltsin is likely to join in chest-thumping about the rights and greatness of the Russian state from time to time. But that does not mean that he will retreat on any of the fundamentals that have governed his relations with the outside world—and particularly with the U.S." Primakov, the paper concluded, was likely to adapt a more hard-nosed attitude toward the West but was not a risk taker. "Although not pro-Western in the sense that Kozyrev is, Primakov has not shown a proclivity to recklessness, xenophobia or extreme nationalism. He won't be looking for fights with the West; he will simply be less inclined to paper over differences or to be responsive to our positions."[24]

In early February Christopher and Primakov met in Helsinki. Primakov assured the Secretary that Russian foreign policy would not become threatening and urged Washington to treat Moscow as an equal partner. But the new Russian Foreign Minister was adamant in his opposition to NATO enlargement. He resurrected Moscow's old claims that the NATO leaders had promised not to enlarge during the negotiations on German unification. He floated several alternatives to NATO enlargement for Central and Eastern Europe. When Christopher rejected them, Primakov responded: "We will have to find a solution to this issue that is acceptable to Russia, NATO and the Central Europeans or sleep with the porcupine."[25] That evening, Christopher wrote Clinton that "it is clear that for the present we will confront an overt, unyielding, hard line against enlargement from the Russian leadership."[26]

If Washington was holding firm on enlargement, some key allies were showing signs of backsliding. On February 3, German Chancellor Kohl suggested a moratorium on NATO enlargement to Bill Perry. If the West could produce "two years of calm" in relations with Russia, Kohl suggested, "progress in relations" with Russia might again be possible. After the meeting, German National Security Advisor Bitterlich asked whether the U.S. had "gotten the Chancellor's message." Bitterlich reiterated that decisions on enlargement should be taken only after this period of calm and that 1997 should not be used for a NATO enlargement summit, but to further expand PfP. He added that he would float this idea to the British and French as well.[27]

Alarm bells went off in Washington. As a State Department memo put it, the Chancellor's possible change of heart "threatens to disrupt the Western approach to Russia, roil relations with Central Europe, vindicate Russian opponents of NATO enlargement and embroil the Administration in a domestic spat with the Republican internationalists who would accuse us of accommodating Russian pressures."[28] U.S. Ambassador to NATO Bob Hunter reported that his British counterpart had commented over lunch that "the convoy on enlargement seems to be breaking up" as a result of Bonn's changing view.[29] Several days later, British Foreign Secretary Rifkind expressed concern over waning German support for NATO enlargement to Assistant Secretary Holbrooke and made it clear that London was now committed to enlargement and that it would be a disaster if NATO lost its nerve on this issue in the face of Russian pressure.[30]

Bonn quickly backtracked. On February 9, 1996, German Foreign Minister Kinkel tried to take back the Chancellor's "two years of calm" statement, insisting it did not diminish Germany's commitment to NATO enlargement. A senior Chancellery official assured U.S. diplomats that Kohl's comments "only" reflected his concern that public talk about enlargement was strengthening the hands of the nationalists in Moscow in the run up to the Russian elections.[31] Shortly thereafter, Kohl assured Secretary Christopher personally that he was on board for enlargement—and claimed he did not understand how the impression to the contrary had arisen. But he underscored the need to take Russian interests into account and to keep the enlargement issue out of the Russian and U.S. Presidential campaigns.[32]

When Kohl visited Moscow the following week, Yeltsin told him that the two leaders agreed on every issue—except NATO enlargement. At the press conference, Yeltsin denounced NATO enlargement in what the press described as a "furious outburst" and called on NATO to postpone its enlargement plans while an uncomfortable looking Kohl listened to the translation.[33] In a subsequent interview, Kohl stated: "I am now for letting the issue [of NATO enlargement] settle down completely, not for pushing it aside, but letting it calm down, until the elections are over here [in Russia] and the U.S."[34] Kohl called Clinton upon his return from Moscow. He reported that Yeltsin was in good health and spirits for his reelection campaign but strongly opposed to NATO enlargement. He assured Clinton that he had told Yeltsin that NATO would enlarge but that allies were prepared to reach a reasonable settlement on this issue after the elections.[35]

Kohl was not the only European leader getting cold feet on NATO enlargement. U.S. Ambassador to France Pamela Harriman reported that at a diplomatic reception in Paris, President Chirac approached her in the presence of the Russian Ambassador to emphasize to her that the Russian people saw NATO as a threat and that forcing expansion would only aggravate the problem. It could hardly be read as a sign of French enthusiasm for enlargement.[36] Later that spring, Chirac suggested that the Alliance should not move forward on enlargement unless it first had a NATO-Russia agreement in hand.[37] Washington was also nervous about reports that French officials were suggesting that no major steps be taken on NATO enlargement before the Alliance had finished its work on adaptation, thereby potentially holding enlargement hostage to fulfilling Paris' *desiderata* on this issue. Other U.S. diplomatic posts in Europe reported an undercurrent of unease over enlargement among allies.

When Talbott met with Primakov on March 12, he made a pitch for both sides to keep their disagreement on NATO enlargement "manageable."

Primakov agreed but he warned that Moscow would be just as opposed to enlargement after the Russian elections and again urged Washington to reconsider its policy. "What I can't understand," he added, "is that even a guy like you is determined to preserve this element of NATO expansion. This is not just a psychological issue for us. It's a security question." Russia would never have cooperated with NATO in Bosnia, he insisted, if NATO were enlarging. He recalled how he had recently testified before the Duma on strategic arms control issues and found the most reformist deputies insisting that Moscow renounce arms control treaties if NATO expands. He again warned that enlargement would have a devastating impact in Russia politically.[38]

Meanwhile, Primakov was also traveling through Western Europe as well as Central and Eastern Europe, warning about the consequences enlargement could have on Russian reform and on Russia's relations with Europe. He, too, was pursuing a strategy of "negotiate and fight." While negotiating with Talbott and the U.S. about the contours of a possible NATO-Russia deal on the one hand, he was pursuing every possibility to dilute or undercut the Alliance consensus and play on divisions within the Alliance by warning of its possible dire consequences. He probed whether countries such as Poland, the Czech Republic, or Hungary would accept more limited forms of NATO membership—such as a so-called "French solution" whereby new members would join NATO's political but not military structures.[39] In addition, the Russian Foreign Minister tried to draw a second, even firmer line against further enlargement down the road. He hinted that Moscow could perhaps tolerate a limited first round of enlargement, so long as new allies did not allow foreign military forces on their soil, and countries like Ukraine and the Baltic states were excluded from consideration of eventual membership.[40]

In Helsinki, Christopher had warned Primakov that Russian efforts to stop NATO enlargement would only lead the U.S. to become more explicit about its commitment. Washington now decided to send a clear signal that there was no turning back. The Secretary was scheduled to visit Moscow in mid-March to prepare Clinton's upcoming trip. He decided to stop in Central Europe on the way to deliver a major statement on NATO enlargement. As Christopher later wrote in his typically understated manner: "The decision to make this statement reflected the Administration's belief that clarity and firmness concerning the U.S. position were our best assets in managing Russia's lingering opposition to that expansion."[41]

On March 20, Christopher delivered the strongest public endorsement of NATO enlargement yet in Prague. The key sentence in his speech read: "NATO has made a commitment to take in new members and it must not and will not keep new democracies in the waiting room forever. NATO enlargement is on track and it will happen." For the first time he also stated publicly that the first round of NATO enlargement would not be the last and that the

U.S. considered the Baltic states and Ukraine eligible candidates.[42] Meeting with Central and East European Foreign Ministers after his speech, he told them that he had wanted to state the U.S. view clearly and directly given the uncertainty inside Russia and in relations with Russia. The U.S. would enlarge NATO and there would be no pullback and no special deals with Moscow.[43] As Christopher later wrote: "The speech marked a turning point in our policy: after it there was no doubt in Central Europe, among our allies, or in Russia that NATO expansion would take place."[44]

The next day, Christopher arrived in Moscow to confront an enraged Primakov. The Russian Foreign Minister told him that the Prague speech was disingenuous and insulting. There were only two possible interpretations: either there had been a change in U.S. policy or Christopher had been speaking without authority from President Clinton. Christopher went over the speech carefully and pointed out that it was consistent with long-standing U.S. policy that enlargement was going to proceed in a deliberate manner. But Primakov continued his attack. "Russia will not accept NATO enlargement," he told the Secretary of State, "and that's not because it has the right of veto on any such enlargement—it's because Russia will defend its interests in this new, worsening geopolitical situation."[45] As Christopher later noted: "He really let me have it."[46]

When Christopher met with Yeltsin the next day in the Kremlin, however, the atmosphere was completely different. It was, Christopher later told his staff, the best meeting he had ever had with Yeltsin. The two men covered a broad range of issues that included Bosnia, the Middle East, China, the upcoming nuclear and G-8 summits, and Yeltsin's Presidential election campaign. It was clear that Yeltsin wanted a successful summit, not a confrontation with the West. During the meeting he did not even mention NATO enlargement, let alone Christopher's Prague speech. As the meeting was ending, the Russian President told Christopher that there was one issue on his mind that he had not raised: NATO enlargement. "It's now clear that we have at least an agreement to disagree on this point," Yeltsin said.[47]

In the run-up to Clinton's trip to Moscow in April, Christopher and Talbott sent the President a joint memo on what to expect. "You are likely to see in Yeltsin the personification of a Russian bear that is, in its own eyes, a wounded bear, but one bent on recovery and reassertion of its rightful place as a great power." They warned that Primakov and other key Yeltsin advisors "are fueling Yeltsin's darkest suspicions about us." In spite of the rhetoric about partnership, they "hold the very Soviet view that politics and history are a zero-sum game; there are only winners and losers" and "every issue between us becomes a test of wills and wiles." The best way to counter this was to rely on the personal chemistry between the two Presidents to keep the relationship on track. "We came away from our meetings with Yeltsin believing that he has not entirely signed on to the world according to Primakov. Yeltsin resists the worst he is hearing about us and our intentions—because he has a great deal of confidence in you and your personal ties, and because he had rejected the advice of his own isolationists."[48]

Clinton was in Moscow for a so-called P-8 summit arranged to showcase western support for Yeltsin prior to the Russian Presidential elections. When the two Presidents met, Clinton emphasized that the U.S. had no intention of "sidelining" Russia and instead underscored how much the two leaders had already accomplished. "You and I are the first leaders of our two countries after the Cold War. We've done a remarkable job in getting a lot done while being honest about our differences. . . . I want historians fifty years from now to look back on this period and say you and I took full advantage of the opportunity we had. We made maximum use of the extraordinary moment that came with the end of the Cold War."[49] Yeltsin repeatedly referred to the need for a more "equal partnership" but seemed reassured by Clinton's commitment to seek out new ways of working together. The meeting also resulted in an agreement that preserved the Conventional Forces in Europe Treaty (CFE) that would assume a central role in the end game with Moscow on NATO enlargement the following year. Once again, the close personal ties between the two men had helped keep the U.S.-Russian relationship on track.

3. TOUGH LOVE FOR CENTRAL AND EASTERN EUROPE

While enlargement was kept off of the public agenda in the run up to the Russian Presidential elections, behind the scenes the Clinton Administration deployed a "tough love" approach to encourage candidate countries to get as prepared as possible for NATO membership. Enlarging the Atlantic Alliance to Central and Eastern Europe would entail the largest peacetime increase in the U.S. commitment to Europe in half a century. This step would require the support of at least 67 U.S. Senators and would inevitably involve close scrutiny of these countries' qualifications on Capitol Hill. The political stakes were high. Rejection by the U.S. Senate would be a disaster for the country involved, the Clinton Administration and the Atlantic Alliance.

The Administration therefore consciously used the carrot of potential NATO membership as a "golden carrot" to encourage the countries of Central and Eastern Europe to consolidate political and economic reform, resolve minority issues and border disputes, and establish civilian control of the military. To be sure, these countries took these steps just because it was in their own interests. But the desire to rejoin the West, including its premier military alliance, was a powerful reinforcement in terms of validating their western credentials. While many of the reforms these countries were undertaking were also critical to qualify for EU membership, the fact that NATO was prepared to move faster, and the security concerns of these aspirant countries so immediate, put Washington and the Alliance in a position of considerable leverage.

How to exercise that leverage was not always easy to discern. NATO did not have a detailed acquis (or set of detailed criteria) laying out precisely what these countries had to do to qualify as the EU did. NATO's founding fathers had left the Alliance considerable flexibility on this issue. Over the decades, the Alliance had brought in countries at very different levels of political, economic, and military preparedness, and for different strategic reasons. In the course of 1995, the Administration developed what became known as the five "Perry principles," named after the U.S. Secretary of Defense, Bill Perry, democracy, market economies, borders, civilian control of the military, and progress toward compatibility of the armed forces. A version of these had been embraced in the official NATO enlargement study.

But the Alliance's definition of its own strategic interests was also critical. NATO's thinking would crystallize around these two factors — performance and strategic interests — as the benchmarks for Alliance policy and decisionmaking. NSC Senior Director Dan Fried came up with a metaphor that became known as the "Dan Fried SAT Test" in interagency deliberations. Fried compared joining NATO to getting into Harvard, Yale, or another top U.S. university. Meeting the Perry principles, he argued, was like taking the SAT test. If you had an exceptional score, it got your application into the university's admissions office. But a good SAT score alone would not automatically get you into Harvard, and meeting the Perry principles wasn't good enough to get a country into NATO. Solid qualifications helped but at the end of the day Alliance members had to be convinced that a country's admission was in NATO's own best strategic interests. That was a political decision.

But Washington was serious about the performance factor. "NATO membership is not a right," the President had emphasized. "Countries with repressive political systems, countries with designs on their neighbors, countries with militaries unchecked by civilian control or with closed economic systems need not apply."[50] Already in the spring of 1995 Assistant Secretary Holbrooke had been sent to the region to deliver the "tough love" message to these countries that their qualifications would be put under a microscope to see whether they measured up to Western expectations. Holbrooke's message was twofold: The U.S. is committed to enlarging NATO, but it is time for you, too, to roll up your sleeves and get to work if you want to be in the running for an invitation.

At the time the Czech Republic was widely considered the strongest candidate for NATO membership, although it would subsequently lag in meeting NATO standards. Holbrooke had stopped in Prague shortly before becoming Assistant Secretary of State to urge the Czechs to mend their fences with the Germans over the issue of expatriated Germans from the Sudetenland following World War II.[51] Apart from this, Prague was regarded as the farthest along in the region in terms of reform. Many Czech political leaders were pro-Atlanticist—more so than public opinion in general—with President Havel among the most eloquent voices anywhere on NATO's virtues. The country had neither border nor minority problems. They had joined the post-COCOM regime on technology controls. While the Czech military still had a long way to go in terms of defense restructuring and reform, it was hardly unique in this regard. Visiting NATO headquarters in the spring of 1995, Czech Foreign Minister Zieleniec argued that Prague had the best record of any post-communist state and that joining NATO was a "natural" decision given what it had in common with existing Alliance members.[52]

Hungary's case was less certain. Budapest was the first country to literally punch a hole in the Iron Curtain when Prime Minister Gyula Horn opened the border with Austria to allow East Germans to escape to the West in the fall of 1989. It had also led the push to dissolve the Warsaw Pact. Joszef Antall, the country's first post-communist Prime Minister, had been an outspoken Atlanticist who made NATO membership one of his top goals prior to his death in the fall of 1993. At the same time, a cause for concern was the issue of the Hungarian minorities in neighboring countries resulting from the post-World War I peace settlement and dismemberment of the Austro-Hungarian Empire. Under the Treaty of Trianon of 1920, more than two million Hungarians became national minorities in neighboring states. The shadow of Trianon as an "unjust peace" had cast its shadow over Hungarian politics ever since, which had reduced its population and size by about two-thirds. With the collapse of communism, this was precisely one of those ethnic conflicts that Western policymakers feared would again rear its ugly head, and Budapest's initial pronouncements on the issue did not always help inspire confidence.[53]

A new center-left government headed by Prime Minister Gyula Horn came to power in June 1994. Horn and his Foreign Minister, Laszlo Kovacs, pledged to soften Budapest's rhetoric, but they were soon accused by Hungarian conservatives of "selling out" on the minority issue. While Horn and Kovacs were among the most pro-western leaders in the socialist party, they initially seemed less committed to NATO membership. Their economic course also raised doubts about their commitment to reform. Richard Holbrooke, Dan Fried, and David Lipton (from the U.S. Treasury Department) arrived in Budapest in early 1995 to deliver a message that Hungary had to get its house in order if it wanted U.S. support for its NATO candidacy. Horn told Holbrooke he understood what Hungary needed to do to qualify for NATO. He pointed to the introduction of a more austere fiscal and economic policy and a recent ban on arms sales to rogue states and assured Holbrooke that he was committed to resolving the border and minority issues with Slovakia and Romania.[54]

In a separate meeting with Kovacs, the U.S. delegation focused on Budapest's need to resolve its border and minority issues. When Holbrooke tried to make the point that the U.S. respected Hungary's history, Fried broke in to say: "No we don't. We hate it. When you say Trianon we understand the political and emotional content of what you are trying to say but we want to run screaming out of the room." Everyone laughed, but the Hungarians got the point. The last thing the U.S. wanted was to be drawn into modern versions of their age-old ethnic conflicts.[55] Several weeks later, Prime Minister Horn pulled aside the U.S. Ambassador to Hungary, Donald Blinken, at an embassy reception to tell him that he had gotten the message, that negotiations with Slovakia and Romania were on track, and that he was optimistic but could not guarantee that both treaties might be concluded by mid-March 1995.[56] Shortly thereafter, Hungary and Slovakia reached agreement on a new treaty governing minority rights in both countries.

Romania presented even more questions. It lagged behind other Central and East European neighbors and the reform commitment of Romania's first post-communist President, Ion Iliescu, was far from clear. Romanian political life and civil society had been severely damaged by the despotic rule of Nicolae Ceausescu, which now handicapped Bucharest's efforts at reform. The government included several extremist nationalistic and anti-Semitic parties. It was hardly an ideal NATO candidate. But public support in Romania was strongly pro-western and pro-NATO. Bucharest had made EU and NATO membership a top priority and Romanian diplomats were working hard to make the case that their country was "the Poland of the south" in terms of its strategic weight and regional importance. Moreover, they insisted that Hungary and Romania should enter NATO at the same time in order to increase regional stability and avoid exacerbating bilateral relations.

Meeting with Romanian Foreign Minster Teodor Melescanu, Holbrooke assured him that enlargement was not limited to the Visegrad countries and that the Administration did not want to see a new dividing line on the Romanian-Hungarian border. But he also emphasized that all countries could not come in at the same time. Romania's internal reforms and its relations with Hungary would be critical when it came time to consider Romania's candidacy. Unresolved border and minority issues would preclude the admission of both countries, Holbrooke underscored.[57] Later that day Holbrooke asked President Iliescu how he would explain to the U.S. Senate the presence of right-wing extremists in his government. Iliescu responded defensively and treated Holbrooke to a long-winded lecture on just what Romania had actually accomplished and how western countries, including the United States, continued to discriminate against it.[58] It was an early indication of the troubles Washington would have in getting its message through in Bucharest that what counted was performance.

President Clinton became directly involved in helping Hungary and Romania resolve their bilateral issues. Horn and Iliescu were invited to the

White House for visits in June and September 1995, where Clinton emphasized the need to resolve their bilateral differences if they wanted to be considered for NATO membership. Horn told the President that while his priority was getting Hungary invited to join NATO, he would support having Romania and Hungary join at the same time.[59] In his meeting with Clinton in September, Iliescu also made the case that Romania and Hungary should join together.[60] The breakthrough in Hungarian-Romanian relations would not come for another year, however. But the desire to make NATO's list was a key factor that helped convince both Budapest and Bucharest to reach a compromise in the early fall of 1996 so as not to miss NATO's short list for the first round of enlargement.

The key country, however, was Poland. Its size, strategic importance, and history placed it at the heart of the enlargement debate. It had provided the original impetus for the push for enlargement in the West. But it, too, was hardly an ideal candidate. Warsaw did not have effective civilian control of the Polish military. In this case, the problem started with President Lech Walesa. His view of civilian control over the military was simple: he was elected President in a free, open election and since the military reported to him there was civilian control over the military. Walesa wanted the backing of the military, and directly cultivated ties with the senior officers, thereby undercutting the authority of the Defense Minister he had appointed.

The person and personality of General Tadeuz Wilecki, the head of the Polish General staff, also complicated matters. An old-school, former tank commander, Wilecki was determined to protect the Polish military from what he considered misguided civilians or parliamentarians who, in his view, understood little if anything of strategy, Polish history, or the needs of the Polish army. He was suspicious of the West and did not believe it was serious about extending a defense commitment or that such a guarantee, if extended, was credible. Wilecki would often lecture visitors on how Poland had been mistaken to rely on Western powers to come to its defense in the past and sketch out his preferred alternative—a new Central European security confederation from the Baltic to the Black Sea under Polish leadership. He aspired to be a modern-day Pilsudski—and proudly displayed a bust of the Polish leader from the 1920s on his desk.

This was hardly NATO's ideal. The issue came to a head during the fall of 1994 when Walesa attended a dinner at Drawsko, a military training ground in Western Poland. For months Walesa's Defense Minister, former Admiral Piotr Kolodziejczyk, had been trying to bring Wilecki under his control. In the middle of the dinner Walesa polled the Generals regarding Kolodziejczyk's competence. The Generals voted overwhelmingly against the Defense Minister. Polish papers were soon full of accusations of an alleged "coup."[61] While a parliamentary investigation concluded that such allegations were exaggerated, they also concluded that Poland lacked effective civilian control over the military. When the Parliament passed new legislation establishing such control, Walesa refused to sign it. It lay dormant until the new Polish President, Alexsandr Kwasniewski, signed it in early 1996. Wilecki continued to resist the plan and was not removed until shortly before the NATO Madrid summit.

Another question mark over Poland's candidacy for NATO was the Polish post-communist left's commitment, or lack thereof, to the Alliance. Following the left's return to power in the fall of 1993, Walesa had insisted on appointing the foreign and defense ministers to guarantee Poland's pro-western course. In January 1995, Foreign Minister Andrzej Olechowski resigned and claimed that Prime Minister Pawlak favored neutrality and that his post-communist government "simply dislikes the West" and "will never be convinced of the Western option." Russia, he added, was using those in Poland's leftist parties who had business interests or intelligence ties in the East to "disturb our attempts to join NATO."[62] To some observers it raised the specter of the kind of unstable politics that had characterized interwar Central and Eastern Europe and proven damaging to democratic rule.

It was against this background that Holbrooke and Fried arrived in Warsaw. While praising Poland for its overall progress, Holbrooke told Walesa that Poland had an image problem it needed to fix. Political infighting and the lack of civilian control over the military were raising concerns about the country's political stability. Warsaw also needed to stay the course on economic reform and stop arms sales to rogue states. Walesa, unfazed, thanked Holbrooke for his advice and admitted that after 50 years of communism, Poland's democracy might be somewhat less developed than in the U.S. But, he insisted, these were "technical problems" and that the real issue was when the West would abandon its illusions about Russia and enlarge NATO.[63] Pawlak, in contrast, was at pains to make clear that his government remained committed to political and economic reform.[64] Shortly thereafter, Pawlak traveled to Washington to reassure Christopher that the Polish left, too, supported NATO membership. Pawlak also committed to stopping Polish arms sales to rogue states, and an agreement to that effect was concluded later that spring. [65]

In Poland Holbrooke also took part in a ceremony commemorating the fiftieth anniversary of the liberation of the Auschwitz concentration camp. The legacy of the Holocaust was becoming an important issue in the U.S. debate on enlargement. After World War II, few if any of these countries had come to terms with their own role in the Holocaust. Confronting this legacy now became a test of whether these countries shared the common values NATO stood for. Arriving in the U.S. in the summer of 1994, Polish Ambassador Jerzy Kozminski quickly concluded that while no one said it directly, Poland could not get into NATO without tackling these problems. Observing the anniversary of the liberation of Auschwitz, Kozminski watched as an event he believed should have been focused on Germany's past behavior ended up highlighting Polish anti-Semitism.[66] Dealing with the Holocaust would become one of the hardest issues for Poland in the entire NATO enlargement debate.

In April 1995, the first bombshell went off when eight of the most influential American Senators and Congressmen from both the Republican and Democratic parties wrote Secretary of State Christopher to complain about the problems that Americans of Jewish origin and Jewish communities in Central and Eastern Europe were facing regarding the restitution of property confiscated by the Nazis and then nationalized under communism.[67] It was interpreted—correctly—as a sign that Poland and other candidate countries had to deal satisfactorily with this issue if they wanted to get into NATO. A second bombshell went off in early June 1995, when Walesa refused to disassociate himself from anti-Semitic remarks made by a Polish Roman Catholic priest and former Walesa advisor, Father Henryk Jankowski, while the Polish President sat in the congregation.[68] Walesa initially claimed that the "acoustics were bad" in the church and he was not sure what the priest had actually said. When Walesa finally issued a statement condemning the remarks, it was too little too late to quiet the storm in the West.[69]

Walesa was scheduled to meet Clinton in San Francisco, California in July 1995 during the fiftieth anniversary of the establishment of the United Nations. The White House made it clear that Poland had to address this issue if the meeting was to take place. To further complicate matters, Ambassador Kozminski received word that there could be two anti-Walesa demonstrations in San Francisco—the first by American-Jewish groups and the second by local gay groups in response to critical remarks the Polish President had made about homosexuals. NSC Senior Director Fried called Kozminski from U.S. Air Force One to try to defuse the issue. They agreed that Walesa would first meet with American-Jewish leaders who were flying to San Francisco to confront the Polish President. Only then would the President receive Walesa. Walesa met with leaders of the American Jewish Committee (AJC) and condemned anti-Semitism but refrained from criticizing Jankowski. The AJC issued a subsequent press release expressing its "disappointment" with Walesa's remarks, but the meeting with the American President went forward.[70] Kozminski returned to Washington further convinced that Warsaw needed to resolve the lingering issue from the Holocaust to strengthen its NATO candidacy.[71] Kozminski would work diligently over the next three years to resolve many of these issues. His role was critical in building a new, more positive relationship between Poland and the American Jewish community that would eventually culminate in the American Jewish Committee and other American Jewish groups endorsing Polish membership in NATO during the Senate ratification debate.

In November 1995, Walesa was defeated in a bitterly fought Presidential campaign by the socialist candidate, Alexander Kwasniewski. The Nobel

Laureate, who had defeated the Soviets, had now been defeated at the ballot box by a former communist. The alarm bells went off in Washington. Poland was the engine of U.S. strategy in the region and for U.S. public support. With a former communist at the helm, both were now put on hold. When Clinton called Walesa to offer his condolences, the Polish President warned, "You won't be able to count on the communists."[72]

But Kwasniewski had won precisely because he had repackaged himself as a social democrat with economic and foreign policies akin to those of Walesa, including on NATO. During the Polish Presidential debates he had distanced himself from earlier critical remarks on NATO.[73] Kwasniewski and his team immediately assured Washington that Poland's foreign policy goals would not change. When President Clinton called Kwasniewski to congratulate him, the Polish President emphasized that he was just as committed as his predecessor to joining NATO—"not [as] a game directed against Russia" but as a way to improve pan-European cooperation.[74] Speaking before the North Atlantic Council on January 17, 1996, the Polish President concluded an eloquent statement on why Warsaw sought Alliance membership by stating: "Poland will not disappoint NATO. I hope that the Alliance will not frustrate the hopes of the Poles."[75]

Kwasniewski was barely in office, however, when his Prime Minister, Jozef Oleksy, was accused of being a KGB informer. The evidence against Oleksy turned out to be thin, but he resigned amidst fears that Poland was penetrated by Russian intelligence moles. Warsaw was now tainted by accusations of being too close to Moscow, and the seventh Polish Prime Minister in six years had been forced to resign. But Kwasniewski and Foreign Minister Dariusz Rosati stepped up their efforts to show the Clinton Administration that they were just as good Atlanticists as their predecessors.[76] In March, Kwasniewski sent his national security advisor, Marek Siwiec, to Washington for private discussions. Siwiec's message was simple: give Kwasniewski a chance to pass the exam. In April, Foreign Minster Rosati arrived in Washington to meet with senior U.S. officials. Gone was Walesa's tough rhetoric about using NATO enlargement to cage the Russian bear. In its place was a new tone emphasizing enlargement as the means to unify Europe while reaching out to Moscow. It was identical to that of the Clinton Administration.[77]

Washington's rapprochement with Kwasniewski was not complete until the Polish President visited Washington in early July 1996. A day before he departed for the U.S., Kwasniewski invited American Ambassador Nick Rey over for late afternoon drinks. Pressed by Kwasniewski on what he should try to achieve in Washington, Rey said: "Mr. President, you must prove that Commies don't have horns."[78] Kwasniewski passed the test. In the Oval office he told Clinton: "President Reagan helped in bringing about the end of the Soviet Union; President Bush helped reunify Germany. You, Mr. President have the historic challenge of enlarging NATO, thus unifying Europe and completing the changes we began in 1989." He continued: "This is not anything against Russia but for European integration and stability." The Polish President pointed out that whereas the American President had visited the eastern half of a divided Europe as a student twenty years earlier, he had come to the U.S. around the same time as a young Polish student to see what the West was like. "Now we, our generation, can end these divisions once and for all," he told the President.[79] Poland had regained its good name in U.S. thinking and policy.

One country that failed to address its problems and disqualified itself from the first round of enlargement was Slovakia. Following the "Velvet Divorce"— the peaceful breakup of Czechoslovakia in 1993 into separate Czech and Slovak Republics—Slovakia was widely considered to be a front runner in the enlargement race. But the increasingly anti-democratic tactics of Slovakia's first post-independence Prime Minister, Vladimir Meciar, undercut and eventually destroyed his country's chances of joining its neighbors as a candidate for NATO enlargement at the Madrid summit.

In late February 1995, Holbrooke and Fried arrived in Bratislava to deliver the first of several warnings to Meciar about the consequences of his behavior for Slovakia's NATO bid. In a dinner with Holbrooke on February 23, Meciar insisted that he was committed to successfully resolving the Hungarian minority issue and achieving NATO membership. Questioned by Holbrooke and Fried about the anti-democratic methods he was using to fight his political opponents, he argued that he was simply engaging in hard-ball politics. "I know I am a tough opponent but I don't play foul," Meciar claimed, adding that he did not need to "use undemocratic methods" to defeat his political opponents. He told Holbrooke, "I know a club member must respect its rules and that a club must try to prevent anyone from introducing disruption into its ranks. We want to prepare Slovakia to be a reliable partner."[80]

But the evidence of Meciar's undemocratic behavior continued to mount— as did U.S. warnings about the consequences. When Deputy Assistant Secretary of Defense Joe Kruzel and Fried were back in Bratislava for bilateral U.S.-Slovak defense talks later that spring, Slovak President Kovac described how Meciar was telling people that the EU and NATO would turn a blind eye to Slovakia's internal politics. Kruzel and Fried emphasized that such an assumption was "dead wrong."[81] Despite protests from the parliamentary opposition, Slovak civil society, and the West, Meciar's anti-democratic behavior only increased. In August 1995, Kovac's son was kidnapped. Armed thugs halted the younger Kovac's car outside of Bratislava, blindfolded and beat him, poured whiskey down his throat, drove him across the border to Austria and dumped him, unconscious, outside a police station near the Slovak-Austrian border. He was wanted in the West on charges of fraud—but the evidence soon suggested that this was a dirty-tricks operation carried out at Meciar's behest to discredit the Slovak President. In the spring of 1996 a key witness to the kidnapping was killed by a car bomb.

In a meeting with President Kovac in Cedar Rapids, Iowa in August 1995, President Clinton noted that the U.S. did not take sides in political contests and that who won or lost elections was not Washington's business. "But observing the democratic rules of the game is," he emphasized.[82] Later that autumn the EU and the U.S. officially demarched Bratislava over the growing anti-democratic trend in the country. Meciar continued to insist that such criticism would not harm Bratislava's chances of joining the West.[83] But the West was drawing a different conclusion. The U.S. State Department's annual report on human rights detailed "disturbing trends away from democratic principles" in the country.[84] When Assistant Secretary of Defense Frank Kramer and NSC Senior Director Fried returned to Bratislava in the spring of 1996, their message was that NATO enlargement was "values driven" and that Bratislava would not be given "the benefit of the doubt" when it came to decisions on NATO membership.[85]

Slovakia was no longer a credible candidate for NATO membership. While Slovak officials would allege that Bratislava was dropped as part of a "secret deal" with Moscow—an allegation that Meciar made to Ambassador Madeleine Albright in July 1996—the reality is that there never was an official internal U.S. decision to disqualify Slovakia or to take it off some internal list.[86] There was no need to. Slovakia had disqualified itself. By the time the U.S. government started official internal deliberations on which countries it could support for an initial round of enlargement in early 1997, there was nobody left in the U.S. government to support Slovakia's candidacy for NATO at the upcoming summit in Madrid.

4. UKRAINE AND THE BALTIC STATES

The Clinton Administration had pledged that NATO enlargement would enhance security and stability throughout Europe as a whole, including for those countries not invited to join in the first round. Nowhere was the test of that pledge more poignant than in the case of the Baltic states—Estonia, Latvia and Lithuania—and Ukraine. While they were often lumped together in the minds of many Western policymakers as "former Soviet Republics," in reality they had little in common.

The three small Baltic states had been connected to the West through travel and commerce since the days of the Hanseatic League. Rival regional powers had fought to control their ports for centuries, resulting in alternating occupations by the Swedes, Danes, Germans, and Russians. Lithuania had been part of the Polish-Lithuanian commonwealth that had once reigned across the region from the Baltic to the Black Sea. Following the Russian Empire's collapse at the end of World War I, the Baltics emerged as independent states along with Poland and Finland. They were the object of one of the great geopolitical crimes of the 20th century—the Molotov-Ribbentrop Pact signed in 1939 on the eve of World War II. Afterward, they were annexed by Stalin and for forty years Moscow pursued a strategy of forced industrialization that settled large numbers of Russians speaking in Estonia and Latvia. The Baltic desire for independence never died out, however, and the independence movements in these countries played a crucial role in toppling the USSR in 1991. Having escaped Moscow's grasp, these states were determined to do whatever it took to integrate into the West.

Ukraine, on the other hand, had been part of the Russian empire for a century. Kiev was in many ways the cradle of the Russian state, not "just" another imperial possession acquired over time. Even during Soviet times many Russians accepted the fact that the Baltic states were more Western and different. But Ukraine was considered an integral part of Russia proper. While the Baltic states were part of Russia's window to the West, Ukraine was even more significant strategically because of its resources and because it served as a springboard for Russian influence into Europe. As Zbigniew Brzezinski put it: "It cannot be stressed strongly enough that without Ukraine, Russia ceases to be an empire, but with Ukraine suborned and then subordinated, Russia automatically becomes an Empire."[87]

There was one more basic difference. Whereas the Baltic states were united in their desire to integrate with the West, Ukraine was internally unstable and divided on many issues, including its national identity and future geopolitical orientation. Those uncertainties in Ukraine posed some tricky policy challenges for the U.S. and its allies as the Alliance moved forward on enlargement. The last thing NATO wanted was for enlargement to further divide and isolate Ukraine, pushing it back into Moscow's embrace. Occupying a swath of territory nearly 1,000 kilometers wide separating Central Europe from Russia, Ukraine provided the strategic depth that made it possible for NATO to enlarge without the forward deployment of allied military forces.

Kiev's own views on NATO enlargement were a combination of hopes and fears.[88] As Foreign Minister Hennadiy Udovenko put it to Talbott: NATO and Russia are competitors whereas NATO and Ukraine were not.[89] Ukrainian officials supported a strong NATO as a key pillar of European security and a counterweight to Russian pressure that allowed them to consolidate their independence and sovereignty. Publicly, Kiev supported the right of the Central and East Europeans to join NATO. Ukrainian officials underscored that they did not fear NATO's presence on their borders. On the contrary, an enlarged Euro-Atlantic community could facilitate expanded ties with the West. They emphasized that, over time, they wanted their country to become a "European country" in the fullest sense of the word. In private, some Ukrainian officials underscored that their long-term goal was to join NATO but that they did not dare articulate it publicly since it was unrealistic in the foreseeable future and would only further complicate relations with Moscow.[90]

But these long-term hopes were tempered by short-term concerns. Kiev saw itself as the target of Russian political and economic pressure and feared that NATO enlargement could give Moscow a pretext to step up such pressure. It also feared that NATO enlargement, if not handled carefully, could provoke Moscow to deploy additional conventional or even tactical nuclear weapons in the region. Having dismantled its own nuclear deterrent, the prospect of NATO provoking a Russian deployment of additional nuclear weapons on Ukraine's border was a political nightmare. Kiev was also worried about lukewarm Western support for its independence and feared that its own security could be sacrificed as the price for Moscow's acquiescence to NATO enlargement.[91]

As NATO moved forward on enlargement, Kiev tried to come up with a policy that maximized its chances for westward integration yet minimized the dangers of increased Russian pressure. Several Ukrainian desiderata nonetheless emerged.[92] One was that NATO enlargement proceed slowly. As first Deputy Foreign Minister Tarasyuk put it: "the later [the expansion], the better."[93] Another was that the Alliance restrict the military component of NATO enlargement in order to avoid possible Russian pressure for countermeasures. In the summer of 1996 Ukraine tabled a nuclear free zone proposal for Central and Eastern Europe. Finally, Ukraine also wanted to strengthen its own relations with NATO and develop its own "special relationship" with the Alliance in parallel to enlargement. Kiev, in the words of one Ukrainian official, wanted a NATO-Ukraine relationship that would include "everything short of Article V"—that is, everything short of an explicit security guarantee.

As it became clear that NATO enlargement was moving forward, Kiev requested the first of several consultations to discuss the consequences of NATO enlargement on Ukraine. Already in June 1995, President Kuchma had told NATO Secretary General Claes that Kiev was interested in a "special" NATO-Ukraine relationship similar to what was being offered to Russia.[94] As the Alliance completed its enlargement study in the fall of 1995, Kiev forwarded its own first cut of ideas on a NATO-Ukraine relationship.[95] In the summer of 1996, Ukrainian Foreign Minster Udovenko wrote Secretary of State Christopher requesting U.S. support to further institutionalize a NATO-Ukraine relationship "to support regional stability during the expansion of the Alliance and to prevent new lines of division from arising in Europe."[96]

The U.S. response was positive. When Ukrainian National Security Advisor Voloymyr Horbulyn arrived in Washington in September 1996, Talbott assured him there would be "no sign on NATO's door saying that the Baltic states and Ukraine are not welcome" and committed to developing a NATO-Ukraine relationship.[97] In September, the U.S. announced the creation of a U.S.-Ukrainian

Commission modeled after the Gore-Chernomyrdin Commission. In mid-October Foreign Minster Udovenko handed Talbott two non-papers containing Kiev's ideas of how to structure a NATO-Ukraine relationship and in early November Kiev handed over a draft text on a NATO-Ukraine charter to Ambassador Hunter and Secretary Solana.[98] For Washington and its allies, the key questions were how to get Kiev to focus on substance rather than mere symbolism and how to calibrate the NATO-Ukraine relationship so that it had real meat on the bones but was a bit less "special" than the relationship NATO wanted to create with Moscow.

The policy challenge with the Baltic states was different. Swedish Prime Minister Carl Bildt had coined the phrase "the Baltic litmus test" in an article in *Foreign Affairs*.[99] He had written that the Baltic issue was a test of whether Russia had truly become a democratic state. But it was a litmus test for the West as well. Estonia, Latvia, and Lithuania wanted full Alliance membership as soon as possible. These three countries had suffered enormously under Soviet rule. There was hardly a Baltic family that did not have a story about a family member deported to Siberia. Although Soviet troops had withdrawn, the nearest Russian military bases were just across the border. Unlike other Warsaw Pact countries, the tiny Baltic states had to build their militaries from scratch. These states feared they would be the first target if a new neo-imperialist Russian government returned to power. They brushed aside Western arguments that their quest would undercut reform in Moscow and pointed out that if they had followed the same Western advice in 1991, they might have never achieved their independence.

At the same time, there were few countries that were initially less qualified, and whose aspirations for NATO enjoyed less political support in the West. Even the most avid and early supporters of NATO enlargement rarely mentioned the Baltic states. Many in the West worried about strong Russian opposition to Baltic NATO membership. Others worried whether the Baltic states could be defended given their exposed situation. Large Russian-speaking populations in Estonia and Latvia raised doubts over how stable and cohesive these countries were. On a flight to Warsaw from Cracow in January 1995 following the commemoration of the liberation of the Auschwitz concentration camp, Holbrooke asked Estonian Foreign Minister Juri Luik: "Look, are you guys really serious about trying to get into NATO?" Luik responded that while he recognized the hurdles that lay ahead, NATO membership was indeed a top priority for all three Baltic states.

The focal point of Baltic lobbying was Washington. The U.S. was the leading power in NATO. It had never recognized the illegal annexation of these countries and its policies were seen as being shaped less by *Realpolitik* than the major European powers.[100] The Baltic states sent their top diplomats to Washington. They excelled at presenting their countries as the underdog in a

David versus Goliath struggle with Moscow. The Latvian Ambassador to Washington, Ojars Kalnins, was a public relations executive from Chicago. Estonian Ambassador, Tom Ilves, was a former journalist who had grown up in New Jersey before working for Radio Free Europe. Both had given up their U.S. citizenship to work for their homelands. The Lithuanian Ambassador, Alfonsas Eidintas, was a prominent historian as well as an avid basketball player, the latter being Lithuania's national passion. He once showed up to a meeting with Talbott with a broken arm from playing basketball and said: "I got this knocking on NATO's door."

They were assisted by Baltic-Americans, many of whom had returned to their homelands to help rebuild their countries. It was not unusual for U.S. officials to sit down with Baltic delegations and discover that their counterparts were from Cleveland, Chicago, or Los Angeles. The Baltic-American community was small but well organized and worked closely with other groups to build political support for NATO membership. When State Department officials briefed Congress on U.S. policy, they often found that Baltic-American representatives had either just preceded them or were standing outside ready to make the case for the U.S. to provide more security assistance. They were relentless and single-minded in their focus on getting into NATO. As Estonian President Lennart Meri put it to an audience at CSIS following meetings with the President and his national security team: "You are probably wondering what we talked about at those meetings. Well, I'll tell you: security, security, security."[101]

The Baltic states were not the only countries pressing the Administration on how it intended to handle the Baltic issue in connection with NATO enlargement. Their Nordic neighbors were just as keen to know. Nordic support for Estonia, Latvia, and Lithuania was a matter of moral sympathy as well as strategic interest. Nordic leaders were afraid that NATO countries would try to saddle them with the primary responsibility for Baltic security. Suggestions by both British and German officials along these lines set off the alarm bells in the region.[102] Last but by no means least, these countries worried that NATO enlargement, if mishandled, could lead to a new Cold War in Europe that would be disproportionately felt in the Baltic region, where military countermeasures taken by Moscow were most likely to occur.[103]

For all of these reasons, the Nordic countries became nervous as it became clear that the U.S. was moving forward with enlargement. They responded by stepping up their own security assistance to the Baltic states and by speaking out on the right of the Baltic states to join NATO. But they also insisted that only the U.S. and NATO could provide a security guarantee. As Finnish President Martii Ahtisaari told Secretary Christopher: "Some in Europe have suggested that the Nordic states provide security guarantees to the Baltics." But he added "This is not realistic. The Nordics can do much to help the Baltics, but the Nordics cannot realistically guarantee Baltic security.[104] As Swedish Permanent

Undersecretary Jan Eliasson emphasized in a conversation with U.S. Undersecretary of State Peter Tarnoff in early 1996: "It is better to leave to us the non-security measures."[105]

The Clinton Administration knew it needed a Baltic policy. The question was what it should be. In March 1995 Vice President Al Gore had visited Tallinn to underscore American support for Baltic independence and Western integration in principle.[106] But a general assertion that the Baltic states were eligible for NATO membership some day in the future was a first step but not a policy. The real question was what the U.S. was prepared to do to ensure that Baltic security was not undercut in the short-term as enlargement to Central and Eastern Europe took place, and what steps it would take to improve the chances of these countries joining the Alliance at some later date. The closer the Alliance came to launching the enlargement process, the more urgent an answer to these questions became. Yet the Administration remained divided internally. As a State Department memo to Holbrooke noted on April 14, 1995, interagency discussions over how positive Washington should be on the Baltics joining NATO were stalemated.[107] Shortly thereafter, Holbrooke turned to the memo's author, Chris Dell, and told him that the differences in the U.S. government on how to handle the Baltic issue were simply too large. "This is a year too early," he said. "We have to put it aside and come back to it later."

By the end of the year, however, National Security Advisor Lake and Talbott were adamant that the U.S. needed a more clear-cut policy. After yet another round of inconclusive interagency deliberation, NSC Senior Director Dan Fried turned to the State Department's new Office Director for Nordic/Baltic Affairs, Carol van Voorst, and said in frustration: "Carol, you have got to figure this out. We need a policy. Do something." They agreed that van Voorst and Dan Hamilton, a European expert that Holbrooke had brought back with him to Washington from Bonn, would take the lead in drafting a strategy with bilateral and multilateral tracks to help integrate the Baltic states into the West. It would be called the Baltic Action Plan (BAP) and they would use Lake and Talbott to ram it through a hesitant bureaucracy.

About the same time, the first draft of an article that a RAND colleague, Bob Nurick, and I had authored, entitled "NATO Enlargement and the Baltic States," landed on the desks of senior policymakers in Washington. RAND's growing role in the NATO enlargement debate had led a number of Danish and other Nordic diplomats to visit Santa Monica and push us to answer the question of what would happen to the Baltic states if NATO enlarged. Having spent time as an exchange student in Denmark, I was interested in the Nordic and Baltic region but did not consider myself an expert. But the Estonian Ambassador in Washington, Tom Ilves, who had been a colleague of mine at Radio Free Europe in the 1980s, was also pushing us to address the Baltic issue. At the invitation of Danish Defense Minister Hans Haekkerup, Nurick and I toured the Baltic states, and then wrote an article laying out a strawman strategy on how to deal with the issue. We argued that since the Baltic states would not be in the first round of NATO enlargement, it was all the more important for the West to have a strategy. "If mishandled, the Baltic issue had the potential to derail NATO enlargement, redraw the security map in northeastern Europe and provoke a crisis between the West and Russia."[108] To avoid this, the article proposed creating a U.S.-Nordic alliance to implement a five-part strategy to expand Western cooperation with the Baltic states to mute any negative fallout from NATO enlargement. Much to our surprise, the RAND paper had an immediate impact in terms of framing the policy debate. Talbott handed out copies to visitors as an example of the kind of ideas the U.S. was considering and used it to push the government's internal thinking as well.

By the spring of 1996, an initial cut of the Administration's Baltic Action Plan was complete. But the Baltic states were getting more, not less, nervous. A number of Russian press reports speculated that if the Baltic states tried to join NATO, Moscow might retaliate, including with military steps. Two Russian analysts from the Institute of Defense Studies, associated with the Defense Ministry and intelligence circles, published a report suggesting that if NATO enlarged, Moscow should preemptively intervene in the Baltic states.[109] One of the authors subsequently gave an interview to the Estonian daily *Postimees* on April 27, where he warned that Estonian accession would bring about immediate military action by Moscow—and in the meantime Moscow would "nudge our nuclear weapons as close to NATO as possible: to create a "new political-military nuclear curtain."

The Western press also speculated that Baltic exclusion from NATO would be the price Moscow received for acquiescing to NATO enlargement. As the former Finnish diplomat Max Jacobson had warned: "NATO is not going to sign a secret protocol with Russia on dividing Eastern Europe, but the actual outcome of an expansion that admits Poland, Hungary and the Czech Republic—while leaving the three Baltic states indefinitely outside—would be in effect to tell Moscow: 'These are ours, the rest is yours.' That is how the Russians would interpret it."[110] As one Western commentator warned: "NATO Beware—Baltic Iceberg Ahead."[111]

Meeting in Riga in late May, the three Baltic Presidents, Lennart Meri, Guntis Ulmanis, and Algirdas Brazauskas, sent President Clinton a letter asking the U.S. to publicly affirm its commitment to eventual Baltic membership in NATO.[112] In handing the letter over to the U.S. Ambassador in Riga, Larry Napper, President Ulmanis said he was confident that Washington would not sell out the Baltic states but worried that some of Washington's European allies might be tempted to exclude these countries from NATO in the future and urged the U.S. to reign in such proclivities.[113] On June 28, President Clinton met with the three Baltic Presidents in the White House. Ulmanis opened the conversation by stating: "It has been said that in the 20th century God is dead. I nevertheless believe that the values under which Western civilization has united since the Bible have given testimony to a common God. NATO and the EU have come into existence precisely on the basis of those values and with the goal of preserving them."

President Clinton responded that the U.S. wanted to see the full integration of the Baltic states into the West and that there would be no "secret deals" with the Russians. NATO's door would remain open after the first round, he continued. But he left little hope that the Baltic states would be among the first NATO candidates. "Unfortunately I cannot say to you today what you want me to say."[114] When they met with Republican Presidential candidate Bob Dole, he was no clearer on where the Baltics fit into his thinking either. As an editorial in *The Washington Post* noted after the Baltic Presidents' visit, neither the Administration nor the Republicans in Congress had an answer for how to handle the Baltic issue as NATO expanded. "Like the smallest kids on the playground determined to join in the game, the Baltic Republics have repeatedly raised their hand first—first for independence, first to apply to NATO, first to demolish communism and build democracy and send peacekeeping battalions to Bosnia. They are polite, but that is not the same as accommodating. They want to know why they can't play too."[115]

Over the summer, the Administration finalized its Baltic Action Plan. Its premise was clear: U.S. goals for the Baltic states were the same as for Central Europe and Eastern Europe—integration into the West. At the same time, it noted that "for geographical and historical reasons" this goal was more difficult to attain and detailed a three-track approach based on expanded U.S.-Baltic cooperation; greater U.S.-Nordic cooperation in support of Baltic efforts to integrate into the EU and NATO; and enhanced U.S. involvement in helping to manage Baltic-Russian differences. When Deputy Secretary Talbott shared it with the Baltic Ambassadors on August 28, their reaction was cautious and reserved. They knew it was a plan to shelter them from the fallout of NATO enlargement, not one to actually get them into the Alliance. Tom Ilves, the Estonian Ambassador and later Foreign Minister, joked that it should have been called the "Baltic Electoral Plan," since it was unveiled only a few months before the November 1996 U.S. Presidential elections.[116]

That evening the Latvian Ambassador to Washington, Ojars Kalnins, wrote in his journal,

> Once again we are in a position where we can write our own ticket, as long as we have drive, persistence and originality. The Americans have given us their best shot in terms of providing a plan that will address our security needs. Their "best shot" being one that does not provide security guarantees, no hard promises on NATO but a complex of programs and

assistance wherein the hope is that the whole will appear to exceed the sum of the parts and convey the impression of security.

While acknowledging that some of his Baltic colleagues were more cautious and had even dismissed the BAP as a kind of "booby prize," Kalnins wrote:

> I realize that the decision to push full and strong for Baltic membership in NATO is highly unlikely from this or any other administration under the present circumstances. . . . Getting NATO to expand at all will be a battle both in the U.S. and in Europe, and getting the Balts on the front line of expansion merely compounds the problem. Given these realities, we need to squeeze out what we can under the circumstances. Pushing at all times for full NATO membership (we need to do that to maintain maximum leverage) we need to simultaneously nickel and dime the Americans to provide us with programs that will compensate us for the lack of NATO membership.[117]

Shortly thereafter, U.S. Secretary of Defense Bill Perry made it official. Perry was in Copenhagen attending a conference hosted by Danish Defense Minister Hans Haekkerup, perhaps the staunchest supporter of Baltic membership in the Alliance. The U.S. Secretary of Defense was worried that the Baltic states' expectations on enlargement were too high and that the U.S. ran the risk of stringing these countries along, thereby creating an even greater disappointment down the road. As he read his draft speech, he decided the moment had come to tell the Baltics the truth. His staff watched as he rewrote his speech by hand during lunch, wondering what their boss was doing. After lunch, Perry strode to the podium and told the audience that while the United States supported the independence of the Baltic states, "they are not yet ready to take on the Article V responsibilities of NATO membership." He added that they were making progress in that direction and "we should all work to hasten the day that they will be ready for membership." NATO's reply to those countries that had applied for membership but would not be accepted, he concluded, "is not 'no,' it is 'not yet.' "[118]

5. "A LONG DANCE WITH NATASHA"

On June 3, 1996 Lech Walesa visited President Clinton in the White House. The former Polish President described to Clinton a debate he had recently participated in at the University of Chicago on NATO enlargement. He understood that many Americans opposed enlargement—because "they don't want to die for Eastern Europe." He told the President he had tried to persuade his audience that the best way to ensure that Americans would never again risk their lives in Europe was to enlarge NATO but with mixed results. "So it's clear that some Americans are opposed to enlargement and that it is not easy for you," Walesa remarked.

"You know where I stand on this," President Clinton replied. "We should en-large NATO; we will have the support of the American people for this and most Europeans will support us, too. Since we first discussed this, you and I, I've per-suaded most of our European allies that we should move ahead and I've stressed that there will be no veto by Russia nor by anyone else."

Walesa underscored that the key decision lay in Washington's hands. "It all depends on what you in America decide. The Europeans—France, England, the others—will not decide this question. You will. We Europeans complain about you but look to you to decide things," he added. "Without a clear signal Europe will lose its way. That would be terrible because now, for the first time, Europe has a chance, a unique chance, for unity." Walesa added that he knew how important Clinton's support had been. "You have launched this and done a lot. The direction is clear and that is good."

But the Polish President also lamented the fact that, in his view, the West had in the past missed several opportunities to act. "That's because democracy has trouble making the tough decisions; democracy makes easy decisions but not difficult ones." He urged President Clinton to move forward as quickly as possi-ble after the Russian Presidential elections. "Don't waste this opportunity," he told the President." Of course the delays are not America's fault. The Europeans have been slow throughout. And you think, why should we worry about Europe if the West Europeans don't? But you must make the hard choices, even for the Europeans, because the Europeans themselves won't or can't."

Walesa continued that Bosnia had again shown why U.S. leadership was needed. "The Europeans could decide nothing. You had to make the decisive moves. And you did and these were right. He urged Clinton to do the same on NATO enlargement. "Here is where the decisions must be made. Make them and the Europeans will shout for a while but accept them," the former Polish President concluded. Warsaw would support the United States but its patience, too, was wearing thin. "Poland is like a ballet dancer, a beautiful dancer in a theater or a café. Poland has nice legs and Yeltsin is tempted. But we are safer with someone else," Walesa told the President. The key question was: "How long will Poland keep dancing on a thin line, like a ballerina, without knowing with whom to dance? She wants NATO and the EU as her partners. Yeltsin can be very jealous. A jealous Natasha."

"Poland will have a long dance with the right partners, a good dance," the President assured Walesa, adding that "every time I see Boris Yeltsin from now on I'll be sure to think of Natasha." "A jealous Natasha," Walesa emphasized.[119]

On June 7, 1996, NSC advisor Tony Lake handed Secretary Warren Christopher a NSC paper. It was entitled "NATO Enlargement Game Plan:

June 96 to June 97." It contained the White House's game plan for pulling together the different strands of the Administration's efforts at NATO reform culminating in a NATO summit at which the Alliance would announce France's
reintegration with the Alliance, extend invitations to the first new members
from Central and Eastern Europe, and complete an agreement with Moscow
launching a new, cooperative NATO-Russia relationship. The overall theme of
the summit, which would notionally take place in the spring of 1997, would be
the creation of a "new NATO" that had adapted itself for the post–Cold War
era. It was, the paper argued, the culmination of President Clinton's initial call
at the January 1994 NATO summit for the Alliance to recast itself for the new
post–Cold War era.

The historic centerpiece of the summit would be the decision to invite former Warsaw Pact countries to join NATO. "Currently, Poland, the Czech
Republic and Hungary are the aspiring members most frequently cited," the
NSC paper noted. The Baltic states "lack the votes for now" and "the
Romanians are not ready (though it is possible an acceleration of reforms may
compel a second look)." Bulgaria "was not interested" and Slovakia had "fallen
back into the pack" due to Meciar's authoritarian behavior. Slovenia, the authors concluded, was a dark-horse candidate. "Although previously inward-
looking, the Slovenes have recently expressed serious interest in pursuing
NATO membership."

By making the central theme of the Madrid summit "adaptation" as opposed
to "enlargement," the Administration hoped to enlist the support of allies such
as France who considered the Alliance's internal reform more important. It
could also take "some of the sting" out of Russia's response "by demonstrating to
Moscow that NATO has indeed been transformed from its Cold War structure
and is, in fact, becoming increasingly 'European' and focused on new missions
such as peacekeeping and crisis management." The paper concluded: "While
unlikely to fully assuage Russian doubts about enlargement, this shift in emphasis, 'the new NATO,' could help pave the way for a more graceful Russian
acceptance of the inevitable."[120] On July 22, the Deputies Committee endorsed
the NSC's game plan.[121]

The Administration's move did not take place in a political vacuum. With
the U.S. Presidential election campaign approaching, Republican criticism was
getting louder. On June 4, Dole, Gingrich, and Lech Walesa—flanked by a
phalanx of key Republican members of Congress—held a press conference in
the U.S. Capitol to unveil the "NATO Enlargement Facilitation Act."[122]
Gingrich blasted the Administration for "already being several years behind
schedule" on enlargement. "I see no excuse and no reason for blocking this act,
for slowing this act down. Now is the time to do it."[123] Three weeks later, Dole
castigated the Administration for pursuing a foreign policy of "indecision, vacil-
lation and weakness" and called for NATO and a tougher policy toward Russia.

If elected President, Dole promised to bring Poland, Hungary, and the Czech Republic into NATO by 1998—the 6oth anniversary of the betrayal of Munich, the fiftieth anniversary of the communist takeover, and the 39th anniversary of the Soviet invasion in 1968. "It is an outrage," Dole concluded, "that the patriots who threw off the chains of Soviet bondage are told that they must wait."[124]

On July 3, Yeltsin was reelected as President of Russia with nearly 55 percent of the popular vote. Clinton called him on the evening of July 5 to congratulate him: "I'm proud of how hard you fought back after being down in the polls." Yeltsin thanked Clinton for his support: "I appreciate that throughout the campaign up to the last day you said the right things and never sent the wrong signals."[125] Shortly thereafter, Mamedov was in Washington to discuss NATO-Russia issues. Talbott arranged for Mamedov to meet with President Clinton in the Oval Office. Clinton told Mamedov how happy he was with Yeltsin's election victory. "We were dancing in the White House after the results came in," the President said. Mamedov responded: "I can assure you where our sympathies lie in your own election, and you can count on us."[126] As Talbott escorted Mamedov out of the Oval Office, he joked that he hoped the Deputy Foreign Minister would keep the Russian endorsement of Clinton a state secret lest the Republicans hear about it!

With the Russian elections over and Clinton's promise to Yeltsin fulfilled, the Administration moved to implement its agenda of adaptation, enlargement, and NATO-Russia. On August 7, President Clinton wrote Major, Kohl, and Chirac. "Over the course of the next year, I believe we can and must take important decisions in several areas: completing NATO's internal adaptation, moving forward with enlargement and deepening NATO's relationship with Russia and other partner nations. Each of these elements is essential if we are to achieve our goal of an undivided, secure Europe," he wrote. On NATO enlargement, Clinton stressed that the Alliance had to fulfill its promises to Central and Eastern Europe while avoiding the creation of a new division with countries further eastward. "These two goals," the President concluded, "are not only compatible, they are mutually reinforcing. Properly managed, the enlargement of NATO can encourage all the former Communist states to stay on the path of democratization, market economics, cooperative security and integration. Indeed, we may not have fully appreciated the powerful incentive for political and economic reform that has been provided by making these matters a prerequisite for NATO membership."[127]

In early September Christopher delivered a major speech in Germany reinforcing the President's message. The Clinton Administration had considered, and rejected, a Presidential speech at home for fear of being accused of allowing electoral considerations to drive Administration policy.[128] Instead, Christopher spoke in Stuttgart on the same day and stage that U.S. Secretary of State Byrnes had delivered his famous "speech of hope" fifty years earlier. "NATO enlargement is on track and will happen," Christopher now stated and laid out the Administration's vision of an adapted and enlarged NATO working cooperatively with Russia. He now proposed an Atlantic Partnership Council as a replacement for the NACC as a way to expand cooperation and reach out to those countries not joining NATO. But the big news was Christopher's announcement that a NATO summit would be held in mid-1997 at which the Alliance would extend invitations to the first new members.[129]

If the NATO enlargement piece of the Administration's agenda was moving forward, the grand compromise that Washington had hoped to achieve bringing Paris fully back into the Alliance was starting to unravel. Both Paris and Washington had hailed the June 1996 Berlin ESDI compromise as a success.[130] In Lyons in late June Chirac had reassured Clinton that he was "ready, within the Berlin framework, to reenter [NATO] fully and without reservations. There are some technical problems to work out," Chirac noted. "But let us leave it to the experts to think this through. We are ready, as I said, to go all the way into NATO."[131] During July and August, however, the common ground between Washington and Paris started to crumble as it became clear that Chirac's desiderata included the U.S. giving up major command slots in NATO. To this day, it remains unclear whether Paris' upping of the ante was a response to domestic criticism that Chirac was "selling out" French interests in his bid to reenter NATO, or whether the French President had always wanted a major additional step beyond the Berlin compromise.[132]

These differences came to a head over who would occupy the top military command posts in a restructured NATO. Traditionally, the U.S. had filled the position of NATO's two strategic commanders—the Supreme Allied Commander-Europe (SACEUR) and the Supreme Allied Commander-Atlantic (SACLANT). In return, the Europeans had filled the post of NATO Secretary General. Command slots below that level were filled by both Americans and Europeans depending on who provided the most forces for a particular region. Based on this rule of thumb, the Germans had traditionally held key command positions in Central and Eastern Europe and the British in Northern Europe. The U.S. had held the senior job in Southern Europe, in part due to the importance of the Sixth Fleet, stationed in Naples for Mediterranean security.

After reviewing a variety of different options, NATO had proposed the creation of two new regional commands for Northern and Southern Europe— AFNorth and AFSouth—below the level of SACEUR. This reduction from three to two key regional commands now created a major political problem. If the U.S. continued to provide both of NATO's strategic commanders, as well as the commander for NATO's new southern command, it meant that the number of European commanders was being reduced. This ran counter to Chirac's goal of increasing the European profile in the Alliance. In the summer of 1996, therefore, French officials floated the idea of creating a new single, overall NATO strategic commander—a kind of super-SACEUR—with a European SACEUR and a U.S. SACLANT subordinated to him. Another option was to alternate the slots of NATO Secretary General and SACEUR between an American and a European. The third option was to stick to the Berlin compromise of a European Deputy SACEUR but to complement it with Europeans assuming both major regional commands.[133]

On August 28, President Chirac wrote President Clinton noting that it seemed "difficult" for Washington to accept a new American "super-SACEUR." The French President added that he could support the creation of a European Deputy SACEUR and the setting up of two regional commands, but only if both commanders were Europeans. He concluded: "If those proposals could be adopted, France would be willing to take its full place in the renewed Alliance. The adaptation of the Alliance would also allow enlargement to commence under favorable conditions."[134] In Paris in early September, Secretary Christopher told French Foreign Minister de Charette that Washington would insist on keeping NATO's southern command.[135] But Paris would not budge either. When NATO Secretary General Solana visited Paris in late September, Chirac reiterated his interest in a "super-SACEUR" and insisted that, at a minimum, AFSouth be led by a European.[136]

Washington now decided it had to make its position on the AFSouth issue crystal clear. On September 24, Secretary of Defense Bill Perry told French Defense Minister Millon at an informal NATO Defense Ministers Ministerial in Bergen, Norway that there was no flexibility in the U.S. position. He justified the U.S. stance by pointing to the preponderance of U.S. military power in the region and the danger that the American public's commitment to NATO would be undermined if the U.S. was left with no senior commanders on the ground in Europe. Millon was equally inflexible, demanding to know why the U.S. Congress and public were not satisfied with having NATO's two strategic commanders—SACEUR and SACLANT. He also suggested putting the U.S. Sixth fleet directly under SACEUR's command. When Perry would not budge, Millon told him he would call President Chirac immediately. But he warned that if U.S. policy was indeed set, France would have to reconsider its policy of moving back into the Alliance.[137]

Later that day, Perry told Solana he feared that a U.S.-French confrontation was in the making, but that the French threat not to reintegrate would not dissuade the United States from its position.[138] President Clinton also wrote Chirac on September 26 in an attempt to avoid a confrontation. He underscored how far the two countries had come in harmonizing their views, but tried to steer the French President away from the idea of a European AFSouth commander. "The weight of the U.S. force commitment, the stabilizing role of the U.S. presence in the region and the need to maintain public and political support here in the United States for our continued military contribution to the Alliance argue overwhelmingly for the maintenance of a U.S. Commander in AFSouth," the President wrote. At the same time, President Clinton hinted that the U.S. might consider other steps to meet French concerns.[139]

Chirac's response arrived on October 10. The French President repeated his argument for a greater European role in NATO. At the bottom of the letter, the French President wrote by hand that: "The issue of the Southern Command is, in my view, of capital importance."[140] With the U.S.-French fight spilling over into the public, Tony Lake slipped into Paris unannounced on November 1 to see what could be salvaged. Chirac told Lake that he was willing to re-enter NATO if the terms were right in spite of the political risk he faced but only if AFSouth were run by a European. Lake made it clear that the U.S. position on AFSouth would not change but asked that the two sides continue to try find an alternative package that might be attractive to Paris. "We can proceed with NATO enlargement and NATO-Russian relations without French reintegration, but it would be better to do so with it." He held out the prospect of Madrid becoming "a Super-summit" with France's reintegration, enlargement, and a NATO-Russia agreement all taking place. "This would be of huge historic significance," he argued.

Chirac responded: "Regarding the Southern Command, I understand your position—if I were in the United States, I would adopt the same position. What is important in a command system is who is in charge." U.S. policy, Chirac continued, had changed in word but not yet enough in deed. France needed something more: "I am prepared to adopt anything that you propose but not enter the system if there is not a real change. This is not worth a crisis between us. NATO has worked well without France for many years and this will continue." France and the U.S. were working well together in Bosnia without French reintegration. The French President concluded: "I repeat, France is ready to discuss returning to NATO if there is a real change and that means a change in the command structure. If this is not possible, it will not pose any difficulties for France. We just will not rejoin."[141] But the two sides were deadlocked. Soon the public rhetoric over who was to blame for the breakdown in U.S.-French talks started to escalate. Solana now suggested to Christopher that both sides try to de-escalate the situation for the December Foreign Ministers meeting and return to it after the Christmas holidays.[142]

Moscow also continued to make Washington's life difficult. Talbott, the Administration's point person in NATO-Russia talks, was frustrated by the inability to move Moscow beyond its attempts to hinder enlargement and to force it to negotiate seriously. He believed that the way to maximize U.S. leverage was to make it clear that enlargement was going to take place irrespective of whether Russia negotiated a NATO-Russia agreement. For this to be credible, Washington had to first shore up support among the allies. The best way to do so was for Washington to go the extra mile in developing a NATO-Russia pack-age that demonstrated the U.S.'s desire to address Moscow's concerns. If Yeltsin and Primakov turned down the package, it would be clear that failure to reach agreement could not be blamed on Washington. But Talbott emphasized: "We're not going to solve this problem unless we think outside of the box, and unless we are willing to question some of the orthodoxy." The exercise also had to be restricted to a small circle of senior officials on both sides of the Atlantic. In justifying this back channel, Talbott told Christopher: "There is too much neuralgia and theology and turf consciousness for me to want to risk a more tra-ditional intramural or interagency vetting of these ideas at this point."[143]

During the first half of July, Talbott sent Christopher a series of memos lay-ing out a framework for bridging the gap between NATO and Russian positions. There were four core ideas. First, while the Alliance could only accept one class of members, it could unilaterally elaborate on its intention not to deploy nu-clear weapons in the new countries to meet Russian concerns. And both sides could update the CFE Treaty to reach a mutually acceptable understanding about the deployments of conventional forces. Second, the Alliance could give Russia a "seat at the table" in the emerging European security architecture through a NATO-Russia mechanism or a new European Security Directorate under the auspices of the OSCE. Third, Talbott suggested that NATO's door be left open to Russia over the long-term. While nearly every European ally op-posed this, it was important for Yeltsin and domestic reformers in Russia that they not be seen as being *a priori* excluded from the West. Fourth, Talbott wrote that the Alliance needed to package NATO's own adaptation and a greater European role through ESDI to emphasize that NATO was no longer aimed against Russia.[144]

Following consultations with Solana and key allies, Talbott floated the ele-ments of this package as a trial balloon with Primakov in Moscow in mid-July 1996. The Russian Foreign Minister responded: "Your list of topics is interesting. I think it's constructive." But he insisted that Russia needed something more concrete on NATO military infrastructure on the territory of new members. "Your remarks make Russia's desiderata clear," Talbott responded: "But there can only be one class of membership in NATO. We're not going to discriminate against new members or underline the fundamentals of the Alliance." Primakov responded: "You know that we do not want to see the U.S. leave Europe. We think your presence is in our interest." He understood that NATO's adaptation could be used to project a different image of NATO to the Russian public. "Let's think how all these factors can help us resolve the issue. For example, peace-keeping as a mission for NATO is entirely acceptable—indeed welcome—to us."

"What's not acceptable to us," he continued, "is having Poland in the same category as England. The fact is that there are already different classes of mem-bers of NATO. Countries have different limits to which they are subject. With respect to nuclear weapons, Germany has one set of limits. Norway has another." Primakov also warned that Moscow would never accept the Baltics or Ukraine joining NATO. "In reality it is not acceptable to us that NATO is open to everyone," he told Talbott. Moscow had both vertical and horizontal red lines with respect to NATO enlargement. "The vertical ones include such items as infrastructure. The horizontal ones include such issues as the Baltics and Ukraine." Talbott responded that "then we've got a collision of red lines" and the two sides would be "at an impasse if not a train wreck." Primakov backed down and agreed that the overall approach Talbott had suggested made sense and that Christopher and he should try to agree on the way ahead.[145]

By late July, a final version of the Talbott paper, now dubbed "the bible" in interagency discussions, laid out the U.S. strategy for achieving a NATO-Russia accord on Western terms. The "U.S. and its allies," the paper stated, "will make a best effort to work out a NATO-Russia relationship that induces Russia to adjust cooperatively to expansion" by answering Russia's concerns "on what we deem to be its legitimate security concerns and to find ways of accommodating Russia's desire for inclusion and active participation in new/enhanced European security structures, insofar as such arrangements support our overall security and political interests." The paper listed a number of NATO "redlines" that the Alliance could not cross: no veto, no second class NATO membership, no subordination of NATO to other bodies, no dilution in NATO command structures, and no secret deal over the heads of allies or new members.

In a nutshell, the strategy was to convince Moscow that enlargement would take place and that if Russia wanted to be part of a new European security architecture it was going to have to significantly modify its goals. "If Russia wants to maximize its participation in and benefit from the larger evolutionary/integrative process underway in Europe, it should solve the problem of NATO enlargement, not fight it," the paper concluded. At the same time, the paper pointed to two major problems. One was that Moscow still needed to be persuaded "on all counts—and may, in the timeframe we envision, be incapable of accepting our bottom lines." Second, many European allies, especially Germany and France, had doubts about the preferred U.S. pace on enlargement and could therefore be vulnerable to Russian efforts to slow down the pace or block it from happening.[146]

For much of August and September, Talbott shuttled between meetings with Mamedov and consultations with Solana and the NATO allies to hammer out a framework that might be acceptable to both sides. During long hours of debate at the Russian Ambassador's residences in Ottawa and Paris, Talbott and Mamedov argued over the substance of a possible package, and eventually agreed on a framework paper.[147] Talbott was increasingly convinced that there was enough common ground between him and Mamedov to make a NATO-Russia agreement feasible.

But Talbott was also worried that Moscow was playing a double game. On the one hand, Primakov continued to tell Washington that Moscow valued U.S.-Russian cooperation and wanted to work closely to build a new, cooperative NATO-Russia relationship. Mamedov was claiming that Moscow realized that enlargement was going to happen and he had been authorized to "brainstorm" with Talbott on what such a relationship might look like. On the other hand, Primakov continued to attack NATO enlargement, warn of its destabilizing consequences, and probe Washington's European allies for signs of division and weakness. Mamedov's counterpart in the Russian Foreign Ministry responsible for European affairs, Deputy Foreign Minister Nikolai Afanas'evsky, was touring European capitals with a tougher message and a long laundry list of Russian demands designed to tie NATO in knots.

"What we've got it seems," Talbott had written Christopher in late August, "is Primakov letting Afanas'evsky run the European play while Mamedov runs the American one, with Primakov himself reserving on which playbook he will take to Yeltsin this fall."[148] And it was not entirely clear that Primakov's strategy would fail. At the top of Moscow's target list were two allies, Germany and France, whose support for enlargement was essential, whose leaders prided themselves on their own special relationship with Yeltsin, and who had shown their ambivalence about NATO enlargement moving forward absent a NATO-Russia agreement.[149] Primakov's goal was, in Talbott's words, to "keep looking for (and, I fear, finding) weak spots on the NATO front; he'd like to exploit these to see if he can slow down or even stop enlargement, or extract from us concessions that would make a mockery of our determination—that new members of the Alliance have all the rights and protections of current members." Washington had to force Primakov to choose—and to choose the path of NATO-Russia cooperation.[150]

The Deputy Secretary suggested to Christopher that he use his upcoming meeting with Primakov in New York to force the issue and to try to clarify Primakov's position. Christopher agreed. Meeting with the Russian Foreign Minister at the Waldorf Towers on September 23, 1996, the U.S. Secretary of State asked to see Primakov alone. He told him that this was one of the most important meetings they ever had. President Clinton was committed to a positive NATO-Russia relationship, but time was starting to run out. NATO enlargement was going to move forward and if the two sides were going to achieve progress in parallel on NATO-Russia, they needed to move quickly. Washington was receiving mixed signals. If Moscow was prepared to move forward on such a track it was imperative to "clarify the road ahead and provide an impetus to steady, timely progress." Primakov recalled that at their first meeting in Helsinki, he had told Christopher that enlargement would be like "sleeping with a porcupine." The task they now faced, he said, was to "make the porcupine as small as possible."[151]

But Christopher's plea for parallel tracks was not good enough for the Russian Foreign Minister. "What I don't like about parallelism is that it means you're saying that once NATO expansion has started, you would set the conditions and Russia has nothing to say about what happens. . . . That is not acceptable." Pointing to a picture on the wall, he insisted that Russia needed to have more details on just what enlargement as well as NATO-Russian cooperation would entail. "Look at that picture on the wall," he said, "if there's only a frame but no painting in it, what good is it? In addition to seeing the frame, we would at least like to have a rough sketch inside."

By this time, Talbott and Mamedov had joined the two Foreign Ministers. In an attempt to illustrate how the U.S. saw the process moving forward, Talbott took a piece of paper and drew four lines to symbolize NATO enlargement, NATO's internal adaptation, NATO-Russia, and the CFE Treaty moving in parallel. He then drew a line symbolizing Russia's intent to stop or slow down enlargement. "We have a four letter word," he told Primakov, "for what this would amount to: veto." Primakov lost his temper: "You want to expand NATO and tell us that nothing we do or think or say will have any affect on your plans. Yet you also accuse me of wanting to veto it. Are you playing us for fools?" The Russian Foreign Minister regained his composure: "Okay, let's go back to square one: You can't let go of NATO expansion and we can't agree to support it in advance and then applaud it when it happens. That's not a veto. We realize we have no veto power. . . . But that does not mean we have to agree to a scheme that merely provides cover for NATO to expand."

Talbott drew a large oval around the four parallel lines: "This represents a single context in which these parallel processes are going forward," he said. "That context is the post–Cold War evolution of Europe, of NATO, of Russia, of the OSCE, of the European Union. Let's imagine these lines continue out into the mid-21st century. What Europe is like at that point in the future will depend a lot on what Russia is like; what NATO is like will depend a lot on how Russia has developed. And what Russia is like will depend to a significant degree on how its relations with NATO have developed. So, yes, there's connection," Talbott concluded.

"I finally see your point," said Primakov. "When in the year 2050 Russia becomes more democratic and is transformed in fundamental ways, then NATO as an organization will also be transformed. Of course we cannot insist that everything has to happen right now, that all the changes that will happen in the future are pre-programmed right now."

Primakov and Talbott started to debate the nuances in Russian between parallelism and correlation, but Christopher interrupted to say: "I am the only one in this room who does not speak the Russian language but I still understand the issue." He suggested that Talbott and Mamedov continue their work. "Yevgeny," he told Primakov, "don't sell short the importance of this charter serving to indicate the overall direction in which we want to move."[152] It would take another eight months before a NATO-Russia agreement was finalized. And senior Russian officials would hint that Moscow might simply prefer to put relations with NATO on hold until after enlargement had taken place rather than sign an agreement that appeared to give Washington a green light to move forward.[153] But Moscow had finally started to accept that NATO enlargement was going to happen.

On October 22, 1996, two weeks before the U.S. Presidential election, Clinton spoke before a group of foreign policy scholars and Democratic party activists at an election rally in Hamtramck, Michigan. He publicly set a target date for bringing new members into NATO. "By 1999, NATO's fiftieth anniversary and 10 years after the fall of the Berlin Wall, the first group of countries we invite should be full-fledged members of NATO."[154] The Dole campaign alleged that Clinton was "waffling" and "foot-dragging" and concluded: "Under Bill Clinton NATO enlargement will never happen."[155] On November 5, 1996 Bill Clinton was reelected President of the United States. Ten days later, a Principals Committee meeting on NATO policy decided the U.S. should call for a NATO summit to be held no later than July 1997 at which the first invitations to join the Alliance should be extended.[156]

In early December Talbott and Primakov met in Oslo for another go-round on enlargement. Talbott told Primakov that while they had made progress in scoping out the possible content of a Charter, the U.S. side was increasingly unsure whether Russia actually wanted a political accommodation with the West. Primakov complained that the NATO enlargement issue was increasingly permeating the U.S.-Russian relationship and making it difficult to achieve progress on any issue. Talbott responded that he did not believe that the average Russian was concerned about enlargement, but that the Russian political elite was the problem—and that Primakov had fed those fears himself with his harsh rhetoric. "You've worked yourself into a corner. By warning that NATO enlargement will be the end of the world, you've defined the problem in a way that defies solution," he said. Primakov responded: "We need to escape from this dilemma. . . . This is the question of questions."[157]

1. Czechoslovak President Vaclav Havel (seated center left) addressing the North Atlantic Council on March 21, 1991. He apologized to the gathered Ambassadors for the lies the communist authorities told about NATO during the Cold War and thanked the Alliance for its role in saving Europe from totalitarianism. Seated at the table to the right of Havel is NATO Secretary General Manfred Woerner.

2. Czechoslovak President Vaclav Havel (seated center), Hungarian Prime Minister Jozsef Antall (seated right) and Polish President Lech Walesa (seated left) at the Visegrad Summit held in the Prague Castle on May 6, 1992. The three leaders announced publicly for the first time their desire to seek full NATO membership.

3. German Defense Minister Volker Ruehe, the first major western leader to speak out in favor of NATO enlargement, is pictured in Brussels on December 14, 1994.

4. Bill Clinton lighting a memorial flame at the opening of the Holocaust Memorial Museum on April 22, 1993. Clinton met with Central and East European leaders on the margins of the opening where he was confronted for the first time personally with their strong desire to join NATO. To Clinton's right is Elie Wiesel, Nobel Laureate and Founding Chairman of the U.S. Holocaust Memorial Museum,. To his left is Harvey Meyerhoff, Council Chair Emeritus of the Museum.

5. Polish President Lech Walesa welcomes Russian President Boris Yeltsin at the Belvedere Palace on a state visit to Warsaw on August 24, 1993. Walesa convinced Yeltsin to agree to a statement in which Moscow would not oppose Poland's quest for NATO membership. Yeltsin would subsequently reverse his position and Walesa would accuse the West of having missed a major opportunity to expand NATO.

6. RAND headquarters in Santa Monica, where much of the early intellectual work on NATO enlargement took place in the early 1990s.

7. U.S. General John Shalikashvilli, Chairman of the Joint Chiefs of Staff, initially opposed moving forward on NATO enlargement in the summer and fall of 1993 and instead proposed the Partnership for Peace (PfP) to reach out to the countries of Central and Eastern Europe. Here he is pictured with NATO's Supreme Allied Commander, U.S. General George Joulwan, at NATO headquarters in Brussels the spring of 1995.

8. President Clinton with the leaders of the Visegrad group outside the U.S. Ambassador's residence in Prague on January 12, 1994 announcing that U.S. policy on NATO enlargement was "not whether but when." Standing behind Clinton are Slovak President Michal Kovac, Polish President Lech Walesa, Czech President Vaclav Havel and Hungarian President Arpad Goncz.

9. President Clinton playing the saxophone at the jazz club Reduta in Prague on January 11, 1994.

10. Russian Foreign Minister Andrei Kozyrev signs Russia's Partnership for Peace framework agreement in a special ceremony at NATO headquarters on June 22, 1994, following difficult negotiations and in spite of strong opposition back home.

11. A Polish tank commander participating in NATO's first PfP training exercise held in Biedrusko, Poland on September 12, 1994.

12. The close friendship between Deputy Secretary of State Strobe Talbott and then Assistant Secretary of State for European and Canadian Affairs Richard C. Holbrooke was key to the Clinton Administration's ability to pursue NATO enlargement and NATO-Russia cooperation in tandem. Here, the two men are shown horsing around after a briefing for the White House press corps on Bosnia in the fall of 1995. Talbott was armed with a cane because he'd torn a muscle in a family touch-football game.

13. U.S. Secretary of Defense Bill Perry was the last senior holdout against enlargement in President Clinton's inner circle. But Perry was also an enthusiastic supporter of expanded military cooperation with both Central and Eastern Europe and Russia. His personal ties to senior Russian military leaders were crucial to obtaining Russia's involvement in both PfP and on the ground with NATO in Bosnia. Here Perry is pictured with Russian Defense Minister Pavel Grachev, US SACEUR George Joulwan and Russian Bosnia commander Colonel-General Leontiy Shevstov after reaching agreement on NATO-Russia cooperation in Bosnia.

14. Clinton and Yeltsin having coffee at the end of a private lunch in the East Wing of the White House on September 28, 1994 where the U.S. President told Yeltsin for the first time of his intent to move forward on NATO enlargement that fall but assured him that it was not a move aimed against Russia.

15. In spite of the Clinton-Yeltsin conversation in September, the Russian President surprised the U.S. President three months later by publicly exploding in anger over NATO enlargement and warning of a "Cold Peace" at the OSCE summit in Budapest on December 5, 1994.

16. Clinton and his national security team at Franklin D. Roosevelt's estate at Hyde Park on October 23, 1995 during a visit by Yeltsin. Pictured from left to right at the table are Secretary of State Warren Christopher, Deputy Secretary of State Strobe Talbott, National Security Senior Director for Russian, Ukrainian and Eurasian Affairs, Coit Blacker, U.S. Ambassador to Russia Thomas Pickering, and National Security Advisor Anthony Lake.

17. Secretary of State Warren Christopher and Deputy Secretary Strobe Talbott bore the initial brunt of trying to negotiate a NATO-Russia understanding with Moscow and managing what Russian Foreign Minster Yevgeny Primakov called "porcupine" of enlargment. Here Christopher and Talbott are pictured in the Secretary of State's private office in the State Department.

18. NATO Secretary General Javier Solana. Although his nomination was initially opposed by Republican conservatives in Washington, Solana became an especially close and effective ally of the Clinton Administration as NATO Secretary General. This picture shows Solana and Deputy Secretary General Sergio Balanzino at the North Atlantic Council in early December 1996.

19. Presidents Clinton and Yeltsin in Helsinki with Finnish President Maarti Ahtisaari at the Finnish Presidential Residence in March 1997. During bilateral talks Yeltsin made a final effort to stop NATO enlargement but eventually backed down and gave a green light for negotiating what became the NATO-Russia Founding Act.

20. U.S. Secretary of State Madeleine Albright reporting to President Clinton in the Oval Office in the spring of 1997. Pictured from left to right standing behind Clinton and Albright are Vice President Al Gore, National Security Advisor Sandy Berger, NSC Senior Director for European Affairs Sandy Vershbow and Deputy National Security Advisor James Steinberg.

21. Albright and Primakov at a press conference at the Russian Foreign Ministry's Ostankino guest house in Moscow following the conclusion of their talks on May 2, 1997.

22. Presidents Clinton and Yeltsin shaking hands at the NATO-Russia summit in Paris on May 27, 1997 where the Founding Act was signed. In the background is French President Jacques Chirac who hosted the event.

23. Albright on May 29, 1997 at the NATO spring Foreign Ministers meeting in Sintra, Portugal where the U.S. unveiled, for the first time, its preference for a small first round of invitations. To Albright's left is Swedish Foreign Minister Lena Hjelm-Wallen and to her right Bulgarian Foreign Minster Nadezhda Mihailova who were attending the session of the Euro-Atlantic Partnership Council.

24. The author at a press conference in Vilnius, Lithuania with Lithuanian Deputy Foreign Minister Albinas Januszka following the conclusion of the first round of negotiations for the U.S.-Baltic Charter on June 25, 1997

I JUST WONDER IF WE HAVEN'T GONE TOO FAR EXPANDING NATO.

25. This cartoon taken from the *Weekly Standard* in the spring of 1997 captures Western skepticism about bringing Central and Eastern Europe countries into the Atlantic Alliance and just how far NATO enlargement would extend.

26. NATO Secretary General Javier Solana at the NATO Madrid summit, one of the most controversial in the history of the Alliance.

27. French President Jacques Chirac and German Chancellor Helmut Kohl at the NATO Madrid summit on July 8, 1997. In spite of their close personal ties and the importance of the Franco-German axis, Kohl supported Clinton and the United States on limiting the first round of enlargement to three countries and helped steer the Alliance to a balanced compromise regarding the future of its "open door" policy.

28. U.S. President Bill Clinton and Polish President Alexandr Kwasniewski celebrating Poland's invitation to join NATO in Warsaw's Castle Square on July 10, 1997 following the NATO Madrid summit.

29. National Security Advisor Sandy Berger with his "troika" of NSC Senior Directors Dan Fried, Sandy Vershbow and Steven Pifer following the Madrid summit in the summer of 1997.

30. Albright holding hands with Senator Jesse Helms at Wingate University on March 25, 1997. The relationship between Albright and Helms was key to building bipartisan support for enlargement in the U.S. Senate.

31. President Clinton signing the protocols of accession for the Czech Republic, Hungary and Poland after the Senate voted 80-19 in favor of ratification on April 30, 1998. The ceremony took place in the White House Rose Garden on May 21, 1998. The participants in the ceremony include (from left to right): General Wesley Clark, Polish Ambassador Jerzy Kozminski, General Joe Ralston, Hungarian Ambassador Gyorgy Banlaki, Secretary of Defense Bill Cohen, Czech Ambassador Alexandr Vondra, Senator Gordon Smith (R-OR), Secretary of State Madeleine K. Albright, Special Advisor Jeremy Rosner, SNOG Chairman Senator William Roth (R-DE), Senator Joseph Biden (D-DE), Vice President Al Gore, Senator Barbara Milkulski (D-MD), and Senator Richard Lugar (R-IN).

32. Albright holding the signed protocols of accession and posing with Foreign Ministers Jan Kavan of the Czech Republic, Janos Martonyi of Hungary, and Bronislaw Geremek of Poland at the Truman Library in Independence, MO on March 12, 1999.

Book VI

THE NATO-RUSSIA ENDGAME

At noon on January 20, 1997, William Jefferson Clinton was sworn in for his second term as President of the United States. In his State of the Union address two weeks later, he listed NATO enlargement as his top foreign-policy priority. He noted that fifty years earlier "a farsighted America" had led in creating institutions like NATO that had helped secure the West's victory in the Cold War. "Now we stand at another moment of change and choice—and another time to be farsighted. In this endeavor, our first task is to help build, for the first time, an undivided, democratic Europe." To that end, he committed the U.S. to launch the enlargement of NATO at the upcoming NATO summit in Madrid in July with the goal of bringing new members into the Alliance on its fiftieth anniversary in 1999.[1]

With six months to go until Madrid, the Administration faced one of the greatest foreign policy challenges of the Clinton Presidency. On paper, almost everything appeared set. Washington had consulted extensively with its allies. It had laboriously tried to negotiate a new, cooperative NATO-Russia relationship with Moscow. It had awaited the outcome of the U.S. and Russian Presidential elections before moving forward. But enlargement was not yet a done deal. Little if anything was fully locked in. And there were still major differences— both between NATO members and Russia and among countries within the Alliance's own ranks—on the outstanding issues. There was still work to do to complete this project—and ample opportunity for mistakes and failure. The stage was set for one of the most dramatic plays in NATO's history.

In April 1997, I switched from being a RAND analyst and State Department consultant to being a fulltime American diplomat when I joined the Department's European Bureau as a political appointee responsible for NATO issues and European security. Within days, I was off to Moscow as part of the team helping Secretary of State Albright and Deputy Secretary Talbott negotiate what would become the NATO-Russia Founding Act. From the ceremony launching a new NATO-Russia relationship in Paris in late May 1997, we went directly to the Alliance's spring Ministerial in the Portuguese city of Sintra where, for the first time, the latent differences between Washington and some of its allies over the scope of enlargement and its future broke into the open.

In the ensuing weeks, U.S.-French differences over who should be invited to join NATO would escalate into a dramatic diplomatic shoot out between Washington and Paris at the Madrid summit. Following the summit, President Clinton went to Warsaw where he received a jubilant welcome from more than 30,000 enthusiastic Poles. Even more dramatic was the President's reception in Bucharest where an estimated 100,000 Romanians turned out to cheer Clinton and Romanian President Emil Constantinescu—in spite of Washington's rejection of Romania's bid for immediate NATO membership. Clinton wrapped up this week-long tour with a stop in Copenhagen where some 80,000 Danes turned out to cheer him as well. I, in turn, was part of the team accompanying Albright on a tour of Ljubljana, St. Petersburg, Vilnius, and her native city of Prague for an emotional homecoming. Secretary of Defense Bill Cohen completed the Administration's grand tour of Central and Eastern Europe, traveling to Budapest and Sofia, to show the U.S. commitment to building a unified Europe.

Nearly everyone on Clinton's national security team dealing with European security issues had read former Secretary of State Dean Acheson's memoir, *Present at the Creation*, in which he eloquently describes NATO's founding.[2] We shied away from saying it publicly for fear of appearing pretentious, but there was a very real sense of being present at and participating in the birth of a new NATO for a new Europe. Madrid was the culmination of years of political and diplomatic work involving some of the most far-reaching changes in NATO's history. But it was not an easy birth. These six months were filled with drama, diplomatic intrigue, and political confrontation—with the Russians as well as with some of our closest allies. Madrid was one of the most important, and also one of the most contentious summits, in NATO's history.

1. MADELEINE'S VISION

President Clinton's commitment to NATO enlargement was underscored by his decision to nominate Madeleine K. Albright as Secretary of State for his second term. Perhaps no one better epitomized the U.S. commitment to overcome Europe's Cold War divide. A naturalized American citizen born in Czechoslovakia, Albright had come to the United States at the age of eleven after the communist coup in Prague that led her father, Josef Korbel, then the Czechoslovak Ambassador to Belgrade, to flee to the West. Albright was fiercely proud to be an American. Unlike many Democrats of her generation, her intellectual paradigm was Munich, not Vietnam. She did not harbor any doubts about using America's power to pursue U.S. diplomatic goals. Instead, she saw the U.S. as the "indispensable" nation when it came to advancing the cause of peace and democracy.[3]

Albright knew firsthand Europe's tragic recent history. As a child she had witnessed first Hitler and then Stalin's occupation of her native Czechoslovakia. Her academic training was in Soviet and East European studies at Columbia University, where she wrote her doctoral dissertation on Czechoslovakia. Following a stint working as a legislative aide for Senator Edmund Muskie, she worked for Zbigniew Brzezinski's National Security Council staff in the second half of the 1970s, where she was in charge of legislative affairs. From there she went to Georgetown University where she taught U.S. foreign policy and became the President of the Center for National Policy. In the mid-1980s, Albright started traveling back to Central and Eastern Europe where she met many of the dissidents in Prague, Warsaw, and Budapest. She became a friend of and eventually an informal advisor to Vaclav Havel. Following communism's collapse, she was part of a team of experts that examined public attitudes in Central and Eastern Europe and the former Soviet Union.[4] Few Americans knew the region better than she did.

By the time she became Secretary of State, Albright had become an enthusiastic champion of NATO enlargement. She saw it as a historic opportunity to anchor a democratic Central and Eastern Europe to the West once and for all. "The purpose of enlargement," she said in her first statement before the Senate Foreign Relations Committee on January 8, 1997, "is to do for Europe's East what NATO did 50 years ago for Europe's West: to integrate new democracies, defeat old hatreds, provide confidence in economic recovery and deter conflict."[5] Her goal, she once hand-wrote on a memo that U.S. Assistant Secretary of State Marc Grossman had sent her, was to ensure that Europe's future was safer than its past: "Let's develop a 21st century better than the 20th—the bloodiest in Europe's history."[6]

Albright also viewed enlargement as a moral imperative. It was an opportunity to erase the lines drawn by the armies of Hitler and Stalin and accepted by the West at Yalta. Following the Madrid summit, Albright spoke in Prague about how NATO's Madrid summit had framed her life and her life's work. She talked about the three journeys that shaped her commitment to NATO enlargement—her family's journey through war to the safe shores of America; Europe's journey from total war and absolute division to the promise of a new unity; and the Czech nation's journey from independence in 1918 to subjugation in 1948 to taking what she described as "your rightful place in the family of European democracies—fully, finally and forever." NATO enlargement was "a moment of injustice undone, of promises kept, of a unified Europe begun." This single sentence encapsulated the reasons for Albright's commitment to NATO enlargement.[7]

But Albright's commitment to enlargement also reflected her vision of a new U.S.-European relationship. She believed that the U.S. and Europe remained natural partners in the post–Cold War world. NATO enlargement was important to make Europe's eastern half safe and secure. But it was also a stepping stone to modernize the Alliance for a future in which a secure Europe would join the U.S. in dealing with new threats beyond the continent. In the spring of 1997 Albright was reading a biography of former Secretary of State Dean Acheson.[8] In meetings with her senior staff, she often compared the period following the end of the Cold War to the early post-World War II period. In the late 1940s, Truman and Acheson had committed the United States to remain in Europe. They had created NATO as a security umbrella against the very real Soviet threat and as the framework within which European reconciliation and integration could take place. In so doing, they had helped to define fifty years of U.S. international engagement.

The task the U.S. faced, she told us, was to build on that legacy and accomplishment. Sitting with Albright in her private office one day in the spring of 1997, she said to me and other members of her senior staff: "The challenge we face is different than the one Truman and Acheson faced. Thank God we don't face the threat that Stalin posed or the danger of World War III." "But," she continued, "in many ways the questions are still the same. What shape will this new Europe take? What role will the U.S. have? Will we continue to work together to solve the problems of the future?" There was little doubt in her mind what the answer *should* be. America was a European power. It had fought the Cold War not only to defeat communism but to win the peace as well. We had an historic opportunity to lay the foundation for a Europe whole and free in alliance with the United States—and we had to use it.

Albright firmly believed that America's interest and role in Europe transcended the Soviet threat, but that the Alliance had to be reshaped if it was to survive. She believed that NATO needed to be transformed and modernized to meet the challenges of the next fifty years—and the U.S. needed to do so at a time when many questioned whether it was needed at all or if the U.S. should even remain in Europe. "We have a window of opportunity in which to recast the foundation of this Alliance. If we get it right, NATO will last for another fifty years. And we will have succeeded just like the founding fathers of NATO did. If we don't, the U.S. and Europe are likely to slowly drift apart and the Alliance will atrophy," she once told me. The problem, she often repeated to us, was that too many people on both sides of the Atlantic were complacent and took the U.S.-European relationship for granted.[9]

In the spring of 1997, Albright delivered the commencement speech at Harvard University—on the spot where 50 years earlier Secretary of State George Marshall had launched the Marshall Plan. Albright invoked the vision of Marshall and her own life experience to underscore the role that America still had to play in Europe and around the world. She recalled sitting in a bomb shelter in London during World War II praying for American help. But she also recalled the price the West paid for not being vigilant in standing up early enough to Nazi aggression. America, she underscored, had to continue to lead. A new generation again had to make the choice to lead and shape a new world just as Marshall's generation had done in their time.

"Today," she told her audience, "the greatest danger to America is not some foreign enemy; it is the possibility that we will fail to heed the great example of that generation, that we will allow the momentum towards democracy to stall, take for granted the institutions and principles upon which our own freedom is based, and forget what the history of this century reminds us, that problems abroad, if left unattended, will all too often come home to America."[10]

Critics would at times accuse Albright of pushing for too much change too quickly, and hectoring or riding roughshod over our allies. But Albright was convinced the U.S. had a window of opportunity in which to lay the foundation for a new and transformed trans-Atlantic relationship. The danger in her eyes was not that the U.S. was too ambitious, but rather that it would become complacent. She wanted the U.S. to take the lead in consolidating the global triumph of democracy and forging new alliances to keep the peace as effectively as those of the Cold War. "We have a responsibility in our time, as others had in theirs," she said in her Harvard speech, "not to be prisoners of history but to shape history; a responsibility to fill the role of pathfinder, and to build with others a global network of purpose and law that will protect our citizens, defend our interests, preserve our values and bequeath to future generations a legacy as proud as the one we honor today."[11]

Albright's vision of a unified Europe included a democratic Russia. For Albright, the Cold War had been a fight against communism as an ideology, not against the Russian people. Following her nomination as Secretary of State, the Russian press initially portrayed her as a disciple of Zbigniew Brzezinski and an unreconstructed anti-Russian Cold Warrior. They dubbed her *Gospozha Stal* or "Madam Steel"—a label she was actually fond of. But her commitment to bring Russia into the Western community of nations came as a surprise to some of her Russian interlocutors.[12] In her first meeting with Russian President Yeltsin in February, Albright told him that he should not view her as a former Cold Warrior, but as an American version of Primakov—a tough but pragmatic defender of national interests who was committed to building a friendlier U.S.-Russia partnership. When Yeltsin told her that she needed to recognize that there was a new Russia, she asked Yeltsin to recognize that NATO, too, had changed. "I would like you to think," she told Yeltsin, "that there is a new NATO, not one of we versus you or you versus us, but one where we are on the same side."[13]

Some six weeks later, Albright was back in Moscow for a final round of negotiations on the NATO-Russia Founding Act. She met with a group of Russian strategic intellectuals at the Carnegie Moscow Center. Albright made an impassioned plea for them to put aside Cold War stereotypes and bury their distrust of NATO.[14] In the question and answer session, she talked about how both she and many of them had what she termed "Cold War libraries" filled with books on communism, arms control and the history of a divided Europe in the 20th century. "My library at home is a Cold War library. It is filled with books about totalitarianism, communism and arms control," she said. "I want to make it obsolete. I want people to look at these books and think they belong to ancient history because we have so changed our relations for the better."[15]

How important was Albright for NATO enlargement? Her role was critical for three reasons. First, her appointment was widely seen in Europe, Russia, and in the U.S. as confirmation of Washington's determination to see NATO enlargement through. While many conservative critics had openly questioned whether President Clinton was truly committed to enlargement, no one doubted *her* determination to seeing it through. She was the high-level champion on this issue the Administration needed at home and abroad.

Second, while much of the conceptual work and diplomatic foundation was completed prior to her becoming Secretary of State, it was Albright who got the actual job done. Her relationship with Primakov helped broker the final compromises that made the Founding Act possible. She was critical in holding the line in favor of three candidates for NATO's first round at Madrid—and convinced skeptics that Washington's commitment to further enlargement was credible. To use an American football metaphor, she came in as the team quarterback in a red zone offense and put the ball in the end zone—a metaphor of the sort she teased her male colleagues for using.

Third, Albright's passionate ability as a communicator made her the ideal spokesperson on NATO enlargement. She became the public face selling the policy to the U.S. public, to the Europeans, and to the U.S. Senate. She enjoyed taking on NATO enlargement's critics and explaining why, in her words, a bigger NATO was a better one.[16] She could reach across the aisle to conservatives in a way that other Administration officials could not. Republicans who disliked President Clinton liked Albright, her patriotism and her defense of America's role in the world—as shown by her 99-0 confirmation by the Senate. A picture of her holding hands with Senator Jesse Helms became a popular poster during the Senate ratification campaign. While Albright's star as U.S. Secretary of State would subsequently fade as criticism of her and her policies grew, she was at the top of her game during the first years of her tenure when NATO enlargement was implemented.

2. CHANCELLOR KOHL COMES THROUGH

On January 6, 1997, Chancellor Helmut Kohl called Clinton with a firsthand account of his recent trip to Russia where he had met privately with Yeltsin at his country home in Zavidovo on January 4. It was Yeltsin's first meeting with a western leader since heart surgery two months earlier. Kohl had found Yeltsin looking older and frailer than previously. The Russian President had expressed his anger over what he referred to as the "monster" of NATO enlargement that "our friend Bill" had unleashed. Yeltsin appealed to Kohl to help him. "I have to be able to look my people in the eye and tell them that their interests are being protected," he said. "We can't keep cooperating with the West unless I can assure them of that."[17]

Kohl assured Clinton that he had stood firm on enlargement. But he described Yeltsin's position in vivid terms: "His position is quite clear; he is against it. He thinks it is unnecessary and fraught with enormous psychological problems. He is afraid that a new Cold War is imminent and that the people won't understand it." The Chancellor told the President he still supported NATO enlargement, but Western leaders had to deal directly with Yeltsin to reach an understanding and not rely on normal diplomatic channels or the NATO bureaucracy. Absent a deal with Yeltsin before the Madrid summit, he warned, there was a real risk of a breach in the West's ties with Moscow. The German Chancellor asked Clinton to send Talbott to Bonn to meet with him as soon as possible.[18]

Kohl's phone call came at a critical juncture. The wrestling match between Washington and Moscow over NATO enlargement was not over. Although Primakov had signaled to Washington in private that he recognized enlargement was going to happen, Moscow remained adamantly opposed in public. By this time, Yeltsin and Primakov had staked out such strong rhetorical and public opposition to NATO expansion that it was going to be difficult for them to back down without suffering political damage.[19] Meeting with an American official in early 1997, Russian communist party head Gennady Zyuganov noted smugly that whereas in Washington there still appeared to be a range of views on enlargement, in Moscow there was only one view—everyone was opposed.[20]

That opposition continued to be accompanied by ominous hints at possible retaliatory steps. After a Kremlin meeting on NATO enlargement chaired by Yeltsin on January 6, anonymous Defense Ministry sources were quoted in the Russian press as saying that the Russian President's advisors all favored "tough countermeasures" against NATO. "If NATO moves eastward, Russia will move westward," one Kremlin source was quoted as saying. Moscow was also reportedly considering creating an anti-Western alliance with China, Iran, and India. Even if it could not stop enlargement's first round, the same source concluded, Moscow would reserve the right to use "any means" to prevent the Baltic states from "joining the military orbit of the U.S. and NATO."[21]

The endgame was starting. The Madrid summit was scheduled for early July 1997. NATO had six months to try to finalize a NATO-Russia deal and complete preparations for enlargement. But the gap between NATO and Moscow was still large. By this time Talbott had concluded that the only way to induce Moscow to work seriously to bridge that gap was to make it crystal clear that enlargement was going ahead, irrespective of whether NATO and Russia came to terms or not. Only the absolute certainty that enlargement was coming would lead the Russians to shift away from attacking enlargement and instead focus on what kind of relationship they wanted to have with an enlarged NATO. In other words, American diplomacy had to convince Moscow that the timetable and outcome of the Alliance's enlargement plans were set in concrete—and that the real choice facing Russia was whether it would protect its own interests by seeking a closer and cooperative relationship with the Alliance or watch enlargement go ahead without it.

For that strategy to work, Washington needed to be confident that its allies would not blink if negotiations with Moscow stalled. But the U.S. was still not sure how solid Western European allied support was. The Russians had spent almost four years trying to convince the Europeans that expansion would destroy Moscow's relationship with Europe. NATO Secretary General Solana had warned Ambassador Hunter in early November that European support for enlargement remained weak. Faced with conflicting choices, he said, some Europeans seemed prepared to choose Moscow as their first priority.[22] Solana repeated that concern to Senator Bill Roth (R-DE) later that month. If the Europeans had to choose between NATO enlargement and conflict with Russia, the Secretary General said, NATO enlargement might just lose.[23]

The Administration faced a paradox. To get the allies on board it needed a NATO-Russia agreement—or at least to be able to demonstrate that it had done everything possible to try to get one. But to get Moscow to negotiate seriously on a NATO-Russia agreement, it needed to convince Moscow that allied support was solid and enlargement inevitable. The Administration also needed a mechanism for negotiating with Moscow that included the allies but was not overly cumbersome. Kohl had told President Clinton that this issue was too important to be left in the hands of NATO bureaucrats and that he wanted it handled privately among the U.S., the major European powers and the Russians.

Talbott, too, had concluded that the NATO bureaucracy was not agile enough for this effort. He was looking for a vehicle that would put NATO, not the U.S., in front yet still allow Washington to drive the process from behind the scenes. In early January 1997, Solana visited Washington. Talbott proposed empowering him to be the Alliance's point person in dealing with Moscow—with the U.S. playing an active behind-the-scenes-role. While Solana was open to the idea, he emphasized it would only work if the other NATO allies, especially France, went along with it. And Talbott's scheme was not the only one on the table. French President Chirac had suggested that the U.S., France, Germany, and the United Kingdom hold a five-power summit with Moscow to try to hammer out the details of a NATO-Russia agreement. The Administration was not enthusiastic. In talking to Chirac, the President had told him that he did not rule out such a meeting but wanted to try to first make progress in the U.S.-Russia channel.[24]

One week later Talbott departed for London, Paris, and Bonn. His mission was to get Washington's closest allies to agree to the Administration's proposed strategy and mechanism for negotiating a NATO-Russia agreement. He arrived in London on January 13 for meetings with British Foreign Secretary Rifkind and senior British officials. They made it clear to him that London supported Washington's approach and was prepared to let Solana and the U.S. take the lead in hammering out a NATO-Russia agreement. While underscoring the British interest in reaching an agreement with Moscow, London also signaled that it was prepared to go ahead with enlargement with or without a NATO-Russia agreement.[25]

Crossing the channel, however, Talbott arrived to a chillier reception in Paris. While President Chirac was more supportive on NATO than his predecessors, Paris' reticence to follow the U.S. lead *en principe* was also well known. From the beginning, France had been the most reluctant of Washington's major allies on enlargement, and Chirac had already floated the idea of postponing the Madrid summit with Polish President Kwasniewski some weeks earlier. Chirac had his own, often strongly held, views on how to deal with Moscow, too. Complicating matters, the White House and the Elysée were conducting quiet back-channel talks between Sandy Berger and Jean-David Levitte, President Chirac's diplomatic advisor, to explore a compromise that would still bring France back into NATO's integrated military command by Madrid. It was a delicate moment in U.S.-French relations.

In the Elysée, the French President listened politely as Talbott argued that only a clear and unified allied position would induce Moscow to seriously negotiate a NATO-Russia agreement before Madrid. Chirac's response made it clear that he saw the problem lying not only in Moscow, but in Washington as well. The problem was a "fundamental lack of understanding between Russia and the United States," the French President said. He disapproved of what he termed a lack of American "finesse" in dealing with the Russians. "My conviction is that the U.S. does not take full account of Russian sensitivities," he said.

"The Russian people are profoundly hostile to NATO enlargement. It reflects a fear of encirclement—a traditional fear of the Russians—as well as a fear of humiliation." He recalled running into a busload of forty Russian *babushkas* in Paris who had told him that NATO was encircling Russia and had asked: "What will Yeltsin do when American nuclear weapons start falling on Moscow and St. Petersburg?"

Chirac warned that if Washington simply went ahead and enlarged NATO, the consequences could be the collapse of the Yeltsin government. "If one imposes NATO enlargement on the Russians, the Yeltsin regime will not be able to resist the public reaction and will not remain in power for very long," the French President suggested. Washington could not simply impose NATO enlargement on Russia and not worry about consequences that would be felt first and foremost by the Europeans. "Do not forget that it is we Europeans who are Russia's neighbors and who are most concerned about the consequences," Chirac concluded. "You should not blind yourself to the possibility that this could lead to a resurgence of deep-rooted Russian nationalism."

Instead, Chirac wanted France and Germany to step in and act as an honest broker. "Yeltsin needs a meeting with me and Helmut Kohl because Russia knows that France and Germany understand the situation better than others." The French President returned to the idea of a Big Five summit with Moscow. It was also an attempt to reduce Washington's role and leverage. And it completely cut out NATO Secretary General Solana from any official role. When Talbott asked what the summit's goal would be, Chirac responded that "whatever solution we arrive at must not be imposed on the Russians." It was the opposite of what Washington wanted.

Talbott asked what France would do if such a strategy failed. Was Paris prepared to go ahead and enlarge NATO if it proved impossible to conclude a NATO-Russia agreement? Chirac dodged the question: "I can't imagine failure. If we failed, it would raise questions in France as to whether we were back to square one. We will not fail if we approach the issue with finesse. So failure is unthinkable. If there were some fundamental reasons why the Russians were opposed to enlargement, we would have to confront some serious questions. But surely most of the problem is based on misunderstandings."

Washington and Paris were clearly not on the same wavelength. Talbott disagreed with Chirac's analysis—of Russia, of the U.S.-Russia relationship and of the tactics on how to deal with Moscow in the months ahead. He told the French President that he thought it was quite possible that Russia would not be willing or able to negotiate a NATO-Russia deal by July—even if it wanted to, which was not at all clear. "The Russian side is all screwed up," Talbott told Chirac, having "gone through one of the greatest traumas in history, with more sudden change in their internal order, external relations and ideology, and in their definition of statehood, than any country which has not lost a major war."

President Clinton, he continued, was "thinking about what we would do in that situation: faced with the prospect of Madrid but no NATO-Russia deal, and what signal we would send about that all-too-imaginable possibility." Washington's view, he continued, was that Madrid had to take place even absent a deal with Moscow. "If we were to allow the Russian's discontent, or their inability to come to terms, to determine whether we go ahead with NATO enlargement then enlargement will stop in its tracks and never go forward," Talbott went on. "If we make it a condition for enlargement that Russia be completely satisfied and that their satisfaction be written into the terms of a NATO-Russia deal, we will have made enlargement hostage to the Russians and have given them a veto. It will take 100 years—or if you're an optimist 50 years—for the Russians to be completely confident in themselves and the vision that you and President Clinton have for an undivided Europe."

Chirac countered that NATO and Russia could reach an accommodation—so long as the U.S. showed the proper degree of finesse. "You must start," he lectured Talbott, "by understanding Yeltsin." The Russian President, he continued, "is a man who did not attend *les Grandes Ecoles*; he didn't go to Harvard. He is, nonetheless, a man of sensitivity, although not someone who was trained to think in terms of 'one, two, three' in Cartesian fashion. That is why you need a warmer approach to him." In all frankness, Talbott responded, he had been dealing with the consequences of Chirac's previous "warmth" toward Moscow and his statement that the Alliance needed to first agree with Moscow before enlarging. He explained how Primakov had repeatedly distorted France's position to try to slow down and postpone enlargement in talks with him.

The Deputy Secretary concluded by saying: "If we convey any qualifications or ambiguity about our resolve with regard to enlargement, the Russians will conclude that NATO will postpone enlargement, and that will be the end of it. It will never happen. They will have won the game." Chirac replied that he found Talbott's view "a bit abrupt, a bit too black and white." The allies, the French President concluded, needed to look at what he called the "cost-benefit analysis." "I repeat that to impose something on Russia would be a big risk. NATO enlargement is not urgent—although I would never say that in public, of course. We need to look at the cost-effectiveness of proceeding. My conviction is that there is a 99 percent chance that we will resolve this problem if we use the proper skill."[26]

Talbott left Paris worried that Chirac was not on board. He arrived in Bonn the next day with some trepidation. On the one hand, the German Chancellor had made it clear that he viewed Poland's integration into the West and Polish-German reconciliation as a historical task on a par with the rapprochement between France and Germany that his political mentor, Konrad Adenauer, had brought about with Charles de Gaulle. At the same time, Kohl had on several occasions also made it clear that enlargement was only worth doing if it could be accomplished without a confrontation with Yeltsin's Russia, and had also floated his own proposal for postponing enlargement only one year earlier. Given the close political ties between Paris and Berlin, a Franco-German coalition in favor of postponing enlargement could not be excluded. It would have been a disaster for U.S. policy.

As Talbott entered the Chancellor's office along with Assistant Secretary of State John Kornblum, he found Kohl reviewing a German transcript of his conversation with Chirac from the previous day with the key sections underlined with a yellow highlighter. The Chancellor was clearly well informed. But the contrast between the views of Paris and Bonn could not have been more obvious. One of Kohl's cardinal principles was to avoid having to choose between Washington and Paris. And the Chancellor was careful not to utter a single word that could have been interpreted as discord between Paris and Bonn. But his message was the opposite of Chirac's. "I want to stress: I am absolutely against postponing the summit," he told Talbott. Whatever doubts the Chancellor had harbored on NATO enlargement were now gone. He was committed to enlarging NATO—and doing so at Madrid. "If we were to postpone it, it would only make things more difficult. We must have a clear vision and nerves of steel. Aware that Paris had at times suggested that its support of enlargement was tied to a successful resolution of the AFSouth issue, he said: "I know that internal adaptation of NATO is also important, but enlargement must be the number one priority."

In contrast to Chirac's push for European solidarity to balance Washington's approach, Kohl emphasized that the key to success was close U.S.-German cooperation. He told Talbott that he had been thinking a good deal in recent days about the United States and the importance of U.S.-German cooperation. He had supported Clinton during the recent Presidential elections and considered him a friend. Clinton, he noted, was different from previous American leaders. "I appreciate a President who can listen. He understands that while the U.S. is important, it needs genuine partners, not subordinates." Yeltsin trusted the U.S. President, too, he added: "He trusts Clinton—he thinks he is the best American leader. He has great mistrust of others, especially some in Congress whom he calls warmongers."

The Chancellor underscored that Washington and Bonn were at a "historical crossroads" in European security comparable to the Euromissile crisis of the early 1980s or German unification. It was again imperative that Washington and Bonn work together closely. "I must tell you that in our country, or elsewhere in Europe, there is an undertone of anti-Americanism," the Chancellor continued. Failure on NATO enlargement would only encourage that trend. "If we fail," Kohl concluded, "others will say that the Americans have not done a good job, then they will say that Helmut Kohl was asleep and should never have let it happen. Finally the French will say that they knew better all the time but the Americans would not listen."

He did not want that to happen, Kohl added. "If NATO enlargement fails now, we will have a dismal situation for many years. Again the Americans will be blamed and the President will be blamed. Certain circles will make much of the failure. Please tell Bill Clinton as a friend: I don't want that to happen. I want to use these four years to capitalize on American leadership."

Kohl now told Talbott that the time to enlarge NATO had arrived. "We can't tell the Poles and the Czechs that they are not welcome [in the West] after what they did to survive communism." But NATO enlargement was also a question of German national interest, especially in terms of Germany's relations with neighboring Poland, Kohl added. "This is not just a moral issue," he said, "it's in our self-interest to have this development now and not in the future."

Kohl was well known for his strong European credentials. European integration, he underscored, was of "existential" importance to Germany. Many in Western Europe, he added, were hypocritical about their support for Central Europe, especially in the EU. "If there were today a truly secret vote among my EU colleagues, I am not sure we would have a majority for expansion." The Chancellor brushed aside arguments that EU membership could serve as a substitute for NATO. "Even if the EU could manage expansion, it would not be enough to stabilize Central and Eastern Europe. My clear position is that EU is no substitute for NATO enlargement. It is important that you understand that this is our clear position."

"Time is running out," the German Chancellor continued. There were two key reasons why the Alliance had to act now. The first was that trends in Russia were pointing in the wrong direction. "The situation in Russia is getting more difficult all the time, both concerning NATO and in other areas. New waves of nationalism are mounting in Russia." The problem was the psychology of the Russian people trying to recover from the debris of seven decades of communism. "You can make politics with a people's psychology—just look at 20th-century Germany."

The second reason was that it was not clear how much longer Yeltsin would be around. Yeltsin was "the best of the current political figures that might come to power" in Russia—but not the only one imaginable. "I don't think Yeltsin will last out his term," Kohl said. He recalled how moved Yeltsin had been to see him and how the Russian President had confided in him that he had underestimated the severity of his illness and was not sure how long he would live. His last meeting with the Russian President in Moscow had been an emotional one. "I am no doctor but I believe we should make good use of the time remaining. If the chances are going to be good, it is now."

The Chancellor was flexible on the modalities for moving forward. The key thing was that Western leaders worked together in a small group with Yeltsin. He underscored the importance of giving France and Chirac a special role, but made it clear he was not opposed to using Solana as NATO's lead negotiator if

Moscow accepted that approach. The important thing was to move while Yeltsin was in office and make him feel included in the decisionmaking process. "We have to give priority to embracing Yeltsin in the positive sense of the word—and we have to do so before July, well before July. Time is running out on us." Yeltsin should be able to say afterwards, Kohl concluded, "that he played a special role in the process. He can say: 'I helped decide. I am a big guy.' That's very important to him." If Yeltsin knew that NATO would proceed with or without a NATO-Russia agreement, he would "join us rather than turning his back to us or letting himself be left behind as Europe moved forward without him."[27]

Talbott left Bonn relieved. The German Chancellor had endorsed the essence of Washington's strategy. Chirac and France would still require special handling, but Washington had enough support from Solana and key allies to launch the effort. The U.S. Deputy Secretary returned to Washington on January 16 to report to the President and his national security team in the Cabinet Room on his trip. Sandy Berger, now sitting opposite President Clinton at the cabinet table as the President's National Security Advisor, warned the President that the road ahead would be difficult. Managing the twin commitments to enlarging NATO and sustaining cooperation with Russia, he said, was going to be like Scylla and Charybdis and among the most difficult foreign policy challenges Clinton would face as President.[28]

3. THE ROAD TO HELSINKI

Clinton and Yeltsin were scheduled to meet in Helsinki in March. Over the next two months a frenzied set of negotiations took place in Moscow, Brussels, and Washington. In late January Talbott and Gore's national security advisor, Leon Fuerth, visited Moscow for three days of intense discussions. "Our conclusion is that, after three years of fighting the problem of NATO, the Russians may finally be prepared to join us in solving it," they wrote upon their return. "This is partly because they seem to have realized that despite their opposition to enlargement and their best efforts to derail the process, Madrid is a fixed point on the horizon—and on the calendar—and they must navigate accordingly."

Russian attitudes had not changed, Talbott and Fuerth noted. "From the Russians' perspective, what will happen in Madrid remains a thoroughly ugly fact. But they are no longer devoting quite so much energy to trying to talk us out of enlargement, or to split us from our Allies. Nor are they quite so baldly threatening to restart the Cold War in retaliation for enlargement." Instead, Moscow seemed to be groping for a way to insulate the U.S.-Russia relationship and its ties with the West from the fallout of enlargement.

"The devil, however, is not just in the details—it's in the fundamentals," the memo continued. Moscow was still insisting on demands that were complete non-starters. Left to their own devices, Primakov and Rodionov were unlikely to negotiate a deal on NATO's timeline. They were too interested in haggling over the details, especially regarding the military details of enlargement. But the good news was that Chernomyrdin and Yeltsin were increasingly involved—and they had different concerns that were easier for the U.S. to address. Their priority was that they "credibly be able to claim to their own people this spring that they have defended Russia's security and honor in the face of a looming development that their domestic political adversaries will characterize as a defeat and humiliation."[29]

Shortly thereafter, Yeltsin sent out the first feelers suggesting he wanted a deal. In a letter to Clinton on January 30, the Russian President underscored the need to ensure that the U.S.-Russian partnership remained "irreversible." He noted that both sides were "deadlocked" on the issue of NATO expansion, but recalled President Clinton's past assurances that enlargement would be carried out in a fashion not inimical to Russia's interests. "I believe you, and trust that our justified concern will, as you said, not simply be noted but will be taken into account in a clear and precise form," Yeltsin wrote. "It would be best if this were done, as you yourself stated publicly, in the form of an official agreement between Russia and NATO."[30]

They were not the words of a leader about to break off relations with the West. In a closed briefing to the Duma in early February, Primakov stated that Moscow had decided to try to negotiate a NATO-Russia deal in the hope that "the West will take into account our objective, serious concerns related to NATO enlargement."[31] When Chernomyrdin arrived in Washington in early February, he took a tough line at the official GCC meetings, but was more conciliatory in private. Meeting with Clinton, Chernomyrdin made it clear that Moscow did not want a confrontation with the West. But he underscored that the communist-led opposition in the Duma "will take advantage of anything" to try to "change the whole regime."[32] Flying to Chicago with Gore the next day, Chernomyrdin told him: "I understand that the decision [on enlargement] has been made; and we know you can't reverse it. But we need help on managing our own domestic politics on the issue." Gore responded: "Victor, we'll do that, so long as you can find a way to declare victory in what we can offer."[33]

It was now clear that Moscow wanted to negotiate with the U.S., not Paris or other European capitals. For all of his previous efforts to exploit divisions between Washington and its European allies, Primakov now referred to Solana and Washington's NATO allies with contempt. He would continue to talk to others, he told Talbott, but he considered Solana a "stool pigeon" and the role of countries like France "ornamental." Moscow knew who was making the real decisions. "That's why we'd rather talk directly with you. We're not so naïve as to think that you don't call the shots. Sure, I'll keep talking to Solana, but just so we all understand that a deal depends on the U.S. and Russia coming to terms—and that means our two Presidents when they meet."[34] When he received Albright on February 21 during her first visit to Moscow as Secretary of State, Yeltsin made the same point: "Russia and the United States have problems to discuss which can only be resolved by the Presidents. If we are to come to closure on NATO, he and I are the ones who will decide."[35]

To maximize Washington's ability to manage this process, Talbott assembled a team of trusted aides to serve as his brain trust in bridging the remaining divide between NATO and Moscow. In the State Department, this team consisted of Eric Edelman, Talbott's chief of staff; Lynn Davis, Undersecretary of State and the key advisor on arms control issues; John Bass, a young and talented foreign service officer who served as the primary drafter of our position papers; Victoria Nuland, my counterpart in the State Department's bureau dealing with the Newly Independent States (S/NIS); Craig Dunkerley, the U.S. envoy for conventional disarmament negotiations, and myself. Sandy Vershbow was the head figure at the NSC. The key figures at the Defense Department were Walt Slocomb, Undersecretary of Defense for Policy, his deputy Jan Lodal, and Assistant Secretary of Defense Frank Kramer. Lieutenant General Richard B. Myers was the representative of the Chairman of the Joint Chiefs of Staff. He was later replaced by Lieutenant General "Doc" Vogelsong as the senior military representative on the team.

The gap between what NATO was proposing and what Russia was seeking was still huge in conceptual and practical terms. The short-term U.S. goal was to prevent a rupture in the West's relations with Russia over enlargement. One did not need to be a strategic genius to understand that if Russia saw NATO as responsive to its legitimate concerns, it was more likely to be a constructive partner than one that felt rejected and isolated. But the broader, long-term U.S. goal was more ambitious: namely to build a cooperative relationship that, in spite of our disagreement over enlargement, would chip away at Russian hostility toward the Alliance through concrete cooperation. The Administration did not see this as a negotiation simply to "compensate" Russia for acquiescing to enlargement. Instead, the objective was to create a relationship that would, over time, build greater trust and help change Russian attitudes toward NATO.

At the same time, the U.S. wanted to protect the Alliance's decisionmaking autonomy and its military ability to act. Internally, it used two benchmarks to evaluate proposals for NATO-Russia cooperation. The first was whether the idea made sense on its own merits and could be justified even if NATO were not being enlarged. The second was to avoid anything that would hinder the Alliance from being able to carry its commitment to defend new members in case they were threatened. This mix was summed up as the "three yes's" and "the five no's." The U.S. and NATO were saying "yes" to a new partnership with Russia, "yes" to institutionalized consultations, and "yes" to expanded cooperation. The U.S. wanted Russia, as a major European actor, to be included and have a voice in deliberations on European security.

At the same time, the Administration also had five red lines it would not cross. It would reject any proposals that might give Russia a direct or implicit veto over Alliance decisionmaking, subordinate the Alliance to another institution such as the UN, slow down the enlargement process, create second-class members in Central and Eastern Europe, or close the door to future enlargement to countries such as the Baltic states. These five "no's" framed a pentagon within which NATO-Russia talks could take place. The Administration wanted to make this package look as attractive as possible to Moscow. It was prepared to be forward leaning on symbolism, but determined to remain firm on substance.

In one sense a NATO-Russia agreement was simply the next logical step in what NATO was already doing. Already under President George Bush in the early 1990s, NATO had declared that Russia was no longer an enemy and established the first NATO-Russia links. NATO and Russian Foreign and Defense Ministers were already meeting regularly. And Moscow had established a presence at NATO headquarters through PfP. But by proposing to institutionalize and take such links to the next level, the Administration was crossing important political and psychological thresholds that made people nervous—in Washington, Western Europe, and especially in Central and Eastern Europe.

The Administration's critics at home suggested that closer NATO-Russia consultations were a slippery slope that would lead to Moscow having a de facto veto. No one was more vocal or adamant in his criticism of Administration policy on this point than former Secretary of State Henry Kissinger.[36] Talbott was confident NATO could devise an arrangement that ensured that it was the Alliance, not Russia, that would be in the driver's seat and control the scope and pace of cooperation. In March 1997, he addressed Kissinger's critique in a note to Albright. A NATO-Russia agreement, he wrote, should be viewed as a form of "time release medicine" with the U.S. and its allies controlling the dosage and when it was administered. NATO's opening to Moscow would be both gradual and conditional—and depend on Russia's own behavior in the NATO-Russia Council as well as its own democratic transformation. He wrote that the Charter:

> will create a foundation on which we can construct a closer relationship—over time, in a deliberate process, the pace and contents of which will remain very much under our control. Additional measures will require the good intentions and hard work of both parties. Think of it as a pay-as-you-go plan—with the Russians under a reciprocal obligation to "pay" in the coinage of good behavior—as opposed to one that requires a big down payment on our part. There are no fixed deadlines by which we

commit ourselves to begin the activities that are of interest and benefit to the Russians. Rather, we commit to general undertakings, with no mention of how quickly—or slowly—they will occur.[37]

Moscow, of course, had very different objectives—and we knew it. It hoped to use this dialogue to accomplish its goals by other means à la Clausewitz. Once Moscow accepted that it could not stop enlargement, it still sought to limit it numerically and geographically and hollow it out militarily. It tried to restrict the Alliance's ability to deploy military equipment beyond its old borders, limit the activities of new members to the Alliance's political tasks, and prevent them from fully participating in alliance military planning. It wanted a ban on nuclear weapons, conventional forces, or "infrastructure" to the territory of new NATO members. It wanted to make sure that a first round of NATO enlargement would be the last. Most critically, it wanted to maximize Russian influence over the Alliance through what it referred to as "co-decision making," which was a euphemism for getting as much say as possible over future NATO actions.

One of Moscow's demands on enlargement had been that NATO leaders not exclude Russia from eventual membership. Clinton had obliged Yeltsin on this point, while making it clear that this was not a realistic prospect any time soon. Internally, I often told my staff that we had the 10, 25, and 50-year plans. The first was for Central and Eastern Europe, the second for Ukraine, and the third for Russia. At the same time, both we and our allies were nervous that Moscow might try to use this offer by NATO to create mischief by actually applying for membership. In the summer of 1996, Primakov suggested to Talbott that Russia was thinking about applying for NATO membership. After Talbott responded that Russia would have to get into the same queue and meet the same criteria as other candidates, Primakov acknowledged that he was not really interested in membership. "In reality," he continued, "it is not acceptable to us that NATO is open to everyone." Referring to the Baltic states and Ukraine, he stated that "this is an issue that could disrupt or destroy everything. We must be very, very careful."[38]

In the run up to Helsinki, Primakov again warned Talbott about the Baltic issue: "If any countries of the former Soviet Union are admitted to NATO, we will have no relations with NATO whatsoever. I know this can't be in the NATO-Russia document but it must be a common understanding." Both Vietnam and Cuba had wanted to join the Warsaw Pact, he insisted, but Moscow had not taken them in. Washington, he suggested, now needed to show similar restraint. Talbott reminded him that the U.S. never recognized Moscow's annexation of the Baltic states. "But the more general point" he continued, "is that we don't accept the idea of any sovereign independent state being told by someone else that it can never join an international organization or alliance. The Russian Foreign Minister dismissed what he referred to as "high theory and legalisms." If NATO expanded to the Baltic states, he insisted, the Yeltsin government would have no chance of weathering the ensuing storm in the Duma.[39]

The question was whether the Clinton Administration could somehow reconcile these two very different agendas—and package that common ground in a document Yeltsin would be willing to sign before Madrid. In late January, Talbott's team drew up a NATO-Russia scorecard that laid out where we disagreed and why, areas where compromise might be possible, and areas where there was no give in the NATO position.[40] As the spring unfolded, this scorecard would be regularly updated as both sides resolved some issues and clarified what they could, or could not, agree on. We also outlined a draft NATO-Russia document with five sections: a preamble, the principles governing the relationship, the consultation mechanism both sides were creating, a list of areas and topics where NATO and Russia would seek to cooperate, and military issues. It drew as much as possible on themes and language agreed to in other contexts and which could now be tailored to create a foundation for NATO-Russia cooperation.

But there were a multitude of issues over which the two sides simply disagreed. They included what the document would be called, which key principles would be highlighted, and how the newly formed NATO-Russia Council would operate. Moscow, for example, wanted language underscoring how NATO was changing since it wanted to argue domestically that a new, more political Alliance was emerging. The NATO allies were willing to consider language along these lines, but wanted reciprocal language on how *both* the Alliance and Russia had evolved after the end of the Cold War. The Alliance, in turn, wanted language from the OSCE Charter of Paris recognizing the rights of countries to determine their own alliances. Although Moscow had signed these documents, it was loath to put that language into what became the NATO-Russia Founding Act for fear that this would be interpreted as its acquiescing to NATO enlargement.

Establishing the rules for a NATO-Russia consultative mechanism was harder. The Alliance was willing to give Russia a voice, but not a veto, in NATO deliberations. This meant that NATO was prepared to consult with Moscow— but as an alliance and only after the allies had consulted with each other and reached a common position. In diplomatic parlance, this was referred to as a relationship of "16 plus 1." Moscow initially insisted on some version of co-decisionmaking in which it would be part of the consultation process before NATO had closed ranks. It demanded a voice in any NATO actions beyond its borders. And it wanted the Alliance to be subordinate to the United Nations, which given Moscow's seat on the Security Council would also ensure that it could not act without Moscow's consent. On these issues, the U.S. and its allies simply had to hold firm.

The most contentious issues were the military ones—or what soon was referred to in shorthand as Section V of the NATO-Russia draft. Moscow insisted upon a complete ban on the deployment of NATO nuclear weapons, troops, and infrastructure on the soil of new members. That was unacceptable to NATO. At the same time, the Alliance had flexibility in terms of how it carried out Article V guarantees when it came to its own strategy. The withdrawal of Russian military power eastward, the strategic depth provided by an independent Ukraine, and the ongoing erosion in Moscow's military capabilities had left NATO with conventional superiority in military terms. There was no cookie cutter model for how NATO carried out its security guarantees. The Alliance had defended countries in different ways over the years depending on a wide range of factors. Some allies had foreign forces on their soil, but others did not. Some countries had deployed nuclear weapons on their soil but this was not a precondition for membership.[41]

The NATO enlargement study from 1995 had established the principle that there was no *a priori* requirement for the deployment of either nuclear or conventional forces on the territory of new members. Both U.S. and NATO military authorities were comfortable relying on the capability to project military power to these countries in a crisis to carry out NATO's defense commitment to new members. Such a strategy assumed that new members would provide for their own national defense in the initial stage of a conflict until reinforcement arrived—and that the infrastructure existed that would allow NATO troops to deploy quickly and operate effectively thereafter. The Alliance had no intention of initiating a major military build-up in Central and Eastern Europe.

The question was whether NATO could articulate this in a fashion that addressed Russian concerns without arbitrarily tying the Alliance's hands. NATO allies were prepared to lay out Alliance thinking to reassure Moscow on this point, but politically, the allies could only do so if such statements were, and were seen as, voluntary Alliance decisions acceptable to new members and not the results of "concessions" given in NATO-Russia talks. Such constraints also had to be conditional. The Alliance needed to be able to abandon them if the security environment took a turn for the worse. If Moscow were to resort to its previous imperial ways or initiate its own military build-up, all bets were off.

Both sides now turned to the Vienna arms control negotiations on Conventional Forces in Europe (CFE) as a way to manage the military modalities of enlarging NATO. Politically, it was an acceptable forum because the prospective new members of the Alliance were at the table and had a full voice in these deliberations. Whatever restrictions were agreed to would be blessed by all the parties involved. Above all, the CFE negotiations were a two-way street. NATO's willingness to codify how many forces it would or would not deploy also depended on what kinds of restrictions Moscow would agree to for the forces on its territory. It also provided Moscow with the firm legally binding agreements it was looking for.

By now, Washington and its allies had agreed to scrap the old CFE framework and work on a new structure replacing the old treaty's group limits with separate national limits. NATO planners realized that this offered a way to square the circle with Moscow on enlargement's military consequences. To meet Alliance standards, the NATO candidate countries were building smaller militaries more in line with those of the West Europeans. The combination of these lower national force levels, plus planned NATO reinforcements, was still below the existing level of entitlements under the CFE treaty. In other words, NATO could enlarge and meet its obligations to defend new Alliance members. While highly technical in nature, these negotiations held the key for a possible deal. The Alliance could show that NATO enlargement, far from leading to a new military build-up that Moscow feared, was actually taking place in conjunction with a military draw-down. Moscow, in turn, could tell its public that it would not be facing a single additional Western tank after enlargement.

An even thornier issue was what the Russian side called "infrastructure." Moscow wanted a ban on what it called "offensive" infrastructure. This, too, was a non-starter for NATO for several reasons. No previous arms agreements had ever provided a working definition of "defensive" or "offensive" infrastructure, and it was probably not possible to come up with one at all; and certainly not on the timeline NATO and Russia were working on. More importantly, there was an inverse relationship between forward deployed troops and infrastructure. NATO could limit one or the other—but not both without being rendered militarily impotent and creating de facto second-class allies. If NATO refrained from the forward deployment of conventional forces on the territory of new members, it needed to have the infrastructure to project power quickly into these countries.[42]

In December 1996, NATO took the first in a series of steps to reassure Moscow about the military consequences of enlargement for Russia. At the NATO December Foreign Ministers meeting, the Alliance reaffirmed that its nuclear umbrella would be extended to new members but that enlargement would "not require a change in NATO's current nuclear posture and, therefore, NATO countries have no intention, no plan and no reason to deploy nuclear weapons on the territory of new members."[43] In mid-February, NATO tabled a CFE proposal that was clearly designed to show that NATO enlargement would not lead to an eastward shift or to a build-up of NATO conventional forces.[44]

By early March, these military issues had moved to the forefront of NATO-Russia talks. Meeting with Talbott in Brussels on March 5, Solana told him that he could see his way through to an acceptable compromise on most of the political issues. But the one where he was making the least headway with Primakov was on the issue of conventional forces.

Was there a way, Solana asked, to take the model that NATO had used to address the nuclear issue and apply it to conventional forces? It was a tricky issue. The Alliance had always retained the option of small deployments of conventional forces for new members. While Solana and Talbott talked, NSC Senior Director Sandy Vershbow scribbled out a sentence that captured the essence of the Alliance's thinking and handed it to Talbott. It read: "In the current and foreseeable security environment, the collective defense of the Alliance and the participation of all its members in the Alliance's military activities will be based on interoperability and a capability for reinforcement rather than on the permanent stationing of substantial, large combat units where they are not currently deployed."

Talbott quickly dubbed it the "sentence from hell" and it soon became known as the SFH.[45] While it hardly would qualify as a literary breakthrough, the meaning was sufficiently clear. As long as Russia did not threaten its neighbors in Central and Eastern Europe with new military steps, NATO would not deploy large numbers of troops on the soil of new allies, and rely instead on its reinforcement capability to make them feel secure.

When Talbott informally floated the idea with Mamedov in Moscow a few days later, the Russian Deputy Foreign Minster immediately responded: "This could be what we're looking for." He asked Talbott to repeat the sentence and carefully wrote it down. He wanted Talbott to define "large" and "substantial," but the Deputy Secretary demurred. The next day a well-briefed Primakov also pushed Talbott for greater specificity. "We need to be able to explain to the Russian public that there will be no nuclear weapons, no forces, no troops moving closer to Russia's borders."

Talbott responded that Moscow had to stop defining partial success as failure. "You must stop trying, in both what you're saying and what you're doing, to nullify the military dimension of membership for the countries that will be coming into NATO as new members. You've got to accept that these countries are coming into the Alliance as genuine equal members, including in the military dimension."[46] During a refueling stop on his way back to Washington, Talbott nonetheless called Solana to report that the "sentence from hell" had clearly elicited Russian interest and looked like a promising way to proceed.

But first the U.S. had to make sure the Central and East Europeans would not interpret this step as a sellout. These countries had been following the quickening pace of NATO-Russia talks with mixed feelings. While they supported them in principle, they feared that some of their own interests might be short-changed in the rush to reach an agreement. This, they feared, could result in them joining the Alliance but as "second-class" members. As one senior Polish official put it: "The smell of Yalta is always with us."[47] The Alliance had consulted closely with them in crafting its new CFE proposal to regulate the military side of NATO enlargement in a way that respected their sensitivities.

But as rumors of NATO issuing a second unilateral statement on its conventional posture spread, they grew nervous.

In Washington, Polish Ambassador Kozminski had caught wind of the fact that a NAC statement on NATO's future conventional force posture in an enlarged alliance was in the works. By this time the original SFH had gone through several iterations. Kozminski saw an early version containing the phrase "new members." Alarm bells started to go off. He feared that such language would violate Poland's own "red lines." These were simple: no second-class membership or limits that would discriminate against Poland in the Alliance or singularize it in ways that would create a domestic backlash. And for the Administration, keeping Poland happy was key for many reasons, not least of which was that it was the best key to keeping Republican critics at bay.

Kozminski arranged for Polish Foreign Minister Darius Rosati to fly to Washington to see Albright and other senior U.S. officials before the Helsinki summit. At meetings with the officials on March 13, Rosati argued that the proposed U.S. statement was unlikely to placate Russian concerns but would instead be pocketed by Moscow, which would then ask for more. He added that it also ran the risk of creating a second-class status for Warsaw that could produce a negative backlash in Polish public opinion. NSC Senior Director Fried was the first to meet with Rosati over lunch at the Mayflower Hotel. Fried took him through the logic of Washington's approach and explained how it protected the Alliance's ability to come to Poland's defense in a crisis. Rosati was not persuaded. After lunch, Fried called Edelman to warn that he had made little headway. Edelman responded: "That's ok. You are our blast shield—and you've absorbed the first Polish blast."

Later that afternoon Rosati met with Deputy National Security Advisor Jim Steinberg at the White House, as well as Albright and Talbott at the State Department. They walked Rosati through the sentence, again pointing out the protections and qualifications that were built into it. But Rosati was still opposed. Albright reassured him that NATO's proposal was merely a repackaging of things already said many times and that its purpose was to preempt Russian efforts to impose unacceptable limits on NATO by having the Alliance close ranks around a statement that did not cross the Alliance's own red lines. Rosati replied that Moscow was trying to make NATO militarily irrelevant by "pulling out its teeth" and that the U.S. approach looked like "appeasement," a charge that Albright vehemently rejected.[48] Afterwards, Albright confessed to Talbott that it had been easy for her to empathize with Rosati since she sympathized with the Central and East European concerns "in my bones and in my genes."[49]

On March 14 NATO unilaterally issued a simplified version of the "sentence from hell" in which it unilaterally defined its policy on the forward deployment of troops on the territory of new members. It read: "In the current and foreseeable security environment, the Alliance will carry out its collective defense and other missions by ensuring the necessary interoperability, integration and capability for reinforcement rather than by additional permanent stationing of substantial combat forces."[50] The next day Albright met with Primakov in Washington. While the two Foreign Ministers were officially negotiating a bilateral U.S.-Russian statement on European security for the Helsinki summit, everyone understood that the upcoming Clinton-Yeltsin meeting was critical if there was to be a breakthrough in the talks on a NATO-Russia Charter.

Primakov started out the conversation by noting that the two sides had nearly resolved their differences on the first four parts of the draft Charter—the preamble, the principles guiding the relationship, the nature of the NATO-Russia Council and the areas for possible NATO-Russia cooperation. But the key issue was Section V, the military implications of NATO enlargement. The Russian Foreign Minister insisted that there was one question that needed to be resolved. Otherwise there could be no Charter. NATO's statement from the previous day was "totally unacceptable," he insisted. There had to be a permanent ban on the deployment of NATO forces and new infrastructure. The Alliance could deploy troops temporarily for the purpose of exercises or for peacekeeping operations, but that was it. A clear statement along these lines in the Charter was a *sine quo non* for Moscow.

The Secretary responded that NATO's policies were not negotiable with non-NATO countries, especially Russia. Washington would not agree to anything that would make new members second-class allies. Primakov countered that NATO already had allies who had accepted restrictions imposed on them, such as Germany. In addition, Denmark and Norway had voluntarily agreed to restrictions. This showed, he insisted, that NATO could, in fact, agree to special conditions for certain members. "Look Yevgeny," Albright responded, "Neither the President nor I are going to negotiate over the heads of the Central Europeans about their security arrangements. That's been done in the past and it is not going to happen again, not on my watch."

When Primakov continued to push the Russian position that Washington had previously rejected, Albright cut him off and said: "We've said 'no' to all this stuff before, and if you've come here simply to hear me say 'no' again, I'm happy to do so."

"Madeleine," Primakov countered, "why aren't you willing to meet us halfway."

"Halfway? Halfway," Albright responded, "You keep going back to square one!" Primakov, in response, threw up his hands and said: "I don't really think we can have an agreement."

"Well," Albright snapped, "so be it." Frankly, she continued, the U.S. could live without the Charter. NATO enlargement would move forward on its own. The U.S. supported a Charter because it believed such a document could provide a roadmap for improving NATO-Russia relations. But if Primakov insisted on trying to negotiate NATO policy, it would not work.[51]

Talbott decided it was time for another private chat with Mamedov. While Secretary Albright and Primakov exchanged rather forced closing courtesies, he pulled Mamedov aside to invite him to his house for an off-line review of the bidding. The next morning Mamedov sat down with Talbott and Berger in Talbott's home. Mamedov said that Primakov and he had put their heads together and came up with an outline for a joint statement for Helsinki. The Russian side, he insisted, had finally done what Talbott had been urging them to do—to work with what Washington was offering to construct an attractive package that would address Moscow's concerns but would not cross the United States' "red lines." Looking at the draft, Talbott saw that it was an improvement. Yet it still took all the things the Russians wanted while ignoring several issues high on the U.S. wish list. Above all, it allowed Russia the option of continuing a war of words on enlargement to try to squeeze out additional concessions down the line.

Berger and Talbott therefore told Mamedov that there had to be an agreement in advance that the harsh Russian rhetoric against enlargement would cease, starting with Yeltsin at Helsinki. They also underscored that the agreements on the military aspects of enlargement would have to be codified at the official CFE negotiations that included the Central and East Europeans. Mamedov told Talbott that Albright and Primakov would have to finalize the understanding that evening over dinner and that the Russian Foreign Minister would, on his return to Moscow, give Yeltsin an assessment of what it would take to get a NATO-Russia charter before Madrid. Yeltsin would then have to decide whether it was worth the price.[52]

That evening, Albright and Primakov, along with Mamedov and Ambassadors Jim Collins and Yuri Vorontsov, arrived at the Talbott residence where Talbott's wife, Brooke Shearer, had prepared a wonderful Italian meal. Albright explained that she would have invited the group to her Georgetown townhouse, but that it was being exterminated for termites. "Aha!" said Primakov. "Like NATO, your exterminators are pre-positioning infrastructure on new territory!" "Just as NATO did long ago in Norway," said Albright. And so it continued: a new metaphor was born. Madeleine interpreted Primakov's attempt to reopen issues the U.S. regarded as non-negotiable as the result of "termites" in the Russian bureaucracy bent on preventing a NATO-Russia deal before Madrid. In response, Primakov proposed a "joint ministerial extermination of all termites on both sides." The two Foreign Ministers went back and forth over the joint statement all evening. Primakov kept gnawing away on core issues which required Albright to review, with mounting impatience, U.S. objections and counter-proposals. But by the end of the evening they had agreed on way ahead.[53]

The next morning the Russian side returned to the official negotiating table with new flexibility. Following a three-hour drafting session between Albright, Talbott, and Primakov, a joint text was agreed upon. Later that day, Primakov met with President Clinton to review the understanding that had been reached. Clinton told the Russian Foreign Minster that the text was acceptable but that Moscow needed to tone down the anti-NATO rhetoric lest it undercut and devalue the impact of a possible NATO-Russia agreement. "If the strategy is to set up the notion that Russia has achieved something meaningful and important to alleviate Russia's concerns, then that's okay. I don't mind getting beaten up in the meanwhile. But after Helsinki, the tone and rhetoric has to change to create the impression of partnership, as in Bosnia." Primakov agreed.[54]

Talbott took it as a good sign that Primakov had not raised the issue of the Baltic states in meetings with Clinton and Albright. In the car on the way to Andrews Air Force base for his flight home, however, the Russian Foreign Minister told him that Yeltsin was going to suggest an agreement to exclude the Baltic states from NATO enlargement. Talbott warned Primakov that such a proposal ran the risk of ruining the summit. But Primakov responded angrily that the two sides then had a real problem. "There are some things that can't be fixed at our level. They're in the hands of the gods—or at least of Presidents."[55]

4. BREAKTHROUGH AT HELSINKI

When Presidents Clinton and Yeltsin sat down in Helsinki on March 21, they had met nearly a dozen times. They liked each other and had an open and frank relationship. In the opening plenary session at the Finnish President's residence, both Clinton and Yeltsin launched their discussions by going straight to the most difficult issue—European security and NATO enlargement. Yeltsin said: "Our position has not changed. It remains a mistake for NATO to move eastward. But I need to take steps to alleviate the negative consequences of this for Russia. I am prepared to enter into an agreement with NATO, not because I want to but because it's a step I'm compelled to take. There is no other solution for today."

The one condition he had, the Russian President continued, was that the U.S. promise that NATO would not bring "former Soviet republics" into the Alliance. It was a clear reference to the Baltic states. He proposed that they reach "an oral agreement—we won't write it down" to that effect. "This would be a gentlemen's agreement that won't be made public," he underscored. Clinton initially sidestepped Yeltsin's suggestion and instead sketched out his vision of a grand signing ceremony, somewhere in Europe, before Madrid, at which a NATO-Russia Charter would be concluded that would allow Clinton and Yeltsin to "say to the world that there really is a new NATO and there really is a new Russia."

"I agree," said Yeltsin.

"Good," the President continued. "But I want you to imagine something else. If we were to agree that no members of the former Soviet Union could enter NATO, that would be a bad thing for our attempt to build a new NATO. It would also be a bad thing for your attempt to build a new Russia. I am not naïve. I understand you have an interest in who gets into NATO and when. We need to make sure that all these are subjects that we can consult about as we move forward. 'Consult' means making sure that we're aware of your concerns, and that you understand our decisions and our positions and our thinking. But consider what a terrible message it would send if we were to make the kind of supposedly secret deal you're suggesting. First, there are no secrets in this world. Second, the message would be, 'We're still organized against Russia—but there's a line across which we won't go.' In other words, instead of creating a new NATO that helps move toward an integrated, undivided Europe, we'd have a larger NATO that's just sitting there waiting for Russia to do something bad."

"Here's why what you are proposing is bad for Russia," the U.S. President argued. "Russia would be saying, 'We've still got an empire, but it just can't reach as far West as it used to when we had the Warsaw Pact.' Second, it would create exactly the fear among the Baltics and others that you're trying to allay and that you're denying is justified. A third point: the deal you're suggesting would totally undermine the Partnership for Peace. It would terrify the smaller countries that are now working well with you and with us in Bosnia and elsewhere."

Pointing out that they were meeting in Helsinki, the U.S. President recalled what Finnish President Martti Ahtisaari had told him the previous evening—that the U.S. was doing the right thing by ensuring that NATO's door remained open in the future. "He said that Finland hasn't asked to be in NATO, and as long as no one tells Finland it can't join NATO, then Finland will be able to maintain the independence of its position and work with PFP and with the U.S. and with Russia."

"Under no circumstances," the U.S. President continued, "should we send a signal out of this meeting that it's the same old European politics of the cold war and we're just moving the lines around a bit." Yeltsin's proposed gentlemen's agreement, President Clinton insisted, "would make us both look weaker, not stronger. If we made the agreement you're describing it would be a terrible mistake. It would cause big problems for me and big problems for you. It would accentuate the diminishment of your power from Warsaw Pact times. The charter will be a much more powerful and positive message. It's without precedent, it's comprehensive, and it's forward looking, and it's hopeful. It will move us toward a situation that's good for both of us."

"Bill," Yeltsin conceded, "I agree with what you've said. But look at it from my standpoint. Whatever you do on your side, we intend to submit this document to the Duma for ratification. But the Duma will take two decisions. First, it will ratify the document, then it will attach a condition that if NATO takes in even one of the former republics of the Soviet Union, Russia will pull out of the agreement and consider it null and void. That will happen unless you tell me today, one-on-one—without even our closest aides present—that you won't take new republics in the near future. I need to hear that. I understand that maybe in ten years or something, the situation might change, but not now. Maybe there will be a later evolution. But I need assurances from you that it won't happen in the nearest future."

"Come on, Boris," said Clinton, "if I went into a closet with you and told you what you wanted to hear, the Congress would find out and pass a resolution in-validating the NATO-Russia charter. Frankly, I'd rather that the Duma pass a resolution conditioning its adherence on this point. I'd hate for the Duma to do that, but it would be better than what you're suggesting. I just can't do it. A pri-vate commitment would be the same as a public one. I've told you—and you have talked to Helmut and Jacques, you know their thinking—that no one is talking about a massive, all-out, accelerated expansion. We've already demon-strated our ability to move deliberately, openly. But I can't make commitments on behalf of NATO and I'm not going to be in the position myself of vetoing any country's eligibility for NATO, much less letting you or anyone else do so. I'm prepared to work with you on the consultative mechanism so as to make sure that we take account of Russia's concerns as we move forward."

Clinton also pointed to Bosnia as an example that was important for the fu-ture. "That's the worst conflict in Europe since World War II. The Europeans couldn't solve it. The U.S. was finally able to take an initiative there, and Russia came in and helped. It took me years to build support. What if, sometime in the future, another Bosnia arises? If the NATO-Russia understanding is done right, then Russia would be a key part of the solution, working with the U.S. and Europe. But if we create a smaller version of the larger standoff that existed dur-ing the cold war, there won't be the needed trust. This process of integrating Europe is going to take years. We need to build up the OSCE. It's not going to happen overnight. But if we make a statement now that narrows our options in the future, it will be harder to do the other good things we want to do."

"I know what a terrible problem this is for you," he continued, "but I can't make the specific commitment you are asking for. It would violate the whole spirit of NATO. I've always tried to build you up and never undermine you. I'd feel I had dishonored my commitment to the alliance, to the states that want to join NATO, and to the vision that I think you and I share of an undivided Europe with Russia as a major part of it."

Yeltsin responded: "Okay, but let's agree—one-on-one—that the former Soviet republics won't be in the first waves. Bill, please understand what I'm dealing with there: I'm flying back to Russia with a very heavy burden on my shoulders. It will be difficult for me to go home and not seem to have accepted NATO enlargement. Very difficult."

The President replied: "Look, Boris, you're forcing an issue that doesn't need to drive a wedge between us here. NATO operates by consensus. If you decided to be in NATO, you'd probably want all the other countries to be eligible too. But that issue doesn't arise. We need to find a solution to a short-term problem that doesn't create a long-term problem by keeping alive old stereotypes about you and your intentions. If we do the wrong thing, it will erode our own position about the kind of Europe we want. I hear your message. But your suggestion is not the way to do it. I don't want to do anything that makes it seem like the old Russia and the old NATO." At this point, Yeltsin appeared to simply give up. "Well," he said, "I tried."[56]

Later that afternoon, Clinton and Yeltsin reviewed what they would say to the press. Clinton suggested both leaders avoid using the word "concessions." "I don't want people to score this as you versus me; I don't want them to say that Boris won on three issues and Bill won on two." NSC Adviser Sandy Berger then played the role of the journalist. He asked the two Presidents the tough questions. One of them was: "Have you made any secret deals here in Helsinki?" With a smile Yeltsin replied: "My answer will be: 'We wanted one but were rejected.'" As the two Presidents got up to face the press corps, Yeltsin grabbed Clinton by the hand and said; "Bill, we have done powerful work."[57]

At the press conference later that afternoon, Clinton led off by explaining why he supported NATO enlargement. "NATO is the bedrock of Europe's security and the tie that binds the United States to that security." That is why, he continued, the U.S. had led the way in adapting and enlarging the Alliance for the post–Cold War era. "We are building a new NATO just as the Russian people are building a new Russia," he added. "I am determined that Russia will become a respected partner with NATO in making the future for all of Europe peaceful and secure."

While he and Yeltsin did not agree on NATO enlargement, there was an overriding agreement between the two Presidents: "We agreed that the relationship between the United States and Russia and the benefits of cooperation between NATO and Russia are too important to be jeopardized," Clinton said. In response to a question, Yeltsin added: "We believe that the eastward expansion of NATO is a mistake and a serious one at that. Nevertheless, in order to minimize the negative consequences for Russia, we decided to sign an agreement with NATO, a NATO-Russian agreement."[58]

In the aftermath of Helsinki, Russian officials put on a brave face. Foreign Minister Primakov called the summit a "breakthrough" and argued that President Yeltsin had successfully defended Russian interests.[59] In private they were more reserved. As Yeltsin told Finnish President Ahtisaari, he had tried to get Clinton to agree to no NATO expansion to former parts of the Soviet Union. "But," the Russian President admitted, "I failed."[60] For President Clinton and his national security team, it was *the* breakthrough. It was as if Yeltsin's opposition to NATO enlargement had evaporated in front of their eyes. Following his visit to Moscow shortly after the Helsinki summit, NATO Military Committee Chairman Klaus Naumann reported to the North Atlantic Council in Brussels that his Russian military counterparts, for the first time, seemed resigned to the fact that enlargement would take place.[61]

5. PLAYING BOTH SIDES OF THE CHESSBOARD

At Helsinki, Yeltsin had finally accepted that NATO enlargement was going to happen and had decided to seek a NATO-Russia understanding to protect Moscow's interests. He had also agreed that NATO and Russia should sign a document *prior* to Madrid at a separate summit involving heads-of-state. The best time to hold such an event would be in late May, when President Clinton was already scheduled to be in Europe. The tentative date was penciled in for May 27. Out of deference to Chirac, the site envisioned was Paris. Both sides had two months to finalize a NATO-Russia charter.

But Clinton and Yeltsin had not agreed on the content of a charter at Helsinki. Many of the differences that still separated NATO and Russia had merely been papered over. In the weeks following the summit Russian diplomats seemed reticent to engage in resolving these outstanding issues. John Tefft, the U.S. chargé d'affaires in Moscow, reported that while Yeltsin had committed in principle to complete an understanding by the late May deadline, the foreign policy bureaucracy lacked the authority to make the compromises required to seal the pact. It was also not clear if Moscow understood how far it still had to move in order to meet NATO's bottom line, or if Yeltsin could overcome Duma opposition to any agreement that NATO would find acceptable.[62]

It was yet another example of how dysfunctional the Russian national security bureaucracy was as well as the antipathy toward closing any deal with NATO that sanctioned enlargement. If a deal was going to be reached, the final push would have to come from the U.S. and NATO. On the plane to Moscow for U.S.-Russia consultations in late April, Talbott said to me: "You have to think in terms of playing a game of chess—but one where you are playing both sides of the chessboard. After you make your move, you run over to the other side of the board and tell your opponent who is really your partner in this game: 'Move your piece there.' That's the only way we are going to get this thing done." In the hectic days that lay ahead, Talbott was the U.S. official coordinating NATO policy with Solana and his counterparts in allied capitals as well as working with Primakov and Mamedov to steer the Russian side toward possible common ground.

Solana and Primakov held another round of consultations in Moscow on April 15, 1997. Afterwards the Secretary General reported to the NAC that his just-concluded talks with the Russian Foreign Minister had been the toughest so far. While the first four sections of the draft charter were, in his words, "90% complete," the two sides remained deadlocked on the core issues in Section V.[63] In parallel, Primakov had sent Mamedov to Washington where he handed over a Russian draft charter to Talbott. It was unacceptable as it crossed several of our "red lines." It would have created second-class NATO allies in Central and Eastern Europe, and prevented further enlargement at a later date. Buried in the technical details of CFE adaptation was Russia's attempt to freeze NATO deployments, numerically and geographically. Moscow was making one last effort to limit any extension of the Alliance's military reach eastward.

It demonstrated again the gap in our respective approaches. The U.S. and NATO viewed enlargement as part of an overall European integration strategy that would transcend the old Cold War bloc-to-bloc divide that projected stability eastward. We had said that NATO and Russia were no longer enemies, but partners. While for us a NATO-Russia agreement was the basis for long-term cooperation, Moscow never made the leap to this new integrationist thinking. It continued to think in terms of blocs and spheres of influence. While Moscow, too, said that NATO was no longer an enemy, such proposals suggested that Russia still viewed NATO enlargement as the extension of a hostile bloc to their borders. We had not bridged this gap and time was getting short.

Talbott now told Mamedov that they were getting nowhere with the Russian draft and that the gains of Helsinki were in danger of unraveling. If Moscow's bottom line was a desire to show that an enlarged NATO would not pose a greater military threat to Russia than the Cold War, then Washington disagreed with the philosophy but could nonetheless think about ways in which this could be accommodated. But Moscow was going about it in a way that was forcing Washington to say no. Mamedov asked Talbott to provide him with an alternative. Talbott, in turn, asked Undersecretary for Arms Control and International Security Affairs Lynn Davis to draft a short paper showing how the current NATO-CFE proposal could produce an outcome where the overall level of forces in an enlarged NATO was not greater than the old NATO collective ceiling. This had to be done in a way that did not cross any of NATO's "red lines."

During a walk in Washington, D.C.'s Rock Creek Park later that day with Talbott and his dog, Mamedov told the Deputy Secretary they might be getting somewhere and that he would try to sell the paper back home in Moscow. The two men soon dubbed the document "the walk with the dog" paper—a play on the "walk in the woods" compromise that the U.S. diplomat Paul Nitze and his Russian counterpart Yuli Kvitsinski had developed to break the impasse on Intermediate-range Nuclear Forces (INF) talks in the mid-1980s, which Talbott had written about as a journalist.[64]

Talbott and Albright were scheduled to travel to Moscow at the end of the month. The trip was set up so that Talbott and his team would get to Moscow first and try to make progress, with Albright arriving a day later to try to clinch a deal. A phone call with President Yeltsin had also been arranged so that Albright could appeal to the Russian President to give Primakov the flexibility needed to close the gap on the outstanding issues. In preparing for the trip, we created three scenarios for what Albright might encounter in Moscow. Three factors were singled out as being crucial. The first was how committed Yeltsin and Primakov were to getting a deal. The second was what kind of deal and whether Moscow, at the end of the day, would accept a deal which met NATO's criteria but would be difficult to defend in the Duma, or whether it would insist on something that might be acceptable to the Duma but was unacceptable to the allies. And the third factor was whether Moscow now believed that, absent a Paris deal, the allies would proceed with enlargement at Madrid.

The three scenarios were called: "The Good, the Bad and the Ugly."[65] The first scenario, The Good, assumed that after difficult talks and Yeltsin's interventions the two sides would manage to resolve all their differences before Paris. The second scenario, The Bad, assumed that Primakov would stonewall, receive instructions from Yeltsin to hold firm, and the two sides would not reach agreement but nonetheless work out a damage limitation strategy for managing Madrid without a NATO-Russia agreement. The third scenario, The Ugly, assumed that the two sides could not agree, but that negotiations would go down to the wire, severely testing Alliance cohesion, and maybe even require the personal involvement of head-of-states at Paris. Talbott added a fourth scenario that he called "Uglier Still," in which the Russian side, after failing to reach agreement, would launch a campaign to blame the breakdown on the U.S. to shake up the allies and pressure us to make more concessions.

The U.S. delegation arrived in Moscow on a warm spring day. We made little progress during the first day of talks. While Primakov had shown a clear willingness to engage, all of his proposals were variations on the some theme — a desire to impose a collective limit on the forces of an enlarged NATO, place restrictions on any permanently stationed forces, and limit NATO infrastructure on the territory of new members. The Russian Foreign Minister was, in effect, trying to close the loopholes the Alliance had deliberately left itself in its unilateral statements of restraint on conventional forces. As the U.S. delegation broke up into working groups with their Russian counterparts for a final round of talks, I accompanied Talbott back to his hotel to help draft a note to Albright who was departing from Andrews Air Force Base. We agreed that, based on the results thus far, we were headed toward "The Ugly" scenario.[66] The Russian proposal for a collective ceiling, Talbott said, was like a vampire. Every time the U.S. side thought they had killed it, it rose again. He joked that we had to drive a stake though its heart once and for all.

Over dinner that evening with Mamedov, however, Talbott made progress in sketching out a fallback compromise the Russian side might be able to live with. He had suggested to Mamedov that the two sides, in the interest of getting an agreement, scale back their ambitions and instead shoot for a more general and limited "framework argument" on CFE. Mamedov was noncommittal but had agreed to take this idea back to Primakov. Talbott sent Albright a midnight update from Moscow with better news. He sensed that while he had made little concrete progress, the Russians were increasingly "in a bind between Yeltsin's publicly stated desire to go to Paris and their wish to put every conceivable block on enlargement, permanent stationing, infrastructure, etc." He laid out two alternative scenarios for the Secretary: either Primakov would agree to a fairly general "element of a framework" statement that could be first incorporated into a NATO-Russia agreement and then finalized in CFE talks in Vienna, or he would hold firm on Moscow's desiderata even if that jeopardized a NATO-Russia summit.[67]

Albright arrived in Moscow the next morning, May 1, descending the steps of her Air Force plane wearing a red Stetson. Although a small crowd of anti-NATO demonstrators was gathered in front of our hotel when she arrived, most of Moscow was out in the countryside enjoying the national holiday. It was another reminder of how the Russian elite were preoccupied with the NATO enlargement issue but average Russians were not. Albright and Primakov spent a long session going around and around the same issues that had proven so difficult the previous day, but did not reach a breakthrough.[68] Albright placed her prearranged phone call to Yeltsin, who was in his countryside dacha. He told Albright how eager he was to go to Paris and how much he was counting on his friends, including President Clinton, to make sure the meeting went well. As the day unfolded, it was increasingly clear to the U.S. side that Primakov was under instructions from Yeltsin to get a deal.

That evening Primakov invited Albright and part of the U.S. delegation to dinner at his apartment, an unusual gesture of friendship and hospitality for a senior Russian official. After dinner, Albright and Talbott sat down with Primakov for what was supposed to be the final negotiating session. Primakov said that if the U.S. did not yield on the remaining points, he would "become a pessimist" about getting a deal in time for a NATO-Russia summit in Paris. "Me too," said Madeleine, "and in that case, we'll just have to skip Paris and keep negotiating on a charter after Madrid." Primakov sighed heavily and suggested that they hold one more unscheduled meeting the following morning prior to her departure.[69]

During the night, the U.S. and Russian sides worked on compromise language along the lines of an "elements of a framework" that Talbott and Mamedov had discussed. The next morning Albright and Primakov held two hours of grueling final discussions in the Russian Foreign Ministry. Finally, Albright, accompanied by Talbott and Lynn Davis, retreated into Primakov's private office. Primakov was accompanied by Colonel-General Leonid Ivashov, well known in the U.S. as the most publicly outspoken anti-NATO figure in the

Russian Ministry of Defense. Albright and Primakov finally agreed on a text. When Ivashov criticized it, Primakov overruled him—and everyone dashed off to the airport.[70] That evening, Albright wrote the President: "If the partial understanding I reached with Primakov holds, it means we are entering the endgame in the negotiation of a charter." But the clock was ticking. Albright noted that they probably needed to decide by May 12 whether or not Paris was on.[71]

Solana was scheduled to meet with Primakov on May 6 in Luxembourg. At NATO headquarters, diplomats poured over the Albright-Primakov language on CFE and eventually blessed it with minor changes.[72] At a meeting on May 6, prior to Solana's departure for Luxembourg, the NAC authorized Solana to explore compromise language on the outstanding issues: the name of the document, the chairmanship, as well as to explore the possibility of NATO adding additional language further clarifying its position on both nuclear and conventional forces.[73] To support Solana on the military issues, U.S. Air Force Lieutenant General Keogh was added to the Secretary General's team. In parallel, Talbott sent Mamedov a letter underscoring the need for any restriction on forces in Central Europe to be reciprocal and not single out new NATO members, and the need to reach agreement soon if Paris was to happen.[74]

Despite four-and-one-half hours of talks, Solana and Primakov could not close the deal. While dropping its insistence on the sufficiency rule, the Russian side still insisted on limiting the temporary deployment of allied forces on the soil of new members to one brigade for peacekeeping purposes and pushed for constraints on infrastructure. Solana again rejected the Russian proposals and reiterated that the fact that NATO was not forward deploying troops meant that it would have to maintain adequate infrastructure for reinforcements. At the end of their meeting, Primakov handed over a new Russian draft for Section V of the draft charter. It was still a long way from being acceptable to the Alliance.[75] There was now less than a week to go before the Alliance's internal deadline expired. Solana and Primakov agreed to one last session in Moscow on May 13.

NATO officials scrambled to prepare for this last session and to come up with final steps that could still produce an agreement.[76] In addition to the official guidance sent to Ambassador Hunter, Talbott wrote Solana a letter with some suggestions on how to close the deal. He suggested offering interpretive language on both nuclear and conventional forces that would be an extrapolation of the Alliance's previous statements, as opposed to new statements, on these issues. The language clarified that NATO's three nuclear no's encompassed nuclear storage facilities, thereby addressing a Russian demand. He told Solana that Washington was prepared to live with limits on deployments on the territory of new members under certain conditions. If these could be met, Washington was also prepared to add a statement that the Alliance intended to build infrastructure commensurate with the military tasks outlined in the March 14 statement if Moscow dropped further demands along these lines.

In parallel, Talbott tried to play the other side of the chessboard as well. He wrote Mamedov on May 8 to suggest what Moscow needed to do to close the deal. He told Mamedov that the draft Primakov had given Solana was a step backward, not forward. He also told the Deputy Russian Foreign Minster where Solana was going to be able to show flexibility and where he was not—hinting at the kinds of compromises NATO was going to table but avoiding the details.[77] When U.S. chargé d'affaires John Tefft delivered Talbott's letter the next morning, the Deputy Foreign Minister asked him to pass a message back to the Deputy Secretary on what he called the "really, truly honestly Russian bottom line." The most important and sensitive issue for the Russian side was the nuclear issue, he told Tefft. Moscow also needed some flexibility on the language on translating the CFE flank agreement to a new adapted treaty. On the question of infrastructure, Mamedov said that Primakov had come up with a possible solution but refused to divulge the details.[78]

Talbott had also promised Solana he would send NSC Senior Director Sandy Vershbow to Moscow to provide on-the-spot assistance for the final round of talks. The Russian side was delighted. Vershbow arrived in Moscow before the Secretary General and was immediately whisked off to see Primakov. His mission was to float some of the proposals Solana was bringing on nuclear and conventional forces to see if Primakov would bite. As Solana's motorcade was approaching the Foreign Ministry, Vershbow snuck out by a side exit and called Solana in his car to give him a readout of what Primakov appeared receptive to. He remained in cell phone contact with Solana that evening through the Secretary General's chief of staff, Jorge Domecq, and then joined up with the Secretary General at 1:00 A.M. to plot strategy for the next morning. Vershbow then phoned Eric Edelman, Talbott's chief-of-staff in Washington, for final instructions.[79]

The next morning the same scene was repeated. Vershbow privately met with Primakov at the Russian Foreign Ministry guest house. He again left by a side door as Solana arrived for the final round of talks to avoid being seen by the cameras—and again called the Secretary General on his cell phone to provide him with some last-minute tips on how to close on the final issues. Several hours later Solana and Primakov had an agreed text. Solana rushed back to Brussels to present the agreed text to the North Atlantic Council for its final blessing.

Later that day in Washington, President Clinton went before the press in the Rose Garden to state, "Today in Moscow, we have taken a historic step closer to a peaceful, undivided democratic Europe for the first time in history." In response to a reporter's question on the details of the agreement and why it was important, the President pointed to the bigger picture and urged his audience to look at the agreement in a new light. "Keep in mind," he said, "that we are all

trying to change the . . . whole pattern of thought that has dominated the international politics of Europe for 50 years."[80] In a background briefing later that
day, National Security Advisor Sandy Berger called the Founding Act "a win-
win-win agreement" for the U.S., Europe and Russia—and proof that "a new
NATO would work with a new Russia to build a new Europe."[81]

On May 19 President Yeltsin wrote Clinton to congratulate him "on our
common victory." The Paris agreement would not have been possible without
Helsinki and the close relationship the two men had, he wrote. "Now," he continued, "we must demonstrate to everybody, both to the supporters of the agreement and its opponents, that it works."[82] Two weeks later, NATO leaders and
Russian President Yeltsin gathered in Paris to sign the Founding Act. Meeting
with Albright over dinner the evening before the signing, Primakov told her that
negotiating the Founding Act was one of "the biggest achievements of my political life." They also compared notes to see which of them had received more
criticism at home for the document.[83]

The next day, at an ornate ceremony in the Elysée Palace, NATO leaders got
up one by one to praise Boris Yeltsin as a democrat and a reformer willing to
turn the page and start a new relationship with NATO. When it came to his
turn, President Clinton said: "I know that some still see NATO through the
prism of the Cold War," and that critics viewed the Alliance's decision to enlarge as creating "a Europe still divided, only differently divided." He continued,
"I ask them to look again. For this new NATO will work with Russia, not against
it." The U.S. and its allies had created a new NATO-Russia relationship, "because we are determined to create a future in which European security is not a
zero-sum game—where NATO's gain is Russia's loss, and Russia's strength is
our alliance's weakness. That is old thinking, these are new times."[84]

All eyes were on Boris Yeltsin. When it came time for him to sign the
Founding Act on behalf of the Russian Federation, he wrote his signature with a
flourish and gave Solana a bear hug and a kiss on both cheeks. In his remarks,
Yeltsin stated that this document would "protect Europe and the world from a
new confrontation and will become the foundation for a new, fair and stable
partnership." Russia still opposed enlargement, the Russian President reminded
his audience. But he added that he wanted to "pay tribute to the readiness ex-
hibited by NATO countries, despite these difficulties, to reach an agreement
with Russia" that took Moscow's interests into account.[85]

Yeltsin then looked around the room. Everyone sensed he was about to im-
provise. Journalists were waiting expectantly for another Yeltsin one-liner that
would make the nightly news. The Russian President announced: "Today, after
having signed the document, I am going to make the following decision: everything that is aimed at countries present here, all of those weapons are going to
have their warheads removed." No one knew what it meant. Albright and
Primakov, who were sitting next to each other, were talking intensely, but the

Russian Foreign Minister did not seem to have a clue either. On this slightly surreal note, the NATO-Russia Founding Act was launched.

Meeting with Clinton later that day, Yeltsin repeated: "Today I am very glad and satisfied with the results. There are opponents. I have some, and Primakov does as well. But still, we managed to find a solution. I said I would never use the word 'compromise'—what we reached is a balanced result and that is very helpful. It is important for NATO and Russia and the world." NATO will enlarge, Yeltsin continued, "and everyone knows it. My position remains that bit-by-bit we will overcome our differences." He pointed to Albright and Primakov and described them as "allies" who had done "immense work" to complete the document.[86]

Book VII

HEAD-TO-HEAD AT MADRID

The ink was barely dry on the NATO-Russia Founding Act when the Clinton Administration faced its next fight—this time with some of our closest allies. The issue was which Central and East European candidate countries would receive invitations to join NATO at the Madrid summit. Related, and equally contentious, was how firm a commitment the Alliance would make to continue the enlargement process in the future. The Czech Republic, Hungary, and Poland were the leading candidates to receive invitations. Slovenia and Romania were, for different reasons, longer shots but each had launched its own aggressive lobbying effort to make the Alliance's short list. Prime Minister Vladimir Meciar's strong-arm authoritarian tactics had taken Slovakia out of the running.[1] No one in NATO was seriously pushing to include the Baltic states for the first round of enlargement, but disagreements over how to address their future prospects added to the mix of issues dividing the allies.

Having led the Alliance enlargement debate for nearly three years, the United States now found itself outflanked by France, Italy, and other allies who argued that a larger round of enlargement including Romania and Slovenia would provide better geopolitical balance and help stabilize southeastern Europe. Washington opposed this larger group on the grounds that they were not yet qualified, that their inclusion would damage the prospects for further enlargement down the road, especially to the Baltic states, and that a larger group could endanger prospects for enlargement's ratification in the U.S. Senate. The stage was set for a head-to-head confrontation between Washington and Paris and one of the most contentious summits in NATO's history.

1. SINTRA

Two days after the signing the Founding Act in Paris, NATO Foreign Ministers met in the Portuguese coastal town of Sintra for their annual spring meeting. The agenda included the first official discussions on which countries should be invited to join NATO at Madrid. Earlier in the year Solana had asked all allies to avoid public debate on this issue and refrain from campaigning on behalf of their favorite candidate countries. Instead, he proposed quietly starting discussion of this issue at Sintra at the Foreign Ministers lunch that was traditionally set aside for informal, candid discussion of sensitive issues. Solana had also scheduled so-called "confessionals" to sound out allies regarding their views on who should be invited. This Catholic tradition had been imported into trans-Atlantic diplomacy from the EU as a way to privately ascertain the true bottom line of member countries before coming up with a common position acceptable to all.[2]

Behind this was the desire to minimize what Albright referred to as the "beauty contest" syndrome—i.e., a situation where candidate countries spent nearly all of their time competing and lobbying Western allies as opposed to doing their own homework to prepare for membership. NATO had set two overall benchmarks to guide its decisionmaking on taking in new members—performance and the Alliance's overall strategic interests. Yet both of these benchmarks had been kept quite general. At the end of the day this was going to be a political decision—and everyone knew it.

Avoiding lobbying for candidate countries was one of those ideas that was great in theory but impossible to sustain in practice. The stakes were simply too high. Candidate countries felt they could leave no stone unturned in showcasing their accomplishments. Indeed, the shakier the record, the more these countries tried to compensate with an intense lobbying campaign. Allies, too, found it all but impossible not to champion their favorite candidate countries, especially if this played well domestically. American and European commercial firms were also often in intense competition in the region. Many were trying to benefit by suggesting that if a business deal were closed with them, it might help a candidate country's chances of making the short list at Madrid—irrespective of whether it was actually true.

The U.S. was in a unique position in this debate. Although NATO decisions were made by consensus, the reality was that the U.S. vote counted for more than any other ally. NATO enlargement was seen as an American project. The Clinton Administration had led the process and done most of the heavy lifting diplomatically. U.S. military might was the backbone of new Article 5 security guarantees to Central and Eastern Europe. But for the previous three years, Washington had strictly hewed to the line that no decisions on the "who" had been made and refused to tip its hand on which candidate countries it preferred. Indeed, National Security Advisor Tony Lake had forbidden any official meetings on the "who" issue in the Administration in the course of 1996 for fear that the results would leak and launch an early debate with the allies.

Washington still viewed overall European support for enlargement as tepid. Several allies had privately floated proposals to Washington suggesting limiting the first round to only one or two countries—e.g., Poland or the Czech Republic, or both. It was an attempt to find a way to fulfill the Alliance's commitment to enlarge while doing as little as possible. Support for future rounds of enlargement seemed weak as well. When Washington tried to get a simple statement at the December 1996 Foreign Ministers Ministerial that enlargement would not be a one-time deal, the allies balked. Against this background, it was perhaps not surprising that Washington saw itself as leading the pack in defining the scope of enlargement.[3]

In the spring of 1997, however, an important shift in European thinking took place. A number of European allies who had previously been lukewarm about enlargement now suddenly came out in support of a larger first round than the U.S. was comfortable with. Leading this shift was France, which now stepped up its advocacy of Romania's candidacy. In the fall of 1996 Paris had started to raise the issue of including Romania in a first round of NATO enlargement. French officials insisted that Romania was considered to be a Francophone country that Paris felt historically close to, and that Paris could not accept Hungary without Romania. While they did not say so explicitly, U.S. officials sensed that Paris also wanted to bring in a country it considered more pro-French to balance the pro-American sentiments of a country like Poland.

Romania's prospect for NATO membership had been considerably strengthened by the election of a new pro-reform government led by President Emil Constantinescu in November 1996. Domestically, he was committed to making a clear break with the country's nationalist and xenophobic past and to mending fences with the Hungarian minority. In foreign policy terms, he was pro-Western and determined to anchor his country to the West as well. Constantinescu was an impressive figure and these were admirable goals, but Bucharest's economic backwardness left it with little chance of being included in the first round of EU enlargement. The exclusion of Romania from both the EU and NATO, Constantinescu now argued, could be a politically disastrous double whammy that would undercut pro-reform forces and strengthen the nationalists and communists.[4] Since the EU was beyond reach, it was imperative that Bucharest be included in NATO enlargement, Romanian officials insisted. When Chirac paid a state visit to Bucharest later that month, he publicly pledged to "do everything possible" to include Romania in NATO's first round of enlargement.[5]

French support for Romania was reinforced by the more general sense, shared by other Southern European NATO members, that the Alliance was paying insufficient attention to the southern region. Conflict in the Balkans had underscored how potential conflict in post–Cold War Europe had shifted southward. NATO enlargement to the Visegrad countries, they contended, looked like a U.S.-German project to consolidate stability in an already fairly stable Central Europe. Therefore, NATO enlargement had to be more "balanced," they insisted. The fact that the candidate countries in southeastern Europe were often less developed and ready for membership was secondary to the broader need to stabilize Europe's southern flank.

The signing of the NATO-Russia Founding Act also reinforced this shift in European views. By removing the specter of a confrontation with Moscow over enlargement it emboldened allies that had previously been cautious to come out in favor of a bigger enlargement round. Some allies saw it as a window of opportunity of Russian acquiescence, the duration of which was uncertain. In private several allies urged Washington to take in as many countries as possible. Who knew, they asked, whether or when there would be another chance to enlarge. A number of southern European allies wanted to keep the candidacies of Slovenia or Romania as separate as possible from the Baltic issue. Russian opposition to the Baltic states joining NATO was well known. And our southern European allies did not want decisions regarding their favorite candidates linked or held hostage to that difficult issue.

Italy joined France in pushing for a larger first round and now stepped forward as the leading supporter of Slovenia. Even close U.S. allies such as Turkey went from being skeptics of enlargement to supporters of a large first round. Reports started to trickle in to Washington that France and Italy had set up a senior level working group in their respective Foreign Ministries to coordinate their respective lobbying efforts in favor of Romania and Slovenia. Several allies informed us about various offers Paris had floated in trying to enlist their support. Solana's plea for allies to avoid publicly lobbying for their favorite candidates was not holding.

All eyes were on Washington for clues on how American thinking was developing. In late March, Ambassador Hunter sent in a cable assessing the line-up in the Alliance. "Debate within the Alliance ranges between three and five countries to be invited to join at Madrid," he wrote. "Poland and the Czech Republic are favored by all allies; Hungary is also, with the qualification of at least one ally." Slovenia, he continued, "has the active backing of Italy and would likely be accepted if the U.S. wants. Romania is the most debated. France actively supports it, Turkey backs it as well (as well as Bulgaria), and Italy, Spain and Portugal support it to please France, but are not wedded to this candidacy. The U.S. attitude—whether we are prepared to make the essential strategic commitments—will be key to both Slovenia and Romania."[6]

But the U.S. government was reaching a conclusion different from that of France and other European nations. One of the first tasks Albright and Talbott entrusted me with when I joined the State Department in April was to be their working-level point person on this issue. In my first weeks on the job, Talbott and I exchanged a series of memos in which we debated the merits of inviting a small or a large first group. By early May Albright, Talbott, and I had reached a meeting-of-the-minds on an approach that we called "small is beautiful" plus "robust open door." Making fun of our government's propensity to reduce everything to an acronym, we referred to it in shorthand as SIBROD.

The premise was that the best way to maintain the Alliance's integrity and to ensure the continuation of the enlargement process was to make certain that the first round was an unambiguous success. And the best way to guarantee that was to invite only those candidates that we were fully confident were ready and where we had a strong moral and strategic case that could be explained to the American public and ratified in the U.S. Senate. A small first round was also seen as protecting us against the charge that by enlarging NATO we were diluting it. At the same time, it was the best guarantee that NATO's door would remain open in the future since it maximized the number of allies who had a stake in enlargement continuing.

The argument that we should bring a country into NATO because it could not get into the EU was anathema to the Administration. It made NATO membership sound like a kind of consolation prize. Our strategy was just the opposite: we wanted to be in a position to argue that we were only bringing in the *strongest* countries that would strengthen the Alliance. Washington was just as concerned as Paris about the stability of a country like Romania. But we were not prepared to jettison the performance principle to meet the short-term political needs of a specific government even if we admired it. If a country's argument for getting into NATO was that it would self-destruct if it did not, that was a reason not to invite it. We also had in mind the example of Slovakia, which had been a leading candidate but had disqualified itself. What if the same happened elsewhere?

A small first group would also avoid exacerbating the dilemma of the Baltic states. Protecting the Baltic states and ensuring that they, too, had a chance to join NATO down the road was a key consideration in our thinking. A country like Estonia was much further along in terms of reform than Romania and, arguably, at about the same level as Slovenia. Bringing in Romania but excluding Estonia ran the risk of making a mockery of the principle of performance or our insistence that Russia did not have a veto over Alliance decisions. How would President Clinton look Estonia's President Lennart Meri in the eye and explain such a decision?

Shortly after my arrival at the State Department, NSC staffers Sandy Vershbow and Dan Fried invited me over for a private talk. On the phone Vershbow hinted that the subject was the infamous "who." As I sat down in Vershbow's NSC office, he said to me: "I need to know where you are on the who—and what Madeleine and Strobe think." Talbott, in turn, had asked me to check on the thinking of Sandy Berger and his deputy, Jim Steinberg. The three of us laid our cards on the table. We all favored inviting three countries at Madrid.

The U.S. would later be criticized for acting in a heavy-handed fashion and not thinking enough about the wishes of our European allies or the consequences of our decision on the stability of the countries whose candidacy was rejected. But the Administration did not make these decisions lightly. From Albright on down, many of us had spent a good part of our professional careers studying Central and Eastern Europe. We had great sympathy for the people in these countries and, in particular, for the new Romanian government. But our primary responsibility was to think about what was best for the U.S. and NATO. Poland had a reform track record of seven years whereas Romania's was only seven months. Romania was not yet ready for NATO—and we were not ready for it.

Slovenia was an even tougher call. It was arguably as far along in terms of political and economic reform as the Czech Republic, Hungary or Poland. Bill Perry had returned from a visit to Ljubljana in July 1996 enormously impressed by the progress that country had made. It later became clear to us that the Slovenes may have over-interpreted Perry's comments at the time as suggesting official U.S. support for their country as a first round candidate.[7] Not everyone in Washington shared Perry's enthusiasm. There were several question marks that made others hesitate. One was Slovenia's defense performance. All the Central and East European candidates were struggling to reform their militaries, but Ljubljana's track record in this area was viewed as especially spotty.

It was also important that future members demonstrated a willingness to contribute to stability beyond their own borders. We were not confident that Ljubljana had this attitude which, in our view, was central to being a good ally. A number of us felt the country was in denial about having once been part of the former Yugoslavia and was shunning its regional responsibility in the Balkans. If Ljubljana refused to accept responsibility for its local neighborhood, what did that say about its willingness to be a good ally in other areas or future crises? We feared it wanted to join NATO to validate its Europeaness, not because it wanted to help us in stemming future European conflicts. We were already nervous we had one potential free rider candidate with the Czech Republic, whose performance already showed signs of slipping. We didn't want to risk a second one. We decided it was better to be safe than sorry and to recommend that Slovenia wait.

Starting in late April, a series of senior inter-agency discussions took place on how to think about the open door and other outstanding issues for Madrid.[8] It soon became apparent that there was no one at the table prepared to support an invitation to Romania for the first round. On Slovenia, there were different views in the Administration. The Defense Department initially favored the inclusion of Ljubljana, while the NSC and the State Department opposed it. But DoD was not willing to go to the mat for its view. The absence of Bill Perry may have made a difference. His successor, William Cohen, was more cautious.

On May 19, the Deputies Committee decided to support extending invitations to the Czech Republic, Hungary, and Poland. The case for Romania and Slovenia, Deputies decided, was less compelling. Romania "still has a considerable way to go in implementing internal reforms," they concluded. Slovenia was judged to be lagging "badly behind the others militarily and, possibly, in its ability to make a political contribution." Beyond these individual country weaknesses, four broader considerations shaped this recommendation. First, a small-group approach was consistent with the long-held U.S. view of enlargement as a steady deliberate process. Second, it was more prudent from a military viewpoint to start with a small group of invitees. Third, a small group was seen as helpful in allaying domestic and congressional concerns over the costs of enlargement and a possible "dilution" of the Alliance. Finally, a small group approach, Deputies concluded, would maximize allied support for a strong open door package for countries not in a first enlargement round.[9]

The next day, May 20, Berger, Albright, and Cohen endorsed the approach. Albright was authorized to make it clear at Sintra that the U.S. favored a small-group approach, along with the reasons why, but to avoid detailed discussions on specific countries. Above all, Albright was to underscore that the President had not yet made a final decision. Later that day, Talbott laid out our general thinking and the philosophy behind our policy in a speech before the Atlantic Council.[10]

By this time the French and Italian lobbying effort in favor of Romania and Slovenia had developed a considerable head of steam. If we were going to stop that momentum, it was time to lay down a marker on where the U.S. stood. Albright, Berger, and Cohen were aware that our stance would provoke another U.S.-French quarrel. No one wanted it, especially as we still held out hope of finding a final compromise bringing Paris back into the NATO integrated command by Madrid. But neither was the U.S. government prepared to back Romania for the first round of enlargement.

Having made that decision, we had little choice but to blunt the rising expectations that a first round of enlargement could include Romania and Slovenia. As Ambassador Hunter wrote to Albright on the eve of the Sintra Ministerial, everyone was waiting for a signal where the United States stood on Romania and Slovenia. "If we do not want this outcome, especially regarding

Romania," Hunter wrote, "we need to give some indication soon about our preferences; indeed, it will be important to start laying the groundwork at Sintra. The French campaign for Romania is gaining momentum, and we could soon face a difficult problem in turning it off."[11]

There was a sense of anticipation in the air—reinforced by humidity and the fact that the air conditioning had broken down at the conference site—when we arrived at Sintra. Everyone knew that the debate on who to invite to join NATO was about to start. Vershbow and I stayed up late refining Albright's talking points for the lunch and incorporating a number of points the Secretary had asked us to emphasize. After the opening plenary discussion, the Foreign Ministers retreated to their informal lunch for their discussion on the "who."[12]

At the lunch, Albright spoke last, but made a simple straightforward case. She underscored that the U.S. had not made a final decision but that Washington saw substantial arguments in favor of a small group. As her talking points stated: "From the beginning, the U.S. had emphasized that enlargement should be a deliberate, step-by-step process in order to ensure that NATO maintains its military effectiveness and political cohesion. For this reason," Albright emphasized, "we need to start with the strongest candidates." Since NATO's security guarantee was "irreversible," allies had to be convinced that these countries were irreversibly committed to the values NATO was pledged to defend. The Alliance had to avoid the perception it was pursuing an overly ambitious enlargement, "one that appears to put political goals ahead of hard-nosed security considerations."

NATO was a military alliance, not a charity or a political club, she said. A smaller first group would be safer, cost less, and was more likely to ensure that a first round was successful. But the U.S. felt equally strong about the need for a credible open door policy: "We should view our decisions on the 'who' and the 'open door' as two sides of the same coin," and parts of a single-policy package. She pointed out that if the Alliance were to admit countries that were close calls based on their performance to date, it could undercut other candidate countries that were just as qualified but for whom there was not an Alliance consensus. It was a reference to the need to protect the Baltic states.

Albright's view was not widely shared around the table. Nine of the Foreign Ministers who had spoken before her had suggested they were prepared to consider a larger round. Only British Foreign Secretary Robin Cook and Icelandic Foreign Minister Halldór Ásgrímsson had argued in favor of a small group—with the UK favoring four countries including Slovenia. Clearly, France had been more successful than Washington had realized in lining up support for its position. While the lunch proceedings were supposed to be confidential, within minutes reporters were calling us. The French delegation, they reported, was claiming that Albright had been isolated at the lunch and that a majority of NATO allies supported the French position in favor of five new invitees. Would we confirm or deny the story? Paris had scored a point on us in the public relations battle as well.[13]

In the course of the day, several European delegations told us that they actually agreed with the U.S. position but had not spoken up more clearly because they either lacked instructions on their own position, were waiting to see what the U.S. had decided, or were reluctant to take on France. For Albright, the Sintra experience ended up convincing her that the decision in favor of a small group of initial candidates was the right one. As she wrote President Clinton that evening: "My experience at the NATO Ministerial in Sintra convinced me that we are right to push for a small first tranche of new members—but we've got our work cut out for us over the next several weeks to bring the rest of the allies around to our view." Paris, she noted, was on an "all-out campaign" on behalf of Romania and had successfully lined up support from the NATO southern flank allies.

The U.S. was not as isolated as it looked at first glance, Albright noted. "We should keep in mind that this was the first time that the U.S. had tipped its hand—and the first time the Alliance held a systematic discussion of the issue." Now that the allies knew where the U.S. stood, some of them were likely to review their positions. "One reason we decided to lay down a marker in favor of a small first tranche in Sintra," Albright reminded the President, "was that we knew momentum for a larger group had been building. I wanted to stop it from becoming a juggernaut." Many allies, she noted, were staking out initial positions that were essentially cost free—"and, yet again, waiting for us to lead and play the heavy." Once they knew the U.S. was committed, "the ground will undoubtedly shift in our favor," she predicted.

Above all, she had found many of the arguments put forth by her European colleagues in favor of a larger group unconvincing. "The arguments in favor of this larger group were remarkably narrow and short sighted (i.e., rooted in domestic political calculations or in a reluctance to offend with the Romanians, Slovenians or French)," she wrote. Few allies were looking at the big picture or what was right for the Alliance. "No ally," Albright continued, had a good counter to the basic U.S. argument that a small round would keep the Alliance strong and was the best guarantee for a credible open door policy. European preoccupation with the ostensible need for "geographic balance," she wrote, "is traditional EU thinking but not very germane to the serious business of extending permanent security guarantees."

Albright had no illusions about what lay ahead. "There will be a lot of heavy lifting and it could get pretty nasty with the French," she predicted. At the same time, she sensed that this was just the latest example of what has become a pattern in Washington's dealing with the allies on NATO enlargement. "At each stage of the enlargement process we have had to exert leadership, withstand grandstanding and grumbles and insist that big picture considerations prevail over parochialism." NATO, she noted, must be decided by consensus. "There is now a clear consensus for the Czech Republic, Hungary and Poland. So that much *is* decided. We'll go beyond that only if the U.S. makes a conscious decision to do so, a course I would not at this point recommend."[14]

2. PLAYING THE HEAVY

Sintra was nevertheless a public relations disaster. While we achieved what we had wanted diplomatically, we paid a heavy price politically for what was widely characterized in the European press as American arrogance and heavy-handedness. In one sense such stories were inaccurate and unfair. We had simply laid out our national predisposition—something France, Italy, and others had done months earlier. Moreover, while our critics accused us of acting prematurely and short-circuiting NATO's consultation process, the reality was that a number of allies had urged us to finally indicate what the U.S. position would be. While the French immediately claimed to speak on behalf of Europe, and sought to give the story a "U.S. vs. Europe" spin, the real lineup in the Alliance was more complicated—as would soon become evident.

The backlash we faced after Sintra underscored another challenge—what Albright and Talbott referred to privately as the "hegemon problem." During Clinton's first term in office, the U.S. economy had turned around and was now booming. The increase in American confidence and influence that flowed from this turn around was considerable. Whereas only a few years earlier the European press had been full of reports worrying that the U.S. was in a state of decline, now the surge in American political and economic strength had them concerned that the U.S.-European relationship was becoming so lopsided that it was unhealthy and dangerous. French Foreign Minister Hubert Védrine had coined the phrase "hyperpower" to describe the amount of power the United States had accumulated.

There was a certain irony to this criticism. President Clinton was strongly pro-European and popular in Europe. His Administration was strongly internationalist and believed in strengthening American alliances as opposed to going it alone. Many of us in the President's national security team found it a bit strange to be criticized at home for being too multilateral and Euro-centric, but criticized on the other side of the Atlantic for ostensibly being hegemonists. There was also often a difference between the private views of these governments and their public stances. On Romania, for example, a number of allies privately urged us to hold the line on not extending an invitation but then demurred when it came to speaking out in public when our actions were criticized as heavy-handed. When asked why, the explanation offered was simple: they still had to live and deal with Paris the next day in an EU meeting whereas we did not.

Albright and Talbott spent a great deal of time discussing the "hegemon issue" issue and whether we had misplayed our hand on NATO enlargement with their senior staff. Perhaps the sagest counsel was provided by an old friend, German State Secretary and later Ambassador to the U.S., Wolfgang Ischinger, who gave Talbott this advice on how to handle our European allies: "Be firm but nice." We simply had to make the best policy judgments we could and not compromise our policies simply to avoid the criticism of the day. Looking back several years later, nearly everyone involved in the U.S. decision to limit a first round of enlargement to three countries would still feel that we had made the right decision.

But the accusations of American hegemonic behavior would only get worse in the weeks ahead as the NATO enlargement fight escalated. Having put down a marker at Sintra, we had to decide whether we would persist and play the heavy, or adjust our policy to accommodate France and Italy even though we disagreed with their approach.

While no senior officials inside the Administration favored a larger round, there were key Senators on Capitol Hill who supported both Slovenia and Romania. Slovenia in particular enjoyed the support of Delaware's two Senators, Roth (R) and Biden (D). Senator Gordon Smith (R-OR), the Chairman of the European Subcommittee of the Senate Foreign Relations Committee (SFRC), was supportive of Romania's case. Even though no longer in the Administration, Dick Holbrooke lobbied hard privately in favor of Romania and Slovenia and, as always, was a forceful advocate of his case.

In early June, the Administration sat down in the wake of Sintra to review its position in favor of a small group, in particular the pros and cons of Romania and Slovenia. Once again, no one was willing to extend an invitation to Romania. Bucharest was simply not considered ready for NATO membership. The Romanian argument that the country would be destabilized if we did not bring them into the Alliance only hardened Washington's resolve to be cautious. It was as if Bucharest was putting a gun to its head and threatening to commit suicide if they did not receive an invitation. Politically, it was a disastrous argument.

There was discussion about whether the U.S. should reconsider its view on Slovenia. However, the Administration decided to hold firm in opposing an invitation to Slovenia as well. Two arguments tipped the scales against Slovenia. One was the U.S. military's judgment that the Alliance did not need the geographic contiguity that Slovenia provided with Hungary to extend an Article 5 guarantee to Budapest. The other factor was the judgment that supporting four countries was likely to be an untenable compromise position and would instead only expose us to even greater pressure to take five. The fact that France and Italy had entered a pact to support both Romania and Slovenia made it all but impossible that one would be able to enter without the other. Slovenia's fate was tied to Romania's — not by us, but by the confidential understanding France and Italy had reached the previous winter.[15]

The Deputies concluded it was time to finalize the U.S. decision. Since we were not going to change our mind, we needed to make that clear and start to build a consensus around the U.S. view. Ambassador Hunter was scheduled to have his "confessional" on the U.S. position with Solana the following week. The issue needed to be taken to Clinton for a final decision on the way ahead. A meeting of the Principals Committee was scheduled for June 10, after which Albright, Berger and Cohen would officially put forward their final recommendation to President Clinton. He, in turn, would consult with the Congressional leadership before making a final decision.

Clinton was fully aware of the drama playing out within the Alliance — and was increasingly involved in the diplomacy as well. He had already spoken to Blair, Chirac, and Kohl in early June. He was especially interested in Kohl's view. The two leaders had discussed the issue of three versus five new members in a phone conversation in late May and agreed to return to it during Kohl's visit to Washington in early June.[16] On June 4, Clinton and Kohl met for dinner in Georgetown at their favorite Italian restaurant, Filomena's. While a written record of their conversation does not exist, the President came away convinced that he had Kohl's personal backing for the U.S. approach. The next day Bitterlich told Assistant Secretary Kornblum that he thought the arguments for three were better than five, but that he had reservations about how the decision was being made and how to arrange a soft landing with France on the issue.[17]

On June 10, Albright, Berger and Cohen met to reaffirm the U.S. decision to hang tough in favor of three candidates and to push for a strong open door package. With a NATO Defense Ministers meeting scheduled for June 12 in Brussels, they recommended that Cohen convey the U.S. position to Solana in person. They also approved a diplomatic strategy to build support for the U.S. position in Europe. That strategy was centered on solidifying support from the United Kingdom, Germany and the Nordic countries, and then trying to address the concerns of France, Italy, and other southern European countries with a strong open door commitment along with stepped-up engagement with Romania and Slovenia.

President Clinton now received the official recommendation of his national security team to support extending invitations to three countries at Madrid.[18] He scheduled a meeting to consult with Congressional leaders on June 11 before making a final decision. That same day Cohen left for Brussels for his first visit as U.S. Secretary of Defense to a NATO Defense Ministerial. On the plane he gave a press briefing. While Cohen was careful to say that President Clinton had not yet announced a final decision, he confirmed that the U.S. thinking had not changed since Albright laid it out in Sintra. The media instantly reported that the U.S. decision was for three.[19]

Later that day in Washington, the White House announced President Clinton's decision after a meeting with the Senate NATO Enlargement Observer Group. Clinton wrote his NATO counterparts and Albright phoned several of her allied colleagues to deliver the news. In Brussels, Cohen laid out the reasons for the U.S. decision with his NATO colleagues.[20] Talbott called in the Washington-based Central and East European Ambassadors to explain the U.S. decision. The Czechs, Poles, and Hungarians were ecstatic; and the Romanian and Slovenian Ambassadors, while not surprised, were nonetheless dejected. The three Baltic Ambassadors were relieved, as they understood that the decision for a small group was also meant to protect them.

The U.S. was subjected to another wave of fierce criticism in the European press. The next day, Chirac and Kohl met in Poitiers, France, for a Franco-German summit where the French leader complained bitterly that important alliance decisions affecting Europe were being dictated by Washington and lobbied Kohl to support extending invitations to five new members with him.[21] When Albright called Védrine to suggest bilateral consultations to avoid a U.S.-French confrontation, he made it clear that Chirac would not relent and would press the issue all the way to Madrid.[22] Washington concluded that Chirac was calculating that either the U.S. would back down and he would get his way, or else that he would score points domestically by simply standing up to "the Americans." It left the U.S. with little choice but to prepare for a fight with Paris.

But France's ability to push its case was also limited. It had never been a strong supporter of NATO or of enlargement. Nor was it part of the Alliance's integrated military command. As one French diplomat admitted, "it's hard to press for an enlarged NATO without France being fully part of it.[23] Chirac had stated in public that he would not pay one franc for the costs of NATO enlargement, making him the most ambitious and most stingy leader on the issue. Cohabitation hurt as well as it was clear that France's new socialist-led government was also less supportive. Foreign Minster Védrine, for example, had previously been an open critic of NATO enlargement, labeling it an American plan to keep Europe under U.S. tutelage. All of these factors undercut Paris' own case and leverage.

In spite of the European cries about an alleged American *diktat*, the reality was that NATO was divided right down the middle. Approximately half of the allies supported the French view. But the other half supported us. This was less a case of the "U.S. vs. Europe," as France would have had it, but rather of different European allies lining up on both sides of the issue. The real lineup became evident when Solana shared with NATO Ambassadors the result of his first round of "confessionals" on June 19. He announced that seven countries wanted enlargement limited to three countries, six countries preferred five, and two countries preferred more than five. One ally had not yet decided. Ten allies said they could accept a consensus of three. Another ten said they could accept five. Nine, in theory, could have accepted four countries but could not agree on the fourth candidate. Three preferred Slovenia and four preferred Romania.[24]

The annual G-8 summit took place June 19–20, 1997 in Denver. It was the last chance for Clinton to meet his European counterparts face-to-face prior to Madrid. Clinton and Chirac had a final opportunity to explore a compromise that could prevent a U.S.-French clash at Madrid. But the two men could not find any common ground. "I understand," Chirac told Clinton, "that Romania is very far from the United States, but it is close to France." The U.S. position, he said, was an "error in political and moral terms" that could destabilize Romanian democracy. The French President also stated that Paris would never accept Slovenia's entry without Romania. But Chirac also proposed a compromise. Would the U.S. consider bringing in the first three candidates now and the second two at the next NATO summit in 1999?

Clinton responded by laying out his reasons for supporting three candidates. While he supported Romania and Slovenia in principle, he did not think they were ready for Alliance membership now. "We should take in new countries as they become qualified," he said, and added that taking in five countries would exacerbate the Baltic issue at a time when the West was not yet ready to confront it. Unfortunately, he could not accept Chirac's demands. "If we said the three will get in right away and identified the next two at the same time, there would be no substantial difference than if we took five." But Clinton tabled his own compromise proposal. Would Chirac consider joining him in visiting Bucharest after Madrid where the two leaders could assure Romanians that if they continued to perform well they would be among the strongest candidates for the next wave? Chirac also refused.[25]

All eyes now turned to Bonn. Germany's official position was that it would support consensus in the Alliance. Kohl's National Security Advisor, Joachim Bitterlich, had explained that this meant that Bonn would support the U.S. position for three *if* that became the consensus view at Madrid. But Germany would not allow itself to be put in a position where it had to publicly disagree with France or veto another country from joining the Alliance.[26] When Albright called German Foreign Minster Kinkel in mid-June to inform him of the final U.S. decision, he told her that Germany could not give the U.S. its full support at this point given the pressure it was under from Romania and Slovenia and divisions in the German government on how many candidates it should support.[27] Two weeks later on June 26, Kinkel stated to the Bundestag that Germany could support three candidates—but that it could also support four or five. Meanwhile, Defense Minister Ruehe continued to support the U.S. position. From Washington's perspective, it was not exactly a show of decisive German leadership.[28]

Washington, too, was under pressure from both the Slovenes and the Romanians to reconsider its view. The U.S. position at Sintra had caught

Slovenia by surprise and plunged it into a mini-crisis. Prime Minister Janez Drnovsek had launched an all-out-come-from-behind effort to get a NATO invitation at Madrid. While Albright's message at Sintra had poured cold water on their hopes, it did not deter Ljubljana from pressing on. On May 31, Prime Minster Drnovsek told U.S. Ambassador Vic Jackovich that if there were to be a compromise between three and five, he would continue his campaign and try to get Washington to change its mind and position on Slovenia as "everybody's fourth candidate."[29]

On June 11 Prime Minister Drnovsek wrote Clinton to make the case that Slovenia should be included in the first round of enlargement.[30] By the time the letter arrived, the President's final decision in favor of three had been announced. When informed by Ambassador Jackovich on the morning of June 13 of the final U.S. decision, the Slovene Prime Minister expressed his anger and disbelief and asked whether it was perhaps true that Slovenia was being excluded as a part of a secret U.S.-Russia deal, as some rumors had alleged.[31] He claimed that he would not be deterred by the U.S. decision and instead continued his country's campaign for NATO membership to the bitter end. Two weeks later, Drnovsek wrote Clinton again to urge him to reconsider his earlier decision.[32]

Slovenian President Milan Kucan was equally blunt in his initial assessment, describing the U.S. decision as "devastating." He complained that his country was unfairly being held hostage to a broader set of factors beyond its control. He told Ambassador Jackovich that he did not believe there would ever be a second round of enlargement, and feared Slovenia would be confined to a gray zone of insecurity for a long time to come.[33] Meeting with Jackovich a week later, however, Kucan was more reflective and self-critical. "We lost the battle for NATO right here at home," Kucan suggested, admitting that the Slovene government had at times been "arrogant" and had not adequately prepared its people for the responsibilities of NATO membership by refusing to have anything to do with the other Visegrad candidates and its Balkan neighbors.[34] Both the Slovenian Foreign and Defense Ministers eventually resigned, in large part because of Ljubljana's failure to receive an invitation.

Our discussions with Romania were even more difficult. With one foot in Central Europe and the other in the Balkans, Bucharest suffered from an inferiority complex when it came to Europe, believing—with some justification—that many in the West had considerable doubts about its European and Western credentials. Romanian political and civic life had suffered enormously under the destructive rule of Nicolae Ceaucescu, perhaps the most despotic communist leader in the region but one the West had backed because of his "autonomy" from Moscow.

Yalta cast a long historical shadow here as well. Many Americans visiting Bucharest were surprised to discover their interlocutors raising the issue of how

Washington had allegedly sold them out at the end of World War II by not standing up to Stalin. As Romanian President Constantinescu told U.S. Undersecretary of Defense Walt Slocombe on January 9, "Romania has been waiting ever since for the Americans. And now if Romania does not get into NATO in the first grouping, Romanians will again see it as American treachery."[35]

By now the new Constantinescu government in Romania had made getting into NATO a matter of "national honor." Nearly 90 percent of the public supported joining NATO—a number matched only in Poland. The U.S. Ambassador in Bucharest, Al Moses, experienced just how deeply rooted Romania's desire to join NATO was during a visit to the famous Putna monastery in the spring of 1997. He described the scene in a diary he kept. Following breakfast, he and his sister were escorted to their car: "Kisses on both cheeks was a mere prelude to a five-minute plea by the Father Superior, first for Christian fellowship, then to preserve Romania from his Slavic neighbors and the familiar words about NATO. Even the clergy is singing the NATO chant," Moses wrote. "The scene had to be seen to be believed. A Romanian Orthodox priest and an American Jewish lawyer standing in a four-handed handshake, eyes meeting, a group surrounding us and the priest in a soft Romanian, translated by Mihai Carp, making a traditional plea for understanding of Romania's unique position in Europe."[36]

Washington recognized the strategic case for Romanian membership in NATO. It was the largest and most pro-American country in southeastern Europe, French claims notwithstanding. Anchoring Romania to the West also had broader regional implications. We admired the new Constantinescu government's commitment to make a clear break with the country's nationalist and xenophobic past and to mend fences with the Hungarian minority. But the new Romanian government had only been in power a matter of months and its track record was still too spotty. When Romanian Foreign Minster Adrian Severin came to Washington in late April, Albright and Talbott explained that the U.S. recognized his country's regional importance and the strategic case for NATO membership, but Bucharest needed a longer track record of successful reforms. Poland, it was pointed out, had a reform track record of several years, whereas Romania's was several months. They urged him not to raise expectations at home that Washington could not fulfill.[37]

Albright's announcement at Sintra that the U.S. favored a small group did not stop Bucharest's campaign, however. When Ambassador Moses visited the Romanian President the day after Albright unveiled the U.S. view at Sintra, an obviously disturbed Constantinescu, referring to press reports that Albright's stance in favor of three had only been supported by the Icelandic Foreign Minster, said: "Tell me Mr. Ambassador, what did Romania ever do to Iceland?" When the U.S. announced Clinton's final decision in favor of three countries two weeks later, Bucharest issued a measured public statement noting that the U.S. did not speak for NATO as a whole. The government's private reaction, as described by Ambassador Moses in a cable to Washington, was one of anger and defiance—"full speed ahead, damn the torpedoes."[38]

Bucharest was caught between Washington and Paris, uncertain whether it should bet on France to champion its case and run the risk of alienating the U.S., or accept that an invitation was not in the cards and work with Washington to get the best possible open-door package. Increasingly, the Romanian government was also divided internally over whether it should fight to the last minute or recognize that an invitation was no longer in the cards. Foreign Minister Severin was urging the former whereas Romania's gifted Ambassador in Washington, Mircea Geoana, was recommending to President Contantinescu and Prime Minister Ciorbea the latter. In mid-June, Albright agreed to a visit by Romanian Prime Minster Victor Ciorbea. But she set a precondition that Ciorbea would not try to reopen the issue of a Romanian invitation but instead focus on the way ahead and how to build a stronger U.S.-Romanian bilateral partnership. Ciorbea agreed to these terms but, at the airport in Bucharest before his departure, he confessed to Ambassador Moses that he had changed his mind and wanted to again raise the issue of a Romanian invitation in Washington. Fortunately, Moses managed to convince him to stick to the agreed upon script.

On June 18–19, Ciorbea was received by Vice President Gore as well as Secretary Albright and Talbott. The U.S. message was that its response to Romania's NATO aspiration was not "no," but "not yet." Ciorbea emphasized that he wanted to be part of the solution, not the problem, at Madrid. But he tabled exactly those demands that we had already rejected with Paris—a set date for a second round and an explicit commitment to bringing in Romania at that time. We agreed to the notion of a U.S.-Romanian "strategic partnership," which recognized Romania's potential leadership role in Southeastern Europe, and provided Bucharest with a list of what we thought that partnership might entail.[39] Ciorbea had barely left town for New York, however, when part of his delegation returned to ask for a second confidential meeting with Talbott to make a final plea for Romanian membership. Shortly thereafter, Bucharest came back with its own wish list. It was wildly unrealistic as it proposed creating a major U.S. military base in the country along with economic assistance of more than $2 billion. By this time, everyone in the Administration was becoming increasingly fed up with Bucharest's tactics. It was a reminder that Romania still had one foot in the Balkans.

3. A BALTIC CHALLENGE

One of the responsibilities Albright and Talbott entrusted me with when I joined the State Department was the Baltic states. They both had a special interest in the issue. If NATO enlargement was about creating a Europe whole and free and undoing historical injustice, then there was no doubt in Albright's mind that the Baltics qualified on both counts. One of her favorite sayings about Estonia, Latvia, and Lithuania was that one did not have to be located in Central Europe to have Central Europe in one's heart. Along with the subjugation of her native Czechoslovakia in 1938, Albright considered the Hitler-Stalin Pact and the illegal annexation of these three states by the USSR among the great injustices of the 20th century.

Albright saw the Baltic issue as a litmus test of NATO enlargement. If enlargement was part of an integrationist strategy to remove Russia's imperial temptation and alter old patterns of zero-sum thinking, nowhere was this antidote more needed than in the Baltic states. One day shortly after I joined the State Department, Albright told me of her dismay that so many people were trying to simply ignore the Baltic issue. "We can't ignore this problem" she said. "It is a test of whether we can succeed in changing the way people think about the politics of post–Cold War Europe. We shouldn't run away from it," she continued. "I want to try to tackle it. I want to make it the litmus test of our whole strategy." And she was looking to Talbott and me to help her come up with that strategy.

During a trip to Vilnius to meet with the three Baltic Presidents after the Madrid summit, Albright would say in public what she had told me earlier in private: "Perhaps no part of Europe has suffered more from the old pattern of European politics than the Baltic states. You lost your security, your freedom, your independence, your prosperity—everything but your spirit and your spine." No one would benefit more, she argued, if we could create "a new pattern of politics in Europe." The United States, she made clear, supported Baltic aspirations to join NATO and would not discriminate against them. "We will not punish you in the future because you were subjugated in the past."

But Albright did not just want to reassure the Balts about our commitment to their Western integration. She wanted to use the carrot of eventual NATO membership to help them transform and Westernize their own societies. This included encouraging countries like Estonia and Latvia to integrate their Russian-speaking minorities and become multi-ethnic democracies. Albright was willing to stand up and defend the Baltics against Moscow's pressure. But she also wanted them to change their own zero-sum thinking and reach out to Russia as they became part of the West. "The quest for security is not a zero-sum game in which Central Europe must lose if Russia gains and Russia must loose if Central Europe gains" she stated in a major speech in Vilnius. The process of NATO enlargement "is not about escaping West, it is about gaining the confidence to look East in a spirit of cooperation."[40]

Talbott, too, had a deep interest and commitment to the Baltic states dating back to his days as a journalist covering the former Soviet Union. He often told the story of how he had sat with Lennart Meri, then still a quixotic filmmaker, dissident, and chronicler of the native peoples of the Soviet far North, on a steamer between Tallinn and Helsinki debating the future of the Baltic states. Talbott was one of the strongest advocates of an open door policy that protected the Baltic states—and left open the possibility that countries further to the east might one day join NATO as well. At a Deputies Committee meeting in spring 1997 Talbott passionately made the case for SIBROD because of the need to protect the Baltic states. Several colleagues around the table in the White House Situation Room looked stunned. Finally, Undersecretary of Defense Walt Slocombe broke the silence and said: "Strobe, you are supposed to be against all of this stuff." Everyone laughed. But it was another example of the contrast between the public caricature of Talbott's thinking and what he advocated in reality.

No one knew better than Talbott how deeply rooted Russia's neuralgia on the Baltic issue was and how hard it would be to change that mindset. It was one reason why he was so adamant that the U.S. position on NATO's open door be clear and consistent. His view was that Western strategy needed to be clear in saying that the Baltic states would one day join NATO. But he also believed the West, including the Baltic states, had to simultaneously reach out to Russia, co-operate with it, and address its sensitivities where they were legitimate. Just as the West needed to offer Moscow a vision of a new cooperative NATO-Russia relationship, Talbott believed that Washington needed a vision of how Baltic membership in NATO was part of a broader, cooperative framework around the Baltic Sea in which Russia, too, would have its place.

Derek Shearer, the U.S. Ambassador in Helsinki, Eric Edelman, Talbott's Executive Assistant, and I resurrected the idea of the Hanseatic League as an image or metaphor for what we had in mind. By reaching into the region's past, we hoped to show that it had once been possible for these countries to have the kind of normal, alternative future we were striving for in which Russia, as a Baltic littoral country, was connected to these countries by commerce and travel. Talbott liked it so much he asked us to read up on the history of the Hanseatic League and to look for modern-day parallels. When I brought back a book on the Hansa from the Hanseatic Museum in Bergen, Norway, he had the CIA blow up one if its maps into a chart which he kept in his office and would bring out to engage visitors on Baltic-Russian relations.

At a conference at Stanford University in the fall of 1997, Talbott spoke about how the U.S. needed to manage the dilemma of supporting the legitimate Baltic aspirations to reintegrate into the West and join NATO with Russia's fear and loathing that they might succeed in doing so. "Quite bluntly," Talbott told his audience,

> Russians need to get over their neuralgia on this subject; they need to stop looking at the Baltic region as a pathway for foreign armies or as a buffer zone, not just because such old think offends and menaces the Balts but

because it doesn't make sense, since there are no would-be aggressors to be rebuffed.

In the final analysis, Russia will have to make that adjustment herself, by its own light and for its own reasons. But we and our European partners can help. One way is to make the idea of commercial, political and environmental and other forms of collaboration among the states along the littoral of the Baltic Sea a centerpiece of our own activity there—and an important part of our dialogue with Russia as an important regional power.

Our message to Moscow is this: if you Russians insist on looking at the 13th century for models applicable to the 21st, then you should dwell less on the image of Alexsandr Nevsky defeating the Swedish knights on the ice and think instead in what might be called "Hanseatic" terms—that is think about the Baltics not as an invasion route inward, but as a gateway outward.[41]

The Clinton Administration's Baltic commitment took many people by surprise. And not everyone was happy. Primakov hated it and repeatedly warned us against taking steps to bring the Baltic states closer to NATO. It was unpopular with some of our key European allies as well. The exception was our Nordic allies who were, if anything, even more supportive in word and deed than the U.S. We looked to them for advice and ideas on how to craft our strategy. They knew the region better than we did and understood the importance of getting the U.S. more involved—and often lobbied for more U.S. involvement vis-à-vis more skeptical Europeans. The convergence of U.S.-Nordic thinking on the Baltic issue led to a kind of implicit strategic alliance and cooperation in the region that would, in turn, play a key role at the NATO Madrid summit.

The Clinton Administration was often accused of pursuing a strong Baltic policy for domestic political reasons. The reality was that we were being criticized at home from both the right and the left. I would sometimes amuse my Nordic and Baltic counterparts by explaining the U.S. political lineup on this issue with four wine glasses at dinner. My staff soon dubbed it the "Asmus Four Glass Theory on the Politics of Baltic NATO Membership." As I described it to Talbott in a memo, "Right-wing Republicans want to bring them in now, Bush Republicans and Democratic defense hawks say never; Democratic internationalists such as you and me say yes in principle but not now; and liberal Democratic arms controllers say it is not worth risking the arms control agenda with Moscow because of the Baltic issue."[42] Fashioning the two-thirds majority required for Senate ratification required a good strategy and enough time.

This was why the United States had proposed a U.S.-Baltic Charter. We needed a strategy to create the conditions that would make it possible to one day bring the Baltic states into NATO—not as a precipitous, isolated act that would sour relations with Moscow but as part of an overall strategy for building security and stability in the region. But for that strategy to work, we first needed to agree with leaders of the Baltic states on what we were trying to achieve, embrace a common strategy on how to achieve it, and create the mechanisms to follow up with practical steps.

The Baltic states did not trust us either, at least not initially. Although we were in many ways their strongest supporters, the fear of betrayal by the West ran deep. Our Baltic interlocutors were uncomfortable with the slow, deliberate course we had charted on enlargement and they considered our approach to addressing Russian concerns naïve. Like Lech Walesa in Poland, they believed that the best approach was to simply enlarge NATO and create facts on the ground—the sooner, the better. Moscow's attitude, they believed, would change only once they were in NATO, not beforehand.

As a Democratic political appointee, I took some refuge in the fact that this distrust was bipartisan. The people of the Baltics had never forgiven Roosevelt for Yalta; and many of them still considered Democrats almost congenitally naïve about Russia. But they did not trust the Republicans either. One could hardly spend an evening in a pub in Tallinn, Riga, or Vilnius without someone bringing up the fact that President George Bush had hesitated in recognizing Baltic independence in 1991 for fear of undercutting Soviet leader Mikhail Gorbachev. At the time, President Bush had stated that: "When history is written, nobody will remember that we took forty-eight hours more than Iceland or whoever it is" that recognized them first.[43] But they did. I was constantly reminded that the U.S. was number 34 in the list of countries recognizing the regaining of Baltic independence.

Vytautis Landsbergis, the first post-independence Lithuanian head of state, in many ways epitomized Baltic distrust of the U.S. He was a Lithuanian hero—the man who had led his nation to independence and rallied the nation to stand up to Moscow in 1991, when the Soviets had started to intervene and killed a number of Lithuanians in front of the parliament. An ethno-musicologist by training, Landsbergis was stubborn and proud. He had pursued Lithuania's independence, which would help catalyze the collapse of the Soviet Union, over the advice and objections of many Western governments and friends who had urged him to adopt a more moderate course. He, and Lithuania, had won as a result.

I met Landsbergis while working at RAND in the mid-1990s and developed a candid relationship with him even though we did not see eye-to-eye on many issues. When I once tried to explain the reasons why the U.S. could not bring the Baltics into NATO right away, he brushed my comments aside as irrelevant. Landsbergis thought the U.S. was a naïve but powerful country that sometimes had to be forced to do the right thing. It was the lesson he had drawn from dealing with the Bush Administration. Landsbergis's view was simple. U.S. policy should be to enlarge NATO as fast as possible to remove any lingering Russian imperial temptations. Like the Nike commercial, his motto was: "Just do it." Landsbergis wanted a security guarantee and he wanted it now—from the United States. All other issues regarding Lithuania's qualifications could be sorted out later.

To varying degrees, this view was shared throughout the three Baltic states. These countries looked to Washington because we were a superpower and because they believed the U.S. policy had more of a moral component to it than the *Realpolitik* practiced by many Europeans. At the same time, they also thought that Americans in general, and the Clinton Administration in particular, were not hard headed enough when it came to dealing with the Russians and their security. While respecting American power, they were determined to do whatever it took to get a security guarantee for their countries. If need be, that included pushing and even humiliating the U.S. into doing the right thing.

In the spring of 1997, Baltic anxiety was at an all-time high. The Baltic press was full of speculation about a possible sellout of the Baltic states as the price for Russian acquiescence to enlargement in the context of negotiations over the Founding Act. To make matters worse, Yeltsin had stated to the Russian press that he reserved the right to revise the Founding Act if any former Soviet republics were ever admitted to NATO. As Latvian Foreign Minister Valdis Birkavs had put it: "NATO says the door is open, but the Russian dog is sitting in the entrance barking at us not to go in."[44] Knowing that Baltic anxieties were on the rise, Talbott invited the Presidents of all three Baltic states to a meeting to reassure them that no deals had been cut at their expense.

The meeting took place in The Hague on May 28, 1997 where President Clinton was commemorating the fiftieth Anniversary of the 1947 Marshall Plan. While welcoming the signing of the NATO-Russia agreement in Paris the day before, Latvian President Guntis Ulmanis and Estonian President Lennart Meri had expressed their fears that their nations' security was being sacrificed in the attempt to accommodate Moscow. Ulmanis told Talbott that he was "no longer sure" where his country fit in the U.S. vision of Europe's future.

President Meri was more dramatic. He started by telling Talbott that the last week had been one of the most difficult in recent memory for the Estonian nation. The combination of the signing of the NATO-Russia Founding Act along with several U.S. policy moves had sent "the wrong signals to our immediate neighbors." He had "expected more" from the United States and was disappointed. There were "illusions" in Moscow about the Baltic states that needed to be dispelled and only Washington could do that. He was concerned for the fate of the Estonian people. He compared himself to an Estonian Moses who had been chosen, "in a biblical sense," to lead his people back out of bondage to freedom and to Europe. And he felt personally betrayed—including by us.

Talbott looked at Edelman and me for help. But at first we did not know what Meri was talking about. Then it clicked. He was referring to a U.S.-led military exercise named "Baltic Challenge." As part of our effort to reassure the Baltic states, we had agreed to a series of military exercises in these countries over a three-year timeframe. In mid-April we had moved the dates of the exercise and scaled it back in size after someone realized it was going to take place *during* the Madrid summit. We did not think that 2,500 U.S. Marines landing on Baltic beaches was an ideal backdrop for the summit. All the participants, including the Estonians, had agreed to these changes. But somehow the story had become twisted that the rescheduling was in response to Russian pressure. The second complaint was that a U.S. spokesperson had mistakenly referred to the U.S.-Baltic Charter as a "cultural agreement." It was an honest mistake by someone not up to speed on what we were doing. But it was taken as evidence that the U.S. was about to sell these countries out.

Talbott's temper flared. Looking at Meri, he told him that they had known each other for many years and had always spoken openly and honestly to one another. If it were not for the U.S. commitment and this President, NATO enlargement would not have happened. Similarly, if it were not for Washington's leadership, enlargement would surely have been capped after a single round and the Baltics would have been excluded. The President had defended the right of the Baltic states to join NATO with Yeltsin at Helsinki and there was nothing in the Founding Act "in large print, fine print or between the lines" that in any way discriminated against the Baltic states or closed the door to their entry into NATO. Estonian accusations on the Baltic Challenge were "just plain wrong."

The Balts did not have a better friend in the West than the United States and the Clinton Administration, Talbott continued. The distrust of American intentions Meri had shown would be a great disappointment to President Clinton and Secretary Albright. The Deputy Secretary challenged Presidents Meri and Ulmanis to name a single instance where the U.S. had failed to do what it had promised. Moses, he pointed out, also had a little bit of help. While making no claims to divinity, he told the Baltic Presidents that the U.S. was just as committed to leading the Baltic states back to Europe as they were.[45]

His outburst was met by silence. It was the low point in our relations with the Baltics. After the meeting broke up, Edelman put his hand on Talbott's shoulder and said, "Remember what he and those people have been through. Besides, Moses was probably a pain in the ass too after forty years in the wilderness." But the meeting proved to be cathartic. The distrust and anger on both sides had been vented and the air cleared of the former acrimony. We moved quickly to make a new start. At Sintra, Estonian Foreign Minster Ilves and Defense Minister Luik visited me in my hotel, looking slightly chagrinned. Talbott dropped by and we started to patch things up over drinks.

Over the next two years, our dialogue with all three Baltic states would grow extremely close. As they started to believe that we were indeed committed to using American influence to guarantee them the perspective of eventual NATO membership, they started to relax and focused on doing their homework to get ready. Lithuania took the lead in trying to improve relations with Moscow and working regionally with Kaliningrad. Talbott and I would grow close to the leaders of all three countries, but especially to Meri and the Estonians. In the summer of 1999, Talbott and I spent a day as Meri's guest at the Estonian President's retreat on the Baltic coast—taking a sauna, swimming in the Baltic Sea, and talking politics into the dark hours of the morning. In the helicopter on the way back, Talbott said to me: "You know we talk more openly to these guys than even some of our current allies." It was a dramatic shift from the scene in that Dutch hotel room in May 1997.

Back in Washington, I had assembled a small team to draft a U.S.-Baltic Charter. A lot of good legwork had been done, especially by our Ambassador in Riga, Larry Napper. But the bigger questions about what we were trying to achieve had not yet been answered. With a mandate from Albright and Talbott, I took over the process. My basic idea was simple. The Charter would convey in clear terms that we had a common vision of Europe, that they were part of that vision, that NATO enlargement was part of a broader strategy of building this unified Europe, and that our goal was to integrate them into the institutions of this new Europe, including NATO. Politically, we were not willing to agree to any language that implied a surrogate U.S. security guarantee in lieu of NATO. But we were willing to underscore our enduring interest in their independence and sovereignty and the fact that we would not consider our vision complete unless and until we had brought them in.

At the same time, the Charter was not just about NATO. We wanted to use it to encourage the Baltic states to accelerate their internal reforms as well as to embrace policies that would contribute to our broader vision for the region—including an improved relationship with Russia. We therefore insisted on strong language on the need to build multi-ethnic democracies and the integration of Russian-language speakers, as well as support for regional cooperation with Moscow. It was far easier for these countries to make such pledges in a document with the U.S. than in any other context. We also wanted to back up these pledges with concrete tools to implement them. We proposed creating a Partnership Commission that would meet once a year. It would have two working groups on economic and military issues that would report to the Commission. It would be chaired by Talbott and the Baltic Foreign Ministers, respectively.

The goal was to use the commitment of the U.S. government to identify and resolve problems that would, in turn, accelerate the integration of these countries into Western institutions, including NATO. Our philosophy was captured in a metaphor I used with my Baltic interlocutors. I told them that they would have to complete the marathon to get into NATO, but that we saw ourselves as their coach. While they would have to run the race themselves, we would use America's influence to guarantee that there was a level playing field and that they were not handicapped because of geography or history. We would also be on the sidelines, offering practical advice and be cheering them on until they crossed the finish line.

The next step in clarifying our Baltic policy came in mid-June on the day we announced the President's decision in favor of inviting three countries to join NATO at Madrid. Several days earlier, Edelman and I had joined Talbott for a quick visit to a Starbucks. Talbott was practically addicted to cappuccinos and enjoyed sneaking out of the office for a quick caffeine fix. His secretary would call to say that the Deputy Secretary needed me to join him immediately for a meeting. I would drop what I was doing and run up the stairs to his office only to discover it was time to sneak out for a caramel macchiato. The drive on the way over was often used to plot strategy and think out loud about future policy.

It was during one of these covert trips to Starbucks in early June that Talbott asked Edelman and me how we envisioned actually bringing the Baltic states into the Alliance. We ran though various scenarios on how the Baltics might actually join NATO and debated the pros and cons of the countries coming in individually, as a group, or in conjunction with other Nordic countries. We concluded that the day when any of this would be feasible was probably still a long way off. But we agreed it was important that the Baltics understood our goal was to eventually bring them in, and that the strategy we were proposing was designed to make that possible.

Several days later on June 12, I joined Talbott in his office as we prepared to inform the three Baltic Ambassadors about Clinton's decision to invite three countries to join NATO at Madrid. As we went through his talking points, Talbott hinted that he had decided to clarify our long-term intentions on the Baltic issue. During the subsequent conversation with the three Ambassadors he stated: "We will not regard the process of NATO enlargement as finished or successful unless or until the aspirations of the Baltic states are fulfilled. We are aware of the implications of that, in the near term, the middle term and the long term." No U.S. official had previously made such a statement. It had not been in his talking points either. As we walked out of his office I turned to the Department's Baltic desk officer, Trevor Evans, who had been the notetaker, and said: "I want that sentence inscribed in that memcon. It is now U.S. policy."[46]

By mid June, Talbott and I had worked through several versions of a draft Charter to our satisfaction. We had promised the Balts we would start negotiations on the Charter before Madrid so that they had a clear sense of what we wanted to achieve. Getting the entire U.S. government to close ranks around the philosophy and strategy we had developed was not easy, however. I often had to invoke both Albright and Talbott to overcome the ingrained skepticism and reluctance of various parts of the U.S. government to take on any new obligations, especially on a sensitive issue like this one.

Finally, we were down to one last clearance—the White House. National Security Advisor Sandy Berger and his Deputy, Jim Steinberg, were uncomfortable with a couple of key sentences in the draft. Although much of the language was a repackaging of things we had previously said in other contexts, we had deliberately put it together in a way that sent a clear and powerful message. That was the idea. But Berger and Steinberg were nervous that the Balts might over-interpret the language and suggested that we had given them a quasi security guarantee. I appealed, arguing that not to repeat language previously used would be seen as a step back and that I could get assurances from these countries that they would not over-interpret such language. I was in a cab on my way to the airport to fly to the region when Talbott reached me from Denver on my cell phone, where he was attending the G-8 summit. He gave me my final negotiating instructions. I had nearly all the language I had requested.[47]

On June 23, 1997, I arrived in Tallinn for the start of a negotiating tour through all three Baltic capitals. I insisted that we ensure strict confidentiality of our talks. I had no intention of negotiating the content of this document with the Baltic press or, even worse, the Baltic-American community and press looking over our shoulders and judging who had made what compromise. It was also important that we send a clear and common message to our respective publics on what the purpose of this exercise was. We believed it was not a negotiation over a security guarantee or a precommitment to NATO membership. We saw it as a discussion among friends on how we could build our common vision of Europe, the principles underlying that vision and how the U.S. and the three Baltic countries could work together to achieve our common goals.

In Tallinn, I paid a courtesy visit to Meri. By this time I had developed my own personal relationship with the man I had come to view as a kind of Havel of the north. He was known for playing practical jokes on his staff and friends. As I shook his hand, he looked at me with a twinkle in his eyes, reached up and touched the lapel on my suit and asked: "Ron, have you brought the security guarantee?" It was his way of reminding me that he was determined to use every ounce of his political capital and energy to make sure his country would be safely anchored in the West.

The Estonians were pleasantly surprised by our draft which, they admitted, was much better than they had expected. The Latvians were supportive as well, and especially grateful that we were proposing mechanisms to turn the rhetoric of the Charter into practical steps on the ground. The Lithuanians were more skeptical. Not only did they want a separate document, they also wanted more clarity on NATO membership than our draft offered. In essence, they wanted an implicit security guarantee. I detected the guiding hand of Landsbergis as the *éminence grise* behind the scenes as I negotiated with my Lithuanian counterparts.[48]

I explained the limits of our policy and warned them not to overplay their hand and run the risk of destroying the goodwill Washington was offering. The U.S. would not be pushed into offering them a security commitment through a back door that it was not prepared to offer through NATO's front door. It had to evolve through the building of trust, cooperation, and performance. The Charter was the first step in that process. I knew my counterparts understood the message. But I also knew that they were under instructions to get more. They were not going to get it. One of the Lithuanian negotiators was suffering from a bad back. I saw a dark sweat stain spreading across his shirt. I told him I hoped it was because of his back and not my message. He smiled weakly and said he had to go back to the parliament and brief Landsbergis on our talks. I encouraged my Lithuanian counterpart at our press conference, Albinus Januszka, to say that the Charter would not contain a security guarantee and that Vilnius had not asked for one.

Upon returning to Washington, I sent Talbott a memo on the week's results: "I believe that we have finally succeeded in moving the Baltics, including the Lithuanians, beyond the point where they somehow view NATO membership as an "entitlement" or something we owe them. Instead, they increasingly acknowledge that this will be a long haul and that we are one of their closest friends and strongest supporters." We had come a long way, I wrote, since our disastrous meeting in The Hague one month earlier.

The challenge we now faced was the risk that it would have to compromise our open door policy at Madrid by agreeing to a package on Romania and Slovenia to accommodate the French that discriminated against the Baltic states. "At each stop I was repeatedly questioned about how committed the U.S. was to these measures and whether we wouldn't agree to compromises with the allies that would, in turn, compromise Baltic security as well. I assured them we would not. I hope I'm right."[49]

4. MADRID

The days preceding the Madrid summit were like the calm before the storm. The U.S. had decided to stick to its decision in favor of three invitees—and ride out French and other European accusations that we had imposed a *diktat* on the Alliance. Paris had made it equally clear that Chirac wanted to make the case for inviting five countries in person and in public at Madrid. When Solana suggested a Foreign Ministers meeting on the eve of the summit to try to resolve the issue, French Foreign Minster Hubert Védrine declined, citing other pressing business. Clearly, France had opted for a high stakes public fight with the U.S. It thought it was in a win-win situation. Either Chirac would succeed in getting us to change our mind at Madrid or obtain language putting Romania at the head of the queue for the next round of enlargement. In either case, he was claiming to speak for European interests against the arrogant Americans, a posture that would play well in French politics.

The U.S. strategy was not to budge from our position on extending only three invitations and try to channel the desire for a larger round into a strong commitment to future enlargement. At the same time, we wanted to avoid naming specific countries or language that would be a kind of pre-selection for the next round.[50] But it was increasingly clear that pressure was building to give Romania and Slovenia some kind of preferential treatment. This, however, threatened to create another problem on the Baltic issue. Our Nordic allies were urging us to hang tough and not agree to language that prejudiced the future chances of the Baltic states. We agreed in principle but we also needed to avoid a train wreck with France. Clinton had made it clear that he wanted a result that did not jeopardize the U.S.-French relationship or his ties with Chirac.

We were reasonably confident the U.S. position on only inviting three new members would prevail. NATO's game rules played in our favor. Alliance decisions were made by consensus, not majority vote. There was a consensus for three new countries and not for five. We knew that, with the exception of France and Italy, much of the support for Romania and Slovenia was shallow. So long as we had the United Kingdom, Germany, and the Nordic countries solidly on our side, we were safe. Our only concern was how solid the German support was. While German Defense Minister Ruehe was solidly behind us, Foreign Minister Kinkel was all over the map on the issue. President Clinton seemed confident that Chancellor Kohl would support him. But Kohl had yet to take a public position. And France, too, was invoking its special relationship with Bonn to gain German support.

In the State Department we were focused on what we could still do to de-escalate the situation. One day in mid-June, Romanian Ambassador Geoana came to visit Talbott to discuss how best to preserve a strong U.S.-Romanian relationship in spite of our rejection of the country's quest for NATO membership. Sitting in Talbott's private study, Geoana floated the idea of a Clinton visit to Bucharest immediately following Madrid. It was a way to show that America still stood behind Romania's effort to join the West. Geoana and I had discussed the idea among ourselves, but I had not fully briefed the Deputy Secretary on it. It was a bold proposal but not one without risks. Talbott's eyebrows arched in surprise and he looked at me. I could see what was going through his mind. Was this a brilliant or foolish idea? What if the President was booed in the streets of Bucharest? We all laughed and agreed that, while risky, it was certainly worth pursuing. When it was proposed to President Clinton, he liked it and agreed to go.

Romanian President Constantinescu was scheduled to visit Bonn on July 4, three days before the start of the Madrid summit, to make a final pitch for

German support for Romania's candidacy. Védrine was scheduled to arrive in Bonn the day after. The French and Romanians were making one last run at the Germans. Constantinescu's Bonn visit on July 2 ran late into the evening. Our chargé in Bonn, J. D. Bindenagel, went to bed assuming he would have plenty of time to report on the meeting in the morning before American officials arrived in their office given the time difference between Europe and the U.S. About 3:00 A.M., Bindenagel was awakened by a call from Talbott. The Deputy Secretary had a press report that Kohl was supporting Romania's entry into NATO. The chargé admitted that he not seen the statement but promised Talbott to look into it immediately.

Bindenagel immediately turned on his computer and did an Internet search. He found an AP piece reporting that Kohl's press spokesman had said the Chancellor supported early Romanian membership in the Alliance. At the opening of business he got a copy of the German press release, which spoke of the Chancellor's support for the "early entry" of Romania in NATO. The German phrase was ambiguous. Bindenagel called Kohl's National Security Advisor, Joachim Bitterlich, for an explanation.[51] But Bitterlich played coy and asked if there was a translation problem. The U.S. chargé replied that he understood the German but wanted to know the phrase's political meaning. Had Bonn's position changed? Would the Chancellor still support a consensus position of three if the U.S. stuck to its guns? Bitterlich responded by saying: "That's your interpretation."

Bindenagel immediately reported on the conversation and suggested that Clinton call Kohl to check on what the Chancellor really thought.[52] At a lunch later that day with Fred Kempe, a leading journalist from the *Wall Street Journal*, Bindenagel received a second call on his cell phone from Talbott. This time Berger was also on the line. They asked Bindenagel for his personal assessment of what was going on. Bindenagel repeated his belief that Kohl would support the President if he stuck to extending invitations to only three countries. A somewhat nervous Talbott replied: "You better be right."

Later that day I received a read-out from the NSC on a phone call Clinton had made to Kohl. Bindenagel was right. After checking with Clinton to make sure the U.S. position in favor of three had not changed, Kohl said: "I think we can pursue it that way, but we simply need to give a message opening up a perspective for Romania and Slovenia." President Clinton agreed. "I think we ought to say," he told Kohl, "that these three are the most ready, but that we have an interest in building NATO's southern flank, and that we'll review it in 1999. Then we can send a clear signal to the individual countries that if they can keep their democracies going and stay on the path of reform, they will be excellent candidates." The President added, however, that it had to be done in a way "that doesn't create another problem for us with the Baltic states."[53] The devil, however, would be in the details.

The Madrid summit started the evening of July 7 with an opening dinner for the NATO heads of state. Clinton met with Solana prior to the start of the official festivities. Solana thanked the President for the help he had received from the U.S. side in the run-up to the summit. "I hope I can say the same thing in two days," he quipped. He then laid out his thinking on how to manage the next day. He hoped that senior officials would finalize the communiqué that evening with the exception of the open door section. He had proposed that the heads of state go straight into a restricted working session the next morning to avoid a lengthy *tour de table* where they would simply repeat their established positions and posture for the audience. After about one hour in a restricted session, Solana would ask the Foreign Ministers to try to come up with compromise language—with the goal of finishing by lunch.

"I think the Germans are the key," President Clinton said. "I think so as well," Solana responded. But he noted that if Kohl said he preferred three but could live with four or five that would only encourage Chirac to fight on. "It would be better if he said he preferred three and urged that allies work on the open door," Solana concluded. The President agreed but also made clear he was willing to be flexible on the open door language to accommodate Chirac. "I think we will need more to help the French get out of the hole. I want a result in which Jacques Chirac can say that he won. We do not need it to look like a defeat."[54]

It was easier said than done. France refused Solana's request to go immediately into a restricted heads of state session the next morning. Chirac wanted exactly what the Secretary General hoped to avoid—a public *tour de table* that forced countries to take sides. It was France's way of maximizing the pressure on us. Moreover, negotiations among senior NATO officials on the communiqué that evening were deadlocked. French officials were clearly under instructions not to give anything to the U.S. on any issue—and the U.S. team, headed by Assistant Secretary John Kornblum, was more than capable of holding its own. It quickly was becoming a U.S.-French standoff.

Around 4:00 A.M., NATO's Assistant Secretary General for Political Affairs, Gebhardt von Moltke, called it a night so that he and other senior officials could get a catnap before briefing their Prime and Foreign Ministers on where things stood at breakfast. Kornblum sent me back to compose a brief memo on the state of play for Albright and Berger while he took a brief nap as well. His guidance was to write something that would keep the Secretary of State calm. I remember staring at my computer screen at 5:00 A.M. trying to find the right words to tell Albright and Berger that we were in fine shape—except that there were nearly a dozen key issues unresolved in the communiqué. I was not sure whether that memo was more fact or fiction. As I handed it to Alex Wolff, Albright's executive assistant, for her morning reading, the sun was rising.

Several hours later on July 8, Solana opened the summit's first full plenary session. Following opening remarks by the Secretary General and Spanish

Prime Minister Aznar, President Clinton took the floor. "Three-and-one-half years ago, we began to construct a new NATO for a new Europe, a Europe that at last could be undivided, democratic and free" he said. On enlargement, he laid out the American position in favor of inviting three countries. These countries had a track record of reform "long enough to give us the confidence that they are irreversible. Just as our offer of NATO membership is irreversible." Clinton continued, "I think it is quite important we remember that, when we make a decision about who to be invited to be a part of this, we have no precedent for uninviting someone because of their reversal of freedom or capacity of their country." A smaller group would be easier to integrate, would help keep down the costs of enlargement, and would create momentum for future rounds of enlargement.

French President Chirac and Italian Prime Minister Prodi made the case for five countries. The Romanian people, Chirac argued, had made a clear choice in favor of democracy and market economy. Public support for NATO in Romania was overwhelming, and indeed higher than in the Czech Republic or Hungary. Romania was critical for stabilizing NATO's southern flank and Bucharest had shown its commitment to the Alliance by contributing to operations in Bosnia and Albania. They were just as qualified as the Czech Republic, Hungry, and Poland, the French President insisted. Above all, it was important, he emphasized, that the Alliance, in attempting to overcome the old East-West divide, did not create a new North-South divide on the continent.

Italian Prime Minister Prodi followed by arguing that Slovenia's inclusion would also provide geographic contiguity and greater cohesion in NATO's southern flank. "Moreover, I insist on the southern region, the Balkans and beyond. I must state that this is the area in which actual and potential risks are the greatest. This is the area where NATO has been more heavily and so far successfully engaged since the end of the Cold War. We need to expect future challenges to emerge from this area rather than any other areas. Italy believes therefore that the inclusion of Romania and Slovenia in the first round at this stage is the logic of enlargement and will fully correspond to the fundamentals of the Alliance. Enlargement must be a geographically balanced process, and to not include those areas that are crucial to all of us in order to prevent instability on the European continent would not be a rational decision."

In the ensuing *tour de table*, the U.S. President's position in favor of three was supported by the leaders of the United Kingdom, Denmark, Norway and Iceland. Other allied leaders—Canadian Prime Minster Chrétien, Portuguese Prime Minster Guterres and Spanish President Aznar—supported five but also underscored the need for consensus and indicated a willingness to fall back to three. One head of state did not take a position in his first go around: German Chancellor Helmut Kohl. The Chancellor declined the opportunity to speak, saying this would only prolong the discussion, which was not going to produce results in any case. He would hold his comments for the restricted session. If Kohl was going to have to choose between Washington and Paris, he was not going to do it in a large, quasi-public setting but in the smaller, restricted session.[55]

As soon as the heads of state had moved into a smaller, restricted session Solana turned to Kohl. The German Chancellor would prove himself, once again, to be President Clinton's close political ally. The Madrid summit, the Chancellor began, was very important for NATO's reputation and for himself as a German. NATO stood for freedom and peace. Without it the history of the postwar period would have been very different and Germany would never have been reunified. The world had changed dramatically for the better, not least because of NATO. It had been a beacon of hope in a fairly gloomy world. He urged his colleagues to think in terms of what was right for NATO rather than in terms of posturing and national prestige.

"One miracle has already come true," Kohl said. "There is agreement on the membership of Poland, Hungary and the Czech Republic. Two or three years ago such an agreement would not have been a simple matter of course." But clearly, "there would not be agreement on more than three countries," the Chancellor continued. With that single sentence he ended any chance France might have had to box through a decision in favor of five. Instead, he urged his colleagues to focus on the public message the Alliance wanted to convey.

Kohl recalled his own terrible experience dealing with the Ceausescu regime in Romania. The Romanians had liberated themselves from that terrible past and were putting enormous efforts into building a democracy. They needed a clear message opening up the perspective of future membership. The same approach should be adopted for Slovenia.

But Germany, the Chancellor noted, also had a special responsibility to the Baltic states. Germans could never forget that Hitler had betrayed these countries. Their torturous past could not be forgotten either. Therefore, NATO also had to send a clear signal that it would be open to them as well at some point in the future. The allies should also not forget that enlargement would have to be ratified by the Nordic allies who had a direct link to the Baltic states. Kohl suggested that the Alliance couple extending invitations to Poland, Hungary and the Czech Republic with language encouraging the reform efforts of other partners along with a review of further admissions at the next Alliance summit in 1999.

Kohl was followed by Tony Blair. The decision to take in three new members, the British Prime Minister argued, was already a huge step for NATO. Decisions on who should join the Alliance should not be seen as a test of political wills, but should be made based on the performance of each country and hard-headed realism. NATO was a military alliance, not a political club. He reminded his colleagues that the terms of an Article 5 commitment were clear and worth rereading. It would be a big challenge to integrate even three new members and it was important that the Alliance not be weakened in the process. He was certain new members would want to join a strong, not a weakened, Alliance.

Taking in Romania and Slovenia would be another huge step, Blair emphasized. He wondered whether the Alliance was prepared for it. Not bringing them into NATO now did not mean that the Alliance did not welcome the enormous progress these countries had made. While the UK did not support extending Romania an invitation at this juncture, it was among Bucharest's greatest supporters in other ways. The United Kingdom was spending more on defense assistance in Romania than in any other Central European country—and more than those allies urging its admission to NATO in the first wave. Bucharest was making great progress and it needed to be given hope for the future, Blair concluded, but it was not yet ready for membership.

But Chirac was not prepared to give up. The problem, he countered, was of a political nature. Therefore, it needed to be resolved with an eye toward European "harmony." The Alliance needed a balanced approach that embraced Romania and Slovenia. NATO's southern flank and security in the Balkans would be enhanced by bringing these two countries into the Alliance. In terms of costs, there was little difference between taking in three or five members, he insisted. If Romania and Slovenia could not be brought in immediately, the Alliance needed to send a clear message that they would be included in a second round in 1999. Chirac had tabled his fallback position: he wanted a NATO commitment that Romania and Slovenia would get in at the next summit in 1999.

Clinton spoke next. He urged his colleagues to also consider the impact of what was being proposed for Romania and Slovenia on the Baltic states. A large group of five invitees, he continued, would increase tension in the Baltic region. Some would say to these states that they would never get into NATO because Russia would never accept it, the President noted. However, the future was unknown and so much had already been accomplished. It would be wrong to signal that the Alliance might exclude them.

Clinton returned to the irreversibility of any enlargement decisions. Had they met two years earlier, they would in all likelihood have invited Slovakia to join NATO. But what had since happened in that country was a reminder of why they needed to be absolutely certain a country was on the right path. What would they do, the President asked, if in Romania, anti-democratic extremists and nationalists returned to power in the future? He supported Romania and Slovenia, but their NATO candidacies required more time.

Danish Prime Minister Poul Nyrup Rasmussen also spoke out on the Baltic issue. Denmark could not support Chirac's proposal to invite three countries now and name two additional countries to be invited at a later time. Such a move could destabilize the Baltic states and send the wrong signal to Moscow.

Naming just Romania and Slovenia would leave the Baltic states vulnerable and subject to Russian pressure. The only way forward, he insisted, was to either name all candidate countries or none at all. He was supported by the Norwegian Prime Minister Thorbjorn Jagland and Icelandic Prime Minister David Oddson.

But Chirac and Prodi insisted that the problems of the Balkans and the Baltics were very different and could not be treated in the same fashion. Romania and Slovenia needed to be explicitly mentioned in the communiqué with a date mentioned for their inclusion in 1999. Prodi insisted that the problem of the southern flank was more urgent. If the communiqué did not name a date for Slovenia and Romania, they could be pushed out of consideration forever, he believed. It was another reminder how little confidence people had in the open door. Following the completion of the *tour de table*, Solana concluded the restricted session and sent the Foreign Ministers off to negotiate compromise language for the communiqué while the heads of state worked on other issues.

5. THE FINAL COMPROMISE

But the political battle was now simply transferred into another setting. It was clear that three countries would be invited to join NATO. Now the fight would be over how NATO described its open door policy and which countries would receive the kind of favorable mention that could put them at the head of the queue for the next round. Specifically, the issue was what the Alliance would say about the chances for Romania and Slovenia and what, if anything, would be said about the Baltic states.

The Alliance's lineup was clear. The British were the most cautious on the open door—they wanted to say as little as possible. The U.S. wanted to be forward leaning on the open door in principle, but to avoid language that either tied its hands for the future or created a de facto pecking order of preferred future candidates. The French and Italians were at the other end of the spectrum. They wanted a firm commitment to bring in Romania and Slovenia in 1999 while avoiding any mention of the Baltic states. The other Southern European states supported the Franco-Italian position while the Nordics were in our corner out of a shared desire to not discriminate against the Baltic states.

For the next three hours the Foreign Ministers haggled over two short paragraphs in an effort to find a compromise. Tempers flared as Ministers argued their respective cases. Italian Foreign Minister Dini was the most vocal in insisting on stronger language for Romania and Slovenia and insisting that the Baltic states not even be mentioned. Danish Foreign Minster Niels Helveg Petersen led the fight for equitable language for the Baltic states. At one point it looked as if the two Ministers were about to shout at one another.

Albright hung back in her comments. Having born the brunt of stopping the French-led campaign for five, she feared that if the U.S. also took the lead in pushing for language on this issue it would only have a polarizing affect. When the Danish delegation inquired whether we would speak out on the Baltic states, we told them that their Foreign Minister would have to take the lead in proposing language and that the U.S. would then support them. At one point there was a compromise on the table that included positive language on Romania and Slovenia, but no mention of the Baltic states. The chair, Canadian Foreign Minster Lord Axworthy, asked whether all allies could live with such language. The Danish Foreign Minister refused to accept it. After a brief pause, German Foreign Minster Kinkel also spoke out to support the Baltic states too. Albright then added her voice in support and the Ministers went back to the drawing board.

Gradually, a new compromise emerged with three elements—agreement to a review of enlargement at the next NATO summit in 1999, recognition of the progress that Romania and Slovenia had made, and a more general acknowledgement that the Baltic countries were also candidate countries that had made important progress as well. In an exercise that demonstrated a Talmudic wisdom, the language crafted was sufficiently strong to convey a sense of commitment to future enlargement yet not too strong as to tie the Alliance's hands in any meaningful way. And the language describing the progress of Romania and Slovenia, while stronger than that used for the Baltic states, was largely descriptive, not prescriptive.

Finally, at about 3:00 P.M., the Foreign Ministers had an agreed-upon text. With a sense of exhaustion, the delegations emptied the room. But the first signs of trouble became evident as we headed down the corridor and back to the plenary hall where the heads of state would gather. Ahead of us, Foreign Minster Védrine was standing in a small huddle with President Chirac. Suddenly, we heard Chirac say an emphatic "Non." He was visibly angry and Védrine looked humbled. The French President stalked off looking more determined than ever. Word quickly spread through the corridors that Chirac had rejected the compromise. A sense of tension hung in the air as the heads of state again gathered to review the new text.

Danish Prime Minister Rasmussen turned to his Ambassador at NATO, Gunnar Riberholdt, and asked what he now thought was going to happen. Using a soccer analogy Riberholdt told him: "At some point Chirac is going to take the ball and kick it way out of the stadium. And someone is then going to have to go get the ball and put it back into play. And that person is going to be you. And you will have to do it alone." As Solana reconvened the meeting, Chirac immediately asked for the floor. The text, as it stood, was not acceptable to France, he said. However, it could be made acceptable by simply reordering the text.

What sounded like an innocent change, however, had real political implications. The French President wanted a single paragraph on Romania and Slovenia and a second one on the Baltic states. In doing so, the positive language the Foreign Ministers had agreed to concerning the progress of these countries and the Alliance's recognition of their aspirations to join NATO was now in the first paragraph but not the second, thereby creating the impression that it applied only to Romania and Slovenia but not the Baltic states. Chirac was not bashful about his intent. He told his colleagues that there should be no linkage between Slovenia and Romania on the one hand and the Baltic region on the other. They were two different problems in his view.

Danish Prime Minister Rasmussen immediately asked for the floor. He could have accepted the Foreign Ministers' proposed compromise but not Chirac's proposal, which discriminated against the Baltic states. He reiterated what he had said earlier in the day; that either all candidates should be treated equally or they should not be mentioned at all. Several heads of state now broke in with their own wording suggestions. The meeting threatened to turn into chaos. Chirac proposed suspending the session for ten minutes and asked Solana to come up with a new compromise text. The proceedings were halted to give him time to do so. He was soon surrounded by a number of NATO leaders, including Chirac and Kohl, and Rasmussen, who seemed intent on guiding his pen. Clinton, for his part, stayed away form the fray and started to walk around the table. He stopped at the Belgium delegation and, looking at the commotion at the other end of the room, said: "Isn't this great? That's democracy."

After a short break, Solana reconvened the session and read his proposed compromise. He had accepted Chirac's proposal of two separate paragraphs but had added stronger language to the Baltic paragraph on the Baltic countries recognizing them as "aspiring members." He had given Chirac what he wanted in form but not in substance. Kohl immediately supported Solana's proposed compromise. Prodi, however, rejected it and read out a new Italian version. Kohl immediately interjected that this language was actually a step backward and would never be accepted by the Nordic states. Chirac, however, supported Prodi's proposal and again insisted that the problems of the Balkans and the Baltics could not be treated on the same level.

Kohl asked to speak again. As U.S. National Security Advisor Berger later recalled: "The place was absolutely silent. While Kohl was formally talking to the entire gathering of leaders around the table, in reality he was addressing Chirac. It was a pivotal moment." Kohl said that he regretted having to contradict his Italian and French colleagues, but that the Prodi proposal weakened the language on the Baltic states compared to Solana's text. He, too, was supportive of Romania and Slovenia but Solana's proposal was one all of the allies could accept whereas Prodi's was not. Dutch Prime Minister Kok chipped in to remind his colleagues that they all, including Chirac, had given Solana a mandate to find a compromise. He seconded Kohl's proposal that they accept the Chairman's proposal. Solana then officially asked the heads of state to approve his text. Neither Chirac nor anyone spoke—and Solana quickly gaveled the decision to a close. One of the most contentious NATO summit meetings in history had finally come to an end.

The following day, July 9, the Madrid summit concluded after the inaugural meeting of the NATO-Ukraine Council and a lunch gathering of more than fifty leaders represented in the Euro-Atlantic Partnership Council (EAPC). Both steps were designed to underscore the vision of a Europe free, secure, and undivided. Clinton and Albright sat at a giant oval table with the representatives of other nations, arrayed in alphabetical order. Directly across from the U.S. were the Albanian, Armenian, and Azerbaijani delegations; next to Clinton was the President of Uzbekistan. It was one of those moments when we realized that we were trying to create a new Europe where all countries, big and small, would have a voice.

Protocol called for a *tour de table*, with every delegation invited to give a short speech. At the luncheon meeting of the EAPC, the U.S. President spoke. As often was the case, he had rewritten his speech on the spur of the moment. "I would like to ask that all of us just take a moment to look around this room. It is a remarkable collection of people. People have come together in a new and very different way with a new vision of a transatlantic community in the 21st Century. We have here not a few great powers cavalierly deciding the fate of smaller nations, ignoring the hopes and dreams of ordinary citizens but instead a community of free democratic states at peace with each other committed to building a future of free, undivided, democratic nations in the European continent."[56]

That evening Albright and Talbott went to the Prado. They spent most of an hour in the basement, viewing Francisco Goya's paintings—an eloquent if dark reminder of the tragedy of modern-day Europe. Albright drew the connection with the events that had unfolded during the day. She commented to Talbott how the paintings symbolized the dark demons of European history that the U.S. and its allies had tried through NATO enlargement to consign forever to history earlier in the day.

Following Madrid, President Clinton left for a series of emotional and triumphal visits to Warsaw, Bucharest, and Copenhagen. At each stop he was greeted by enthusiastic crowds. In Warsaw, we celebrated at an elaborate state dinner held in the same room where Solidarity had negotiated the peaceful transfer of power from the communist party one decade earlier. The next day an emotional crowd greeted the President on Castle Square. Many of my Polish friends were in tears. I watched as one of my military colleagues in uniform was kissed by several Polish girls to thank the United States for what it had done. The headline in the daily *Gazeta Wyborcza* read: "You have changed the course of history." Another Polish newspaper declared that Madrid marked the "funeral of Yalta."

The most emotional visit, however, was to Bucharest on July 11. The President's decision to go to Bucharest was made not without trepidation. Given America's refusal to back Romania's entry at Madrid, we arrived not knowing what to expect. Starting outside the airport, Romanians were lining the street to catch a glimpse of the President. At first we were not sure whether they were friendly or angry. But they started waving to us and it soon became clear that they were simply trying to express their desire to connect with America and the West.

Clinton met with Romanian President Constantinescu who was gracious and eloquent in expressing his country's desire to be part of the West.[57] The U.S. President was scheduled to give a speech with Constantinescu at University Square in downtown Bucharest. The crowds were now lined three and four deep along the main boulevard leading to the square. By the time we got there, more than 100,000 people had gathered. It was a remarkable scene as the two Presidents were greeted by shouts of "Clinton, Clinton, Clinton." As the two leaders spoke, I watched a middle-aged Romanian standing close to Talbott and me with tears running down his cheeks. It was a vivid testimony of Romania's desire to become part of the West. As I listened to Clinton's speech, I realized that he was tiptoeing beyond the carefully crafted sentences on NATO enlarge-ment worked out with his speechwriters. Talbott looked over to me with an arched eyebrow as the crowd cheered. "There's your next tasking," he said above the roar of the crowd.[58]

In the limousine on the way back to the airport, President Clinton asked Ambassador Moses whether he agreed with the decision not to extend an invi-tation to Romania. Moses said he thought Romania needed another two years of successful reform. The President agreed, noting that if Romania could stay the course, the U.S. would work to present it as a logical candidate for the next round of NATO enlargement. But it was up to Romania to perform, he added. President Clinton flew off to Copenhagen where the largest crowds since John F. Kennedy turned out to greet a U.S. President. Secretary Cohen traveled to Budapest, Sofia, and Kiev to carry the message that NATO's door remained open. Secretary Albright, in turn, flew to Ljubljana, St. Petersburg, and Vilnius before returning to an emotional homecoming in her native Prague.

Many on the American side would look back at Madrid as one of those oc-casions where the U.S. had asserted its influence—for the right reasons and with the right results. In Washington, the Madrid summit was welcomed as a tri-umph of American diplomacy in the noble cause of building a unified Europe. Yet there were bruised feelings in parts of Western Europe. As a commentary in *Le Figaro* put it: "Washington's hegemony is bitterly resented in many European capitals, starting with Paris." Clinton would be forever grateful to

Helmut Kohl for the role he played at the Madrid summit. In a meeting with German President Roman Herzog in Washington later that month, Clinton bubbled over with praise for the German Chancellor. "I would do anything for Chancellor Kohl—even jump off this building—since he has done so much for the United States," the President gushed.

Clinton said that some in Europe were criticizing the U.S. for the way it had handled NATO expansion, and that the French were feeding that feeling. "All that I can tell you," he said, "is that I have supported a strong European Union, a European defense identity within NATO, and the expansion of the European Union. On occasions, there will be differences, but I have no interest in trying to use the fact that, at the moment, we are doing well economically. I have to deal with an isolationist Congress but my goal is not to throw our weight around. I favor partnership," the President said. "Therefore, I invite you to treat us as friends with whom you can be honest and not to see us as a country that is trying to be both isolationist and arrogant at the same time. I regret how some of the issues played out, but please understand that I see our future in continued partnership, shared responsibility and shared decision-making."[59]

Book VIII

THE POLITICAL BATTLE

One major hurdle remained. NATO enlargement required ratification by all the allies. In the United States, this meant a two-thirds majority vote in the U.S. Senate. While the U.S. was the NATO ally most committed to enlargement, it was also paradoxically the country where enlargement was most vulnerable politically. The U.S. constitution, by requiring a two-thirds Senate majority, set a higher bar for ratification than that faced by most other allies. And the independent traditions of the Senate inevitably made the task even harder.

At first glance, the Administration had several key advantages. Both Republicans and Democrats supported NATO enlargement in their party platforms and several votes on nonbinding resolutions on the Senate floor had produced a solid majority in favor of enlargement.[1] The final 80–19 Senate vote suggested an overwhelming victory over enlargement opponents. But the actual political fight was closer and harder fought than those numbers suggested. The Administration's support was broad but often shallow and was not locked in until late in the game. One week after the final vote in the spring of 1998, President Clinton admitted to Italian Prime Minister Romano Prodi that the final vote was "a little misleading" and that the outcome of the enlargement battle was closer than it looked. "A lot of people who voted with us were reluctant," the President said.[2]

The reasons were apparent. NATO enlargement to the Czech Republic, Hungary, and Poland involved the biggest increase in the U.S. security commitment to Europe in decades. The Clinton Administration also insisted that the first new members would not be the last and that enlargement could eventually embrace countries from the Baltic to the Black Sea. This ambitious agenda was put forward at a time when foreign policy was seen as a less pressing national priority, and when the American public appeared skittish about new commitments abroad and Congress was less prepared to be deferential to the President. Generational turnover and the decrease in the authority of the key Congressional committees had also undermined the traditional levers for the Senate leadership to ensure building bipartisan support on Capitol Hill.[3]

While both Democrats and Republicans supported enlargement in principle, there were also important differences between them that needed to be reconciled. The Clinton Administration had embraced enlargement as part of a broader overhaul of the Alliance to help unify Europe and create a new trans-Atlantic partnership oriented toward new threats. It emphasized that enlargement was part of a broader effort to create a "new NATO" for a new era. In contrast, many Republicans were inclined to support enlargement as a geopolitical hedge against Moscow. They were suspicious of, if not opposed to, negotiating the NATO-Russia Founding Act. They were skeptical about NATO assuming new missions such as peace support operations and uncomfortable that the Administration put emphasis on such missions beyond NATO's borders. Lurking behind these questions was the broader issue of why the U.S. remained in Europe after the end of the Cold War and what NATO was for in the future.

Partisan politics was also a factor—and increasingly so. The President's avoidance of the draft, his handling of gays in the military, and what Republicans perceived as his unsteady record on the use of force had all contributed to Republican criticism of Clinton's handling of foreign affairs. The bitter debates over Bosnia policy had also left political scars on both sides. While the Monica Lewinsky scandal would not break until early 1998, the increasingly bitter tenor of Washington politics made it difficult to knit together bipartisan cooperation in any area, including foreign policy. After the end of the Cold War, politics no longer stopped at the water's edge, if it ever had. Even Republicans inclined to support enlargement nevertheless asked why they should help the Clinton Administration achieve a major foreign policy victory.

Opposition to enlargement was also passionate. The opponents included many well-known and respected figures in the U.S. foreign policy establishment. George Kennan, a key architect of post–World War II containment policy, attacked the decision to enlarge NATO as "the most fateful error of American policy in the entire post–Cold War era."[4] John Lewis Gaddis, the well-known diplomatic historian, wrote: "I can recall no other moment in my own experience as a practicing historian at which there was less support, within the community of historians, for an announced policy position."[5] The *New York Times* issued one editorial after another opposing enlargement and urging Congress to do the same. Critics openly predicted that support would collapse once it was exposed to public scrutiny. Some suggested that enlargement would never be ratified. The stage was set for a major political battle.

1. CREATING A COMMAND POST: THE BIRTH OF S/NERO

Recognizing the challenge the Administration faced, President Clinton and Secretary Albright decided to create a special NATO Enlargement Ratification Office to spearhead the ratification effort. Like everything in the State Department, it had to be reduced to an acronym—S/NERO—which in State Department-ese meant that it answered directly to the Secretary of State. But the acronym led to more than one quip about whether we truly wanted a name that many people associated with the hubris and fall of the Roman Empire. While located in the State Department, this office was to be the command post for coordinating the entire Administration's political effort to ensure enlargement's ratification.

The Administration turned to Jeremy Rosner to head this office. Rosner had been a senior NSC aide in charge of legislative affairs and speechwriting in Clinton's first term and had written the President's January 1994 Prague speech on enlargement. After leaving the White House, he had gone to the Carnegie Endowment, a leading Washington-based think tank, to write a book on why some foreign policy issues become relatively easy successes on Capitol Hill and others fail.[6] One of the first books Rosner read was Stull Holt's *Treaties Defeated by the Senate* which traced the history of the Senate's handling of treaties in explaining the demise of the Treaty of Versailles after World War I.[7]

Rosner immediately saw parallels between the League of Nations' defeat and the looming battle over NATO enlargement. In both cases, the Administration was trying to push a treaty through the Senate involving a major new U.S. commitment following victory in a war but at a time when there were real pressures to retrench from international commitments and refocus on domestic issues. Rosner was convinced enlargement ratification was a winnable proposition and that public support for it existed. But the more Rosner looked at the parallel between the League of Nations and NATO enlargement, the more convinced he became that the Administration could lose this battle if it adopted a "business as usual" approach in the uncertain political environment of the post–Cold War era—a point he made in an article in *Foreign Affairs* and pressed with both Lake and Berger in private in the fall of 1996.[8]

Rosner believed that the main political danger facing the Administration was on the right. Democrats seemed less enthusiastic about enlargement at first glance but at the end of the day were unlikely to desert their President on this issue in spite of their qualms. Republicans, in contrast, seemed more supportive on paper but, Rosner noted, they were deeply uncomfortable with the Administration's enlargement rationale, its policy on Russia, and the implications for NATO's effectiveness as a military alliance. In a memo to Berger in early 1997, Rosner laid out four scenarios detailing how the Administration might lose the ratification battle. In the first scenario, Republicans defected from the pro-enlargement coalition because the Administration was viewed as having gone too far in accommodating Moscow's concerns. In a second scenario the pro-enlargement coalition splintered over cost and burden-sharing issues. A third scenario envisioned Republicans deserting the President because Democrats tried to monopolize the political credit for enlargement. Rosner's final scenario foresaw the Senate turning down enlargement because it felt it had not been given an adequate say in the process, as was the case in part with the League of Nations.[9]

To avoid these pitfalls, Rosner believed the Administration had to reach out to the conservative Republicans and pursue a "center out" as opposed to "left in" strategy. In other words, it had to start by locking in political support among both internationalist Democrats and Republicans in the center and then build out toward both political extremes. On February 26, 1997, Rosner sent Berger and Albright a private memo outlining his strategy. The stakes involved were high, he argued. Success "would give NATO, Europe and general U.S. foreign policy an important boost." But a loss "would be League of Nations II with grim consequences for NATO and the ability of the U.S. to pursue its goals abroad." The Administration therefore needed a "good win" in the Senate "on a comfortable, larger-than-expected margin rather than simply winning 67 votes by the skin of our teeth."[10]

To get this "good win," Rosner concluded, the Administration had to pursue the ratification effort "aggressively, broadly and doggedly" and knit together a coalition spanning divergent groups — "hawks and doves, Russo-phobes and NATO-philes, Democrats and Republicans." It also had to recognize just where its political Achilles' heel was: "While most of the votes we need to pick up at this point are from Democrats on the left, the most serious prospect for defeat entails a broad defection by Republicans on the right." This meant that a focal point of our strategy had to be winning over conservative Republican figures like Trent Lott and Jesse Helms, hardly beloved figures for most Democrats. Some senior White House officials initially strongly opposed the notion of giving Senate Republicans preferential treatment. One week later, however, Rosner received a copy of his memo dated March 3 with a handwritten note scrawled on it by National Security Advisor Berger: "I agree with this approach."

Rosner's strategy required three ingredients if it were to work. The first was a close working relationship with the Republican Senate leadership, especially the Senate Foreign Relations Committee, which had formal jurisdiction over the issue. That meant dealing with the Committee's Chairman, Senator Jesse Helms (R-NC). Albright was already working hard to establish that relationship. In her confirmation testimony, she had pledged to be nonpartisan, joking that she had had her partisan political instincts surgically removed when she became Secretary of State. Albright journeyed to Wingate, North Carolina in late March 1997 to visit Helms on his home turf where he had attended college. A picture of Helms and Albright holding hands on the stage at Wingate University would later become a popular poster of the U.S. Committee to Expand NATO in the campaign for Senate ratification with the slogan: "Let's Do It Right. Secure the Peace. Expand NATO."

Helms was an especially harsh critic of the Clinton Administration. But he liked Albright's straightforward style and her anti-communist credentials. He was inclined, at least initially, to give her the benefit of the doubt. But Helms was not yet locked in as a supporter of enlargement. While he had voted in favor of several nonbinding resolutions supporting NATO enlargement, his staff also made it clear that he was reserving final judgment and that he had concerns that needed to be addressed. Pro-freedom and anti-Yalta, he was also skeptical of entangling alliances and overseas commitments. Indeed, during the actual Senate vote on ratification, Helms would say to one of his top aides, Steve Biegun: "You don't know how big a shift this was for me. I was a supporter of the Mansfield amendment"—a reference to the attempt to pull U.S. troops out of Europe in the mid-1970s."[11]

The Administration also needed a mechanism for generating bipartisan support for enlargement in the Senate and spanning the five different committees that could potentially claim a stake in the issue. It got it when on March 21, 1997 Majority Leader Senator Trent Lott announced the creation of a Senate NATO Observers Group (SNOG) for what he called "the painstaking effort" to build support for ratification.[12] Lott had been a member of the Arms Control Observer Group as a member of the House, which in turn served as a model for the SNOG. The idea of creating such a group had originally been floated with the Administration by Ian Brzezinski, an aide to Senator William Roth (R-DE), in December 1996. Roth, who was also President of the North Atlantic Assembly (NAA), became chair of the SNOG. It started work on April 22, 1997 with 28 Senators as members.

Other private groups also stepped forward to reach across the political aisle. Perhaps the most important was the U.S. Committee to Expand NATO (USCEN). It was the brainchild of several Republican supporters of enlargment who had worked together in the Dole Presidential campaign: Bruce Jackson, a former Defense Department official in the Reagan Administration who had become a Vice President at Lockheed Martin; Steve Hadley, a lawyer and well-known figure in the strategic community who had been Assistant Secretary of

Defense in the first Bush Administration and would become Deputy National Security Advisor in the second Bush Administration; and Julie Finley, a prominent Republican philanthropist and fundraiser whose foreign policy views had been shaped by the late Senator Henry M. Jackson (D-WA). Along with Paula Dobriansky, Paul Wolfowitz, and Bob Zoellick, they had helped ensure that the Dole campaign and the Republican Party platform took a strong stance in favor of NATO enlargement in the summer and fall of 1996 and defeated the more isolationist sentiments in the GOP.

Once it became clear that Clinton was going to be reelected, Finley, Hadley, and Jackson reached out to centrist Democrats to create what they envisioned as a bipartisan "citizen's initiative" to support NATO enlargement.[13] They approached Greg Craig, a well-known Democratic lawyer at the law firm of Williams & Connolly who had worked for Senator Ted Kennedy and would become Albright's first head of Policy Planning before going on to defend President Clinton during his impeachment hearings. They asked Craig to join them in a bipartisan effort to support enlargement. On November 1, 1996 the Committee was established with a bipartisan Board of Directors and a group of senior advisors, including strategic heavyweights like Richard Holbrooke, Anthony Lake, as well as Wolfowitz and Zoellick. On November 12, 1996, one week after Clinton's reelection, Jackson sat down with NSC Senior Director Dan Fried at the Metropolitan Club to discuss the Committee's plans to help build bipartisan support for enlargement.[14]

Jackson became the Committee's President. He had initially been skeptical about NATO enlargement, but Hadley had convinced him that it was the logical extension of Ronald Reagan's support of Solidarity in Poland in the 1980s and George Bush's unification of Germany in NATO.[15] Jackson had been involved in the bitter fights within the Republican Party between the internationalist and isolationist wings prior to Pat Buchanan's departure from the Party. He believed the key to ensuring Republican support for enlargement was to lock in conservative stalwarts like Senator Helms and Senate Majority Whip Don Nickles (R-OK) to form a firewall against isolationists within his own party. In a memo to the members of the Committee Board in March 1997, he wrote that "the greatest threat to a successful ratification of a treaty expanding NATO lies in the potential defection of conservative Republicans" led by "national security conservatives and Rocky Mountain unilateralists."[16]

Jackson also believed that NATO enlargement ratification required freezing out the isolationists in both political parties. He called it the "wing nut strategy." It meshed well with the "center-out" approach Rosner was developing. As a Reaganite Republican, Jackson also had the credentials to bring conservative Republicans on board in favor of enlargement. When Senator Bob Smith (R-NH) said he would "never" vote for any initiative pushed by "that———Arkansasan," Jackson told him that "you may be shooting at Clinton but you are hitting Reagan." In the spring of 1998, he went to see Nickles to follow up on a commitment the Senator had made the previous year to support enlargement. Jackson reminded him of his pledge and underscored how critical his support was in securing conservative support. Nickles told Jackson he was a man of his word and the Committee could count on his vote. But he added: "Young man, don't ever come back in my office asking for a favor for Bill Clinton."[17]

In early 1997 the Committee hosted the first of many dinners at Finley's residence. At the suggestion of Kozminski, it invited Adam Michnik to be the guest of honor at a dinner designed to showcase Poland's case for Alliance membership. Michnik was a well-known former Polish dissident who had gone on to become editor-in-chief of Poland's first independent newspaper, *Gazeta Wyborcza.* The dinner was held on February 18. Finley and Jackson waited nervously for Michnik to arrive for a dinner of red wine and lamb chops with a select group of Washington's power elite. Michnik arrived late, dressed in blue jeans and a leather jacket—and having clearly already had a few drinks. He proceeded to sit down and, while chain-smoking cigarettes and drinking scotch, mesmerized his audience with a two-hour discourse on Poland's tragic history, his own incarceration and torture by the communist police, and how NATO membership was the logical culmination of Solidarity's struggle for democracy and freedom. The audience was overwhelmed.

Finley's stately home on Woodland Drive soon became a kind of salon where both Republican and Democrat activists rubbed shoulders with Central and East European intellectuals-turned-diplomats and former freedom fighters. Political gossip was exchanged on who was on board and who was not and NATO enlargement lobbying efforts were coordinated. Central and East European Foreign Ministers vied with one another for invitations to meet Senators and members of Congress to make the case for their entry into NATO. Craig noted jokingly in a fax to Finley on March 6, 1997 after receiving requests from several Central and East European Foreign and Prime Ministers for dinner during the same week: "Well, now I know (finally) what it is like to be in demand. We are really where it is at in Washington these days!"[18]

Jackson became a well-known figure who could almost always be found at the Metropolitan Club after work comparing notes and discussing tactics with Administration officials and Central European diplomats on the most recent twist and turn in the debate. At a time when partisanship in Washington was on the rise, the Committee was one of the few examples of bipartisan foreign policy in practice. At a time when the Administration needed to shore up support on the Hill, the Committee members helped reach out to the target audience the Administration needed most—conservative Republican Senators. By early June 1997, the Committee had met one-on-one with some 25 Senators, along with the staff of 15 others.[19]

The third piece of Rosner's strategy was to make it easy for Senators to vote in favor of enlargement. One way to do that was to signal that this was a top

Administration priority that the President was prepared to go to the mat over. By sending that message early and often, the Administration wanted to deter potential opposition. NATO enlargement was the topic of Clinton's only foreign policy speech during the 1996 Presidential campaign and listed as the first priority in Clinton's January 27, 1997 State of the Union speech. Along with the creation of a special envoy, these steps were also designed to underscore that the Administration's commitment was serious.

Another way was to line up as many public endorsements of enlargement as possible. The debate over enlargement was always going to be predominantly an elite issue. But Rosner was determined to change the face of the issue — from its perceived image as an "ethnic issue," into a broad-based "American" issue by lining up a broad and diverse set of supporters. When a Senator subsequently focused on the issue, he or she would almost inevitably take a look at who was in favor and who was against. If the list included groups whose views the Senator considered important, it eased the way for that Senator to join the "yes" column.

Rosner's first step in setting up S/NERO was to hire as his right-hand man Dr. Cameron Munter, a talented foreign service officer who had served in Poland and the Czech Republic. Munter was not only Rosner's eyes and ears but also the point person in organizing a domestic coalition supporting NATO enlargement. S/NERO staff crisscrossed the country doing briefings on NATO enlargement for state and local politicians, business councils, etc. They accompanied religious, ethnic, and veterans leaders on visits to the candidate countries; arranged for Administration representatives to go on public call-in radio shows; and worked tirelessly to enlist support from veterans' groups, business associations, labor leaders, local politicians, as well as the American Jewish community and other representatives of the religious and values community.

By the time of the Senate vote in the spring of 1998, S/NERO staffers had visited more than 40 states to brief local leaders and editorial boards, and to meet with a variety of groups representing different segments of American society. When, in the spring of 1998, opponents would claim that enlargement had not been debated and did not have the support of the U.S. public, they were confronted with evidence of public support in the form of endorsements from more than 60 organizations. In a flyer circulated to Senators, the Committee estimated that these organizations represented more than 10 million Americans.

In early March 1997, however, the Administration still had a long uphill struggle ahead of it. Much of the foreign policy establishment was still skeptical of, if not hostile to, the Administration's policy. In a widely publicized debate at the Council on Foreign Relations in December 1996 between former Assistant Secretary Holbrooke and NATO enlargement critic Michael Mandelbaum, an informal vote taken at dinner following the debate clearly favored the opponents of enlargement.[20] As Richard Cohen wrote in *The Washington Post*,

"Holbrooke lost the debate—not to mention, on occasion, his temper." Whether the audience was predisposed to oppose enlargement or won over by Mandelbaum's arguments was not important: "Whatever the case, NATO lost—and lost big," Cohen noted. "If a bunch of internationalists feel this way, how's NATO expansion going to play in Peoria?"[21]

Support on Capitol Hill was also broad but often shallow. The Senate had overwhelmingly passed several non-binding resolutions in favor of enlargement, but these were precisely that: non-binding. They were important as a barometer of sympathy and an indication of which way Senators were leaning. But at the end of the day they did not mean that the Administration had the votes of these Senators locked in. A closer look at the views of the heads of several key committees revealed that the Administration still had work to do, even among its own party faithful. The ranking Democrat on the Senate Foreign Relations Committee, Senator Joe Biden (D-DE), signaled his unease with the Administration's policy in January 1997 as well. "I have serious reservations about NATO enlargement," Biden told *New York Times* columnist Tom Friedman. Anyone assuming that Congress was on board for enlargement, the Senator emphasized, "was making a big mistake."[22]

In early March Rosner set up shop in a dingy State Department office. He and Munter put up a calendar on the wall mapping out what needed to be accomplished by when. On March 5, Rosner's first day in the job, Albright called him up to her office. The Secretary had testified on Capitol Hill earlier that day and had found herself criticized from both the left and the right and by Democrats and Republicans on NATO enlargement. Albright was no newcomer to the job of dealing with Congress, having worked as Seantor Ed Muskie's chief legislative assistant and having been NSC Senior Director for legislative affairs in the Carter White House. Her message to Rosner was clear: we're behind the curve on this. She emphasized to Rosner the need to develop a clear and crisp message on enlargement and to have answers for the barrage of questions she was being confronted with—and quickly.[23]

2. THE CAMPAIGN STARTS

The Administration's campaign to sell enlargement started in earnest in late April 1997 when Albright and Cohen were scheduled to testify before the Senate Armed Services Committee. Albright had asked Rosner and me to arm her with the best arguments in favor of enlargement. We had both joined the Administration within weeks of each other with the same mandate: to successfully enlarge NATO. We both believed that this debate was not just about adding new members to an existing Alliance. Instead, it would be about why the U.S. should remain in Europe following communism's demise and what kind of NATO made sense in the post–Cold War era. Even before joining the State

Department, we had discussed at length how to integrate the policy and politics of enlargement. We often joked that my office did the "engineering" of enlargement while Rosner's did "sales." Our staffs would work together closely and avoid the normal bureaucratic frictions and rivalries that often plagued policy-making in the Department.

Albright wanted to clearly lay out the Administration's vision of Europe and our rationale for enlargement as the centerpiece of a broader Alliance overhaul. Whereas critics were portraying enlargement as a radical and potentially dangerous step, the Administration saw it as the logical adaptation of the Alliance to a new Europe. Albright also wanted us to convey our view that if the Alliance did not adapt to the needs of modern-day Europe, it was doomed. Rosner and I decided on an approach that drew on an argument I had picked up at RAND—namely posing and then answering the question of what kind of NATO we would want if we were building it over from scratch. It was an attempt to get people to think beyond the status quo. If NATO did not exist, would we create it and what would it look like?[24]

Our answer was that of course we would still want to have a strategic alliance between the U.S. and Europe to defend our common interests against future threats. But it was also obvious that such an alliance would look quite different—and would have new members and be focused on a different set of missions. Ergo, enlargement was part of the natural transformation and modernization of NATO for a new era. Albright liked the argument and asked us to work it into her testimony. It was a way to underscore that the changes we were making in NATO were a commonsensical adaptation of the Alliance to a new post–Cold War world.

On April 23 Albright and Cohen appeared before the Senate Armed Services Committee. Albright led off her testimony by stating that the Administration's goal was "to build, for the very first time, a peaceful, democratic and undivided trans-Atlantic community" that would do for the eastern half of the continent what the Alliance had previously done for the western half—namely provide peace and prosperity. But Albright immediately framed the issue of enlargement as the centerpiece of a broader effort to transform the Alliance for a new era. "The debate about NATO enlargement is really a debate about NATO itself. It is about the value of maintaining alliance in times of peace and the value of our partnership with Europe."

"Clearly, if an institution such as NATO did not exist today, we would want to create one," Albright insisted. "Just as clearly, if we were creating a new alliance today, we would not make the old Iron Curtain its eastern frontier. We would not leave a democratic country out in the cold because it was once, against the will of its people, part of the Warsaw Pact." The key question, she said, was the following: "Which democratic nations in Europe are important to our security and which are willing and able to contribute to our security?" She urged the Senators not to be confined by the old thinking of the Cold War and to think in terms of what an Alliance between the United States and a Europe whole and free should look like.

Albright listed four reasons why NATO enlargement was in America's interest. First, it was the best way to prevent another war in Europe. Second, it was the best way to consolidate Europe's gains toward democracy, peace, and integration. Third, it was needed "to right the wrongs of the past" and to allow Europe's new democracies to join the old ones as American allies. Finally, the Secretary insisted that enlargement would also strengthen NATO by adding new, capable allies. The issue, she concluded, was "whether the people who knocked the teeth out of totalitarianism in Europe and who helped to liberate us from the Cold War are worthy members of history's greatest democratic alliance."[25]

But the responses of many of the Senators were skeptical. One Senator after another now asked whether enlargement would not create a new dividing line in Europe, whether it wouldn't weaken and dilute NATO and who would pay for it. The Chairman of the Committee, Senator John Warner (R-VA), summed up his concerns at the end of the hearing by saying: "I come from the school 'if it's not broken, why try and fix it?'" By the end of the hearing Albright was forced to concede: "In listening to you," she said, "there is no question that we have a very difficult job ahead of us." [26] *New York Times* columnist and enlargement opponent Tom Friedman gloated that the Administration had run into bipartisan skepticism from some of the Senate's most knowledgeable defense experts. "Imagine," he wrote, "what happens when the 'know nothings' in Congress start debating expansion."[27]

The committee hearings were also a reminder of the tensions within the coalition we were trying to knit together. Democrats on the left were worried that enlargement would damage Russian democracy and arms control. The Administration's most effective political weapon in addressing these latter concerns was Talbott, whose commitment to Russian democracy and reform was beyond question. Throughout the spring of 1997 he met with numerous Democratic Senators and Members of Congress to explain why the Administration believed it could pursue both NATO enlargement and support Russian reform in tandem. Talbott corresponded privately with a number of critics, including George Kennan, to explain Administration policy. Diplomatic breakthroughs at Helsinki and the NATO-Russia Founding Act helped lock-in Democratic support, including that of Senator Joseph Biden (D- DE), the ranking Democrat on the SFRC.

But Republican critics now lashed out at the Administration for going too far in NATO's relations with Russia. Perhaps no one was more outspoken than former Secretary of State Henry Kissinger. Whereas the Administration saw the NATO-Russia Founding Act as a major accomplishment that preserved our relations with Moscow, shored up support for enlargement among the allies, and secured our liberal political flank at home, many Republicans, led by Kissinger, belittled these accomplishments and accused the Administration of granting Moscow too much say in the Alliance's inner workings and trying to turn it "into a U.N.-style system of collective security."[28] The former Secretary of State's argument that enlargement was a good idea done wrong was exactly the kind of critique that Rosner feared could lead to the defection of conservative Senators.

But Albright fought back, defending the Administration's approach. She told one visitor after another: "Henry just has his facts wrong on this one." Administration officials fanned out to meet with key Senators and other influential Washington individuals to explain the safeguards we had built into the NATO-Russia Founding Act. We also got some help from Czech President Vaclav Havel who defended the Administration's attempt to shift NATO away from a focus on a Russian threat in *The New York Times*. "Some people simply want to continue fighting the cold war and consider Russia their chief enemy; they see the threat of Russia as the reason to enlarge NATO," he wrote. Such thinking, Havel underscored, underestimated the range of dangers facing the Euro-Atlantic region. NATO needed to focus on these new threats or else it would turn "into a hopelessly antiquated club of cold war veterans."[29]

The Administration was also determined to blunt suggestions that it was afraid to talk about the risks enlarging NATO involved, above all the pledge to go to war to defend Central and Eastern Europe if need be. There was no better way to kill this argument than to have President Clinton address the issue himself. The venue chosen was the U.S. military academy at West Point. After all, it would be these young cadets who were likely to command the U.S. troops who might be called upon to defend Central Europe at some point in the future. Addressing the graduating class of West Point on May 31, 1997, Clinton told them that he was proposing to expand NATO "to make it less likely that that you will ever be called to fight in another war across the Atlantic." But, looking directly at the graduating cadets, the President acknowledged that enlargement was not risk free and that enlargement "means that you could be asked to put your lives on the line for a new NATO member, just as today you can be called upon to defend the freedom of our allies in Western Europe."[30]

But nowhere was the President more effective than in dealing directly with key Senators himself. On the evening of June 11, the SNOG leadership was invited to the White House for consultations before Clinton made a final decision on the countries the U.S. would support inviting to join NATO at Madrid. But it was also an opportunity for the President to gauge the overall level of support among the Senators on enlargement. Clinton opened the session by laying out his arguments in favor of inviting just three countries—the Czech Republic, Hungary, and Poland. "You know from press reports that I favor a smaller expansion," he told the Senators. "These three countries are the best prepared.

Extending a security guarantee is important. No NATO member has ever been attacked." He also underscored the need to avoid creating a new dividing line in Europe that could jeopardize the Baltic states or Ukraine.

"If you take a smaller number, we have a better chance to keep the Europeans in line for a second round of admissions. It will also keep people from going nuts on the Baltic issue. We need to keep a certain amount of ambiguity here. If we take five, we are just creating a new dividing line. But we want to keep the door open," Clinton told the group. "The Europeans originally did not like enlargement," the President added. "But now they think it is their idea. They think the easier thing to do is to just let everyone in. But if we listen to the JCS and their arguments, I'm tilting to three. I know there's a lot of support for Slovenia and maybe even Romania. But I'd like to hear your views."

Roth, as Chairman of the SNOG, responded first. He supported four candidates including Slovenia—and handed Clinton a letter signed by 11 Senators backing that small Balkan country's candidacy.[31] Biden also supported Slovenia and argued that including it would have a positive effect on stability in the Balkans. But he agreed that Romania was not ready and would be a problem on the Hill. "If Romania is the price for Slovenia, I wouldn't do it," he concluded. The President thanked Roth and Biden. Noting that the two SNOG leaders both came from the small state of Delaware, the first to ratify the Constitution, he quipped: "All of us who come from other states appreciate that Delaware supported enlargement in the United States."

Senator Helms was next. "Mr. President, I think you have sized it up just right." He was unimpressed with the argument that the Alliance had to bring Romania in because it was fragile. "That is not a good reason to bring them in. NATO is not a therapy group. Romania's reforms are great, but they are not yet locked in. It would be very tough politically to do 4 or 5." As they went around the table, there were a variety of views. Senators Gordon Smith (R-OR) and Dan Coats (R-IN) underscored their support for Romania.

The President then turned to Senator Strom Thurmond (R-SC). Thurmond, the 95-year-old Senator who had recently broken the Senate's record for the longest term in office, responded with remarkable succinctness: "I'd stay with three and do it quickly and by doing that it will lend hope to the others." There was a wave of laughter, as everyone marveled at his insight and brevity. The President quipped: "Strom, this is the first time I have spoken to you since you broke the longevity record. If I could say so much so briefly, they'd repeal the 22 amendment!"—a reference to the two term limit for Presidents.

But several Senators fired warning shots across the President's bow on the wisdom of enlarging NATO at all. The strongest warnings came from Republican Senators Warner and Ted Stevens (R-Alaska). As Chairman of the Senate Armed Services and Appropriations Committees respectively, each was a political powerhouse in his own right. Each of them had traditionally been a strong proponent of NATO throughout their careers in Congress. They were potentially dangerous opponents if they publicly opposed enlargement. And both were leaning in that direction.

Warner told the President that he had come to learn. "But I have strong concerns," he added, signaling that he was not on board. "We have to make sure we're not ruining the best military alliance in history." Stevens echoed that sentiment. He asked how we could be expanding U.S. commitments at the same time we were shrinking the size of the military and our defense budgets. The way the debate was being conducted made it sound like joining NATO was joining a political club, Stevens continued. "I have not opposed enlargement publicly," he added, but he feared it would ruin the Alliance. A younger generation of U.S. politicians would not pay for it. He was also not convinced it was in the U.S. interest to go forward with enlargement in light of other global defense commitments, particularly those in Asia, a region that the Senator from Alaska had long urged the U.S. to pay more attention to.

The President responded first to Warner. "What's the option if we don't expand? If you believe that we and the Canadians have an interest in staying engaged in Europe, I guess we could dress up PfP and leave that as our strategy. But one thing I learned as a result of Bosnia is that the bottom line for us is that we should have the broadest and deepest alliance with the democracies of Europe."

Addressing Stevens, Clinton said. "Your point is that we may need our defense resources in Asia. I agree with that. We need to be honest about providing what we need to fund defense, including in Asia. But my thought has been that if we could get a good deal with Russia, strengthen NATO and PfP, then we could eliminate the possibility of a major upheaval in Europe. Even if things happen on the edges of Europe—like in Bosnia—we would have a mechanism, the allies and the resources to handle them. So I see this as freeing up resources for Asia. But you are right we have to be honest about the defense dollars."

But Stevens warned: "I expect another Mansfield amendment [on withdrawing U.S. troops from Europe]. If Europe is ready to have a collective defense mechanism, why not let them do it without us. They all talk to me about interoperability, but it only means more U.S. dollars." Berger broke in to say: "We're more vulnerable to the Mansfield Amendment if we freeze NATO in Cold War amber. I think we are more likely to have public support if we keep it as a strong collective defense pact but one which is also helping to bolster new democracies." Clinton agreed that the Europeans should do more for their own defense. "That's why we support ESDI," he said. "But," he told Stevens, "if we were not there, Bosnia would still be going on."[32]

Meanwhile, Rosner was also looking for a way to put a human face on the enlargement issue. He had asked both Munter and Roger Kaplan in the Defense Department whether Polish or Czech forces had fought alongside the

U.S. during World War II. They pointed him to John Keegan's *Six Armies in Normandy* which describes a battle where U.S. and Polish forces fought side by side in Normandy after the D-Day invasion. Outside the French city of Chambois, several German tank divisions were encircled when the U.S. Army's 90th Infantry Division met up with the Polish 1st Armored Division to close the last escape route—the so-called Falaise Gap. Over the next few days, the Polish units held their ground against a series of bloody German counterattacks while awaiting Canadian reinforcements. In the days after the battle, the bodies of 325 Polish soldiers were buried in makeshift graves. A Canadian unit subsequently placed a sign in English on the French farmland that read "A Polish Battlefield."[33] .

Rereading Keegan, Rosner realized this battle could offer a way to remind an American audience that Poles had already proven their worth as allies in Europe's last great war. The American soldier who had made the first contact with the Polish 1st Armored Division in closing the Falaise Gap had been U.S. Army Captain Laughlin E. Waters. Rosner asked Kaplan in the Pentagon's Public Affairs Office to track him down. They found Waters in Los Angeles, where the 82-year-old Waters was a retired federal judge—and a Republican. Rosner called him to inquire whether he would be willing to introduce President Clinton at a NATO enlargement event at the White House. "That's a pretty broad invitation to extend to a Republican," quipped Waters, but he agreed to do it.[34]

On July 3, Judge Waters introduced President Clinton at a ceremony in the East Room of the White House. In his remarks, the President noted that for more than five decades U.S. soldiers had labored for the goal of an undivided, democratic and peaceful Europe. That goal, he noted, was now "within reach" as the Alliance prepared to expand to Central and Eastern Europe. "Judge Waters," the President concluded, "your presence here today 53 years later reminds us of the character of these we are about to add to NATO." Taking on those critics who claimed that adding these countries as allies would weaken NATO, the President added: "They, too, have fought and died for freedom and democracy, for ours as well as their own. Our ties have been forged in blood. And just as they were strong allies in World War II, they will be again."[35]

But the opposition was organizing as well. On June 16, the first news wire reports crossed our desks announcing that a group of prominent foreign policy figures were denouncing NATO enlargement in an Open Letter to the President. Led by Susan Eisenhower, the granddaughter of the late President Dwight Eisenhower and the ultimate icon of America's ties with Europe, the group consisted of nearly 50 foreign policy experts, retired diplomats, senators, and senior military officers spanning the political spectrum from left to right. Among the signatories were former Senators Bill Bradley, Gary Hart, Gordon Humphrey, Mark Hatfield, and Sam Nunn, as well as former Secretary of Defense Robert

McNamara, Ambassadors Paul Nitze and Jack Matlock as well as Professors Michael Mandelbaum and Richard Pipes.

The letter attacked NATO enlargement "as a policy error of historic proportions." It claimed enlargement would undercut Russian reform, degrade NATO's primary mission of self-defense, diminish the security of countries not in enlargement's first round, and extend a U.S. guarantee "to countries with serious border and national minority problems and unevenly developed systems of democratic government." The letter concluded by stating that enlargement was "neither necessary nor desirable and this ill-conceived policy can and should be put on hold."[36] Several signatories made their case at a press conference on June 26. Matlock, former U.S. Ambassador to the USSR, warned that an enlarged NATO would be too "preoccupied with its own navel and its expanding waistline" to carry out its mission. Asked whether it was not too late to stop enlargement, Mandelbaum insisted that the end of the Cold War meant that U.S. credibility was no longer on the line in the same way. "The world is now safe for the United States to recognize its errors and correct them."[37]

Even more worrying was a letter to President Clinton dated June 25, 1997 and signed by 20 Senators. It had been organized by enlargement skeptic Senator Kay Bailey Hutchison (R-TX). While careful not to explicitly oppose enlargement, it listed more than one-and-a-half pages of concerns and questions that could not be read as anything but a warning light. The letter was signed by twice as many Republicans as Democrats.[38] The most troubling name on the list was that of Senator Helms. The doubts of Warner and Stevens as the Chairmen of the Armed Services and Appropriations Committees were known to the Administration, but Helms's signature came as a surprise. The conservative *bête noire* was thought to be in the pro-enlargement camp. His defection would have been a major boost for the opposition. Along with Warner and Stevens, it would have meant that the Chairmen of all three key Senate Committees on foreign, defense, and appropriations opposed enlargement.

Jesse Helms's shadow seemed to follow us on the road as we departed for the Madrid summit. As part of its outreach effort, the President had invited a SNOG delegation led by Senator Lott to accompany him to Madrid. We had also arranged for SNOG Chairman Roth to address the summit in his capacity as head of the North Atlantic Assembly. After Madrid, the President arrived in Warsaw for a stop intended to be the trip's emotional highlight. President Clinton and the entire U.S. delegation received an emotional reception from a crowd of more than 30,000 Poles in Warsaw's Castle Square. I watched as Poles spontaneously went up and hugged a U.S. military officer who was in the crowd.

Our jubilant mood was punctured when, on the morning of July 9 we woke up in Warsaw to read an op-ed by Senator Helms in the European edition of *The Wall Street Journal*. In it, he launched a frontal assault on our NATO policy by throwing almost every conceivable conservative criticism at us. The Administration was accused of pursuing a "dangerous and ill-considered plan for NATO transformation" that was a combination of "nation building," and "an exercise in the appeasement of Russia." The editorial ended on a threatening note: "If the Clinton Administration views NATO not as a tool to defend Europe, but as a laboratory for social work, then NATO should not only eschew expansion, it should declare victory and close shop." Helms's op-ed demanded that "dramatic changes must be made" before he would support enlargement—and listed nine conditions that the Administration had to meet to gain his support. [39]

We were stunned. Had Helms defected to the opposition? Or was he merely firing a warning shot across our bow? Rosner called Helms's press spokesman, Marc Thiessen, from his cell phone while standing on Warsaw's Castle Square. He told Thiessen that the President and Secretary Albright had read the Senator's op-ed, but were also seeing news reports suggesting that the Senator had come out against NATO enlargement. Rosner asked whether the latter reports were accurate. As Thiessen wrote in an email to Bud Nance later that day: "I told him the news reports were inaccurate, and that Helms's position is what he wrote in the op-ed: he is inclined to support expansion but has a number of serious concerns that need to be addressed." Rosner, Thiessen wrote, had responded that he thought the Administration could "meet Senator Helms's conditions." When Senator Helms saw Thiessen's e-mail, he wrote in hand on it: "Bud, Marc handled this just right."

It was the start of a careful dance between the Administration and Senator Helms that would lead to a set of understandings that, in turn, became a cornerstone of the Senate ratification effort. We needed Helms's seal of approval, both as Chairman of the Senate Foreign Relations Committee and as a conservative icon to lock in conservative Republican votes—and he knew it. We were willing to address his concerns—but not at the expense of reversing core policy decisions, alarming the allies or reopening the NATO-Russia Founding Act with Moscow. Given the other tensions in the pro-enlargement coalition, we had to be careful that whatever moves we made in the direction of Helms did not alienate those Democratic Senators whose votes we needed, too.

3. DANCING WITH JESSE HELMS

We returned to Washington from the President's Madrid trip to find the critics of enlargement keeping up a steady drumbeat of attacks.[40] The Council for a Livable World, a liberal anti-nuclear group that opposed enlargement, issued a vote count showing 49 Senators leaning in favor of enlargement, 26 against and the rest undecided. It underscored that in spite of the Madrid summit the opposition was only 8 votes shy of the 34 votes needed to defeat enlargement.[41]

Especially worrisome were signs of erosion of support in Republican ranks more generally.[42] Senator Richard Lugar (R-IN), one of the staunchest supporters of enlargement, sent National Security Advisor Sandy Berger a private memo warning that the Administration was in danger of losing the battle in the Senate.[43]

In late July, Rosner sat down to assess where the Administration stood politically. Paris and Madrid had consolidated support among some Senate Democrats. The Senate Republican leadership was still solidly behind enlargement although there were signs of erosion in Republican support. Rosner himself counted fewer than 40 Senators as confirmed supporters. The danger the Administration faced, he wrote Albright, was that Senators with very different concerns would coalesce into a bloc to provide the 34 votes needed to defeat enlargement.[44] But the first fruits of the Administration's outreach strategy were also starting to come in. In late June, the U.S. Conference of Mayors and the American Jewish Committee endorsed enlargement. Throughout the summer and early fall a series of veterans organizations came out in favor as well—the Reserve Officer's Association, the Veterans of Foreign Wars, Jewish War Veterans and the American Legion.

In early September the Administration got a major boost when the New Atlantic Initiative (NAI) issued a pro-enlargement letter signed by more than 130 figures from the foreign policy establishment—including former secretaries of state, five former national security advisors, six former secretaries of defense, eight former senators, and two former vice presidents. It was presented in early September by Republicans Jeane Kirkpatrick and Paul Wolfowitz, along with Democrats Tony Lake and Richard Holbrooke, in the Andrew Mellon Auditorium of the State Department.[45]

But the key to the Administration's strategy was the Senate Foreign Relations Committee, which would make the initial recommendations to the Senate as a whole and draft the resolution of ratification, and in particular Senators Helms and Biden. . With the Armed Services and Appropriations Committees chaired by skeptics, we needed Helms and Biden to cheerlead enlargement in the Senate. Over the summer Rosner met regularly with Helms's and Biden's chiefs of staff, Bud Nance and Ed Hall, as well as the key European-foreign-policy aides of the two Senators—Steve Biegun and Mike Haltzel. Randy Scheuneman from Majority Leader Lott's staff and Ian Brzezinksi from Senator Roth's staff also played a key role. We agreed to a series of fall hearings focusing on the rationale for enlargement, new members' qualifications, and burden-sharing as well as NATO-Russia relations.

On August 28, Rosner reported to Albright on how the planned hearings fit into the Administration's strategy. He underscored Albright's crucial role in aggressively addressing Helms's concerns during the hearings—while at the same time working to bring skeptical Democrats on board. NATO planned to sign the protocols of accession at its Foreign Ministers meeting in December. The tentative window for the vote in the Senate was in March 1998. The clock was starting to tick. Therefore, the autumn hearings were key to locking in the Senators' support.[46]

The following week, Helms' staff sent him a parallel memo proposing the fall hearings as initiating the formal process of Senate advice and consent. The Senator agreed to chair the hearings, and circled on his copy of the memo the issue of burden-sharing and writing: "This should be number one."[47] But Helms was still being lobbied by conservative opponents of enlargement to reconsider his position. On September 2, Helms wrote Jude Wanniski, a friend of the Senator and patron saint for conservative supply side economists, denying that he had irrevocably committed himself to expansion. "My only firm public position is that I do not favor further soaking the American taxpayer for any NATO expansion (and I do favor diminishing our enormous outlays as quickly as may be possible)."

When Helms' staff saw the letter, they realized their boss had still not yet fully made up his mind. They requested a meeting with the Senator to clarify his views on enlargement. In preparation for that meeting, they sent him a memo on September 8 arguing that enlargement was a conservative idea that came from anti-communist leaders like Lech Walesa and Vaclav Havel who feared Russian encroachment. They noted that it was supported by key U.S. conservative figures such as Jeane Kirkpatrick, Richard Perle, and Dick Cheney and had been part of the Republican "Contract with America." The message was clear: enlargement had a solid Republican pedigree. The Clinton Administration, the memo alleged, had initially opposed enlargement for fear it would offend Russia. "Clinton political advisors," it noted, had "belatedly accepted the issue of NATO enlargement and tried to claim credit for the initiative." But the memo admitted that Albright's appointment as Secretary of State "has put the United States on a clear course toward NATO enlargement."

Republicans, the memo noted, had three concerns about the Administration's handling of enlargement. One was the Clinton Administration's reticence to justify NATO enlargement as a military response to a residual Russian threat. The second was the NATO-Russia Founding Act's provisions on potential joint decisionmaking. The third was the costs of enlargement. "Notwithstanding some of the unfavorable inclinations of the Clinton Administration, NATO enlargement can be done right," the memo concluded. "For the somewhat moribund though still formidable military alliance of NATO, enlargement will be a certain improvement. For the legacy of Yalta it will be a reversal, and for the future stability of Europe it can build upon the fifty years of the NATO alliance which kept the United States *out* of yet another world war in Europe."[48]

Helms signed off on the memo—and in favor of enlargement. One week later Helms went public with his support—but also with his qualifications. In a letter to Secretary Albright, he wrote: "I have arrived at my decision to support enlargement based on my belief that this is a worthwhile endeavor. However, my support remains conditioned upon our ability to work together to include proper safeguards." Those safeguards, he continued, needed to include "a clear, military rationale for NATO enlargement," agreement in advance on the costs of enlargement, and assurances to U.S. taxpayers as to costs, and clearly delineated limits to Russia's role in NATO decisionmaking. The letter concluded by stating: "The alternative is for the process of NATO enlargement to fail upon the very concerns that I have outlined above. *We must not let that happen*" [emphasis in original].[49]

Rosner and I were greatly relieved. While each condition required meshing different political impulses, we felt the Administration could meet them. In terms of the military rationale for NATO enlargement, the Administration recognized that a revanchist Russia might someday again threaten Central and Eastern Europe. We thought the chances of that happening were low and that engaging Moscow through a cooperative NATO-Russia relationship could make that probability even lower. We also wanted a rationale for NATO that went beyond a hedge against Russia and that was based on what we were *for*, not only what we were *against*. We thought NATO should focus on all the possible threats to its allies. Russia was one of those but not the only or even the most likely one.

Republicans, in contrast, saw enlargement primarily as a hedge against Russia. They thought the Administration was ducking the issue of Russian neo-imperial ambitions and too focused on new missions like peacekeeping. Many Republicans were comfortable with NATO assuming a more active war-fighting role out of area, but wanted to avoid messy and at times ambiguous peacekeeping operations—i.e., they wanted an Alliance that could deploy to the Persian Gulf but not get bogged down in Bosnia. In contrast, the Administration saw peace support operations as important in their own right *and* as a stepping stone for our allies to embrace other, more ambitious post–Cold War missions. There was common ground here between Republicans and Democrats. But finding it in the politically heated context of the NATO enlargement debate was not always easy.

Republican skepticism on Russia lay behind Helms' demand that clear limits be set on the NATO-Russia Permanent Joint Council. Above all, Helms wanted it to be clear that NATO would always have a common position before it sat down in the PJC to talk with Russia. Helms wanted this safeguard on the record in a clear way. He and his staff repeatedly told us that they wanted to tie not only our hands, but those of future Administrations as well. One day in mid-September Steve Biegun from Helms' staff called Rosner with the idea of a choreographed exchange between Albright and Helms to clarify what the PJC would and would not do. Among other things, the exchange would underscore that NATO would always have an agreed position before sitting down with Moscow. He then proceeded to read a question slowly so Rosner could take down every word. Rosner came to see me and we spent the next couple of days clearing an answer Albright could give Helms. When we first showed Albright our proposed answer, she said, "It's not tough enough," and added several sentences drawing the line even more firmly against Russia having too strong a voice in the North Atlantic Council (NAC).

Shortly thereafter, however, Talbott, who was out of town, called in to complain that our proposed response sounded too anti-Russian. So we added yet another paragraph that addressed his concerns as well. Rosner then called Biegun back: "Of course, you understand that I can't predict what the Secretary will necessarily say, but what do you think the reaction would be if her response was as follows?" He then read the carefully scripted response. Biegun responded: "I think if the Chairman asked that question, and the Secretary gave that answer, the response would be very positive." The day before the hearings Biegun faxed Rosner a piece of paper with the question he had provided Helms. "This is what we gave the Senator," he wrote on the fax. "I *cannot* guarantee 100 percent that he will ask it" [emphasis in original].[50]

The third of Helms' concerns was on the costs of enlargement. Here the Administration was in a quandary of its own making. NATO did not have an agreed upon methodology for measuring the costs of enlargement. Initial studies by RAND and the Congressional Budget Office (CBO) had produced a wide spectrum of estimates ranging from as little as $10 billion to more than $100 billion.[51] A Defense Department study issued in February 1997 had estimated the costs of enlargement—for the United States, other current allies, and the new members—to be between $27–35 billion over a ten year period. This estimate was premised on the assumptions of the NATO enlargement study—i.e., that no immediate military threat existed and that NATO could rely on a reinforcement capability to carry out new commitments. It also made the point that such costs spread out over a 10-year period were modest in an Alliance where European allies spent $160 billion per year on defense—and were in any case much lower than what these countries would spend if they were providing for their own national defense.[52]

Politically, these numbers nonetheless created sticker shock across the continent—and promised to hand our opponents at home an issue with which to attack us. Allies were under pressure to meet the fiscal criteria for the European Monetary Union and in no mood to increase defense spending. They accepted U.S. thinking on the military requirements for enlargement—i.e., what kind of forces were needed to defend these countries—but not our methodology for costing out those requirements. Instead, they wanted to limit those costs to what

NATO would spend on its common budget on for infrastructure. This was less than half of one of the categories the Administration had identified in its cost study. They wanted to stretch even those costs over a longer period and fund them through reprioritization and reallocation. At Madrid, we squeezed a statement out of our allies that they would provide the resources needed for enlargement—but it had been like squeezing blood out of a stone.[53]

The Administration had a political problem. Isolated in NATO, it had little choice but to give in to the allies. As a result, NATO's official cost estimates were going to be a fraction of what DoD had estimated some eight months earlier. We had to explain why the Administration had decided to go with new, much lower numbers measuring a different, and much smaller, piece of the NATO enlargement pie. Such an approach promised to make the cost numbers so small that they ceased to be an issue for some—but it also opened us up to the charge of either having been incompetent in grossly overstating the costs initially or as having capitulated and accepted lower figures under political pressure from free-riding allies.

On the eve of Albright's committee appearance, Rosner and I laid out our private thoughts in a memo to her. "The set of hearings you will kick off on Tuesday offer an enormous opportunity, but also distinct dangers. If we handle the hearings right, we could be well on our way to generating the momentum we need to assure both the ratification of NATO enlargement and the absence of harmful reservations. You are the key asset, because you can speak with great credibility to the concerns of both the anti-communist-right and the too-worried-about–Russia-left." Momentum was building in our favor, we emphasized, but events were still fluid and there was plenty of room for mistakes. We still had less than fifty confirmed votes in our favor.

The vote count was not our only concern, however. "The danger here is not simply falling short of 67 votes, although that remains possible. The larger danger is that we will face a raft of reservations and conditions, and each of which only needs 51 votes to become binding." While some amendments were unobjectionable, others were potential "killer" amendments we would need to defeat—and would need a bloc of cohesive voters to do so. "Thus, the stakes are high," the memo concluded. "If this month's hearings go badly, we will face a long sustained fight, particularly over reservations. But if you hit a home run, we could start to see more critics folding their hands, more undecideds declaring support, and more reporters and observers concluding that this fight may not be much of a fight after all."[54]

On October 7, the Senate Foreign Relations Committee kicked off the first of nine full committee hearings on enlargement over the next thirty days before three different Committees—Foreign Relations, Appropriations, and the Budget Committee. Albright led off the first hearing before the Foreign Relations Committee on the morning of October 7. In her testimony, she directly addressed the concerns that Helms had laid out in his letter the previous month. Why, she asked, was the U.S. so focused on enlarging NATO at a time of relative peace when there was no immediate military threat in Europe? "The answer," she said, "is that we want the peace to last. We want freedom to endure, and we believe there are still potential threats to our future emanating from European soil."

"Let us not deceive ourselves," she said. "We are a European power. We have an interest in the fate of the 200 million people who live in the nations between the Baltic and the Black Sea. We waged the Cold War in part because these nations were held captive. We fought World War II in part because these nations had been invaded. If there were a major threat to the security of their region, we would want to act, enlargement or no enlargement. Our aim must be to prevent that threat from arising."

One of the threats NATO enlargement was designed to address, she told Helms, was Russia's uncertain future. "We want Russian democracy to endure. We are optimistic that it will. But one should not dismiss the possibility that Russia could return to the patterns of the past. By engaging Russia and enlarging NATO, we give Russia every incentive to deepen its commitment to peaceful relations with neighbors, while closing the avenue to more destructive alternatives." While there was no way to predict what dangers might arise in or to Europe in the decades ahead, we did know the following, she said: "whatever the future may hold, it will be in our interest to have a vigorous and larger alliance with those European democracies that share our values and our determination to defend them." "A larger NATO," she concluded, "will make America safer, NATO stronger and Europe more peaceful and united. That is the strategic rationale."[55]

Helms then read Albright the exact question on the NATO-Russia relationship that Biegun had previewed with Rosner, adding, "A pretty hefty question but I know you can handle it." Albright reiterated that the NATO-Russia Permanent Joint Council did not give Russia "any role in decisions the Alliance takes on internal matters, the way NATO organizes itself, conducts its business, or plans, prepares for and conducts those missions which affect only its members." The independence of the North Atlantic Council was sacrosanct, she underscored. Russia would never have a veto over internal NATO decisions and NATO-Russia consultations would only take place after NATO had first set its own policies. After she finished, Helms replied: "That is a very good answer to my question and I appreciate it."

Senator Biden made it clear that he, too, supported enlargement, but that the Administration still had to convince the American public that enlargement was needed. Americans wanted to know, he insisted, why NATO was still needed after the end of the Cold War. "The thing I hear my colleagues say is, 'Damn it, Joe, why can't they do it?' "

"I believe very strongly," she responded, "that this is a very smart additional preventive measure because history has shown us that we will go into Europe when we see massive wars that involve people we are closely related to, and when it involves our economic and strategic interests."

Other Senators asked Albright a series of questions about different aspects of enlargement, but it was also clear that the majority of Senators on the Committee were now inclined to support the Administration. After the hearings Biden said: "I think I've got the votes but I'm not sure."[56]

In the following weeks, critics of enlargement such as Ambassador Jonathan Dean, Ambassador Jack Matlock, and Michael Mandelbaum also had their say before the Committee. But they received a critical reception from both Helms and Biden. Biden in particular dismissed the arguments of Dean and Mandelbaum against enlargement as "dead wrong." He described the suggestion that U.S.-Russian arms control agreements could be in trouble because of enlargement as "a perversion of recent history" and suggested that to not enlarge NATO because there was no immediate Russian threat was "a prescription for paralysis." There was no longer any doubt on which side of the issue the Democratic Senator from Delaware stood.[57]

The Albright-Helms exchange also took much of the sting out of conservative complaints about the NATO-Russia Founding Act. In a special session set aside to explore the NATO-Russia issue, Henry Kissinger stated that he was reassured by the Albright-Helms exchange on the PJC and that enlargement should proceed with bipartisan support.[58] When Moscow was briefed by American diplomats about the restrictive interpretation of the Founding Act that the Administration and the Senate had agreed to, it was not pleased.[59]

The cost issue, in turn, was tackled on October 21 before Senator Ted Stevens' Appropriations Committee, where Albright appeared along with Secretary of Defense William Cohen. Stevens had called the hearing because he believed the Administration's assumption on both costs and troop deployments was too rosy. He believed that the demands on U.S. forces would be greater and that the end result would be a further erosion of U.S. military readiness when the main strategic threats to the U.S. were in Asia. Shortly before the hearing started, Cohen turned to Albright and said "Let me handle this. I know these guys and can talk to them." It was one of many moments where Cohen's credentials and support were invaluable in terms of winning over skeptical Republican Senators. A Republican and former member of the Armed Services Committee himself, he enjoyed great respect among his former colleagues.

Stevens opened the hearing by reading Albright Dean Acheson's unfortunate response to Senator Bourke B. Hickenlooper (R-Iowa) at the 1949 hearings when Acheson had stated that the U.S. did not intend to deploy substantial numbers of U.S. troops in Europe on a more or less permanent basis.[60] Stevens now asked whether Albright could assure him that the U.S. was not repeating the same mistake. Albright responded by carefully explaining why NATO did not see the need to deploy any additional U.S. troops in Europe in the existing environment—and argued that enlargement was the best way to lock in the peace and prevent the U.S. from fighting a future European war.

But it was Cohen who bore the lion's share of the burden in explaining why the Administration's cost estimates had changed so dramatically. He put his prepared statement aside and addressed the Senators as their former colleague. He laid out the reasons why the initial U.S. estimate was so high and why NATO's own estimates were going to be lower. He explained that NATO assessment teams had found that the infrastructure in these countries was in better shape than expected. And he assured the Senators that, based on his discussions with his colleagues in NATO, that the allies would pay their fair share.[61] Cohen concluded by quoting President Eisenhower that a soldier's pack is not as heavy as a prisoner's chains. "That is something that these three countries have endured for too many decades." They have had to carry around the weight of prisoner's chains. They now have an opportunity to join the most successful military institution in the history of the world, and to secure their security, and to promote their prosperity and stability. That is in our vital interest and we should ratify for those reasons alone."[62]

At a final hearing before the SFRC in early November, nongovernmental and other organizations were offered an open mike to go on the record either supporting or opposing enlargement. Representatives of some fifteen groups testified, including the Atlantic Council, Freedom House, the American Jewish Committee, trade unions, veterans and ethnic groups—with twelve of the fifteen supporting enlargement. The broad-based coalition of enlargement supporters was starting to come together. S/NERO's work in encouraging many of these groups to get involved was paying off. Bipartisan support was growing—and Senators were starting to pay attention.[63]

4. NEW MEMBERS AND NEW MISSIONS

In mid-November Helms and Biden issued a joint "Dear Colleague" letter summarizing the SFRC hearings. "We are convinced more than ever," the two Senators wrote, "that the enlargement of the North Atlantic Treaty Organization to include Poland, the Czech Republic, and Hungary is the correct policy for the United States to pursue." Many of the principles upon which the Administration's policy was premised, they noted, had gone largely uncontested in the hearings. But their concluding paragraph was the key one politically: "We believe that NATO enlargement, arguably the most important foreign policy initiative for the country in many years, is an issue that transcends partisan politics. Both of us are firmly convinced that enlargement is squarely in the American national interest and we anticipate that the Senate debate before the ratifications vote early next year will validate our conclusion."[64]

With this seal of approval from the leadership of the Senate Foreign Relations Committee, a cornerstone of the Administration's strategy was in place. A month later, Albright joined her NATO colleagues in Brussels to officially sign the protocols of accession. Albright signed the document using her full name: Madeleine Korbel Albright. Afterward she turned to Rosner and me and noted that she rarely signed her name that way but wanted to do so on this document as it would bring the homeland of her father into NATO. We returned home to find on our desks the most recent vote count of the Committee to Expand NATO from mid-December. It showed 66 Senators inclined to vote yes, 13 inclined to oppose, and 21 undecided. We had turned the corner and were well on the way to consolidating the two-thirds majority we needed in the U.S. Senate.

In the meantime, an important piece of our open door strategy had also fallen into place with the completion of negotiations on a U.S.-Baltic Charter. On her plane after visiting Vilnius during the Administration's post-Madrid tour of Central and East European capitals, Albright had turned to me and said: "Ron, that was a great speech but where is the strategy to turn it into reality?" With a direct mandate from Albright, I had spent much of the summer working with my colleagues at State, the Defense Department, and the White House to develop our Baltic strategy. If the Charter were going to provide the perspective of NATO membership, we needed an action plan. Major General "Buzz" Kievenaar at DoD took the lead in developing a plan to help the Baltic states reform their militaries so that they would become NATO compatible. In early September, Assistant Secretary of State Marc Grossman had unveiled a new U.S. "Northern European Initiative" at a meeting with Nordic and Baltic Foreign Ministers in Bergen, Norway which embraced the idea of an expanding regional cooperation around the Baltic Sea, including with Russia.[65] It was a part of a broader strategy to help re-create the spirit of the old Hanseatic League, where all of those countries were connected by commerce and regional cooperation.

In mid-October, a final round of negotiations between the U.S. and the Baltic states held in the State Department produced a common text. The distrust from the previous spring had dissipated as we all sat around a table with a Thesaurus looking for the right adjectives to resolve final wording issues. When the White House schedulers postponed the initial signing date for the Charter, National Security Advisor Berger called in the three Baltic Ambassadors to reassure them that everything was on track. To everyone's surprise, he revealed that his ancestors were from Riga and quipped that he was the first Baltic-American National Security Advisor of the United States.

In an emotional ceremony held in the White House on January 16, 1998, President Clinton and the Presidents of the three Baltic states met to sign the U.S.-Baltic Charter. Clinton pledged to the three Baltic Presidents that the U.S. would never consider Europe to be fully secure until they, too, were secure. He underscored the importance of NATO's open door policy and underscored that the United States was "determined to help create the conditions under which Estonia, Latvia and Lithuania can one day walk through that door."[66] Albright turned to Grossman and me and said: "It doesn't get much better than this. This is what we all signed up for." At a reception at Blair House, conservative Republican supporters of the Baltics mixed with Democrats, another sign of the bipartisan support that was starting to emerge.

At the same time, the Senate hearings from the fall and the public debate on NATO were changing. Increasingly, we were no longer confronted solely or even primarily with questions on the pros and cons of enlargement. Instead, the debate was shifting from the question of NATO's future roster to rationale—i.e., what was an enlarged NATO for and what would its future mission be? The question was not a new one. The Administration had fought bitter fights over whether the Alliance should intervene in Bosnia and whether U.S. troops should be deployed as part of a peacekeeping mission on the ground. More generally, the Administration had argued that in a post–Cold War world the Alliance had to be prepared to intervene beyond its borders to defend its members against new and different threats.

This debate over NATO's future missions had been percolating in the strategic community. In early 1997 a group of RAND analysts published a book putting forth the thesis that the U.S. and Europe should embrace a new global partnership in which NATO should refocus on threats to common trans-Atlantic territory and interests that could come from beyond Europe in the form of weapons of mass destruction or terrorism. The argument was simple but controversial: as Europe became increasingly stable and the Russian threat continued to wane, the traditional U.S. role of defender of Europe was becoming less relevant. As opposed to viewing Europe as a place the U.S. had to defend, we needed to think of it as a partner with which we tackled new threats to our common interests *together*. This meant that NATO had to shift its focus away from Russia to the most likely military threats of the future—many of which were likely to be beyond Europe.[67] Prior to joining the State Department, I was among those arguing for NATO's "double enlargement" of new members and new missions.[68]

At the time, such views were dismissed by many in the U.S. government as beyond the pale in terms of what the U.S.-European relationship could handle or our European allies would ever embrace. But Albright was open to this kind of rethinking. It resonated with her belief that we had to modernize NATO for a new world in which we would confront very different threats than during the Cold War. That view was also shared by her new Assistant Secretary for European Affairs, and my new boss, Marc Grossman, who had arrived to take up the reigns of the State Department's European Bureau that summer. Grossman had spent much of his diplomatic career going back and forth between diplomatic assignments in Europe and the Middle East. As Ambassador to Turkey, he had seen how events in one region increasingly affect the other, and how the neat bureaucratic distinction between European and Middle Eastern or Persian Gulf security often broke down in the real world and how events in one region increasingly affected the other.

Within the State Department, Albright's new chief of Policy Planning, Greg Craig, was also pushing for a more radical rethink of NATO's core missions in conjunction with enlargement. Craig was one of the founders of the Committee to Expand NATO and had independently come to the same conclusion that NATO needed to be overhauled if it was to remain relevant.[69] Grossman encouraged me to pursue my ideas in private, as well as in collaboration with Dan Hamilton from Craig's staff. A strong advocate of enlargement, Grossman nonetheless realized that size was not the same as purpose. Madrid had clarified NATO's future roster, but not its future role. Grossman wanted NATO to remain a strong and effective military alliance. He had started his career as the special assistant to NATO Secretary General Lord Carrington and had remained a staunch Atlanticist. One day he confided to me that his nightmare was that we would wake up in ten years and find that NATO had begun to look like the EU or the OSCE as it competed with these institutions for something meaningful to do.

In the fall of 1997 and early 1998, Grossman and I exchanged a series of notes in which we debated those issues. Should the prime focus of U.S. policy be simply to continue the enlargement process eastward? Or was it more important to refocus the Alliance on addressing new threats of instability in the south, including potential threats from weapons of mass destruction coming from beyond Europe? Or should we try to do both in parallel? Grossman called it the "mega-question" in U.S. policy on NATO.[70] We concluded that we needed a NATO that both helped to build a Europe whole and free that also served as a stepping-stone for a broader partnership. The question was how both to enlarge the Alliance and to reorient it to face the missions of the future—and prevent it from becoming a politically weak and militarily impotent organization as it grew in numbers.

The best way to avoid this dilemma, Grossman believed, was to make sure NATO was focused on real military missions in a new post–Cold War environment. NATO, he emphasized, had to remain focused on what it did best—deterring and, if need be, fighting wars. If those threats came from new sources or beyond Europe, the Alliance had to reorient itself to meat them. The U.S., he believed, should view NATO as "the institution of choice" when the U.S. and Europe would have to act together militarily. If the residual Russian threat continued to wane, NATO had to focus on the new threats to our territory and interests. This meant the Alliance had to rethink what Article 5 meant in a new era and prepare for missions that would take the Alliance beyond its own territory. But it had to do it in a step-by-step fashion that did not fracture the Alliance's consensus.

At Madrid the Alliance had decided to rewrite its strategic concept. In the fall of 1997 the Administration was starting to define its own goals for this exercise. At first there was little appetite in the U.S. government for an ambitious rewrite of the strategic concept as it promised to be divisive with the allies. But Albright firmly believed that NATO had to start to tackle such issues as Saddam Hussein and his attempt to acquire weapons of mass destruction. At the December NAC, she publicly called on NATO to "start a discussion" on the challenge posed by the growing spread of weapons of mass destruction to the Alliance and the need to think about new threats to Alliance security that could come from beyond Europe. Those remarks dominated the headlines of the December 1997 Foreign Ministers' meeting but it was clear that most of our allies were not yet ready for such a discussion.[71]

Following our return from the December Foreign Ministers meeting, Grossman raised the need to focus on the issue of NATO's future missions in a memo to Albright.[72] In parallel, he asked me to prepare a presentation for him to make at Albright's annual strategic retreat in early January.[73] In making our case, we were joined by Craig. Grossman and Craig made their pitch to Albright on January 9, 1998 at the Secretary's annual retreat with her senior advisors. Albright was supportive and asked us to develop our views further.

On January 15, Grossman sent her a note suggesting the U.S. consider using 1999 to define a new U.S.-European bargain for the 21st century premised on the U.S. and Europe working together in an expanded trans-Atlantic framework to solve problems both in *and* outside of Europe. This would require a new NATO with expanded missions, the reorientation of US-EU relations to global challenges, and a retooled OSCE to promote democracy throughout the Euro-Atlantic region. Grossman suggested using major summits that each of these institutions had scheduled for 1999 to push for this new U.S.-European bargain. He had a name for it—the trifecta. Albright wrote back on the note: "Good idea. Let's develop a 21st century better than the 20th—Europe's bloodiest."[74] It was a green light to make this a top policy priority—but after the ratification vote. We wanted to avoid provoking a debate on this sensitive issue prematurely.

In mid-December, National Security Advisor Sandy Berger sent President Clinton a memo laying out an endgame strategy for NATO enlargement ratification. It emphasized that the Administration was in good shape in the Senate, but pointed to the failure to obtain fast-track authority for a new free trade round as an example of the need not to take things for granted. Even though a two-thirds majority in the Senate appeared increasingly likely, the memo warned that support for enlargement in the Senate was still tepid; the Administration would face battles over key amendments. It urged early Presidential involvement to strengthen the Administration's hand early in the endgame, generate political momentum, and create the solid victory that would strengthen Clinton's future prerogatives and those of his successor.[75]

President Clinton kicked off the campaign by highlighting his commitment to enlargement in the State of the Union address in late January. On February 11, he officially transmitted the protocols of accession from the executive branch to the Senate. He was joined by the three Foreign Ministers and the Senate leadership for a ceremony in the ornate Franklin Room of the State Depart- ment. The President delivered his remarks in front of a full-size photo replica of the Berlin Wall, which Rosner had borrowed from the Pentagon for the event. As he finished his remarks, the President pointed to the display and said: "Behind me is a picture of the wall that for so long represented the false and forced division of the European continent. NATO cannot maintain the old Iron Curtain as its permanent frontier. It must and can bring Europe together in se- curity, not keep it apart in instability." As they left the ceremony, Vice President Gore reminded Senator Biden that it was the fiftieth anniversary of the end of the Yalta conference that had started to cement the original division of Europe—and that the West was now overcoming.[76]

Events were now breaking our way. In late January the AFL-CIO came out publicly in favor of the Administration's policy, following meetings between both Albright and Clinton with the organization's president, John Sweeney.[77] A few days later, a group of sixty senior retired military commanders—including five former Chairmen of the Joint Chiefs of Staff—endorsed enlargement in an effort organized by Steve Hadley of the Committee to Expand NATO.[78] It all seemed almost too good to be true. On January 20, Polish Ambassador Jerzy Kozminski sat down to write a cable identifying what could still go wrong for Warsaw. He sketched out several scenarios in which NATO enlargement might still be derailed.

The first was a crisis with Russia in the Balkans or elsewhere that would lead Western leaders to rethink enlargement. The second was a crisis in one of the candidate countries that might disqualify it or lead to new doubts about their qualifications. A third was something happening in the U.S. that damaged the President's ability to get enlargement through the Senate. The next day, January 21, 1998, Rosner walked into my office with a copy of *The Washington Post* and pointed to a story alleging that President Clinton had had an affair with a young intern by the name of Monica Lewinsky and had tried to cover it up. We were probably the only people in the world thinking about the connections between Lewinsky and NATO enlargement. We were lucky that the President's impeachment hearings, as well as the war in Kosovo, did not unfold until one year later. Ratifying enlargement against that backdrop of either would have been much more difficult and perhaps impossible.

The opposition had not given up either. In late January, we received reports about a new anti-enlargement group, the Coalition Against NATO Expansion (CANE). It consisted of political groups from both ends of the political spectrum, from the Free Congress Foundation and Eagle Forum on the right to the Union of Concerned Scientists and Council for a Livable World on the left. CANE's Founding Declaration claimed that NATO enlargement amounted to a "Gulf of Tonkin" resolution that would entangle the U.S. in ethnic conflicts in Central and Eastern Europe and soak the U.S. taxpayer of billions of dollars. Claiming that enlargement was being driven by Washington elites out of touch with the American public, they called for exhaustive hearings and an extensive floor debate with no vote before mid-1998, alleging that plans for an earlier vote were "railroading the issue."[79] Similarly, we also picked up reports of growing internal debate and opposition to enlargement within conservative Republican circles and the board rooms of think tanks such as the Heritage Foundation who officially supported enlargement. Both ends of the political spectrum, it seemed, had their own Russia-firsters.

Later that spring CANE was joined by the Business Leaders for Sensible Priorities (BLSP) whose President, Ben Cohen, was a co-founder of the Ben and Jerry's ice cream empire. BLSP was committed to shifting U.S. government spending from defense to domestic needs. It would fund a series of ads that opposed enlargement and showed the mushroom-shaped clouds of nuclear explosions and warned that NATO expansion could alienate Russia and rekindle Cold War tensions. They were focused in states where Senators had yet to announce their positions on NATO enlargement. But the opposition was unable to make significant political inroads—either in the Senate or in the broader public. They were not well organized politically, too disparate in their ideological composition, and unable to put together a broad-based coalition. Above all, they could not enlist a critical mass of political leaders, neither on Capitol Hill, nor more generally from the political center—which the Administration had assiduously cultivated.

By this time S/NERO had become a kind of a political rapid reaction SWAT unit. Every time Rosner received a report that a Senator might be wavering, he immediately arranged for a phone call from the President or from Albright, Cohen, or Berger addressing his or her concerns. A team of senior officials was often dispatched to follow-up with a briefing for the Senator or staff. Rosner and I met regularly with the Ambassadors of the three invited countries over breakfast to compare notes and were on the phone several times a day with USCEN exchanging notes on how to counter the critics. Rosner joked it was like playing the game "whack-a-mole"—every time an opponent popped up, the Administration tried to bat down what it considered a bad idea.

But it was a two-front struggle. While waging the public battle, the Administration was also engaged in intense and at times contentious talks with the Republican staff from the Senate Foreign Relations Committee over the language of the resolution of ratification. It was the vehicle through which Senators could attach reservations or amendments that could constrain future Administrations or, in the worst case, force the Administrations to abandon the treaty. By mid-February we had had several difficult rounds of contentious talks but were finding common language on many key issues: Russia, costs and burden-sharing, the open door, CFE, intelligence sharing with new members, POWs, and Jewish property restitution. On February 19, Helms' staff sent him an updated draft resolution of ratification. Helms sent it back with his comment: "Looks good to me!" Two days later, Rosner and I sent our assessment to Talbott concluding that we could work with the SFRC draft as well.[80]

5. THE ENDGAME

The SFRC was scheduled to hold the last in a series of seven hearings concluding the formal testimony record on NATO enlargement on February 24. The day before, February 23, we got the SFRC's latest draft of the resolution of ratification. We were narrowing the gap.[81] That same day the results of a new poll on U.S. public attitudes on enlargement showed that public support was high and unchanged from the fall of 1996. It belied the argument of the critics that once Americans became more familiar with the issue support would fall. The poll showed that 61 percent of Americans supported adding the first three members, and 50–43 percent supported adding additional states after the first three. As Rosner underscored in an e-mail, virtually all the pro-enlargement arguments tested had gained support whereas nearly all the anti-enlargement arguments had lost support.[82]

The next morning Albright made her final appearance before the SFRC. In addition to repeating the Administration's arguments in favor of enlargement, she took aim at some of the proposed amendments that enlargement opponents were starting to circulate. The signing of the U.S.-Baltic Charter two weeks earlier had opened another line of attack from enlargement critics who now claimed the Administration's open door strategy was reckless. In a *New York Times* editorial in early February, four well-known opponents of enlargement— Howard Baker, Sam Nunn, Brent Scowcroft, and Alton Frye—called for "a definite if not permanent pause in this process" after the first enlargement round.[83] It was quickly embraced by Senator Warner in the form of an amendment.[84]

The Administration believed that a "pause" on enlargement was unnecessary because the U.S. already had a de facto veto over further invitations, and it was dangerous because it could undercut democratic reforms in the region. Albright, who was already on record opposing the amendment before Warner officially offered it, wanted to lay down a marker that we were going to fight hard against Warner in her final testimony.[85] She pointed out that NATO had already enlarged several times in its history and had become stronger, not weaker, each time. She insisted that an open door policy was "central to the logic" of a new Alliance that would help knit Europe together. "A mandated pause," Albright told the gathered Senators, "would be heard from Tallinn in the north to Sofia in the south as the sound of an open door slamming shut. It would be seen as a vote of no confidence in reform-minded governments from the Baltics to the Balkans."[86]

The Senate Foreign Relations Committee convened on March 3 to vote on the resolution of ratification. The vote was 16–2 in our favor. Rosner's "center-out" strategy had worked. We had the support of all but the most conservative and liberal Senators on the Committee—Republican John Ashcroft (R-MO) and Democrat Paul Wellstone (D-MN). But several Senators had made it clear that they were uncomfortable over where NATO was headed. In a memo to Albright that evening, Rosner and I wrote: "Today's meeting of the Senate Foreign Relations Committee on NATO enlargement was intellectually and politically fascinating, and holds many lessons. The 16–2 margin clearly bodes well for the final tally. But the substance of the Committee's deliberations suggest the debate has gone beyond the merits of enlargement to these first three states, and has moved to broader issues: NATO's future orientation and new missions; future rounds of enlargement and the European security strategy beyond NATO."

We warned Albright that a number of Senators still had concerns and were likely to try to use amendments to put their imprint on enlargement. "Today's meeting," the memo stated, "does nothing to diminish our confidence that we will obtain the needed two-thirds vote. But it does suggest that if the ultimate vote is going to stand as a broad affirmation of our vision for NATO and Europe, we have work to do."[87] The next morning, March 4, the USCEN issued an informal vote count that had 72 Senators voting yes, 13 opposing and 15 undecided. By this count, we had crossed the hurdle of 67 votes required for ratification. We could now focus on the endgame. In a subsequent memo we underscored: "How this ends—the final margin, the amendments that prevail, the post-mortems by the press—will all color our ability to pursue the next phase of policy toward NATO and Europe."[88]

The Senate Foreign Relations Committee vote was a major victory for the Administration. The critics were furious. The *New York Times* charged that, "Rarely has such an important matter seemed headed for approval with so little enthusiasm or attention."[89] Tom Friedman accused the SFRC of putting on a "shameful performance." In a column in *The New York Times*, he complained, "Senators Jesse Helms, Joe Biden & Co. rolled over like puppies having their bellies rubbed when Clinton officials explained their plans for NATO expansion by dodging all the hard questions."[90] Other major newspapers, including *The Washington Post*, praised the SFRC vote.[91] And on March 13, *The Chicago Tribune* reversed its previous position opposing enlargement and now came out in our favor—a reversal that followed an intense effort by S/NERO to get at least one major editorial board opposed to enlargement to change its position.[92]

Sensing that momentum was rapidly building on our side, enlargement opponents urged a postponement of the final Senate vote. Seventeen Senators sent Lott and Daschle a letter asking that the vote be delayed until June 1. Former Senators Sam Nunn and Howard Baker also wrote the Senate Armed Services Committee criticizing the SFRC resolution and calling for additional hearings and a delay in the vote.[93] When Albright heard about their request, she rolled her eyes and reminded us that during the four years we had been debating enlargement the founding fathers of NATO had not only created the Alliance but also already enlarged it once. Pro-enlargement Senators countered with their own letter, and President Clinton weighed in with Lott to urge him to stick to the planned schedule.[94] Helms, in turn, defended his handling of enlargement in an op-ed.[95]

The Senate floor debate on enlargement started on March 18 but then, faced with the need to address a pending education bill, Lott postponed it until after the Senate's Easter recess. While disappointed, this was a pause we could live with. With the final floor fight now scheduled for late April, we had a chance to step back and review the order of battle. The fight was now over amendments. More than a dozen Senators had signaled their intention to offer amendments, often more than one. The amendments we worried about most were those proposed by Ashcroft, Harkin, Hutchison, Levin, Moynihan, Stevens, and Warner. They were proposing amendments ranging from restricting bilateral assistance to new members, a cap on U.S. contributions to NATO budgets, limits on new missions, creating a new conflict resolution process within the Alliance for Central Europe, to a suggestion that we create a way to eject allies from the Alliance if they did not meet our standards.[96]

While the Administration was determined to fight each of them, two were at the top of our list of "must wins." The first was Senator Warner's "pause" amendment. The second was an amendment Senator John Ashcroft had announced to limit any future out of area role for NATO. The Senator from Missouri was considering a run for the Presidency and positioning himself as the candidate of the right wing of the Republican Party. He had launched a mean-spirited attack mischaracterizing Albright's views on NATO's new missions. Albright had written him explaining in detail why his characterization of her views was wrong, but Ashcroft had ignored her explanation and instead accused the Administration of trying to distort the intent of the Washington Treaty.[97]

But Ashcroft had his history wrong—and the consequences of his amendment were potentially far-reaching and dangerous. The Washington Treaty was clear that NATO's collective defense commitment was limited to the North Atlantic area as defined in the treaty in geographic terms. But it had left open the option of NATO members coming together voluntarily under other articles of the Treaty to defend their common interests outside of that area. Acheson had made these points quite clearly in March 1949 in public interviews in which he had explained each Article of the Washington Treaty. We had dug the Department's summary of those interviews out of the archives and circulated it as part of our effort to defeat the Ashcroft amendment, which we feared would prevent NATO from being able to address new threats from beyond Europe in the future.[98]

On April 21 Albright met with the Democratic Caucus to shore up their support. She told the gathered Senators that the enlargement vote was one of the most important they would cast. It was a chance to truly end the Cold War—"to put it in concrete"—and to overcome Europe's divide. "I hope you would view it as an honor to vote for enlargement—to make these three countries part of the best Alliance in the world," she told them. Even at this late stage, however, it was clear that a number of Senators still had doubts centering largely on enlargement's impact on Russia and arms control. Albright went out of her way to address them: "I want you to know how committed the President and I are to making our relations with Russia work." The Russians did not like enlargement but they had accepted that it was going to happen, Albright said. There were still problems in U.S.-Russian relations, but it was a mistake to blame them on enlargement. "That's like blaming everything on El Nino," she quipped. A number of Senators said they were going to support the President—but without enthusiasm.[99]

On April 24, 1998 Senators Roth, Lieberman, and McCain sent around a "Dear Colleague" letter urging their colleagues to vote in favor of enlargement. They noted that enlargement enjoyed wide bipartisan support and had been endorsed by three former Presidents, eight former secretaries of state, seven former secretaries of defense, five former national security advisors and sixty former senior flag officers in the U.S. military. In addition, enlargement had been endorsed by 13 state Senates and House of Representatives, the U.S. conference of Mayors, the National Governor's Association, the Council of State Governments, the AFL-CIO, numerous veterans groups, and 26 ethnic, religious and humanitarian organizations. "These endorsements," they concluded, "are a powerful reflection of the broad consensus affirming that NATO enlargement is in America's national interest and deserves the full support of the Senate."[100]

The final floor debate opened on a slightly nervous note on April 27, 1998. Only a few days earlier Senator Lott had publicly urged the Administration not to take anything for granted. "I told the White House for the third and last time, 'If you don't pay attention to this bill this thing could get away from us,'" the Mississippi Republican told reporters. "The odds are we're going to get over 70 votes, but there's not a lot of enthusiasm in here," he warned.[101] The pro-enlargement forces were led by Senator Biden who took over the role of floor manager and became in many ways the key figure in managing the Senate debate. The opposition was *de facto* led by Senator John Warner. By the evening of the first day some fifteen Senators had spoken—ten for, five against and one undecided.

Behind the scenes, the President, Albright, Cohen and Berger worked the phones to line up the votes to defeat the amendments the Administration was fighting. SACEUR General Wes Clark pitched in by calling a number of Republican Senators to explain why the Ashcroft amendment was damaging to NATO. The rest of us spent most of the day working with SFRC staff to answer the concerns of individual Senators and to field requests for last-minute phone calls to help get them on board. A Democratic whip count found that there was almost no support among Democrats for the Ashcroft amendment—but that there was support for the Warner "pause" amendment. Secretary of Defense Cohen met privately with Senator Stevens to convince him to withdraw his amendment.

The first amendments came to the Senate floor for votes on April 28. Senator Harkin's amendment proposing limits on bilateral assistance to the new members was defeated 76–24. Senator Jon Kyl (R-AZ) offered an amendment suggesting guidance for the rewrite of the strategic concept which made clear that NATO's future missions would not be limited to peacekeeping. It was a vehicle to deflect support away from Ashcroft by allowing Senators to underscore their support for NATO's core mission of collective defense and to note their reservations about peacekeeping while keeping open the option of more ambitious out-of-area war fighting missions. The Administration eagerly supported it. It passed overwhelmingly 90–9. We also enlisted the support of Zbigniew Brzezinski and senior Republican strategists to lobby against the Ashcroft amendment. In a memo written late on the evening of April 28, Rosner wrote: "Today was a good day."

The political battle was now being fought on the editorial pages of the major U.S. newspapers. *The New York Times*' ongoing opposition to enlargement was relentless.[102] Anticipating that the *Times* would issue a final blast against the Administration on the day of the vote, Albright submitted her own editorial making the case for enlargement. On April 29th, we woke up to see the two contrasting editorials on *The New York Times* editorial page. As expected, the *Times*' editorial attacked enlargement as a mistake of historic proportions. "It is delusional," they wrote, "to believe that NATO expansion is not at its core an act that Russia will regard as hostile."[103] In contrast, Albright entitled her editorial "Stop Worrying about Russia"—and urged her readers to stop viewing Central Europe through the prism of Russia but instead think of these countries as independent nations who wanted to be America's allies. Enlarging NATO, she argued, would be a sign that we understood the world had changed and the Cold War was over.[104]

A group of us headed over to the Senate to help head off any last-minute surprise challenges before the final vote. A highlight came when Dan Fried, who had since moved on to become U.S. Ambassador in Warsaw, phoned to tell us about an amusing incident he had experienced earlier in the day. While visiting the Jasna Gora monastery in southern Poland, the home of the famous Black Madonna icon, Fried had been approached by one of the Fathers—complete in white robe and cell phone—who said: "We know you are having some problems in the Senate." He then pointed to the ceiling and said: "We're willing to provide a little help."

The day was filled with political skirmishing before the final vote. In the Senate, a series of last-minute maneuvers was underway. At one point enlargement opponents suggested that the vote be put off because Helms was scheduled to undergo surgery the next day. But Helms called their bluff by saying he was prepared to debate through the night if necessary. Lobbying by Biden along with Berger and Talbott helped convince Democratic Senators Leahy (D-VT) and Bingaman (D-NM) to withdraw amendments on CFE and the Baltic states. Biden and Helms urged their colleagues to fold as many other amendments as possible into a single manager's amendment to get to a final vote. But we still faced a number of potentially dangerous amendments, above all those being pushed by Ashcroft, Moynihan, Stevens, and Warner. When David Gompert, a senior NSC official responsible for European affairs in the Bush Administration, wrote an op-ed criticizing Ashcroft, we made sure it was faxed to every Republican Senator's office.[105]

Voting on amendments started at 3:30 P.M. There were now seven of them. Ashcroft and Warner had each asked that their amendments be considered last. It was an attempt to gather the protest votes of those Senators who had supported enlargement but still wanted to signal that their support of our policy was not *carte blanche*. But the momentum was now clearly on the Administration's side. Moynihan's amendment linking EU and NATO enlargement was defeated 83–17 in spite of an emotional warning from the New York Senator that the U.S. was re-creating the hair-trigger tensions that existed at the height of the Cold War.[106] Senator Hutchison's amendment on a new conflict dispute resolution was defeated 62–37. Warner continued to argue against enlargement as committing the U.S. to a "blank check" for an ill-defined military alliance. "We'd be creating through this expansion a 911 organization," he argued claiming that NATO was in danger of becoming "Dial a cop, dial a soldier." But his "pause" amendment also went down to defeat, 59–41.[107]

Throughout the day Ashcroft bargained with Lott over how much debate time should be set aside for his amendment. Lott wanted to wrap up the vote that evening and became increasingly irritated with Ashcroft's demand for several hours of debate at prime time when other Senators were getting much less. Finally, fed up with Ashcroft's tactics, he walked over to ask Senator Biden to move to table Ashcroft's amendment. It was a parliamentary maneuver to kill it before it even reached the floor. Biden agreed—but only if Lott would second his motion to make it clear that this was not a partisan move. After hesitating for a minute, Lott concurred. As Ashcroft walked back into the Senate chamber, he saw his amendment, which the Administration feared would be the most dangerous and closely-voted amendment, go down to defeat 82–18 without ever having reached the Senate floor.

At 8:30 P.M. the final floor debate commenced. The vote started at 10:25 P.M. Senator Robert Byrd (D-WVA), invoking an old Senate tradition for votes on grave matters of state, insisted that the Senators remain at their desks and rise one at a time to have their votes registered. There was a hushed silence in the chamber as each Senator rose with his "yea" or "nay." The final vote was 80–19 with 45 Republicans and 35 Democrats in favor. Rosner was called into another room to take a congratulatory call from the President. Senators Lugar and Biden came over to congratulate us. Standing outside the visitor's galley in the corridors of the Senate, we saw the 84-year-old Jan Nowak walking toward us swinging his cane like a spry youngster with a big smile on his face. "I never thought," he said, "that I would live to see the day when Poland is not only free—but safe."

The next day Secretary Albright issued a statement on the vote. "The Senate has done the right thing at the right time. For this is a moment of relative peace in Europe, a time when freedom is ascendant. Now we can be that much more confident that peace and freedom will endure." Albright underscored the broader implications of the vote for U.S. foreign policy. "Today's vote sends a message to our old and new allies that America will continue to defend its interest in the peace and security of Europe. It will reassure all of Europe's new democracies that we are not going to treat them as second class citizens in the future just because they were subjugated in the past. It is a signal that America will defend its values, protect its interests, stand by its allies and keep its word."[108]

CONCLUSION

At NATO's founding on April 4, 1949, President Harry S. Truman described the creation of the Atlantic Alliance as a neighborly act taken by countries deeply conscious of their shared heritage as democracies that had come together determined to defend their common values and interests from those who threatened them. The Washington Treaty was a very simple document, he noted. But it was a treaty that might have prevented two wars had it existed in 1919 or 1939. Its goal was to establish a zone of peace in an area of the world that had been at the heart of those two wars. Protecting this area, the President said, was an important step toward creating peace in the world. And he predicted that the positive impact of NATO's creation would be felt beyond its borders.[1]

Fifty years later, NATO decided to extend that zone of peace and stability from Western to Central and Eastern Europe following the collapse of communism and the end of the Cold War. It opened its door to the Czech Republic, Hungary, and Poland as part of a strategy of uniting Europe and recasting the Alliance for the post–Cold War era. By underscoring that NATO's door remained open to other European democracies willing and able to meet the criteria set out in the Washington Treaty, allied heads of state affirmed their wish to extend that zone even further in the future. NATO enlargement, in President Clinton's words, was designed to ensure that the eastern half of the continent would become as secure as its western half and that Europe's future would be better than its past.

By opening NATO's door to new members, the Clinton Administration saw itself as fulfilling the vision President Truman had articulated decades earlier. Rather than disengage from Europe in the wake of the collapse of communism and Soviet power, the U.S. opted to use its influence to help consolidate democracy in Central and Eastern Europe and to expand the zone of peace and stability on the continent. To do that, it initiated some of the farthest reaching changes in NATO strategy since its founding and one of the largest increases in the U.S. security commitment to the old continent in decades. The Alliance not only embraced new members in Central and Eastern Europe but also deployed its forces beyond its borders in the Balkans to halt ethnic cleansing and genocide. Originally established as an instrument to defend Western Europe from a Soviet threat, NATO was being recast into a tool to promote Europe's unification, manage security across the continent, and defend common trans-Atlantic values and interests beyond its borders.

The enlargement of NATO was neither inevitable nor preordained. It took place because the United States, as the lead ally in the Alliance, made it a top strategic priority that it pursued in the face of strong Russian opposition, at times tepid European support, as well as significant criticism at home. Although the idea of opening NATO's door originated in Central and Eastern Europe, it became an American project after the Clinton Administration embraced it. It flowed from an American vision of a Europe whole and free in permanent alliance with the United States. That vision was rooted in the belief that the U.S. interest in Europe and its security transcended communism and the former Soviet threat, and that the destinies of America and Europe were increasingly intertwined. From that conviction came the conclusion that stabilizing democracy and extending stability to Central and Eastern Europe was just as critical to America's own security as that process had been to Western Europe in the preceding half century. And from this view logically flowed the conclusion that it was necessary to open those Western structures and institutions that had so successfully guaranteed peace and security in Europe's western half to aspiring democratic nations in the other half.

U.S. policy in the 1990s was driven by a second conviction—the importance of adapting America's alliances to meet the needs of an increasingly interdependent and globalized world. The Clinton Administration believed that Europe was America's key partner and NATO its premier alliance. In its view, consolidating democracy and winning the peace in Europe was not only an important strategic interest, but also had broader consequences for America's position around the world. Confident that Europe was secure, the U.S. would be much better off if and when it had to confront other major threats beyond Europe. Achieving a Europe whole and free also made it more likely that

America's allies on the continent would now join the U.S. in working together to meet new challenges beyond Europe.

In other words, the Clinton Administration believed that America's interest in an alliance with the old continent was enduring—both to keep Europe secure and as part of a post–Cold War partnership to tackle new challenges to common interests. In its view, there was perhaps no part of the world with which the United States had as much in common and with which a strategic alliance was more important. U.S. policy therefore had to shift from simply viewing Europe as a place to defend and instead start to view it as a partner with which the U.S. worked together to meet those challenges. A unified Europe, as Secretary of State Albright often put it, could become America's geopolitical base in a new strategic partnership that could address the new threats of a new century.

From the outset, therefore, the Clinton Administration saw an enlarged NATO as part of a broader effort to reshape the Alliance in a radically different strategic context. Washington was not simply enlarging the old NATO, Administration officials repeatedly emphasized, but building a new NATO for a new era. Because NATO's rationale as well as its roster was being updated to reflect new realities, enlargement was matched by a parallel effort to update NATO's missions and shift the focus of the Alliance toward dealing with new post–Cold war threats. The goal was to modernize NATO—to make it as effective in meeting future threats to the trans-Atlantic community of nations as it had been in countering the USSR during the Cold War.

That vision and strategy was not the product of a single decision or a sudden epiphany. Instead, it evolved over the course of President Clinton's two terms in office into an increasingly coherent policy in response to events on the ground and as the Administration's own views matured. President Clinton and his national security team did not come into office with a grand vision for the future of the Alliance or the U.S.-European relationship. On the contrary, the President was initially focused on his domestic agenda. His initial top foreign policy priority was not Europe, but bolstering American support for democratic reform in Russia.

But by the end of Clinton's first year in office, the issue of NATO's future had nonetheless landed at the center of the Administration's foreign policy deliberations and agenda. It was put there by Central and East European leaders such as Havel and Walesa as well as influential Western voices such as Volker Ruehe, Richard Lugar, and RAND. But events on the ground played an equally key role. The spreading conflict in Bosnia, growing instability in Russia, and a slowdown in the European integration process combined to create a sense that Europe was at a potentially dangerous turning point. It convinced the Clinton Administration that it had to step forward with a new vision for the Alliance that would help anchor Central and Eastern Europe to the West and in which U.S. power and influence would be harnessed to project stability across the continent as a whole in order to secure a new post–Cold War peace.

It was against this background that President Clinton took the initial steps in opening NATO's door to new members in the East. In January 1994, he told the Visegrad heads of state in Prague that enlargement was no longer a matter of "whether but when and how." That statement in and of itself did not fully resolve the fight in the Administration's ranks over the wisdom of enlargement. After all, the issues of "when and how" went to the core of the differences that still divided the Administration. Proponents of enlargement nonetheless seized this statement as a mandate to move forward. In the spring, National Security Advisor Lake asked his staff to come up with a game plan that contained, in rudimentary form, the key elements of what would become a full-fledged U.S. strategy—a rationale, a list of initial candidates, a target date when they might join, as well as a strategy for addressing Russian concerns.

During a visit to Warsaw in July 1994, Clinton pushed the ball forward by publicly suggesting it was time for NATO to take the next steps on enlargement. Over the summer Dick Holbrooke was brought back to Washington to implement the shift in U.S. policy and to bring the allies on board. In September Clinton also told Russian President Boris Yeltsin for the first time that he intended to move forward with enlargement but wanted to do so in a way that would not rock the boat in U.S.-Russian relations. At the same time, the Administration's push coincided with growing pressure from Newt Gingrich and Republicans on Capitol Hill, as reflected in their Contract with America, to more clearly embrace enlargement.

This shift in U.S. policy had a cascading effect on attitudes across the European continent. Allies in Western Europe, taken by surprise, were initially reticent to follow the U.S. lead. The result was a compromise reached at a NATO Foreign Ministers meeting in December 1994 to launch a study on enlargement to start the process. Even this modest step, however, elicited an angry outburst from Yeltsin several days later at the OSCE summit in Budapest. Moscow's hostile reaction, in turn, led Secretary of Defense Bill Perry, the remaining enlargement skeptic in the Administration's ranks, to make a final appeal to the President to reverse course. But Clinton stood by the decision to press forward.

Washington had crossed its own internal Rubicon in deciding to enlarge NATO. But this did not mean that enlargement was a done deal. Officially, Washington was pursuing a dual track approach in which preparations for NATO enlargement would be matched with the building of a cooperative NATO-Russia relationship. As the Administration labored to put the building blocks for this strategy in place, opposition to NATO enlargement was growing. Nowhere was this more true than in Moscow, where enlargement was opposed with growing vehemence across the political spectrum. As a result, Yeltsin started to back away from his assurances to Clinton that enlargement was an issue the two men could manage. Instead, it became clear that enlarging NATO was becoming a major obstacle in Russia's relations with the West and could undercut Russian reform. While enlarging NATO and building a cooperative NATO-Russia relationship in tandem made great sense on paper, but was increasingly elusive in practice.

Moscow's growing hostility, in turn, reinforced skepticism about enlargement in Europe and the United States. The Administration now found itself in a growing crossfire of criticism between those who wanted it to move faster on enlargement and adopt harder-line policies vis-à-vis Moscow and those who did not want it to move ahead on enlargement at all. In the spring of 1995 Clinton reached a private understanding with Yeltsin to put off further decisions on enlargement until after the Russian Presidential elections in the summer of 1996 if Moscow would move forward with NATO-Russia ties. It was intended to help Yeltsin politically and give the two sides time to defuse at least some of Moscow's concerns.

The Alliance had an additional, more pressing issue it also needed to fix before it could enlarge. It was what Warren Christopher had called "the problem from hell"—stopping the war and bloodshed in Bosnia. The Dayton peace agreement, signed in late 1995 following NATO air strikes that helped turn the tide against the Bosnian Serbs, finally brought peace to that war-torn country. It also helped clear the way for NATO to enlarge. It restored a much-needed sense of unity and purpose across the Atlantic and strengthened the case that NATO had to act to consolidate stability beyond its old borders. And the U.S.-brokered deal on Russian participation in IFOR moved the idea of NATO-Russia cooperation from the realm of theory to reality on the ground.

But the drama surrounding NATO enlargement only continued to grow. Andrei Kozyrev's replacement by Yevgeny Primakov as Russian Foreign Minister in January 1996 signaled a tougher-edged Russian approach. With Alliance decisions on enlargement put on hold for the Russian and U.S. Presidential elections, Primakov pursued a strategy best described as "negotiate and fight." While exploring with the U.S. the contours of a NATO-Russia agreement that might allow Moscow to live with enlargement, the Russian Foreign Minister also pushed the European allies to roll back NATO's plans by repeatedly warning of the dire consequences for Russian democracy and Moscow's relations with the West.

Such threats from Moscow were not entirely without effect. In private, key allies such as Germany and France wondered out loud whether NATO might consider postponing its enlargement plans or, alternatively, that the Alliance only move forward if an agreement with Russia could be worked out in advance. But the U.S. held firm to its commitment to move ahead. Following Yeltsin's reelection in July 1996, Clinton wrote his key allied counterparts to confirm his determination to move forward. In September, Christopher announced that NATO would hold a summit in the first half of the following year where the first invitations to new members would be extended. In November, President Clinton publicly confirmed his commitment to move ahead with enlargement early in his second term.

The Administration made the implementation of its vision for a new NATO a top foreign policy priority during Clinton's second term in office. The President's appointment of Madeleine Albright as Secretary of State underscored the priority attached to this goal. The early months of 1997 saw a frenzied burst of diplomatic activity as the U.S. now took its enlargement plans off of the drawing board and started to turn them into reality.

The key diplomatic breakthrough that smoothed the way to NATO enlargement was the Helsinki summit between Presidents Clinton and Yeltsin in March 1997. With Helmut Kohl now firmly on his side, President Clinton held his ground against Yeltsin's last attempt to convince him to drop enlargement or at least to limit its future scope. The Russian President now gave a green light to negotiate the details of a NATO-Russia agreement, leading to a frenzied round of negotiations involving NATO Secretary General Javier Solana and Russian Foreign Minister Primakov with the United States playing a key behind-the-scenes role to achieve a final outcome.

The ink was barely dry on the NATO-Russia Founding Act when the U.S. faced a fight with some of its closest allies over which Central and East European countries to invite at Madrid and how firm a commitment NATO would make to future enlargement. The U.S. was now confronted by France and other allies who argued that a larger round of enlargement including Romania and Slovenia would provide a better geopolitical balance and help stabilize southeastern Europe. Washington's opposition to this larger group set the stage for one of the most historic yet contentious summits in NATO's history. At the end of the day, the Czech Republic, Hungary and Poland received invitations and the allies reached a compromise highlighting NATO's commitment to future enlargement to southeastern Europe but in a manner that did not prejudice the chances of other counties such as the Baltic states.

For the United States there was one final hurdle—Senate ratification. At home NATO enlargement had sparked one of the most passionate debates on any national security issue since the end of the Cold War. Opposition to enlargement was real and often passionate. While the political platforms of both parties had embraced enlargement in the 1996 Presidential campaigns, influential Senators in each continued to oppose it. Many influential figures in the U.S. foreign policy community, as well as the media, were also strongly opposed. The intellectual battle was fought in dueling op-eds, journal articles and in debates at leading think tanks in the strategic community. The stage was set for a major political battle over ratifying enlargement.

While the U.S. was the NATO ally leading the push for enlargement, a two-thirds majority vote for ratification in a politically independent Senate meant the Administration had to meet a higher bar than other allies. Democrats and Republicans had important differences on how to approach enlargement that needed to be ironed out before a true bipartisan consensus could jell. Partisan politics was also a factor, and increasingly so. Even Republicans inclined to support enlargement sometimes asked why they should help the Clinton Administration achieve a major foreign policy victory.

But in the end Republicans and Democrats came together in a remarkable display of bipartisan cooperation to ratify NATO enlargement. In doing so, they affirmed a long tradition of support across the aisle for the Atlantic Alliance. While the final vote tally of 80–19 in the spring of 1998 gave the President a comfortable victory, ratification was nevertheless harder fought—and the Administration more vulnerable to defeat—than those numbers suggested, as the President himself confessed to the then Italian Prime Minister, Romano Prodi, the week after the final Senate vote.

With the Senate vote ratifying the entry of the Czech Republic, Hungary, and Poland as NATO members, the curtain came to a close on one of the most important and far-reaching chapters in NATO's history. The United States and its European allies had extended the Alliance's security umbrella to Central and Eastern Europe, the source of so much conflict in Europe's turbulent past. They had done so in a time of peace, not war. And they had done so as an act of integration to help build a more democratic and unified Europe, not as an act of aggression or confrontation.

In doing so they had redrawn the political map of Europe and taken a major step in overcoming Europe's Cold War divide. As Polish President Aleksandr Kwasniewski had put it, if the great accomplishment of Ronald Reagan was to help bring down the Soviet empire, and that of George Bush was to unify Germany in NATO, then Bill Clinton's legacy was to have brought these three countries into NATO to complete the changes in Central and Eastern Europe that began with the triumph of Solidarity and the Velvet Revolution in 1989.

Historians often debate the degree to which historical outcomes are shaped by the actions of individual leaders or more objective underlying trends. In the case of NATO enlargement, future diplomatic historians may well debate the degree to which the events described in these pages were determined by people or the more anonymous forces of history and whether the outcome that occurred was or was not inevitable. As a witness to and participant in many of the events described in these pages, it is hard to escape the conclusion that people and choices—intellectual, diplomatic, and political—made the key difference. What in many ways remains remarkable about the history of NATO enlargement is how an idea that initially encountered such strong opposition actually became U.S and NATO policy, and was then successfully implemented in practice without the cataclysmic consequences that critics and opponents predicted.

Looking back upon this period, the United States' handling of three challenges stand out as crucial for enlargement's success. The first was dealing with Russia. The challenge Washington faced was not only or even primarily a matter of asserting U.S. or Western strength. By the early 1990s it was increasingly clear that the West enjoyed economic and military superiority over a weakened Russia. Instead, the key issue was how to enlarge NATO in a way that did not appear as part of a punitive peace, reminiscent of Versailles, or which produced an anti-Western backlash. President Clinton's vision of a Europe free, democratic, and undivided was open to a democratic Russia, too. The Administration did not see Yeltsin's Russia through the prism of a residual threat but rather as a potential partner. President Clinton believed that "getting Russia right" after the end of the Cold War was as important as integrating Germany had been following World War II.

Thus, when President Clinton embraced NATO enlargement, he did so as part of an effort to consolidate democracy and project stability to Central and Eastern Europe, not as a strategic response to a real or imagined Russian threat to the region. He believed that there was enough overlap between his vision of an undivided Europe and what Yeltsin was seeking for Russia that NATO enlargement did not have to be a zero-sum game where the integration of Central and Eastern Europe into the West had to come at Russia's expense. The American goal was not only to anchor Poland and its neighbors to the West, but to integrate a democratic Russia into a larger European framework as well. From the Administration's perspective, an enlargement of NATO that secured Poland but led to a train wreck in U.S.-Russian relations would have been a failure.

Avoiding a rupture with Russia was also critical to shoring up European support for enlargement. Chancellor Helmut Kohl's statement that enlargement was only worth doing if it did not lead to a confrontation with Moscow was a view many allies shared. Negotiating the right NATO-Russia deal was also important to obtain the broad-based domestic political support needed to ensure Senate ratification. While Republican conservatives wanted Clinton to enlarge faster, Democrats worried about the impact on Russia. The Administration therefore had to simultaneously address Republican suspicions that it was giving Moscow too much influence in NATO on the one hand, and Democratic concerns that enlargement could derail Russian reform, arms control, and spark a new U.S.-Russia confrontation on the other. Many Senators did not fully commit to NATO enlargement until it was clear that a confrontation with Moscow had been avoided.

The challenge of integrating a country the size of Russia into the West was of a different magnitude than integrating Central and East European countries. When Administration officials spoke of the possibility that Russia might one day itself be eligible for NATO membership, it was meant as a political signal that the West supported Russia's westernization in principle, not a short-term issue of operational diplomacy. Secretary of State Albright, when asked about the possibility of Russia one day joining NATO, often responded that if we ever reached the point where Russia aspired to and qualified for NATO, then it would be a different Russia, a different Europe, and both Russia and the West would have succeeded beyond our wildest dreams. Under such circumstances, NATO's future would have to be rethought once again—but those would be the problems of success.

The issue, therefore, became how to enlarge NATO to Central and Eastern Europe while creating a parallel cooperative NATO-Russia relationship that would give Moscow a voice in European security but not over the Alliance's own internal affairs or decisionmaking. Washington made it clear that it was prepared to build a close NATO-Russia relationship that could grow over time.

But the U.S. was also prepared to enlarge over Moscow's objections if it had to. American policy was to work for success with the Russians but to be prepared for failure. NATO enlargement was designed as part of a strategy of integration that could potentially include Russia. At the same time, it also functioned as a hedge in case trends in Moscow moved in the wrong direction. While pledging to enlarge slowly, U.S. officials made it clear to Moscow that this process could be accelerated if events in Russia took a turn for the worse. And when it came to the details of NATO military strategy, the U.S. and its allies were careful to ensure that the Alliance had the flexibility to provide a credible defense for these countries if Russia ever again became a threat.

It was on Russia that the Administration parted ways with other enlargement supporters, ranging from Lech Walesa to leading Republican conservatives. Many of them believed that Moscow did pose a threat to Central and Eastern Europe and that NATO should enlarge as a hedge against Russian neo-imperialism—the sooner the better. They felt the Administration had a naïve view of Russian intentions and its ability to change age-old Russian geopolitical habits. They feared that by moving slowly and seeking to work with Moscow, the Administration was frittering away a window of opportunity to lock-in the security of these countries and giving Russia a chance to reassert its influence. Conservative critics believed that the better strategy was to enlarge NATO quickly, create facts on the ground, and deal with Moscow's concerns later. In Walesa's words, the West had to first "cage the bear" before trying to tame it.

The Clinton Administration rejected this approach out of concern that it could become a self-fulfilling prophecy that would turn Moscow into a new strategic rival. It believed that the U.S., by simultaneously championing Russia's overall integration with the West, could enlarge the Alliance without a rupture in Russia's relations with the West. It opted to enlarge NATO gradually and in tandem with an offer to build a cooperative NATO-Russia relationship. This approach was designed to coax Moscow into a dialogue where NATO could address legitimate Russian concerns and bring Moscow to the point where, even if it disliked enlargement, it would remain engaged and not take steps that would seriously damage East-West relations.

Diplomatically, this was easier said then done. While Russians had accepted the fact that NATO was going to remain in existence after the end of the Cold War, the argument that enlarging it to Central and Eastern Europe could solve the age-old problems of security on Russia's western borders was a bridge too far for most Russian leaders. At a time of rising nationalist and anti-Western sentiment, many Russians came to see enlargement as a western attempt to exploit Moscow's weakness and vehemently opposed it. Many senior Russian officials, first and foremost Foreign Minister Kozyrev, knew better and would admit in private that NATO enlargement was largely a political and not a strategic issue. But such voices soon faded in Moscow.

At least initially, President Yeltsin did not strongly oppose NATO enlargement. His early conversations with Clinton on the issue suggested that this was an issue the two men could manage together. As the anti-Western and anti-NATO mood in Moscow grew, however, Yeltsin was increasingly driven to oppose NATO enlargement, too. At the same time, Yeltsin hesitated to embrace the harder line voices urging him to take tougher steps to deter the U.S. and its allies from moving forward. In replacing the pro-Western Kozyrev with Primakov, Yeltsin gave a green light to a more vigorous political effort to stop enlargement, and undoubtedly would have been delighted if the Russian Foreign Minister had succeeded. But he was careful to ensure that Primakov's tactics did not spill over to the point where they could directly threaten on the overall U.S.-Russia relationship or his personal ties with President Clinton.

Washington was therefore stymied in its early efforts for far-reaching NATO-Russia cooperation. It concentrated on creating a NATO-Russia relationship that would allow enlargement to move forward and that would lay the foundation for further cooperation down the road. Achieving even this more limited goal became a matter of diplomacy at the highest levels. It was not until the fall and winter of 1996, however, that Foreign Minister Primakov began to indicate that he knew that Moscow's campaign to stop enlargement was failing—a point Yeltsin finally conceded to Clinton at the Helsinki summit in March 1997. It nevertheless took two more months of carefully orchestrated diplomacy at the highest levels led by NATO Secretary General Javier Solana to reach closure on the NATO-Russia Founding Act. At the end of the day, the personal relationship between Clinton and Yeltsin and their key advisors were essential ingredients in ensuring this soft landing and laying the foundation for future NATO-Russia cooperation.

The second major challenge the United States had to surmount to successfully enlarge NATO was with Europe. Washington had to build a consensus in Western Europe behind the decision to enlarge and then translate that decision into a set of practical policies on the modalities of enlargement that all allies could support. In parallel, the Administration had to convince candidate and partner countries in Central and Eastern Europe that the Alliance's overall approach was sound and that they, too, were better off with a measured approach that gave both sides time to prepare and do their homework and that kept the door open for further enlargement down the road.

While the first major Western political figure to call for enlargement was a European, German Defense Minister Volker Ruehe, overall European support was scattered at best. The instincts of many of America's European allies were not to turn to NATO as the instrument to embrace Central and Eastern Europe and knit the continent back together. A majority of European countries initially thought that the EU was a more logical candidate for the job. They only turned to NATO after it became clear that the United States was serious about pursuing enlargement, that the EU was too weak to take on the challenge in the near term, and that the clear top priority of many Central and East Europeans was to join the Alliance first.

Even then, European support was often tepid and remained so through much of the debate. Among Washington's major allies, London supported enlargement, but less due to strategic conviction than a desire to preserve its influence with Washington. France was skeptical from the outset, fearing it would strengthen American influence in Europe, distract from European integration and antagonize Moscow, although President Chirac's Gaullist instincts made him more open to the vision of a broader Europe than his predecessor, François Mitterrand. Support was the strongest in Germany, but even there Chancellor Helmut Kohl remained very cautious, caught between the historical desire to integrate Poland and the need to avoid steps that would lead to a confrontation with Moscow. Several smaller European allies were at times more supportive of enlargement but it was clear that Washington would be expected to do the diplomatic heavy lifting.

Once the decision in principle to enlarge had been made, Washington moved to gradually firm up support on the continent by answering the key questions Europeans had and addressing their concerns. Those concerns related not only to Russia's reaction, but also to what was expected from existing members to carry out new commitments and how enlargement would impact on the vitality and effectiveness of the Alliance. NATO committees worked their way through a maze of practical problems ranging from how these countries would be defended to how costs would be assessed. As those concerns were addressed and answers found, the political will to move forward with enlargement started to grow as European allies could see just how it could be accomplished without damaging their own interests.

Perhaps the key question was whether the consensus across the Atlantic would hold if a real crisis with Moscow started to unfold. Until very late in the game, Washington was not sure how deep the Alliance consensus was and whether it would hold if Moscow opted for an all-out effort to prevent enlargement. That was exactly the strategy that some harder-line voices in Moscow had advocated. And NATO Secretary General Solana had warned Washington on more than one occasion that he was not sure what choice allies would make were they forced to choose between enlargement and Russia. Fortunately, the signing of the NATO-Russia Founding Act meant that this question was never put to the test. Sometimes success in diplomacy is best measured by the questions one never has to address.

It is therefore somewhat ironic that the issue where Alliance consensus would break down was over which Central and East European countries would be invited to join the Alliance at Madrid and what the prospects for further enlargement down the road would be. The original impetus for NATO enlargement was the strategic need to anchor Poland and to secure Germany's eastern frontier. Indeed, many of enlargement's original proponents in the West saw it as a move limited to Warsaw and its neighbors. While they supported expanded NATO cooperation with other countries in the region, not everyone saw such cooperation leading to full membership.

That changed once the Clinton Administration and other allies made it clear that the vision of an enlarged NATO applied to the continent as a whole—and that *all* countries from the Baltic to the Black Sea were potential members. However, this only underscored the need for a credible and transparent process for adjudicating who would receive invitations, when, and why. The U.S. was determined to ensure that performance and not just geopolitical considerations were the basis for enlargement decisions. Washington wanted to use the incentive of eventual NATO membership as a kind of golden carrot to encourage Central and East European countries to reform themselves into more attractive candidates. The goal was not only to get these countries into NATO, but also to use the process to fix as many internal or bilateral issues as possible, thereby improving European security.

Many Central and Eastern European countries were at first uncomfortable with the Administration's approach. Candidate countries initially had little understanding of what NATO membership entailed and the homework that needed to be done, both by them and the Alliance. They harbored fears that NATO would raise the bar to a point where they could no longer meet it. Yet in many ways NATO's approach turned out to be a blessing in disguise. Many countries figured out how to use the goal of NATO membership to justify difficult reform decisions at home or fix minority or border issues that otherwise might have festered. As they came to understand the requirements of NATO membership involved, they were often grateful they had more time to prepare.

But while NATO's benchmarks and criteria were good enough to motivate Central and East European countries, they were insufficient when it came to harmonizing allied views on who would be invited at Madrid. The U.S. approach was to embrace the widest possible open door in principle, but to insist on keeping NATO's performance standards high as a safeguard. That preference was driven by the desire to keep NATO strong militarily, to ensure that NATO's open door approach was credible, and to maximize the chances of a successful ratification in the U.S. Senate. But European allies had other preferences and made their own political calculations. If the U.S. had its eye on Capitol Hill, other European allies had their eye on the likely lineup of candidates in the EU or their own bilateral relations with major European powers who they did not dare alienate because they needed cooperation on other issues.

What appeared to one country to be a clear-cut case of a candidate qualifying or not qualifying for membership was hotly contested by another. In the final analysis NATO's standards were too loose, the national interests of different allies too divergent, and the temptation to lobby for favorite candidates too strong to avoid what Secretary Albright had termed the "beauty contest." As a result, the decision on who to invite was driven to the highest levels, where it became a brutal test of political clout in which Washington ultimately prevailed. Looking back, most of the U.S. officials involved in those decisions would have few regrets and would argue that the U.S. stance was proven right by the subsequent events in the region. Yet the Madrid summit goes down in history less as a case of far-sighted U.S. leadership than as an example of how a summit where Washington got its way in the end but paid a political price in doing so.

If there is one political relationship that stands out as key in bridging U.S.-European differences on these issues, it is the tie between Washington and Bonn, and especially the bond between Bill Clinton and Helmut Kohl. The U.S.-German relationship was not only a key motor behind enlargement's first round, but the German Chancellor showed himself to be the President's closest confidant and ally not only in handling Russia but also in brokering the key compromises at Madrid. It was Kohl's dramatic intervention in the heads-of-state meeting that ensured that only three countries would receive invitations, and his subsequent intervention with Jacques Chirac that ensured that the open door compromise balanced the needs of Romania and Slovenia with a perspective for the Baltic states.

U.S. leadership was important in one final area — ensuring that NATO's open door pledge was credible. Washington had pledged to enlarge NATO in a manner that would enhance the security for all countries in Europe, not just those who received the first invitations. It was determined to make sure that enlargement to some Central and East European countries not simply draw another line further eastward that would undercut others, as critics alleged. On more than one occasion Albright, Talbott, and other senior U.S. officials would remark that the problem of what to do with those countries not receiving invitations was as, if not more, difficult than dealing with the countries that were going to get one.

The answer was to embrace practical policies and steps both inside and outside the Alliance that reached out to these countries. By pushing increasingly deeper integration through the Partnership for Peace within the Alliance and by negotiating the Baltic Charter or a separate strategic partnership with Romania bilaterally, the U.S. helped to put meat on the bones of the Alliance's open door policy. Other allies joined in with their own matching efforts. The success of this policy was demonstrated when countries such as the Baltic states supported the first round of enlargement moving forward even though they did not receive invitations, thereby undercutting the argument of the critics that a limited enlargement to a handful of countries was a mistake because it ran the risk of destabilizing those countries not included.

The third major policy challenge the United States had to surmount was embedding NATO enlargement within a broader vision and sense of purpose for an Alliance that was being modernized for a new era. If one had asked the average American or European during the Cold War what NATO was for, the reply would have been that the Alliance had been founded and designed to deal with the Soviet Union and the Warsaw Pact. By the early 1990s that state and alliance were gone and so was the threat that they posed. For many the symbol of NATO's purpose during the Cold War had been the Fulda Gap—a small town in Germany where the Soviet invasion of Western Europe was expected to start and where U.S. forces formed an initial line of defense.

What was NATO's purpose in a world where its previous adversary, Soviet communism, had disappeared? It was a question that confronted President Clinton from his first day in office. The President's early embrace of reform in Russia as his top foreign policy priority underscored his desire to treat Moscow as partner, not a former adversary. At the same time an out-of-control war in Bosnia and the desire of the countries of Central and Eastern Europe to be anchored to the West through the Alliance showed clearly that while the old threat from Moscow was gone, the continent was not yet secure and that new threats on the continent could still undermine European security.

Intellectually, the issue was framed in the slogan that NATO had to go "out of area or out of business." It was a catchy way of pointing out that the strategic challenges of the day all lay beyond NATO's West European borders, and that the Alliance had the choice of exporting security to address them or it would run the risk of importing new insecurity. And the best way to export security was to expand the zone of stability by embracing those countries willing and able to become members as well as being ready to use force to stem conflicts such as those in the Balkans.

What seems pretty straightforward in retrospect was a paradigm shift at the time for an Alliance that for forty years had focused solely on preparing to defend Alliance territory in Western Europe from external aggression. Suddenly, the Alliance was being urged to expand to the territory of former adversaries and deploy forces in peacekeeping and peace support scenarios potentially across the continent. Often the need to act on the ground in response to the real world ran ahead of official NATO theology as evidenced in the remark by one senior French official who, after an agreement on an action in Bosnia, remarked that it would work fine in practice but he was not sure how to square it with Alliance theory.

The Clinton Administration was determined to define a purpose for NATO that was future-oriented, politically sustainable in the U.S. Congress and with the American people, and which was not tied primarily to the danger that democratic reform in Russia might fail. As Albright frequently put it, the U.S. needed to answer the question about what NATO was going to do for the next fifty years, not why it had been important for the previous five decades. President Clinton wanted a rationale for NATO that fit with his own vision of Europe, of America's internationalist role, and of the value of U.S.-European partnership in a new era.

In articulating that purpose, the Administration returned to first principals, at times literally going back to the words and texts of NATO's founding fathers to capture the essence of what the Alliance was all about. The answer it came up with was a simple one, namely that NATO's core purpose was to defend the freedom, territory, and interests of its members from whatever threatened them. In 1949 it was Stalin and Soviet communism that had posed that threat. But in the post–Cold War world the threats to those goals were different. The Alliance had to adopt an approach recognizing that NATO in the future would have to respond to threats from potentially many different directions and sources. Taking on new missions in response to those new threats was fulfilling NATO's original purpose in a new strategic context, not a radical break from the intent of the Alliance's founding fathers.

The closer the U.S. came to completing the first round of enlargement and launching the NATO-Russia Founding Act, the more pressing the question of the Alliance's longer-term purpose and strategic direction started to become. What was NATO going to become in a world where Europe was increasingly peaceful and secure, Russia was becoming a partner, and where the greatest threats to our future security came from Europe's periphery or beyond? At the same time, it was also starting to become clear that the threat to both sides of the Atlantic from weapons of mass destruction and rogue states beyond the continent was growing and could, over time, become a far greater threat to our nations. During the course of the Senate debate on NATO enlargement r atification the issue of the Alliance's future rationale become the focal point of questioning and debate. Indeed, many of the final amendments the Administration battled on the Senate floor had little to do with the first round of enlargement. Instead, they reflected a growing questioning over NATO's future strategic direction.

The Administration's victory in the Senate marked the conclusion of the political battle over the first round of NATO enlargement. But it did not end the debate over NATO's future or the Administration's efforts to reform the Alliance. Albright, in particular, came away convinced that the Administration needed to take on this issue and that NATO had to start to confront issues such as weapons of mass destruction in the hands of hostile states beyond Europe that could nonetheless threaten NATO members. Following the vote in the Senate, the Administration decided that its top priority for the NATO fiftieth anniversary summit scheduled for Washington in the spring of 1999 had to be setting NATO's future rationale and that it was better to defer decisions on future enlargement pending agreement with our allies on NATO's role in a broader and updated U.S.-European partnership.

The United States would therefore spend much of 1998 and the spring of 1999 seeking to articulate a new vision for the trans-Atlantic partnership, in which the U.S. and Europe would, while completing the job of building a Europe whole and free, increasingly start to look beyond the confines of the continent and develop a common agenda on new challenges and threats beyond Europe. These two goals—building Europe whole and free and working together beyond Europe—were seen as mutually reinforcing. As part of this new partnership, NATO's role was seen as the natural institution of choice the U.S. and Europe would turn to when they had to act militarily.

To prepare the Alliance for this role, the U.S. came up with a package of proposals for the Washington summit in the spring of 1999 designed to highlight its view of a new NATO for the new century. The core of that package was a new strategic concept that emphasized an enlarged NATO assuming new missions to project stability beyond its immediate borders as one central pillar of a new Euro-Atlantic community. To back up that concept, the Alliance adopted a series of initiatives to retool its military forces to better address a broad spectrum of new threats ranging from instability on Europe's periphery to threats from weapons of mass destruction.

The need for NATO to assume military missions beyond its borders was reinforced by the escalating violence in Kosovo as Slobodan Milosevic unleashed his campaign of violence and terror against Kosovar Albanians. After months of efforts at a diplomatic solution, NATO launched its air campaign against Milosevic's forces only weeks before the Washington summit in the spring of 1999. The ensuing months were among the most dramatic in NATO's history as the coalition strained to keep together and sustain the military pressure in Milosevic and his army. Moscow broke off ties with NATO in protest and the PJC was put on ice. After 78 days of the NATO air campaign, the Serbian dictator capitulated. One year later, he was toppled by a pro-democracy movement in Serbia, thereby bringing an end to the series of wars in the Balkans that he himself had instigated at the beginning of the decade.

NATO's victory in the Balkans, along with its successful enlargement to Central and Eastern Europe, underscored how the Alliance had remade itself into the security guarantor of the continent as a whole.

As the Clinton Administration left office, it could look back at a Europe and a NATO that were very different than when it took office. The cornerstones of its vision of a Europe whole and free in alliance with the United States and in partnership with Russia had been laid. The entry into NATO of the Czech Republic, Hungary, and Poland had helped put Central and Eastern Europe on track for being integrated into the West. The Baltic states had successfully moved out of the shadow of the former Soviet Union and were increasingly credible candidates for EU and NATO membership. In southeastern Europe, the Balkan wars had been stopped and those countries now had the chance to rejoin the European and trans-Atlantic mainstream. Europe was safer, freer, and more secure. NATO's door remained open for additional qualified members and the Alliance had remade itself for a new era.

Building on that foundation would be left to the next President of the United States and his European counterparts. The need to complete the job was underscored by the terrorist attacks on America on September 11, 2001, which led NATO to invoke Article 5 of the Washington Treaty for the first time in its history — not in response to a Soviet attack against Europe but a terrorist attack against the United States. In a dramatic way, this tragedy underscored the importance of completing the job of enlarging the Alliance to secure peace in an undivided Europe at a time when the U.S. faced great threats elsewhere in the world. But the September 11 attacks also underscored the importance of allies and alliances to fight the war on terrorism—while reinforcing that fact that NATO had to continue to change so that it could be as effective in meeting the threats of the future as it had been in helping win the Cold War. More than anything else, the events of September 11 confirmed the need for NATO to complete the job of reshaping itself for a new era—and for the U.S., in cooperation with its NATO partners, to continue to lead the way.

NOTES

BOOK I. THE ORIGINS

1. See A. W. DePorte, *Europe Between the Superpowers: the Enduring Balance* (New Haven: Yale University, 1979), p. vii.

2. See John Lewis Gaddis, *The Long Peace: Inquiries Into the History of the Cold War* (New York: Oxford University Press, 1987).

3. On German unification see Philip Zelikow and Condoleeza Rice, *Germany Unified and Europe Transformed: A Study in Statecraft* (Cambridge: Harvard University Press, 1995).

4. Philip Zelikow, "NATO Expansion Wasn't Ruled Out," *International Herald Tribune*, August 10, 1995.

5. See "Memcon from 2/9/90 meeting w/USSR Pres. Gorbachev & FM Shevardnadze, Moscow, USSR." This exchange is also described in Zelikow and Rice, pp. 182–83.

6. See Valentin Falin, *Politische Erinnerungen* (Munich: Droemer Knaur, 1993); and Julij A. Kwizinskij, *Vor dem Sturm* (Berlin: Siedler Verlag, 1993).

7. The argument that Baker and Gorbachev were talking in their capacity as representatives of the Quadripartite powers with residual responsibility for Germany resulting from World War II was underscored by Assistant Secretary for European Affairs, John Kornblum. See the memorandum from Assistant Secretary of State for European Affairs John Kornblum and acting S/NIS Director John Herbst entitled "NATO Enlargement: Russian Assertions Regarding the Two-plus-Four Agreement on

German Unification. The memo was sent to our U.S. Embassies in Europe as the official U.S. position in February 1996.

8. Krzysztof Skubiszewski, "Polska I Sojusz Atlantycki w latach 1989–1991," *Sprawy Miedzynarodowe*, no. 1 (1999), p. 18.

9. See Adam Michnik's 1976 essay entitled "The New Evolutionism" reprinted in Adam Michnik, *Letters from Prison and Other Essays* (Berkeley: University of California Press, 1985), pp. 135–148.

10. See Milan Kundera, "The Tragedy of Central Europe," *The New York Review of Books*, April 26, 1984.

11. See "Letter from Gdansk Prison" in Michnik, *Letters from Prison and Other Essays*, pp. 96–97.

12. See Gyorgy Konrad, *Antipolitics: An Essay* (New York: Harcourt Brace and Jovanovich, Publishers, 1984), pp. 1–10.

13. See Vaclav Havel's essay on Central and East European attitudes toward the peace movement in his essay "The Anatomy of a Reticence" in *Vaclav Havel, Open Letters: Selected Writings, 1965–1990* (New York: Vintage Books, 1992), pp. 291–322.

14. The Prague Appeal was issued on March 11, 1985 as a message to the International Conference on Nuclear Disarmament scheduled to take place in Amsterdam that summer. It was signed by the then Charter 77 spokespersons Jiri Dienstbier, Eva Kanturkova, and Petuska Sustrova. It is reprinted in the *East European Reporter* (London) 1, no. 1 (Spring 1985): 27–28.

15. For an eyewitness account of the 1989 revolution, see Timothy Garton Ash, *The Magic Lantern: The Revolution of '89 Witnessed in Warsaw, Budapest, Berlin and Prague* (New York: Vintage Books, 1993).

16. For further details on the Polish-Soviet troop negotiations and how these shaped overall Polish thinking at the time on broader security issue, see Grzegorz Kostrewa-Zorbas, "The Russian Troop Withdrawal from Poland" in Allan Goodman, ed., *The Diplomatic Record 1992–1993* (Bolder, CO: Westview Press, 1995), pp. 113–138.

17. For press coverage of the Budapest conference, see Blaine Harden, "Warsaw Pact Disbands Military Union," *The Washington Post*, February 26, 1991. See also Celestine Bohlen, "Warsaw Pact Agrees to Dissolve its Military Alliance by March 31," *The New York Times*, February 26, 1991.

18. With the exception of Romania, the former members of the Warsaw Pact refused to agree to this language bringing negotiations to a deadlock that was not broken until after the failed Soviet coup attempt in the fall of 1991. For further details see F. Stephen Larrabee, *East European Security After the Cold War* (Santa Monica, CA.: RAND, 1993), pp. 154–156.

19. See "Warsaw Pact Now Part of History," *The Chicago Tribune*, July 2, 1991.

20. The Conference on Security and Cooperation in Europe (CSCE) was renamed the Organization for Security and Cooperation in Europe (OSCE) at the Budapest Summit, December 5–6, 1994. The official title took effect January 1, 1995. The European Community (EC) member states and their territories agreed on November 1, 1993 to be subsequently be known as the European Union (EU). For the purposes of this book, the OSCE and EU will be used throughout.

21. See "Memorandum on the European Security Commission" by the government of Czechoslovakia, Prague, April 6, 1990.

22. According to Havel. "It seems that NATO, as a more meaningful, more democratic and more effective structure, could become the seed of a new European security system with less trouble than the Warsaw Pact. But NATO, too, must change. Above all, it should—in the face of today's reality transform its military doctrine. And it should soon—in view of its changing role—change its name as well. The present name is so linked to the era of the Cold War that it would be a sign of a lack of understanding present-day developments if Europe were to unite under the NATO flag." For the Vaclav Havel speech at The Council of Europe, Strasbourg, May 10, 1990, see "Responsibility, Safety, Stability: Vaclav Havel Concerning NATO," *Selected Speeches, Articles and Interviews 1990–1999*, pp. 6–14. Authors signed private copy.

23. See Jiri Dienstbier, "Central Europe's Security," *Foreign Policy*, Summer 1991, p. 121.

24. For a firsthand account of U.S. policy toward Europe during the period 1989–1992 see Robert L. Hutchings, *American Diplomacy and the End of the Cold War: An Insider's Account of U.S. Policy in Europe, 1989–1992* (Baltimore: The Johns Hopkins University Press, 1997).

25. See "Charter of Paris for a New Europe," Conference for Security and Co-operation in Europe, 1990 Summit, Paris, November 19–21, <http://www.osce.org/docs/english/1990–1999/summits/paris90e.htm>. The Paris summit agreed to create a standing Council with accredited Ambassadors, which would meet once a year in Ministerial session; a Committee of Senior Officials that could be convened in the interim; and a secretariat. It also created special offices to monitor elections as well as a new conflict prevention center.

26. For further details see James B. Steinberg, *An Ever Closer Union* (Santa Monica, CA: RAND, 1993).

27. See "Dans un entretien à Radio-France internationale Les pays d'Europe centrale n'adhéreront pas à la CEE avant 'des dizaines d'années déclare M. Mitterrand,'" [Mitterrand declares in a Radio-France international interview that the countries of Central Europe will not become CEE members for dozens of years], *Le Monde*, June 14, 1991. See also William Drozdiak, "France Clouds EC Prospects; Mitterrand Urges Confederation Plan," *The Washington Post*, June 13, 1991.

28. In his speech at the conference Havel said that the security link across the Atlantic "is and will remain inevitable, logical and legitimate on the historic and geopolitical level." He added: "Even if it proves, over time, that it is possible to loosen it, even if the alliance transforms itself into a looser treaty, even if one day there is no reason for a last American soldier to remain in Europe, this would change nothing in the spiritual and political closeness across the Atlantic and the need for a close connection." See Henry Kamm, "Havel, in Rebuff to Paris, Backs U.S.-Europe Ties," *The New York Times*, June 13, 1991.

29. Alexandr Vondra—confident of Havel, former dissident, Deputy Foreign Minister and subsequently Czech Ambassador to Washington—described Czech motivations to join NATO in the following terms: "We trusted America as a nation—and

we felt our aspirations were understood in the White House. We did not trust the West Europeans. NATO enlargement was as much about involving the Americans in our part of the world to achieve a balance within Europe as it was about balancing the Russians." Interview with Alexandr Vondra, November 25, 2000.

30. A good summary of the discussion at that conference is contained in Ronald D. Asmus and Thomas S. Szayna, *Polish National Security Thinking in a Changing Europe* (Santa Monica, CA,: RAND, 1991).

31. See Jiri Dienstbier, *From Dreams to Reality: Memoirs from the Years 1989–1999*, p. 32 (Prague: Lidove Noviny, 1999).

32. For Vaclav Havel speech at NATO Headquarters, Brussels, March 21, 1991, see "Responsibility, Safety, Stability: Vaclav Havel Concerning NATO," *Selected Speeches, Articles and Interviews 1990–1991*, pp. 15–24. Author's signed private copy. See also <http:www.hrad.cz/president/Havel/speeches/1991/2103_uk.html>.

33. See Clifford Krauss, "Bush Greets Walesa With Debt Relief," *The New York Times*, March 21, 1991. See also Andrew Borowiec, "Soviets' ex-satellites warming up to NATO," *The Washington Times*, March 25, 1991.

34. As quoted in Robert Kupiecki, "Atlanticism in Post-1989 Polish Foreign Policy" in Roman Kuzniar, *Poland's Security Policy 1989–2000* (Warsaw: Foundation of International Studies/Scholar Publishing House, 2001), p. 245.

35. See Michnik's interview entitled "I am immensely afraid of an Epidemic of Populism," in *Lidove Noviny*, June 15, 1993 reprinted in JPRS-EER-93–081-S, August 11, 1993. See also his article "Nationalism," *Social Research*, No. 4, (Winter 1991): 757–763.

36. For a description of the failed coup, see Chapter 10, "The Revolution," in Leon Aron, *Yeltsin: A Revolutionary Life* (New York: St. Martin's Press, 2000), pp. 439–493.

37. See Skubiszewski, "Polska I Sojusz Atlantycki," p. 11.

38. See the "Declaration of the Highest Representatives of the Triangle," adopted at their Prague Meeting on May 6, 1992.

39. See Kupiecki, "Atlanticism in Post-1989 Polish Foreign Policy," p. 253.

40. See "Speech by the Secretary General of NATO at the Seminar on Security in Central Europe, March 12, 1992. Author's private copy.

41. See "Statement By Deputy Secretary of State Lawrence S. Eagleburger," North Atlantic Council Ministerial Meeting, Oslo, June 4, 1992. Author's private copy.

42. Interview with Robert Hutchings, November 15, 2001 At the time Hutchings was working as a Director for European Affairs on the National Security Council with responsibility for Central and Eastern Europe.

BOOK II. THE DEBATE BEGINS

1. See Warren Christopher, *In the Stream of History: Shaping Foreign Policy for a New Era* (Palo Alto: Stanford University Press, 1998), p. 36.

2. See "The Three Pillars of U.S. Foreign Policy and Support for Reform in Russia," Address Before the Chicago Council on Foreign Relations, the Executives' Club of Chicago, and the Mid-America Committee, Chicago, Illinois, March 2, 1993, reprinted in Christopher's *In the Stream Of History*, pp. 40–60. The quote is from p. 46.

3. See "A Strategic Alliance with Russian Reform," Prepared Remarks of President William J. Clinton to the American Society of Newspaper Editors, Annapolis, Maryland, April 1, 1993, <http://clinton6.nara.gov/1993/04/1993-04-01-presidents-speech-to-am-soc-of-newspaper-ed...o>.

4. As Secretary of Defense Bill Perry and former Assistant Secretary of Defense Ash Carter later described the work of the GCC: "These twice-yearly meetings, begun in 1993 under the auspices of U.S. Vice President Al Gore and Russia's Prime Minister Viktor Chernomyrdin, were remarkable affairs. Virtually the entire U.S. cabinet would sit along one side of a giant meeting table and their Moscow counterparts would sit along the other: the U.S. secretary of health and human services across from Russia's health minister, the head of NASA across from the head of the Russian space program, the secretary of energy across from the minister of atomic energy, the director of the Environmental Protection Agency across from the environment minister and so on. Each pair would report on their progress in crafting joint projects that pooled the technology of each country for the good of both." See Ashton B. Carter and William J. Perry, *Preventive Defense: A New Security Strategy for America* (Washington, DC: Brookings Institution Press, 1999), p. 25.

5. See U.S. Senate Armed Services Committee, *Confirmation Hearing for Rep. Les Aspin (D-WI) as Secretary of Defense*, Afternoon Session, *Federal News Service*, January 7, 1993.

6. See Richard C. Holbrooke, "America: A European Power," *Foreign Affairs* 74, no. 2 (March/April 1995): 40.

7. Clinton compared Bush's policy on the former Yugoslavia to his "indifference at Tiananmen Square and his coddling of Saddam Hussein" and stated, "once again the administration is turning its back on violations of basic human rights and our own democratic values." See "Governor Bill Clinton, Democratic Presidential Nominee Speech on Foreign Policy Before the Los Angeles World Affairs Council," Los Angeles, California, *Federal News Service*, August 13, 1992.

8. See Elaine Sciolino, "U.S. Declines to Back Peace Plan as the Balkan Talks Shift to UN," *The New York Times*, February 2, 1993. For Owen's recollections, see David Owen, *Balkan Odyssey* (New York: Harcourt Brace, 1995).

9. There is a growing literature on the development of the Clinton Administration's policy on Bosnia and the Balkans, including just how chaotic and erratic foreign policy decisionmaking on Bosnia was in the early months of the Administration. See Ivo Daalder, *Getting To Dayton: The Making of America's Bosnia Policy* (Washington, DC: Brookings Institution Press, 2000); Elisabeth Drew, *On The Edge: The Clinton Presidency* (New York Simon & Schuster, 1994); and David Halberstam, *War in a Time of Peace* (New York: Scribner's, 2001).

10. Drew, *On the Edge*, p. 150.

11. See Colin L. Powell, *My American Journey* (Random House, 1995), p. 576.

12. Drew, *On the Edge*, p. 156.

13. As quoted in Raymond Seitz, *Over Here* (London: Phoenix, 1998), p. 329.

14. See Halberstam, *War in a Time of Peace*, p. 228.

15. See Daniel Williams and John M. Goshko, "Administration Rushes to 'Clarify' Policy Remarks by 'Brand X' Official," *The Washington Post*, May 27, 1993.

16. See James Chace, "Exit, NATO," *The New York Times*, June 14, 1993.

17. See "Address by Elie Wiesel at the Dedication of the Holocaust Memorial Museum," Washington, DC, April 22, 1993.

18. An interesting account of the atmosphere surrounding the Holocaust Memorial Museum opening and how the Holocaust and the history of the region shaped the discussions regarding Central and Eastern Europe's future is contained in an oral history recorded by State Department diplomat J.D. Bindenagel. In the spring of 1993 Bindenagel was the Director of the Office of Central Affairs. Ambassador Bindenagel was later prompted to be the Department's Special Envoy for Holocaust Issues. See the transcript of Bindenagel's oral history recorded on September 24, 1999 and contained in the State Department's archives.

19. See "President Clinton's Meeting with President Havel," State 137029, May 5, 1993.

20. See "Meeting with President Lech Walesa of Poland," State 134465, May 4, 1993.

21. Interview with Anthony Lake, July 10, 2000.

22. Interview with Sandy Berger, December 20, 2000.

23. See "The President's News Conference," June 17, 1993 in *Public Papers of the Presidents of the United States: William J. Clinton, Book 1, January 20 to July 31, 1993*, (Washington, DC: GPO, 1994), pp. 867–875.

24. Dutch Ambassador Adriaan Pieter Roetert Jacobovits de Szeged presented his credentials to the President on June 23, 1993. J.D. Bindenagel was in the meeting and wrote up a note summarizing what the President had said for Assistant Secretary of State for European and Canadian Affairs Stephen Oxman.

25. See Anthony Lake, "From Containment to Enlargement," Johns Hopkins University School of Advanced International Studies, Washington, D.C., September 21, 1993. Author's private copy. For background on the Administration's efforts to define a post-containment doctrine during this first year see Douglas Brinkley, "Democratic Enlargement: The Clinton Doctrine," *Foreign Policy* 106 (Spring 1997): 111–127.

26. See "Memorandum of Conversation from the President's Meeting with Italian Prime Minister Carlo Ciampi," September 17, 1993.

27. The one exception is when Morris, in the spring of 1995, at his own initiative and without consulting the President, included a question on enlargement in a poll testing what concessions Americans might be willing to support in order to get Russia to stop its nuclear cooperation with Iran. That poll was conducted in the spring of 1995 prior to Clinton's visit to Moscow. The results showed that the American public strongly opposed postponing enlargement. According to Morris: "One of the great myths about NATO enlargement is that the President cared about it for domestic political reasons." Interview with Dick Morris, August 8, 2000.

28. Interview with Sandy Berger, December 20, 2000.

29. Interview with Tony Lake, July 10, 2000.

30. See Janne E. Nolan, ed., *Global Engagement: Cooperation and Security in the 21st Century* (Washington, DC: The Brookings Institution, 1994).

31. See Carter and Perry, *Preventive Defense*, pp. 23–24.

32. See, for example, the memo from Assistant Secretary of State for European Affairs Tom Niles to Secretary of State Christopher entitled "Your Meeting with NATO Secretary General Manfred Woerner Brussels, Belgium, February 26, 1993, 9:15 AM," February 11, 1993; and the cable "Your February Meeting with NATO Foreign Ministers, USNATO 00790, February 15, 1993. For Christopher's NAC discussions see "February 26 Special NAC Ministerial — Interventions by Ministers and SYG Woerner; Secretary's Closing Remarks," USNATO 001019, March 3, 1993.

33. See Les Aspin, Department of Defense, *Report on the Bottom Up Review,* October 1993, Washington, D.C.

34. See "NATO: June 6 Permreps' Lunch Details Athens Ministerial Agenda," USNATO 002532, June 8, 1993.

35. See "Letter from the Secretary to NATO Foreign Ministers," State 170901, June 6, 1993.

36. See "Intervention by Secretary of State Warren Christopher Before the North Atlantic Council Ministerial Meeting," Nafsika Hotel, Athens, June 10, 1993.

37. See the "Talking Points" used by Secretary Christopher at the Foreign Ministers lunch at the Ministerial.

38. See "Bosnia, NATO & American Leadership," Excerpts from Secretary Christopher's Press Conference After NATO Foreign Ministers Meeting," June 10, 1993, *Foreign Policy Bulletin* (September/October 1993): pp. 23–24.

39. For Weisser's recollections see Ulrich Weisser, *NATO ohne Feindbild* (Bonn: Bouvier Verlag, 1992), pp. 158–159.

40. Ruehe explained his support for NATO enlargement in a Bundestag debate on enlargement in the following terms: "The opening of the Alliance to the East is in our vital interests. One does not have to be a strategic genius to understand this. I have often been surprised how little our debate on this issue has been guided by a clear analysis of German interests. A situation where we are at the border of stability and security — stable here but unstable east of us, prosperity on this side but poverty on the other side of the border — such a situation is not tenable in the long-run. It is for this reason that Germany's eastern border cannot be the border of NATO and the European Union. Either we will export stability or we will end up importing instability." See Ruehe's speech delivered in the parliamentary debate on the NATO summit in the Bundestag in January 1994; reprinted in *Das Parlament*, No. 3, January 21, 1994.

41. As Ruehe once put it: "We owe them in a negative sense for what we did to them during the war. And we owe them in a positive sense for their courage in the 1970s and the 1980s. Their liberating themselves was really the key to overcoming the division of Europe. We need to understand that there would have been no Leipzig without Gdansk." As quoted in Frederick Kempe, *Fatherland: A Personal Search for the New Germany* (New York: Putnam, 1999), pp. 111–112.

42. See Volker Ruehe, "Shaping Euro-Atlantic Policies: A Grand Strategy for a new Era," *Survival* 35, no. 2 (Summer 1993): pp. 129–137.

43. As quoted in Ulrich Weisser, *Sicherheit fuer ganz Europa*, (Stuttgart: Deutsche Verlags-Anstalt, 1999), p. 34.

44. See Senator Richard Lugar, "NATO: Out of Area or Out of Business. A Call for U.S. Leadership to Revive and Redefine the Alliance," Overseas Writers Club, Washington, D.C., June 24, 1993.

45. See Ronald D. Asmus, Richard L. Kugler and F. Stephen Larrabee, "Building a new NATO," *Foreign Affairs* 72, no. 4 (September–October 1993): 28–40.

46. See the draft "Framework Paper" prepared by the State Department's European Bureau for the IWG and circulated on July 2, 1993; as well as the NSC paper circulated by NSC Senior Director Jennone Walker on July 4 as a guide to discussions on NACC outreach, entitled "NATO, NACC and Security in the East."

47. A variety of proposals were floated in these brainstorming meetings. They included upgrading the NACC into a semi-autonomous pan-European body with its own Charter with which NATO, and potentially other regional subgroups, would cooperate; creating a new senior slot in the NATO structure to be filled by an East European charged with peacekeeping. A good overview of the state of play and thought in the interagency process can be found in the paper entitled "NATO Summit Preparations," circulated by State Department Deputy Assistant Secretary of State Thomas Weston as comments on the NSC summit concept paper and in response to the Defense Department's proposal for a NACC "Charter of Association with NATO" circulated on July 23 in anticipation of an IWG meeting on July 29, 1993.

48. General Shalikashvilli's thinking is reflected in a paper outlining his views circulated interagency on August 2, 1993, entitled "Strengthening Outreach to the East."

49. As Charlie Kupchan, who worked in the NSC's European Directorate at the time, later wrote: "The Partnership was deliberately designed to enable member states to put off questions of formal enlargement and of NATO's ultimate disposition in post–Cold War Europe." See Charles Kupchan, "Strategic Visions," *World Policy Journal*, vol. 11 (Fall 1994), p. 113.

50. Interview with Thomas Donilon, July 28, 2000.

51. Hans Binnendijk was Principal Deputy Director of Policy Planning and one of the earliest U.S. advocates of enlargement. See Hans Binnendijk, "NATO Can't Be Vague About Commitment to Eastern Europe," *International Herald Tribune*, November 8, 1991. Flanagan had stayed on in the Policy Planning staff after the Clinton Administration took office. He, too, was an early supporter of NATO enlargement, having laid out his views publicly in the spring of 1992. See Stephen J. Flanagan, NATO and Central and Eastern Europe: From Liaison to Security Partnership," *The Washington Quarterly*, Vol. 15, no. 2, pp. 141–151.

52. See Oxman to Christopher, "NATO Expansion to the East," July 23, 1993.

53. See Oxman's address before The Atlantic Council of the United States, "NATO: In Business to Stay," Washington, DC, August 12, 1993.

54. See Davis to Christopher, "Expanding and Transforming NATO," August 12, 1993.

55. See "Russian foreign minister warns of consequences of Eastern Europe joining NATO," *BBC Summary of World Broadcasts*, August 26, 1993.

56. The Joint declaration was signed August 25, 1993. For key excerpts from the Russian-Polish Declaration, see "Officials Seek To Clarify Position on NATO Expansion," *FBIS Trends*, September 29, 1993, p. 45. See also Sergei Parkhomenko,

"Neighbors: Russia Gives Poland Leave to Join NATO," August 27, 1993, as translated in *The Current Digest of the Post-Soviet Press*, September 22, 1993.

57. Press Conference, "Polish and Russian presidents welcome signing of agreements," as translated in *BBC Summary of World Broadcasts* from Polish TV1, Warsaw, in Polish 0901 GMT, August 25, 1993.

58. Interview with Richard Lugar, July 24, 2000. See also "NATO-Mania Greets Senator Lugar in Poland," Warsaw 12545, August 27, 1993.

59. For U.S. Embassy coverage of this event see "Russia Will Not Oppose Poland in NATO," Warsaw 12390, August 25, 1993; and "The Yeltsin Visit: Remembering the Past, Looking to the Future," Warsaw 12734, September 1, 1993.

60. As quoted in Jane Perlez, "Yeltsin 'Understands' Polish Bid for a Role in NATO," *The New York Times*, August 25, 1993.

61. For Yeltsin's comments see "Yeltsin would not bar Czech Republic from NATO, *CTK National News Wire*, August 26, 1993.

62. See "Suchocka on Delay in NATO Membership," FBIS-WEU-93–168, September 1, 1993, p. 36.

63. The U.S. eventually decided to leave it to NATO Secretary General Woerner to perform the awkward task of answering the Polish President. Woerner finally wrote Walesa on September 23, 1993 on behalf of all allies. He stated that he had received Walesa's letter with "great interest" and appreciated Walesa sharing his views with him on Poland's desire to join NATO "with all clarity." The Secretary General simply noted that "The issue addressing in your letter of still further enhancing the ties between NATO and Poland will be carefully considered in the Alliance" in the run up to the NATO summit. See Woerner's letter to Polish President Walesa, September 23, 1993.

64. See "The Secretary's Meeting with Manfred Woerner, March 3, 1993," State 67584, March 3, 1993.

65. See "NATO SYG Manfred Woerner Discusses the NATO Summit," US NATO 03245, August 6, 1993.

66. Interview with Klaus Scharioth, September 16, 2000.

67. See "Woerner on Expanding Membership," USNATO 03586, September 3, 1993.

68. See speech by Manfred Woerner entitled, "NATO's Role in a Changing Europe," September 10, 1993 delivered at the International Institute for Strategic Studies 35th Annual Conference, "European Security After the Cold War," Brussels, September 9–12, 1993. Author's private copy.

69. Davis's memo to Secretary Christopher is from September 7, 1993, entitled "Strategy for NATO's Expansion and Transformation."

70. Gati's paper was dated September 3, 1993 and entitled "Apropos Polish Elections: Central Europe's Uncertain Future and What We Can Do About It."

71. Davis' paper was officially circulated to the interagency process on September 14, 1993. See the memo from State Department Executive Secretary Marc Grossman to his counterparts entitled "State Department Paper on the NATO Summit," September 14, 1994.

72. Strobe Talbott, *The Russia Hand: A Memoir of Presidential Diplomacy* (New York: Random House, 2002), p. 95.

73. In a January 8, 1999 letter to Prof. George Grayson, author of a book on NATO enlargement entitled *Strange Bedfellows*, Talbott wrote: "I believed that while new members were an important part of the new NATO, they were not the only dimension; there was also the issue of new missions—and new relationships with former adversaries. . . . I felt that the arguments in favor of admitting new members outweighed those against. But I believed that enlargement should be pursued in parallel with the development of cooperative relations with Russia and Ukraine in particular." Author's private copy of the letter.

74. Edelman wrote up his arguments and sent them to Talbott as a memo in September 1993 entitled "Phone Notes for Strobe on NATO expansion."

75. See Talbott letter to Grayson, January 8, 1999.

76. See, "NATO Expansion: Now is Not the Time," Moscow 31886, October 8, 1993.

77. As quoted in "NATO Expansion and the FSU," Ankara 11443, September 14, 1993.

78. See the description of the meeting in the memo from Assistant Secretary of State for European Affairs Steve Oxman to Undersecretary of State for Political Affairs Peter Tarnoff, "Your Deputies' Meeting on the NATO summit Wednesday, September 15, 1993, 11:00 A.M.," September 14, 1993.

79. See "Christopher-Kozyrev Meeting on September 13," State 284802, September 17, 1993.

80. See "Talbott/Burns Delegation: Meetings At NATO," USNATO 003804, September 21, 1993. See also Talbott's memo and trip report to Secretary of State Christopher entitled "My September Trip to the Caucasus and Central Asia," September 20, 1993.

81. See Hurd's speech entitled "The Role of NATO in the Post Cold War World," the Carlton Club Political Committee, London, June 30, 1993.

82. See Rifkind's comments from the House of Commons Hansard debate of October 18, 1993 on the Ninth Report from the Defence Committee on the Statement on the Defence estimates 1993 at <http://www.parliament.the-stationer . . . 3/cmhansrd/1993–10–18/Debate-1.html>, pp. 9–10.

83. As quoted in David S. Yost, *NATO Transformed: The Alliance's New Roles in International Security,* (Washington, D.C.: United States Institute of Peace Press, 1998), pp. 112–113.

84. See "NATO: Ambassador Hunter's 9/16 Lunch with French PermRep Blot," US NATO 03764, September 17, 1993.

85. See "Meeting with Helmut Kohl," Bonn 27340, September 30, 1993.

86. See "Possible Yeltsin Letter on NATO," Moscow 028107, September 3, 1993.

87. See "Early Visegrad-Four Membership in NATO: Russia's Likely Response," Moscow 028212, September 7, 1993.

88. See "Kozyrev on Possible NATO Expansion: Russia First," Moscow 029067, September 13, 1993.

89. See "Russian President Boris Yeltsin's Letter To US President Bill Clinton," September 15, 1993, Stockholm International Peace Research Institute, *SIPRI Yearbook* (Oxford: Oxford University Press, 1994), pp. 249–250.

90. For excerpts of the study, see "NATO Report Summarized," FBIS-SOV-93–226, November 26, 1993.

91. For Primakov's public statement, see "Head of Foreign Intelligence Service's report on plans to expand NATO," *BBC Summary of World Broadcasts*, November 30, 1993.

92. See "Yeltsin-Woerner Bilateral—Russia Should Join NATO or EE States Should Stay Out," USNATO 005029, December 9, 1993.

93. An overview of the state of play on the enlargement issue is contained in the memo background materials prepared for the DC meeting on September 15, 1993. See A/S Oxman to Undersecretary Peter Tarnoff "Your Deputies' Meeting on the NATO Summit, Wednesday, September 15, 1993, 11:00 A.M.," September 14, 1993.

94. See the OSD paper circulated interagency in mid-September entitled "Partnership for Peace with General Link to Membership."

95. See Walker's note to Lake simply entitled "To: Tony" and "From: Jennone," dated September 23, 1993.

96. See "Secretary Christopher's Lunch with NATO SYG Woerner and German FM Kinkel," October 5, 1993," State 309312, October 8, 1993.

97. Davis's Note to the Secretary is dated October 15, 1993.

98. See the updated talking points based on the results of the Saturday meeting included as an attachment to a memo from Assistant Secretary of State Steve Oxman to Christopher dated October 18, 1993.

99. See Hunter's cable entitled "The NATO Summit and the Eastern Question," USNATO 004194, October 16, 1993.

100. Talbott's memo to Christopher is simply entitled "Note To: the Secretary" and dated October 17, 1993.

101. See "Summary of Conclusions for Meeting of NSC Principals Committee, October 18, 1993" circulated on October 27, 1993.

102. See "Letter from the Secretary to NATO FONMINS," State 319425, October 20, 1993.

103. See "Aspin News Conference of 10/20/93," Travemuende, Germany, EUR405, Tracking Number 308616.

104. See the paper entitled "Partnership for Peace" distributed by the U.S. delegation at the Travemuende informal Defense Ministers meeting on October 20, 1993.

105. See Weisser, "Sicherheit fuer Europe," pp. 49–51.

106. See "NATO ministers back 'partnerships' idea," *The Washington Times*, October 22, 1993.

107. See Lippman's account in Thomas Lippman, *Madeleine Albright And The New American Diplomacy* (Boulder, CO: Westview Press, 2000), pp. 311–312.

108. For Lake's remarks, see "Background Briefing by Senior Administration Official," October 22, 1993, <http://www.pub.whitehouse.gov/uri-res/I . . . di://oma.eop.gov.us/1993/10/22/3.text.1>.

109. The letter was delivered to the White House on October 6, 1993. See "Letter from President Antall to President Clinton on NATO Enlargement," State 310005, October 9, 1993.

110. "Christopher, Jeszenszky Hold Joint Press Conference," Budapest, Hungary, EUR504, Tracking Number 308839.

111. See Christopher, "In the Stream of History," pp. 92–93.

112. See "Secretary Christopher's Meeting with President Yeltsin, 10/22/93, Moscow," Secto 17027, October 25, 1993.

113. See Christopher, *In the Stream of History*, pp, 93—94.

114. See David B. Ottaway and Peter Maass, "Hungary, NATO Grope Toward New Relationship," *The Washington Post*, November 17, 1993.

115. See Jeszensky's lecture, "The Lessons of Appeasement," delivered at the School of Slavonic and East European Studies, University of London, December 6, 1993, as reprinted in *The Hungarian Observer*, January 1994.

116. See Budapest 11646, "A/S Oxman Briefs Visegrad Four on Partnership for Peace," October 29, 1993.

117. Interview with Andrzej Ananicz, May 3, 2000.

118. For two essays that capture the Central and East European mood in the summer and fall of 1993, see Przemyslaw Grudzinski and Andrzej Karkoszka, "East Central Europe in an Uncertain World," pp. 9–38, and Martin Palous "Weaving A Security Net: East Central Europe and the Structures of International Peace and Security," pp. 39–60, in Jeffrey Laurenti, ed., *Searching for Moorings: East Central Europe in the International System* (New York: United Nations Association of the United States of America, 1994). The quote from Grudzinski and Karkoszka is on p. 38.

119. As quoted in Daniel Williams, "U.S. Trying to Sell NATO Partnership; Ex-East Bloc Countries Want Full Seat," *The Washington Post*, January 1, 1994.

120. This objective is reflected in a "non-paper" circulated by Warsaw in late November 1993. See "Polish Non-Paper on Partnership for Peace," Warsaw 017122, November 29, 1993. (A non-paper is term used to describe a "food for thought" paper that does not [yet] have official status.)

121. See "The Secretary's Meeting with Polish FM Olechowksi," State 383575, December 23, 1993. Olechowski made these points in public as well. See his statement entitled "Seven Statements on Poland's Security" delivered at the Center for Strategic and International Studies (CSIS) on December 15, 1993.

122. As quoted in "Central Europe's Disappointment and Hopes," Alfred A. Reisch, *RFE/RL Research Report* 3, no.12, March 25, 1994, p. 25.

123. See Olechowski's letter to Secretary of State Christopher dated December 22, 1993.

124. Interview with Nicholas Rey, April 23, 2000.

125. See Jan Nowak, *Courier From Warsaw* (Michigan: Wayne State University Press, 1982).

126. See Rowland Evans and Robert Novak, "Ghost of Yalta," *The Washington Post*, November 22, 1993.

127. For the role of ethnics in the NATO enlargement debate, see Bruce Stokes, "NATO's Facing a Winter of Discontent," *The National Journal* 25, no. 43 (October 23, 1993): 25–41. An overview of the Polish American Congress' lobbying campaign can be found at <www.polamcon.org/poland%20%20nato.html>.

128. This description of the conversation is drawn from a memo of the discussion written by Dr. Brzezinski following the meeting.

BOOK III. ACROSS THE RUBICON

1. For further background see James M. Goldgeier, *Not Whether But When: The U.S. Decision to Enlarge NATO* (Washington, DC: Brookings University Press, 1999); and George W. Grayson, *Strange Bedfellows: NATO Marches East* (University Press of America, Inc., 1999).

2. Interview with Sandy Berger, December 22, 2000.

3. See "Secretary's Letter to Central and East European Foreign Ministers, State 0019, January 3, 1994.

4. See "Polish Foreign Minister on Prague Summit," Warsaw 00121, January 4, 1994.

5. See John Pomfret, "Walesa Warns Communism Could Reemerge in Europe: Polish President pleads for West to Include E. Europe in NATO," *The Washington Post*, January 3, 1994.

6. See "Special White House Briefing With Chairman of the Joint Chiefs of Staff General John Shalikashvilli," The Press Room, The White House, Washington, D.C., *Federal News Service*, January 4, 1994.

7. See "Walesa Waffles on PfP with Albright Delegation; Urges NATO to 'Leap Now' to Expand," See Warsaw 00308, January 7, 1993.

8. See "Amb. Albright's Meeting with Polish FM: GOP Seeks Predictability, Fears Abandonment," Warsaw 00312, January 8, 1993.

9. Geremek's Democratic Union was created in 1990 and later merged with the Liberal-Democratic Congress to form the Freedom-Union Party in 1994.

10. See "Ambassador Albright's January 7 Dinner with Polish Foreign Minister Olechowski," Warsaw 00490, January 11, 1994.

11. For Gore's speech, see "Remarks By The Vice President in Foreign Policy Speech," Pabst Theater, Milwaukee, Wisconsin, January 6, 1994, <http://www.pub .whitehouse.gov/uri-res/I2R?urn:pdi://oma.eop.gov.us/1994/1/6/2.text.1>.

12. As Berger subsequently recalled the Milwaukee meeting: "Fried and I met with a rather skeptical and extremely sophisticated coalition of leaders from the ethnic communities. I knew then that the President wanted to enlarge. But they never believed we would do it. They believed that in the final analysis the Russian card would trump the enlargement card. They believed that as a matter of power in the final analysis Central Europe would once again be sold out like it had been sold out before. We went on for hours and we still did not convince them. They were also pressing quite hard on questions such as 'who would come in' and criteria questions to which we did not yet have answers." Interview with Sandy Berger, December 22, 2000.

13. Obtained from Strobe Talbott's personal papers.

14. See "Remarks By the President to Multinational Audience of Future Leaders of Europe," Gothic Room, Hotel De Ville, Brussels, Belgium, January 9, 1994, < http:// www.pub.whitehouse.gov/uri-res/I2R?urn:pdi://oma.eop.gov.us/1994/1/9/6.text.1>.

15. See "Remarks by the President at Intervention for the North Atlantic Council Summit," NATO Headquarters, Brussels, Belgium, January 10, 1994, <http://www .pub.whitehouse.gov/uri-res/I . . . pdi://oma.eop.gov.us/1994/1/10/1.text.1>.

16. See "Polish Statement Accepting PfP Participation," Warsaw 000393, January 10, 1994.

17. See the Memcon entitled "The President's Meeting with Czech Leaders," January 11, 1994 5:30 P.M., -7:00 P.M., Prague Castle.

18. See "Press Conference by the President With Visegrad Leaders," U.S. Ambassador's Residence, Prague, Czech Republic, January 12, 1994, <http://www.pub.whitehouse.gov/uri-res/I-pdi://oma.eop.gov.us/1994/1/13/3.text.1>.

19. See President's Bilateral With Polish President Walesa, Premier Pawlak," Bonn 00904, January 12, 1994.

20. See the Memorandum of Conversation entitled "President's Dinner With President Yeltsin, January 14, 1994."

21. See "Press Conference by President Clinton and President Yeltsin," Kremlin Press Center, Moscow, Russia, January 14, 1994.

22. Interview with Anthony Lake, July 10, 2000.

23. Interview with Bill Perry, August 21, 200.

24. See Albright to the President, "PfP and Central and Eastern Europe," January 26, 1994.

25. For a good summary of PfP's start up see Gebhardt von Moltke, "Building a Partnership for Peace," *NATO Review* 42, no. 3 (June 1994): 3–7; and George A. Joulwan, "NATO's Military Contribution to Partnership for Peace: The progress and the challenge," *NATO Review* 43, no. 2 (March 1995): 3–6.

26. For a list of PfP signature countries and dates, see NATO Partnerships: Signatures of Partnership for Peace Framework Document, <http://www.nato.int/pfp/sig-cntr.htm>.

27. As quoted in Rick Atkinson, "Poland Hosts Mission Improbable—NATO Games with Ex-Warsaw Pact," *The Washington Post*, September 13, 1994.

28. As quoted in Jane Perlez, "Biedrusko Journal; the Cold War Armies Meet, Just to Link Arms," *The New York Times*, September 15, 1994.

29. See Ivan Rodin, "NATO's Program is Not Entirely to the Liking of the State Duma," *Nezavisimaya gazeta*, March 18, 1994. As summarized in *The Current Digest of the Post-Soviet Press*, April 13, 1994.

30. See Ivashov's interview conducted by Vyacheslav Kockerov and published under the title of "Partnership—for What?" in *Rossiiskaya Gazeta*, March 25, 1994. Summarized in *The Current Digest of the Post-Soviet Press*, April 20, 1994. The U.S. Embassy in Moscow reported frequently on the depth of Russian opposition to PfP during the spring months of 1994. For Washington's guidance on how to respond see "Russian Concerns About PfP," State 109220, April 26, 1993.

31. See "Secretary/Kozyrev Memcon of March 14, 1994," State 076059, March 24, 1994; and Christopher's Note to the President entitled "My Meeting with Kozyrev in Vladivostock," March 15, 1994.

32. See "May 12 Kohl/Yeltsin Talks," Bonn 11493, May 13, 1994; and "Yeltsin's May 11–13 Visit to Germany: Kozyrev's Comments on PfP," Bonn 12613, May 26, 1994.

33. On the Perry-Grachev relationship see Ashton B. Carter and William J. Perry, *Preventive Defense: A New Security Strategy For America* (Washington, D.C.: Brookings Institutions Press), pp.26–27.

34. Interview with Ashton Carter, November 6, 2000.

35. See Fred Hiatt, "Russia Speeds Plan for Link to NATO, *The Washington Post,* March 17, 1994.

36. For the text of Grachev's speech see "Meeting of Defense Ministers with Cooperation Partners, 25 May 1994: Statement by Russian Defense Minister Grachev," USNATO 02177, June 2, 1994.

37. See "NATO: May 30 PermReps' Lunch—the NATO/Russian Relationship," USNATO 002105, May 31, 1995.

38. See "Secretary's Meeting with Russian Foreign Minister Kozyrev, June 10, 1994, Istanbul, Turkey," State 160602, June 16, 1994.

39. For Kozyrev's NACC intervention, Author's private copy. See also "NACC Istanbul Ministerial—June 10, Morning Session," USNATO 002360, June 16, 1994. For the afternoon session see "NACC Istanbul Ministerial—June 10, Afternoon Session," USNATO 02372, June 16, 1994.

40. As quoted in Bruce Clarke, "Russia looks to closer western ties soon: meeting of NATO and former Warsaw Pact Ministers becomes trench warfare," *The Financial Times,* June 11, 1994.

41. See "Summary of Conclusion," Discussions between the North Atlantic Council, and the Foreign Minister of Russia, Andrei Kozyrev, Brussels, June 22, 1994, <http://www.nato.int/docu/comm/49095/c940622a.htm>. Shortly thereafter, Kozyrev wrote an article in *NATO Review* detailing his proposals for NATO-Russia cooperation. See Andrei V. Kozyrev, Minister of Foreign Affairs of the Russian Federation, "Russia and NATO: A Partnership for a United and Peaceful Europe," *NATO Review* 42, no. 4 (August 1994): 3–6.

42. See Steven Greenhouse, "Russia and NATO Agree to Closer Military Links," *The New York Times,* June 23, 1994; and Daniel Williams, "Russia Joins NATO Plan," *The Washington Post,* June 22, 1994.

43. See "NATO: Russia Signs PfP Framework Agreement," USNATO 002458, June 22, 1994.

44. As quoted in Daniel Williams, "Russia Joins NATO Plan; Clinton-Yeltsin Summit in DC is Set," *The Washington Post,* June 23, 1994.

45. Graham Brown, "Russia signs NATO's partnership for peace," *Agence France Presse,* June 22, 1994.

46. For a summary of the briefing see, "NATO Expansion: The Next Steps," *Survival* 37 (Spring 1995): 7–33.

47. Deputy Secretary Strobe Talbott, "The Crooked Timber: A Carpenter's Perspective," Address at All Souls College, Oxford University, Oxford, England, January 21, 2000, <http://www.state.gov/www.policy_remarks/2000/000121_talbott_oxford.html>.

48. See "Official Informal: Uncleared Memcon of Deputy Secretary's Meeting in Warsaw with President Walesa," Warsaw 005124, April 12, 1994.

49. Interview with Nicholas Rey, April 23, 2000.

50. I was one of several individuals to whom Talbott reached out to discuss enlargement strategy. Although I had declined a job offer to work for the State Department, I did become a consultant to him and our exchange of ideas on NATO and

European security issues continued. It was clear to me that Talbott was increasingly open to the argument that NATO enlargement could help build a more unified Europe and was looking for the way to reconcile it with the Administration's approach to Russia. We stayed in touch and corresponded regularly. That relationship would grow and by the spring of 1997 I would go to work for him.

51. As Holbrooke recalls in his book: "When I laid out this 'lose-lose' dilemma to Strobe, he laughed. 'We assumed you will be aggressive,' he said. 'That's why we need you. We'll back you up.' This time it was my turn to laugh. How long have you been in Washington? I asked, amused. 'Anyway,' Strobe said, 'I'll back you up—and you'll finally be part of our team.'" See Richard Holbrooke, *To End A War* (New York: The Modern Library, 1998), p. 57.

52. Holbrooke wrote in a letter-to-the-editor in the *World Policy Journal* that "When I arrived in Germany in September 1993, I believed that EU membership was more important and would arrive first. What turned me around was the realization that the EU, mired in its own Euro-mess . . . was not going to invite any of these countries in, at the earliest, before 2003. . . . In short, they were vulnerable to a number of different scenarios that would have sent them back into new darkness. I concluded it would be irresponsible and potentially dangerous to leave these countries outside the "West" for so long after the fall of communism." See Richard Holbrooke, "Marooned in the Cold War"—An Exchange, *World Policy Journal* (Winter 1997/98): 100.

53. Holbrooke, "Marooned," p. 101.

54. See Talbott memo to Christopher entitled "The Future of European Security," September 12, 1994.

55. Interview with Sandy Berger, December 22, 2000.

56. See "Foreign Minister Urges President Clinton to Focus on Polish Security During Visit," Warsaw 009178, June 24, 1994. Olechowksi would be even more emphatic on this point when he met Christopher on the margins of President Clinton's trip several weeks later. There was a danger that they would turn to the East if the western option was seen as failing again. He said that his country's trust in the U.S. and the West was at risk and that there was growing talk in Poland of looking for alternatives to integration with the West. See "The Secretary's Meeting with Polish Foreign Minister Olechowski; Warsaw, July 7, 1994," SECTO 014005, July 11, 1994.

57. See "New Polish Ambassador Urges Polish Membership in NATO to Acting Secretary," State 166385, June 22, 1994.

58. See "Remarks by the President to the Sejm," Parliament Building, Warsaw, Poland, The White House, Office of the Press Secretary, July 7, 1994.

59. See "Remarks by President Clinton and President Walesa After Their Meeting," Residential Palace, Warsaw, Poland, July 6, 1994, <http://www.pub.whitehouse.gov/uri-res/I...pdi://oma.eop.gov.us/1994/7/8/13.text.1>.

60. Interview with Anthony Lake, July 10, 2000.

61. The President traveled to Berlin following Warsaw. In a press conference with Chancellor Kohl and French President Jacques Delors, he stated in response to a question on enlargement: "To the Poles I will say to you what I said to them directly—they have certainly shown the greatest interest in this issue, the greatest determination to do their full part, and I think they have virtually assured that they are at the front of

the line as NATO will be expanded. We just have to get together and work out the details." For full text of remarks, see "Remarks By President Clinton, Chancellor Kohl, and President Delors in Press Availability," East Hall, Reichstag, Berlin, Germany, July 12, 1994, <http://www.pub.whitehouse.gov/uri-res/I . . . di://oma.eop.gov.us/1994/7/15/11.text.1>.

62. See the memo from Alexander Vershbow to Tony Lake entitled "NATO Expansion –Next Steps," July 15, 1994.

63. Roth, for example, introduced a resolution as early as February 1992 supporting NATO enlargement. See Senate Concurrent Resolution 90—Relative to the Role of the North Atlantic Treaty Organization, 102nd Cong, 2nd sess., S.Con.Res. 90, Congressional Research, (February 4, 1992). This resolution was the first evidence in Congress of a member pushing for NATO enlargement. Several months later Senator Lieberman joined Roth in a second proposed resolution that called for NATO to step up its role in Central and East European countries as well as to reorient its mission to deal with future contingencies outside of Europe. In September, Roth and Lieberman proposed an amendment to the National Defense Authorization Act for Fiscal Year 1993 (bill S. 3114, supra). See Roth (and Lieberman) Amendment No. 3055, Congressional Record (September 18, 1992): p.S14129. All three amendments died in Committee.

64. Interview with Newt Gingrich, September 8, 2000.

65. The NATO Participation Act passed the House and Senate as Title II of the International Narcotics Control Corrections Act of 1994, and became law on November 4, 1994. See NATO Participation Act, 103rd Cong., 2nd sess., part II, Congressional Record, (October 7, 1994): S14883, <http://www.congress.gov/cgi-lis/query/D?r103:4:./temp/~r103Tkqo::> .

66. See Senator Brown's Floor Statement in the Congressional Record, "Is Congress Irresponsible? You Be The Judge," S. Amendment No. 2248, (July 14, 1994), <http://www.congress.gov/cgi-lis/query/D?r103:1:.//temp/~r103DkXyax:e465751:>.

67. See Congressman Gilman's "Dear Colleague" letter from April 22, 1994 in which he invites other Congressmen to co-sponsor H.R. 4210 entitled the NATO Expansion Act of 1994.

68. See House Rep. Benjamin Gilman of New York speaking before the Committee on Rules Regarding Amendments to H.R. 4426, Foreign Operations Appropriations Act, 1995, 103rd Cong., Congressional Record (May 24, 1994).

69. NATO Revitalization Act (Introduced in the House), 103rd Cong., 2nd sess., H.R. 4358, Congressional Record, (May 5, 1994), <http://thomas.loc.gov/cgi-bin/query/z?c103:H.R.4358:>. The bill died in Committee.

70. See Rep. Newt Gingrich, Rep. Dick Armey and the House Republicans, *Contract With America: The Bold New Plan by Rep. Newt Gingrich, Rep. Dick Armey and the House Republicans, To Change the Nation* (New York: Time Books and the Republican National Committee, 1994).

71. *Contract With America*, pp. 112–113.

72. The Republican Party Platform statement issued in Philadelphia in July 2000 states that "As the new democracies of Central Europe chose freedom, America was ready to respond. Republicans made the enlargement of NATO part of our Contract

With America. Their firm stand before the American people and in the Congress finally succeeded in bringing Poland, the Czech Republic, and Hungary into the North Atlantic Alliance." Author's private copy.

73. Interview with Newt Gingrich, September 8, 2000.

74. Ibid.

75. See Roger Cohen, "Taming the Bullies of Bosnia" *The New York Times*, December 17, 1995.

76. See "Hearing of the Senate Foreign Relations Committee: Confirmation of Richard Holbrooke to be Assistant Secretary of State for European and Canadian Affairs," August 10, 1994.

77. See Vice President Al Gore, "U.S.-German Relations and The Challenge of a New Europe," Conference on New Traditions, Berlin, Germany, September 9, 1994. Obtained from the US Department of State Dispatch, Bureau of Public Affairs, vol. 5, pp. 1–2.

78. See Ruehe's remarks at the U.S.-Embassy sponsored "Conference on New Traditions" in Berlin on September 9, 1994. Obtained from the U.S. Department of Sate Dispatch, Bureau of Public Affairs, vol. 5. For press coverage see Josef Joffe, "Nach dem Zapfenstreich Neue Traditionen," *Sueddeusche Zeitung*, September 13, 1994.

79. The paper was entitled "NATO Expansion: Concept and Strategy" and was circulated to members of the IWG on September 19, 1994.

80. See the "Memcon of Meeting with Paris Mayor Jacques Chirac, September 21, 1994."

81. See Boris Yeltsin, *Midnight Diaries* (New York: Public Affairs, 2000), pp. 134–135.

82. According to a senior U.S. official, Clinton planned to tell Yeltsin that he "is fully committed to the integration of Europe and a Europe that is undivided and whole but one in which the question of NATO expansion is something that we contemplate and indeed expect to occur." See "Background Briefing by Senior Administration Officials," September 21, 1994, < http://www.pub.whitehouse.gov/uri-res/I2R?urn:pdi://oma.eop.gov.us/1994/9/21/3.text.1>.

83. See Prime Minister John Major's letter to President Clinton dated September 25, 1994.

84. See the Memcon entitled "Second Clinton/Yeltsin One-on-One," 1:00 P.M–2:30 P.M., September 28, 1994.

85. See "British Thinking on NATO Expansion," London 014877, September 19, 1994.

86. See "British Discuss NATO Expansion with A/S Holbrooke," London 016422, October 17, 1994. Foreign and Commonwealth Office (FCO) Political Director Pauline Neville-Jones told Talbott in Washington shortly thereafter that London was willing to go along with what she called a "Russia-friendly" discussion of enlargement so long as it avoided the issues of timetable, candidates or criteria. See "The Deputy Secretary's October 20 Meeting with FCO Political Director Neville-Jones," London 016663, October 21, 1994.

87. See "Undersecretary Davis' July 20–21 Paris Discussions: NPT Extension, Fissile-Material Cutoff, North Korea, NATO Expansion, Ukraine Rwanda," Paris 20200, July 25, 1994.

88. See "U/S Tarnoff's Paris Visit: Discussions on Haiti, NATO, EU Stability Pact, Aegean Issues," Paris 25538, September 19, 1994.

89. See "French Thinking on NATO Expansion," Paris 28401, October 14, 1994.

90. See "Chancellor Kohl: NATO and EU Enlargement, The Future of Europe," Berlin 002793, September 10, 1994.

91. See the NSC paper entitled "Moving Toward NATO Expansion," October 12, 1994.

92. See, for example, "British Reactions to USG Presentation on NATO Expansion," London 017382, November 2, 1994; "Inter-Agency Presentation on NATO—Germany," Bonn 26966, November 3, 1994.

93. For further details on the rift in the Alliance in general in the fall of 1994, and the issue of Bihac in particular, see Daalder, *Getting to Dayton*, pp. 31–34.

94. See, for example, Dmitry Gornostayev, "Republican Control on Congress Could Lead to Cooling of Relations Between Washington and Moscow," *Nezavisimaya gazeta*, November 10, 1994, as summarized in *The Current Digest of the Post-Soviet Press*, December 7, 1994.

95. See "NATO: Ambassador Churkin Zeroes In on NATO Expansion in Courtesy Call on Ambassador Hunter," USNATO 004251, November 14, 1994.

96. See Christopher's Night Note to President Clinton from October 20, 1994.

97. This quote comes from a Talbott memo to Secretary of State Christopher, excerpts of which Christopher, in turn, attached to his own Night Note to the President from October 20, 1994.

98. See "Final Communiqué" issued at the Ministerial Meeting of the NAC, NATO Headquarters, Brussels, December 1, 1994, < http://www.nato.int/docu/comm/ 49–95/c941201a.htm>.

99. See "Secretary's meeting with Polish Foreign Minister Olechowski, December 2, 1994," SECTO 028008, December 4, 1994. For the positive remarks of other Central and East European Foreign Ministers see "Secretary's Meeting with Central European/Baltic Foreign Ministers," SECTO 028010, December 4, 1994.

100. Interview with Andrzej Olechowski, December 18, 2000.

101. See "Foreign Minister on NATO Expansion," *CTK National News Wire*, December 2, 1994.

102. NATO and Russia were also scheduled to officially sign Russia's so-called Individual Partnership Program (IPP) in PfP as well as a second paper entitled "NATO-Russian Relations Beyond PfP."

103. See "Russia Fails to Approve IPP and NATO-Russia Relationship in 16-plus-I Ministerial, USNATO 04586, December 2, 1994. For coverage of Kozyrev's public remarks see Leonid Velekhov, "Russia-NATO Betrothal Didn't Happen: Andrei Kozyrev Awaits Explanation of 'Ambiguous Communiqué' From Counterparts in North Atlantic Alliance," *Sevodnya*, December 3, 1994. As summarized in *The Current Digest of the Post-Soviet Press*, December 28, 1994.

104. See Mikhail Karpov, "The Ceremony That Wasn't Held: After Russia's Renunciation of Program for Cooperation With NATO, Success of Budapest Forum is Problematic," *Nezavisimaya gazeta*, December 3, 1994. As summarized in *The Current Digest of the Post-Soviet Press*, December 28, 1994.

105. For Yeltsin's speech at the CSCE summit in Budapest, see "At CSCE Summit, Yeltsin Warns of 'Cold Peace,'" as translated from *Rossiiskaya gazeta*, December 7, 1994 in *The Current Digest of the Post-Soviet Press*, January 4, 1995.

106. Asked if Russia would view NATO enlargement differently if it were asked to join, he responded: "You know we have already discussed this issue several times in our Security Council, at the ministry and with the Foreign Minister and it is our opinion that at some point we may become ready for the political part of NATO." Asked by the interviewer if Russia was not ready now, Yeltsin responded: "Not as yet. Not for the political part. It is quite possible that we shall enter a political alliance with NATO and then at least we have not been kept apart from the issues which all European countries will be discussing if they all suddenly become members of NATO. We too must prepare some way of retreat." Interview by Sergey Medvedev with President Yeltsin during the "Vesti" newscast on Moscow Ostankino Television First Channel Network, 1800 GMT, December 10, 1994 as reprinted in FBIS-SOV-94-238, December 12, 1994.

107. See "December 15 Talbott-Ryurikov Meeting on NATO, Chechnya," Moscow 036374, December 16, 1994.

108. Talbott's conversations with Kozyrev are summarized in a long private memo to Christopher describing his Moscow trip entitled "The Vice President's trip to Russia," December 19, 1994.

109. See "Vice President-Chernomyrdin Breakfast 12/15," Moscow 036923, December 23, 1994.

110. Gore gave this account of that meeting in the White House on December 21, 1994. This description is drawn on notes taken by NSC Senior Director Nick Burns. For further details, see Talbott memo, pp. 144–145.

111. Interview with William Perry, August 21, 2000.

112. For Perry's recollection of the meeting see Carter and Perry, *Preventive Defense*, pp. 31–32.

113. Ibid., p. 32.

114. Interview with William Perry, August 21, 2000

115. See the notes from the December 21, 1994 meeting taken by NSC Senior Director Nick Burns.

116. See Talbott's untitled memo to Christopher dated January 2, 1995.

117. See President Clinton's letter to President Yeltsin dated December 24, 1994.

118. See the letter from Russian President Boris Yeltsin to President Clinton dated December 29, 1994.

BOOK IV. ESTABLISHING THE DUAL TRACK

1. See "NATO Expansion: Getting from Here to There," USNATO 000287, January 25, 1995.

2. See President Clinton's "Remarks at the White House Conference on Trade and Investment in Central and Eastern Europe in Cleveland, Ohio," *Public Papers of the Presidents*, January 12, 1995. See also "Address by Secretary of State Warren Christopher at the John F. Kennedy School of Government," Cambridge, Massachusetts, January 20, 1995, <http://dosfan.lib.ic.edu/ERC/briefing/dossec/1995/9501/950120dossec.html>. See also Remarks by Secretary of Defense William J. Perry to the Wehrkunde, Munich (Germany) Conference on Security Policy, "The Enduring, Dynamic Relationship That Is NATO," Feb. 5, 1995, <http://www.defenselink.mil:80/speeches/1995/s19950205-perry.html>, and Remarks by Perry at the George C. Marshall European Center for Security Studies, Garmisch, Germany, "Beginning the World Anew Through Partnership for Peace," May 24, 1995, <http://www.defenselink.mil:80/speeches/1995/s19950524-perry.html>.

3. See Richard Holbrooke, "America; A European Power," *Foreign Affairs* 74, no. 2 (March/April 1995): 38–51.

4. See Strobe Talbott, "Why NATO Should Grow," *The New York Review of Books*, August 10, 1995, pp. 1–6.

5. See "January 18 US-UK Security Talks: MOD Views on NATO Expansion and other European Security Issues," London 000542, January 11, 1995.

6. See "Secretary's Meeting with UK Foreign Secretary Hurd, January 16, 1995, Washington, DC," State 016931, January 23, 1995.

7. See Foreign Secretary Hurd's speech before the London Business School on January 19, 1995. See "Bilateral Meeting, SecDef, UK MOD Rifkind, Wehrkunde Conference, 4 February 1995," State 043701, February 22, 1995.

8. See the Memorandum of Conversation of the meeting Between Chancellor Helmut Kohl and Bill Clinton, February 9, 1995.

9. See "Moving Ahead on NATO Enlargement," State 042708, February 19, 1995.

10. One anonymous French diplomat was quoted as saying: "NATO enlargement is a mistake but no one wants to say 'No' because of the bad experience over Bosnia and the need to keep the U.S. engaged in Europe." As quoted in Lionel Barber, "Europe steps up efforts to strengthen ties with US," *The Financial Times*, February 20, 1995.

11. French Foreign Minster Juppé was the representative of the EU Presidency which France held during the first six months of 1995. See "The Secretary's Meeting with EU Presidency/Foreign Minister Juppé and European Commissioner Brittan, January 26, 1995 at the State Department," State 025603, February 1, 1995.

12. See speech by Foreign Minister Alain Juppé, "20ème Anniversaire du Centre D'Analyse et de Prevision-Intervention du Ministre Des Affaires Étrangères, M. Alain Juppé," Paris, January 30, 1995, <http://www.doc.diplomatie.fr/BASIS/epic/www.doc/DDW?W = CLE = 980107267>.

13. See "NATO Enlargement Study: Where Are We?," USNATO 000842, March 2, 1995.

14. See, for example, the joint paper produced by Principal Assistant Deputy Assistant Secretary of State John Kornblum and Principal Deputy Assistant Secretary of Defense Frank Miller entitled "NATO Expansion—Nuclear Aspects," March 17, 1995.

15. See "NATO Expansion: U.S. Views on Military Implications," State 052655, March 3, 1995. See also "NATO: NMA Contributions to Chapter III, V and VI of Enlargement Study, USNATO 000906, March 6, 1995.

16. The outstanding issues included France's objection that the study explicitly stated that new members should join NATO's integrated military structures; the precise language to be used on the issue of NATO conventional or nuclear forces on the territory of new members; and whether Russia should be explicitly ruled in or out as a candidate for membership. There were also disagreements over NATO's strategy to deal with these countries not included in the first round of enlargement and, specifically, whether new members should pledge not to block the accession of possible subsequent candidates for membership, a reference to the strained relations between Hungary and Romania. See "NATO Enlargement Study: Where Are We?," USNATO 000842, March 2, 1995.

17. See Holbrooke's note on the memo from Jim Cunningham to Holbrooke and Kornblum from March 30, 1995 updating him on the status of the enlargement study.

18. See the "Memorandum of Conversation between President Clinton and NATO Secretary General Willy Claes, March 7, 1995."

19. The Foreign Ministers communiqué simply noted that the allies were "satisfied" with progress on the study and that it would be completed in accordance with the agreed upon timetable. See the "Final Communiqué," as issued by the North Atlantic Council in Ministerial Session at Noordwijk, The Netherlands, May 30, 1995, <http://www.nato.int/docu/comm/49–95/c950530b.htm>.

20. See "NATO Enlargement: September 28 Collective Briefing to Partners," USNATO 003817, September 29, 1995.

21. See the NSC paper entitled "NATO Enlargement: Road Map for 1996" circulated on September 22, 1995 for the Deputies Committee on October 2, 1995. The results of the meeting are contained in "Summary of Conclusions" issued by the NSC on October 6, 1995.

22. See "Memorandum of Conversation: The President's Working Lunch with Prime Minister Kok, February 28, 1995."

23. See "Deputies Committee Meeting on NATO-Russia Relationship and Christopher-Kozyrev Meeting" dated January 7, 1995.

24. See Talbott's Memorandum of Conversation of his discussion with Mamedov in Brussels, January 10, 1995.

25. See Talbott's note to Secretary Christopher from January 11, 1995.

26. See Talbott's memo to Secretary Christopher entitled "Preparing for Geneva" dated January 12, 1995.

27. See "Hurd Meeting with Kozyrev in Stockholm, February 14," London 002522, February 16, 1995.

28. See the speech by Secretary of Defense William J. Perry at the Wehrkunde Munich Conference on Security Policy, February 5, 1995. Author's private copy.

29. For an excellent account of the shift in Russian attitudes against NATO in the spring of 1995, see the paper delivered by Alexei Pushkov at the 1995 NATO symposium in Washington, D.C., entitled "NATO Expansion: A Russian Perspective." See

also Alexander Velichkin, "NATO As Seen Through the Eyes of the Russian Press," *NATO Review* 43, No. 2, March 1995.

30. Obtained from Strobe Talbott's personal papers.

31. See "Mamedov Visit: February 22 Sessions of the U.S.-Russian Strategic Stability Group," State 062120, March 14, 1995.

32. See the letter from President Clinton to Yeltsin dated March 15, 1995.

33. According to Russian press reports, Yeltsin criticized the Foreign Ministry for focusing too much on the conditions under which Russia would accept enlargement. See Alexei Pushkov, "When A Minister Refutes the President," *Moscow News*, no. 19, March 19–26, 1995. See also "Presidential Aide Says Yeltsin Angered Over MFA Mishandling of NATO Expansion Issue," Moscow 009356, March 21, 1995.

34. See "Mamedov Reiterates Russian Sensitivities Over NATO Expansion," Moscow 009127, March 18, 1995.

35. See the Memorandum of Conversation Between Secretary of State Warren Christopher and Russian Foreign Minister Andrei Kozyrev, Geneva, March 23, 1995.

36. See Christopher's "Night Note," March 23, 1995.

37. See Steven Erlanger, "Russia Says Sale of Atom Reactors To Iran Is Still On," *The New York Times*, April 4, 1995; and Charles Hecker, "Perry Visit Marked by Rebuffs," *The Moscow Times*, April 5, 1995.

38. See Thomas Urban: "Yesterday's Enemy, Tomorrow's Enemy," *Sueddeutsche Zeitung*, April 19, 1995; and "General Lebed threatens third world war if Czechs and Poles join NATO," Czechoslovak Press Agency, as translated in *BBC Summary of World Broadcasts*, April 14, 1995.

39. See Talbott's untitled Memo to Christopher from March 24, 1995.

40. Ibid.

41. See "Summary of Conclusions of Deputies Committee Meeting on NATO Enlargement and NATO-Russian Relations," April 25, 1995.

42. See "Memorandum of Conversation of the President's Working Lunch with Prime Minister Major," April 4, 1995.

43. Obtained from Strobe Talbott's personal papers.

44. Ibid.

45. See "Secretary Christopher's Meeting with Andrei Kozyrev, April 26," State 106418, May 12, 1995.

46. Ibid.

47. See the transcript of the telephone conversation between President Clinton and Russian President Boris Yeltsin from April 27, 1995.

48. See Talbott's note entitled "May 10: The Moment of Truth."

49. See the transcript of the conversation between President Clinton and Russian President Boris Yeltsin, Moscow, May 10, 1995.

50. See "Remarks By President Clinton and President Yeltsin In a Joint Press Conference," Press Conference Hall, The Kremlin, Moscow, Russia, May 10, 1995, <http://www.pub.whitehouse.gov/uri- . . . oma.eop.gov.us/1995/5/10/10.text.1>.

51. See President Clinton's letter to Yeltsin from May 23, 1995.

52. See, for example, the press conference with Oleg Lobov, Russian Federation

Security Council Secretary, on the results on the Security Council meeting of May 24 entitled "NATO expansion and other Topics," *Staraya Ploshchad Press Center,* 13:30, May 24, 1995. For comments in U.S., see U.S. Department of State Daily Press Briefing, Wednesday, March 24, 1995.

53. See Pavel Felgengauer, "Russia's Defense Ministry Has Got The Upper Hand Over The Foreign Ministry," *Segodnya,* May 31, 1995.

54. Yeltsin's letter confirming the understanding is contained in "Letter from President Yeltsin," Moscow 016992, May 26, 1995.

55. See the English language text of Russian Foreign Minister Andrei Kozyrev at the 16+1 Meeting with the North Atlantic Council at Noordwijk, The Netherlands, May 31, 1995, distributed by the Russian delegation.

56. See "A Russian grunt," *The Economist,* June 3, 1995.

57. See Christopher's Night Note to President Clinton entitled "Note from the Netherlands," May 3, 1995.

58. The conference was held June 24–25, 1995, and was co-sponsored by the Institute for East-West Studies and the Russian Center for National Security Problems and International Relations. See "Russian Policymakers Send Sharp Message on NATO During Moscow Academic Conference," Moscow 020252, June 28, 1995.

59. The so-called "Karaganov Theses" were first published in *Nezavisimaya Gazeta* on June 21, 1995. They were signed by more than forty Russian academics and policymakers. For the full text in English see "Russia and NATO: Theses of the Council on Foreign and Defense Policy," *Comparative Strategy,* No. 15, 1996, pp. 91–102.

60. See "Karaganov Elaborates on His Russia-NATO Theses: But No Give on Expansion," Moscow 020261, June 298, 1995.

61. For Senator McConnell's (R-KY) questioning of Talbott see his February 9 hearing, "Hearing of the Foreign Operations Subcommittee of the Senate Appropriations Committee," Chaired by Sen. Mitch McConnell, *Federal News Service,* February 9, 1995. See also "Prepared Opening Statement of Sen. Mitch McConnell Before the Senate Appropriations Committee Subcommittee on Foreign Operations," *Federal News Service,* February 16, 1995.

62. As quoted in William Safire, "Baltics Belong in a Big NATO," *The New York Times,* January 16, 1995.

63. For remarks by Rep. Gilman, see "National Security Revitalization Act," House of Representatives, January 4, 1995 <http://thomas.loc.gov/cgi-bin/query/D?r104:44:./temp/~r104mm7sEZ::>. For a summary of the NSRA see "H.R. 7—The National Security Revitalization Act: Congress's Defense Contract with America," January 19, 1995.

64. See McConnell's hearing, February 9, 1995, cited above, note 61. On March 23, 1995, Brown tabled the NATO Participation Act Amendments of 1995, S. 602. This legislation would have expanded eligibility to participate in the NATO Participation Act of 1994 to any country emerging from communist domination that participates in the Partnership for Peace program. See Senator Lugar's speech delivered at the CSIS Conference on "NATO's Role in European Security," March 3, 1995. Lugar chaired the first Senate Foreign Relations Subcommittee (SFRC) hearing on the future of

NATO on April 27, 1995. He chaired the second hearing on May 3, 1995, which explored the paths and impediments to NATO enlargement, and the interests of Allies, Russia, and aspirant countries.

65. See the Memcom "Working Lunch with Prime Minister Jean-Luc Dehaene of Belgium." February 11, 1995.

66. See "Winning the Peace: American Leadership and Commitment," Remarks by Senate Majority Leader Bob Dole at the Nixon Center for Peace and Freedom Policy conference, March 1, 1995.

67. See the press release from Senator Helms' office on March 20, 1995 entitled "Helms Calls Decision to Attend Moscow Summit a Mistake."

68. Henry Kissinger, "For U.S. Leadership, a Moment Missed," *The Washington Post*, May 12, 1995.

69. See "Ambassador Nitze on NATO: The Case Against Expansion," *SAIS Calendar*, The Paul H. Nitze School of Advanced International Studies, Johns Hopkins University, February 1995. See also Fred C. Ikle, "How to Ruin NATO," *The New York Times*, January 11, 1995.

70. See Harold Brown, Transatlantic Security," *The Washington Quarterly* 18, no. 4 (Autumn 1995): 77–86. See also Lee H. Hamilton, "Don't Rush NATO Enlargement," *The Christian Science Monitor*, August 30, 1996.

71. The original letter addressed to Secretary of State Warren Christopher is dated May 2, 1995. This group sent Secretary Christopher additional letters throughout the spring and summer of 1995 as their number grew from 15 to 18. As former U.S. Ambassador to Poland, Richard Davies, wrote on July 5, 1995, "the eighteen signatories represent over 550 years of services in the international-relations and national-security agencies of the government and over 150 years of experience in significant executive and policy-making positions in these agencies." Author's private copy.

72. See Michael Mandelbaum, "Preserving the New Peace: The Case Against NATO Expansion," *Foreign Affairs* 74, no. 3 (May/June 1995): 9–13; Michael Brown, "The flawed Logic of NATO Expansion," *Survival* 37, no. 1 (Spring 1995): 34–52.

73. See Charles A Kupchan, "It's A long Way to Bratislava," *The Washington Post*, May 14, 1995.

74. See "NATO, Then and Now," *The New York Times*, May 9, 1995.

75. See Thomas L. Friedman, "Eye On the Prize," *The New York Times*, May 10, 1995.

76. See "Testimony May 03, 1995 Joseph R. Biden, Jr. Senator Senate Foreign Relations European Affairs: Enlarging the Size of NATO," Federal Document Clearing House Congressional Testimony.

77. See "The Future of NATO in an Uncertain World," Speech to the SACLANT Seminar 95, June 22, 1995, Norfolk, Virginia. Author's private copy.

78. See "Memorandum of Telephone Conversation Between the President and German Chancellor Kohl," May 26, 1995.

79. One example of this nervousness was the "Poland-NATO: Report," by Andrzej Ananicz, Przemyslaw Grudzinski, Andrzej Olechowski, Janusz Onyszkiewicz, Krzysztof Skubiszewski, Henryk Szlajfer (Warsaw: Institute of Public Affairs, 1995).

80. Interview with Ambassador Jerzy Kozminski, December 19, 2000.

81. Bartoszsewski had been quoted in *The Financial Times* on July 18, 1996 saying that "all progress on relations with Russia has been made under Republican Presidents—from Nixon, Reagan and Bush—not the Democrats." See "Demarche: Polish FonMin Bartoszewski on NATO," State 172376, July 19, 1995. Bartoszewski claimed to have been misquoted. See "Bartoszewski and the Clinton Administration: What the Foreign Minister Meant to Say," Warsaw 009923, July 19, 1995.

82. See "Clinton-Kohl Telcon of September 23, 1995," State 233388, September 30, 1995.

83. See "Memorandum of Conversation Between the President and President Havel of the Czech Republic on October 21, 1995."

84. See statements by Senators Hutchinson and Nunn, "NATO Expansion," October 10, 1995, <http://thomas.loc.gov/cgi-bin/query/D?r104:8:./temp/~r104X3Ligm:eo:>.

85. Richard Holbrooke, *To End A War* (New York: The Modern Library, 1998), p. 365.

86. See Ian Davidson, "Unwrap the Package: The political effects of the Bosnian Peace Plan should force a rethink of the agenda for the intergovernmental conference," *The Financial Times*, November 29, 1995.

87. For detailed accounts of U.S. policy on Bosnia, see Ivo Daalder, *Getting to Dayton: The Making of America's Bosnia Policy* (Washington, DC: The Brookings Institution Press, 2000); Richard Holbrooke, *To End A War*; Anthony Lake, *6 Nightmares: Real Threats in a Dangerous World and How America Can Meet Them* (New York: Little, Brown 2000); Bob Woodward, *The Choice* (New York, New York: Simon & Schuster, 1996); David Halberstam, *War in a Time of Peace: Bush, Clinton, And the Generals* (New York: Scribner's, 2001).

88. As Lake recalls, the President was "furious at what was happening on the ground, frustrated by the restrictions imposed by the UN and our NATO allies, embarrassed by congressional attacks on his policies in both parties and pushed by his political advisors who reported that Bosnia was hurting his standings (in the polls) on other issues." *6 Nightmares*, pp. 145–146.

89. Holbrooke, *To End a War*, p. 70.

90. See Woodward, *The Choice*, p. 261.

91. As quoted in Daalder, *Getting to Dayton*, p. 114.

92. For Holbrooke's personal account of the accident, see Holbrooke, *To End a War*, pp. 10–14.

93. Ibid., p. 93.

94. See Dawid Warszawski, "Menetekel fuer Osteurope" [The Handwriting is on the Wall for Eastern Europe], *Die Zeit*, July 28, 1995.

95. See Donald Blinken, "How NATO Joined Hungary," *European Security* 8, no. 4 (Winter 1999): 111.

96. Interview with Laszlo Kovacs, February 5, 2001.

97. See Blinken, "How NATO Joined Hungary," pp. 109–129.

98. Ibid., p. 119.

99. On Hungarian public opinion and the impact of the IFOR deployment, including on the region around Taszar see the essay by Ferenc Somogyi, "NATO

Accession and Hungarian Public Opinion" in Rudolf Joo, ed., *Hungary: A Member of NATO* (Budapest: Ministry of Foreign Affairs, 1999), pp. 70–87.

100. See Carla Anne Robbins, "Hungary's NATO Bid Illustrates the Hopes, Risks in Central Europe," *The Wall Street Journal*, January 2, 1996.

101. See Steven Erlanger, "Politics on His Mind, Yeltsin Warns West on Bombing in Bosnia," *The New York Times*, September 8, 1995.

102. As quoted in Talbott's memo to Christopher on his conversations with Kozyrev, September 14, 1995.

103. Ashton B. Carter and William J. Perry, *Preventive Defense: A New Security Strategy for America* (Washington, D.C.: Brookings Institution Press, 1999), p. 38.

104. Ibid., p. 41.

105. Ibid.

106. Ibid., pp. 44–45. General Shevtsov wrote his own account of these events in "Russia-NATO Military Cooperation in Bosnia: A Basis for the Future?," *NATO Review*, March 1997, pp. 17–21.

107. See George A. Joulwan, "When Ivan Meets GI Joe," *The Washington Post*, April 28, 1996.

108. See "Remarks by the President at the Harry S. Truman Library Institute Legacy of Leadership Dinner," National Building Museum, October 26, 1995.

109. See the "Memorandum of Conversation of the President's Meeting with Prime Minister John Major of the United Kingdom," November 29, 1995.

110. See Talbott, *The Russia Hand, p. 188.*

BOOK V. TOWARD A NEW NATO

1. See "Intervention By Secretary of State Warren Christopher At The North Atlantic Council, Brussels, Belgium, December 5, 1995," <http://dosfan.lib.uic.edu/ERC/briefing/dossec/1995/9512/951205dossec1.html>.

2. See Christopher's "Night Note from Brussels," December 7, 1995.

3. As French Foreign Minister Hervé de Charette told the North Atlantic Council on December 5th, "France has decided from now on to participate much more fully in all NATO bodies." See "Session ministérielle du Conseil de l'Atlantique nord—Intervention du ministre des Affaires étrangères, M. Hervé de Charette," Bruxelles, 5 Decembre 1995, in *La Politique Étrangère de la France, Textes et Documents*, Novembre–Decembre 1995 (Paris, France: Ministere des Affaires Étrangères), pp. 185–186.

4. Ibid.

5. For a good overview of the factors behind this shift in French policy see Robert P. Grant, "France's New Relationship with NATO," *Survival* 38, no. 1 (Spring 1996): 58–60.

6. See "France weighing Greater Participation in NATO," Paris 25201, October 18, 1995.

7. See Address by Jacques Chirac, President of the French Republic, as Delivered before the Congress of the United States (Washington, D.C., Vital Speeches 269, City News Publishing Company Inc.).

8. See "Memorandum of Conversation of the Presidents: February 1 Meeting with President Jacques Chirac of France," State 030140, February 15, 1996.

9. See "Memorandum of Conversation Between the President and NATO Secretary General Javier Solana," February 20, 1996.

10. See "February 28 U.S.-French Consultations on NATO," Paris 5031, March 6, 1996.

11. See "Memorandum of Conversation Between the President and NATO Secretary General Javier Solana," February 20, 1996.

12. As the December Foreign Ministers had defined them: "Interested Partners will learn more about the specific and practical details of Alliance membership; they can review their efforts in terms of the various precepts and principles included in the enlargement study. NATO, in turn, will learn more about what individual partners could or could not contribute to the Alliance and could begin to identify areas for additional work." See Final Communiqué from the Ministerial Meeting of the North Atlantic Council held at NATO Headquarters, Brussels, December 5, 1995, <http://www .nato.int/docu/comm/49–95/c951205a.htm>.

13. The 1996 Congressional Budget Office (CBO) study, "Congressional Budget office Estimates on the Cost to Expand to Visegrad States: Poland, Hungary, Czech Republic, and Slovakia, 1996–2010" estimated that over a ten-year period, the total costs of the first round of enlargement would rise above the $100 billion mark. See also Ronald D. Asmus, F. Stephen Larrabee, and Richard L. Kugler, "What Will NATO Enlargement Cost?," Survival 38, no. 3 (Autumn 1996): 5–26.

14. See the memo from Acting Assistant Secretary for European Affairs John Kornblum to Christopher entitled "Berlin NAC—Adaptation as Message from May 4, 1996. See also Ambassador Hunter's cable entitled "The Berlin NAC Ministerial," USNATO 002222, May 31, 1996.

15. See "Remarks by Secretary of State Warren Christopher to the North Atlantic Council," Intercontinental Hotel, Berlin, Germany, June 3, 1996, <http://dosfan .lib.uic.edu/ERC/briefing/dossec/1996/9606/960603dossec2.html>. See also Final Communiqué of the Ministerial Meeting of the North Atlantic Council, Berlin, Germany, June 3, 1996, <http://www.nato.int/docu/pr/1996/p96–063e.htm>.

16. According to de Charette: "France is satisfied because for the first time in alliance history Europe will really be able to express its personality. . . . If this process is completed, France regards with interest this new alliance and declares itself ready to participate fully according to a new status." See "Conseil ministériel de l'OTAN— Intervention du ministre des Affaires étrangères, M. Hervé de Charette, Berlin, 3 Juin 1996, and "Conseil ministériel de l'OTAN—Point de presse du ministre des Affaires etrangères, M. Herve de Charette," in La Politique Etrangere de la France: Textes et Documents, Mai–Juin 1996 (Paris, France: Ministere des Affaires Étrangères).

17. See "Memorandum of Conversation Between President Clinton and Yeltsin on 1/26/96," State 19590, February 12, 1996.

18. See the Letter from Russian President Boris Yeltsin to President Clinton delivered on January 26, 1996.

19. See President Clinton's letter to Russian President Boris Yeltsin from February 8, 1996.

20. See Talbott's assessment of Primakov, and how different he was from Kozyrev, in his untitled Memo to Christopher from March 16, 1996.

21. Ibid.

22. See "Secretary's Conversation with FM Primakov," State 003144, January 11, 1996.

23. Obtained from Strobe Talbott's personal papers.

24. See the strategy paper entitled "Managing U.S.-Russian relations in a Year of Challenge," January 23, 1996.

25. See "The Secretary's Helsinki Meetings with Russian Foreign Minister Primakov, February 9–10," State 29302, February 14, 1996.

26. See Christopher's Memorandum to the President entitled "Note on Helsinki Meetings with Primakov," dated February 12, 1996.

27. See "Chancellor Kohl Suggests More Deliberate Approach to NATO Enlargement," Bonn 01572, February 5, 1996.

28. See the memo to Christopher from Acting Assistant Secretary for European Affairs Richard Hecklinger entitled "Your Telephone Conversation with German Chancellor Kohl," February 9, 1995.

29. See "British Suspect Germany is Slowing Down on NATO Enlargement," USNATO 000849, February 9, 1996.

30. See "February 14 Dinner with Foreign Secretary," London 001951, February 16, 1996.

31. See "Chancellor Kohl's Russia Policy Turns Cautious," Bonn 001892, February 9, 1996.

32. See "Secretary's Conversation with Chancellor Kohl," State 028088, February 13, 1996.

33. See "German Chancellor's Visit to Moscow; Chancellor Kohl and President Yeltsin address news conference after talks," *The British Broadcasting Corporation*, February 21, 1996.

34. As quoted in "Public Statements by Kohl and Yeltsin on NATO Enlargement during Kohl Visit to Moscow," Bonn 02426, February 20, 1996.

35. See "Telcon with Chancellor Helmut Kohl of Germany," February 28, 1996.

36. See "Chirac: Protector of Russia," Paris 00761, January 12, 1996.

37. On May 1, President Chirac told Ambassador Pamela Harriman that NATO enlargement should not move forward without an agreement on adaptation and a NATO-Russia agreement in place. See "Responding to President Chirac's Call for an Agreement with Russia Prior to NATO Enlargement," State 092972, May 4, 1996.

38. Talbott met with Primakov on March 12, 1996. See his memo on the talks dated March 16, 1996.

39. See the memo from Rudolf Perina, Acting Assistant Secretary of State for European Affairs, and John E. Herbst, Acting S/NIS entitled "Primakov's Recent Statements on NATO Enlargement," March 15, 1996.

40. See the Memorandum from Acting S/NIS John Herbst to Secretary Christopher entitled "Scope Paper—Your Trip to Moscow," March 18, 1996.

41. Christopher, *In the Stream of History*, p. 399.

42. See Address by Secretary of State Warren Christopher, "A Democratic and Undivided Europe in Our Time, Cernin Palace Prague, Czech Republic March 20, 1996, <http://dosfan.lib.uic.edu/ERC/briefing/dossec/1996/9603/960320dossec2.html>.

43. See "Secretary's Lunch with Central European Foreign Ministers, March 20, 1996, Prague," State 059734, March 27, 1996.

44. See Christopher, *In the Stream of History*, p. 399.

45. See "Secretary Christopher's Meeting with Russian FM Primakov, March 21, 1996," April 3, 1996.

46. See Christopher, *In the Stream of History*, p. 401.

47. See "Secretary Christopher's Meeting with Russian President Yeltsin, March 22, 1996," State 068798, April 3, 1996.

48. See the memo to the President from Warren Christopher and Strobe Talbott entitled "Your Meeting with Yeltsin," April 18, 1996.

49. See the "Memcon of Conversation Between President Clinton and Russian President Boris Yeltsin, April 21, 1996.

50. See "Remarks at the White House Conference on Trade and Investment in Central and Eastern Europe in Cleveland, Ohio," *Public Papers of the Presidents*, January 12, 1995.

51. See "Ambassador Holbrooke's Meeting with Foreign Minister Zieleniec," Prague 006126, August 18, 1994.

52. See "Czech Foreign Minister Zieleniec Addresses NATO Membership with PermReps," USNATO 001259, March 29, 1995.

53. For example, George Schoepflin, one of the West's leading scholars on the region, had called the Hungarian minority issue "the second most sensitive security issue in Central and Eastern Europe after the war of Yugoslav succession." See George Schoepflin, "Hungary and Its Neighbors," *Chaillot Papers*, No. 7 (Paris: Institute for Security Studies of the West European Union, May 1993), p. 1.

54. See "PM Horn Welcomes NATO Expansion Plan and Asks that Russia's Concerns be Considered," Budapest 002061, March 3, 1995.

55. See "Holbrooke and Kovacs: A Meeting of the Minds," Budapest 002063, March 3, 1995.

56. See "Dialogue with Prime Minister Horn at Spanish Embassy," Budapest 002116, March 6, 1995.

57. See "EUR A/S Holbrooke's Meeting with Romanian Foreign Minister Melescanu," Bucharest 002061, February 27, 1995.

58. See "EUR Assistant Secretary Holbrooke's Meeting with President Iliescu," Bucharest 002218, March 2, 1995.

59. See "Memcom of Conversation: The President's June 6 Meeting with Gyula Horn," State 143442, June 13, 1995. See also *The Washington Post*, "Hungary in NATO in 1997?," June 7, 1995 and "President [Iliescu] outlines Romanian reforms in Washington speech," *BBC Summary of Word Broadcasts*, September 30, 1995.

60. See "Memcom: President Clinton's Meeting with President Iliescu," State 234298, October 3, 1995.

61. On the Drawsko affair, see Jeffrey Simon, "Central European Civil-Military

Relations and NATO Expansion," National Defense University, *Strategic Forum*, Institute for National Strategic Studies, March 1995, No. 22.

62. See Olechowski's interview with Adam Michnik and Edward Krzemien in the leading Polish daily, *Gazeta Wyborcza*, "Russian Fists & Polish Scissors," January 19, 1995.

63. See "A/S Holbrooke Sketches Out NATO Expansion Process for Walesa; Warns on Democracy," Warsaw 02289, February 17, 1995.

64. See "A/S Holbrooke Briefs PM Pawlak on NATO Expansion; Urges Greater Political Stability," Warsaw 001304, January 30, 1995. See "US For Poland's Joining NATO," *Polish News Bulletin*, January 27, 1995. See also "Holbrooke Tells Pawlak About U.S. Support for Joining NATO," *PAP News Wire*, January 26, 1995.

65. See "the Secretary's Meeting with Polish PM Pawlak," State 031006, February 7, 1995.

66. See, for example, the editorial entitled "Remembering Auschwitz," *The New York Times*, January 26, 1995. See also Gustav Niebuhr, "Whose Memory Lives When the Last Survivor Dies?," *The New York Times*, January 29, 1995.

67. The letter was signed by Senators Bob Dole (R-KS), Jesse Helms (R-NC), Claiborne Bell (D-RI) and Thomas Daschle (D-SD), as well as by Representatives Newt Gingrich (R-GA), Richard Gephardt (D-MO), Ben Gilman (R-NY) and Lee Hamilton (D-IN). It stated that the response of Central and East European countries on this matter "will be seen as a test of their respect for basic human rights and the rule of law, and could have practical consequences on their relations with our country." As quoted in Jay Bushinsky, "E. Europe Bristles at D.C. Demand," *Chicago Sun-Times*, April 24, 1995.

68. Jankowski had gained international fame during the heyday of Solidarity but had become increasingly nationalistic and anti-Semitic by the mid-1990s. In his sermon he had stated that the "Star of David is implicated in the swastika as well as the hammer and sickle" and that Poles could no longer "tolerate" governments made up of "people who have not declared whether they come from Moscow or Israel"—a slight that many assumed was directed at Walesa's opponent in the upcoming Presidential election, the socialist candidate Alexander Kwasniewski. See "Walesa urged to condemn priest's remarks on Jews," *The Jerusalem Post*, June 15, 1995. See also "Walesa Disappoints Clinton," *Sacramento Bee*, July 20, 1995.

69. For Walesa's statement see "President: Star of David is Great Sign of Jewish Faith," PAO, June 20, 1995. See also Jane Perlez, "10 Days Later, Walesa Rebukes Anti-Semitism, but Not Priest," *The New York Times*, June 22, 1995.

70. See the AJC's Press release "American Jewish Committee Meeting with Polish President 'Inconclusive;' Walesa Broadly Condemns anti-Semitic Message but not the Messenger," June 27, 1995. On the President's meeting with Walesa see "Memcom of President Clinton's Meeting with President Walesa in San Francisco, June 26," State 159630, July 3, 1995.

71. At the top of that list were the issues of communal and private property that had been first taken by the Nazis and then nationalized by the communists. Negotiating an agreement on communal property would take nearly three years and a final agreement

would be reached only in February 1998, shortly before the U.S. Senate was scheduled to vote on NATO enlargement ratification.

72. See "Telcon with Polish President Lech Walesa," November 21, 1995.

73. See "Walesa, Kwasniewksi hold TV Debate," *PAP News Wire*, November 13, 1995.

74. See "Telcon with President-elect Aleksander Kwasniewski of Poland," November 21, 1995. See "Change in Style Not Substance in Poland's Campaign for NATO Membership," Warsaw 016130, December 8, 1995.

75. See Kwasniewski's statement before the North Atlantic Council from January 17, 1996. Author's private copy.

76. See, for example, "Rosati Pledges No Changes in Polish Foreign Policy: Seeks Early Kwasniewski Trip to U.S.," Warsaw 00412, January 11, 1996.

77. See "Foreign Minister Rosati's U.S. Visit: Heavy on Security Questions," Warsaw 004254, April 16, 1995; and "Polish ForMin Rosati and Acting Secretary Talbott Discuss NATO Enlargement and Regional Relations," State 0979984, May 11, 1996.

78. Interview with Nick Rey, April 23, 2000.

79. See "Memorandum of Conversation with President Kwasniewski of Poland," from July 8, 1995. See also *PAP*, July 9, 1995.

80. See "Slovak PM Meciar: "I Know a Club Member Must Respect Its Rules," Bratislava 000425, February 28, 1995; and "A/S Holbrooke's Dinner with Slovak PM Meciar: NATO Expansion, Russian Concerns," Bratislava 000426, February 28, 1995.

81. See "5/24 Meeting of DoD Deputy Assistant Secretary Kruzel and NSC Senior Director Fried with Slovak President Kovac," Bratislava 001179, May 25, 1995.

82. See "Memorandum of Conversation between the President and President Michal Kovac of Slovakia," October 21, 1995. That message was reinforced on Capitol Hill when Senator Jesse Helms introduced an amendment noting that consideration of Slovakia for NATO should be judged based on the country's political performance. On July 31, 1995, Senator Helms submitted Amendment No. 1927 to the Foreign Relations Revitalization Act of 1995, S.908, which he introduced to the Senate on June 9, 1995. Helms' amendment stated that "future consideration of Slovakia for accelerated NATO transition assistance should be evaluated in terms of its government's progress towards freedom of press, representative government and privation." The bill S.908 went to the Senate floor on December 14, 1995, <http://rs9.loc.gov/cgi-bin/query/D?r104:1:./temp/~r1040Mizss::>.

83. If the EU or NATO decided to expand in 1996, he told them, "we still have enough time to deal with our internal problems." See Marian Lesko, "Story of Self Disqualification," in Martin Butora and Frantisek Sebej, eds., 1998, *Slovensko v sedej zone*), p. 42.

84. U.S. Department of State, "The Slovak Republic Country Report on Human Rights Practices for 1996," released by the Bureau of Democracy, Human Rights, and Labor, January 30, 1997, <http://www.state.gov/www/global/human_rights/ 1996_hrp_ reports/slovakre.html>.

85. See "Slovakia: Kramer Tells Kuchar No Benefit of the Doubt for Slovakia on NATO Enlargement," Bratislava 001046, June 17, 1996; as well as "Slovak President to

A/S Kramer: Don't Punish the Country for the Government's Flaws," Bratislava 001048, June 17, 1996.

86. Meciar himself subsequently stated that he had told Albright he knew of such a deal on July 6, 1996. See Martin Butora and Frantisek Sebej, eds., 1998, *Slovensko v sedej zone?*, p. 51.

87. Zbigniew Brzezinski, "The Premature Partnership." *Foreign Affairs*, 72, no. 2 (March–April 1994): 80.

88. On Ukrainian views see F. Stephen Larrabee, "Ukraine's Balancing Act," *Survival*, 38, no. 2 (Summer 1997): 143–165; and Sherman W. Garnett, *Keystone in the Arch* (Washington: Brookings Institution Press, 1997).

89. Foreign Minster Udovenko's comments were made to Deputy Secretary Talbott in a meeting in the State Department on October 21, 1996.

90. As First Deputy Foreign Minister Boris Tarasyuk told a senior U.S. diplomat in late February 1995, Ukraine's public position was not to block membership. In private, however, they were much more open to NATO membership. According to Tarasyuk: "No matter what we say publicly, I can tell you that we absolutely want to join NATO." See "DFM Tarasyuk Discusses PfP, GOU Internal Problems, Kiev 01752, March 6, 1995. But as Tarasyuk said in an interview, it did not make sense for Ukraine to ask for NATO membership at a time when NATO's answer would clearly be negative: "Seeking membership now would only devalue our position in Europe: the door is not opening so why should we lose respect and ask for membership? If we can be sure that the door will open, then we can think about membership. But that process will take time and we should [meanwhile] find a proper form of cooperation between Ukraine and NATO." See the interview with Boris Tarasyuk, "A New Concept of European Security," *Transition* 1, no. 13 (July 28, 1995): 19.

91. As one Western scholar noted: "Deep down, many Europeans are unsure whether Ukraine is a 'real country' or not. They are reluctant to invest major resources in trying to stabilize Ukraine, especially given their own mounting economic problems. Others are concerned that too visible a Western interest in Ukraine could antagonize Russia and complicate relations with Moscow at a time when Russia's relations with the West are already strained over NATO enlargement." See Larrabee, "Ukraine's Balancing Act," p. 144.

92. See "Ukrainian Views on NATO Expansion: Ukraine and PfP," USNATO 000633, February 15, 1995.

93. See the interview with Boris Tarasyuk, "A New Concept of European Security," *Transition* 1, no. 13 (July 28, 1995): 18.

94. See "NATO: Meeting of SYG Claes with Ukrainian President Kuchma, June 1, 1995" US NATO 002513, June 16, 1995.

95. They included regular bilateral consultations in a 16+1 framework, creating a NATO presence in Kiev, as well as joint cooperation in nonproliferation, arms control, and other defense-related areas. See the draft agreement presented by Foreign Minster Udovenko at NATO headquarters on September 14, 1995. Author's private copy. 16+1 refers to the then-16 NATO member states plus Ukraine.

96. Udovenko's letter is dated August 26, 1996.

97. See "Deputy Secretary's 9/16 and 9/29 Meetings with Ukrainian NSDC Secretary Horbulyn," State 205479, October 2, 1996.

98. Ukrainian Ambassador Offers Draft Agreement on "Special Partnership" between NATO and Ukraine," USNATO 003872, November 6, 1996.

99. Carl Bildt, "The Baltic Litmus Test," *Foreign Affairs* 73, no. 5 (September/October 1994): 72–85.

100. Estonian President Lennart Meri would often tell visitors the story how, while visiting Washington prior to Estonia regaining its independence, he went to look at his nation's flag flying in the lobby of the Department of State. It was the only Foreign Ministry in the West where it was on display.

101. See "Remarks by Mr. Lennart Meri, President of the Republic of Estonia at the Center for Strategic and International Studies, June 17, 1996, Washington, D.C." Author's private copy.

102. At a conference held on the Swedish island of Visby in June 1995, German Defense Minister Volker Ruehe stated that the Baltic states would not be included in an enlarged NATO and should instead seek close security cooperation with the Nordic states. See the article by Siegfried Thielbeer, "Klare Worten an die Baltischen Republiken" [Clear Words Addressed to the Baltic Republics], *Frankfurter Allgemeine Zeitung*, June 30, 1995. In his IISS Alastair Buchan Lecture of March 28, 1996, the British Foreign Secretary suggested a similar approach to Baltic security.

103. Whereas the collapse of the Soviet empire in Central and Eastern Europe had created a *de facto* "double buffer" between Western Europe and Russia, it had paradoxically made Northern Europe more important to Moscow in strategic terms. See Krister Wahlbaeck. "Der unwaegbare Osten: eine schwedische Sicht neuer Sichereitsprobleme," *Europa Archiv*, no. 3, 1993, p. 10.

104. See "Secretary's Meeting with Martii Ahtisaari, President of Finland, February 8, 1996," SECTO 03030, February 10, 1996.

105. See "Undersecretary Tarnoff's Meeting with Swedish MFA Rep Eliasson on European Security, CTBT," State 030285, February 15, 1996.

106. In his Tallinn speech, Gore stated that "President Clinton is leading the way toward the integration of Europe's new democracies into a growing transatlantic community of secure, prosperous and peaceful nations. This will be a community without spheres of influence or arbitrary lines, a community rooted in the values for which you struggled so hard and so successfully." See "Remarks by Vice President of the United States Al Gore," Town Hall Square, Tallinn, Estonia, The Embassy of the United Sates of America, Kentmanni 20, 15099 Tallinn, Estonia, March 13, 1995, <http://www.usislib.ee/algore.html>.

107. See the memo from ROM Director Christopher W. Dell, to Assistant Secretary of State Holbrooke entitled "Baltic Policy" and dated April 14, 1995.

108. See Ronald D. Asmus and Robert C. Nurick, "NATO Enlargement and the Baltic States," *Survival* 38, no. 2 (Summer 1996): 121–42.

109. See the article by Lt. Gen Dementyev and Anton Surikov in *Nezavisimaya Gazeta*, April 11, 1996.

110. See Max Jacobsen, "Envisioning a Possible Deal with Russia on NATO Expansion." *International Herald Tribune*, February 23, 1996.

111. See Anatol Lieven, "Baltic Iceberg Ahead: NATO Beware," *The World Today*, pp. 175–79.

112. See Joint Declaration of the Baltic Presidents on Partnership for Integration, Vilnius, May 28, 1996.

113. See "Latvian President Discusses NATO Enlargement, Urges President Clinton to Meet Baltic Leaders in June," Riga 001672, June 3, 1996.

114. As quoted from the diary of Ambassador Ojars Kalnins.

115. See Fred Hiatt, " . . . And the Three Presidents," *The Washington Post*, June 30, 1996.

116. See "Acting Secretary Briefs Baltics on Action Plan," State 186058, September 7, 1996.

117. This excerpt from Ambassador Kalnin's diary is quoted with his permission.

118. See "Copenhagen Seminar: Secretary Perry, UK and German Defense Ministers say "Not Yet" to Baltic NATO Membership: Russians Don't Show," Copenhagen 005129, October 11, 1996.

119. See "Memorandum of Conversation with Former President of Poland, Lech Walesa," June 7, 1996.

120. See the NSC paper entitled "NATO Enlargement Game Plan: June 96 to June 97," dated June 5, 1996 and circulated interagency on June 7, 1996.

121. See "Summary of Conclusions, Restricted Meeting on NATO Policy, July 29, 1996," July 31, 1996.

122. For transcript of news conference, see "Webwire-Holds News Conference With Speaker Gingrich, Former Polish President Lech Walesa and Others on NATO Expansion," June 4, 1996 (Federal Document Clearing House, Inc., FDCH Political Transcripts, 1996).

123. Ibid.

124. See Bob Dole, Republican candidate for President of the United States, "Leadership for a New Century," Philadelphia World Affairs Council, June 25, 1996.

125. See "Memorandum of Conversation Between President Clinton and President Yeltsin on 7/5/1996."

126. See "The President's Meeting with Deputy Foreign Minister Georgiy Mamedov of Russia," July 9, 1996.

127. The same language is contained in the letters to President Chirac, Prime Minister Major and Chancellor Kohl, dated August 7, 1996.

128. According to Christopher: "President Clinton had considered making the statement himself, but in the thick of his reelection campaign we were concerned that critics at home and abroad would view his announcement of NATO expansion as a political ploy. We hoped that my delivering the speech would help remove our policy from the context of Presidential politics." Christopher, *In the Stream of History*, p. 452.

129. See the speech by Secretary of State Warren Christopher in Stuttgart, "A New Atlantic Community For the 21st Century," September 6, 1996, <http://www.usislib.ee/wchrist.html>.

130. President Chirac gathered his advisors after the Berlin Ministerial and congratulated them on the "victory for France, Europe and trans-Atlantic solidarity"—a

formulation that French officials subsequently used with the press as well. See "Berlin NAC: French Views on Next Steps." Paris 12927, June 12, 1996.

131. See the "Memorandum of President's Meeting with President Jacques Chirac of France," June 27, 1996.

132. French officials involved in these negotiations insist that the Berlin package itself was never sufficient for Chirac. Their American counterparts, on the other hand, underscore that they were surprised by the more ambitious proposals France now demanded, including positions that were unacceptable to Washington and most European NATO allies.

133. See "Consultations With the French MFA on European Security, August 22," Paris 19272, August 27, 1995.

134. See President Chirac's letter to President Clinton dated August 28, 1996.

135. See "Secretary Christopher's Working Lunch with Foreign Minister de Charette, September 5, 1996, State 187939, September 10, 1996.

136. See "President Chirac and NATO SYG Solana Discuss NATO Adaptation, Post-IFOR, NATO Summit," Paris 20377, September 26, 1996.

137. See "Informal Defense Ministers Meeting in Bergen, Norway, SecDef Bilateral with French MOD Millon," USNATO 003452, September 27, 1996.

138. See "Informal Defense Ministers Meeting in Bergen, Norway, SecDef Bilat with SYG Solana, 24 Sep 96," USNATO 003439, September 27, 1996.

139. See President Clinton's letter to President Chirac from September 26, 1996. When the U.S. Deputy Chief of Mission in Paris, Don Bandler, handed Clinton's letter to Chirac's diplomatic advisor, Jean-David Levitte, he was asked whether there was any daylight in the U.S. position. Bandler said that the U.S. was willing to consider making other key positions in the Southern Command European, but not the AFSouth commander. Levitte responded: "Then we have a real problem." See "Initial French Reaction to President's September 26 Letter to Chirac on NATO," Paris 021877, September 30, 1996.

140. See President Chirac's letter to President Clinton of October 10, 1996. A copy of Chirac's letter was subsequently leaked the press. See Reuters, December 2, 1996.

141. See the Memorandum of Conversation entitled "Lake Meeting with President Jacques Chirac of France," November 1, 1996.

142. See "The Secretary's Breakfast Meeting with NATO Secretary General Solana," State 248137, December 4, 1996.

143. See Talbott's Note to Christopher from July 9, 1996.

144. The first version of this paper was sent to Christopher on July 9, 1996. Modified versions were sent on July 12 and on July 18, the latter entitled "NATO/Russia: A Framework for the Next Phase."

145. See the Memorandum of Conversation between Deputy of State Strobe Talbott and Russian Foreign Minister Primakov, Moscow, July 15, 1996.

146. See the paper dated July 29, 1995 and entitled "NATO-Russia: Objectives, Obstacles and Work Plan."

147. See Talbott's summaries of his conversations with Mamedov contained in his untitled memos to Secretary of State Christopher from August 28, 1996 and September

13, 1996, respectively. The framework paper was entitled "Common Elements for the Conduct of a NATO-Russia Dialogue and an Eventual NATO-Russia Charter," and dated September 12, 1996.

148. See Talbott's note to Christopher on his meeting with Mamedov dated August 28, 1996.

149. In the spring Chirac had told U.S. Ambassador Pamela Harriman that NATO should not enlarge until it has a NATO-Russia agreement in hand. Over the summer French officials repeated that view and claimed that it was shared in Bonn. As Ambassador Harriman wrote: "It is precisely the French temptation to play friend in court to Russia that is a potential source of difficulty. We have sought to convince the French that if NATO allies appear divided on enlargement, Russia will exploit these differences to increase its demands. However, Russia, is a deeply personal subject for Chirac. He may well calculate that with Russia, as well as with Iraq, a measure of independence from the United States will win France a special place—without undermining the GOF's special strategic relationship with Washington." See "Scenesetter for Deputy Secretary Talbott's September 11–13 Visit to Paris," Paris 20153, September 10, 1996.

150. As President Clinton had written in his letter to Chirac, Kohl, and Major in early August, Moscow was "looking for signs of divisions or uncertainty on our part in order to slow down or even stop enlargement if they can. . . . The best way to ensure that the Russians work constructively with the Alliance," President Clinton concluded, "is to proceed with enlargement in the steady, unpredictable and transparent way we have done to date. Allowing the Russians to delay the next step would only encourage those in Moscow who still favor a hard line approach."

151. See the Memorandum of the conversation between Secretary of State Warren Christopher and Russian Foreign Minister Primakov, Waldorf Towers, September 23, 1996.

152. Ibid.

153. The idea that Moscow might prefer to slow down NATO-Russia talks until after enlargement to avoid the appearance that it was acquiescing to the Alliance was floated by Presidential foreign policy advisor Dmitriy Ryurikov. See his comments to departing U.S. Ambassador Thomas Pickering as reported in "Ambassador's Farewell Call on Presidential Foreign Policy Advisor Ryurikov," Moscow 030332, October 29, 1996.

154. See "Clinton Remarks to People of Detroit," October 22, 1996, <http://www.usemb.ee/clitond.html>.

155. As quoted in John F. Harris, "Clinton Vows Wider NATO in Three Years; Foreign Policy Stands Defended as challenger Alleges Foot-Dragging," *The Washington Post*, October 23, 1996.

156. The Principals Committee meeting was held on November 15, 1997. See "Summary of Conclusions on NATO Policy," circulated interagency on November 21, 1996.

157. See Talbott's memo to Christopher on his talks with Primakov dated December 4, 1996.

BOOK VI. THE NATO-RUSSIA ENDGAME

1. See Clinton's State of the Union Address, February 4, 1997.

2. Dean Acheson, *Present at the Creation: My Years in the State Department* (New York: Norton, 1969).

3. See "Statement By Secretary of State-Designate Madeleine Korbel Albright Before The Senate Foreign Relations Committee, Wednesday, January 8, 1997.

4. The study was commissioned by the Pew Trust and released in the fall of 1991. See Donald S. Kellerman, Andrew Kohut, and Carol Bowman, *The Pulse of Europe: A Survey of Political and Social Values and Attitudes* (Washington, DC: Times Mirror Center for The People & The Press).

5. See Albright's January 8, 1997 testimony before the U.S. Senate Foreign Relations Committee.

6. See Albright's handwritten comments on Grossman's note to her entitled "Thinking About 1999" and dated January 15, 1998.

7. See Secretary of State Madeleine K. Albright, Address to the People of Prague, Obecni Dum, "A Moment of Celebration and of Dedication," Prague, Czech Republic, July 14, 1997, http://secretary.state.gov/www/statements/970714.html.

8. The book was James Chace's *Acheson: The Secretary of State Who Created The American World* (New York: Simon & Schuster, 1998).

9. As Albright put it in her first speech as Secretary of State at NATO Headquarters in Brussels: "Today we are privileged to live in a time of relative stability and peace. But we know from history that we cannot take the extension of these blessings for granted. Peace is not a gift. It must be earned. And if it is to last, it must be constantly reinforced." See "Statement By Secretary Madeleine Albright At The North Atlantic Council Special Ministerial Meeting," NATO Headquarters, Brussels, February 18, 1997.

10. See "Commencement Address by Secretary of State Madeleine K. Albright at Harvard University," Cambridge, Massachusetts, June 5, 1997.

11. Ibid.

12. In his memoirs, former Russian Foreign Minister Yevgeny Primakov writes that he was initially worried about Albright as U.S. Secretary of State but was pleasantly surprised to discover that she, while a vigorous defender and promoter of American interests, was committed to finding common ground with Russia as well. See Yevgeny Primakov, *Gody v Bolshoy Politike* (Moscow: Sovershenno Sekretno, 1996), p. 272.

13. See the Memorandum of Conversation entitled "The Secretary's Meeting with President Yeltsin," February 21, 1997.

14. See Secretary of State Madeleine K. Albright, "Opening Statement at the Carnegie Roundtable Discussions," Carnegie Moscow Center, Moscow, May 2, 1997.

15. These quotes come from my notes from the meeting.

16. See Madeleine K. Albright, "Why Bigger is Better," *The Economist*, February 15, 1997.

17. Kohl's National Security Advisor, Joachim Bitterlich provided a read out of the conversation to Talbott as well as to the U.S. charge in Bonn, J.D. Bindenagel. See

"Kohl's Telephone Call with the President on January 6"; and "Kohl's suggestion on NATO-Russia Relations," Bonn 00102, January 6, 1997.

18. The phone call took place on January 6, 1997. See Memorandum of Conversation Between the President and German Chancellor Helmut Kohl, January 13, 1997.

19. See "Report Card on Primakov: B Plus on Process, C Minus on Substance," Moscow 01151, January 17, 1997.

20. See "February 21 Meeting with Communist Leader Zyuganov, State 032968, February 22, 1997.

21. The article was written by the pro-communist Duma staffer and security expert Anton Surikov in the January 15 edition of *Pravda Pyat*. See "Duma Staffer Surikov Describes Recent Presidential Meeting on Response to NATO Expansion," Moscow 001403, January 22, 1997.

22. See "SYG Solana on AFSouth, Ministerials, Bosnia," USNATO 003863, November 5, 1996.

23. See "Senator Roth's 11/26 Meeting with NATO Secretary General Solana on NATO Expansion," USNATO 000307, January 31, 1997.

24. See the Memorandum of Telephone Conversation between Clinton and Chirac from January 30, 1997.

25. See "Deputy Secretary's 1/13 Meeting with Foreign Secretary Rifkind and Foreign Office Officials," London 000657, January 17, 1997.

26. See Memorandum of the Conversation between Deputy Secretary Strobe Talbott and French President Jacques Chirac, January 14, 1997.

27. See Memorandum of Conversation between Deputy Secretary Strobe Talbott and German Chancellor Helmut Kohl, January 15, 1997.

28. Strobe Talbott, *The Russia Hand: A Memoir of Presidential Diplomacy* (New York: Random House, 2002), p. 224.

29. See Talbott and Fuerth's Memorandum for the President and Vice President dated January 24, 1997.

30. See Yeltsin's letter to Clinton dated January 30, 1997.

31. See "Primakov Publicly Commits to Negotiations with NATO," Moscow 003619, February 14, 1997.

32. See the Memorandum of Conversation between Clinton and Gore with Chernomyrdin, entitled "Meeting with Russian Prime Minister Viktor Chernomyrdin: March Summit, GCC Results, European security, START, Economics," The Oval Office, February 7, 1997.

33. See Talbott, *The Russia Hand*, p. 233.

34. See the Memorandum of Conversation between Deputy Secretary Talbott and Russian Foreign Minister Primakov, March 6, 1997.

35. See the Memorandum of Conversation entitled "The Secretary's Meeting with President Yeltsin," February 21, 1997.

36. See Henry Kissinger, "Helsinki Fiasco," *The Washington Post*, March 30, 1997.

37. See Talbott's Note to Albright dated March 14, 1997 and entitled "The NATO-Russia Charter as time-released medicine."

38. See the Memorandum of Conversation between Deputy of State Strobe Talbott and Russian Foreign Minister Primakov, Moscow, July 15, 1996.

39. See the Memorandum of Conversation between Deputy Secretary Talbott and Russian Foreign Minister Primakov, March 6, 1997.

40. See the scorecard entitled "A NATO-Russia Understanding" dated January 27, 1997. See also the updated written version from February 8 entitled "From Helsinki to Madrid: A Scenario" which lays out internal U.S. thinking on how to bring NATO-Russia talks to closure in the run-up to the Madrid summit.

41. For background on how NATO strategy has evolved see Richard L. Kugler, *Commitment to Purpose: How Alliance Partnership Won the Cold War* (Santa Monica, CA: RAND, 1993).

42. For an example of Moscow's attempt to define "offensive infrastructure" see "Russians Identify 'Infrastructure'," Vienna 001791, March 11, 1997.

43. See *Final Communiqué* issued at the Ministerial Meeting of the North Atlantic Council, Brussels, Belgium, December 10, 1996.

44. See also NATO/CFE: Feb. 17 HLTF Agrees on NATO Position on Adaptation," USNATO 000509, February 19, 1997.

45. This sentence went through a number of iterations. The version Vershbow wrote on March 5 is quoted verbatim from Talbott's memo to Albright from March 7, 1997. See "My Meeting with Primakov—and Yours," March 7, 1997.

46. Ibid. See also the Memorandum of Conversation between Talbott and Russian Foreign Minister Primakov, March 6, 1997.

47. As quoted in William Drozdiak, "Poland Urges NATO Not to Appease Russia: 'The Smell of Yalta is Always with Us,' " *The Washington Post*, March 17, 1997.

48. See "The Secretary's Meeting with Polish Foreing Minister Rosati," State 056869, March 27, 1997.

49. Speaking before the press with Rosati, Albright underscored that Poland would be a full NATO member: "They will be full allies in every sense of the word. Every important decision which will be made by NATO's 16 allies is made in full consultations with our partners. And there will be nothing about you without you." See Secretary of State Madeleine K. Albright and Polish Foreign Minister Dariusz Rosati, Remarks at photo opportunity, Washington D.C., March 13, 1997, <http://secretary.state.gov/www/statements/970313a.html>.

50. See "Statement by the North Atlantic Council, March 14, 1997," <http://www.nato.int/docu/pr/1997/p97-027e.htm>.

51. See Memorandum of Conversation between Secretary of State Albright and Russian Foreign Minister Primakov, March 15, 1997. This description also draws on Talbott's notes of the meeting.

52. See Talbott's typed up notes of the meeting between Berger and him with Mamedov on the morning of March 16, 1997.

53. Obtained from Strobe Talbott's personal papers.

54. See Memorandum of Conversation Between the President and Russian Foreign Minister Yevgeny Primakov on March 17, 1997.

55. See Talbott, *The Russia Hand*, p. 237.

56. See the memcon entitled "Morning Meeting with Russian President Yeltsin: NATO-Russia, START, ABM/TMD," March 21, 1997.

57. See Talbott, *The Russia Hand*, pp. 241–242.

58. See "Press Conference of President Clinton and President Yeltsin," Kalastafa Torppa, Helsinki, Finland, March 21, 1997. Author's private copy.

59. See "Russian Reaction to Helsinki," Moscow 007281, March 25, 1997.

60. Finnish President Ahtisaari briefed U.S. Ambassador Derek Shearer on his conversation with Yeltsin in Finnish-Russian talks the day after the U.S.-Russian summit had concluded. See "The Morning After: Russian/Finnish Post-Summit Bilaterals Focus on the Baltics," Helsinki 001550, March 26, 1997.

61. Naumann was in Moscow March 23–26, 1997. See "NATO-Russia: CMC Chairman Briefs the NAC on his Russia Visit," USNATO 01212, April 14, 1997.

62. See "Russia's Foreign Policy Malaise," Moscow 010483, April 25, 1997.

63. See "SYG Solana's Debrief of His 4/15 Meeting with FM Primakov," USNATO 1231, April 15, 1997.

64. See Strobe Talbott, *Deadly Gambits: The Reagan Administration and the Stalemate in Nuclear Arms Control* (New York: Random House, 1984).

65. See the paper entitled "A Menu of Scenarios for Your May Day in Moscow: The Good, the Bad and the Ugly," April 25, 1997.

66. Talbott called Albright from Moscow to convey this message to her during the flight. It is also contained in a memo drafted summarizing the first day of talks in Moscow and sent to Albright's plane. See Memorandum to the Secretary From Strobe Talbott in Moscow, April 30, 1997.

67. See Talbott's "NATO-Russia Midnight Update" faxed to Albright on her plane en route to Moscow, April 30, 1997.

68. See "Secretary's Meeting with Russian Foreign Minister Yevgeny Primakov, May 1, 1997, Moscow," State 084836, May 6, 1997.

69. See Talbott, *The Russia Hand*, pp. 244–245.

70. See "Secretary's Meeting with Russian Foreign Minister, Yevgeny Primakov, May 1, 1997, Moscow," State 84836, May 6, 1997. The results of the Albright-Primakov conversation on May 2 are described in a confidential summary of their conversation. Albright also describes the meeting in a Night Note to the President sent later that day. See the Secretary's "Night Note" sent to the President on May 2, 1997.

71. "Night Note," Ibid.

72. See "NATO/HLTF: May 6 HLTF Meeting—Allies Support Albright Primakov Paper on CFE," USNATO 085231, May 6, 1997.

73. See "NATO-Russia: NAC Discusses NATO-Russia relationship Before SYG Meets Primakov," USNATO 1506, May 6, 1997.

74. See "Deputy Secretary's Letter to DFM Mamedov," State 084033, May 6, 1997.

75. See "NATO-Russia: Debrief of May 6 Solana-Primakov Meeting," USNATO 1531, May 7, 1997.

76. For the U.S. instruction to Hunter for the final NAC on May 13 see "NATO-Russia: Guidance on Section V for 5/13NAC, "State 088990, May 13, 1997.

77. See "Letter from the Deputy Secretary to DFM Mamedov," State 86892, May 9, 1997.

78. See the Official Informal from Tefft to Talbott entitled "For Deputy Secretary Only from Chargé," May 12, 1997.

79. See the guidance sent to Vershbow following the Vershbow-Edelman conversation entitled "NATO-Russia: Guidance to Close on March 14 Language/Flank Agreement." State 090106, May 14, 1997.

80. See "Statement by the President on NATO Expansion," The White House, The Rose Garden, May 14, 1997, <http://www.allied.be/usa/president/s19970514b.html>.

81. See "Background Briefing by Senior Administration Officials," The Briefing Room, May 14, 1997. Author's private copy.

82. See Yeltsin's letter to President Clinton from May 19, 1997.

83. See Memorandum of Conversation of a Dinner Meeting Between Secretary Albright and Russian Foreign Mister Primakov, State 110688, June 12, 1997.

84. See "Remarks by President Clinton at the Signing Ceremony of the NATO-Russia Founding Act," Paris, May 27, 1997, <http://www.nato.int/usa/president/s970527.a.htm>.

85. See "Remarks by Russian President Yeltsin at the Signing Ceremony of the NATO-Russia Founding Act," Paris, May 27, 1997, <http://www.nato.int/docu/speech/1997/s970527e.htm>.

86. See the Memorandum of Conversation of the Clinton-Yeltsin meeting held at the American Ambassador's Residence in Paris on May 27, 1997.

BOOK VII. HEAD-TO-HEAD AT MADRID

1. This did not mean that the U.S. had given up on Slovakia. In the spring of 1997 Albright asked Talbott to come up with a strategy to encourage Bratislava to return to a reformist track. See Deputy Secretary Talbott's memo entitled "A Strategy for Slovakia" dated April 21, 1997.

2. In a memo to the NATO Ambassador in February, Solana wrote: "In order to avoid a prolonged public debate before the summit, there should be no formal discussion either in Council or at the spring Ministerial and no recommendations on which country or countries to invite at the summit to start accession negotiations with the Alliance. We should rather aim at a late and quiet process of consensus building between the Sintra Ministerial and the summit. I would be prepared, if you agree, to sound out nations individually by mid-June and present a consolidated overview to Permanent Representatives at a private luncheon or an informal meeting which would allow nations to consult bilaterally on different views. A few days before the summit we should aim to arrive, in an informal meeting, at unanimous recommendations to be submitted to heads of state and government. Any leak or advance notice to the "selected" countries or to the "non-selected" must be strictly avoided." See "NATO: Enlargement Preparations for the Madrid Summit, USNATO 000430, February 12, 1997.

3. At the NATO December 1996 Foreign Ministers Ministerial, the U.S. had been unable to gain acceptance of the relatively anodyne statement: "The first shall not be

the last." See Hunter's assessment of the weakness of allied support for the "open door" policy in "NATO in 1996: Beyond Architecture to Action," USNATO 000056, January 6, 1996.

4. Speaking before the NAC in Brussels on February 4, 1997, President Constantinescu said that his government had promised the Romanian people three things: democratic stability, economic prosperity, and Euro-Atlantic integration. He concluded his speech by saying that if any of these goals were not achieved, quoting Titus, "the day is lost." See "Romanian President Constantinescu Meets the NAC," USNATO 000426, February 12, 1997.

5. But Chirac also noted that "the greatest difficulty" would be to convince the United States to support Romania's candidacy. See "Chirac Visit to Bucharest," Bucharest 001247, February 27, 1997. For an internal assessment of French thinking on Romania in the spring of 1997 see "France and NATO: Plugging for Romania," Paris 010053, May 2, 1997.

6. See "NATO in 1997," USNATO 001053, March 28, 1997.

7. On Perry's trip to Ljubljana see "What A Difference Ten Months Makes: Secretary Perry's July 3 Visit to Slovenia," Ljubljana 000756, July 5, 1996.

8. In order to avoid leaks, these meetings were kept smaller and less formal than normal Deputy Committee meetings and were referred to as "rump DCs." My description draws on my own notes from these meetings.

9. Since these meetings were not official DC meetings, an official "Summary of Conclusions" of the DC process was never produced. The rationale for the U.S. decision is nonetheless contained in the paper entitled "Principals' Checklist of NATO Summit Issues," May 20, 1997.

10. See Deputy Secretary of State Strobe Talbott, "NATO, Russia and Transatlantic Security in the 21st Century," The Atlantic Council, May 20, 1997.

11. See Hunter's cable "The Sintra Ministerials," USNATO 001804, May 26, 1997. See also my note to Albright entitled "What to Watch Out for on Enlargement Issues" dated May 23, 1997.

12. See "Talking Points on Small First Group," May 28, 1997.

13. Albright emerged from the lunch somewhat shaken and angry that she had so little support. Talbott sent me off to draft a memo listing the reasons why we were still in good shape. See my note to Albright entitled "Thoughts on Your Lunch and Aftermath."

14. See Albright's Night Note from Sintra dated May 30, 1997.

15. In a meeting with Italian Defense Minister Andreata, Cohen replied that if Slovenia had not been included by others with Romania, the U.S. decision might have been different. See "Defense Ministers Meeting at NATO HQ, Italian Bilateral, 12–13 June 1997," USNATO 002120, June 19, 1997.

16. The conversation took place on May 22, 1997. Clinton said: "The challenge at Madrid is to make sure the countries invited to join NATO can fulfill their obligations, so that it will be a credible alliance and not purely political." The two leaders agreed on the merits of such an approach in general, but did not discuss individual candidates. See the "Telephone Conversation with Helmut Kohl of Germany," State 107309, June 7, 1997.

17. See "Bitterlich June 5 Readout," State 120928, June 26, 1997.

18. The rationale for the President's decision was contained in "NATO Enlargement—U.S. Decision on New Members," State 111475, June 13, 1997.

19. See DoD New Briefing, "Secretary Cohen: En route Interview with Traveling Press," June 11, 1997, <http://www.defenselink.mil/news/Jun1997/t06131997_t611enrt .html>.

20. See also "U.S. Statement on NATO Enlargement," by Secretary of Defense William S. Cohen, North Atlantic Council in Defense Ministers' Session, June 12, 1997, <http://www.nato.int/usa/dod/s970612c.htm>.

21. See "Deutsch-franzoeischer Motor im Leerlauf," Neue Zuercher Zeitung, June 14, 1997.

22. As Védrine subsequently put it to U.S. chargé, Don Bandler, "You have to accept that there will be discussion of this at Madrid." See "FM Védrine on Denver Summit NATO, Europe and Mideast Issues," Paris 13923, June 19, 1997."

23. As quoted in the brief news summary in the Wall Street Journal entitled "NATO" on June 6, 1997.

24. See "SYG's Enlargement Conversations with PermReps," USNATO 002139, June 20, 1997.

25. See "Memorandum of Conversation Between the President and French President Chirac on June 20, 1997, June 25, 1997.

26. See "Chancellor Kohl and Romania's NATO Candidacy," Bonn 7047, June 12, 1997.

27. See "Secretary's Conversation with German Foreign Minister Kinkel," State 111238, June 13, 1997; as well as "Secretary Albright's Meeting with German Foreign Minster Kinkel," State 119427, June 25, 1997.

28. See "NATO Enlargement: Kinkel Underscores Consensus on Three Initial Entrants, Open Door Policy," Bonn 07834, June 27, 1997.

29. See "Slovenians Grapple with U.S.-European Standpoints on NATO Enlargement," Ljubljana 001318, June 3, 1997.

30. See "Letter to President Clinton from Slovene Prime Minister Drnovsek," Ljubljana 111408, June 11, 1997.

31. To complicate matters, the U.S. Ambassador had not received his official instructions explaining the reasons for the U.S. decision due to a communications error. He was therefore not armed with the latest in Washington's official thinking. See "PM Drnovsek Reacts to Slovene Exclusion from NATO First Round," Ljubljana 001427, June 13, 1997.

32. See "Text of Letter from Slovene Prime Minister Janez Drnovsek to President Clinton," Ljubljana 01537, June 26, 1997.

33. See "Slovenian Officials Register Disappointment Over U.S. Decision on NATO Enlargement," Ljubljana 001431, June 13, 1997.

34. See "Kucan Cites Slovenian Missteps on NATO," Ljubljana 001483, June 19, 1997.

35. See "Visit To Romania by Under Secretary of Defense Slocombe," Bucharest 000175, January 13, 1997. The quote comes from a diary kept by Ambassador Moses and is quoted with his permission.

36. Ibid.

37. See "The Secretary's Meeting with Romanian Foreign Minister Severin," State 097074, May 23, 1997.

38. See "Romanian Foreign Minister Expresses Views/Feelings on U.S. Enlargement Decision," Bucharest 003778, June 16 1997.

39. See "Romanian Prime Minster's Meeting with the Secretary, Deputy Secretary," State 133663, July 17, 1997.

40. See "Secretary of State Madeleine K. Albright, Remarks and Question and Answer Session at Vilnius University, Vilnius University, July 13, 1997.

41. See the Speech by Talbott entitled "The End of the Beginning: The Emergence of a New Russia," Stanford University, September 19, 1997. See also my speech at a conference in Helsinki, Finland on "The New Hanseatic League" on October 8, 1997.

42. See my note to Talbott from July 16, 1997 entitled "The Baltic Hanseatic Strategy."

43. For further details see Michael R. Beschloss and Strobe Talbott, *At the Highest Levels* (Boston, Little, Brown and Co., 1993), pp. 443–444.

44. As quoted in "From the Grapevine: Baltic News Trends and Perspectives," *City Paper*, no. 28, May/June 1997, pp. 7–8.

45. See "Memcon of Deputy Secretary Talbott's Meeting with Estonian President Lennart Meri and Latvian President Guntis Ulmanis, May 28, The Hague." State 110550, June 12, 1997.

46. See "The Deputy Secretary Briefs Baltic Ambassadors on U.S. First Tranche Position," June 13, 1997. State 114913, June 18, 1997.

47. The language in dispute was a description of the U.S. interest in the Baltic states. The Balts wanted to use the phrase "direct and material interest" that Vice President Gore has used in a speech in Estonia in 1995. But putting that phrase in the Baltic Charter was seen as running the risk that it could be interpreted as an actual security guarantee. The second issue was whether the Charter would state that we "supported" Baltic aspirations to join NATO or whether we simply said we "welcomed" their aspirations and "supported" their efforts. See my note to Talbott summarizing these differences on June 17, 1997.

48. See "Positive Estonian Reaction to Draft of Baltic Charter," Tallinn 02159, June 23, 1997; "Latvians Respond Positively and Pragmatically to Draft U.S.-Baltic Charter, Copenhagen 003601, June 30, 1997; and "Initial Lithuania Reaction to U.S.-Baltic Charter Positive." Copenhagen 003463, June 25, 1997.

49. See my note to Talbott, entitled "Baltic Success" from June 27, 1997.

50. For the proposed U.S. draft communiqué language see "Proposal for Close Allies Meeting in Washington Prior to the Denver Summit on NATO Madrid Summit Issue," State 111311, June 12, 1997.

51. The German used in the press release was "baldiger Eintritt" or "early entry."

52. See "German Support for Romania: Finding a Way Toward Consensus at Madrid," Bonn 008087, July 3, 1997.

53. See "President's July 3, 1997 Telcon with German Chancellor Helmut Kohl," State 127943, July 9, 1997. In Bucharest, Ambassador Moses met with Constantinescu

following his return from Bonn. The Romanian President said that he had told the Chancellor he didn't want Romania to become the focal point of dissension in the Alliance but that he needed a specific reference in the communiqué. Otherwise—in his words—"I will have achieved nothing. Romania will be in the same position as Bulgaria. And I will have failed as a leader." See "President Constantinescu's Meeting with Chancellor Kohl," Bucharest 004204, July 3, 1997.

54. See the Memorandum of Conversation entitled "Meeting with NATO Secretary General Solana," July 7, 1997.

55. For a summary of the opening plenary session see "NATO Summit—Plenary Discussion of NATO Enlargement," SECTO 021007, July 10, 1997.

56. See "EAPC Summit, July 9," Secto 021020, July 14, 1997.

57. See "Memorandum of Conversation: President Clinton's Meeting with Romanian President Constantinescu," State 144970, August 22, 1997.

58. See "Remarks by President Clinton and President <http://clinton5.nara.gov/textonly/WH/New/Spain/19970714-15453.html>.

59. See "Memorandum of Conversation Between the President and German President Herzog on July 24, 1997," State 146743, August 6, 1997.

BOOK VIII. THE POLITICAL BATTLE

1. For example, in the summer of 1996 the Senate passed the "NATO Enlargement Facilitation Act" by a vote of 81–16. See Vote Summary, July 25, 1996 on S.Amdt.5058 to H.R.3540, <http://thomas.loc.gov/cgi-bin/bdquery/z?d104:h.r.03654.>.

2. See "Memorandum of Conversation, Expanded Meeting with Prime Minister Romano Prodi of Italy, May 6, 1998, 11:50 A.M.–12:30 A.M., Cabinet Room."

3. On the changing role of the executive branch and Congress see Stanley Sloan, Mary Locke, and Casimir A. Yost, *The Foreign Policy Struggle* (Washington, DC: Institute for the Study of Diplomacy, 2000).

4. See George F. Kennan, "A Fateful Error," *The New York Times*, February 5, 1997.

5. See John Lewis Gaddis, "History, Grand Strategy and NATO Enlargement," *Survival* 40, no. 1 (Spring 1998): 145–151.

6. See Jeremy D. Rosner, *The New Tug-of-War: Congress, the Executive Branch and National Security* (Washington, D.C.: Carnegie Endowment for International Peace, 1995).

7. See William Stull Holt, *Treaties Defeated by the Senate: A Study of the Struggle Between President and Senate Over the Conduct of Foreign Relations* (Baltimore: The Johns Hopkins Press, 1933).

8. See Jeremy D. Rosner, "The Perils of Misjudging Our Political Will," *Foreign Affairs* 75, no. 4 (July 1996): 9–16. On public support for enlargement see Steven Kull and Jeremy D. Rosner, The American public, Congress and NATO enlargement, Part I: "Is there sufficient public support?" and Part II: "Will Congress back admitting new members?" in *NATO Review* 45, no. 1 (January 1997): 9–11 and 12–14, respectively. For the original Kull poll, see Principal Investigator Steven Kull, "Americans on

Expanding NATO: A Study of US Public Attitudes Summary of Findings," Program on International Policy Attitudes (PIPA), October 1, 1996.

9. See Rosner's memo to Berger entitled "Legislative, Public Affairs and Diplomatic Priorities for the Next Six Months," January 16, 1997.

10. See Rosner's memo to Secretary Albright, National Security Advisor Berger, Deputy Secretary Talbott, and Deputy National Security Advisor Steinberg entitled "Initial Thoughts on NATO Enlargement Ratification Strategy," February 26, 1997.

11. Helms's then chief-of-staff, retired Rear Admiral Bud Nance, would play a key role in convincing the Senator to support enlargement. Nance had served at NATO SACLANT headquarters in Norfolk, Virginia. He often remarked to visitors that one lesson he had learned while serving at SACLANT was that NATO's role was not only to deter the Russians, but to keep the peace among the European countries as well.

12. See Trent Lott, "The Senate's Role in NATO Enlargement," *The Washington Post*, March 21, 1997.

13. For a portrait of Julie Finley see Jill Abramson, "The Belle of the Soft Money Soiree," *The New York Times Magazine*, February 20, 2000.

14. The U.S. Committee to Expand NATO was incorporated as a 501 (C) (4) corporation on November 1, 1996 in the District of Columbia. Jackson's role as President and his ties to Lockheed Martin led to accusations that it was a front for the U.S. defense industry to sell weapons to the region. The Committee's article of incorporation and bylaws emphasized the *pro bono* nature of the organization and a prohibition against accepting contributions from corporations or foreign nationals in accordance with the belief of its founders that it was an organization of individual American citizens supporting NATO enlargement. For an example of accusations that the U.S. defense industry was a major supporter of enlargement see Katherine Q. Seelye, "Arms Contractors Spend to Promote an Expanded NATO," *The New York Times*, March 30, 1998.

15. On Jackson's views see Bruce Pitcairn Jackson, "The Conservative Case for NATO," *Policy Review*, no. 94 (April/May 1999): 45–57.

16. See Jackson's memo from March 1997 entitled "A Political Strategy for NATO Expansion" contained in the archives of the U.S. Committee to Expand NATO.

17. Interview with Bruce Jackson, August 16, 2001.

18. Craig's fax went on to say: "You will be pleased to know that this morning I received a call from the Slovenian Ambassador who told me that his Foreign Minister would be in town next week and was free for dinner on Tuesday. I went ahead and scheduled him in—and then, to my shock, recalled that yesterday, I had told the Ambassador from Slovakia, whose Prime Minister is also in town next week, that Tuesday could be his night at the house. Fortunately, the Slovaks—being particularly eager to please—were willing to reschedule to Wednesday. And just now, I got another call, this time from the Estonian Ambassador who was so excited he could hardly get the words out. He wanted to tell me that half the cabinet of Estonia was coming to town, that they were eager to talk to the Committee about NATO enlargement, and that they were free for dinner late Thursday night." Craig's fax to Finley dated March 6, 1997 is contained in the archives of the U.S. Committee to Expand NATO.

19. See the memo from Jackson to the USCEN's Board of Directors dated June 9, 1997 summarizing the USCEN's activities November 1, 1996–May 31, 1997 contained in the archives of the U.S. Committee to Expand NATO.

20. See the transcript of the debate between Richard C. Holbrooke and Michael E. Mandelbaum entitled "Expanding NATO: Will it Weaken the Alliance?" December 9, 1996.

21. See also Richard Cohen, "Endangered Expansion," *The Washington Post*, December 12, 1996.

22. As quoted in "NATO or Tomato?," *The New York Times*, January 22, 1997.

23. See the notes from the meeting by Cameron Munter dated March 5, 1997.

24. This idea came from RAND President Jim Thomson. See JimThomson, "Perspective on NATO; Back to Square 1 With Einstein," *Los Angeles Times*, March 21, 1995.

25. See Secretary of State Madeleine K. Albright's Prepared Statement Before the Senate Armed Services Committee, "NATO Enlargement," Washington, D.C., April 23, 1997, <http://secretary.state.gov/www/statements/970423.htm>.

26. See Senate Committee on Armed Services Hearing on NATO Enlargement, Senator John Warner (R-VA), April 23, 1997, <http://www.fas.org/man/nato/congress/1997/s970423t_warner.htm>.

27. See Thomas L. Friedman, "Held Hostage," *The New York Times*, April 28, 1997.

28. See Henry Kissinger, "Helsinki Fiasco," *The Washington Post*, March 30, 1997 and "The Dilution of NATO," *The Washington Post*, June 8, 1997.

29. See Vaclav Havel, "NATO's Quality of Life," *The New York Times*, May 13, 1997.

30. See "Remarks By the President At The United States Military Academy Commencement," Michie Stadium, West Point, New York, May 31, 1997, Office of the Press Secretary, <http://clinton6nara.gov/1997/05/1997–05–31-president-at-west-point-graduation.html>.

31. See "Dear Mr. President" letter dated June 11, 1997.

32. This account is based on Rosner's notes from the meeting.

33. See John Keegan's *Six Armies in Normandy: From D-Day to the Liberation of Paris , June 6–August 25, 1994* (New York: Viking Press, 1982), Chapter Seven, 'A Polish Battlefield,' pp. 249–282.

34. For further details on the Judge Waters event see George W. Grayson, *Strange Bedfellows: NATO Marches East* (Lanham, MD: University Press of America, 1999), pp. 109–112.

35. See Remarks by President Bill Clinton at Veterans' Event, "NATO Enlargement," The White House, The East Room, Washington, DC, July 3, 1997, *Federal News Service* (Washington, DC: Federal News Service Group, Inc., 1998).

36. See "The Open Letter to the President," June 26, 1997, <http://www.cpss.org/nato/oplet.htm>.

37. See "Center for Political and Strategic Studies News Conference on NATO Enlargement," Speakers: Richard Davies, IISS Consulting Professor, Center for International Security and Arms Control, Stanford University; Stanley Rieser; Jack Matlock, Former Ambassador To The Soviet Union; Michael Mandelbaum, Professor,

Nitze School of Advanced International Studies, Johns Hopkins University, National Press Club, Washington, DC, June 26, 1997, *Federal News Service* (Washington, DC: Federal News Service Group, Inc., 1997).

38. See "Letter to the President" by Senator Kay Bailey Hutchison and others, June 25, 1997.

39. See Senator Jesse Helms, "Enlarging the Alliance: New Members, Not New Missions," *Wall Street Journal*, July 9, 1997.

40. See Thomas L. Friedman, "Clinton's Folly," *The New York Times*, July 31, 1997.

41. See the memo from John Isaacs from the Council for a Livable world dated July 14, 1997, entitled "Senate Vote Count on NATO Enlargement."

42. Memo circulated by the Committee to Expand NATO also warned that the Administration was in danger of losing key Republican supporters. See Jackson's memo entitled "The NATO Debate After Madrid," July 30, 1997.

43. The letter was sent from Senator Lugar to Berger on July 28, 1997 and included a 14-page memo entitled "Strategy for Securing Senate Ratification of NATO Enlargement."

44. See Rosner's memo of July 25, 1997 entitled "Update on NATO Enlargement Ratification."

45. See New Atlantic Initiative statement on NATO Enlargement, September 9, 1997.

46. See memo from Jeremy Rosner to Secretary Albright entitled "Strategy for Achieving Ratification" dated August 27, 1997, and Rosner's outline for the meeting with Albright on August 28 entitled "MKA Meeting: Road Ahead on NATO+ Ratification."

47. See memo from Steve Biegun and Beth Wilson to Senator Helms entitled "Suggested Schedule of Hearings on NATO Enlargement, September 2, 1997.

48. See the memo from Steve Biegun, Beth Wilson and Marc Thiessen to Senator Helms entitled "NATO Enlargement," September 8, 1997.

49. See the letter from Senator Helms to Secretary Albright, September 17, 1997.

50. See the fax sent from Steve Biegun to Jeremy Rosner dated, October 6, 1997 and contained in the S/NERO archives.

51. See Ronald D. Asmus and F. Stephen Larrabee: "What Will NATO Enlargement Cost?," *Survival* 38, no 3 (Autumn 1998): 5–26. See also Ivan Eland, "The Costs of Expanding the NATO Alliance," Congressional Budget Office Paper prepared for the House International Relations Committee, March 1996.

52. See "Report to the Congress on the Military Requirements and Costs of NATO Enlargement, February 1998, <http://www.defenselink.mil/pubs/nato/>.

53. The Madrid Communiqué stated: "Admitting new members will entail resource implications. It will involve the Alliance providing the resources which enlargement will necessarily require. . . . We are confident that, in line with the security environment of today, Alliance costs associated with the integration of new members will be manageable and that the resources necessary to meet those costs will be provided." See Madrid Declaration on Euro-Atlantic Security and Cooperation as Issued by the Heads of State and Government, July 8, 1997, <http://www.nato.int/docu/pr/1997/p97–081e.htm>.

54. See memo from Ronald Asmus and Jeremy Rosner to the Secretary, entitled "Strategy (and one-liners) for SFRC Testimony," October 3, 1997.

55. See Madeleine Albright, "Statement of Hon. Madeleine Albright, Secretary of State," *The Debate on NATO Enlargement, Hearings before the Senate Committee on Foreign Relations,* October 7, 1997, 105 Cong. 1st sess. (Government Printing Office, 1998), pp. 6–39.

56. As quoted in Pat Towell, "Albright Argues NATO Expansion Would Buttress Democracy," *Congressional Quarterly,* October 11, 1997, p. 24.

57. See statement of Dr. Michael Mandelbaum, *Hearings Before the Committee on Foreign Relations United States Senate,* October 9, 1997, 105 Cong., 1st sess. (Government Printing Office, 1998) pp. 72–89.

58. See Henry A. Kissinger, "NATO-Russia Relationship-Part I," *Hearings Before the Committee on Foreign Relations United States Senate,* October 30, 1997, 105 Cong., 1st sess. (Government Printing Office, 1998) pp. 183–206.

59. When U.S. Ambassador to Moscow Jim Collins briefed senior Russian officials informally in late February on the Senate resolution of ratification they were furious about the language. See "Mamedov Reacts Strongly Against Senate NATO Document," Moscow 004932, February 28, 1998.

60. Hickenlooper had asked Acheson whether, under Article 3 of the Washington Treaty in which the parties pledged via mutual assistance to help develop the capacity to resist armed attack, the U.S. was "going to be expected to send substantial numbers of troops over there as a more or less permanent contribution to the development of these countries capacity to resist?" Acheson had replied that: "The answer to that question is a clear and resolute 'No.'" To be fair to Acheson, this exchange took place at a time when the U.S. had no intention of forward deploying U.S. troops in Europe. It was not until a year later that NATO started to think of a unified command structure that could include U.S. defense forces. For Acheson's account see Dean Acheson, *Present at the Creation* (New York: Norton, 1969), p. 285.

61. Cohen's argument was buttressed by an op-ed that appeared the morning of this hearing in which UK Defense Minister George Robertson stated that London would pay its fair share of additional enlargement costs. See George Robertson, "Redesigning NATO," *The Washington Times,* October 21, 1997.

62. See William S. Cohen, "Statement of Hon. William S. Cohen, Secretary of Defense, Department of Defense," *NATO Enlargement Costs, Hearings before the Senate Committee on Appropriations,* October 21, 1997, 105 Cong., 1st sess. (Government Printing Office, 1998) pp. 1, 30, 35–41.

63. See "Public Views on NATO Enlargement," *Hearings Before the Committee on Foreign Relations United States Senate,* November 5, 1997, 105 Cong., 1st sess. (Government Printing Office, 1998) pp. 261–330, 537–552.

64. See letter from Senators Helms and Biden, dated November 10, 1997.

65. See "EUR Assistant Secretary Grossman's Remarks at Bergen Nordic/Baltic Foreign Ministers Meeting," Oslo 04013, September 5, 1997. See also the memo from Grossman to Secretary Albright, "Our New Northern Strategy," August 27, 1997. See also my public remarks on "The New Hanseatic League" delivered at a conference in Helsinki Finland on October 8, 1997 sponsored by the U.S. Embassy and Nordicum.

66. See President Clinton's "Remarks at the Signing Ceremony for the Baltic Nations-United States Charter of Partnership," January 16, 1998, Weekly *Compilation of Presidential Documents*, 34, no. 4 (January 26, 1998): 85–86.

67. See David C. Gompert and F. Stephen Larrabee, eds., *America and Europe* (Cambridge: Cambridge University Press, 1997).

68. See Ronald D. Asmus, "Double enlargement: redefining the Atlantic partnership after the Cold War," in Gompert and Larrabee, ibid., pp. 19–50. See also Ronald D. Asmus, Robert Blackwill, and F. Stephen Larrabee, "Can NATO Survive?" *The Washington Quarterly* 19, no. 2 (Spring 1996): 79–101.

69. Craig view's are contained in a memo to Albright entitled "What Kind of NATO Do We Really Want?," January 8, 1998.

70. See my memo to Grossman "Defining U.S. Interests: The Mega-Question" from September 8, 1998.

71. See Secretary of State Madeleine K. Albright, "Statement at the North Atlantic Council," Ministerial Meeting, NATO Headquarters, Brussels, Belgium, December 16, 1997, <http://secretary. state.gov/www.statements/971216a.html>.

72. See Grossman's memo to Secretary Albright entitled "Thinking About 1998," January 6, 1998.

73. Grossman's briefing to Albright was entitled "NATO After the First Round of Enlargement: Next Steps?"

74. See Grossman's Note for the Secretary entitled "Thinking about 1999," January 15, 1999.

75. See the memo from Samuel Berger and John Hilley to the President entitled "Strategy for Completing Ratification of NATO Enlargement" dated December 17, 1997.

76. See "Clinton Letter Transmitting to the U.S. Senate Protocols to NATO Treaty," The White House, February 11, 1998, <http://fb10cdrom.fb10.uni-bremen.de/cd/infousa/usiaweb/usis/clinlet.htm>. Senator Biden would recall the discussion with the Vice President later that day in a statement on the Senate floor. See *Congressional Record*, February 11, 1998, p.S076.

77. See AFL-CIO endorsement, "A Declaration of Support for NATO Enlargement," January 20, 1998.

78. "The upcoming Senate vote," the statement read, "is fundamentally a test of whether the U.S. will remain engaged in the Europe of the 21st century. Since the end of World War II, our nation has extended an enormous effort to build a Europe of free and democratic states at peace with one another. For the first time there is a realistic possibility of achieving this goal. Now is not the time to turn our back on this great project." See Statement of 60 Retired Military Officers, February 3, 1998.

79. See "Founding Declaration of the Coalition against NATO Expansion," Council for a Livable World Education Fund, *Briefing Book on NATO Enlargement* (Washington, D.C.: Council for a Livable World Education Fund, April 1998), pp. 69–72.

80. See the memo from Rosner and Asmus to Talbott entitled "NATO+ Resolution of Ratification" dated February 21, 1997.

81. See Rosner's memo "Initial Comments and Issues on SFRC's NATO Enlargement Resolution of Ratification, Draft #2," February 23, 1998.

82. See Rosner's e-mail to Ron Asmus, Dan Fried, Jamie Rubin and others, entitled "New NATO+ pollings #s," February 23, 1998.

83. See Howard Baker, Jr., Sam Nunn, Brent Scowcroft and Alton Frye, "NATO: A Debate Recast," *The New York Times*, February 4, 1998.

84. Senator Warner first indicated publicly his support for a "pause" amendment in a statement he put in the Senate record on February 10, 1998 in connection with the NATO expansion amendment. See *Congressional Record*, February 10, 1998, p. S584.

85. In her speech before the New Atlantic Initiative on February 9, 1998, Albright had stated: "This Administration opposes any effort in the Senate to mandate a pause in the process of NATO enlargement." See Albright's "Remarks Before the New Atlantic Initiative Conference: NATO Expansion."

86. See Statement by Secretary of State Madeleine K. Albright, "Testimony Before the Senate Foreign Relations Committee on NATO Enlargement," February 24, 1998.

87. See our memo to Albright entitled "Today's SFRC Hearing on NATO enlargement and the Road Ahead," March 3, 1998.

88. See the memo from Rosner and Asmus to Albright entitled "Status of NATO Enlargement Debate," March 12, 1998.

89. See "NATO Myopia," *The New York Times*, March 5, 1998.

90. See Thomas L. Friedman, "Ohio State II," *The New York Times*, March 3, 1998.

91. See "The NATO Dispute," *The Washington Post*, March 11, 1998.

92. The *Chicago Tribune* initially took a position opposing enlargement in an editorial on February 1, 1998 entitled "A case of less is more with NATO." On March 13, it reversed itself. See "The Case for NATO Expansion," *The Chicago Tribune*, March 13, 1998.

93. See the letter from former Senators San Nunn and Howard H. Baker, Jr. addressed to Senators Thurmond and Levin.

94. See "Dear Mr. Leader" letter from President Clinton, The White House, March 14, 1998.

95. See Jesse Helms, "The New NATO: NATO Expansion Has All the Safeguards it Needs," *The Wall Street Journal*, March 23, 1998.

96. In early April Rosner noted that S/NERO knew of 23 potential amendments. See his memo entitled "Update on Timing of Amendments," April 6, 1998.

97. Albright wrote Ashcroft on March 12 explaining her views and making it clear that Ashcroft had misrepresented her thinking. See Rosner's memo "Letter to Senator Ashcroft (and Contingency Letter to Senator Helms) on NATO Enlargement," March 9, 1998. Ashcroft ignored the letter and instead continued to attack the Administration. Speaking on the Senate floor on March 19, Ashcroft stated: "I will be submitting an amendment for consideration by the Senate to make it clear that collective security will remain the heart of NATO, and that this is the only mission allowable under the treaty." See *Congressional Record*, March 19, 1998, S2284.

98. See the memo from Asmus and Rosner to Secretary Albright entitled "NATO Enlargement and the Ashcroft Amendment," April 23, 1998. See also the paper entitled "Why the Ashcroft Amendment is Harmful to the U.S. and NATO," which was circulated to both Senate staff and influential members of the foreign policy establishment.

99. The description of this meeting is taken from Rosner's notes from the meeting.

100. See the "Dear Colleague" letter signed by Roth, Lieberman and McCain dated April 24, 1998.

101. As quoted in *Reuters*, April 23, 1998.

102. In the run-up to the final vote on April 30, Tom Friedman had dubbed enlargement "Gulf of Tonkin II" and likened enlargement to "a car with no brakes on a slippery slope to trouble." See Thomas L. Friedman, "Gulf of Tonkin II," *The New York Times*, March 31, 1998.

103. See "NATO and the Lessons of History," *The New York Times*, April 29, 1998.

104. See Madeleine K. Albright, "Stop Worrying About Russia," *The New York Times*, April 29, 1998.

105. See, for example, David Gompert, "A Vote Against NATO," *The Washington Times*, April 29, 1998.

106. See Senator Moynihan's statement in the *Congressional Record*, "Protocols to the North Atlantic Treaty of 1949 on Accession of Poland, Hungary and the Czech Republic," Senate, April 27, 1998, p. S3610, <http://thomas.loc.gov/cgi-bin/query/C?r105:./temp/~r105GLJkUF>. See also Senator Moynihan's speech entitled "Could NATO Expansion Lead to Nuclear War?" delivered to the 1fiftieth Anniversary Annual Meeting of the Associated Press in Dallas, Texas on April 20, 1998.

107. For the final vote totals on the amendments see "US. Senate Roll Call Votes," 105th Congress—2nd Session (1998) in *Thomas*, <http://www.senate.gov/ legislative/vote1052/vote_menu.html. >.

108. See Secretary of State Madeleine K. Albright "Statement on the Senate Ratification to NATO Enlargement," Washington, D.C., April 30, 1998, <http://secretary.state.gov/www/statements/1998/980430d.htm.>.

CONCLUSION

1. See President Truman's "Address on the Occasion of the Signing of the North Atlantic Treaty, April 4, 1949," *Public Papers of the Presidents of the United States: Harry S. Truman 1949* (Washington, DC: Government Printing Office, 1964), pp. 196–98.

INDEX

academics, opposition to NATO en-
largement by, 121
Acheson, Dean, 176, 178, 274, 356 n.60
"Advancing our European Security
Agenda" memo (NSC), 73–75, 77–78
Afanassievsky, Nikolai, 172
AFL-CIO, 280
AFNorth command, 167
AFSouth command, 167–169, 342 n.139
Ahtisaari, Martii, 159
Alastair Buchan lecture, IISS, 31–32
Albright, Madeleine K.: Ashcroft and,
284, 358 n.97; Baltic policy, 239;
NATO and, 219, 220–221, 279; NATO-
Russia Founding Act, 205–208;
Partnership for Peace, 62–63, 68–69;
personal history and vision, 176–181,
344 n.9; Poland, 197, 346 n.49; pre-
Helsinki negotiations (March 1997),
198–200; protocols of accession, sign-
ing of, xv, xix–xx; Senate hearings tes-
timony, 259–261, 271, 272–275, 282;
Senate ratification vote, 285, 286–287,

288, 358 n.85; Yeltsin meeting (Feb.
1997), 179–180
American Jewish Committee (AJC), 152
Ananicz, Andrzej, 54
Antall, Jozsef, 9–11, 14, 17, 53, 148
arms control negotiations, Vienna CFE,
194–195
arms sales, Russian, 108, 109
Ashcroft, John, 284–285, 287–288, 358
n.97
Aspin, Les, 21, 45–46, 52
Athens, 1993 NATO Foreign Ministers'
meeting, 28–29
Atlantic Partnership Council, 167
Atlanticism, 148
Auschwitz concentration camp, 151–152
authoritarianism, post-communist threat
of, 43

Baker, James, 4–7
Baltic-Americans, 159
Baltic states: Albright and, 239; Baltic
Action Plan, U.S., 160–163;